March of America Facsimile Series

Number 4

The Decades of
the Newe Worlde or West India

Pietro Martire d'Anghiera

The Decades
of the Newe Worlde
or West India

by Pietro Martire d'Anghiera

ANN ARBOR

UNIVERSITY MICROFILMS, INC.

A Subsidiary of Xerox Corporation

Foreword

The Decades of the newe worlde or west India, printed in London in 1555, is the second book in English containing information about the discoveries of Columbus and other explorations of the New World. Richard Eden, the compiler, included in the volume his own translation of *De rebus oceanicis et orbe novo decades tres* (Basle, 1533), by Pietro Martire d'Anghiera.

The Italian born Peter Martyr, as he was known to Eden, became a member of the Spanish Council of the Indies. His *Decades* consisted of newsletters addressed to various prelates, including Pope Leo X, in which he reported the exploits of voyagers in the service of Spain. Eden had earlier translated part of the *Cosmographiae* of Sebastian Münster, which contained accounts of the explorations of Columbus, Magellan, and Amerigo Vespucci, but the *Decades* was the first comprehensive collection in English of such narratives. To Martyr's work Eden added translations of excerpts from Gonzalo Fernández de Oviedo y Valdes' *Historia general y natural de las Indias* and from writings by Francisco López de Gómara, Amerigo Vespucci, and Antonio Pigafetta, among others. Eden's volume was particularly valuable for its dissemination of information about the Cabot voyage of 1497, upon which the English later based their claim to territory on the North American continent.

Richard Eden attended Queens' College, Cambridge, and it was there that he first read Peter Martyr and developed a keen interest in cosmography and related sciences. In addition to the travel narratives in his *Decades*, he translated therein "The manner of fyndynge the longitude of regions by dyvers wayes after the description of Gemma Phrysius," and in 1561 he published a translation of Martin Cortés' *Breve compendio de la sphera y de la arte de navegar*, a work of incalculable importance in the history of English seamanship.

Eden was a worthy forerunner of the two Richard Hakluyts as a propagandist for English colonization. Since Queen Mary was married to Philip II of Spain when his *Decades* was published, Eden was optimistic that Spain and England could cooperate instead of competing in the settlement of the New World. His preface makes clear that his motive in collecting narratives of Spanish accomplishments was to stir Englishmen to emulate them: "Howe muche...shall this sounde unto owre reproche and inexcusable slothfulnesse and negligence bothe before god and the world, that so large dominions of such tractable people and pure gentiles ...are now knowen unto us, and that we have no respecte neyther for goddes cause nor for owre owne commoditie to attempte summe vyages into these coastes, to doo for owr partes as the Spaniardes haue doone for theyrs, and not euer lyke sheepe to haunte one trade, and to doo nothynge woorthy memorie amonge men or thankes before god, who maye herein woorthely accuse us for the slackenesse of owre dewtie towarde hym.' The combined appeal to commercial profit and Christian zeal was to be sounded again and again by later enthusiasts, most notably by the two Hakluyts.

A detailed analysis of Eden's compilation and his contribution to English exploration is given by Edward Arber, ed., *The First Three English Books on America* (Birmingham, 1885). An assessment of the importance of the *Decades* is also to be found in Franklin T. McCann, *English Discovery of America to 1585* (New York, 1952).

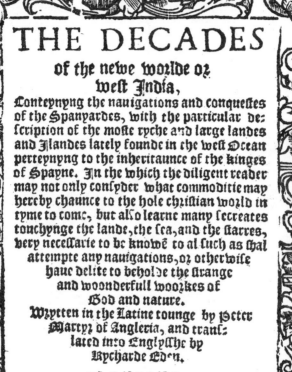

THE DECADES

of the newe worlde or
west India,

Conteynyng the nauigations and conquestes
of the Spanyardes, with the particular description of the moste ryche and large landes
and Ilandes lately founde in the west Ocean
perteynyng to the inheritaunce of the kinges
of Spayne. In the which the diligent reader
may not only consyder what commoditie may
hereby chaunce to the hole christian worlld in
tyme to come, but also learne many secreates
touchynge the lande, the sea, and the starres,
very necessarie to be knowē to al such as shal
attempte any nauigations, or otherwise
haue delite to beholde the strange
and woonderfull woorkes of
God and nature.
Wrytten in the Latine tounge by Peter
Martyr of Angleria, and tranf-
lated into Englysshe by
Rycharde Eden.

¶ L O N D I N I,
In ædibus Guilhelmi Powell,
A N N O. 1555.

¶POTENTISSIMO AC SERE-
NISSIMO PHILIPPO, AC SERENIS=
simæ potentissimæq̃ Mariæ, Dei gratia Regi ac Re=
ginæ, Angliæ, Franciæ, Neapolis, Ierusalem, et Hi=
berniæ: Fidei defensoribus, Principibus Hispania=
rum et Siciliæ, Archiducibus Austriæ, Duci=
bus Mediolani, Burgundiæ, et Brabantiæ,
comitibus Haspurgi, Flandriæ, et
Tirolis, Richardus Edenus
perpetuam optat fœli=
citatem.

VM IN PRIMO VESTRO
ingressu in hanc celeberimam Londini
vrbem (illustrissimi Principes) cerne=
rem quanto omnium applausu, popu
li concursu, ac ciuium frequentia, quã=
to insuper spectaculorum nitore, nobilium virorum
splendore, equorum multitudine, tubarum clango=
re, cæterisq̃ magnificis pompis ac triumphis, pro
dignitate vestra accepti estis dum omnes φ sui est
officij facere satagebant, vbi in tanta hominum tur=
ba vix vnus reperiatur qui non aliquid agendo ad=
uentum vestrum gratulabatur, cœpi et ego quoq̃ a=
liorum exemplo (propius presertim ad me acceden=
tibus

tibus Celſitudinibus veſtris) tanto animi ardore ad
aliquid agendum accendi ne ſolus in tanta hominum
corona otioſus viderer, ꝙ vix me continebam quin
in aliquam extēporariam orationem temere erupuiſ-
ſem, niſi et præſentiæ veſtræ maieſtas, et mea me ob-
ſcuritas a tam audaci facinore deterruiſſent. Verum,
cum poſtea penitius de hac re mecum cogitaſſem,
conſyderaſſemꝗ quam hæc omnia alioqui per ſe lau
de digna, veſtris tamen meritis ac regiæ dignitatis e-
minentiæ comparata, plebeia ac ludicra videantur,
cœpi denuo cum animo meo reputare qua in re ita
cum immortali rerum memoria fœliciſsimum veſtrū
aduentum gratularer, vt inde nominis veſtri fama et
ſplendor, non vllis ſpectaculorum temporarijs oſten
tis, ſed rerum geſtarum gloria, ad poſteros perpetuo
emanaret. Excutio ſtatim diuitias meas. Perſcrutor
ſi quid ex penu meo depromere poſſum ꝙ me ad aliquid agendum veſtris heroicis virtutibus dignum
excitet. Sed cum penes me nihil tale reperio, agnoſ-
co nuditatem meam, atꝗ ad vos confugio. Patrum,
auorum, proauorum, atꝗ atauorum vitas et facta
recolo. Syluam rerum geſtarum video, totꝗ precla-
riſsimorum principum propagines, vt merito ab ip-
ſis heroibus, Saturno videlicet, Ioue, ac Hercule,
cæteriſꝗ theanthropis, originem duxiſſe videantur.
Quod

Quod cum ita ſit, non aliunde profecto quam ex hac
ſylua materies mihi petenda erit quo in mentibus ho
minum et æterna rerum memoria, perpetua ſpecta=
cula rerum a vobis et progenitoribus veſtris præcla=
re geſtarum, in mundi theatro ab omnibus cum ſū=
ma nominis veſtri fama ac veneratione cernantur.
Cum itaqʒ inter cætera a maioribus veſtris præclare
geſta, nihil ſit admirabilius aut maiori laude dignū,
quam qʒ incredibili fiducia et plus quam Herculeis
laboribus ſuperato Oceano, fœliciſsimo tandem euē=
tu, Indiæ Occidentalis ditiſsimas Inſulas atqʒ Con=
tinentis ampliſsimas regiones, mortalium primi in=
uenerunt, in quibus infinitas incolarum myriades ad
fidem Chriſti conuerterunt (quo nihil auguſtius aut
Chriſtianis principibus magis dignum excogitari
poteſt) viſus ſum mihi qʒ non alia in re magis poſſe
fœlicitati veſtræmerito gratulari, quā ſi noſtris quoqʒ
hominibus quibus hæc hactenus nihil aut parum
cognita ſunt, innoteſcere faciam, vt perſpectis illo=
rum ſimul et veſtrorum ampliſsimis imperijs non ſi=
ne diuina prouidētia (vt credere par eſt) ad ipſos vſqʒ
Antipodes et PLVS VLTRA terminatis,
omnes boni, ipſa rerum magnitudine in admiratiōe
ducti, vos ament et venerentur: Malis vero et impro
bis, os obſtruatur ſi quam in maledicendo volupta=

tem

tem capiunt. Hæc dum cogito, venit mihi in mentē
ꝙ olim adoleſcens perlegi Decades de Nouo Orbe
a Petro Martyre ab Angleria, illuſtriſsimi Ferdinãdi
regis Catholici, ac tui (Sereniſsime rex) proaui ora=
tore, Latine conſcriptas, atꝗ ſacræ Cæſariæ maie=
ſtati patri tuo dedicatas. Tanti itaꝗ autoris fide et
eruditione motus, eum præ cæteris in noſtram lin=
guam traducendum ſuſcepi, ꝙ non ſolum vt hiſtori=
cus res Indicas cum ſumma fide ſcriptis mandauit,
ſed etiam vt philoſophus (ꝙ in cæteris ſcriptoribus
deſyderatur (naturalium rerum occultas cauſas red=
dit, ac admirabilium naturæ operum (quibus hæc
veſtra India plena eſt) rationes inueſtigat. Atꝗ vt
huius Indiæ poſterior ſtatus cognoſcatur, quantulꝗ
theſaurus auri, gemmarum, aromatum, aliarumꝗ
ditiſſimarum mercium ac annui cenſus inde quotan=
nis in Hiſpaniam aduehitur, adiunxi doctiſsimi vi=
ri Gonzali Ferdinandi Ouiedi libellum quem ille
Indicæ hiſtoriæ generalis Summarij titulo inſcripſit,
eiuſdemꝗ illuſtriſsimi Caroli Imperatoris patris tui
nomini conſecrauit: Cæteraꝗ plurima ex recentio=
ribus ſcriptoribus excerpſi, que mihi in tam immen=
ſa rerum memorabiliū bibliotheca, præcipue adno=
tanda videbantur. Quæ, quanta et qualia ſunt, quā=
tiſꝗ paraſangis, omnium heroum ac Argonautarū
res

res geſtas toto terrarum orbe tantopere celebratas
ſuperent,næc mea ſequens præfacio vulgari ſermone
ad huius hiſtoriæ lectores populumcჳ Anglicū con-
ſcripta,ſatis prolixa oratione indicabit,adeo vt idem
hic repetere ſuperuacaneum ſit, minimecჳ neceſſari-
um, quandoquidem Anglica lingua tibi Sereniſſi-
ma Regina vernacula eſt,idemcჳ illuſtriſsimo Regi
cჳ tibi ſcriptum aut dictum exiſtimen, non ſolum cჳ
diuino vinculo vnum ſitis in carne vna, ſed etiam cჳ
eadē animi lenitate, humanitate, affabilitate,cæteriſ-
cჳ virtutibus, non minus animi moribus quā carnis
vinculo vnum ſitis. Sed necჳ hic opus eſt vt ego La-
tino ſermone veſtras virtutes. animi moderationem,
clementiam, religionem, pietatem, educationē, caſti-
tatem fœlicitatem, fortunas, opes, munificentiam,
victorias, imperia, ſtemmata, cæteracჳ huiuſmodi
multa enumerē,cum præſertim vir nobilis et doctus
Leonhardus Goretius Polonus de his omnibus decჳ
fœliciſsimo veſtro matrimonio, orationæ ſatis fuſa
tractauit,in qua nihil pretermiſit cჳ ad Celſitudinis
veſtræ et progenitorum veſtrorum gloriam virtute
partam, pertineat. Cæterū cum regiæ veſtre virtutes
nominiſcჳ ſplēdor ac regnorum amplitudo alias per
vniuerſa Chriſtiani orbis imperia ſatis nota ſint,niſi
forte ibi minime vbi maxime nota eſſe deberēt, nem-
pe in

pe in hoc Angliæ regno, ideo operepræcium et ren
omnibus bonis gratam, quodǫ mei eſt officij erg:
Celſitudines veſtras me facturum exiſtimaui, ſi hæ
noſtris (vt dixi) hominibus, noſtraǫ lingua ob ocu
los contemplanda propoſuero. Quod quam fœli
citer aut dextre a me factum ſit, aliorum eſto iudici.
um. Quam vero fideliter, ſyncere, ac animo in Ma
ieſtatis veſtras propenſo hoc idem aggreſſus ſum,
teſtis eſt mihi conſcientia mea in conſpectu illius qu
hominum corda et renes ſcrutatur. Macte igitur vir
tutis iſtius animi veſtri eſtote Sereniſsimi Principes
atǫ Diuino auxilio freti, pergite ea qua cœpiſtis ſi
ducia, huius deploratæ ac collapſæ reipub.noſtræ ſta
tum, priſtino decori reſtituere, id ǫ omnes a vo
bis expectant atǫ efflagitant, pollicentes inſuper vo
bis in eo negotio ſuam operam in nullo defuturam,
Ne terreat vos quorūdam canum latratus qui boni:
omnibus oblatrant, et tunc deſinent latrare cum de
ſinent viuere. Vulgatiſsimum ſemper fuit improbos
homines viris probis vel propter inuidiam vel prop:
ter diſsimilitudinem, ſolere latrare. Et tamen ille pro
bus ſemper habitus eſt, quem peruerſi maxime im
probauerint. Non eſt igitur curandum quid de no:
bis homunculi, ſed quid viri boni loquantur. Cogi
tate (Sereniſsimi Principes) ǫ magnanimitate ac ma
iorum

orum infignijs, aquilis et leonibus fimiles eftis. A=
quilæ natura eft, alta petere, et aduerfus folis radios,
n altum volare. Leonis proprium eft paccere fub=
ectis et debellare fuperbos. Generofus equus per
plateas incedens, canes vt animalcula imbella prætes
it non perturbatus. Virtus non exercita (inquit Se=
neca ad Neronem) paruam laudem meretur. Non
admodum magnificum fuerit mediocrem fortunam
probe adminiftrare: Sed tanta rerum omnium licen=
ia non abuti, hoc vero admirabile eft: Multo autem
admirabilius in iuuenili ac lubrica ætate cui accedat
ætas magiftra: hijs præfertim qui contumelia lacef=
cuntur, quæ alioqui homines vel placidifsimos folet
de gradu deijcere. Sed (vt fupra dixi) non eft hic
mei propofiti (Serenifsimi Principes) veftras laudes
pro meritis decantare, aut exprimere quo modo in
fummo rerum faftigio vos humiles præbuiftis, de
quare fufius in præfacione ad lectores tractaui. Iam
itaqʒ vt huic epiftolæ dedicatoriæ finem imponam,
rogo Serenifsimas Maieftates veftras vt has meas
lucubrationes in hijs autoribus vertendis, (quas ve=
ftro nomini confecraui) ea humanitate ac fauore fuf=
cipiatis, quibus omnes beneuolo animo ad vos ac=
cedentes, facile admittitis ac neminem reijcitis, Quē=
admodum enim qui pomarium aut vineam planta=

b.i.   uit

uit ac maturos inde fructus collegit, illi merito primi
tias ſoluit a quo prima ſemina primaſ㧝 arborum in
ſitiones habuit, ita et ego qui a maiorum veſtrorum
rebus geſtis primis ſumptis ſeminibus, hos qualeſ
cum 㧝 ftuctus ædidi, videor profecto mihi, debito
veſtro honore vos defraudaſſe, niſi eoſdē veſtro
nomini ac numini obtuliſſem. Deus. Opt.
Max. Celſitudines veſtras perpetuo ſer=
uat incolumes, faxit㧝 vt fœcunda
ſobolis propagine, ſumma㧝 pace
ac trāquillitate, huius regni ha=
benas ad Diuini nominis
gloriam, diu gu=
bernetis.

FINIS.

⁋ The table of the contentes of this booke.

Belyde the Decades (the table of whose contentes yow may reade in the ende of the booke) are conteyned furthermore in this boooke these thynges folowynge.

b. ii.　　　　A discourse

The Table,

Of

The Table.

The Table,

FINIS.

¶ The interpretacion of cer-teyne woordes.

¶ Continente (that is) the firme lande not inclosed with water, or no Jlande.
A Carauel or Caruel, a kynde of shyppes.
Hemispherium, the halfe globe of the earth and water.
Pesus, a ducate and a halfe.
Equinoctial, the line that diuideth the heauen and the earthe in the myddest betwene the two poles, in the which when the sonne commeth, the days & nyghtes are of equal length
Clime, is a portion of the worlde betwene north and south.
Paralleles, are lines whereby the sonne passynge causeth variation of tyme.
Gatti Mammoni, Monkeys.
Schoenus, is a space of. xl. furlonges.
Werst, is an Italian mile.
Colonie, an habitacion.

The Jndian language.

¶ Canoa, a boate or barke.
Caciqui, kynges or gouernours.
Zemes an Jdole.
Tupra, the deuyll.
Machana, a swordе.
Areitos, songes or balades.
Tona, the moone.
Tonatico, the soonne.
Buines, prestes.
Chiuy, a man.
Jra, a woman.
Boa, a house.
Cauni, golde.
Mapani, nothynge. &c.
¶ Note that the Jlande of Hispaniola, is nowe cauled San Domingo by reason of the chiefe citie so named. Also saynte Johns Jlande cauled sancti Johannis, or Burichena, is otherwyse cauled Boriquen.

Rycharde Eden to the reader.

He moſte famous ozatoure and learned Phylo:
copher Marcus Tullius Cicero, wzyteth, that
in all conſultations as touchynge owre beha:
uoure and ozder of lyupnge amonge men, it be:
houeth vs euer to beare in mynde howe farre
the dignitie of mans nature, excelleth the con:
dition of bzute beaſtes. Foz they, beinge ruled altogether by
ſence, delyte in nothynge but beaſtely appetites, whercunto
they runne headlonge as to theyz onely felicitie. But the
mynde of man, beinge of moze noble nature, is nuryſhed
with knowleage, and taketh pleaſure in diuiſynge oz excogi:
tatynge ſume honeſt thynge, whereby it not onely leaueth a:
monge men a memoze of his immoztall nature, but alſo en:
gendereth the lyke affection in other that delyte to ſee and
heare ſuch thinges as are commendable in theyz predeceſſours
And this ſurely thynke J to bee the cauſe that eyther the fa:
mous factes of woozthy men, oz ingenious inuentions of ex:
perte artificers, haue not onely nobilitate the autours and di:
uiſers of the ſame, oz ſuch to whom they haue byn dedicate,
but alſo that parte of theyz commendations haue redounded
to all ſuche as haue ſpente theyz tyme and taken peynes in il:
luſtratynge and ſettynge furthe theyz doynges. Foz who
ſhulde at this daye haue knowen Mauſolus the kynge of Ca:
ria, with his wyfe Artemiſia, oz theſe famous artificers, Sco:
pa, Bzyaces, Timotheus, Leochares, oz Pythis, if the won:
derfull and ſumptuous woozke of the ſepulcher whiche Arte:
miſia made foz kynge Mauſolus her huſband (beinge of ſuch
woozkemanſhyppe that it was accompted foz one of the mar:
ueyls of the woozlde) had not geuen vnto all theſe immoztall
fame, whereas neuertheleſſe it coulde not defende it ſelfe a:
geynſt thiniurie of tyme conſumynge all thynges. There re:
mayneth at this daye no token of the laboziouſ Tabernacle
whiche Moiſes buylded, oz of the renoumed and marueilous
Temple that was buylded in Dieruſalem by Salomon and re:
newed by Eſdias. ye ſhall the name of the excellente artifi:
cers Doliab and Beſeleel, and Hyzam the kynge of Tyrus,

Commendati
on of noble
factes.

Mauſolus.

Cunnynge ar:
tificers.

The Taber:
nacle of Moſ:
ſes.
The Temple
of Salomon.

Hyzam.

a.l.   lyue

lyue foz euer in the memozy of men. Furthermoze alſo, Salomon hym ſelfe, although he were many other wayes famous,
yet gaue he a greate parte of his glozy to that pzincely buyldynge. But certeynely the moſt trewe and permanent gloze,
pzocedeth of ſuch monumentes as bzynge ſume great and notable cōmoditie & pzofite to the lyfe of men, rather then of the
hugious heapes of ſtones of the Pyzamides of Egypt, wherin
is nought els to ſee but the fonde & barbarous oſtentation of
ſuperfluous riches: Oz of the Mazes cauled Labyzinthi, oz of
hozzyble great Images cauled Coloſſi, of knottes inexplica-
ble, of bzaſen caudzons of monſtrous byggeneſſe, of hauens
with echo ſeuen tymes reboundynge, and dyuers ſuche other
poztentous inuentions, the which as they do delite vs in conſiderynge the maruelous arte and witte of ſuche artificers as
diuiſed and made the ſame, ſo are they otherwyſe vnpzofita-
ble: And bzynge rather a fame to theyz inuentoures, then
trewe gloze. Perillus was famous by diuiſynge his bzaſen
bulle: yet ſo, that it had byn better foz hym to haue byn obſcure and vnknowen. They haue therefoze deſerued moze
trewe commendation whiche in buyldynge of cities, townes,
foztreſſes, bzidges, cundites, hauens, ſhyppes, and ſuche o-
ther, haue ſo ioyned magnificence with pzofecte, that bothe
may remaine foz an eternal teſtimonie of abſolute gloze, whoſe
perfection extendeth to the gratifynge of vniuerſal mankind
as farre as mans moztalitie wyll permit. The whiche thinge
whyle I conſider, and caule to memozie howe Cicero defineth
trewe gloze to bee a fame of many and greate deſertes eyther
towarde owre citizens, owre countrey, oz towarde all man
kynde, and the ſame to bee of ſuch excellencie that the owlde
poetes foz ſume effecte fayned it to bee the ſweete Ambzoſia
and Nectar wherwith the goddes are fedde, and that of ſuch
foze that who ſo may dzynke therof, ſhal alſo become a god,
(that is to ſay inmoztall and happy) mee thynke verely that
(yf man maye be a god to men as holy ſcripture ſpeaketh of
Moiſes and other) the kynges of Spayne of late dayes (if I
may ſpeake it without offence of other) may ſo much the moze
foz theyz iuſt deſertes and good foztune be compared to thoſe
goddes made of men (whom the antiquitie cauled Heroes and
foz theyz manyfolde benefites to man kynde honoured theym
with diuine honoure) as theyz famous factes ſo farre excell al
other

other, as I dare not speake to such as haue not yet harde oz
redde of the same, least the greatnesse therof shulde at the first
bzunte so muche astonyshe the reader that he myght gene the
lesse credite to the autoure of this booke, who neuerthelesse
hath moste faythfully wzytten this hystozye of suche thynges
wherof he hath seene a greate parte him selfe (as being by the
moste catholyke and puissaunt kynge Ferdinando appoynted
a commissionarie in thaffayzes of India) and gathered the residewe partly by infozmation and partly out of the wzytinges
of such as haue byn (as Wyrgyll wzyteth of Aeneas, *Et quorum*
pars magna fui) that is, doers and parte of such thynges as are
conteyned in the hystozie: as Gouernours, Lieutenauntes,
Capitaynes, Admirals, and Pylottes, who by theyz painefull
trauayles and pzowes, haue not onely subdued these landes
and seas, but haue also with lyke diligence commytted thozder therof to wzytinge: And not this onely, but foz the better
tryall of the trewth herein, haue and yet doo in maner dayly
sende from thense into Spayne such monumentes as are most
certeyne testimonies of theyz doynge, as yow may reade in dyuers places in this boke. This newe wozlde is nowe so much
frequented, the Ocean nowe so well knowen, and the commodities so greate, that the kynge erected a house in the citie of
Siuile (cauled the house of the contractes of India) perteynynge onely to thaffayzes of the Ocean, to the which al such
resozte foz necessaries as attempte anye vyage to this newe
wozlde, and lykewyse at theyz returne make theyz accompte
to the counsayle foz the Indies foz the golde and suche other
thynges as they bzynge from thense. It is therefoze apparent that the heroicall factes of the Spaniardes of these days,
deserue so greate pzayse that thautour of this booke (beinge
no Spanyarde) doth woozthely extolle theyz doynge aboue
the famous actes of Hercules and Saturnus and such other
which foz theyz glozious and vertuous enterpzyses were accoumpted as goddes amonge men. And surely if great Alexander and the Romans which haue rather obteyn.d then deserued immoztall fame amonge men foz theyz bluddye victories onely foz theyz owne glozy and amplifyinge theyz empire
obteyned by slawghter of innocentes and kepte by violence,
haue byn magnified foz theyz doinges, howe much moze then
shal we thynke these men woozthy iust commendations which

The certentie
of this hystory

The house of
the contractes
of India.

The counsayl
foz the Indies

The heroicall
factes of the
Spanyardes.

Great Alexan-
der.

The Spany-
ardes warres
in the Indies.

in theyr mercyfull warres ageynst these naked people haue so vsed them selues towarde them in exchaungynge of benefites for victorie, that greater commoditie hath therof ensewed to the vanquisshed then the victourers. They haue taken no thynge from them but such as they them selues were wel wyl lynge to departe with, and accoumpted as superfluities, as golde, perles, precious stones and such other: for the which they recompensed theym with suche thynges as they muche more esteemed. But sum wyll say, they possesse and inhabyte theyr regions and vse theym as bondemen and tributaries, where before they were free. They inhabite theyr regions in deede: yet so, that by theyr diligence and better manurynge the same, they maye nowe better susteyne both, then one before. Theyr bondage is suche as is much rather to be desired then theyr former libertie which was to the cruell Canibales rather a horrible licenciousnesse then a libertie, and to the innocent so terrible a bondage, that in the myddest of theyr fere full idlenesse, they were euer in daunger to be a pray to those manhuntynge woolues. But nowe thanked be God, by the manhodde and pollicie of the Spanyardes, this deuelysshe generation is so consumed, partely by the slaughter of suche as coulde by no meanes be brought to ciuilitie, and partly by reseruynge such as were ouercome in the warres, and conuer tynge them to a better mynde, that the prophecie may herein bee fulfylled that the woolfe and the lambe shall feede toge ther, and the wylde fieldes with the vale of Achor, shalbe the folde of the heard of gods people. Moises as the minister of the lawe of wrath and bondage geuen in fyer & tempestes, was commaunded in his warres to saue neyther man, woman, nor chylde, and yet brought no commoditie to the nations whom he ouercame and possessed theyr landes. But the Spaniardes as the mynisters of grace and libertie, brought vnto these newe gentyles the victorie of Chrystes death wherby they be inge subdued with the worldely sworde, are nowe made free from the bondage of Sathans tyrannie, by the myghty poure of this triumphante victourer, whom (as sayth the prophet) god hath ordeyned to be a lyght to the gentyles, to open the eyes of the blynde, and to delyuer the bounde owt of pryson and captiuitie. What other men do phantasie herein, I can not tell: but sure I am, that lyke as the slowe and brutysshe wyttes

Marginal notes:

The benefites that the Indiens haue receaued by the Spanyardes.

Lybertie.

The Canibales,

Fearful idlenesse.

Isai. 65.

The warres of Moises.

The Indians subdued to the fayth.

Isai. 42.

The preface to the reader.

wyttes, foz the felenderneffe of theyz capacitie and effeminate hartes, do neuer oz feldome lyfte vp theyz myndes to the contemplation of goddes wozkes and maieftie of nature, but lyke bzute beaftes lookynge euer downewarde, thynke the wozlde to be in maner no bygger then theyz owne dungehylles oz cagies, lyttle paffynge whether the Chzyftian fayth do fpzeade thzough the wozlde, oz bee dzyuen to one cozner: Euen fo al good wyttes and honeft natures (J doubte not) wyl not onely reioyce to fee the kyngedome of God to bee fo farre enlarged vppon the face of the earthe, to the confufion of the deupll and the Turkyffhe Antichzyfte, but alfo do the vttermoft of theyz poure to further the fame. Foz furely, as Gonfalus Ouiedus wzyteth to the Emperours maieftie in his hyftozie of the Wefte Jndies, that he thynketh hym no trewe Spanyarde whiche reioyceth not in the good foztune of theyz kynges by whofe ayde and godly zeale this myghtie poztion of the wozlde hath byn added to the flocke of Chzyftes congregation, Euen fo do J thinke them no trewe Chzyftian men that do not reioyce with the Angels of heauen foz the deliuerie of thefe owre bzootherne, owre fleffhe, and owre bones from the handes of owre commune enemie the oulde ferpente who hath fo longe had them in hys poffeffion, vntyll the fulneffe of the gentyles be accomplyffhed accozdynge to the time pzefinite by hym, who vnto the yeare after his incarnation. M. CCCC. lxxxxii. hath fuffered the greate ferpente of the fea Leuiathan, to haue fuche dominion in the Ocean and to cafte fuch myftes in the eyes of men, that fence the creation of the wozlde vntyll the yeare befoze named, there hath byn no paffage from owr knowen partes of the wozld to thefe newe landes, wheras nowe the fame are mofte certeynely knowen to be not paft. xxx. dayes faylynge from Spayne. Neyther yet had the church of Europe any knowleage of the myghtie Chzyftian Empire of Pzeciofus Johannes, otherwyfe cauled Pzefbyter Johannes, Emperour of many Chzyftian nations in Æthiope, vntyll the yeare of Chzyfte. M. CCCC. xxxiii. as largely appeareth in the nauigations of the Poztugales, and efpecially in the booke of Damianus a Goes, wzytten to the byffhop of Rome, Paule the thyzde of that name, of the fayth and religion of the Æthiopians which they haue hadde fence the tyme of the Apoftles, A thynge certes moft woonderfull

The contemplation of gods wozkes.

The Chzyftian Empire enlarged.

The conuercion of the gentyles.

Leuiathan.

Pzefter John the Chzyftian Emperour of Ethiope.

derfull, and suche, that yf the same were not hydde hetherto by gods vnsercheable prouidence, J can not but thynke much negligence or ignorance in owr forefathers and predicessours vntyll the dayes of the ryght noble, prudent, and Catholike

Don Ferdinando kynge of Aragon.

kynge of Aragon Don Ferdinando grandfather to Themperours maiestie by his eldest dowghter, & to the queenes hyghnesse by his seconde dowghter the most vertuous lady Queene Catherine her graces moother : J prince doubteleffe of suche nobilitie, prowes, magnificence, and all other vertues commendable in a prince, that who so shall indifferently way all his doinges and good succeffe in all his affayles, comparinge the same to thenterprifes and doinges atchyued by suche famous princes in whome the Greekes and Romans haue so greatcly gloryed, maye with one eye perceaue not onely howe farre his noble factes do surmount theyrs, but also wel confyder what noble braunches of iffhewe were lyke to sprynge owt of so wooɾthy a stocke. And suerly if sence the begynning

The fauour of god knowen by his benefites.

of the woɾlde, the fauour of god toward men hath byn knowen by such benefites and bleffynges as he hath geuen to men, it seemeth to me that in maner (onely Chryste excepted) there neuer lyued man to whom god hath geuen greater benefites and shewed moɾe fauoure.   Great doubteleffe was the fauour and mercie that god shewed vnto Noe, by whom he saued the remanent of mankynde beinge but fewe in number. But much

What god hath wɾought by kynge Ferdinando.

greater was the grace which he shewed to kynge Ferdinando vnder whom and by whose meanes he saued not onely the bodies but also the soules of innumerable millions of men inhabytynge a great part of the woɾlde heretofoɾe vnknowen and dɾowned in the deluge of erroure. What shulde J here speake

Abɾaham.

of Abɾaham the father of fayth whose proɱyses were great, and he cauled the frende of god ? Dyd he oɾ his posteritie see

Spirituall Israell.

Jsraell increase to such multitudes and nations as kyng Ferdinandos posteritie may see thincrease of this spirituall Jsraell vnto whome as a seconde Abɾaham he was the father of

Moises.

fayth ? Moises was so great in the syght of god that he difclosed vnto hym his secreate name, and miraculously caused a coɾner of the sea to open at his prayer.   But howe greater a myɾacle was it that he opened vnto the nauie of Don Ferdinando the greate Ocean thowght befoɾe that tyme to bee without ende, where neuertheleffe he and his posteritie the

kynges

The preface to the reader.

kynges of Spayne haue nowe planted a newe Israell muche greater then that whiche Moises ledde throughe the red sea. It were here superfluous to speake of Dauid whom Godds founde a man accordynge to his hartes desyre: and yet maye it be doubted whether his plages and scourges were greater then his benefites? His sonne Salomon for al his inconstant and wauerynge wysedome and his great ryches obteyned by his nauigations to Ophir, yet was there at this tyme no knowleage of Antipodes, neyther dydde any of his shyppes sayle about the hole worlde, perce the Ocean, and trauerse the Equinoctial lyne to thinferiour hemispherie or halfe globe of the earthe and sea as dyd the famous shyppe Uictoria sent furth by Themperours maiestie. A thyng doubtlesse so strange and marueylous that as the lyke was neuer done before, so is it perhaps neuer lyke to be done agepne: so farre haue the nauigations of the Spanyardes excelled the vyage of Jason and the *Argonautes* to the region of Colchos, or all that euer were before. And although in the booke of kynges and Paralipomenon it bee hyperbolically wrytten that in the dayes of Salomon golde & syluer were in Hierusalé in maner as plentiful as stones, & that his seruantes broughtt from Ophir foure hundreth & fiftie talentes of gold, yet do we not reade that any of his shyppes were so laden with golde that they soonke, as dyd a shyppe of kynge Ferdinandos as yow maye reade in the last booke of the fyrste Decade. Neyther was the dominion of Salomon extended from the ryuer of Euphrates to the lande of the Philistians and thextreme confines of Egypte to be compared with the large Empire whiche the kynges of Spayne haue in the west Judies: Nor his ryches of golde to be thought much in respect of that which hath byn broughtt from thense into Spayne as shall playnely appere to al suche as wyll seeke to knowe the truth hereof. But to let passe to speake any further of the myracles which god hath wrought by the handes of this noble prince in this newe world among these newe gentyles. Is it not well knowen to all the world what a defence and brazen wall he hath byn to all Chrystendome in that he hath quite dryuen out of Spayne the Moores or Sarasens and Jewes which so many hundreth yeares possessed a greate parte of Spayne to no smaule daungioure of the hole Christian Empire, and yet coulde neuer before bee clean

Dauid.

Salomon.

Ophir. Antipodes.

The nauigation rounde about the worlde.

The dominion of Salomon. Paral. 9.

The Judies.

The warres of kynge Ferdinando agaynst the Sarasens.

cleane vanquyſſhed vntyll the dayes of this noble and Catho
lyke prince ſo named for his warres ageynſte the infidelles,
whom God rayſed for a Capitayne of his people as an other
Gedion vnder whoſe banner they myght ouercome theyr enemies and pourge his vineyarde from ſuche wycked weedes.
The which thynge doubtelesſe may ſeeme ſo much the greater
and more difficulte, foraſmuch as in the myddeſt of the chiefe
heate of his chargeable warres ageynſte the Moozes of Gra-
nada, he euen then and at the ſame tyme ſente furth ſhyppes

The conqueſte
of the Indies

for the conqueſtynge of the Indies, as thowgh he and the na
tion of the Spanyardes had byn appoynted by god eyther to
ſubdue the enemies of the fayth or to bringe theym to Chriſtes
religion. The ſelfe ſame kynge Ferdinando alſo abowte the
yeare of Chriſt. 1503. ſent a nauie of ſhyppes into Italy, where

The conqueſte
of Naples.

they vanquyſſhed, chaſed, and ſlewe the Frenchemen, and
recouered the kyngedome of Naples with all the dominions
belongynge thereunto. By which noble victory, his ſucceſſion and poſteritie as themperours maieſtie and nowe his ſonne
the kynge owre maſter and ſoueraigne lorde haue euer ſence
enioyed thinheritaunce of the ſame as of antiquitie by iuſt and
ryght tytle dewe to them and theyr predeceſſours. And as it
is the nature of god not only to ſhewe his loue and fauour to
ſuch as haue pleaſed hym, but alſo to poure furth the plentie
of his grace vppon theyr ſucceſſion from generation to gene-

The Empe-
rours maieſtie

ration, ſo hath he with lyke fecilitie proſpered the reigne of
Themperours maieſtie who by his wiſdome and prowes hath
not onely pollitikly gouerned, but alſo augmented and inlar-
ged ſuch dominions as fel to hym by diſcente of inheritaunce.
What ſhuld I ſpeake of his warres and conqueſtes in India,
in Aphrike, in Italie, in Fraunce, in Germanie, and in Flaun
ders : all the which to be declared accordyngely wolde rather
require hole volumes then fewe ſheetes of paper. yet hath one
in fewe woordes effectually expreſſed his dominions and con
queſtes in theſe verſes folowynge.

The preface to the reader.

Imp iger expauit rapidas tranfire per vndas
  Oceani Alcides: continuitᴢ gradum.
Maximus at Cæfar, PLVS VLTRA tendere curfum
  Aufus, et ignotis eft dare iura locis.
Et domita aurifera nunc victor gente reuerfus,
  Cætera fub fceptro ponat vt ipfe fuo.
Nam pater omnipotens vt famam terminet aftris
  Iufsit, et imperium fineat Oceano.

**⊂ An other alfo bꝛeefely hath declared the
  fame in thefe verfes.**

Confortem Imperij voluit quia Iuppiter orbis,
  Aftra Deo cedunt, Carole terra tibi.

And certes who fo well confidereth the pꝛogenie of kynges
that in fo ſhoꝛte a time haue linially defcended from Don Fer
dinando, and howe many kyngedomes they poffeſſe, may fee
that God hath fulfylled in hym alfo the pꝛomifes and bleffynges of Abꝛaham, as to make hym the father of many nati ***Gen. 17.***
ons, and his feede to growe great vpon the earth : Alfo that
many kynges ſhulde come furth of his loynes, and to make a
perpetuall league and conuenaunt with hym and his pofteritie to bee theyꝛ god foꝛ euer. And here to omytte to fpeake of
other : Was there euer better hope oꝛ moꝛe likenes then now,
that thefe blefſynges and pꝛomfes of god ſhulde continewe
in this pꝛincely pꝛogenie, fyth the vertues and felicitie of thē
al doo fo ſhyne and floꝛiſhe in owr noble and gracious pꝛince ***The kinges***
kynge Phylyppe, to whom euen in his youth his father (oc ***maieftie.***
cupied in the warres of Italye and Aphꝛike) commytted the
hole gouernaunce of the kyngedomes of Spayne and the Indies. Of his behauour in Englande, his enemies (which canker, vertue neuer lacked) They I fay (if any fuch yet remaine)
haue greateſt caufe to repoꝛte well : ye fo well, that yf his nab.i.   tural

The preface to the reader.

turall clemencie were not greater then was theyr vnnaturall indignation they knowe them selues what myght haue folowed. The properties of fooles and wyse men are declared in these olde verses.

Quid stulti proprium ? Non posse et velle nocere.

Quid sapientis opus : Non velle et posse nocere.

That is to say : What is the propertie of a foole ? To wyl to doo hurte and can not. What is the woorke of a wyse man ? Not to wyll to hurte though he may. But whether he hath lacked poure or wyll, it is knowen to barbers and blere eyde men. Who lamented theyr folly more then he ? Who more humbly admytted theyr sutes and supplications ? ye who obteyned theyr pardon but he ? Beynge a Lion he behaued hym selfe as a lambe, and strooke not his enemie hauynge the swoorde in his hande. Stoope Englande stoope, and learne to knowe thy lorde and master, as horses and other brute beastes are taught to doo. Be not indocible lyke Tygers and Dragons, and such other monsters noyous to man kynde. God by the mouth of Isaias the prophet reproueth the Israelites that they knewe not so well theyr dewtie towarde hym as dyd the brute beastes : he mangiers of theyr masters. The ore and the asse (sayth he) knoweth the mangier of theyr master, but Israell knoweth not me. For shame let vs not be woorse then oxen and asses, & lyke vnto horses and mules in whom is no vnderstandynge. But O vnthankeful! Englande and voyde of honest shame: Who hath geuen the the face of a hoore and toonge of a serpent withowt shame to speake venemous woordes in secreate agaynst the annoynted of god. O paynted hoore that hast Christe in thy mouth and the deuyl in thy harte. Hath not the pocks of thy licentiousnesse brusse furth in maner to thyne owne destruction. Howe longe wylt thou nuryshe in thy bosome that serpente whose nature is to deuoure her moother ? Take a vomyte in tyme least thy disease become vncurable. What neede I rehearse vnto the thy manyfolde infirmities and deformities whiche thou arte faulen into by thyne owne owtragiousnesse ? If the greefes of them bee to thee vnsensible by reason of thy feeblenesse and longe sickenes, take vnto the that glasse wherin thou glozyest with the Iewe and thynkest that thou seest al thynges and canst iudge all mysteries, Looke I say in that pure glasse and be-

Apostrophe to Englande.

Isai. i.

holde thy owne deformities, which thou canste not oz wylte
not feele. I feare greatly that if thou looke therein diligently
and looke euen throughe thy selfe, then wylte abhozre thy
selfe to see howe many monsters lye hid in the vnder the shape
of man. There is euen nowe great talke of them in the mouthes **Monstrous byzthes.**
of all men that thou hast of late yeares brought furthe many
monsters and straunge byzthes, wherof dyuers men make dyuers interpretacions moze monstrous then the monsters theim
selues. But shall I bzeefely and simply declare vnto thee the **The significa- tions of mon- strus byzthes.**
signification of thy monsters? Fyzst then consyder that they
are monsters of mankynde and not of other beastes. Secunda-
rlp marke well that in them al, the headde is perfect, so that
the monstrositie groweth owt of the body, although not owt
of the hole body but certeyne partes therof. But not to go to
farre. Consyder agayne that disozder of the partes is a defoz-
mitie to the hole. One hath well interpzeted that such mon- **The deformitie of monstrous myndes.**
strous byzthes signifie the monstreus and defozmed myndes
of the people myshapened with phantastical opinions, disso-
lute lyuynge, licencious talke, and such other vicious beha-
uoures which monstrously defozme the myndes of men in the
syght of god who by suche signes dooth certifie vs in what
similitude we appere befoze hym, & thereby gyueth vs admo-
nition to amende befoze the day of his wzath and vengeance.
What defozmed beastes are moze monstrous then lyinge, rebellion, strife, contention, pziuie malice, slaunderynge, mutte-
rynge, conspiraces, and such other deuilpshe imaginations.
But O Englande whyle tyme is gyuen thee, circumcise thy
harte. But to onely thy good wyll, and thou mayste fynde
grace and fauoure to recouer thyne aunciente bewtie whiche
hath so longe byn defaced. Thou haste nowe a kynge and **The kyng and Queene.**
queene that desyze thee to remember thy dewtie, and holde
theyz armes abzode to embzace thee yf thou wylt dzawe nere
vnto them. They are sozy to occupie the whyppe yf thou migh-
test otherwyse bee bzought to obedience. But yf thou take
pleasure to persist in frowarde stoobbernesse, knowe thou that
they are Lyons whelpes and conquerours of monsters wherof thou hast had suche experience, that proudely trustynge in
thyne owne strengthe, and attemptynge lyke an other Nem-
roth to buylde a newe towze of confusion, the woozkes of thy
giantes were miraculously ouerthzowne by a woman who de-
                    b.ii.   liuered

The preface to the reader.

liuered thee from that captiuitie, whereby thou oughtesse to
knowe the daungiour thou wass in, and bee thankefull to th
deliuerer. Beware therefore leasse whyle thou contemne th
praceable princes that god hath sent che, thou bee lyke vnto
Æsopes frogges to whő for theyr vnquietnesse, Jupiter sen
a heaton to picke them in the hedes. Consider what benefite
thau mayss recceaue at theyr handes if thou doo thy dewtie to
warde them. Consyder ageyne that as they are able, so ma
thy gentelnesse make them wyllynge to recompense the same
Stoppe thyne eares from vayne fables as from the inchaun
tynge Mermaydes. For as manye speake of Robbyn Hood
and of his bowe that neuer shot therin, so doo fooles prate o
such thynges as they knowe not. But O god? what phanta
sies are nowe in the heades of men? Howe redy they are to in
uent lyes and tales? and of howe smaul sparkes they kyndle
greate flames? Summe are so curious to fynde faute in other
that for lacke of iust matter woorthy reproche in them whon

How curious
summe are to
fynde fauts in
other.

they despre to depraue, they speake euyll of theyr parentes
kynred of whom they knowe as lyttle. And not so satiffyed
they dispise and with lyinge dispraayse theyr hole nation an
countrey. Ye sum take such pleasure herein, that if they ca
fynde nought els to displaayse, they wyll fynde faute in such
as they fauour not, bycause they weare not theyr apparell a
they doo, or perhappes are not so effeminate as they, or eat
not as they eate, or fight not as they fyght, so parciall is th
iudgement of fooles in theyr owne rudenesse, thynkyng then

Lyes Imagi
ned.

selues the better for dispraysynge of other. Spayne is a beg
gerly countrey sayth one: Themperour is but poore sayth an
other: He is deade sayth an other: The Indies haue rebelle
sayth an other, and eyther there commeth no more golde from
thence, or there is no more founde nowe: with suche other
false and licentious talke diuised by vnquiet braines in whos
heades the hammers of sedition sease not to forge iugens o
iniquitie. If I shulde here answere to all these querels parti
cularly and as the woorthynesse of the thynge requireth,
myght fynde matter sufficient to make a volume of iuste quan
tiric and perhappes be tedious to summe. Yet not to passe o
uer so great a matter vntouched, and partely to stoppe th

Commendati=
ons of Spain

mouthes of suche impudente lyers, I haue thought good te
speake sumwhat hereof, Fyrst therefore to speake of Spayne
an

The preface to the reader.

by the teſtimonie of oulde autours to declare the commoditꝛes therof: Plinie a graue & faythful autour, in the laſt boke laſt chapiture of his natural hiſtoꝛy greatly commendynge, gealy aboue al other contreys, giueth the ſecond pꝛayſe vnto Spaine, aſwel foꝛ al ſuch thynges as in maner the heuen can geue & the earth bꝛynge furth foꝛ the commoditie of this lyfe, as alſo foꝛ the excellente wittes of men & Ciuile gouernaunce. Alſo Diodoꝛus Siculus in the ſixt booke of his Bibliotheca ſpeakynge of Spayne (cauled of the Greekes Iberia) wꝛiteth that when in the mountaines named Pyꝛinei thinhabitantes **Ryche ſyluer mynes in Spayne.** burnte vp the wooddes, there ranne owt of the mountaynes as it were dyuers ſtreames of pure ſyluer molten by the heate of the fyꝛe. But the eſtimation and pꝛice of ſyluer beinge at thoſe dayes to them vnknowen, the Phenician marchauntes bought the ſame of them foꝛ thynges of ſmaule value: And carynge it into Grecia, Aſia, and other countreys, got great ꝛycheſſe therby. Foꝛ the deſyꝛe of gaynes (ſayth he) ſo greatly moued the marchauntes, that when moꝛe ſyluer remayned then myght lade theyꝛ ſhyppes, they tooke the leade frome theyꝛ ankers, and put ſyluer in the place therof. The Phenices by this gaynes beinge made very ryche, dyd aſſigne many colonie ꝛ both in Sicilie and the Ilandes there abowt, and alſo in Libya, Sardinia, and Iberia. But after many yeares when the Iberians (that is the Spaniardes) knewe the pꝛice of ſyluer, and applyed them ſelues to the ſeckynge of metals, and founde great plentie of ſyluer, they obteyned greate ryches therby foꝛaſmuch as in maner al that earth of the mountaynes is ſo replenyſſhed with ſyluer that it is a marueylous thynge to conſyder the nature of the region and the continual laboure of the wooꝛkemen in thoſe mynes. Lykewyſe when afterwarde the Romans ſubdued the Iberians, the Italians **The Romans inriched by the ſyluer of Spayne.** which foꝛ the deſyꝛe of gaynes ſearched thoſe metals, gotte great rycheſſe by the ſame. Foꝛ they deputed to that laboure a multitude of bowght ſeruauntes, whiche ſearchynge the vaynes of metals in dyuers places, and peꝛcyng the earth dyuers wayes foꝛ the ſpace of many furlonges, bꝛowght furthe great plentie of golde and ſyluer. But the rycheſſe of theſe mynes was fyꝛſt founde at ſuch tyme as the Carthaginenſes **The Carthaginenſes ... of Spayn.** (the enemies of the Romane Empire) had the Iberians in ſubjection: which was the cauſe that theyꝛ poure afterwarde increaſed

creafed. Fo2, with monye hyzinge the beft and mofte expert
fouldiers, they kepte greuous warres ageynft they2 enemies
And not vfynge the ayde eyther of they2 owne fouldiers o2
they2 affociates, they were a terrour to the Romanes, Sici
lians, and Libyans, whom they b2owgh: into great daungi
our by reafon they paffed them al in abundaunce of golde and
fyluer. With better fo2tune therefo2e, and greater hope of
gayne are ryche metals fought in Spayne, the goodneffe of
whofe foyle yeldeth cloddes of earth conteynynge much golde
and fyluer. And thefe be the very wo2des of Disdo2us Sicu
lus, which the later w2yters doo alfo confirme. Fo2 Iulius
Solinus in his Polyhifto2, compareth Spayne to the beft con
treys in plentie of grayne, byrtaples, oyle, fyluer, golde, and
Iron. Likewyfe Strabo, Statius, and Claudius, do no leffe
commende it. It were to longe here to fpeake of the greate
plentie of fine woolles lyttle inferiour vnto owrs: alfo abun
daunce of fugar, vines, pome granates, limondes, and o2an
gies in fuch plentie that they fuffice not only Spayne, but al
fo in maner all Europe: whereas the apples and crabbes of
Englande are fcarfely able to ferue it felfe. And althowgh
here fumme wyll obiecte, that they lacke co2ne, woodde, and
certeyne other thynges, yet are they2 commodities fo greate
otherwyfe, that al fuch thynges are b2owght them owt of o2
ther countreys fo2 they2 wares: and that in fuch plentie, that
they are there better chepe then euer they were in Englande
fince the figne of the fteeple the poo2e mans Inne was pulled
downe in all places. Summe fo2 lacke of other matter, fynde
greate faute that in trauaylynge in Spayne, men fhalbe fer
ued with halfe a henne, and go to the cookes fo2 they2 meate
and to the tauerne fo2 they2 d2ynke. And what then I pray
yow? What inconuenience enfueth hereof? Is it not better
fo to doo then to pay th2yfe fo2 one thinge as is the maner te
doo in fumme of owre Innes and in tauernes where all that
eate rofte meate are beaten with the fpitte, as where they that
of late in Barthelmewe fayre payde fo2tie pence fo2 a pygge
where the good man of the houfe was not a fhamed to make
his vaunte that he had made foure fhyllynges of a pygge, and
had in one day taken foure pounde fo2 pygges. But if I fhuld
here particularly and at large declare howe Englande is in
fewe yeares decayed and impoueryffhed, and howe on the
contra

The commodities of Spain

The fygne of the fteeple.

*nd was
decd,
of infi*

The preface to the reader.

contrary parte Spayne is inryched, I shulde perhappes dis-
please moze in descrybyng the myserie of the one, then please
other in expressynge the glozyThynge state of the other, which
by all reason is lyke dayly to increase, aswell foz the great rychesse that are yearely bzowght thyther from the Indies, as
also foz the ryche sylver mynes that are founde of late in
Spayne in the countrey of Asturia as I was credably infozmed by the wozthy and lerned gentelman Augustinus de Ce-
catta, Contadoz (that is) the auditour of the kynges myntes
who had longe befoze byn surveyoure of the golde mynes of
Peru, and bzowght from thense and from Rio de Plata. xiii.
thousand pounde weyght of sylver which was coyned to the
kinges vse in the towze of London where never so much hath
byn seene at once as suche as have byn owlde officers in the
mynte doo affirme. What shulde I heare speake of the golde
which themperours maiestie receaueth frome all the Indies,
wheras onely in the two meltynge shoppes of the gold mines
of the Ilande of Hispaniola, is molten yearely thzee hundzeth thousande pounde weyght of. viii. vnces to the pound,
wherof the fyfte parte is dewe vnto hym, whiche amounteth
to thzee scoze thousande weyght yearely. yet doo I not here
speake of the golde mines of the other Ilandes and the firme
lande reachynge. viii. thousande myles from the nozth to the
south: Neyther of the ryche Ilandes of the south sea cauled
Mare del Sur, where the kynge of one lyttle Ilande named
Tararequi, Margaritea, oz de las Perlas, lying in the goulfe
of Saynt Michael, payeth yearely foz his tribute a hundzeth
pounde weight of perles: Neyther yet of the fyfte parte of o-
ther thynges, as pzecious stones, bzasile, gossampine cotton,
spices, and dyvers other thynges, wheras also the ryche I-
landes cauled the Maluchas perteyne to the inheritaunce of
Castile, althowgh the kynge of Poztugale enioy them foz certeyne yeares by composition. But the Indies have rebelled
(say they) and there commeth no moze golde from thense. But
what if summe of them have rebelled? dooth it therby felowe
that there commeth no moze gold from the other that lyve vnder obedience? But if thou wylte say that they have al rebelled at once, thou must pzoue that thou sayest eyther by hystorie oz wytnesse of such as know the truth herof, as I (having
made diligent searche foz the same) am able to pzoue the contrarie,

Sylver mines
founde of late
in Spayne.

Sylver
bzowght from
Peru into
Englande.

Thèperours
reuenues from
the Indies.

The Ilandes
of the Southe
sea.

The Ilandes
of Maluca.

trarie, and that suche talke is onely imagined by busie head
des. Ageyne: what if they haue rebelled in summe prouin
ces? dooth it folowe that they maye not ageyne be browgh
vnder subiection as were oftentymes the prouinces of the Ro
manes and as were in owre dayes dyuers countreys of Eng
lande whiche haue byn sore afflicted with that plage. Bu
whether the sandes of the ryuers and the mountaynes of th
Indies bee so emptied with golde that no more can be found
there, I thinke it here superfluous to answere to this obiecti
on, forasmuch as it is hereafter confuted in the booke of me
tals where yow shall fynde by experience that metals grow
and increase, and that after certeyne yeares, suche owlde ca
ues of the mynes as haue byn dygged, are ageyne replenys
shed with vre: Also that the sprynges of suche mountaynes
turnynge theyr course and breakynge furth in other places
brynge with them greate plentie of such golden sande as is
founde in the ryuers into the which they faule. What impu
dencie is it therfore with woordes of reproche to caule hym
poore whose poure is so greate, his treasure so infinite, and
his doinges so chargeable, that I beleeue that when so eue
it please almyghtie God to caule hym frome this lyfe to th
greate domage of all Chrystendome, it shalbe harde to fynd
an other that shall in all poyntes bee so well able to supply
that roome and mayntayne thimperiall dignitie. Let al hone
natures therfore learne to speake well of prynces accordyng
to the sentence De *Principibus nil nisi bonum*, forasmuch as they ar
the ministers of god who hath theyr hartes in his hande an
ruleth the same as seemeth beste vnto hym. For there is n
poure neythar good nor badde, but of god: and he that resp
steth or speaketh euyll of the poure, resisteth and speaketh
euyll of god. Thou shalt not speake euyll of the prynce or ru
ler of thy people saith saint Paule.

The nauiga
tions of the
Spanyardes
But wheras nowe by the poure of Neptunus (I wot ne
with what wynde) I haue byn dryuen thus farre from my na
uigations, I haue thought good to turne my sayles and t
folowe the ordinarie course which I beganne, and by thex
emple of this woorthy capitayne kynge Ferdinando, encou
rage al other to theyr poure to attempte the lyke vyages: A
touchynge the which in fewe woordes to declare my oppny
on, if any man shulde aske me what I thynke these thinge
wyl

wyll growe to in tyme, J wyll anſwere as dooth the autour
of this booke, that when J conſyder howe farre owre poſſeſ
ſitie ſhall ſee the Chriſtian religion enlarged, J am not able
with tounge oʒ penne to expreſſe what J conceaue hereof in
my mynd. yet one thyng J ſee which enforceth me to ſpeake
lament, that the harueſt is of great & the woʒkemen ſo few.
the Spanyardes haue ſhewed a good exemple to all Chriſtiꝰ
a nations to folowe. But as god is great and woonderfull
all his woozkes, ſo beſyde the poʒtion of lande perteynyng
the Spanyardes (beinge eyght tymes bygger then Jtalye
yowe maye reade in the laſte booke of the ſeconde Decade)
d beſide that which perteineth to the Poʒtugales, there yet
mayneth an other poʒtion of that mayne lande reachynge
warde the noʒtheaſt, thought to be as large as the other,
d not yet knowen but only by the ſea coaſtes, neyther inhaꝛ
ted by any Chriſtian men : whereas neuertheleſſe (as wʒyꝛ
th Gemma Phʒiſius)in this lande there are many fayʒe and
utefull regions, hygh mountaynes, andfayʒe ryuers, with
undaunce of golde and dyuers kyndes of beaſtes.   Alſo
ties and towres ſo wel buylded and people of ſuch ciuilitie,
at this parte of the woʒlde ſeemeth lyttle inferiour to owre
urope,if thinhabitauntes had receaued owre religion. They
e wyttie people and refuſe not barterynge with ſtraungers.
theſe regiōs are cauled Terra Floʒida and Regio Baccaleaꝛ
m oʒ Bacchallaos of the which yow may reade ſumwhat in
his booke in the vyage of the woozthy owlde man yet lyuing
ebaſtiane Cabote, in the. vi. booke of the thyʒde Decade.
But Cabote touched only in the noʒth coʒner and moſt barba
us parte hereof, from whenſe he was repulſed with Jſe in
he moneth of July. Neuertheleſſe, the weſt and ſouth partes
f theſe regions haue ſence byn better ſearched by other,and
unde to bee as we haue ſayde befoʒe. The chiefe citie in the
uthweſt partes of theſe regions, is cauled Temixtetan, oʒ
Jexico in maner vnder the circle cauled Tropicus Cancri,and
rongely defended by the nature of the place. Foʒ it ſtandeth
t a very great lake hauynge abowt it innumerable bʒidges,
nd buyldynges to be compared to the wooʒkes of Dedalus.
Thinhabitauntes alſo can wʒyte and reade, Summe wʒyters
onnecte this lande to the firme lande of Aſia: But the truth
ereof is not yet knowen. And althoughe the Spanyardes
haue

c.i.

Marginal notes:

Jtali is. 1c2o
myles in leng
the and. 126.
in breadthe.

The lande
cauled Terra
floʒida,& regio
baccalearum.

Looke the laſt
booke. thirde
Decade.

This region
is now cauled
Noua Hiſpa=
nia .Sum
thinke that
this citie is
Quinſai of
marcus Paue
lus.
Looke the laſt
booke of the
3.decade, and
the begꝛning
of the booke
of the landes
lately found.

haue certeyne colonies in that part of this lande that is nowe
cauled Noua Hispania, yet are the people for the moste part
Idolatours. Howe much therfore is it to be lamented, and
howe greatly dooth it sounde to the reproche of all Christen
dome, and especially to such as dwell nerest to these landes
(as we doo) beinge muche nearer vnto the same then are the
Spanyardes (as within, xxb. dayes saylinge and lesse) howe
muche I saye shall this sounde vnto owre reproche and iner
cusable slothfulnesse and negligence bothe before god and the
worlde, that so large dominions of such tractable people and
pure gentiles, not beinge hytherto corrupted with any other
false religion (and therefore the easyer to bee allured to em
brase owres) are nowe knowen vnto vs, and that we haue
no respecte neyther for goddes cause nor for owre owne com
moditie to attempte summe vyages into these coastes, to doo
for owr partes as the Spaniardes haue doone for theyrs, and
not euer lyke sheepe to haunte one trade, and to doo nothyng
woorthy memorie amonge men or thankes before god, whe
maye herein woorthely accuse vs for the slackenesse of owr
dewtie towarde hym. Saynt Paule the doctoure of the gen
The godlye zeale of. S. Paule.
tiles (to whose Apostelshippe also these newe gentiles do
perteine) was of such zeale toward the Jewes whom god had
reiected, that he wisshed hym selfe to bee accursed of god for
theyr sakes. He went from Damascus to Arabie, preached
the gospell in Grecia, came prisoner to Rome, was scourged
and stoned, and suffered thryse shypwracke, what then think
yow he wold do if he were now aliue? Is it to be thoughte tha
he wolde not aduenture. xxb. dayes saylynge to come to suc
a marte of soules in such rednesse to bee easely obteyned? I
beleue verely that neyther death, nor the deuyll, nor Leuia
than, nor the worlde, shulde let hym but that he wolde gen
thonset ageynst them all in hope of victorie by hym by whom
he sayth he can doo all thynges. He was not negligent in his
office nor ignorant of his rewarde, but trusted to the promess
of him that sayde by the mouth of the prophet Isai: Of them
Isai. 66.
that shalbe saued, I wyl sende sum to the gentyles in the sea
into Aphrike and Libia, Italie, and Grecia, and into the I
landes a farre of, to them that haue not harde of me, and haue
not seene my glorie. The like zeale that Paule had, and pro
ssadynge of the same spirite, hath euer sence Chrystes tyme
mous

moued not only the Apostles, but also many other famous and
godly men (as superuisours of his testamente) to sende owte
preachers into dyuers partes of the worlde to shewe furth the
gladde tydynge of the gospell. By this zeale dyd Gregorye   *Gregorie the*
byshoppe of Rome and fyrste of that name, when he sawe   *First.*
Englyshe mens chyldren in Rome and askeb what nation
they were, when answere was made hym in the laten tounge
that they were Angli, (that is, Englyshe men)he sayd (allu=
byng to the similitude of the worlde) that they myght wel be   *Thoffice of*
cauled Angeli, that is, Angels : Meanyng therby that lyke as   *byshoppes.*
god had done his part in geuyng them bodies of natural bew
tie and comelynesse, so it apperteyned to his office beinge the
cheefe pastoure of goddes stocke,to prouyde that theyr soules
might be made woorthy to inhabite such bodies and the hole
nation consecrated vnto god by baptisme. For he sayde fur=
thermore : It is meete that vnto these also,the gospell of life   *England con=*
bee preached: And hereuppon immediatly sent preachers into   *verted to the*
Englande whereby the hole nation was in shorte tyme conuer   *faith of christ.*
ted to Christes faith, although sum had receaued the gospell
longe before euen from Chrystes tyme by the preachyng of Io
seph of Arimathia who asked the body of Chryste of Pilate,
and buryed it reuerently.I wolde to god that there were now
many mo such Gregories in the worlde:And that there might
lyke zeale and gentelnesse bee founde in vs Englyshe men to=
warde other nations, as we haue founde in other towarde
vs. Owre predicessoures were not vtterlye vnmyndefull of
these benefites, but applyed them selues lykewise to spreade
the gospell in other nations. For Uadianus in his booke
De tribus terræ partibus, wryteth, that more then seuen hundrethe   *This vnifride*
yeares after the death of Chryste,one Unefride an Englyshe   *was after*
man and byshoppe of Mogunce (nowe cauled Mense) was   *warde named*
the fyrste that taught the fayth of Chryste amonge the Ger=   *Boniface.*
maynes, at such tyme as the Frankes and Almaynes had pas
sed ouer the ryuers of Rhene and Danubius,and by puttynge
the garrysons of the Romans to flight, had possessed a great
parte of theyr moste notable prouinces. For albeit that these
rude and barbarous nations then accustomed onely to warre
and robberie did hardly admitte that holsome doctrine at the
beginning.yet by the pollicie and wisedome of the Frankes,
it came so to passe that in maner through owt all Germanie,

The preface to the reader.

greate increase of the Christian religion folowed there most
ample victories, as the lyke successe is also scene in these ba[r]
barous nations subdued by the Spanyardes. Whereby it [is]
apparent, that although sum holde opinion that none ow[ght]
to bee compelled to the faythe, yet we see by experience tha[t]
withowt disputynge of opinions (lesse the pacientes shuld
dye before the phisitians agree of the remedie) these enterpr[i]
ses haue taken good effect to the great glory of god who ca[l]
leth men vnto hym by dyuers meanes and at dyuers ages [in]
the declinynge worlde, otherwyse nowe then in the tyme [of]
Chryste and his Apostles when the poure of miracles was g[i]
uen vnto men to confirme the newe fayth which had yet pr[e]
uailed no where in the worlde. Albeit, I beleue verely, tha[t]
if we wolde take the matter in hande accordyngly, god wol[d]
not forget to ayde vs with miracles if it shald so be requisite
as yowe may reade in this booke howe he wrought miracle[s]
by the fayth of a simple mariner euen in thinfancie of fayth.
And suerlye, lyke as there is no cause why we shalde any[e]
thynge doubte of goddes goodnesse in this behalfe if the fa[ult]
be not in owre selues. Euen so, if we wolde fyrste sette ow[r]
handes to the plowe, we ought to hope that he wolde giu[e]
encrease and woorke with vs as he hath doone with other[s]
by whose prosperous successe we may plainely see that it wa[s]
his wyll that suche thynges shulde go forwarde.   For eue[n]
Israell to whom promesse was made by signes and miracle[s]
that they shulde possesse the lande so thinheritaunce wherof
the sea opened it selfe to giue them free passage, yet were the[y]
commaunded by the poure of the swoorde to make way, wit[h]
greate losse and slaughter of men and by force of armes to o[b]
teyne the lande promysed to theyr fathers, whiche neuerth[e]
lesse fewe of them possessed that first fought for the same, b[ut]
lefte theyr carkeses in the wildernesse. Is it not also wrytte[n]
of the Iumes which repayred the walles of the citie of Hier[u]
salem after theyr captiuitie in Babilon, that Nehemias they[r]
capitaine set the people in order with swoordes, speares, an[d]
bowes to defende the woorkemen ? And that also euen th[e]
Princes of Iuda wrought vppon the walles and caried bur[r]
dens ? lykewyse that they wrought with one hande and hel[d]
theyr swoordes in the other ? And if it were lawful for Isra[e]
ell accordynge to the fleshe, to vse all meanes and pollicie[s]

        t[o]

Whether any
may bee com-
pelled to the
faythe.

The tyme of
miracles.

Miracles of
late dayes.

Howe Israell
possessed the
lande of
promesse.

Esdra. 2.
fol. 4.

The buyldyng of spirituall Hierusalem.

o buylde vp the walles of earthly Hierusalem, howe muche
moze then ought the spirituall Israelites to vse all possible
meanes to buylde vp the walles and temples of spirituall Hie
rusalem, whose fundation is Chzifte, wyllynge all the nati=
ons of the wozlde to bee buylded vppon the same. It is the
propertie of a wyse buylder to vse such tooles as the woozke
requireth. And not at all tymes oz in all woozkes to vse one
oole. Foz that that serueth in softe tymber, wyll not serue
in knottie pieces, noz yet foz stones. The expert phisitian vseth
vhement remedies foz desperate diseases : And cunninge sur=
gians vse burnynge and cuttynge if the case so require, as in
cuttynge of the fynger to saue the hande, oz in cuttyng of the
hande to saue the hole body. ye it hath sumtymes so chaun
ced that wheras men haue entēded hurt, there hath good pzo=
ceaded therof in fine : As he that wolde haue slaine Pzome=
theus, wounded his wenne with his swoozde, whereby he
was healed of that disease. So is god able to turne euyll in=
to good, and to make thynges that are not, as thynges that
are. Euen so although summe wyll obiecte that the desyze of
golde was the chiefe cause that moued the Spanyardes and
Poztugales to searche the newe founde landes, trewly albeit
we shulde admitte it to bee the chiefe cause, yet dooth it no=
folowe that it was the only cause, fozasmuch as nothyng let=
teth but that a man may bee a warrier oz a marchaunte, and
also a Chzistian. Therefoze what so euer owre chiefe intente
bee, eyther to obteyne wozldely fame oz rychesse, (althoughe
the zeale to encrease Chzistian religion ought chiefly to moue
vs) I wolde to god we wolde fyzst attempte the matter : And
then I doubte not but that it wolde so comme to passe with
vs as it dyd with them who of longe time after the beginning
of the wozlde befoze menne were accustomed to eate flesshe,
thought it first sufficient so to vse them selues amonge beastes
that they were not hurte of them : but shoztly after, vsed them
oz theyz commoditie : Then begunne to weare theyz skinnes:
And in fine, fell to eatynge of theyz flesshe, and to vse certeine
partes of thē foz remedies agenst diseases. Euen so may these
barbarians by the only conuersation with the Chzistians, (al=
though they were enfozced therto) be bzought to such famili=
aritie with ciuilitie and vertue, that not onely we maye take
greate commoditie thereby, but they may also herewith im=

bibe

imbibe trewe religion as a thing accidental although neyther they nor we shulde seeke the same. For lyke as they that goe much in the soonne, are coloured therewith although they be not for that purpose, So may the conuersation of the Christians with the gentyles induce theym to owre religion, where there is no greater cause of contrarye to resyste as is in the Iuwes and Turkes who are alredy drowned in theyr confirmed erroure. But these simple gentiles lyuinge only after the

The conuersion of the gentiles.

lawe of nature, may well bee lykened to a smoothe and bare table vnpainted, or a white paper vnwritten, vpon the which yow may at the fyrst paynte or wryte what yow lyste, as yow can not vppon tables alredy paynted, vnlesse yow rase or blot owt the fyrste formes. They may also thestyer bee allured to

The christian faythe.

the Christian fayth, for that it is more agreable to the lawe of nature then eyther the cerimonious lawe of Moises, or portentous fables of Mahometes Alcharon. If we were therfore as desyrous to enlarge the fayth of Chryste as to seeke worldly gooddes, why do we deferre to aduenture that wherin we may doo bothe. We muste not nowe looke for a newe Paule or doctoure of the gentiles to bee conuerted by heauenly reuelations: Or for a newe Moises to leade men through the sea: Or for an Angel to cary men in the ayer from one place to an other as Habacucke the prophete was caryed by the heare of

Isai. 41.

his heade from Iudea to Babilon: Or as Phylippe thappostle was caryed by the spirite from Gaza to Azotus: but muste (as sayth the prophete Isaias) euery man exhorte his neyghboure, and bid his broother be of good chere: That the mason and carpenter may buylde togyther, and say to the glewe or cemente, it is good and faste byndynge. What negligence and slackenesse hath hytherto byn in Christian men in this kynde of buyldynge of goddes lyuely temple, the great clerke Erasmus hath declared in his booke intiteled Ecclesiastes, whose woordes for the woorthynesse of the autoure, I haue here thowght good to rehearse as they are wrytten by hym in the laten toungue in the fyrste booke of the sayde woorke, He wryteth therfore as foloweth.

Augustia Christianæ ditionis.

Audimus quotidianas queremonias deplorantiũ col lapsã Christianã religionẽ, eamcp ditionẽ quæ quon dam complexa est vniuersum terrarum orbem, in

has angustias esse contractam. Hoc igitur quibus
ex animo dolet, eos decet ardentibus assiduisq3 votis
flagitare a Christo vt operarios dignetur mittere in
messem suam, aut (vt melius dicam) seminatores mit
tere in segetem suam. Deum immortalem, quantum
in orbe patet agrorum in quibus aut non dum iactū
est semen Euangelicum, aut ita iactum est, vt plus
sit zizaniarum quam tritici. Orbis minima pars est
Europa: Omnium florentissima pars est Græcia et
Asia minor in quam magno successu primum a Iu=
dæa demigrauit Euangelium. At hæc fere tota, non=
ne tenetur a Mahumetanis et ijs qui Christi nomen
habent inuisum? Iam in Asia maiore quæ latissime
patet, quid obsecro nostrum est? quum ipsa Palesti=
na vnde primo effluxit lux Euangelica, seruiat Allo=
phylis? In Aphrica vero quid nostrum est? Nec du
bitandum est quin in tanta vastitate regionum sint
populi rudes et simplices qui facile possent ad Chri=
stum alici, si mitterentur qui facerent bonam semen=
tem. Quid quod quotidie regiones hactenus in=
cognitæ reperiuntur, ferunturq3 superesse quo nul=
lus adhuc nostratium peruenit. Omitto nunc infi=
nitam Iudæorum vim nobis admixtam : omitto plu
rimos qui titulo Christi tegunt Ethnicos : omitto
tantas schismaticorum et hæreticorum phalanges.
Quantus in his esset prouentus Christo, si guaui ac
fideles

The preface to the reader.

fideles mitterētur operarij qui iaciant semen bonum
qui reuellant zizaniam, qui plantent plantulas bo-
nas, malas exterpent, qui extruant domum Dei, de
moliantur structuras non innitentes petræ Christo
deniq̃ qui metant maturam segetem, sed Christo me
tant non sibi, et animas Domino colligant, non o-
pes sibi. Nuper Aethiopiæ rex quem vulgus appel-
lat Presteian, per oratorem suum submisit se sedi Ro
manæ, non nihil expostulans cum pontifice quod
ea gens quum a fide Christi non sit aliena, tam di
fuerit a tocius orbis pastore neglecta. Quidam vir
boni, et propagandæ religionis studiosi, queruntu
Pilapios Scythiæ septentrionalis populum mire sim
plicem ac rudem, a nescio quibus principibus Chri
stianis teneri ditione, sed ita duro premi iugo huma
no, vt eis non imponatur suaue iugum Christi, atq
ita spoliari bonis externis, vt non ditentur opibu
euangelicis. Pulcherrimum, Deoq̃ gratissimum e
rat dare potius quā accipere ijs quos studemus Chr
sto lucrifacere, ac sic eos in ditionem nostram recipe
re vt gaudeant se subiectos esse principibus sub quo
rum imperio commodius degant quam ante dege
bant. Nouimus cicurare bestias feras et horribiles
vel ad voluptatem, vel ad vsum vulgarem : et non
nouimus mansuefacere homines vt seruiantChristo.
Monarchæ alunt qui doceant elephantos ad saltan
du

Presteian Aethio-
piæ rex.

Pilapij.

ium,qui doment leones ad lusum,qui dement lynces
et leopardos ad venatum : et monarcha ecclesiæ non
inuenit quo homines alliciat ad amabile Christi ser=
uicium ? Scio vix vllam reperiri beluam domitu diffi=
iliorem quam est Iudæus obstinatus, et obduratus
hæreticus : quanquam nullum est animal tam immi
te quod non cicuretur beneficentia et suauitate. E re=
mertis regionibus euehitur aurum et gemmæ : Sed
triumpho dignius erat illuc inuehere Christianam
sapientiam auro preciosiorem, ac margaritum euan=
gelicum quod omnibus diuenditis benæ compara=
tur. Dominus iubet suis rogare dominum messis
vt extrudat operarios quod messis esset ampla, ope=
rarij pauci. Non minus opus est nunc rogare deú
vt in tam late patentes agros eijciat operarios, Sed
excusant omnes, alius aliud. Atqui Christiana di= *Franciscani sera=phici.*
tio tot habet myriadas Franciscanorum in quibus
probabile est quamplurimos esse qui vere flagrant *Dominicani Che=rubici.*
igni seraphico : nec pauciores sunt myriades Domi=
nicanorum, et in his consentaneum est permultos
esse Cherubici spiritus. Ex his cohortibus eligantur
viri, mundo vere mortui, Christo viui, qui syncere a= *Linguæ imperitia*
pud barbaras gentes doceant verbum Dei. Excusa=
tur linguæ imperitia. Atqui principes ob humanas
legationes inueniunt qui varias linguas perdiscant : *Miracula*
Lt Themistocles Athenienses vno anno sic didicit

d.i. sermo=

sermonem Asiaticum vt absɷ interprete cum rege lo
qui posset: An idem non studebimus in tam sublimi
negocio? Inter barbaras et ignotas nationes Aposto
li inuenerunt victum et amictum: et Deus pollicitus
est nihil defuturum quærentibus regnum Dei. Nec
miracula quidem defutura sunt si res postulet, modo
ad sit syncera fides cum seraphica charitate. &c.

Damianus a Goes

Furthermore Damianus a Goes, wryteth in his booke *De de-
ploratione Lappiane gentis*, that he was the fyrst that moued Erasmus to speake sumwhat hereof: And that he (Erasmus I
meane) was determined to wryte a full volume of this matter
yf he had not byn preuented by death. Albeit (sayth Damianus) in his booke entiteled Ecclesiastes, he did not keepe silence of so wicked an vngodlynesse, whiche surely is suche,
that it may in maner make all Christian men (and especiallye

**To the christi-
an princes.**

suche vnto whom god hath gyuen poure and knowleage) giltie
of so heyghnous a crime, that he may take vengeance of them
in the day of iudgement before the iuste iudge Christ. Nowe
therfore (sayth he) let the Christian Monarches take heede
what accompte they shall make before the tribunall of Christe
at the laste day, when neyther fauoure, nor pardon, or flatte-
rie can take place to bee any excuse for the losse of so manye
soules. And these be the very woordes of the woorshipful and
lerned man Damianus a Goes, wrytten to the byshoppe of
Rome Paule the thyrde of that name, whom he further char-
geth to looke diligently hereunto, as a thynge moste chiefely

**The sheepe of
Europe.**

perteynynge to the office of Christian prelates. Wee thynke
verely that the sheepe of Europe shulde by this tyme be so well
fedde, that they shulde by good reason be so stronge and migh
tie in Christes religion (excepte they be infected with the dy-
sease which the phisitians caule Cachexia, beinge an euyl disposition of the body whereby the more they are fed the worse
they lyke) that many sheppardes myght well bee spared to bee

**The doctoure
of diuinitie**

sent to other sheepe which ought to be of the same foulde. For
this purpose the doctoure of diuinitie when he commenseth,
hath his scapular cast ouer his headde in token that he hathe
forsaken

The preface to the reader.

forsaken the worlde for Christes sake : And his bootes on his legges in token that he shall euer bee in a redinesse to go forwarde in preachynge the gospell, as I doubte not there bee many in Englande wolde gladly doo euen amonge these new gentyles if they were therto mainteyned by the ayde of the secular poure as in this case it shalbe requisite for the furniture of necessaries hereunto apperteynynge, I must nowe therfore An admonitiõ to riche men. appele vnto yow, yow riche men and rulers of the worlde, to whom god hath giuen gooddes as thynges neyther good nor badde of them selues, but onely as they are vsed wel or euil. If yow vse them well, they are the gyftes of god wherwith yow may doo many thynges acceptable both to god and men. And if yow vse them otherwyse, yowe possesse not them, but they possesse yow, and theyr canker and ruste (as sayethe the Apostle) shalbe a testimonie ageinst yow in the day of the great audit. Thinke not therfore that this thynge perteyneth not vnto yowe, if yowe perteyne vnto Christe and looke to haue any parte with hym. Consyder with yowre selues if it were onely to get worldely ryches, howe redye and greedy yowe The marchaunt wolde bee to venture a greate deale to get a thyrde part, with owt castynge of any perell by lande or by sea, as the wyttie poet Horale hath in fewe wordes descrybed the marchauntes despre and aduentures to obteyne rychesse.

Impiger extremos currit mercator ad Indos,

Per mare pauperiem fugiens, per saxa, per ignes.

    The which verses are thus much to say in effecte.
The marchaunt in hope greate rychesse to fynde,
By fyer and by water passeth to Inde,
By the burnte line or Equinoctiall,
To flye from pourtrie and hasarde all.

As the poet hath in these verses, by the marchaunt declared the despre that couetous men haue to obteyne slippery riches, The despre of wordely fame. the lyke affection to obteyne worldly fame and honour, maye we see in valiant and noble capitaynes in the warres where they contende to put them selues forwarde to the moste daungerous aduenture as to haue the forewarde of the battayle : a token surely of much nobilitie and manly corage. But oh immortall god? Is it not to bee lamented that men can be so valiant, stowte, and in maner desperate in theyr owne pryuate

D.ii.   matters

matters, perteynyng onely to theyr bodies, and yet so coulde, negligent, and fearefull in goddes cause and thynges touchynge the health of theyr soules? If there were neyther deuyll nor lawe to accuse men before god in this case, shall not theyr owne consciences bee a lawe of condemnation ageynste theym in that they haue not shewed that loue to mankynde, which the very lawe of nature moueth brute beastes to shewe one to an other in theyr generations? But what hope is there (excepte god wolde in maner by myracle conuerte the hartes of such men) what hope is there I say, that they wyll departe with any of theyr gooddes, muche lesse aduenture theyr bodies, to the furtheraunce of Christes religion in these regions beinge so farre from them, wheras many shewe lyttle loue, charitie, or liberaltie (if not rather crueltie, tyrannie, and oppression) to theyr poore neighbours and brootherne dwelling euen at home at theyr owne elbowes. But as this couetousnesse is to bee reproued, so is the liberalitie of such to be commended as haue byn at greate coaste and charges in settynge forwarde suche vyages: wherein not onely the marchauntes of London, but also diuers noble men and gentlemen aswell of the counsayle as other, which bothe with theyr money and furtheraunce otherwyse haue furnyshed and sent furth certeyne shyppes for the discouerynge of such landes and regions as were heretofore vnknowen, haue herein deserued immortall fame, for as much as in such attemptes and daungerous vyages, they haue shewed no smaule liberalitie vppon vncerteyne hope of gayne: wherein they haue deserued so much the greater prayse as theyr intent seemed to bee rather to further honest enterpryses then for respecte of vantage. And here certeynely in the mention of these vyages I myght seeme vngratefull if I shulde omitte to giue dewe commendations to the two chiefe capitaynes of the same as the woorthy knyght syr Hugh Wylloby and the excellent pilotte Rycharde Chaunceler who haue therein aduentured theyr lyues for the commoditie of theyr countrey: Men doubtlesse woorthye for theyr noble attemptes to bee made knightes of the Ocean or otherwyse preferred if euer god sende them home ageyne although they fayle of theyr purpose. For as suche haue obteyned absolute glory that haue brought great thynges to passe, so haue they deserued immortall fame which haue only attempted the same

fame : forafmuch as fortune (who fumtymes fauoureth the
vnworthyeſt) is not in the poure of man. Xerſes obteyned glo
rie in makynge a bridge ouer the ſea Helleſpontus ioynynge
Europe to Aſia, and Darius ouer Boſphorus when he paſſed
with his armye towarde the Scythians. No leſſe fame and
commendacion (although not lyke glory) deſerued Demetrius,
Ceſar, Calligula, and Seleucus Nicanor, whiche attempted
to cutte in ſundre certeyne places cauled Iſthmi, (beinge na=
rowe portions of lande ſo diuidynge twoo ſeas, that there is
no paſſage from the one to the other) and yet neuer finiſſhed
that they tooke in hande, beinge hyndered eyther by deathe,
warres, or other chaunces. The auncient Romans & Greekes
gaue ſuch glorye vnto them that had eyther well deſerued of
the common weltche, or otherwyſe attempted ſuch great enter
priſes as might bee profitable for mankynde, that after theyr
death they cauſed Images of golde, ſyluer, braſſe, Iuery, and
marble to bee made to theyr lykeneſſe, and the ſame to be pla
ced in theyr ſolemne haules, palaices, or temples, with cer=
teyne verſes made to the commendation of them whom the I=
mages repreſented. And this no leſſe to prouoke and enco=
rage other forwarde natures to themulation of their vertues,
then alſo to geue them the due honoure of theyr iuſt deſertes.
And ſurely if euer ſence the begynnynge of the worlde any en
terpryſe haue deſerued greate prayſe as a thynge atchyued by
men of heroicall vertue, doubtleſſe there was neuer any more
woorthy commendation and admiration then is that whiche
owre nation haue attempted by the north ſeas to diſcouer the
mightie and riche empire of Cathay, by which vyage not on=
ly golde, ſyluer, precious ſtones, and ſpices, may be browght
hether by a ſafer and ſhorter way, but alſo much greater mat=
ters may hereof enſewe in tyme if it ſhall pleaſe God to gyue
vnto Chriſtian men ſuch paſſage into thoſe regions, whereby
ſuch familiaritie may further growe betwene the Chriſtiã prin
ces of Europe and the greate emperoure of Cathay, that (as
wryteth Haytho De ſocietate Chriſtianorum et Tartarorum) there can
nothynge be imagined more effectuall for the confuſion of the
Turke if the great Cham of Cathay and the Sophie of Per=
ſia on the one ſyde, and the Chriſtian Princes on the other
ſyde, ſhulde with one conſent inuade his dominions, as dyd
Tamburlanes Themperoure of the Tartars who abowte the

yeare

The rewardt
of noble enter=
priſes.

The vyage to
Cathay by the
north ſeas.

Societie be=
twene the Tar
tars and the
Chriſtians.
The Turke.
The Sophie.

Tambulanes.
Baiaſetes.

yeare of Chrifte. M. CCC. lxxxviii. toke prifoner Baiafetes Ottomanus Themperoure of the Turkes and flewe.xx. thoufande of his men in one battayle befyde many other great victoꝛies, as yowe may further reade in this booke in the hyftoꝛie of Paulus Iouius. And to haue fayde thus muche in maner of a preface it may fuffice.

¶ To the moſte noble Prince and Catholike kynge, Charles, Peter Martyꝛ of Angleria wyſheth perpetuall felicitie.

The largenes of the Ocean vnknowen to this day.

He diuine pꝛouidence, frome the tyme that he fyꝛſte created the woꝛlde, hathe referued vnto this day the knowleage of the great and large Ocean fea: In the which tyme he hath opened the fame, chiefely vnto yowe (moſte mightie Prince) by the good foꝛtune and happie fuccefle of yowr grandfather by yowr mothers fyde. The fame pꝛouidence (I knowe not by what deſtenie) hath bꝛought me owt of my natiue countrey of Milane, and owt of the citie of Rome (where I continued almoſt. x. yeares) into Spaine, that I myght particularlye collecte, thefe marueylous and newe thynges, which ſhoulde otherwyſe perhappes haue line dꝛowned in the whirlepoole of obliuion: foꝛafmuch as the Spanyardes (men wooꝛthy greate commendation) had onely care to the generall inuentions of thefe thynges. Notwithſtandinge, I doo not chalenge vnto me only, the thankes of the trauaile beſtowed herein, wheras the chiefe rewarde therof is due to Afcanius vicounte Cardinal, who perceauynge that I was wyllinge to departe owt of the citie to be pꝛefent at the warres of Granatum, diſſuaded me from my purpofe. But feing that I was fully refolued to departe, exhoꝛted and required me to wꝛyte vnto hym fuch newes as were famous in Spayne and wooꝛthy to be noted. I tooke therfoꝛe my ioꝛney into Spaine chiefely foꝛ the defyꝛe I had to fee therpedition whiche was pꝛepared ageynſt the enemies of the fayth: foꝛafmuche as in Italye, by reafon of the diſſention amonge the Princes, I coulde fynde nothynge wherewith I myght feede my wytte, beinge a younge man defyꝛous of knowleage and experience of thynges. I was therefoꝛe pꝛefente at the warres: frome whenfe I wꝛitte to Cardinal Afcanius, and by fundꝛy epiſtels

Cardinal Afcanius.

The warres of Granatum ageynſt the Moores.

certified

The epistle of Peter Martyr.

certifyed hym of such thynges as I thought moste woorthye to be put in memorie. But when I perceaued that his fortune was turned from a naturall moother to a steppedame, I ceased from wrytynge. yet after I sawe, that by thouerthrowe of the enemies of owre faythe, Spayne was pourged of the Moores as of an euyll weede plucked vp by the rootes, Leaste I shulde bestowe my slippery yeares in vnprofitable Idlenesse I was mynded to returne to Italie. But the singuler benignitie of bothe the Catholyke kynge and queene nowe departed, and theyr large promises towarde me vppon my returne frome my legacie of Babilon, detayned me frome my purpose. yet dooth it not repent me that I drewe backe my foote: Aswel for that I see in no other place of the worlde at this time the lyke woorthy thinges to bee done: As also that in maner throwgh owt all Italy, by reason of the discorde of the Christian Princes, I perceaued all thynges to runne headelonge into ruine, the countreys to be destroyed and made satte with humane bludde: The cities sacked, virgines and matrones with theyr gooddes and possessions caried away as captiues and miserable innocentes without offence to be slayne vnarmed within theyr owne houses. Of the which calamities, I dyd not onely heare the lamentable owtcryes, but dyd also feele the same. For euen the bludde of mine owne kinsfolkes and frendes, was not free from that crueltie. As I was therfore musynge with my selfe of these thynges, the Cardinal of Arragonie, after that he had seene the two fyrste bookes of my Decades wrytten to Ascanius, required me in the name of kynge Frederike his vncle, to put foorth the other eyght epistell bookes, In the meane tyme also, whyle I was voyde of all care as touchynge the matters of the Ocean, the Apostolicall messengers of the byshopppe of Rome Leo the tenth, (by whose holsome counsayle and autoritie we truste the calamities of Italy shalbe fynysshed) raysed me as it were frome sleape, and encoraged me to proceade as I had begunne. To his holynesse I wrote two Decades comprysed in short bokes after the maner of epistels, and added them to the fyrst, which was prynted withowt myne aduise, as shall further appeare by the preface folowynge. But nowe I returne to yow (most noble Prince) from whom I haue sumwhat digressed. Therfore wheras yowr graundefathers by yowre moothers syde,

haue

The autour was sent ambassadour to the Soltane of Alcayr in Egypte.

Italy disquieted with warres.

The sequeles of warre.

Kynge Frederike.

Leo the tenth, byshoppe of Rome.

Spayne subdued from the Moores.

The epistle of Peter Martyr

The kyngdome of Naples.

haue subdued all Spayne vnder yowr dominion except onely one corner of the same, and haue also lefte yowe the kynges dome of Naples with the frutefull Ilandes of owr seas, it is suerly a greate thynge and woozthy to be noted in owre cronacles. But not offendynge the reuerence due to owre predicessours, what so euer frome the begynnynge of the worlde hath byn doone oz wzytten to this day, to my iudgement seemeth but lyttle, if we consyder what newe landes and countreys, what newe seas, what sundzy nations and tounges, what goldempnes, what treasuries of perles they haue lefte vnto yowre hyghnesse, besyde other renenues. The whiche, what they are and howe greate, these thzee Decades shall declare. Come therfoze moste noble Pzince elected of God, and enioy that hyghe estate of thynges not yet vnderstode to men. We offer vnto yowe the Equinoctiall line hetherto vnknowen and burnte by the furious heate of the soonne and vnhabitable after the opinion of the owlde wzyters a fewe excepted: But nowe founde to bee most replenisshed with people, faire, frutefull, and moste foztunate, with a thowsande Ilandes crowned with golde and bewtifull perles, besyde that greate poztion of earth supposed to bee parte of the firme lande, excedynge in quantitie thzee Europes. Come therfoze and embzase this newe wozlde, and suffer vs no longer to consume in despize of yowr presence. From hense, from hense I saye (mooste noble younge Pzince) shall instrumentes be pzepared foz yow, whereby al the wozlde shalbe vnder yowr obeysaunce.

Note, frome the begynning of the worlde

The temperature of the Equinoctial vnknowen to the owlde wzyters.

Continente oz firme lande surpasynge thze Europes

Ryches are the instrumentes of conquestes.

And thus I byd yowr maiestie farewell: To whose taste if I shal perceaue the fruites of this my pillage to be delectable, I wyll hereafter doo my endeuoure that yowe maye receaue the same moze abundauntly. From Madzid. The day befoze the Calendes of October, In the yeare of Chzyste. M. D. XVI.

FINIS.

¶THE FIRSTE BOOKE OF THE DECADES
of the Ocean, written by Peter Martyr of Angleria,
Mileneſe, counſiler to the kyng of Spayne and
Protonotarie Apoſtolicall, To *Aſcanius
Sphorcia*, vicount Cardinall. ꝛc.

THE REVERENDE AND thanckefull
antiquite was accuſtomed to eſteme thoſe men
as goddes, by whoſe induſtrie and magnanimitie ſuche Landes and Regions were diſcouered, as were vnknowen to theyr prediceſ-
ſoures. But vnto vs hauynge onely one god
whom we honour in triplicitie of perſon, this
reſteth, that albeit we do not wꝛoꝛſhip that kind of men with
diuine honoure, yet do we reuerēce them, and woꝛꝛthely mar
uell at theyr noble actes and enterpꝛiſes. Vnto kynges and
pꝛinces we gyue due obeyſaunce, by whoſe gouernaunce and
furtheraunce they haue bin ayded, to perfurme theyr attemptes. we commende bothe, and foꝛ theyr iuſt deſertes woꝛthe-
ly extoll them. Wherfoꝛe, as concernyng the Ilandes of the
weſt Ocean, lately diſcouered, ⁊ of the auctours of the ſame,
(whiche thynge you deſyꝛe by your letters to knowe) I wyll
begynne at the fyꝛſt auctoure therof, leſte I be iniurious to a-
ny man. Take it therfoꝛe as foloweth.

¶ *Chriſtophorus Colonus* (other wiſe called *Columbus*) A gentilman
of Italy, boꝛne in the citie of *Genus*, perſwaded Fernando and
Elyzabeth, catholike pꝛynces, that he doubted not to fynde
certayne Ilandes of *India*, nere vnto owre Ocean ſea, if they
wolde furnyſche hym with ſhyppes and other thynges apperteynynge. Affyꝛminge that therby not onely the Chꝛiſtian religion myght be enlarged, but Spayne alſo enryched by the
great plentie of golde, pearles, pꝛecious ſtones, and ſpices,
whiche might be founde there. At the lengthe thꝛee ſhyppes
were appoynted hym at the kinges charges: of the which one
was a great caracte with deckes: and the other twoo were
light marchaunte ſhyppes without deckes, whiche the Spaniardes call *Carauelas*. Thus he departed from the coſtes of
Spaine about the calendes of September, in the yere of Chꝛiſt
1492. and ſet foꝛward on his viage, being accompanied with
CL.xx. Spanyardes. The foꝛtunate Ilandes (as manye
　　　　　　　　　A.i.　　　　　　　thynke

*The reward
of Vertue*

*The Ilandes
of the weſte
Ocean.*

*Chriſtopho-
rus Colonus.*

India.

*The fyrſt vi-
age of Colo-
nus.*

The Ilandes
of Canarie.
Gades or
Cals mals.
A leaque,
what it con-
teyneth by
sea.
the fortunate
Ilandes.

Cabouerde.

The seuen I-
landes of Ca-
narie.
Betanchor A
frenche man
subdued the
Ilandes of
Canarie.
Lancelotus.
Fortiuetura.
Ferrea.
Gomera.
Grancanaria.
Palma.
Tenerifen.

Alphonsus
Lugo.

thinke them to be, whiche the Spaniardes call Canaria, founde
but of late dayes) are distaunte from the Ilandes of Gades, a
thousande and twoo hundreth myles, accordyng to theyr accompte : for they say they are distant three hundreth leaques :
wheras such as are expert sea men, affyrme that euery leaque
conteyneth foure myles, after theyr supputations . These I-
landes were called fortunate, for the temperate ayre whiche
is in them. For neyther the coldenesse of wynter is sharpe vnto them, nor the heate of sommer intollerable . yet some men
are of opinion, that those were in olde tyme called the fortunate Ilandes, whiche the Portugales call Capo Verde . Colonus
therfore sayled fyrste to the Ilandes of Canarie, to the intente
there to refresshe his shyppes with fresshe water and fuell, before he committed him selfe to this so laborious a vyage. And
bycause I haue here made mention of the Ilandes of Canarie.
It shall not be muche from my purpose to declare howe of vnknowen they became knowen, and of saluage and wilde, better manured . For by the longe course of manye yeres, they
were forgotten, and remayned as vnknowen.

These seuen Ilandes (therfore) called the Canaries, were foũde
by chaunce by a frenche man, called Betanchor, by the permis-
sion of queene Katharine, protectrixe of kyng John her son,
while he was yet in his nonage, about the yere of Christe .
M. CCC. V. This Betanchor inuaded twoo of these Ilandes called Lancelotus and Fortisuentura, whiche he inhabited and
brought to better culture. He beinge deade, his son and heire
solde bothe the sayde Ilandes to certayne Spaniardes.
After this, Fernandus Peraria and his wyfe, inuaded Ferrea and
Gomera . The other three were subdued in our tyme . Grancanaria,
by Petrus de Vera, citezen of the noble citie of Xericium, and Michaell of Moxica . Palma and Tenerifen, by Alphonsus Lugo, at the
kynges charges . Gomera and Ferrea were easely subdued: But
the matter wente harde with Alphonsus Lugo . For that naked
and wylde nation, fyghtinge onely with stones and clubbes,
droue his armie to flighte at the fyrste assaulte, and slewe a-
boute foure hundreth of his men . But at the length he ouercame them . And thus all the Ilandes of Canarie were added
to the dominion of Spayne . From these Ilandes Colonus directynge his viage towarde the weste, folowinge the fallinge
of the sonne, but declining somwhat towarde the left hande,
sayled

ſayled on forwarde. xxxiii. dayes continually, hauynge onely
the fruition of the heauen and the water. Then the Spanyardes whiche were accompanied with hym, beganne fyrſte to
murmure ſecretely among them ſelues : and ſhortly after with
wordes of reproche ſpake euyll of Colonus theyr gouernoure,
and conſulted with them ſelues, eyther to rydde hym out of
the waye, orelles to caſt hym into the ſea : Ragyng that they
were deceyued of a ſtraunger, an outlandiſhe man, a Ligurian
a Genues, and brought into ſuche daungerous places, that
they myght neuer returne ageyne. And after. xxx. days were
paſte, they furiouſely cryed out againſte him, and threatned
him that he ſhulde paſſe no further. But he euer with ientyll
wordes and large promyſes, appeaſed theyr furie, and pro-
longed day after day, ſome tyme deſyring them to beare with
hym yet a whyle, and ſome time putting them in remembrance
that if they ſhulde attempte any thinge agaynſt him, or other
wiſe diſobey hym, it wolde be reputed for treaſon. Thus after a fewe dayes, with cherefull hartes they eſpied the lande
longe looked for. In this fyrſt nauigation, he diſcouered. vi.
Ilandes, wherof twoo were exceding great : Of whiche, the
one he called Hiſpaniola, and the other Iohanna. But at that
tyme he knewe not perfectely that Iohanna (other wyſe called
Cuba,) was an Ilande. As they coaſted alonge by the ſhore
of certayne of theſe Ilandes, they harde nyghtingales ſynge
in the thycke woodes in the month of Nouember. They foũd
alſo great riuers of freſhe water, and naturall hauens, of capacitie to harborowe greate nauies of ſhippes. Saylinge by
the coaſtes of Iohanna, from the northe poynte to the weſt, he
rode lyttell leſſe then eyght hundreth miles (for they call it a
hundreth and foure ſcore leaques) ſuppoſyng that it had byn
the continent or fyrme land, bicauſe he coulde nother fynd the
landes ende, nor any token of the ende, as farre as he coulde
iudge with his eye : wherfore he determined to returne backe
agayne, beyng therto partly enforced by the roughneſſe of the
ſea. for the ſea banckes of the Ilande of Iohanna, by ſondrye
wyndinges and turnynges, bende them ſelues ſo muche towarde the Northe, that the northnortheaſte wynde roughely
toſſed the ſhyppes by reaſon of the wynter. Turnynge therfore the ſtemmes of his ſhyppes towarde the Eaſte, he affyrmed that he had founde the Ilande of Ophir, whyther Salo-
　　　　　　A. ii.　　　　　　mons

Colonus men
rebel againſt
hym.

Faire wor-
des and pro-
miſes.

Hiſpaniola.
Iohanna.

Nightinga-
les ſynge in
Nouember.

The Ilande
of Ophir,

mons shyppes sayled for golde . But the description of the
Cosmographers well considered, it seemeth that bothe these,
and the other Ilandes adioynyng, are the Ilandes of Antilia.
This Ilande he called Hispaniola : on whose northe syde as he
approched nere to the lande, the keele or bottome of the big-
gesse vessell ranne vpon a blynde rocke couered with water,
and cloue in sunder . But the playnenesse of the rocke was a
helpe to them that they were not drowned . Makynge haste
therfore with the other two ships to helpe them, they brought
awaye al the men without hurte . Here comming fyrst a land,
they sawe certayne men of the Ilande : who perceauynge an
vnknowen nation comminge towarde them, flocked together
and ranne al into the thycke wooddes, as it hadde byn hares
courced with grehoundes . Owre men pursuing them, tooke
onely one woman, whom they brought to the shyppes : where
fyllinge her with meate and wyne, and apparelinge her, they
let her departe to her company . Shortly after a greate multitude of them came runnynge to the shore to beholde this newe
nation, whom they thought to haue descended from heauen .
They cast them selues by heapes into the sea, and came swim-
minge to the shyppes, bryngyng golde with them, which they
chaunged with owre men for erthen pottes, drinking glasses,
poyntes, pynnes, hawkes belles, lokinge glasses, and suche
other trifles. Thus growing to further familiaritie, owre men
were honorably enterteyned of the kynge of that parte of the
Ilande, whose name was Guaccanarillus : for it hath many kynges, as when Eneas arriued in Italy, he founde Latium diuided into many kyngedomes and prouinces , as Latium, Mezeuti-
um, Turnum, and Tarchontem, which were seperated with narow
boundes, as shall more largely appere hereafter . At the euen
tyde about the faulyng of the sonne, when owre men went to
praier, and kneled on their knees after the maner of the Christians, they dyd the lyke also. And after what maner so euer
they sawe them praye to the crosse, they folowed them in all
poyntes as well as they coulde . They shewed much humanitie towardes owre men: and helpen them with theyr lighters
or small boates (whiche they call Canoas) to vnlade theyr broken shyppe : And that with suche celeritie and cherefulnesse,
that no frende for frende, or kynseman for kynseman, in suche case moued with pitie, coulde do more. Theyr boates are
made

Marginal notes (left column):

The ilandes of Antilia.

A shypwrack

The people of the ilande.

Naked peo-ple.

Expert swim-mers.
gold for erth and glasse.

Many kinges

Relygious & humaine peo-ple.

Canoas.

made only of one tree, made holow with a certain sharpe stone (for they haue no yron.) And are very longe and narowe. Many affirme that they haue sene some of them with fortie ores. The wylde and myscheuous people called *Canibales*, or *Caribes*, whiche were accustomed to eate mannes flesshe (and called of the olde wryters, *Anthropophagi*) moleft them excedyngly, inuadynge theyr countrey, takynge them captiue, kyllyng and eatyng them. As owre men sayled to the Jlandes of these meke and humayne people, they lefte the Jlandes of the *Canibales*, in maner in the middeft of theyr viage towarde the south. They complayned that theyr Jlandes were no lesse vexed with the incurtions of these manhuntyng *Canibales* when they go forth a rouynge to seeke theyr praye: then are other tame beaftes, of Lyons and Tigers. Such chyldren as they take, they geld to make them fat as we doo cocke chikyns and younge hogges, and eate them when they are wel fedde: of suche as they eate, they fyrst eate the intralles and extreme partes, as handes, feete, armes, necke, and heade. The other moste fleshy partes, they pouder for ftore, as we do peftelles of porke and gammondes of bakon. yet do they abfteyne from eatynge of women and counte it vyle. Therfore suche younge women as they take, they keepe for increace, as we doo hennes to leye egges. The olde women, they make theyr drudges. They of the Jlandes (which we may nowe caul owres) bothe the men and the women when they perceaue the *Canibales* coming, haue none other shyfte but onely to flie: for althoughe they vse very sharpe arrowes made of reedes, yet are they of small force to reprefle the furie of the *Canibales*: for euen they them felues confefle, that tenne of the *Canibals* are able to ouercome a hundreth of them if they encountre with them. Theyr meate is a certeyne roote which they cal *Ages*: muche lyke a nauew roote in fourme and greatnefle: but of fweete tafte, muche lyke a greene cheftnutte. They haue also an other kynde of rootes, whiche they call *Iucca*, wherof they make breade in lyke maner. They vse *Ages* more often rofted or fodden, then to make breade therof. But they neuer eate *Iucca*, excepte it be firfte fliced and prefled, (for it is ful of lycoure) and then baked or fodden. But this is to be marueled at, that the iuyce of this roote is a poyfon as ftrong as *Aconitum*, fo that if it be dronke it caufeth prefent death, and yet the breade made of the mafle

A. iii.   therof

Monoxyla.
They haue no Iren.

Canibales or Caribes Anthropophagi.

The crueltie of the Canibales.

Ages.
Rootes in the fteede of meate.
Iucca.
Breade of rootes.

an herbe of a ftraunge nature.

therof, is of good taſte and holſome, as all they haue proued.
They make also an other kynde of breade of a certayne pulſe,
called Panicum, muche lyke vnto wheate, wherof is great plé-
tie in the dukedome of Mylane, Spayne, and Granatum.
But that of this countrey is longer by a ſpanne, ſomewhat
ſharpe towarde the ende, and as bygge as a mannes arme in
the brawne : The graynes wherof are ſette in a maruelous order, and are in fourme ſomwhat lyke a peaſe . While they be
ſoure and vnripe, they are white : but when they are ripe they
be very blacke . When they are broken, they be whyter then
ſnowe . This kynde of grayne, they call Maizium. Golde is of
ſome eſtimation among them : for ſome of them hange certain
ſmall pieces therof at theyr eares and noſethrilles . A lyttell
beyonde this place, our men wente a lande for freſſhe water,
where they chaunced vpon a Ryuer whoſe ſande was myxed
with muche golde . They founde there no kindes of foure fo-
ted beaſtes excepte three kyndes of lyttell conyes . Theſe I-
landes alſo nouriſhe ſerpentes : but ſuch as are without hurt.
Lykewiſe wylde geeſe, turtle doues, and duckes, much greater then ours, and as whyte as ſwannes, with heades of purple coloure . Alſo Popiniaies, of the whiche ſome are greene,
ſome yelowe, and ſome lyke them of India, with yelowe rynges about theyr neckes, as Plinie deſcribeth them . Of theſe
they broughte fortie with them, of moſte liuely and delectable
coloures, hauyng three fethers entermengled with greene, yelowe, and purple, whiche varietie, deliteth the ſenſe not a litle . Thus muche thought I good to ſpeake of Potingiaies,
(ryghte noble Prynce) ſpecially to this intente, that albeit the
opinion of Chriſtophorus Colonus (who affirmeth theſe Ilandes to be parte of India) dothe not in all poyntes agree with
the iudgement of auncient wryters as touchynge the bigneſſe
of the Sphere and compaſſe of the Globe as concernynge the
nauigable portion of the ſame beynge vnder vs, yet the Po-
pingiaies and many other thynges brought from thence, doo
declare that theſe Ilandes ſauoure ſomwhat of India, eyther
beynge nere vnto it, or elles of the ſame nature : foraſmuche
as Ariſtotle alſo, about the ende of his booke De Cælo et Mundo,
and likewiſe Seneca, with diuerſe other authours not ignorant
in Coſmography, do affirme that India is no longe tracte by
ſea, diſtante from Spayne by the weſte Ocean, for the ſoyle
of theſe

of these Ilandes, bryngeth forthe Mastix, Aloes, and sundrye other sweete gummes and spyces as doth _India_ . Cotton also of the gossampine tree, as in _India_ in the countrey of the people called Seres .

℣ The languages of all the nations of these Ilandes, maye well be written with our Latine letters . For they cal heauen _Turei_ . A house, _Boa_ . Golde, _Cauni_ . A good man, _Taino_ . nothing _Mayoni_ . All other wordes of theyr language, they pronounce as playnely as we doo the Latine tongue . In these Ilandes they founde no trees knowen vnto them, but pyne appe trees, and date trees : And those of maruelous heyght and erceding harde, by reason of the greate moystnesse and fatnesse of the grounde, with continuall and temperate heate of the sonne, which endureth so all the hole yere . They playnely affyrme the Ilande of _Hispaniola_ to be the most fruiteful lande that the heauen compasseth aboute, as shall more largely appere hereafter in the particular description of the same, whiche we intende to sette foorthe when we shall be better instructed.

Thus makynge a leage of frendshyppe with the kynge, and leauynge with hym. xxxviii. men to searche the Ilande, he departed to Spayne takynge with hym. x. of the inhabitauntes to lerne the Spanishe tongue, to the intent to vse them afterwarde for interpretours . _Colonus_ therfore at his returne, was honorably receaued of the kyng and queene : who caused him to sytte in theyr presence, whiche is a token of great loue and honoure amonge the Spaniardes . He was also made Admirall of the Ocean : and his brother gouernoure of the Iland .

Towarde the second viage, he was furnished with. xii. shippes : wherof there were great caractes of a thousand tunne : xii. were of that sorte, whyche the Spaniardes call _Carauelas_ : without deckes : and twoo other of the same sorte somewhat bygger, and more apte to beare deckes, by reason of the gretnesse of theyr mastes . He had also a thousand and two hundreth armed footemen well appoynted : Amonge whiche were many artificers, as smythes, carpenters, myners, and suche other : Certayne horsemen also, wel armed : Likewise mares, shepe, heyghfers, and such other of bothe kindes for incrase. Lykewise all kynde of pulse or grayne and corne, as wheate, barlye, rye, beanes and pease, and suche other, as well for food as to sowe : Belyde vynes, plantes and seedes, of suche trees,

Mastix.
Aloe.
Gossampyne cotton or bombase.
Seres.
The languague of these Indians.

Trees and frutes vnknowen to vs.
Fat & moyste grounde.
Heate continuall and temperate.
The fruitfulnes of Hispaniola

The seconde viage of Colonus.

Corne and sedes to sowe.

Tooles and artillery.

trees, fruites, and herbes, as thoſe countreyes lacke. And (not to be forgotten) ſundry kindes of artillery & iron tooles, as bowes, arrowes, croſſebowes, bylles, hargabuſes, brode ſwordes, large targettes, pikes, mattockes, ſhooueles, hammers, nayles, ſawes, ares, and ſuche other. Thus beynge furniſhed accordyngely, they ſet forwarde from the Ilandes of Gades, (nowe called Cads,) the. vii. day before the calendes of October, in the yere of Chriſte. 1493. and arriued at the Ilandes of Canarie, at the calendes of October. Of theſe Ilandes, the laſte is called Ferrea, in whiche there is no other

water droppyng from a tree continually.

water that maye be drunke, but onely that is gathered of the dewe whiche continually diſtilleth from one onely tree growynge on the higheſt backe of the Ilande, and falleth into a rounde trenche made with mannes hande. We were infourmed of theſe thynges within fewe dayes after his departure. what ſhal ſuccede, we wyl certifie yowe hereafter. Thus fare ye well, from the courte, at the Ides of Nouember. 1493.

⊂ The ſeconde booke of the fyrſte Decade to *Aſcanius Phorcia*, vicounte Cardinall. &c.

YOwe repete (ryghte honorable Prynce) that yowe are deſirous to knowe what newes we haue in Spayne from the newe worlde : and that thoſe thynges haue greatly delyted you which I wrote vnto yowre highneſſe of the fyrſte nauigation, yowe ſhal now therefore

Methymna Campi. Caſtella Vetus.

receaue what hath ſucceded. *Methymna Campi*, is a famous towne in high Spayne in the reſpect from yowe, and is in that parte of Spayne whiche is called *Caſtella Vetus*: beynge diſtante from *Gades* about. xl. myles. Here the courte remayned, when aboute the. ix. of the kalendes of Aprell in this yere of nynetie and foure, there were poſtes ſente to the kynge and queene, certifyinge them that there were. xii. ſhippes come from the newe Ilandes and arryued at *Gades*.

Gades

But the gouernoure of the ſhyppes ſente worde to the kynge and quene that he had none other matter to certifie them of by the poſtes, but onely that the Admiral with fiue ſhyppes and. iiii. ſcore and tenne men remayned ſtyll in *Hiſpaniola*, to ſearche the

ſeacretes

secretes of the Ilande . And that as touching other matters,
he hym selfe wolde shortly make relation in theyr presence, by
worde of mouthe . Therfore the daye before the nones of A-
prel, he came to the courte him selfe . What I learned of him
and other faythefull and credible men whiche came with hym
from the Admirall, I wyl reherse vnto yowe in such order as
they declared the same to me when I demaunded them. Take
it therfore as foloweth . The thyrde daye of the Ides of October, departynge from *Ferrea*, the laste of the Ilandes of *Ca-*
narie, and from the costes of Spayne with a nauie of.xvii.ship-
pes, they sayled. xxi. dayes before they came to any Ilande :
inclynyng of purpose more towarde the lefte hand then at the
fyrst viage, folowyng the northnortheast wynde:and arriued
fyrst at the Ilandes of the *Canibales*, or *Caribes* of which, onely
the fame was knowen to our men. Amonge these, they chaun
sed fyrste vpon one, so beset with trees, that they coulde not
se so muche as an elle space of bare earthe or stony grounde .
this they called *Dominica*, bicause they found it on the sunday.
They taried here no tyme, bycause they sawe it to be deserte.
In the space of these.xxi.dayes,they thynke that they sayled.
viii. hundreth and. xx. leaques, the Northenortheast wynde
was so full with them, and so freshely folowed the sterne of
theyr shyppes . After they hadde sayled a lyttell further, they
espied dyuerse Ilandes replenyshed with sundrye kyndes of
trees, from the whiche came fragrant sauours of spyces and
sweete gummes . Here they sawe neyther man nor beaste, except certayne lisartes of huge bignesse, as they reported whiche went alande to biewe the countrey . This Iland they cau
sed *Galana*, or *Galanta* . From the cape or poynt of this Iland, es-
pyyng a mountayne a farre of, they sayled thyther . Aboute.
xxx. myles from this mountayne, they sawe a ryuer disceding
whiche seemed to be a token of some great and large fludde .
This is the fyrste lande whiche they founde inhabited from
the Ilandes of *Canarie*, and is an Ilande of the *Canibales*, as
they lerned by the interpretours whiche they tooke with them
from *Hispaniola* into Spayne at theyr fyrste viage . Serchynge
the Ilande, they founde innumerable villages of. xx. houses
or. xxx. at the mooste, sette rounde abowte in order, makynge the streete in coompasse lyke a markette place . And for
asmuch as I haue made mention of theyr houses,it shal notbe

B.i.   greatly.

The Iland of
Ferrea.

Ilands of the
Canibales.

The Iland of
Dominica.

viii. hundreth
& xx.leaques
in.xxi. dayes.

Lysertes,

The Ilande
of Galanta.

The Iland of
Guadalupea .

villages of. xx
or.xxx.houses

greatly from my purpoſe to deſcribe in what maner they are buylded . They are made rounde lyke belles or rounde paupylions. Theyr frame is rayſed of excedynge hyghe trees, ſette cloſe together and faſt rampaired in the grounde, ſo ſtandyng a ſlope and bending inward that the toppes of the trees ioyne together and beare one agaynſte an other, hauynge alſo within the houſe, certayne ſtronge and ſhorte props or poſtes whiche ſuſteyne the trees from fallynge . They couer them with the leaues of date trees and other trees ſtrongly compact and hardened, wherewith they make them cloſe from wynde and wether . At the ſhort poſtes or proppes within the houſe, they tie ropes of the cotton of goſſampine trees, or other ropes made of certayne long and toughe rotes much lyke vnto the ſhrubbe called *Spartum,* wherof in olde tyme they vſed to make bondes for vynes and cabuls and ropes for ſhyppes . Theſe they tye ouerthwarte the houſe from poſte to poſte . On theſe they ley as it were certayne mattreſſes made of the cotton of the goſſampine trees, whiche growe plentifully in theſe Ilandes . This cotton the Spaniardes call *Algodon,* and the Italians *Bombaſine* . And thus they ſleepe in hangynge beddes . At the enteraunce of one of theyr houſes, they ſawe two Images of woodde lyke vnto ſerpentes, whiche they thoughte had byn ſuch idoles as they honour . But they lerned afterwarde that they were ſette there onely for coomlyneſſe . For they knowe none other god then the Sunne and Moone, althoughe they make certaine Images of goſſampine cotton to the ſimilitude of ſuch phantaſies as they ſay appere to them in the nyghte . Our men found in theyr houſes, all kyndes of erthen veſſels, not muche vnlyke vnto oures . They founde alſo in theyr kitchens, mannes fleſhe, duckes fleſhe, and gooſe fleſhe, al in one pot : and other on the ſpittes redye to be layde to the fire. Entrynge into theyr inner lodgynges, they founde faggottes of the bones of mennes armes and legges, which they reſerue to make heades for theyr arrowes, bycauſe they lacke iron . The other bones they caſte awaye when they haue eaten the fleſhe . They founde likewiſe the heade of a yonge man faſtened to a poſte and yet bledinge . They haue in ſome villages, one great haule or pallaice, aboute the whiche theyr common houſes are placed . To this they reſort, as often as they come together to playe . When they perceaued the commynge of our men

our men

Marginal notes:

The building of theyr houſes.

So Tampine cotton.

Bombaſe . hangynge beddes.

Images.

Fyne cookery

Arrowe heds of bones.

ur men, they fledde, in theyr houſes they founde alſo about
rr. chyldren and women captiues which were reſerued to be
aten, but our men tooke them awaye to vſe them for inter-
retoures. Searchyng more diligently thynner partes of the
ſlande, they founde. vii. other ryuers, bygger then this whi
he we ſpake of before, runnyng throughe the Jlande, with
ruitefull and pleaſante banckes, delectable to beholde. This
ſlande, they called Guadalupea, for the ſimilitude that it hath
o the mounte Guadalupus in Spayne, where the Image of the
irgin MARIE is religiouſly honored. But the inhabitaun-
es caul it Carucueria, or Queraquiera. It is the chiefe habitation
f the Canibales. They brought from this Jland. vii. Popin-
ayes, bygger then pheſantes, muche differynge from other in
oloure: hauynge theyr backes, brittes, and bealies of purple
oloure, and theyr wynges of other variable coloures. In al
heſe Jlandes is no leſſe plentie of popingiayes then with
s of ſparrowes or ſtarlinges. As we brynge vp capons and
ennes to francke or make them fatte, ſo do they theſe bigger
yndes of popyngaies for the ſame purpoſe. After that they
adde thus ſearched the Jlande and dryuen theſe Canibales to
ſyghte, (whiche ranne awaye at theyr fyrſt approche as ſone
as they had eſpied them)they cauled theyr company together.
And as ſoone as they had broken the Canibals boates or lyghters (whiche they call Canoas) they lowſed theyr ankers the
aye before the Jdes of Nouember, and departed from Guadalupea. Colonus the admirall, for the deſyre he hadde to ſe his
ompanions, whiche at his fyrſt vpage he lefte the yere before
n Hiſpaniola to ſearche the countrey, lette paſſe many Jlandes
othe on his righte hande and lefte hande, and ſayled directly thyther. By the waye, there appeared from the Morthe. A
great Jlande which the captiues that were taken in Hiſpaniola,
cauled Madanino, or Matinino: Affirmynge it to be inhabited only
with wome: To who the Canibales haue acceſſe at certen tymes
of the yeare, as in owlde tyme the Thracians had to the Amazones in the Jlande of Leſbos. The men children, they ſende to
theyr fathers. But the women theye kepe with them ſelues.
They haue greate and ſtronge caues or dennes in the ground,
to the which they flye for ſafegarde if any men reſorte vnto
them at any other tyme then is appoynted. And there defende
them ſelues with bowes and arrowes, agenſt the violence of

The mounte
Guadalupus.

Carucueria.

popyngayes
bygger then
pheſauntes

The Caniba-
les dryuen to
flyght.

Matinino an
Jlande of wo
men.

ſuche as attempte to enuade them. They coulde not at this
tyme approche to this Jlande, by reaſõ of the Northenorth
eaſt wynde which blewe ſoo vehemently from the ſame, whẽ
as they nowe folowed the Eaſteſoutheaſte. After they departed frome *Madanino*, and ſayled by the ſpace of . xl. myles,
they paſſed not farre frome an other Jlande which the captyues ſayde to bee verye peopulous, and replenyſhed with all
thynges neceſſarie foz the life of man. This they cauled *Mons*
Serratus, bycauſe it was ful of mountaynes. The captyues further declared that the *Canibales*, are wonte at ſome tyme to goe
frome theyz owne coaſtes aboue a thouſande myle to hunt
foz men. The daye folowynge, they ſawe an other Jlande
the whiche, bycauſe it was rownde, they cauled *Sancta Maria*
Rotunda. The nexte daye, theye founde an other, which they
cauled *S. Martini*. Which they lette paſſe alſo bycauſe they had
no leaſure to tarye. Lykewyſe the thirde daye they eſpyed
an other, whoſe *Diametral* ſyde extendynge frome the Eaſte to
the weſte, they iudged to bee a hundzeth and fyftie myle.
Theye affirme all theſe Jlandes to be maruelous fayze and
frutefull. This laſte, they cauled *Sancta Maria Antiqua*. Saylyng
yet fozwarde, and leauynge many other Jlandes, after they
had ſayled aboute fortie myle, they chaunced vpon an other
muche bygger then any of the reſte, which thinhabitans caulẽ
Ay Ay, but they named it *Inſula crucis*. Heare they caſt anker to
fetche freſhe water. The Admiral alſo commaunded.xxx.mẽ
to go a lande out of his owne ſhyp, and to ſearch the Jlande
Here they founde fowze dogges on the ſhoze. The Jnhabi-
tants are *Canibales*, and maruelous experte in ſhutinge, as well
women as men : And vſe to infecte theyz arrowes with poyſon : when they had taryed there two dayes, they ſawe a
farre of, a *Canoa*, in the whiche were eight men and as manye
women hauynge with them bowes and arrowes.They fearſly
aſſayled owze men withoute all feare, and hurte ſum of them
with theyz venemous arrowes. Amonge theſe there was a
certen woman to whome the other gaue reuerence and obeyde
as though ſhe were theyz queene. Her ſonne wayted vppon
her, beinge a younge man, ſtrongly made, of terzible & frownynge countenaunce and a lyons face. Owze men leaſte they
ſholde take the moze hurte by beinge wounded a farre of,
thowght it beſte to ioyne with them, Therfoze with all ſpede
ſettinge

The Jlandes of Mons Serratus.

huntinge foz men.

Sancta Maria Rotunda.

Sanctus Martinus.

Sancta Maria Antiqua,

Jnſula crucis An Jlande of the Canibals

The Caniba-les are ex-pert archers.

Arrowes in-fected with veneme.

A conflict with the Ca-nibales.

fettinge foꝛewarde with their oꝛes the bꝛigantine in whiche they were fette alande, they ouerturned their Canoa with a great violence, which beinge ouerwhelmed, they notwithſtondinge, as well the women as the men ſwymminge, caſte theyꝛ dartes at owꝛe men, thicke and thꝛeefowlde. At the lengthe, gatherynge them ſelues together vpon a rocke coueꝛed with the water, they fowght manfully vntyll they were ouercome and taken, one being ſlayne, and the queenes ſonne foꝛe wounded. When they were bꝛowght into the Admirals ſhippe, they dyd no moꝛe put of their fiernes and cruell coun̄ tenances, then do the Lyons of Libia when theyꝛe perceaue the̅ ſelues to be bownde in chaynes. There is no man able to beholwde them, but he ſhall feele his bowelles grate with a certen hoꝛꝛoure, nature hath endewed them with ſoo terrible menacynge, and cruel aſpecte. This coniecture I make of my ſelfe and other which often tymes wente with me to ſee them at Methymna Campi. But nowe to returne to the viage. Proceaꝛ dinge thus further and further, moꝛe then fiue hundꝛethe myles, firſte towardes the Weſteſouthweſte, then towarde the Southweſt, and at the lengthe towarde the Weſte noꝛthe weſte, they entered into a mayne large ſea hauinge in it inꝛ numerable Jlandes, maruelouſlye differinge one frome an oꝛ ther, foꝛ ſum of them were verye frutefull and full of herbes and trees. Other ſum, verye dꝛye, barren, and rowgh with high rockye mountaynes of ſtone, wherof ſum were of bꝛight blewe oꝛ aſurine coloure, and other glyſteringe white : wher foꝛe they ſuppoſed them by good reaſon to bee the mynes of metalles and pꝛecious ſtones. But the rowghnes of the ſea, and multitude of Jlandes ſtandinge ſo thicke togyther, hindeꝛ red them ſoo, that they cowlde caſte no anker leaſte the bigꝛ ger veſſelles ſhulde runne vppon the rockes. Therefoꝛe they deferred the ſearchinge of theſe Jlandes vntyl an other tyme They were ſo manye and ſtoode ſo thicke, that they coulde not number them. Yet the ſmauler veſſelles which dꝛewe no greate depthe, entered emonge them and numbered foꝛtie and ſyxe Jlandes. But the bigger veſſelles, kepte aloofe in the mayne ſea foꝛ feare of the rockes. They caule the ſea where this multitude of Jlandes are ſituate, Archipelagus. Frome this tracte pꝛoceadinge foꝛrewarde, in the mydde waye there lyeth an Jland which thinhabitantes caule Burichena, oꝛ Buchena.

B.iii. But

The fierceꝛ nes and terriꝛ ble counteꝛ naunce of the Canibales.

Methymna Campi.

Jnnumerable ſlandes.

The mynes of Metales pꝛecious ſtoꝛ nes.

The ſea cauꝛ led Archipeꝛ lagus.

Infula. S. Jo:
hannes or Bu
chena.

But they named it *Infula. S. Iohannis,* Dyuers of theym whom
we had delyuered frome the *Canibales,* fayde that they wer
borne in this Jlande:affirminge it to be very peopulous an
frutefull, hauinge alfo manye fayre wooddes and hauens.
There is deadly hatred and continual battayle betwene then
& the *Canibales,* They haue no boates to paffe from their own
coaftes to the *Canibales.* But if it bee their chaunce to ouercom
them,when they make incurfion into theyr countreye to fek
their praye (as it fumtyme happeneth, the fortune of warr
beinge vncerteyne)they ferue them with like faufe,requiting

Death for
deathe

deathe for deathe. For one of theym mangeleth an other i
pieces, and rofte them and eate them euen before their eyes.
They taryed not in this Jlande. yet in the wefte angle the
of, a fewe of them went a lande for frefhe water,and fown
a greate and high howfe after the maner of their bpuilding

The moun:
taynes are
coulder then
the playnes.

hauinge.xii.other of their vulgare cotages placed abowte th
fame : but were all lefte defolate, whether it were that the
reforted to the mountaynes by refon of the heate which wa
that tyme of the yeare, and to returne to the playne when th
ayre waxeth cowlder, or els for feare of the *Canibales* whic
make incurfion into the Jlande at certen feafons. In al
this Jlande is only one kinge. The fouth fyde hereof exten
deth abowte two hundrethe myles.Shortlye after,they cam

From Domini
ca to Hifpani=
ola fyue hun:
drethleagues

to the Jlande of *Hifpaniola,* beinge dfftante frome the firft
Jlande of the *Canibales,* fyue hundrethe leagues. Here the
fownde all thynges out of order, and theyr felowes flayn
which they lefte here at their fyrfte vpage. In the begin
ninge of *Hifpaniola,* (hauinge in it many regions and kynge

The Spany:
ardes lefte in
the Jland are
flayne.
kynge Guac:
canarillus re
belleth).

domes as we haue fayde)is the region of *Xamana* whofe king
is named *Guaccanarillus.* This *Guaccanarillus* ioyned frendefhipp
with owre men at the fyrfte viage, and made a league with
them : But in the abfence of the Admirall, he rebelled,& wa
the caufe of owre mens deftruction, althowgh he diffimule
the fame, and pretended frendfhip at the Admirales returne
As owre men fayled on yet a litle further,they efpied a long

Two Images
of goulde.

Canos with many ores, in which was the brother of *Guaccanari
lus* with only one man waytinge on hym. He browght with
hym two Jmages of goulde, which he gaue the Admirall i
the name of his brother. And towlde a tale in his languag
as concerninge the deathe of owre men, as they proued afte
warD

oarde, but at this tyme had no regarde to his communicati=
on foz lacke of interpzetours, which were eyther all deade,
oz eſcaped and ſtoulne awaye when they dzewe nere the Jlan
es. But of the.r.vij. dyed by change of ayze and dyet. The
nhabitantes of theſe Jlandes haue byn euer ſoo vſed to liue
t libertie, in playe and paſtyme, that they can hardely away
with the yoke of ſeruitude which they attempte to ſhake of
by all meanes they maye. And ſurely if they had receaued
oure religion, J wolde thinke their life moſte happye of all
nen, if they might therwith enioye their aunciente libertie.
A fewe thinges contente them, hauinge no delite in ſuche ſu=
erfluites, foz the which in other places men take infinite
aynes and commit manie vnlawfull actes, and yet are neuer
atiſfied, wheras many haue to muche, and none inowgh.
But emonge theſe ſimple ſowles, a fewe clothes ſerue the na
ed : weightes and meaſures are not needefull to ſuch as can
not ſkyll of crafte and deceyte and haue not the vſe of peſtife=
ous monye, the ſeede of innumerable myſcheues. So that if
we ſhall not be aſhamed to confeſſe the truthe , they ſeeme to
pue in that goulden wozlde of the the which owlde wzyters
peake ſo much : wherin men lyued ſimplye and innocentlye
without infozcement of lawes, without quarellinge Judges
and libelles, contente onely to ſatiſfie nature, without fur=
her veration foz knowelege of thinges to come. yet theſe na
ed people alſo are tozmeted with ambitio foz the deſyzethey
yaue to enlarge their dominions:by reaſon wherof they kepe
warre & deſtroy one an other:frõ the wh ch plage J ſuppoſe
the golden wozld was not free. foz euen thenalſo, *Cede, non
edam*, that is, gyue place, & J wyll not giue place, had entred
emonge men. But nowe to returne to thematter frõ which we
yaue digreſſed. The admiral deſyrous to knowe further of
he death of his men, ſen tfoz *Guaccanarillus* to come to him to
his ſhip, diſſimulinge that he knew any thinge of the matter.
After that he came aboozd ſhyp, ſalutinge the Admiral & his cõ
pany gyuing alſo certẽ golde to the Capetaynes and offycers,
turned him to the wome captiues which not longe before our
mẽ had deliuered frõ the *Canibales*. And erneſtly beholdinge one
of them whome owre men cauled Catharyne, he ſpake gentel
ly vnto her. And thus when he had ſeene and marueyled at
the hozſes and ſuche other thinges as were in the ſhyppe, vn=
knowen

Libertie and idlenes.

A happy kind of lyfe.

Superfluite.

many haue to much and none inough.

The goulden woulde

Naked men troubled with ambicion.

Gyue place.

The Admiral ſendeth for the kynge.

No hozſes in the Jlandes

knowen to them, and had with a good grace and metelye aſ=
ked leaue of the Admirall, he departed. yet ſum there were
which counſeyled the Admirall to kepe hym ſtyll: that if they
might by any meanes proue that he was conſentinge to the

A tyme for all
thynges.

deathe of owre men, he might bee puniſhed accordinglie. But
the Admirall conſidering that it was yet no tyme to incenſe
thinhabitantes myndes to wrathe, dyſmyſſed hym. The next
daye folowing, the kinges brother reſortyng to the ſhyppes,
eyther in his owne name or in his brothers, ſeduced the wo=
men. For on the next nyght about mydnight, this Katherine

A deſperate
aduenture of
a woman.

aſwell to recouer her owne libertie as alſo her felowes, being
ſuborned therto eyther by the kinge or his brothers promiſes
attempted a much more difficulte and daungerous aduenture
then dyd *Cloelia* of Rome, which beinge in hoſtage with other

Cloelia of
Rome.

maydes to the kynge *Porcena*, deceaued her kepers, and rode
ouer the ryuer *Tiber*, with the other virgins which were pled=
ges with her. For wheras they ſwamme ouer the ryuer on
horſebacke. This Katharyne with ſeuen other women, tru=
ſtynge onlye to the ſtrengthe of theyr owne armes, ſwamme
aboue three longe myles: and that alſo, at ſuche tyme as the
ſea was ſumwhat rowghe. For euen ſoo farre of frome the
ſhore, lay the ſhippes at rode, as nigh as they could coniecture
But owre men folowinge them with the ſhippeboates, by the
ſame light ſeene on the ſhore wherby the women were ledde,
tooke three of them: ſuppoſinge that Katharyne with the o=
ther foure, wente to *Guaccanarillus*. For in the ſpringe of the
morninge, certen meſſengers beinge ſente to hym by the Admi=
rall, had intelligence that he was fledde with all his familie
and ſtuffe, and the women alſo. which thinge miniſtred fur=
ther ſuſpection that he was conſentinge to the death of owre
men. Wherfore the Admirall ſente forthe an armye of three
hundrethe men, ouer the which he appoynted one *Melchior* to
be capitayne, wylling hym to make diligent ſearche to fynde

Guaccanaril=
lus is ſought.
Melchior.

owte *Guaccanarillus*. *Melchior* therfore with the ſmauleſte veſſels
enteringe into the countreye by the ryuers and ſcouringe the
ſhores, chaunced into certen croked goulfes defended with. v
lyttle & ſtiepe hilles, ſuppoſinge that it had byn the mouth of
ſum greate ryuer. He founde here alſo a verye commodious
and ſafe hauen, and therefore named it *Portus Regalis*. They
ſaye that the enteraunce of this is ſo crooked and bendinge,
that

that after the ſhippes are once within the ſame, whether
they turne thē to the lefte hand, oz to the ryght, they can not
perceaue where they came in vntyll they returne to the mouth
of the ryuer: Although it be there ſo bzode that thzee of the
byggeſte veſſels may ſayle together on a froont. The ſharpe ⁊
high hilles on the one ſyde and on the other, ſo bzake the
wynde, that they were vncerten howe to rule theyz ſayles. In
the myddle gulfe of the ryuer, there is a pzomontorie oz point
of the lande with a pleaſaunte groue full of Popingayes and
other byzdes which bzeede therein and ſinge verye ſweetlye.
They perceaued alſo that two ryuers of no ſmaule largenes
fell into the hauen. Whyle they thus ſearched the lande betwene bothe, Melchior eſpied a high houſe a farre of, where
ſuppoſinge that Guaccanarillus had lyne hyd, he made towarde
it. And as he was goynge, there mette hym a man with a
frownynge countenaunce and a grymme looke, with a hundzeth men folowynge hym, armed with bowes and arrowes,
and long and ſharpe ſtaues like iauelynnes, made harde at
the endes with fyze. Who appzochyng towardes owre men,
ſpake owte alowde with a terryble voyce, ſayenge that they
were Taini, (that is) noble men, and not Canibales. But when
owre men had gyuen them ſignes of peace, they lefte bothe
theyz weapons and fiercenes. Thus geuynge eche of them
certen haukes belles, they tooke it foz ſo greate a rewarde,
that they deſyzed to enter bondes of nere frendeſhyppe with
vs, and feared not immediatly to ſubmitte them ſelues vnder
owre power, and reſozted to our ſhyps with theyz pzeſentes.
They that meaſured the houſe (beinge made in rounde fourme
fownde it to be from ſyde to ſyde. xxxii. greate paces, compaſed abowte with .xxx. other vulgare houſes, hauinge in them
many beames croſſe ouer, and couered with reedes of ſundzy
colours, wzethed and as it were weaued with maruelous art
When owre men aſked ſum of them where they myght fynde
Guaccanarillus. They aunſwered that that Region was none of
his. But theyz kynges beynge there pzeſente. Yet they ſayde
they ſuppoſed that Guaccanarilllus was gone from the playne to
the mountaynes. Makynge therfoze a bzotherly league with
this Caccicus, (that is to ſaye a kynge) they retourned to the Ad
myzall to make relation what they hadde ſeene and harde.
whervppon he ſent foozth dyuers other Centurians with their

*Popingayes
and byrdes.*

Taini.

*haukes bel-
les.*

A large houſ

*Reedes of ſū-
dzy colours.*

Caccius.

hundrethes to searche the countrey yet further. Emonge th
which were *Hoiedus* and *Gorualanus*, noble younge gentlemen
of great courage. And as they went towarde the mountaine
to seeke *Guaccanarillus*, dyuidinge the mountaynes betwene th
one of them fownde on the one syde therof foure ryuers fau
lynge frome the same mountaynes : and the other founde. ii
on the other syde. In the sandes of all these ryuers is fownt
great plentye of goulde, which thinhabitantes of the same
lande which were with vs, gathered in this maner. Makin
holes in the sande with theyr handes, a Cubette deape, ant
takynge vp sande with their lefte handes from the botome o
the same, they picked out graynes of goulde with their ryḡ
handes withowte any more arte or cunnynge. And so deliue
red it to owre men : who affirme that many of them thus ga
thered, were as bygge as tares or fytchis. And I my self
sawe a masse of rude goulde, (that is to say, suche as was n
uer molten) lyke vnto suche stones as are founde in the bot
tomes of ryuers, weighinge nyne ownces, which *Hoiedu* hin
selfe fownde. Beinge contented with these signes, they retu
ned to the Admirall to certifie him hereof. For the Admira
had commaunded vnder payne of punyshement that they shul
meddle no further then their commission : which was only t
searche the places with their signes. For the fame went tha
there was a certeyne kynge of the mountaynes from when̄s
those ryuers had their faule, whom they caule *Cacicus Caunabo*
that is, the lord of the house of golde. For they caule a hous
Boa, goulde, *Cauni* : and a kynge or Lorde, *Cacicus*, as we hau
sayde before. They affirme that there can noo where be foun
better fysshe, nor of more pleasant tast, or more holsome the
in these ryuers: also the waters of the same to be most holson
to drynke. *Melchior* hym selfe towld me, that in the moneth o
December, the days and nyghtes bee of equal length amon̄
the *Canibales*. But the sphere or circles of the heauen, agreeti
not therevnto. Albeit that in the same moneth, sume byrdes
make their nestes, and sume haue alredy hatched their egge
by reason of the heate beinge rather continuall then extreme
He towlde me also when I questioned with hym as concer
nynge the eleuation of the pole from the horizontal lyne, tha
al the sterres cauled *Pleshrum* or charles wayne, are hydde vn
der the Northe pole to the *Canibales*. And surely there retur
ned none from thense at this viage, to whome there is mor

Hoiedus and
Gorualanus.

Golde in ry-
uers faulinge
from moun-
taynes.

The maner
of gatheringe
golde.
Graynes of
golde.
A masse of
rude golde
weighinge.ix
ounces.

Caunaboa,
kynge of the
house of gold

Holsome wa
ter and plen-
tie of fysshe.
The day and
nyght of e-
qual length
in December.
Byrdes breed
in December

The eleuati-
on of the pole
The sterres
are cauled
gardina of
the pole.

redit to be gyuen, then to this man. But if he had byn ſkil
full in Aſtronomye, he ſhulde haue ſayde that the day was al
moſte equall with the night. For in no place towarde the ſtay
of the ſonne (cauled *ſolſticium*) can the night be equall with the
day. And as for them, they neuer came vnder the Equinoctiall,
or aſmuch as they had euer the northe pole theyr guyde, and
uer eleuate in ſight aboue the Horixontal. Thus haue J briefely written vnto yowre honoure, as muche as J thought ſufficiente at this tyme. And ſhall ſhortly hereafter (by Gods fauoure) wryte vnto you more largely of ſuche matters as ſhalbe dayly better knowen. For the admirall hym ſelfe (whome
J vſe famylyerly as my verye frende) hathe promyſed me by
his letters, that he wyl gyue me knowlege of al ſuch thynges
as ſhall chaunce. He hath nowe choſen a ſtronge place where
he may buyld a Citie nere vnto a comodious hauen. And hath
alredy buylded many houſes and a chapell in the whiche (as
in a newe worlde heretofore voyde of all religion) god is dayly ſerued with.xiii. preeſtes accordinge to the maner of owre
churches. When the tyme nowe approched when he promyſed to ſende to the kynge and queene, and hauynge proſperous wynde for that purpoſe, ſent backe the. xii. Carauelles
wherof we made mencion before it was no ſmaul hynderance
and greefe, vnto hym : Eſpecially conſyderynge the death of
his men whom he lefte in the Jlande at the fyrſt vyage, wherby we are yet ignorant of many places & other ſecretes wherof we might otherwyſe haue had further knowleage. But as
tyme ſhall reueale them ageyne, ſo wyll J aduertyſe yowe of
the ſame. And that you may the better knowe by conference
had with the Apothecaries and marchaunt ſtrangers Sirophenici-
ans, what theſe Regions beare, and howe hotte theyr ground
is, J haue ſent you all kyndes of graynes, with the barke &
inner partes of that tree whiche they ſuppoſe to bee the Cinamome tree. And yf it be your pleaſure to taſte eyther of the
graynes, or of the ſmaule ſeedes the which you ſhoulde perceaue to haue fawlen from theſe graynes, or of the wodde it
ſelfe, touch them firſte ſoftely mouinge them to your lyppes.
For although they bee not hurtefull, yet for theyr exceſſe of
heate, they are ſharpe and byte the tongue, yf they remayne
any whyle theron. But if the tongue be blyſtered by taſtynge
of them, the ſame is taken away by drynkynge of water. Of

C.ii,   the

Marginal notes:

The Equinoc-
tial lyne.

A chapel and
preeſtes.

Marchauntes
Sirophenici:
a.is.

The Cyna-
mome tree.

the coꝛne alſo wherof they make theyꝛ bꝛeade, this bꝛynge
ſhall delyuer ſume graynes to your Loꝛdeſhyppe bothe whyte
and blacke : And therwith alſo, a Trunke of the tree of Aloes.
The which if you cutte in pecces, you ſhall feele a ſweete ſa
uoure to pꝛoceade from the ſame. Thus fare you hartely wel
Fꝛom the courte of Methimna Campi. The thyꝛde day befoꝛe the
Calendis of May. Anno. Domini, M. CCCC. XCIIII.

Xiſoaloes oꝛ lignũ Aloes. (margin)

☞ The thyꝛde boke of the fyꝛſt Decade, to Lodouike Cardinall of Aragonye and Neuie to the kynge.

The fable of Phaeton. (margin)

Owe deſyꝛe that folyſhe Phaeton ſhulde ageine
rule the Chariotes of the Sunne : And con
tende to dꝛawe ſweete lycoures out of the
harde ſlynte, wheras you requyꝛe me to dys
ſcribe vnto you the newe woꝛlde, fownde i
the weſte by the good foꝛtune & gouernaunc
of the Catholike Pꝛinces Ferdinandus and He

kynge Ferdi=nandus and queene Helizabeth (margin)

liſabeth, your Uncle and Aunte : ſhewyng me alſo the letter
of kynge Frederike your vncle, wꝛytten to me in the ſame be
halfe. But ſythe you haue layde this burden on my backe, i
whoſe power it is to commaunde me to take vppon me moꝛ
then I am wel able. ye bothe ſhal receaue this pꝛecious ſtone
rudely cloſed in leade after my maner of woꝛkemanſhyppe.
Wherfoꝛe when you ſhall perceaue the lerned ſoꝛte frendelye
The malicious, enuiouſly : And the backebyters, furiouſly, t

Hereides. He meaneth the Ilandes. (margin)

bende theyꝛ ſclaunderous dartes ageynſt owre fayꝛe Nimphe
of the Ocean, you ſhall freely pꝛoteſte in howe ſhoꝛt tyme, an
in the myddeſte of what troubles and calamities, you haue en
foꝛced me to wꝛyte of the ſame. Thus fare you well frome
Granata the ninthe day befoꝛe the Calendes of May.

Hiſpaniola. (margin)

☞ We haue declared in the boke here befoꝛe, howe the Admi
rall paſſed by the coaſtes of the Canibales to the Ilande of Hiſpa=
niola with his whole nauie. But nowe we entende further to
ſhewe what he fownde as concernynge the nature of this I
lande, after that he had better ſearched the ſeacreates of the
ſame : Likewyſe of the Ilande of Cuba nere vnto it which he
yet ſuppoſed to bee the firme lande. Hiſpaniola therfoꝛe (which

Ophir whe= (margin)

he affirmeth to bee Ophir, wherof we reade in the thyꝛde boke
of

of the kynges) is of latitude, fyue southe degrees : hauynge
the northe pole eleuate on the northe syde.xxvii.degrees:And
on the Southe syde (as they saye) xxii. degrees. It reacheth
in length from the Easte to the Weste, seuen hundrethe and
foure scoze myles. It is distant from the Ilandes of *Gades* (cau
led *Cales*) xlix. degrees, and moze as sum saye. The forme of
the Ilande, resembleth the leafe of a chesnutte tree. Uppon
a high hyll on the North syde of the Ilande, he buylded a ci
tie, bycause this place was most apte for that purpose by rea=
son of a myne of stones which was nere vnto the same, ser=
uynge well bothe to buylde with, and also to make lyme. At
the bottome of this hyll, is there a great playne of thzee scoze
myles in lengthe: and in bzedth sumwhere .xii. sumwhere.xx.
myles where it is bzodest, and.vi. myles where it is narowest
Thzough this playne runne dyuers fayze ryuers of holsome
waters.But the greatest of them which is nauigable, faulleth
into the hauen of the citie for the space of halfe a furlonge.
Howe fertile and fruitfull this valley is, you shal vnderstand
by these thynges which folowe. On the shoze of this ryuer,
they haue lymyted and enclosed certeyne grounde to make
gardeynes and ozchiardes, in the which al kyndes of bygger
herbes, as radyshe, letuse, colewoztes, bozage, and such o=
ther, waxe rype within. xvi. dayes after the seede is sowen.
Lykewyse Melones, Gourdes, Cucumers, and suche other,
within the space of.xxxvi. dayes. These garden herbes, they
haue fresche and greene all the whole yeare. Also the rootes
of the canes oz reedes, of the lycour wherof, suger is made,
growe a cubette high within the space of. xv. dayes : but the
lycoure is not yet hardened. The lyke they affirme of plantes
oz shzouddes of younge vines : And that they haue the second
yeare gathered ripe and sweete grapes of the same. But by
reason of to muche rankenes, they beare but fewe clusters.
Furthermoze, a man of the countrey sowed a lyttle wheate a
bout the Calendes of Febzuary, and bzought with hym to
the citie a handefull of the rype eares of the same the thyzde
day befoze the calendes of Aprell: which was that yeare the
bigile of the Resurrection of owre Lozde. Also, al kyndes of
pulse, as beanes, peason, fytches, tares, and suche other, are
rype twyse in the yeare, as all they which come from thense,
affirme with one voyce: yet that the grounde is not vniuer=

sally apte to beare wheate. In the meane tyme whyle the
thynges were doinge, the Admirall sent owte a companye o
xxx. men to searche the Region of Cipanga, otherwyse cauled

**The Region
of Cipanga or
Cibana.
Golde.**

Cibana. This Region is full of mountapnes and rockes: An
the myddle backe of the hole Ilande in the whiche is grea
plentie of goulde. When they that went to searche the Reg
on, were returned they reported maruelous thynges as to
chinge the great ryches of this Region. Frome these mou

**Foure greate
ryuers.**

taynes, descende foure greate ryuers, which by the maru
lous industrye of nature, deuided the hole Ilande into fou
partes, in maner equall, ouerspreadinge and wateringe th
hole Ilande with their braunches. Of these foure ryuers, th
one reacheth towarde the Easte. This the inhabitantes cau
Iunna: An other, towarde the Weste, and is cauled Attibunicu
The thirde towarde the Northe, named Iachem: the laste re
cheth into the Southe, and is cauled Naiba. The daye befo

**The golden
region of
Cibana.**

the Ides of Marche, the Admiral him selfe with al his hor
men and foure hundreth footemen, marched directly toward
the South syde of the goulden Region. Thus passinge ou
the ryuer, the plaine and the mountayne which enuironed th
other syde of the playne, he chaunced vpon an other vale th

**Uales and
mountaynes.**

which a ryuer muche bygger then the fyrste, and many oth
meane ryuers runne throwgh. When he had also conueighe
his armye ouer the ryuer and passed the seconde vale which
was in no part inferiour to the firste, he made away throug
the thirde mountayne, where was no passage before, and de

**The vale of
Cibana.**

cended into an other vale which was nowe the beginninge o
Cibana. Through this also runne many fluddes, and ryuers
out of euery hyll, and in the sandes of theym all, is fownd
great plentie of goulde. And when he had nowe entered thre
score and twelue myles into the goulden region from the cit
he entended to buylde a fortresse vppon the toppe of a hyll
standing by the shore of a certeyne great ryuer, that he migh
the better and more safelye searche the secreates of the inne
partes of the Region. This he cauled the fortresse of saynt
Thomas. The which in the meane tyme whyle he was buyl

**Golde for
haukes bels.**

dynge, thinhabitantes beinge desirous of haukes belles an
other of owre thinges, resorted dayly thyther. To whom th
Admirall declared, that if they wolde brynge goulde, the
shulde haue what so euer they wolde aske. Forthwith tu
nynge

inge theyr backes and runnynge to the ſhoꝛe of the next ryz
er, they returned in a ſhoꝛt tyme, bꝛyngynge with them their
handes full of goulde. Amongeſt al other, there came a owld
man bꝛingynge with him two pybble ſtones of goulde weigh=
inge an vnce, deſyꝛynge them to gyue him a bell foꝛ the ſame
who when he ſawe oure men maruell at the byggenes therof,
he made ſignes that they were but ſmaule and of no value in
reſpecte of ſume that he had ſeene. And takynge in his hande
oure ſtones the leaſt wherof was as bygge as a walnut, and
the byggeſt as bygge as an oꝛange, he ſayde that there was
ſownde peeces of goulde ſoo bygge in his countrey, beynge
but halfe a dayes iourney from thenſe, and that they hꝭ no
regarde to the gatheringe therof. Whereby we perceaue that
they paſſe not muche foꝛ goulde in aſmuch as it is goulde on=
ly, but ſo farre eſteeme it, as the hande of the artificer hathe
faſhioned it in any coomely fourme. Foꝛ who doth greatly
eſteeme rowgh marble oꝛ vnwꝛought Iuerye. But if they be
wꝛought with the cunninge hande of *Phidias* oꝛ *Praxiteles*, and
ſhaped to the ſimilitude of the fayꝛe nimphes oꝛ fayeres of the
ſea (cauled *Nereiades*) oꝛ the fayꝛes of the wods, (cauled *Hamadri
des*) they ſhal neuer lacke byers. Beſyde this owld man, there
came alſo dyuers other, bꝛyngynge with them pypple ſtones of
gold weighiug .x. oꝛ .xii. dꝛammes: And feared not to confeſſe,
that in the place where they gathered that golde, there were
found ſuꝼtyme ſtones of gold as bygge as the heade of a chyld,
When he had taryed heare a fewe dayes, he ſent one *Luxanus*,
a noble younge gentylman with a fewe armed men to ſearche
all the partes of this Region. Who at his returne, repoꝛted
that thinhabitantes ſhewed him greater thynges thē we haue
poken of here befoꝛe. But he dyd openly declare nothynge
herof: which they thought was doone by the Admirales com
maundement. They haue wooddes full of certeyne ſpyces:
but not ſuche as we commonly vſe. Theſe they gather euen
as they do golde: that is as much as wyl ſerue foꝛ theyꝛ pur
poſe, euery man foꝛ hym ſelfe, to exchange the ſame with the
inhabitantes of other countreys adioyninge to them, foꝛ ſuch
thinges as they lacke, as dyſches, pottes, ſtooles, and ſuche
other neceſſaries. As *Luxanus* returned to the Admiral, (which
was about the Ides of Marche) he fownde in the wooddes,
certeyne wylde vines, rype and of pleaſaunt taſte. But thin=
habitans

Graynes and pipple ſtones of golde.

They paſſe not foꝛ golde, in that it is golde onely but. &c.

Stones of golde as byg as the heade of a chylde.

Spyces.

Wylde vines of pleaſaunte taſte.

habitantes paſſe not on them. This Region though it bee full of ſtones and rockes(and is therfoʒe cauled Cibana, which is as muche to ſaye as a ſtone) yet it is well replenyſhed with trees and paſtures. ye they inſtantly affirme, that if the graſſe of theſe mountaynes bee cutte, it groweth ageyne within the ſpace of foure dayes, higher then wheate. And foʒ as muche as many ſhowers of rayne doo faule in this Region, whereof the ryuers and ſluddes haue their increaſe, in euery of the which, golde is fownde myrte with ſande in all places, they iudge that the golde is dʒyuen from the mountaynes, by the behement courſe of the ſtreames which faule from the ſame, and ʒunne into the ryuers. The people of this Region are gyuen to Idelnes and playe. Foʒ ſuche as inhabyte the mountaynes, ſyt quakynge foʒ coulde in the wynter ſeaſon, ⁊ had rather ſoo wander vppe and downe Idelly, then take the peines to make them apparell, wheras they haue wooddes full of goſſapine cotton. But ſuch as dwel in the vales oʒ plaines feele no coulde in wynter. When the Admirall had thus ſearched the beginninge of the region of Cibana, he repayʒed to Iſabella (foʒ ſo he named the citie) where, leauinge the gouernance of the Ilande with his deputies, he pʒepared hym ſelfe to ſearch further the lymettes of the Ilande of Cuba oʒ Iohanna, which he yet doubted to bee the firme lande, and diſtant from Hiſpaniola. onely thʒee ſcoʒe and ten myles. This dyd he with moʒe ſpeedy expedicion, caulynge to ʒemembʒaunce the kinges commaundement, who wylled hym fyʒſt with all celeritie to ouer runne the coaſtes of the newe Ilandes, leaſte any other pʒince ſhulde in the meane tyme attempte to inuade the ſame. Foʒ the Kynge of Poʒtugale affirmed that it pertyened only to hym to diſcouer theſe vnknowen landes. But the byſhop of Rome Alexander the. vi. to auoyd the cauſe of this diſcenti on, graunted to the Kynge of Spayne by thauctoʒitie of his leaden bulles, that no other pʒince ſhulde bee ſo boulde as to make any biages to any of thoſe vnknowen regions, lyenge without the pʒecinct of a directe lyne dʒawe from the Noʒth to the Southe a hundʒeth leaques weſtwarde without the parallelles of the Ilandes cauled Capud Viride. oʒ Cabouerde, which we thynke to bee thoſe that in owlde tyme were cauled Heſperides,. Theſe perteyne to the kynge of Poʒtugale. And frome theſe, his pylottes whiche doo yearely ſearche newe coaſtes and

Fruitful moūtaynes

Colde in the landes of ʒyuers faulinge from the moū taynes.

Libertie and Idelnes. The mountaynes are coulde.

The Ilande of Cuba.

Leaſt any oʒ ther prince. ⁊c

Diſcenciõ betweene the poʒtugales and Spaniardes.

The Ilandes of Cobouerde oʒ hiſperides

and regions, directe their courſe to the Eaſte, ſaylynge euer
towarde the lefte hande by the backe of Aphrike and the ſeas
of the Ethiopians: Neyther to this day had the Portugales
at any tyme ſayled Southwarde, oʒ Weſtwarde from the I=
landes of *Cabouerde*.Preparyng therfoʒe thʒee ſhippes, he made
haſte towarde the Ilande of *Iohanna* oʒ *Cuba* whyther he came
in ſhoʒte ſpace, and named the poynt therof where he fyʒſt ar=
ryued, *Alpha* and O: that is, the fyʒſte and the laſte: foʒ he
ſuppoſed that there had byn thend of owre Eaſte bycauſe the
ſonne fauleth there: And of the weſte, bycauſe it ryſeth there.
Foʒ it is apparente, that weſtwarde, it is the beginninge of
India beyonde the ryuer of *Ganges*: And Eaſtewarde, the fur=
theſt ende of the ſame:which thinge is not contrary to reaſon
foʒaſmuche as the Coſmographers haue lefte the lymites of
India beyonde *Ganges* vndetermyned: where as alſo ſume were
of opinion that *India* was not farre frō the coaſtes of Spaine
as we haue ſayde befoʒe. Within the pʒoſpecte of the begyn=
nynge of *Cuba*, he founde a commodious hauen the extreme
angle of the Ilande of *Hiſpaniola*. Foʒ in this part, the Iland
receaueth a greate goulfe. This hauen, he named ſaynt Ny=
colas poʒte, beinge ſcarſely .xx. leaques from *Cuba*. As he de
parted from henſe and ſayled weſtwarde by the ſouth ſyde of
Cuba, the further that he went, ſo muche the moʒe the ſea ſee=
med to bee extended in bʒeadth & to bende towarde the ſouth.
On the ſouth ſyde of *Cuba*, he fownde an Ilande which thin=
habitantes caule *Iamaica*. This he affirmeth to bee longer and
bʒoder then the Iland of Sicilie:hauyng in it only one moun
tayne, which on euery parte begynninge from the ſea, ryſeth
by little and little into the myddeſt of the Ilande: And that
ſoo playnely without rowghnes, that ſuche as goo vp to the
toppe of the ſame, can ſcarſely perceaue that they aſcende.
This Ilande he affirmed to bee very fruitfull and full of peo=
ple as well in thinner partes of the ſame as by the ſhoʒe: And
that thinhabitantes are of quicker wytte then in the other I=
landes, and moʒe experte artificers and warrelyke men. Foʒ
in many places where he woulde haue arryued, they came ar=
med ageynſt him and foʒbodde him with thʒeatening woʒdes
But beinge ouercome, they made a league of frendeſhip with
hym. Thus departynge from *Iamaica*, he ſayled towarde the
Weſte with a pʒoſperous wynde foʒ the ſpace of thʒeeſcoʒe &

tenne dayes

Alpha and O

The ende of
the Eaſte and
Weſt.

Note.
India not far
frō Spayne.

Saynt Nyco=
las poʒte.

The Iland of
Iamaica.

Iamaica.

Quicke wyt=
ted people.

The compa=
ſſinge of the
earth.

Aurea Cher-
soneſus, oꝛ
Malaccæ.

A ſecreate of
Aſtronomᵭa.

The ryuer of
Ganges.

Daungerous
ſtreightes by
reaſon of many Jlandes.

The Admi-
ral gaue na-
mes to ſeuen
hundꝛethe J-
landes.
thꝛe thouſãd
Jlandes.

A large hauē

Roſted fyſſhe
and ſerpents
of .viii. foote
longe.

tenne dayes: thinkinge that he had paſſed ſo farre by the cõ-
paſſe of the earth being vnderneth vs, that he had byn ner
vnto *Aurea Cherſoneſus* (nowe cauled *Malaccha,*) in owre Eaſte J-
dia beyonde the beginninge of *Perſides.* Foꝛ he playnely beleued that he had lefte onely two of the twelue howꝛes of th
ſonne, which were vnknowen to vs, foꝛ the owlde wꝛyter
haue lefte halfe the courſe of the ſonne vntouched, where a
they haue but onely diſcuſſed that ſuperficiall parte of th
earth which lyeth betwene the Jlandes of Gades and the ry
uer of Ganges: oꝛ at the vttermoſte, to *Aurea Cherſoneſus.* J
this nauigation, he chaunced on many furious ſeas, runnin
with a faule as it had byn the ſtreames of fluddes: Alſo man
whoꝛlepooles, and ſhelfes, with many other daungers, an
ſtreyghtes by reaſon of the multytude of Jlandes, which le
on euery ſyde. But not regardinge all theſe perelles, he dete
myned to pꝛoceade vntyl he had certaine knowledge whethe
Cuba were an Jlande oꝛ firme lande. Thus he ſayled foꝛwar
coaſtinge euer by the ſhoꝛe towarde the weſte foꝛ the ſpace o
CC.xxii. leaques, that is, abowte a thouſande and thꝛee hu
dꝛeth myles: And gaue names to ſeuen hundꝛeth Jlandes b
the waye: Leauynge alſo on the lefte hande (as he feared no
to repoꝛte) thꝛee thouſande here and thꝛee. But let vs now
returne to ſuche thinges as he fownde woꝛthy to be noted i
this nauigation. Saylinge therfoꝛe by the ſyde of *Cuba*, an
ſearchinge the nature of the places, he eſpied not farre from
Alpha and O, a large hauen of capacitie to harboꝛowe many
ſhippes: whoſe enteraunce is bendinge, beinge incloſed o
bothe ſydes with capes oꝛ poyntes which receaue the water
This hauen is large within, and of exceadinge depthe. Say
linge by the ſhoꝛe of this poꝛte, he ſawe not farre frome th
ſame, two cotages couered with reedes, and in many place
fyer kyndeled. Here he ſente certeyne armed men owte of th
ſhippes to the cotages: where they fownde nother man no
woman, but roſtemeate enowgh. Foꝛ they fownde certeyne
ſpyttes of woodde lyenge at the fyꝛe, hauinge fyſhe on theyn
abowt a hundꝛeth pownde weight, and two ſerpentes of .vii
foote longe a piece, wherat maruaylinge, and lokynge abow
if they coulde eſpye any of thinhabitantes, and that none ap
peared in ſyght (foꝛ they fledde all to the mountaynes at th
comminge of owꝛe men) they fell to theyꝛ meate, and eate th
fyſſh

fyſhe taken with other mens travayle: But they abſteyned frō the ſerpentes, which they affirme to differ nothinge from Crocodiles of Egypt, but onely in byggenes. For (as *Plinie* ſayth) Crocodiles haue ſumetymes byn fownde of. xviii. cůbettes longe. But of theſe the byggeſt were but of. viii. fote. Thus beinge well refreſſhed, they entered into the next woodde where they fownde many of the ſame kynde of ſerpentes hangynge vppon bowghes of trees: of the which, ſume had theyr mouthes tyed with ſtrynges, and ſume theyr teethe taken owte. And as they ſearched the places nere vnto the hauen, they ſawe abowte. lxx. men in the toppe of a hyghe rocke, whiche fledde as ſoone as they had eſpied owre men. Who by ſignes and tokens of peace, caulinge them ageyne, there was one which came nere them and ſtoode on the toppe of a rocke, ſeemynge as thowgh he were yet ferefull. But the Admiral ſent one Didacus to hym, a man of the ſame countrey, whom he had at his fyrſte vyage taken in the Ilande of *Guanahaini*, beinge nere vnto *Cuba*: wyllinge hym to come nere and not to bee afrayde. When he harde Didacus ſpeke to him in his owne tonge he came bowldly to hym: and ſhortly after reſorted to his cōpany, perſuadinge them to come without all feare. After this meſſage was doone, there deſcended frome the rockes to the ſhippes, abowt three ſcore and ten of thinhabitantes, profferinge frendeſhippe and gentelnes to owre men: whiche the Admirall accepted thankefully, and gaue them dyuers rewardes: And that the rather, for that he had intelligence by Didacus thenterpretoure, that they were the kynges fyſſhers, ſent of theyr lorde to take fyſſhe ageynſt a ſolemne feaſte which he prepared for an other kynge. And wheras the Admirales men had eaten the fyſſhe whiche they lefte at the fyre, they were the gladder therof, bycauſe they had lefte the ſerpentes. For there is nothinge amonge theyr delicate dyſſhes, that they eſteeme ſo muche as theſe ſerpentes: In ſoo muche that it is no more lawfull for the common people to eate of them, then peacockes or pheſantes amonge vs. As for the fyſſhes, they doubted not to take as many more the ſame nyght. Beynge aſked why they fyrſt roſted the fyſſhe which they entended to beare to their kynge. They anſwered, that they might bee the freſſher and vncorrupted. Thus ioyninge handes for a token of further frendeſhip, euery man reſorted to his owne. The

Crocodiles of Egypte.

Didacus thinterpretour

The kynges fyſſhers.

Serpentes eſteemed for delicate meat Ophiophagi.

Admiral

Admirall went forwarde as he had appoynted, folowing the
faulinge of the sonne from the beginninge of *Cuba* cauled Alpha and O. The shores or sea bankes euen vnto this hauen, albeit they be ful of trees, yet are they rowgh with mountains.

Blossomes & fruites bothe at one tyme.
Of these trees, sume were ful of blossoomes and flowres, and
other laden with fruites. Beyonde the hauē the lande is more
fertile and peopulous, whose inhabitantes are more gentyll
and more desyrous of owre thinges. For as sone as they had
espied owre shippes, they flocked all to the shore, brynginge
with them suche breade as they are accustomed to eate, and
gourdes full of water, offeringe theym vnto owre men, and

Trees which beare gourds
further desyringe them to coome alande. In all these Ilandes
is a certeyne kynde of trees as bygge as elmes, whiche beare
gourdes in the steade of fruites. These they vse only for drin-
kynge pottes, and to fetche water in, but not for meate, for
the inner substance of them, is sower then gaule, & the barke
as harde as any shelle. At the Ides of Maye, the watche men

A multitude of Ilandes.
lokinge owte of the toppe castell of the shyppe towarde the
Southe, sawe a multitude of Ilandes standinge thicke together, beynge all well replenished with trees, grasse, and herbes, and wel inhabyted. In the shore of the continent, he chaū-

Hotte water.
ced into a nauigable ryuer whose water was soo hotte, that
no man myght endure to abyde his hande therein any tyme.
The day folowinge, espying a farre of a Canoa of fysher men
of thinhabitantes, fearinge least they shulde flye at the syghe
of owre men, he commaunded certeyne to assaple them pryuily
with the shyppe boates. But they fearinge nothinge, taryed
the comminge of owre men. Nowe shal you heare a newe kind

A straunge kynde of fys- shynge. A huntynge fysshe.
of fysshinge. Lyke as we with greyhoundes doo hunte hares,
in the playne fieldes. So doo they as it were with a huntyng
fysshe, take other fysshes. This fysshe was of shape or fourme
vnknowen vnto vs: but the body therof, not muche vnlyke a
greate yele: hauinge on the hynder parte of the heade, a very
towgh skynne, lyke vnto a greate bagge or purse. This fysshe
is tyed by the syde of the boate with a corde lette downe soo
farre into the water, that the fysshe maye lye close hyd by the
keele or bottome of the same, for shee may in no case abyde the
sight of the ayer. Thus when they espie any greate fysshe, or

Abundance of tortoyses.
tortoyse (wherof there is great abundance bygger then great
targettes) they let the corde at lengthe, But when shee feeleth
                                                              her

her selfe loosed, shee enuadeth the fyshe or tortoyse as swift-
ly as an arrowe. And where she hath once fastened her howld
shee casteth the purse of skynne wherof we spake before: And
by drawyng the same togyther, soo graspeleth her pray, that
no mans strength is sufficient to vnloose the same, excepte by
lyttle and lyttle drawinge the lyne, shee bee lyfted sumwhat
aboue the brymme of the water. For then, as sone as she seeth the brightnes of the ayer, shee lettethe goo her howlde.
The praye therfore, beinge nowe drawen nere to the brymme
of the water, there leapeth soodenly owte of the boate into
the sea soo manye fysshers, as maye suffice to holde faste the
praye, vntyll the reste of the coompany haue taken it into the
boate. Which thinge doone, they loose soo muche of the cord,
that the hunting fysshe, may ageyne returne to her place with
in the water : where by an other corde, they let downe to her
a piece of the praye, as we vse to rewarde greyhoundes after
they haue kylled theyr game. This fysshe, they caule *Guaicanil*,
But owre men caule it *Reuersum*. They gaue owre men foure
tortoyses taken by this meanes : And those of such byggenes
that they almoste fylled theyr fysshinge boate. For these fysshes are esteemed amonge them for delicate meate. Owre men
recompensed them ageyne with other rewardes, and soo lette
them departe. Beinge asked of the coompasse of that lande,
they aunswered that it had no ende westewarde. Most instant
ly desyringe the Admirall to coome alande : or in his name to
seude one with the to salute their *Cazicus*, (that is) their kinge:
Affirmynge that he wolde gyue owre men many presentes, yf
they wolde goo to hym. But the Admiral, leaste he shulde bee
hyndered of the vyage which he had begunne, refused to goo
with them. Then they desyred to knowe his name, and towld
owre men lykewyse the name of theyr kyng. Thus saylling on
yet further euer toward the West, within fewe dayes he came
nere vnto a certeyne exceding high mountayne, wel inhabyted
by reason of the great fertilitie of the same. Thinhabitauntes
of this mountayne, browght to owre shippe, breade, gossampine cotton, cunnies, and sundry kyndes of wyldfowle : demaundynge relygiously of thinterpretoures, if this nation des
cended not from heauen. The kynge of this people, and dyuers other sage men that stoode by hym, informed hym that
that lande was no Ilande. Shortly after, enteringe into one

Marginal notes:

Fyssher men.

The fysshe Guaicanum.

humaine peo ple.

A mountaine fruitefull and well inhabi ted.

of the Ilandes beinge on the lefte hande of this lande, they fownde no body therin : for they fledde al at the commyng of owre men. yet fownde they there fowre dogges of maruelous deformed shape, and suche as coulde not barke. This kynd of dogges, they eate as we do goates. Here is great plentie of geese, duckes, and hearons. Betwene these Ilandes and the continente, he entered into soo narowe streyghtes, that he coulde scarsely turne backe the shippes : And these also so shalowe, that the keele of the shyps sumtyme rased on the sandes The water of these streyghtes, for the space of fortie myles, was white and thycke lyke vnto mylke, and as thowgh mele had byn sparkeled throwgh owte al that sea. And when they had at the lengthe escaped these strayghtes, and were nowe coome into a mayne and large sea, and had sayled theron for the space of foure score myles, they espyed an other excedinge hygh mountayne, whyther the Admirall resorted to store his shyppes with fresshe water and fuel. Heare amonge certeyne wooddes of date trees, and pyneable trees of excedyng height he fownd two natiue sprynges of fresshe water. In the meane tyme whyle the woodde was cuttynge and the barrelles fyllyng, one of owre archers went into the wood to hunt: where he espyed a certeyne man with a whyte vesture, soo lyke a fryer of thorder of saynt Marye of *Mercedis*, that at the fyrste sight he supposed it had byn the Admiralles preeste which he browght with hym, beyng a man of the same order. But two other folowed hym immediatlye owte of the same wooddes, shortly after, he sawe a farre of a hole coompany of men clothed in apparel, beinge abowte.xxx.in nomber. Then turning his backe and cryinge owte to his felowes, he made haste to the shyppes with all that he myght dryue. These apparelled men, made signes and tokens to hym to tary and not to bee afraynde. But that notwithstandinge, he ceased not to flye. The Admirall beinge aduertised hereof, and not a lyttle reioysynge that he had fownde a ciuile people, incontinently sent forth armed men, with commaundement, that yf neede shoulde soo requyre, they shulde enter fortie myles into the Ilande, vntyl they myght fynde eyther those apparelled men, or other inhabitantes of that countrey. When they hadde passed ouer the woodde, they came into a greate playne full of grasse and herbes, in which appeared no token of any pathe way. Here attemptinge

attemptinge to goo throwgh the graſſe and herbes, they were
ſoo entangled and bewrapte therin, that they were ſcarſely a
ble to paſſe a myle, the graſſe beinge there lyttle lower then
owre rype corne. Beinge therfore weryed, they were enforced
to returne ageyne, fyndyng no pathe way. The day folowing
he ſent foorth.xxv. armed men an other way : Commaunding
them to make diligent ſearche and inquiſition what maner of
people inhabited the land. Who departinge, when they had
fownde not farre from the ſea ſyde certeyne ſteppes of wylde
beaſtes, of the which they ſuſpected ſum to bee of Lyons feete
being ſtriken with feare, returned backe ageyne. As they came
they fownde a woodde in the which were many natiue vines
here and there crepinge abowte highe trees, with many other
trees bearinge aromaticall fruites and ſpyces. Of theſe vines
they browght with them into Spaine many cluſters of grapes
very ponderous and full of lycoure. But of the other fruites,
they browght none bycauſe they putrified by the waye in the
ſhippe, and were caſte into the ſea. They ſaye alſo that in the
laundes or medowes of thoſe wooddes, they ſawe flockes of
greate cranes twyſe as bygge as owres. As he went forward
and turned his ſayles towarde certeyne other mountaiues, he
eſpied two cotages on the ſhore, in the whiche he ſawe onely
one man : who beinge browght to the ſhyppe, ſignified with
heade, fyngers, and by al other ſignes, that he coulde deuiſe
that the lande which lay beyonde thoſe mountaynes, was ve=
ry full of people. And as the Admirall drewe nere the ſhore of
the ſame, there mette hym certeyne Canoas hauinge in them ma
ny people of the countrey, who made ſignes and tokens of
peace and frendeſhyp. But here Didacus thinterpretour whiche
vnderſtoode the language of thinhabitantes of the beginning
of Cuba, vnderſtode not them one whyrte, wherby they conſp=
dred that in ſundry prouinces of Cuba, were ſundry languages
He had alſo intelligence, that in the inlande of this Region,
was a kynge of greate power, and accuſtomed to weare appa
rell. He ſayth that all the tracte of this ſhore, was drowned
with water and full of mudde, beſette with many trees, after
the maner of owre maryſſhes, yet whereas in this place they
wente alande for freſſhe water, they fownde many of the ſhel
fyſſhes in the whiche pearles are gathered. But that coulde
not cauſe the Admirall to tracte the tyme there, entendinge at
this

Margin notes:

graſſe almoſt as hyghe as corne.

Steppes of wyld beaſtes feete.

Natiue vines

Trees bea=ringe ſpyces and ſweete fruites.

Greate Cranes.

Dyuers lan=guages in the Jlande of Cuba.

Pearles in ſhelfyſſhes.

this viage, only to proue howe many landes & ſeas he coulde
diſcouer accordinge to the kynges commaundement. As they
yet proceded forwarde, they ſawe here and there al the waye
alonge by the ſhore, a great ſmoke ryſinge, vntyll they came
to an other mountayne foure ſcore myles diſtant. There was
no rocke or hyll that coulde be ſeene, but the ſame was all of
a ſmoke. But whether theſe fyers were made by thinhabitantes for their neceſſary buſynes, or as we are wont to ſette
beacons on fyre when we ſuſpecte thapproche of owre enemies, thereby to gyue warninge to theyr neyghbours to bee in a
redines, and gather togyther if perhappes owre men ſhulde
attempte any thinge ageynſt them, or otherwyſe as ſeemethe
moſt lykely, to cauſe them togyther as to a wonder to behould
owre ſhippes, they knewe yet no certentie. In this tracte, the
ſhores bended ſumetyme towarde the Southe, and ſumetyme

The ſea en-
tangeled
with Jlandes

towarde the Weſte and weſteſouthweſt: And the ſea was euery where entangeled with Jlandes: by reaſon whereof, the
keeles of the ſhippes often tymes raſed the ſandes for ſhalow
nes of the water: So that the ſhyppes bringe very ſore bruſed
and appayred the ſayles, cables, and other tacklinges, in ma
ner rotten, and the vytayles, (eſpecially the byſkette breade)
corrupted by takynge water at the riftes euyll cloſed, the Admirall was enforced to turne backe ageyne. This laſte poynte

Euangeliſta.

where he touched of Cubs (not yet beinge knowen to be an
Jlande) he cauled *Euangeliſta.* Thus turning his ſayles toward
other Jlandes lyinge not farre from the ſuppoſed continente,

A multitude
of great tor-
toyſes
A goufe of
whyte water
Humaine peo-
ple.

he chaunced into a mayne ſea where was ſuche a multitude of
greate tortoyſes, that ſumetyme they ſtayed the ſhyppes. Not
longe after, he entered into a gulfe of whyte water, lyke vnto that wherof we ſpake before. At the lengh fearing the ſhelfes of the Jlands, he returned to the ſhore of Cubs by the ſame
way which he came. Here a multitude of thinhabitantes, as
well women as men, reſorted to hym with cheerefull countenaunce and without feare: bringynge with them popingayes

Stock doues
of more plea-
ſaunt taſt then
partriches.

breade, water, and cunnyes: But eſpecially ſtocke doues much
bygger then owres: which he affirmeth, in ſauour and taſte,
to bee muche more pleaſaunt then owre partryches. Wherfore
where as in eatinge of them he perceaued a certeyne ſauoure
of ſpyce to proceade from them, he commaunded the croppe to
bee opened of ſuche as were newely kylled, and fownde the
ſame

same full of sweete spyces, whiche he argued to bee the cause of theyr strange taste. For it standeth with good reason, that the fleshe of beastes, shulde drawe the nature and qualitie of theyr accustomed nuryshemente. As the Admirall harde masse on the shore, there came towarde hym a certeyne gouernoure, a man of foure score yeares of age, and of great grauitie, although he were naked sauinge his pryuie partes. He had a greate trayne of menne waytinge on hym. All the whyle the preeste was at masse, he shewed hym selfe verye humble and gaue reuerente attendaunce with graue and demure countenaunce. When the masse was ended, he presented to the Admirall, a baskette of the fruites of his countrey, delyueringe the same with his owne handes. When the Admirall had gentelly interteyned hym, desyringe leaue to speake, he made an oration in the presence of *Didacus* thinterpretoure, in this effecte. I haue byn aduertised (moste mighty prince) that you haue of late with greate power subdued many landes and Regions hytherto vnknowē to you : and haue browght no little feare vppon all the people and inhabitantes of the same. The which your good fortune, you shal beare with lesse insolencie, if you remember that the soules of men haue two iourneyes after they are departed from this bodye. The one fowle and darke, prepared for suche as are iniurious and cruell to man kynde : The other pleasaunt and delectable, ordeyned for thē which in theyr lyfe tyme, loued peace and quietnes. If therefore you acknowleage your selfe to bee mortall, and consyder that euery man shall receaue condigne rewarde or punyshemēt for such thinges as he hath done in this life, you wyl wronge fully hurte no man. When he had sayde these wordes and other lyke, which were declared to the Admirall by thinterpretour, he marueylinge at the iudgemente of the naked owlde man, answered, that he was gladde to heare his opinion as touchinge the sundry iourneys and rewardes of sowles departed from theyr bodyes : Supposinge that nother he, or any other of thinhabitantes of those Regions, had had any knowleage thereof. Declaringe further that the chiefe cause of his comminge thyther was to instructe them in suth godly knowleage and trewe religion : And that he was sente into those countreys by the Christian kynge of Spayne (his lorde and maister) for the same purpose : And specially to subdue and

C.i. punysshe

The humanitie of a reuerende owlde gouernour.

An oration of the naked go uernour.

Theyr opiniō of the icul of man.

Desyre of golde founde that which religion coulde not fynde. *Virtus post num̄mos.* &c.

punishe the Canibales and such other mischeuous people: And to defende innocentes ageynst the violence of such euyl doers wyllynge hym and all other such as embrased vertue, in no case to bee afrayde : But rather to open his mynde vnto him, if eyther he, or any other suche quiete men as he was, hadde susteyned any wronge of theyr neyghbours: and that he wold see the same reuenged. These comfortable wordes of the Admirall soo pleased the owlde man, that notwithstandyng his extreeme age, he woulde gladly haue gone with the Admiral as he had doone in deede, if his wyfe and chyldren had not hyndered hym of his purpose. But he marueyled not a lyttle, that the Admirall was vnder the dominion of an other : And muche more, when thinterpretour towlde hym of the glorye, magnificence, pompes, greate powers. and furnymentes of warre of owre kynges, and of the multitudes of cities and townes which were vnder theyr dominions. Intendyng ther fore to haue gonne with the Admirall, his wyfe and children fell prostrate at his feete, with teares despyynge hym not to forsake them and leaue them desolate. At whose pytifull requestes, the worthy owlde man beinge moued, remayned at home to the comfort of his people and famylie, satisfyenge ra ther them then hym selfe. For not yet ceasinge to woonder, and of heauy countenaunce bycause he myght not departe, he demaunded oftentymes if that lande were not heauen, which browght foorth suche a kynde of men. For it is certeyne, that

The Ilandas common as the sunne and water.

amonge them, the lande is as common as the sonne and wa ter : And that Myne and Thyne (the seedes of all myscheefe) haue no place with them. They are contente with soo lyttle, that in soo large a countrey, they haue rather superfluitie the scarsenes. Soo that (as wee haue sayde before) they seeme to

The golden worlde.

lyue in the goulden worlde, without toyle, lyuinge in open gardens, not intrenched with dykes, dyuyded with hedges, or defended with waules. They deale trewely one with an o ther, without lawes, without bookes, and without Iudges.

prouisió with out care.

They take hym for an euyll and myscheuous man, which ta keth pleasure in doinge hurte to other. And albeit that they delyte not in superfluities, yet make they prouision for thin

Simple diete

crease of suche rootes, wherof they make theyr breade, as Mi- izium, Iuccss, and Ages, contented with suche simple dyet, wher by health is preserued, and dyseases auoyded. The Admirall
therfore

therfore departinge from thenſe, and myndinge to returne a-
geyne ſhortly after, chaunced to coome ageyne to the Jlande
of Iamaica beinge on the ſowthe ſyde therof: and coaſted all a
longe by the ſhore of the ſame, from the Weſte to the Eaſte.
From whoſe laſt corner on the Eaſt ſyde, when he ſawe to-
wardethe Morth on his lefte hande, certeyn high mountains
he k newe at the length that it was the ſowthe ſyde of the J-
lande of Hiſpaniola, which he had not yet paſſed by. Wherfore
at the Calendes of September, enteringe into the hauen of
the ſame Jlande, cauled ſaynt Mycolas hauen, he repayred
his ſhippes to thintent that he myght ageyne waſt and ſpoyle
the Jlandes of the Canibales, and burne all theyr Canoas,
that thoſe raueninge wolues myght no longer perſecute and
deuoure the innocent ſheepe. But he was at this tyme hyndered of his purpoſe by reaſon of a dyſeaſe which he had gotte
with to muche watchinge. Thus beinge feeble and weake, he
was ledde of the maryners to the citie of Iſabella, where, with
his two brytherne which were there, & other his familiers, he
recouered his health in ſhorte ſpace. yet coulde he not at this
tyme aſſayle the Canibales, by reaſon of ſedicion that was ryſen of late amonge the Spanyardes which he had lefte in Hiſpaniola, wherof we wyll ſpeake more heareafter. Thus fare ye
wel.

The margin notes:
The Jland of Jamaica.

Hiſpaniola.

The Cani-bales.

Sickenes of to much wat-chinge.

The fourth booke of the fyrſt decade to Lodouike Cardinall of Aragonie.

Olonus the Admirall of the Ocean, returning
(as he ſuppoſed) from the continent or firme
lande of Eaſt Jndia, had aduertiſement that
his brother Boilus & one Peter Margarita, an owld
familier of the kinges, and a noble man, with
diuers other of thoſe to whom he had left the
gouernemét of the Jland, were of corrupted
mynde ageynſt him, departed into Spayne. Wherfore as wel
to purge him of ſuch crimes as they ſhuld ley to his charge, as
alſo to make a ſupply of other men in the place of them which
were returned, & eſpecially to prouyde for vitailes, as wheat,
wyne, oyle, and ſuch other which the Spanyardes are accuſtomed to eate, bycauſe they coulde not yet well agree with
ſuch meates as they fownde in the Jlandes, determined ſhort
ly to

The margin notes:
Eaſte Jndia.

The Spany-ardes rebelle in the Admi-rals abſence.

E.ii.

ly to take his vyage into Spayne. But what he dyd befor
his departure, I wyll briefely rehearse.

The kynges of the Ilandes which had hytherto lyued quiet
ly and content with theyr lyttle whiche they thowght abun
The kynges
of the Ilande
rebell.
dante, wheras they nowe perceaued that owre men began to
fasten foote within theyr Regions and to beare rule amonge
them, tooke the matter so greuously, that they thowght no
thynge elles but by what meanes they myght vtterly destroy
them, and for euer abolysshe the memory of theyr name. For
that kynde of men (the Spanyardes I meane which folowed
The Spani=
ardes misbe=
hauour.
the Admirall in that nauigation,) was for the most parte vn
ruly, regardynge nothinge but Idlenes, playe, and libertie
And wolde by no meanes absteyne from iniuries: Rauysshyng
the wome of the Ilandes before the faces of their husbandes
fathers, and brethrene: By which theyr abhomynable mysde
maynour, they disquieted the myndes of all thinhabitantes
In so much that where so euer they fownde any of owre men
vnprepared, they slewe them with suche fyercenes and glad
nes, as thowgh they had offered sacryfyce to God. Inten
dynge therefore to pacifie their troubled myndes, and to pu
nysshe them that slew his men before he departed from thense
he sent for the kynge of that vale, which in the booke before
we descrybed to bee at the foote of the mountaynes of the R
gion of Cibaua. This kynges name was Guarionexius: who, th
Guarionexius
the kynge of
the greatvale
Didacus the
interpretour
more streyghtly to concyle vnto hym the frendeshyppe of th
Admirall, gaue his syster to wyfe to Didacus, a man from hi
chyldes age browght vp with the Admiral, whom he vsed fo
his interpretoure in the prouinces of Cuba. After this, he sen
for Caunaboa, cauled the lorde of the howse of goulde: that is
Caunaboa,
the kynge of
the house of
goulde.
of the mountaynes of Cibaua, For this Caunaboa, he sent one c
pitayne Hoieda, whom the ditionaries of Caunaboa had enforce
to keepe his howlde bysiegeinge for the space of. xxx. dayes
the fortresse of saynte Thomas, in the which Hoieda with hi
Capitayne ho
ieda.
fyftie souldiers, stoode at theyr defence, vntyll the comming
of the Admirall. Whyle Hoieda remayned with Caunaboa, ma
ny ambassadours of the kynges of dyuers Regions were sen
to Caunaboa, persuadinge hym in no condicion to permitte th
Christians to inhabite the Ilande, except he had rather seru
then rule. On the other partie, Hoieda aduertised Caunaboa t
goo to the Admirall, and to make a league of frendeshyp wit
hyr

ym. But the ambaſſadours on the contrary part, thꝛeatened
ym, that yf he wolde ſoo doo, the other kynges wolde in=
ade his Region. But *Hoieda* aunſwered theym ageyne, that
wheras they conſpired to maynteyne their libertie, they ſhuld
by that meanes be bꝛowght to ſeruitude & deſtruction if they
ntended to reſiſt oꝛ keepe warre ageinſt the Chꝛiſtians. Thus
Caunaboa on the one ſyde and the other, beinge troubeled as it
were a rocke in the ſea, beaten with contrary fluddes, & much
moꝛe vexed with the ſtoꝛmes of his gyltie conſcience foꝛ that
he had pꝛiuilie ſlaine .xx. of owre men vnder pꝛetence of peace
eared to coome to the Admirall. But at the length, hauing ex
ogitated this deceyte, to haue ſlayne the Admirall and his
oompany vnder the colour of frendſhippe if opoꝛtunitie wold
oo haue ſerude, he repayꝛed to the Admiral with his hole fa
milie and many other wayting on hym, armed after theyꝛ ma
er. Beinge demaunded why he bꝛowght ſoo greate a rout of
men with hym, he aunſwered that it was not decente foꝛ ſoo
reat a pꝛince as he was, to goo fooꝛth of his howſe without
uche a bande of men. But the thinge chaunced much other=
wyſe then he looked foꝛ. Foꝛ he fell into the ſnares which he
ad pꝛepared foꝛ other. Foꝛ wheras by the way he began to
epente hym that he came fooꝛthe of his howſe, *Hoieda* with
many fayꝛe woꝛdes and pꝛompſes, bꝛowght hym to the Admi
all: At whoſe commaundement, he was immediatly taken &
ut in pꝛiſon: So that the ſowles of owre men were not longe
rom their bodies vnreuenged. Thus *Caunaboa* with all his fa
milie beinge taken, the Admirall was determined to runne o=
er the Ilande. But he was certified that there was ſuch fa=
mine amonge thinhabitantes, that there was alredye fyftie
houſande menne deade therof: And that they dyed yet dayly
s it were rotten ſheepe: The cauſe wherof was wel knowen
o bee theyꝛ owne obſtinacie and frowardnes. Foꝛ where as
they ſawe that owre men entended to chooſe them a dwelling
lace in the Ilande, ſuppoſinge that they myght haue dꝛiuen
em from thence if the vytailes of the Ilande ſhoulde fayle,
ey determyned with them ſelues, not only to leaue ſowing
nd plantyng, but alſo to deſtroy and plucke vp by the rootes
uery man in his owne region, that whiche they had alredye
owen of both kyndes of bꝛeade wherof we made mencion in
e fyꝛſt booke, But eſpecially amonge the mountaynes of

E.iii. Libaua

kynge Cauna
boa, had ſlain
the Spany=
ardes.

Caunaboa cō
ſpireth the
Admiralles
death.

Fayꝛe woꝛds
make fooles
fayne.

Famine inthe
Ilande of hiſ
paniola.

The hunger
of golde cau=
ſeth great
famine.

Cibaua, otherwyse cauled Cipanga, for as muche as they hadde knoweleage that the golde whiche abundeth in that Region, was the cheefe cause that deteyned owre men in the Ilande. In the meane tyme, he sent foorth a Capitayne with a bande of men to searche the sowthe syde of the Ilande. Who at his returne, reported that throwghe out all the Regions that he trauayled, there was suche scarsenes of breade, that for the space of .xvi. dayes he eate nowght elles but the rootes of herbes, and of younge date trees, or the fruites of other wylde trees, But Guarionexius, the kynge of the vale lyinge beneth the mountaynes of Cibaua, whose kyngedoome was not soo wasted as the other, gaue owre menne certeyne vytayles.

Within a fewe dayes after, bothe that the iourneys myght bee the shorter, and also that owre men myght haue more safe places of refuge, if the inhabitantes shuld hereafter rebell in lyke maner, he buylded an other fortesse (whiche he cauled the towre of Conception) betwene the citie of *Isabella* and saint Thomas fortresse, in the marches of the kyngdome of this *Guarionexius* within the precincte of Cibaua vpon the syde of a hyll, hauynge a fayre ryuer of holsome water runnynge harde by the same. Thus when the inhabitantes sawe newe buyldynges to bee dayly erected, and owre shippes lying in the hauen rotten and halfe broken, they beganne to despayre of any hope of libertie, & wandered vp and downe with heuie chere. From the towre of Conception, searchynge diligently the inner partes of the mountaynes of Cibaua, there was a certeine kyng whiche gaue them a masse of rude golde, as bygge as a mans fyst, weighing .xx. vnces. This golde was not fownde in the banke of that ryuer, but in a heape of drye earthe: and was lyke vnto the stone cauled *Tofus*, whiche is soone resolued into sande. This masse of golde, I my selfe sawe in Castile, in the famous citie of *Methymna Campi*, where the courte lay all that wynter. I sawe also a great piece of pure *Electrum*: of the whiche belles and apothecaries morters, and many suche other vessels and instrumentes maye bee made, as were in owlde tyme of copper of the citie of *Corinthus*. This piece of E*lectrum*, was of such weight, that I was not onely with bothe my handes vnable to lifte it from the grownde, but also not of strengthe to remoue it eyther one waye or an other. They affyrmed that it wayde more then three hundreth pownde weight

The towre of conception.

A masse of gold weighinge. xx. ounces.
Tofus.

Electrum is a metall naturally mixt of one portion of golde & another of siluer beinge of propertie to be:

weight, after. biii. vnces to the powmde. It was folwnde in
the howfe of a certen prynce, and lefte hym by his predecef=
fours. And albeit that in the dayes of thinhabitantes yet li=
uynge, *Electrum* was no where digged, yet knewe they where
the myne therof was: but owre men with muche adoo, coulde
hardely caufe them to fhewe them the place, they bore then
fuche priuie hatred. yet at the length, they browght theym
to the myne, beyng nowe ruinate and ftopped with ftones and
rubbiffhe. It is muche eafier to dygge then is the iren myne:
and myght bee reftored agein, if myners and other woorke=
men fkylfull therin, were appoynted therto. Not farre from
the towre of Conception, in the fame mountaynes, is fownd
great plentie of Amber: and owte of certen rockes of the fame
diftilleth a fubftance of the yelowe coloure whiche the payn=
ters vfe. Not farre from thefe mountaynes are many greate
wooddes, in the which are none other trees then braffile, whi
che the Italians caule *Verzino*. But here perhappes (right no
ble prynce) yowe wolde afke what fhoulde be the caufe, that
where as the Spanyardes haue brought owte of thefe Ilan=
des certen fhyppes laden with braffile, fumwhat of goffam=
pine cotton, a quantitie of amber, a lyttel golde, and fum fpi
ces, why they haue not broughte fuche plentie of golde and
fuche other ryche marchaundies as the fruitfulneffe of thefe
regions feeme to promiffe. To this I anfwere, that when
Colonus the admirall was lykewife demaunded the caufe here=
of, he made anfwere that the Spanyardes whiche he tooke
with him into thefe regions, were gyuen rather to flepe, pley,
and ydleneffe, then to laboure: And were more ftudious of fe=
dition and newes, then defyrous of peace and quietneffe: Alfo
that beynge gyuen to lycencioufnes, they rebelled & forfooke
hym, fyndynge matter of falfe accufations agaynft hym, by=
caufe he went aboute to repreffe theyr owtragioufnes.
By reafon wherof he was not yet able to breake the power of
the inhabytantes, and freely to poffeffe the full dominion of
the Ilande. And thefe hynderaunces to be the caufe that hi=
therto the gaynes haue fcarfely counternaypled the charges.
Albeit, euen this yere whyle I wryte thefe thynges at owre
requefte, they gathered in twoo moonethes the fumme of a
thoufande and twoo hundreth poundes weight of golde. But
bycaufe we intende to fpeake more largely of thefe thynges
in theyr

wray poyfon, and was ther fore in owlde tyme in grea ter eftimacion then golde.

The myne of Electrum.

An other kynde of am ber is taken out of greate whale fifhes

Orpement or oker.

wooddes of braffile trees.

Caufes of hinderance.

Licenciufnes of to much li bertie

And this on ly gathered & not digged out of the bo di of the mine

in theyr place, we wyll nowe retourne from whenſe we hau
digreſſed. When the inhabitantes perceaued that they coul
by no meanes ſhake the yoke from their neckes, they made h
ble ſupplication to the Admirall that they myght ſtande t
theyr tribute, and apply them ſelues to reincreaſe the fruite
of theyr countrey, beinge nowe almoſte waſted. He graunte
them theyr requeſte: and appoynted ſuch order that euery R
gion ſhulde paye their tribute, with the commodities of they
countreys, accordinge to theyr portion, and at ſuche tyme a
they were agreed vppon. But the violent famine dyd fruſtra
all theſe appoyntmentes. For all the trauayles of theyr b
dyes, were ſcarſely able to ſuffice to fynde them meate in th
wooddes, wherreby to ſuſteyne theyr lyues, beinge of long
tyme contented with rootes and the fruites of wylde trees
yet manye of the kynges with theyr people, euen in this e
treme neceſſitie, browght parte of theyr tribute: Moſte hum
bly deſpringe the Admirall to haue compaſſion of theyr cala
mities, and to beare with them yet a whyle, vntyll the Ilan
were reſtored to the owlde ſtate. Promyſinge further, th
that which was nowe wantinge, ſhulde then bee dowble r
compenſed. But fewe of the inhabitantes of the mountayne
of Cibaus, kepte theyr promyſe, bycauſe they were ſorer o
preſſed with famine then any of the other. They ſaye, th
the inhabitantes of theſe mountaynes, differ no leſſe in m
ners and language from them which dwel in the playnes, t
amonge vs, the ruſticalles of the countrey from gentylmen
the courte: wheras notwithſtandinge, they lyue bothe as
were vnder one portion of heuen, and in many thinges, muc
after one faſſhion, as in nakednes, and rude ſimplicitie. B
nowe lette vs returne to Caunabos, the kynge of the howſe
golde, beinge in captiuitie. When he perceaued him ſelfe to
caſte in pryſon, fretinge and gratinge his teethe as it had b
a lyon of Libia, and dayely and nyghtlye deuiſinge with hy
ſelfe howe he myght bee delyuered, begannne to perſuade t
Admirall, that for as muche as he had nowe taken vnto h
dominion the Regio of Cipanga or Cibaus (wherof he was kin
it ſhulde bee expedient to ſende thyther a garryſon of Chriſt
an men, to defende the ſame from the incurſions of his ow
enemyes and borderers. For he ſayde, that it was ſignyfi
vnto hym, that the countreye was waſted and ſpoyled wi
ſu

The people
make ſuppli-
cation to ſtãd
to their tri-
bute.

Famine.

The nature
of the Region
diſpoſeth the
maner of the
people.

kynge Cauna
boa in captiu-
itie.

The perſuaſi
on of Cauna-
boa.

uche incurſions. By this crafty deuiſe, he thought to haue
wought to paſſe, that his brother whiche was in that regy=
on, and the other his kynſefolkes and frendes with their ad=
herentes, ſhoulde haue taken, eyther by ſleyghte or force, as
many of owre men, as myght haue redeemed hym . But the
Admyrall vnderſtandynge his crafty meanynge, ſente Hoieda
with ſuche a coompany of men, as might banquiſhe the Ciba=
nians, if they ſhulde moue warre ageynſte them . Owre men
had ſcarſely entered into the Region, but the brother of Cau=
naboa came agenſte them with an armie of fyue thouſande na=
ked menne, armed after theyr maner with clubbes, arrowes
 typte with bones, and ſpeares made harde at the endes with
fyre . He ſtole vpon owre men beyng in one of theyr howſes :
and encamped rownde about the ſame on euery ſyde. This Ci=
auian, as a man not ignorant in the diſciplyne of warre, a=
bowte the diſtance of a furlonge from the howſe, diuided his
campe into fyue bataples, appoyntinge to euery of them a cir=
cuite by equal diuiſion: And placed the froont of his owne ba=
taple, directlye ageynſt owre men. When he had thus ſet his
bataples in good array, he gaue certeyne ſignes that the hole
campe ſhulde marche forwarde in order with equal paces, and
with a larome freſſhly aſſaple theyr enemies, in ſuch ſort that
none might eſcape. But owre men iudginge it better to en=
counter with one of the bataples, then to abyde the brunt of
the hole army, gaue onſet on the mayne bataple arangedin
the playne, bycauſe that place was moſt commodious for
the horſemen. When the horſemen therfore hadde gyuen the
charge, they ouerthrewe them with the breſtes of theyr hor=
ſes, and ſlewe as many as abode thende of the fyght. The re=
due beinge ſtryken with feare, diſparcled, and fledde to the
mountaynes and rockes : from whenſe they made a pytifull
houlynge to owre men, deſyringe them to ſpare them : prote=
ſtinge that they wolde neuer more rebelle, but doo what ſo e=
uer they woulde commaunde them, if they wolde ſuffer theim
to lyue in theyr owne countrey. Thus the brother of Caunaboa
beinge taken, the Admirall licenced the people to reſorte eue=
ry man to his owne. Theſe thinges thus fortunately atchiued
this Region was pacified. Amonge thoſe mountaynes, the
vale which Caunaboa inhabited, is cauled Magona, and is excee=
dynge fruitfull: hauinge in it many goodly ſpringes : and ry=

*Caunaboa
his brother
rebelleth.*

*A conflict be=
twene the Ci=
bauians and
the Spany=
ardes.*

*The Cibaui=
ans haue the
ouerthrowe.*

A great tempest in the mooneth of June.

Three ships drowned lyinge at anker.

Whyrle wyndes. Furacanes.

The death of kynge Caunaboa and his brother.

Bartholomeus Colonus the leauetenaunt searcheth the golde mines.

uers, in the sande wherof, is fownde great plentie of golde. The same yeare in the mooneth of June, they saye there rose suche a boystous tempeste of wynde from the sowtheaste, as hath not lyghtly ben harde of: The violence herof was such that it plucked vppe by the rootes what so euer greate trees were within the reache of the force therof. When this whirle wynde came to the hauen of the citie, it beate downe to the bottome of the sea, three shippes which lay at anker, & brok the cables in sundre: and that(which is the greater maruail without any storme or rowghnes of the sea, onely turnyng them three or foure tymes abowte. The inhabitantes also af firme, that the same yeare, the sea extended it selfe further i to the lande, and rose higher then euer it dyd before by th memory of man, by the space of a cubet. The people therfore muttered amonge them selues, that owre nation hadde trow bled the elementes, and caused such portentous signes. Thes tempestes of the ayer (which the Grecians caule _Tiphones_, tha is, whyrle wyndes) they caule, _Furacanes_: which they say, do often tymes chaunce in this Ilande: But that neyther they nor theyr great grandfathers euer sawe suche violent and fu rious _Furacanes_, that plucked vppe greate trees by the rootes Neyther yet suche surges and vehement motions on the sea that soo wasted the lande. As in deede it may appeare, for a muche as, where so euer the sea bankes are nere to any plain there are in maner euery where, florishing medowes reaching euen vnto the shore. But nowe let vs returne to _Caunaboa_. A kynge _Caunaboa_ therfore and his brother shoulde haue binn browght into Spayne, they dyed by the waye for verye pen syuenes and anguyshe of mynde. The Admiral, whose shippe were drowned in the forsayde tempeste, perceauinge him self to bee nowe enclosed, comaunded foorthwith two other shippes (which the Spaniardes caule _Carauelas_) to bee made. For he had with hym, all maner of artificers perteyninge therun to. Whyle these thinges were dooinge, he sent foorth _Barthol meus Colonus_ his brother, beinge leauetenaunt of the Ilande with an army of men to searche the golde mynes beinge dy stant three score leaques from the citie of _Isabella_, which wer fownde by the conducte of certeyne people of the Ilande, bee fore the mynes of _Cipanga_ or _Cibaua_, were knowen. In thes mynes, they fownde certeyne deepe pittes which had byn di ge

ed in owlde tyme, owte of theſe pyttes, the Admirall (who
ffirmeth this Flande of *Hiſpaniola* to bee Ophir, as we haue
ayde befoze) ſuppoſeth that Salomon the kynge of *Hieruſalem*
ad his greate ryches of golde wherof we reede in the owlde
eſtamente: And that his ſhippes ſayled to this Ophir by the
oulſe of *Perſia* cauled *Sinus Perſicus.* But whether it bee ſoo oz
ot, it lyeth not in me to iudge, but in my opinion it is farre
f. As the mynets dygged the ſuperficiall oz vppermoſt parte
f the earthe of the mynes, durynge foz the ſpace of .vi. miles,
nd in dyuers places ſyfted the ſame on the dzye lande, they
ownde ſuch plentie of golde, that euery hyzed labourer could
aſely fynde euery day, the weyght of thzee dzammes. Theſe
mynes beinge thus ſearched and fownde, the Lieutenaunte
ertifyed the Admirall hereof by his letters. The which when
e had receaued the .v. daye of the Ides of Marche. Anno.
495. he entered into his newe ſhippes, and tooke his viage
irectly to Spayne to aduertiſe the kynge of all his affayzes,
eauing the hole regiment of the Fland with his bzother the
Lieutenaunte,

The golde
mynes of Sa
lomon.

Golde in the
ſuperficiall
partes of the
earth.

The Admiral
taketh his vi:
age to ſpaine

❡ The fyfte booke of the fyzſt decade, to *Lodouike* Cardinall of *Arzgonie.*

Fter the Admyzalles departyng into Spain
his Bzother the Lieutenaunte, buylded A
foztreſſe in the golde mynes, as he had commaunded hym. This he cauled the golden
towze, bycauſe the labourers fownde golde
in the earth and ſtone wherof they made the
waules of the foztreſſe. He conſumed thzee
monethes in makynge the inſtrumentes wherwith the golde
ſhulde bee gathered, waſhed, tryed, and molten. Yet was he
at this tyme by reaſon of wante of vitayles, enfozced to leaue
all thynges imperfecte, and to goo ſeeke foz meate. Thus as
he with a bande of armed men, had entered thzee ſcoze myles
further within the lande, the people of the countrey here and
there reſoztynge to hym, gaue hym a certen poztion of theyz
bzeade in exchange foz other of owze thynges. But he coulde
not long tary here, bicauſe they lacked meate in the foztreſſe,
whyther he haſted with ſuch as he had now gotten. Leauyng

huntinge houndes.

therfore in the fortreſſe a garryſon of tenne men, with that portion of the Ilande breade whiche yet remayned, leauynge alſo with them a hownde to take thoſe kyndes of lyttle beaſtes which they caule *Vtias*, not muche vnlyke owre conyes, he returned to the fortreſſe of Conception. This alſo, was the

kynge Mani-cautexius.

moonthe wherin the kynge *Guarionexius*, and alſo *Manicautexius*, barthered vnto hym, ſhulde haue brought in theyr tributes. Remaynynge there the hole moonthe of June, he exacted the hole tribute of theſe twoo kinges, and vytayles neceſſary for hym and ſuche as he brought with hym, whiche were abowt foure hundreth in number. Shortely after, abowte the calen-

Uytayles browght frõ Spayne.

des of Julye, there came three Carauels from Spayne, brin-gynge with them ſundry kyndes of vitayles, as wheate, oyle wyne, bacon, and marckelmas beafe: whiche were dpuyded to euery man accordynge as neede required. Sum alſo was loſt in the cariage for lacke of good lookyng too. At the arry-uall of theſe ſhyppes, the lieutenaunte receaued commaunde-ment from the kynge and the Admyrall his brother, that he with his men ſhulde remoue theyr habitation to the ſowthe ſyde of the Ilande, bycauſe it was neter to the golde mynes: Alſo that he ſhoulde make dilygent ſearche for thoſe kynges whiche had ſlayne the Chriſtian men, and to ſende them with theyr confederates, bownd into Spayne. At the nexte vyage therfore, he ſent three hundreth captiues with three Kinges: And when he had diligently ſearched the coaſtes of the ſouth ſyde, he tranſported his habitation, and buylded a fortreſſe there, vpon the toppe of a hyll, neere vnto a ſhure hauen.

Saynt Domi-nikes towre.

This fortreſſe, he cauled ſaynt Dominikes towre. Jnto this hauen, runneth A ryuer of holſome water, replenyſhed with ſundrye kyndes of good fyſſhes. They affyrme this ryuer to haue many benefytes of nature. For, where ſo euer it runneth,

Groues of date trees.

all thynges are excedynge pleaſaunte and fruitfull: hauynge on euery ſyde, groues of date trees, and dyuers other of the Ilande frutes ſo plentyfully, that as they ſayled alonge by the ſhore, often tymes the branches therof laden with flowres & fruites, hunge ſoo ouer theyr heades, that they mighte plucke them with theyr handes. Alſo that the frutefulnes of this grownde, is epther equall with the ſoyle of Jſabella, or better. Jn *Iſabella*, he lefte only certeyne ſicke men and ſhippe

Jſabella.

wrightes, whom he had appoynted to make certeyne carauels

The

The refidue of his men, he conueighed to the fowth, to faint
Dominickes towꝛe. After he had buylded this fortreſſe, leauinge therin a garryſon of.xx. men, he with the remanent of
his ſouldiers, pꝛepared them ſelues to ſearche the inner partes of the Weſte ſyde of the Ilande, hythcrto knowen onely
by name. Therfoꝛe abowte.xxx. leaques, (that is) foure ſcoꝛe
and tenne myles from the foꝛtreſſe, he chaunced on the ryuer
Naiba, whiche we ſayde to deſcende from the mountaynes of
Cibaua, ryght towarde the ſowth, by the myddeſt of the Iland.
When he had ouerpaſſed this ryuer with a coompanye of armed men diuided into. xxv. decurions, that is, tenne in a com
pany with theyꝛ capitaynes, he ſent two decurions to the regions of thoſe kinges in whoſe landes were the great woods
of bꝛaſile trees. Inclyninge towarde the lefte hande, they
fownde the woodes, entered into them, and felled the hygh
and pꝛecious trees, which were to that day, vntouched. Eche
of the decurions ſylled certeyne of the Ilande howſes with
the trunkes of bꝛaſile, there to be reſerued vntyll the ſhyppes
came which ſhulde cary them away. But the Lieutenaunt di
rectinge his iourney towarde the ryght hande, not farre from
the bankes of the ryuer of Naiba, fownde a certeyne kynge
whoſe name was *Beuchius Anacauchos*, encamped ageynſt thinhabitantes of the pꝛouince of Naiba, to ſubdue them vnder his do
minion, as he had doone manye other kynges of the Ilande,
boꝛtherers vnto hym: The palaice of this great kynge, is cau
led *Xaragua*: and is ſituate towarde the Weſte ende of the I-
lande, diſtante from the ryuer of Naiba. xxx. leaques. All the
pꝛynces which dwell betwene the Weſte ende and his palaice,
are ditionaries vnto hym. All that Region from Naiba, to the
furtheſte marches of the weſte, is vtterly withowte golde, althowgh it bee full of mountaynes. When the kynge had eſpied owre men, layinge a parte his weapons, & gyuinge ſignes
of peace, he ſpake gentelly to them, incerteyne whether it
were of humanitie oꝛ feare) and demaunded of thẽ what they
woolde haue. The Lieutenaunte aunſwered: That he ſhulde
paye tribute to the Admirall his bꝛother, in the name of the
Chꝛiſtian kynge of Spayne. To whom he ſayde: Howe can
yowe requyꝛe that of me, whereas neuer a Region vnder my
dominion bꝛingeth fooꝛth golde. Foꝛ he had harde, that there
was a ſtrange nation entered into the Ilande, whiche made

F.iii.   greate

The ryuer of
Naiba

wooddes of
bꝛaſile trees.

kinge Beuchi
us Anacau-
choa.

The palaice
of xaragua.

mountaynes
without gold

Tribute.

greate fearche for golde. But he fuppofed that they defyre
none other thynge. The leauetenaunt anfwered ageyne : Go
forbydde that we fhulde enioyne any man to pay fuch tribut
as he myght not eafely forbeare, or fuch as were not engend
red or growinge in the Region: But we vnderftand that you
Regions brynge foorth great plentie of Goffampine cotton
and hempe, with fuche other, whereof we defyre yowe t
gyue vs parte. When he harde thefe woordes, he promyfe
with cherefull countenaunce, to gyue hym as muche of thef
thynges as he wolde requyre. Thus difmiffinge his army,
fendynge meffengers beefore, he hym felfe accompanyed th
Leauetenaunte and browght hym to his palaice, beinge dy
ftante (as we haue fayde).xxx. leaques. In al this tracte, the
paffed throwgh the Jurifdiction of other princes beinge vn
der his dominion : Of the whiche, fume gaue them hempe, o
no leffe goodnes to make tackelinges for fhippes then owt
woodde. Other fume, browght bread, and fum goffampyn
cotton : And foo euery of them payde tribute with fuche com
modities as theyr countreys browght foorth. At the length
they came to the kinges manfion place of *Xaragua*. Before the
entered into the palaice, A greate multitude of the kynges fe
uauntes and fubiectes reforted to the courte, honorably(afte
their maner) to receaue their kyng *Beuchius Anacauchos*, with th
ftrangers which he browght with hym to fe the magnificenc
of his courte. But nowe fhall yowe heare howe they were in
terteyned. Amonge other tryumphes and fyghtes, two are ef
pecially to bee noted. Fyrfte there mette them a company o
xxx. women, beinge al the kynges wyues and concubines, be
ringe in theyr handes branches of date trees, finginge an
daunfinge : They were all naked, fauynge that theyr pryui
partes were couered with breeches of goffampine cotton. Bu
the virgins, hauynge theyr heare hangynge downe abowt
their fhulders, tyed abowte the forehead with a fyllet, wer
vtterly naked. They affirme that theyr faces, breftes, pappe
handes, and other partes of theyr bodyes, were ereedyng
fmoothe, and well proportioned : but fumwhat inclynyng to
louely browne. They fuppofed that they had feene thofe mo
beawtyfull *Dryades*, or the natyue nymphes or fayres of th
fontaynes whereof the antiquites fpeake fo muche. The bran
ches of date trees which they bore in theyr right handes wh
they

The woolfe
entreateth.
the fheepe.

hempe and
goffampine
cotton.

howe the
Lieuetenant
was recea=
ued at the
kynges pa=
laice.

The kinges
wyues.

well fauered
women.

Dryades.

hey daunced, they delyuered to the Leauetenaunt with lowe
urteſy and ſmylynge countenaunce.　Thus enteringe into
he kynges howſe, they fownde a delycate ſupper prepared
or them after theyr maner. When they were well refreſhed
with meate, the nyght drawinge on, they were brought by
he kynges officers, euery man to his lodginge, accordyng to
is degree, in certeyne of theyr howſes abowte the palaice,
where they reſted them in hangynge beddes after the maner
f the countrey, wherof we haue ſpoken more largely in an
ther place.

¶ The daye folowyng they browght owre men to their com=
non haule, into the whiche they coome together as often as
hey make any notable games or triumphes, as we haue ſaid
efore. Here, after many daunſynges, ſynginges, maſkinges
unnynges, wreſtlynges, and other tryinge of maſtryes, ſoo=
enly there appered in a large plaine nere vnto the haule. ii.
reate armies of men of warre, whiche the kynge for his pa=
tyme had cauſed to bee prepared, as the Spaniardes vſe the
daye with reedes whiche they caule *Iuga de Canias*. As the ar=
nies drewe necre together, they aſſayled the one the other
s fierſely, as if mortal ennemies with theyr baners ſpreade,
hulde fight for theyr goodes, theyr landes, theyr lyues, their
bertie, theyr countrey, theyr wyues and theyr chyldren.
Soo that within the momente of an howre, foure men were
layne, and many wounded. The battayle alſo ſhoulde haue
ontynued longer, if the kynge had not at the requeſt of owre
nen, cauſed them to ceaſe. The thyrde day, the Lieuetenant
onſelynge the kynge to ſowe more plentie of goſſampine vp=
on the bankes nere vnto the waters ſyde, that they myghte
he better paye theyr tribute priuately accordynge to the mul=
itude of theyr howſes, he repayred to *Iſabella* to vyſite the
icke men whiche he had lefte there, and alſo to ſee howe his
woorkes wente forwarde. In the tyme of his abſence.xxx. of
is men were conſumed with diuerſe diſeaſes, Wherfore be=
nge ſore trowbled in his mynde, and in maner at his wyttes
nde what he were beſt to doo, for as muche as he wanted al
hynges neceſſarie as well to reſtore them to healthe whiche
ocre yet acraſed, as alſo vitayles to mayntaine the hole mul=
itude, where as there was yet no ſhippe coome from Spaine,
s at the length he determyned t oſende abrode the ſicke men
　　　　　　　　　　　　　　　　　　　　　　　　　　here

A delicate
ſupper.

hanginge
beddes.

A common
haule.

A pretie
paſtyme.

Foure men
ſlaine in ſport

Prouiſion for
diſeaſed men

The fyrst decade.

here and there to sundrye Regions of the Ilande, and to the castelles which they had erected in the same. foz directly from the citie of Isabella to saynt Dominikes towze, that is, from the north to the south, throwgh the Iland, they had buylded thus many castelles. Fyrste. xxxvi. myles distante from Isabella, they buylded the castell of *Sperantia*, from *Sperantia*. xxv. myles, was the castell of saynte Catharine. from saynte Catharines. xx. myles, was saynt James towze. Other. xx. miles from saynte James towze, was A stronger fortresse then any of the other, which they cauled the towze of Conception: which he made the stronger bicause it was situate at the rootes of the golden mountaynes of Cibaua, in the greate and large playne soo fruitefull and well inhabited as we haue befoze described. He buylded also an other in the mydde waye betwene the towze of Conception & saynt Dominikes towze. The which also was stronger then the towze of Conception, bycause it was within the lymittes of A great kynge, hauing vnder his dominion fiue thowsande men: whose chiefe Citie and heade of the Realme, beynge cauled *Bonauum*, he wylled that the castell shulde also bee cauled after the same name. Therfoze leauynge the sicke men in these castels and other of the Ilande howses nere vnto the same, he hym selfe repayred to saynte Dominikes, exactinge tributes of all the kynges whiche were in his waye. When he had taryed there A fewe dayes, there was a rumoz spredde, that all the kynges abowte the bozders of the towze of Conception, had conspyred with desperate myndes to rebell agenste the Spaniardes. When the Lieutenaunte was certified hereof, he tooke his iorneye towarde them immediately, not beyng discozaged eyther by the lengthe of the waye, oz feeblenesse of his souldyers, beynge in maner forweried with trauayle. As he drewe nere vnto them, he had aduertisement that kynge *Guarionexius* was chosen by the other pzynces to bee the Capitayne of this rebellion: And that he was enforzed therto halfe vnwilling, beynge seduced by theyz persuasions and prouocations. The whiche is moze lykely to be trewe, foz that he had befoze had experience of the power and policie of owze men. They came together at a daye appoynted, accompanied with. xv. thousande men, armed after their maner, once agen to proue the fortune of warre. Here the Lieutenaunte consultynge with

the

Marginal notes:

The castels oz towzes of hispan.ola.

The golden mountaynes of Cibaua.

Bonauum

Tribute.

The kynges rebelle.

Guarionexius capitaine of the conspiracie.

An army of xv thousande Barbarians.

the Capitayne of the fortreſſe and the other ſouldiers of whō
he had the conducte, determyned to ſette vppon them vnwares
in their owne howſes before they coulde prepare they army.
He ſent foorthe therfore to euery kynge, a Centurian, that is,
a capitaine of a hundreth, which were commaunded vppon a
ſudden to inuade they howſes in the night, and to take the
ſleepinge, before the people (beinge ſcattered here and there)
might aſſemble to gyther. Thus ſecreatly enteringe into their
vylages, not fortified with waules, trenches, or bulwarkes,
they broke in vppon them, tooke them, bounde them, and led
away euery man his priſoner accordyng as they were commaun
ded. The Lieuetenaunt hym ſelfe with his hundreth men, aſ
ſayled kynge *Guarionexius* as the woorthier perſonage, whom
he tooke priſoner as dyd the other capitaynes they kynges,
& at the ſame howre appoynted. Fourteene of theym were
browght the ſame nyght to the towre of Conception. Short
lye after, when he had put to death two of the kynges which
were the chiefe autours of this newe reuolte, and had ſubor
ned *Guarionexius* and the other kynges to attempte the ſame:
leaſt the people for ſorowe of they kynges ſhulde neglecte or
forſake their countrey, which thinge myght haue byn greate
incommoditie to owre men, who by thincreaſe of they ſeedes
and fruites were oftentymes ayded, he freely pardoned and
diſmiſſed *Guarionexius* and the other kynges. The people in the
meane tyme flocked togyther abowte the towre, to the nōber
of fyue thowſande withowte weapons, with pytiful houling
for the delyueraunce of they kynges: The ayer thundered, &
the earth trembeled throwgh the vehemencie of they owtcry
The Lieuetenaunt warned *Guarionexius* and the other kynges,
with threatenynges, with rewardes, and with promyſes, ne
uer hereafter to attempte any ſuche thynge. Then *Guarionexius*
made an oration to the people of the great power of owre mē,
of they clemencie towarde offenders, and liberalitie to ſuche
as remayne faithfull: deſyringe them to quiet they myndes:
and from henſefoorth nother in deede nor thowght to inter
pryſe any thynge agaynſt the Chriſtians, but to obeye & ſerue
them, excepte they wolde dayly brynge them ſelues into fur
ther calamyties. When the oration was fynyſhed, they tooke
hym vp and ſet hym on they ſhulders, and ſoo caryed hym
home to his owne palaice. And by this meanes, this Region

The kynges
are taken pri
ſoners.

kynge Guari
onexius is
pardoned.

was pacified foȝ a whyle. But owre men, with heauy coun=
tenaunce wandered vppe and downe, as deſolate in a ſtrange
Lacke of vy-
tayles.
countrey, lackinge vytailes, and woȝne owte of apparell.
wheras .rb. moonethes were nowe paſſed ſence the Admirals
departure: duringe which tyme, they coulde heare nothynge
owte of Spayne. The Leauetenaunt comfoȝted them all thi.
he coulde with fayȝe woȝdes and pȝomyſes.   In the mean=
Beuchius A-
nacauchoa,
the kynʒe of
Xaragua.
tyme, *Beuchius Anacauchoa* (the kynʒe of the Weſte partes of th
Region of *Xaragua* (of whom we ſpake befoȝe) ſente meſſen
gers to the Lieutenaunt to ſignifye vnto hym, that he hadd
in a retyȝnes the goſſampine cotton and ſuche other thin
ges as he wylled hym to pȝepare foȝ the paymente of his try
bute. Whervppon the Lieuetenaunt tooke his ioȝney thyther
and was honoȝably receaued of the kynʒe and his ſyſter, ſu
Queene Ana-
caona, the
wife of kynʒe
Caunaboa.
tyme the wyfe of *Caunaboa* the kynʒe of *Cihaua*, bearing no leſſe
rule in the gouernaunce of her bȝothers kyngedome, then h
hym ſelfe. Foȝ they affirme her to bee a wyſe woman, of goo
maners, and pleaſaunt in company. Shee erneſtly perſuade
her bȝother by theȝample of her huſbande, to loue and obey
the Chȝiſtians. This woman was cauled *Anacaona*. He fownd
rrrii. kynʒes.
in the palace of *Beuchius Anacauchos*. rrrii. kynʒes which hadd
bȝowght theyȝ tributes with them, and abode his comminge
They bȝowght with them alſo beſyde theyȝ trybute a Tigne
them, further to demerite the fauour of owre men, great ple
tie of vytayles: as bothe kyndes of bȝeade, cunnyes, and fyſ
Serpentes
eaten.
ſhes, alredy dȝyed bycauſe they ſhulde not putrifie: Serpen
tes alſo of that kynd which wee ſayd to bee eſteemed among
them as moſt delicate meate, and lyke vnto Crocodiles ſauin
in byggenes. Theſe ſerpentes they caule *Iuannas*, which owr
men learned ſumewhat to late to haue byn engendȝed in th
Ilande. Foȝ vnto that day, none of them durſte aduenture t
taſte of them by reaſon of theyȝ hoȝrible defoȝmitie and loth
ſumnes. Yet the Lieutenaunt beinge entyſed by the pleaſan
ces of the kynʒes ſyſter, determined to taſte of the ſerpentes
But when he felte the fleſhe theȝof to bee ſo delicate to hi
tonge, he fel too, amayne without al feare. The which thing
his coompanyons perceauinge, were not behynde hym in gre
dines: In ſoo muche that they hadde nowe none other talk
then of the ſweetenes of theſe ſerpentes: which they affyȝm
to bee of moȝe pleaſaunte taſte, then eyther owre pheſauntes

oz pertriches. But they lose theyz taste, excepte they bee prepared after a certeyne fashion : as doo peacockes and phesauntes except they bee interlarded beefore they bee rosted. They prepare them therefore after this maner. Fyzst takynge owte theyz bowels euen from the thzote to the thyghes, they make and rubbe theyz bodies very cleane bothe within and withowte. Then rouling them togyther on a cyzcle, inuolued after the maner of a slepynge snake, they thzuste them into a potte of no bygger capacitie then to houlde them only. This doone, puttinge a lyttle water vnto them with a poztion of the Jlande pepper, they seethe thē with a soft fyer of sweete woodde, and suche as maketh no greate smoke. Of the fat of them beinge thus sodde, is made an excedinge pleasaunte bzothe oz potage. They say also, that there is no meate to bee compared to the egges of these serpentes, which they vse to seethe by them selues. They are good to bee eaten as sone as they are sodde : And may also bee reserued many dayes after. But hauinge sayde thus muche of theyz interteynement and daintie fare, let vs nowe speake of other matters. When the Lieutenaunt had fylled one of the Jlande howses with the gossampine cotton which he hadde receaued foz trybute, the kynges pzompsed furthermore to grue hym as muche of theyz bzeade, as he wolde demaunde. He gaue them hartie thankes and gentely accepted their freendly pzofer. Jn the meane time whyle this bzeade was gatheringe in sundzy Regions to bee bzowght to the palaice of *Beuchius Anacauchoa* kynge of *Xaragua*, he sent messengers to Jsabella foz one of the two carauelles which were lately made there : intendinge to sende the same thyther ageyne laden with bzeade. The maryners gladde of these tydynges, sayled abowte the Jlande, and in short space bzowght the shippe to the coastes of *Xaragua*. The syster of kynge *Beuchius Anacauchoa*, that wyse and pleasaunt woman *Anacaona*, (the wyfe sumtyme of *Caunaboa* the kynge of the golden howse of the mountaynes of *Cibaus*, whose husbande dyed in the way when he shulde haue byn caryed into Spayne,) when shee harde saye that owre shyppe was arryued on the shore of her natiue countrey, persuaded the kynge her bzother that they bothe myght goo togyther to see it. Foz the place where the shyppe lay, was not passe vi. myles distante from *Xaragua*. They rested all night, in the mydde way, in a certeyne vyllage

B.ii.   in

The blessing of serpentes to be eaten.

Serpentes egges eaten.

Gossampine cotton.

Queene Anacaona.

In the which was the treasurye oz iewell howse of Anacaona. Her treasure was nother goulde, fyluer, oz piecious stones, but only thynges necessary to bee vsed, as cheyars, stooles, settels, dysshes, potingers, pottes, pannes, basons, treyes, and suche other howsholde stuffe and instrumentes, worke: manly made of a certeyne blacke and harde shyninge woodde which that excellent lerned phisition John baptiste Elisius, af: firmeth to bee hebene. What so euer portion of wytte nature hath gyuen to the inhabitantes of these Ilandes, the same doth most appeare in these kynde of woozkes, in whiche they shewe great arte and cunnyng. But those which this woman had, were made in the Iland of Guanabba, situate in the mouth of the weste syde of Hispaniola. In these they graue the lyuely Images of such phantasies as they suppose they see walke by night which the Antiquitie cauled Lemures. Also the Images of men serpents, beastes, ₊ what so euer other thyng they haue once seene. What wolde yowe thinke (moste noble Pzynce) that they coulde doo, if they had the vse of Iren and steele? For they onely fyzste make these softe in the fyze, and after: warde make them holowe ₊ carue them with a certeyne stone which they fynde in the ryuers. Of stooles and chayers, shee gaue the Lieutenaunt. xiiii. And of vessselles perteynynge to the table and kychen, shee gaue hym thzee scoze, sum of wood and sume of earthe. Also of gossampine cotton ready spunne foure great bottomes of exceedinge weight. The day folowing when they came to the sea syde, where was an other vylage of the kynges, the Lieutenaunt commaunded the shyppe boat to bee bzowght to the shoze. The kyng also had pzepared two canoas, paynted after theyz maner : one foz hym selfe and cer teyne of his gentelmen : an other foz his syster Anacaona and her waytinge women. But Anacaona desyzed to bee caried in the shyppe boate with the Lieutenaunte. When they nowe appzoched nere vnto the shyppe, certeyne great pieces of ozdinaunce were discharged of purpose. The sea was fyl: led with thunder, and the ayer with smooke. They trembled and quaked foz feare, supposinge that the frame of the wozld had byn in danger of fauling. But when they sawe the Lieue tenaunte lawgh, and looke cherefully on them, they cauled ageyne theyz spirites. And when they yet dzewe nerer to the shippe, and harde the noyse of the fluites, shalmes, ₊ dzumes, they

The treasurie of Queene Anacaona.

hebene woodde.

The Ilande of Guanabba

Conninge ar: tificers.

A stone in the steede of Iren

Tunges,

Musical in: strumentes,

they were wonderfully astonyed at the sweete harmony ther=
of. Enterynge into the shyppe and beholdinge the foreshippe
and the sterne, the toppe castel, the maste, the hatches, the ca=
bens, the keele, and the tackelinges, the brother fixinge his
eyes on the syster, and the syster on the brother, they were
bothe as it were dumme and amased, and wyste not what to
saye for to muche wonderynge. Whyle beholdinge these thin=
ges they wandered vp and downe the shippe, the Lieutenaūt
commaūded the ankers to bee loosed, and the sailes to be hoy
sed vp. Then were they further astonyshed, when they sawe
soo greate a mole, to moue as it were by it selfe, without ores
and without the force of man. For there arose from the earth
suche a wynde as a man wolde haue wyshed for of purpose.
Yet furthermore, when they perceaued the shyppe to moue su
tyme forwarde and sumtyme backewarde: sumtyme towarde
the ryght hande and sumtyme towarde the lefte, & that with
one wynde and in maner at one instante, they were at theyr
wyttes ende for to muche admiracion. These thynges fynished
and the shyppes beinge laden with breade and suche other re=
wardes, they beinge also recompensed with other of owre
thynges, he dismissed not onely the kynge *Beuchius Anacauchoa*,
and his syster, but lykewise all theyr seruauntes and women
replenyshed with ioye and woonderinge. After this, he hym
selfe tooke his iorney by foote with his souldiers to the citie
of *Isabella*: where he was aduertised that one *Roldanus Ximenus*,
a naughty felowe, (whom before beinge his seruaunte, he had
preferred to bee capitayne of the myners and labourers, and
after made hym a Iudge in causes of controuersie) had vsed
hym selfe owtragiously and was malyciously mynded agaīst
hym, and further, the cause of much myschiefe in his absēce.
For kynge *Guarionexius* (who a whyle before was pardoned of
his former rebellion, and persuaded the people to obeye the
Spanyardes) was by his naughty vsage, and suche other as
were confethered with hym, so accensed to reuenge the iniu=
ries which they susteyned at his handes, bysyde the abhomi=
nable actes which they folowynge onely the lawe of nature,
abhorred to admytte, that he with his famelie, famylyers, &
ditionaries, of desperate mynde sledde to the mountaynes be=
inge distant from *Isabella* onely tenne leaques Westwarde, to=
warde the north syde of the sea. These mountaynes, and also

Marginal notes:

Ignorance causeth admiration.

Roldanus Xemnus.

The intempe rancie and malice of a seruile witte aduaunced.

Cignaians.

the inhabitantes of the same they caule by one name Ciguaios. The greate kyng of al the kynges and regions of these moun taynes, is cauled *Maiobanexius* : and his courte or palaice is na med *Capronus*. The mountaynes are rowgh, hygh, and suche as no man can passe to the toppes therof. They are also ben dynge : and haue theyr corners reachinge downe to the sea. Betwene bothe the corners of the mountaynes, is there a greate playne, by the which many riuers faule from the moun taynes into the sea. The people are verye fierse and warlyke men, hauing theyr original of the Canybales. For when they descende from the mountaynes to the playnes to keepe warre with theyr boorderers, they eate all suche as they kyll. *Guario nexius* therfore, flyinge to this kyng of these mountaynes, gaue hym many presentes of suche thynges as are wantinge in his countrey : therwith declaringe howe by fleip, byplaynously, and violently, he had byn vsed of owre men: with whom he coulde nothinge preuayle nother by fayre meanes, nor by foule : no ther by humilytie nor by stoutnes. And that to bee the cause of his resortinge to hym at that tyme: moste humbly desyring hym to bee his defence ageynst thoppressions of suche myscheu uous people. *Maiobanexius* here vppon, made hym promese to ayde and helpe hym ageynst the Christians al that he myght. The Lieuetenaunt therfore made hast to the fortresse of Con ception : whyther as soone as he was coome, he sent for Rol danus Xeminus, who with suche as folowed hym, lay in certeyne of the Ilande vylages, twelue miles distant from the fortres At his comminge, the Leauetenaunt asked hym what al these sturres and tumultes ment. He answered without aba pement powre brother the Admirall hath to doo therwith, and shall answere for the same before the kynge. For we perceaue that the kynge hath soo put hym in truste, that he hath hadde no regarde to vs. Here we perythe for hunger whyle we folowe powe : and are dryuen to seeke owre vnhappy foode in the de sertes. Powre brother also, assigned me assistant with powe in gouerninge the Ilande. Wherfore syth powe haue no more respecte vnto vs, we are determyned noo longer to bee vnder powre obedience. When *Roldanus* had spoken these wordes suche other, the Lieuetenaunte wolde haue layde handes on hym : but he escaped his fyngers, and fledde to the weste par tes of the Region of *Xaragua*, hauinge with hym a trayne of three

Maiobaneri us, the great kynge of the mountaynes

The inhaby tantes of the mountaynes.

Guarionexi us rebelleth ageyne.

Roldanus Xe minus rebel leth.

threescoze and tenne men whiche were of his confetheracie. Here this fylthy synke of rebels thus conspired, played their rages and lyued with loose brydels in al kyndes of myschefe robbynge the people, spoylinge the countrey, and rauyshinge bothe wyues and virgines. Whyle these thynges were doing in the Jlande, the Admirall hadde eyght shyppes appoynted hym by the kynge: Of the whiche he sent two laden with vitaples, from *Cales* oz *Gades* of Hercules pyllers, directly to the Lieutenaunt his bzother. These shyppes by chaunce arryued fyzst on that syde of the Jlande where *Roldanus Xeminus* ranged with his coompanyons. *Roldanus* in shozte tyme hadde seduced them: promysinge them in the steade of mattockes, wenches pappes: foz laboure, pleasure: foz hunger, abundance: and foz wearynes and watchinge, sleep and quietnes. *Guarionexius* in the meane tyme, a Temblynge a bower of his freendes and confetherates, came oftentymes downe into the playne, and slewe as many of the Christian men, as he coulde meete conuenientlye, and also of the Jlande menne whiche were theyz freendes: wastynge theyz grounde, destroyinge theyz seedes, and spoylinge theyz vylages. But *Roldanus* and his adherentes, albeit they had knowleage that the Admiral wolde shoztly coome, yet feared they nothynge bycause they had seduced the newe menne which came in the fyzste shippes. Whyle the Lieutenaunt was thus tossed in the middest of these stozmes, in the meane tyme his bzother the Admyzall set fozwarde frõ the coastes of Spayne: But not directly to *Hispaniola*: Foz he turned moze towarde the southe. Jn the which vyage, what he dyd, what csastes both of the lande and sea he coompased, and what newe regions he discouered, wee wyl fyzst declare. Foz to what ende and conclusion the sayde tumultes and seditions came, wee wyll expzesse in thende of the booke folowynge. Thus fare ye well.

Licenciousnes in liberte

Hercules pyllers.

A violente persasion.

The furie of guarionexius

The thyzde vyage of Colonus the Admirall.

❡ The syxte booke of the fyzste decade, to *Lodouike* Cardinall of *Aragonie*.

Colonus the Admyzal, the thyzde day of the Calendes of June, in the yeare of Christe. 1498. hoysed vp his sayles in the hauen of the towne *Barramedabas*, not farre distante from Cales: and set fozwarde on on his vyage with eyght shippes laden with vytayles and o‑ther necessaries. He diuerted from his accustomed rase which was by the Ilandes of *Canarie*, by reason of certeyne frenche‑men pirates and rouers on the sea, whiche laye in the ryght way to meete with hym. In the way frō *Cales* to the Ilandes of *Canarie*, abowte foure score and ten myles towarde the lefte hande, is the Ilande of *Madera*, more southwarde then the citie of *Ciuile* by foure degrees. For the pole artyke is eleuate to *Ciuile*, xxxvi. degrees: But to this Iland (as the mariners saye) only.xxxii. He sayled therfore fyrste to *Madera*. And sen‑dinge from thense directly to *Hispaniola*, the resydue of the ship‑pes laden with vytayles and other necessaries, he hym selfe with one shyppe with deckes, and two marchaunt carauelles coasted towarde the southe to coome to the *Equinoctial* lyne, and so furth to folowe the tracte of the same towarde the West, to thintent to searche the natures of suche places as he coulde fynde vnder or nere vnto the same, leauinge *Hispaniola* on the north syde on his ryght hande. In the myddle of his rase, lye xiii. Ilandes of the Portugales, whiche were in owlde tyme cauled *Hesperides*: And are nowe cauled *Caput Viride*, or *Caboeurde*. These are situate in the sea, ryght ouer ageynst the inner par‑tes of Ethiope, Westwarde two dayes saylinge. One of these the Portugales caule *Bonauista*. With the snayles, or rather tortoyses of this Ilande, many leprous men are healed and clensed of theyr leprositie. Departing sodainly from hense by reason of the contagiousnes of the ayre, he sayled.CCCCLXXX myles towarde the Weste southwest, which is the myddest be‑twene the weste and the southe. There was he so vexed with maladies and heate (for it was the moneth of Iune) that his shyppes were almoste sette on fyre. The hoopes of his barrels cracked and brake, and the freshe water ranne owte. The men also complayned that they were not able to abyde that extremitie of heate. Here the northe pole was eleuate only.v. degrees from the Horizontall. For the space of.viii. dayes in the which he suffered these extremities, only the fyrst day was fayre: but all the other, clowdy and rayny: yet neuerthelesse feruent hotte. Wherefore it oftentymes repented hym not a little that euer he tooke that way. Beinge tossed in these dan‑giours and vexations eyght contynuall dayes, at the lengthe an Eastsoutheaste wynde arose, and gaue a prosperous blaste to

Frenche mē pyrats.

The Iland of Madera.

The Admiral sayleth to the Equinoctiall.

xiii. Ilandes of Hesperides, now cauled Caboeurde.

Healynge of the leper.

Contagious ayre and extreme heate

The pole eleuate.v. degrees.

to his sayles. Which wynde folowinge directly towarde the weste, he fownde the starres ouer that paralelle, placed in other order; and an other kynde of ayer, as the Admirall hym selfe towlde me. And they al affirme, that within three dayes saylinge, they fownde moste temperate and pleasaunte ayre. The Admirall also affirmeth, that from the clime of the great heate and vnholsome ayer, he euer ascended by the backe of the sea, as it were by a hygh mountayne towarde heauen. yet in all this tyme, coulde he not once see any lande. But at the length, the day before the Calendes of July, the watcheman lookynge foorth of the toppecastell of the greatest shyppe, cryd owte alowde for ioy that he espyed three excedynge hyghe mountaynes: Exhortinge his felowes to bee of good cheere, and put away all pensiuenes. For they were very heauy and sorowfull, as well for the greefe which they susteyned by reason of thintollerable heate, as also that their freshe water fay led them, which ranne owte at the ryftes of the barels, caused by extreme heate as we haue sayde. Thus beinge wel conforted, they drewe to the lande. yet at theyr fyrst approche, they coulde not arryue by reason of the shalownes of the sea nere the shore. yet lookyng owte of theyr shyppes, they might well perceaue that the Region was inhabyted and well cultured: For they sawe very fayre gardens, and pleasaunte medowes: frome the trees and herbes wherof, when the mornynge dewes beganne to ryse, there proceaded manye sweete sauoures. Twentie myles distant from hense, they chaunced into a hauen, verye apte to harborowe shippes, but it had no ryuer runninge into it. Saylinge on yet sumwhat further, he fownde at the lengthe a commodious hauen wherin he might repayre his shippes and make prouision of freshe water and fuell. *Arenalis* cauleth this lande *Puta*. They fownd no houses nere vnto the hauen: but innumerable steppes of certein wilde beastes feete, of the which they fownde one deade much lyke a goate. The day folowynge, they sawe a Canoa cominynge a farre of, hauinge in it. xxiiii. younge men of godly corporature & high stature, al armed with targets, bowes & arrowes The heare of theyr heds, was lõge & plaine, & cutte on the for heade much after the maner of the Spanyardes. Theyr priuie partes were couered with fillettes of gossampyne cotton, of sundry coloures enterlaced; And were besyde al ouer naked.

.i.D   Here

The starres placed in other order.

A sea rysyng lyke a mountayne.

heate causeth the barrels to bicke.

Swete sauours proceadynge frome the lande.

The Iland of Puta.

people of ly corporature & longe heare nere the Equinoctiall.

Here the Admirall conſideringe with hym ſelfe the corporature of this people and nature of the lande, he beleaued the
ſame to bee ſoo muchthe neuer heauen then other Regions of
the ſame paralelle, a nd further remoued from the groſſe vapours of the bales and marpſſhes, howe muche the hyghelte
toppes of the byggeſt mountaynes are diſtante from the deepe
bales, ffor he erneſtly affirmeth, that in all that nauigation,
he neuer wente owte of the paralelles of Ethiope : So greate
difference is there betwene the nature of thinhabitantes and
of the ſoyles of dyuers Regions all vnder one clyme or paralelle: as is to ſee betwene the people and regions being in the
firme lande of Ethiope, and theym of the Ilandes vnder the
ſame clime, hauinge the pole ſtarre eleuate in the ſame degree.
ffor the Ethiopians are all blacke, hauinge theyr heare curld
more lyke wulle then heare. But theſe people of the Iland of
Puta (beinge as I haue ſayde vnder the clyme of Ethiope) are
whyte, with longe heare, and of yelowe colour. Wherfore it
is apparente, the cauſe of this ſoo greate difference, to bee
rather by the diſpoſition of the earthe, then conſtitucion of
heauen. ffor wee knowe, that ſnowe fauleth on the mountaynes of the Equinoctiall or burnte lyne, and the ſame to en
dure there continually : We knowe lykewyſe that thinhabitantes of the Regions farre diſtante frome that lyne towarde
the northe, are moleſted with greate heate.

℃ The Admiral that he myght allure the younge men to him
with gentelnes, ſhewed them lokynge glaſſes, fayre & bright
veſſelles of copper, haukes belles, and ſuche other thynges
vnknowen to them. But the more they were cauled, ſo much
the more they ſuſpected crafte and deceate, and fledde backewarde. yet dyd they with greate admiracion beholde owre
men and theyr thynges, but ſtyll hauinge their ores in theyr
handes redy to flye. When the Admirall ſawe that he coulde
by no meanes allure thē by gyftes, he thought to proue what
he coulde do wfth muſicall inſtrumentes : and therefore commaunded that they which were in the greateſt ſhippe, ſhulde
play on theyr drumnes and ſhalmes. But the younge men ſup
poſinge this to bee a token of battayle, lefte theyr ores, and
in the twynlynge of an eye hadde put theyr arrowes in theyr
bowes and theyr targettes on theyr armes : And thus directinge theyr arrowes towarde owre men, ſtoode in expectaciō

The higher
the coulder.

Differencebe
twene people
of one clime.
Ethiopia.

Note the
cauſe of
difference.

Muſicalinſtru
mentes.

to knowe what this noyſe myght meane. Owre men lykewiſe
preparinge theyr bowes and arrowes, approched toward thē
by lyttle and lyttle. But they departinge from the Admirals
ſhippe, and truſtinge to the dexteritie of theyr ores came ſoo
neare one of the leſſe ſhippes, that one of theym plucked the
clooke from the gouernour of that ſhippe, and as wel as they
coulde by ſignes, requyred hym to coome alande, promyſinge
ſeyth that they wolde common with hym of peace. But when
they ſawe hym goo to the Admirals ſhippe whether he went
to aſke leaue that he might common with them, ſuſpectinge
hereby ſume further deceate, they lept immmediatly into the
Canoa, and fledde as ſwyft as the wynde. So that to con=
clude, they coulde by no meanes be allured to familiaritie.
Wherfore the Admirall thowght it not conuenient to beſtowe
any longe tyme there, at this vyage. No greate ſpace frome
this Ilande, euer towarde the weſte, the Admirall ſaith he
fownde ſo owteragious a faule of water, runninge with ſuch
a violence from the Eaſte to the Weſte, that it was nothynge
inferioure to a myghty ſtreame faulynge from hyghe moun=
taynes. He alſo confeſſed, that ſince the fyrſt daye that euer
he knewe what the ſea mente, he was neuer in ſuche feare.
Proceadinge yet ſumwhat further in this daungerous vyage,
he fownde certeyne goulfes of .viii. myles, as it had byn then
teraunce of ſume greate hauen, into the which, the ſayde vi=
olent ſtreames dyd faule. Theſe goulfes or ſtreyghtes, he cau=
led Os Draconis, that is, the dragons mouth. And the Iland
directly ouer ageynſte the ſame, he named Margarita. Owte of
theſe ſtreyghtes, iſſhewed no leſſe force of freſſhe water: whi=
che encounteringe with the ſaulte, dyd ſtryue to paſſe foorth:
Soo that betwene bothe the waters, was no ſmaule conflict.
But enteringe into the goulſe, at the lengthe he fownde the
water therof very freſſhe and good to drynke. The Admyrall
hym ſelfe, and they which were his companions in this vy=
age, beinge men of good credit, and perceauinge my diligence
in ſearchinge for theſe matters, towlde me yet of a greater
thynge. That is, that for the ſpace of .xxvi. leaques, amoun=
tynge to a hundreth and foure myles, he ſayled euer by freſhe
water: In ſo muche, that the further he proceaded, eſpecial=
ly towarde the weſt, he affirmeth the water ſo bee the freſher.
After this, he came to a highe mountayne, inhabited onely

with

The violent
courſe of the
water from
the Eaſte to
the weſte.

The goulſe
cauled Os
Draconis.

A conflict be=
twene the
freſhe water
& the ſalte.

A ſea of freſh
water.

marmaſets &
monkeys,

with moonkeys oꝛ marmaſits on that part towarde the Eaſt
Foꝛ that ſyde was rowgh with rockye and ſtony mountains
And therfoꝛe not inhabyted with men. ẏet they that went a
lande to ſearche the countrey, fownde nere vnto the ſea, ma
ny fayꝛe fieldes well tylled and ſowen : But noo people, noꝛ
ẏet houſes oꝛ cotages. Parhappes they were gone further in
to the countrey to ſowe theyꝛ coꝛne and applye theyꝛ huſban
dꝛy, as wee often ſee owre huſbande men to leaue theyꝛ ſtati
ons and vylages foꝛ the ſame purpoſe. Jn the weſte ſyde of
that mountapne, they eſpyed a large playne, whither they

The fayꝛe ⁊ large region of paria.

made haſte, and caſt anker in the bꝛode ryuer. As ſoone as the
inhabitantes had knowleage that a ſtrange nation was arry
ued in theyꝛ coaſtes, they came flockinge withowte all feare
to ſee owre men. We vnderſtode by theyꝛ ſygnes and poyn
tynges, that this Region was cauled _Paria_ : and that it was
very large: Jn ſo muche that the further it reacheth towarde
the weſte, to be ſo muche the better inhabited and replenished
with people. The Admiral therfoꝛe, takynge into his ſhyppe
foure of the men of that lande, ſearched the weſte partes of
the ſame. By the temperatenes of the ayer, the pleaſauntnes

Temperate ayer and !frut ful grounde.

of the grownde, and the multytude of people which they ſaw
dayly moꝛe and moꝛe as they ſayled, they coniectured that
theſe thynges poꝛtended ſum great matter : As in deede their
opinion fayled them not, as we wyll further declare in his
place. The ſoonne not yet ryſen, but beginninge euen now to

Sweete ſa-uours pꝛocee dynge frome the lande.

ryſe, beinge one day allured by the pleaſauntnes of the place
and ſweete ſauours which bꝛeathed from the land to the ſhip
pes, they went alande. Here they fownde a greater multy
tude of people then in any other place. As owre men appꝛo
ched towarde them, there came certeine meſſengers from their

Cacici,

Cacici, that is, the kynges of the countrey, to deſyꝛe the Ad
mirall in the name of theyꝛ pꝛinces to coome to theyꝛ palay
ces withowte feare, and that they and al theyꝛs ſhulde bee at

Humayne people.

his commaundement. When the Admirall had thanked them
and made his excuſe foꝛ that tyme, there came innumerable

Cheynes and garlandes of gold ⁊ perles

people with theyꝛ boates to the ſhippes: hauyng foꝛ the moſt
parte cheynes abowte theyꝛ neckes, garlandes on theyꝛ hea
des, and bꝛaſelettes on theyꝛ armes of pearles of Jndia : And
that ſo commonlye, that owre women in playes and trymm
phes haue not greater plentie of ſtones of glaſſe and cryſtall
in

n theyꝛ garlandes, crownes, gerdels, and suche other tyꝛe-
mentes. Beinge asked where they gathered them, they poynted to the next shoꝛe by the sea bankes. They signified also by
certeyne scoꝛneful gestures which they made with theyꝛ mou-
hes and handes, that they nothyng esteemed perles. Takinge
also baskettes in their handes, they made signes that the
same might bee fylled with them in shoꝛte space. But bycause
he coꝛne wherwith his shyppes were laden to bee caryed into
Hispaniola, had taken hurt by reason of the salte water, he determined to deferre this matte to a moꝛe conuenient tyme. yet
he sent to lande two of the shippe boates laden with men, to
thintent to fetch sum garlandes of perles foꝛ exchange of our
thynges, and also sumwhat to searche the nature of the Region and disposition of the people. They enterteyned owr men
gentelly: and came flockynge to them by heapes, as it hadde
byn to beholde sume straunge monsters. Fyrste there came to
meete owre men, two men of grauitie, whome the multitude
folowed. One of these was well in age, and the other but
younge. They thinke it was the father with his soonne whi
he shulde succede hym. When the one had saluted and embꝛa-
ced the other, they bꝛowght owre men into a certeyne rownde
howse, nere vnto the whiche, was a greate courte. Hether
were bꝛowght many chapers and stooles made of a certeyne
blacke woodde, and very coonningely wꝛowght. After that
owre men, and theyꝛ Pꝛinces were sette, theyꝛ waytyng men
came in laden, sume with sundꝛy delicate dysshes, and sume
with wyne. But theyꝛ meate, was only fruites: and those of
dyuers kyndes and vtterly vnknowe to vs. Theyꝛ wyne was
both whyte and redde; not made of grapes, but of the lycour
of dyuers fruites, and very pleasaunte in drynkynge. After
his banquette made in the owlde mans howse, the younge
man bꝛowght them to his tabernacle oꝛ manciou place, where
was a greate coompany bothe of men and women, but they
stoode deceauered the one from the other. They are whyte, e-
uen as owre men are, sauynge suche as are much conuersant
in the sonne. They are also very gentyll, and full of humanitie towarde strangiers. They couer theyꝛ pꝛyuie partes with
gossampine cotton wꝛowght with sundꝛy coloures: and are
besyde all naked. There was fewe oꝛ none, that had not eyther a coller, a cheyne, oꝛ a bꝛaselette of golde and pearles,
H.iii. and

Baskettes ful of pearles, I knowe who had bags ful.

Howe the Ad mirals men were enter-teyned.

cheyers and stoles of he-bene.

Fruites and wyne.

wyne of the lycour of fruites.

whyte men nere the Equi noctial.

mountaynes
are the matri
ces of golde.

Canibales

Shalownes
of the ſea,

The vſe of
caruelles o:
bzigantines.

Cumana and
Manacapana
regions ofthe
prouince of
Paria.
Curiana.

A ryuer of
maruelous
depth and
bꝛedth.
A ſea of wee=
des.
Lentiſcus.
Maſtix.

and many had all. Beinge aſked where they had that golde,
they poynted to certeyne mountaynes, ſeemynge with theyꝛ
countenaunce to diſſuade owre men from goinge thyther. Foꝛ
puttinge theyꝛ armes in theyꝛ mouthes, and grynninge as
thowgh they bytte the ſame, ſtylle poyntinge to the moun=
taynes, they ſeemed to inſinuate that men were eaten there:
But whether they mente by the Canibales, oꝛ wylde beaſtes
owre men cowlde not well perceaue. They tooke it exceedinge
greeuouſlye, that they coulde nother vnderſtande owre men,
noꝛ owre men them. When they which were ſente to lande,
were returned to the ſhippes abowte three of the clocke at af=
ter noone the ſame daye, bꝛinginge with them certeyne gar=
landes and collers of pearles, they looſed theyꝛ ankers to de
parte, myndinge to coome ageyne ſhoꝛtly, when all thynges
were ſette in good order in Hiſpaniola. But he was pꝛeuented
by an other, which defeated hym of the rewarde of his tra=
uayle. He was alſo hyndered at this tyme by reaſõ of the ſha
lownes ofthe ſea ꝗ violẽt courſe of the water, which with con
tinual toſſing, bꝛooſed the greateſt ſhip as often as any great
gale of wynde aroſe. To auoyde the daungiours of ſuche ſha=
lowe places, and ſhelfes, he euer ſent one of the ſmalleſt ca=
rauelles befoꝛe, to try the way with ſoundinge: and the byg
geſt ſhyppes folowed behynde. The Regions beinge in the
large prouince of Paria foꝛ the ſpace of, ccxxx, myles, are cau=
led of thinhabitantes, Cumana,, and Manacapana: from theſe re
gions diſtant three ſcoꝛe leaques, is there an other Region
cauled Curiana. When he had thus paſſed ouer this long tract
of ſea, ſuppoſing ſtyll that it had byn an Ilande, ꝗ doutinge
that he might paiſe by the Weſte to the Noꝛthe directlye to
Hiſpaniola, he chaunced into a ryuer of. xxx. cubettes depthe, ꝗ
of ſuch bꝛeadth as hath not lyghtly byn harde of. Foꝛ he af=
firmeth it to bee. xxviii. leaques. A lyttle further toward the
Weſte, yet ſumwhat moꝛe ſowthwarde as the bending of the
ſhoꝛe requyred, he entered into a ſea full of herbes oꝛ
weedes. The ſeede of the herbes whiche ſwymme on the
water, are muche lyke the berryes of the tree cauled Lentiſcus,
which beareth the ſweete gũme cauled Maſtix. They grewe
ſoo thicke, that they ſumetyme in maner ſtayed the ſhippes.
The Admirall repoꝛted, that here there is not one daye tho=
rowghe owte all the yeare muche longer oꝛ ſhoꝛter then an
other

other: And that the Nozthe pole is here eleuate onely fyue
degrees as at Paria, in whoſe tracte all theſe coaſtes lye. Hee
alſo declared certeyne thynges as concerninge the variete of
the nozthe pole: The which becauſe they ſeeme contrarye to
thoppinions of all the Aſtronomers, I wyll touche them but
with a dzye foote as ſayth the pzouerbe. But it is wel know
en (moſte noble pzince)that the ſtarre which we caule the pole
ſtarre, oz nozth ſtarre, (cauled of the Italians *Tramontana*) is
not the very poynte of the pole Artyke vppon the whiche the
ares oz extremities of heauens are turned abowte. The which
thynge may well be pzoued,if when the ſtarres fyzſt appeare,
yowe becholde the pole ſtarre thzowgh any narowe hole. Foz
ſoo,applyinge yowre inſtrument therto in the mozninge ſum=
what befoze the day ſpzinge haue blemyſhed theyz lyght, yf
then yowe looke thzowgh the ſame hole, yowe ſhall perceaue
it to bee moued from the place where yowe ſawe it fyzſt. But
howe it commeth to paſſe, that at the beginnynge of the eue=
nyng twilight,it is eleuate in that Region only fyue degrees
in the moneth of June, and in the mozninge twylight to bee
eleuate. xv. degrees by the ſame quaadzante, I doo not vn=
derſtande. Noz yet doo the reaſons which he bzingeth,in any
poynt ſatyſfye me. Foz he ſayth, that he hereby coniectured,
that the earth is not perfectlye rownde : But that when it
was created, there was a certeyne heape reyſed theron,much
hygher thē the other partes of the ſame. So that(as he ſaith)
it is not rownde after the fozme of an apple oz a bal(as other
thynke) but rather lyke a peare as it hangeth on the tree:And
that Paria is the Region which poſſeſſeth the ſupereminente
oz hygheſt parte therof nereſte vnto heauen. In ſoo muche
that he erneſtly contendeth, the earthly Paradyſe to bee ſitu=
ate in the toppes of thoſe thzee hylles, which wee ſayde bee=
foze, that the watche man ſawe owte of the toppe caſtell of
the ſhippe : And that the outragious ſtreames of the freſhe wa
ters whiche ſoo violentlye iſſhewe owte of the ſayde goulfes
and ſtryue ſoo with the ſalte water,faule headlonge from the
toppes of the ſayde mountaynes, But of this matter, it ſhall
ſuffice to haue ſayde thus muche. Lette vs nowe therfoze re=
turne to the hiſtozye from which we haue dygreſſed. When
he perceaued hym ſelfe to bee thus inwrapped in ſoo greate a
goulfe beyonde his expectacion, ſoo that he had now no hope

*The eleuati=
on of the pole
at paria.*

*Note a ſe=
create as con
cerninge the
pole ſtarre.*

An experiēce

*A maruelous
ſecreate.*

*That the
earth is not
perfectly
rownde.*

*paradiſe is in
the moun=
taynes of pa=
ria.
Looke the
ninth booke
ſeconde de=
cade.*

to fynde any paſſage towarde the northe whereby he myght
ſayle directly to Hiſpaniola, he was enforced to turne backe the
ſame way by the which he came, and directed his viage to H-
paniola by the northe of that lande lyinge towarde the Eaſt.
They which afterwarde ſearched this lande more curiouſlye
Paria is part
of the firme
lande of india
wyll it to bee parte of the continente or firme lande of Jndia
and not of Cuba as the Admiral ſuppoſed. For there are many
which affirme that they haue ſayled rownd abowt Cuba. But
whether it bee ſo or not, or whether enuyinge the good fortune of this man, they ſeeke occaſions of querelinge agaynſt
Tyme reuea-
leth al things
hym, J can not iudge: But tyme ſhall ſpeake, which in tyme
appoynted, reucaleth both truth and falſchod. But whether
Paria bee Continent or not, the Admiral dothe not muche contende. But he ſuppoſeth it to bee Continente. He alſo affir-
paria more
ſouthewarde
then hiſpani-
ola
meth that Paria is more ſouthewarde then Hiſpaniola, by eygt
hundreth foureſcore and two myles. At the length he came to
Hiſpaniola (to ſee his ſouldiers which he left with his brethren
the thyrde day of the calendes of September: Jn the yeare
1498. But (as often tymes chaunceth in humayne thynges,
amonge his ſo many proſperous, pleaſaunte, and luckye affayres, fortune mengeled ſume ſeedes of wormewoodde, and
corrupted his pure corne with the malicious weedes of cocell

C **The ſeuenth booke of the fyrſt decade, to**
the ſame Lodouike Cardinall ꝛc.

The ſpany-
ardes rebell
in the Admi-
rals abſence
Hen the Admirall was nowe coome to the J-
lande of Hiſpaniola, he fownde all thynges confounded and owte of order. For Roldanus (of
whom wee ſpake beefore) refuſed in his abſence to obey his brother, truſtinge to the multitude of ſuch as were confethered with him.
And not onely behaued hym ſelfe proudely a-
geynſt the Admiralles brother and Lieutenaunt ſumtyme his
maiſter, but alſo ſente letters to his reproche to the kynge of
Spayne, therin accuſinge bothe the brethren, leyinge heynous
matters to theyr charges. But the Admirall agayne, ſent mea-
ſengers to the kynge, which myght informe hym of theyr rebellion: Jnſtantly deſyringe his grace, to ſende hym a newe
ſupplye of men, wherby he myght ſuppreſſe theyr licetiouſnes
a

and punyshe them for theyr mischeuous actes. They accused he Admirall and his brother to bee vniust men, cruel enemies nd sheaders of the Spanyshe bludde: declarynge that vppon uery lyght occasion, they wolde racke them, hange them, and eade them: And that they tooke pleasure therin. And that hey departed from them as from cruell tyrantes and wylde eastes reioysinge in bludde, also the kynges enemyes. Affyr-minge lykewyse that they well perceaued theyr intente to bee one other then to vsurpe Thempire of the Ilandes: whiche hynge (they sayde) they suspected by a thousand coniectures. And especially in that they wolde permitte none to resorte to he golde mynes, but only suche as were theyr familiers. The Admirall on the contrary parte, when he desyred ayde of the kynge to infringe theyr insolencie, auouched that al those his ccusers, which had deuised suche lyes ageynste hym, were owghtye felowes, abhominable knaues and vylaynes, the-ues and baudes, ruffians aduouterers and rauishers of women aulse periured vagabundes, and suche as had byn eyther con uict in pryson, or fledde for feare of Iudgment: soo escaping unyshement, but not leauinge vice wherin they styll contynu-d and browght the same with them to the Ilande, lyuinge here in lyke maner as before, in thefte, lechery, and all kyn-es of myscheefe: And soo gyuen to Idlenes and sleepe, that wheras they were browght thyther for myners, labourers, & cullyans, they wolde not nowe goo one furlonge from theyr houses except they were borne on mens backes, lyke vnto thē whiche in owlde tyme were cauled *Ediles Curules*. For, to this office, they put the miserable Ilande men, whom they hande-ed moste cruelly. For leaste theyr handes shulde discontinewe rom sheadinge of bludde, and the better to trye theyr strength and manhod, they vsed nowe and then for theyr pastyme to tryue amonge them selues and proue who coulde most cleanely with his swoorde at one stroke stryke of the heade of an inno-cente. Soo that he which coulde with moste agilitie make the heade of one of those poore wretches to flye quyte and cleane rom the body to the grounde at one stroke, he was the best mā nd counted moste honorable. These thynges and many suche ther, the one of them layde to the others charge beefore the kynge. Whyle these thynges were doinge, the Admirall sente his brother the lieuetenaunt with an army of foure score and

The Spanyardes accuse the Admirall.

The Admiralles answere.

Insolencie & idelnes of libertie.

These had the custodies of the tēples.

A cruel and deuelyshe pastyme.

tenne footemen, and a fewe horſemen, (with three thouſande of the Jlande men which were mortall enemies to the Ciguaⁱ uians) to meete the people of Ciguaue, with Kynge Guarionexiuꝰ theyr gruunde capitayne, who had doone muche myſcheefe to owre men and ſuche as fauoured theym. Therefore when the Lieutenaunt had conducted his army to the bankes of a cerⁱ teyne greate ryuer runnynge by the playne which we ſayd beⁱ fore to lye betwene the corners of the mountaynes of Ciguauⁱ and the ſea, he fownde two ſcoutes of his enemyes lurkinge in certeyne buſſhes: wherof the one, caſtynge hym ſelfe headⁱ longe into the ſea, eſcaped: and by the mouthe of the ryuer ſwamme ouer to his coompanyons. The other beinge taken declared that in the woodde on the other ſide the ryuer, therⁱ lay in campe ſyxe thouſande Cyguauians redy, vnwares to aſſayle owre men paſſynge bye. Wherfore the Lieutenaunt fyndyng a ſhalowe place where he myght paſſe ouer, he with his hole army entered into the ryuer. The which thyng when the Ciguauians had eſpyed, they came runnynge owte of the wooddes with a terrible crye and moſte horrible aſpect, much lyke vnto the people cauled Agathyrſi of whom the poete virⁱ gile ſpeaketh. For they were all paynted and ſpotted with ſundry coloures, and eſpeciall with blacke and redde which they make of certeyne fruites nooryſhed for the ſame purpoſ in theyr gardens, with the ioyce wherof they paynt them ſelⁱ ues from the forheade, euen to the knees: hauing theyr heare (whiche by arte they make longe and blacke if nature deny it them) wrethed and rowled after a thouſande faſſhions. A man wold thynke them to bee deuylles incarnate newly brokⁱ owte of hell, they are ſoo lyke vnto helhoundes. As owre men waded ouer the ryuer, they ſhotte at them and hurled dartes ſeo thicke, that it almoſte tooke the lyght of the ſonne from owre men. In ſo much that if they had not borne of the force therof with theyr targettes, the matter hadde gonne wronge with them. Yet at the length, many beinge wounded, they paſſed ouer the ryuer, which thynge when the enemies ſawe they fledde: whome owre men perſuinge, ſlewe ſume in the chaſe: but not many, by reaſon of theyr ſwyftenes of foote. Thⁱs beinge in the wooddes, they ſhotte at owre men more ſafely. For they being accuſtomed to the wooddes and naked withꝛut any lette, paſſed throwgh the buſſhes and ſhrubbes

a⸗

kynge Guariⁱ
onexius is caⁱ
ptaine of .vi.
thouſand Ciⁱ
guauians.

Vide Agathyrſi.

Naked men
paynted with
the ioyce of
certe fruites.

Heare made
longe & black
by arte.

The vſe of
targettes.

The Ciguauⁱ
ans are dryue
to flyght.

as it had byn wylde bores or hartes : wheras owre men were
hyndered by reason of theyr apparell, targettes, longe iauelens, and ignorance of the place. Wherfore, when he had
ceased there all that nyght in vayne, and the daye folowynge
sawe none steringe in the wodes, he went (by the counsel and
conducte of the other Ilande men which were in his armye)
immediatly from thence, to the montaynes in the which king
Maiobanexius had his cheefe mansion place in the vylage cauled
Capronum, by the which name also, the kynges palaice was cau-
ed, beinge in the same vylage. Thus marchinge forwarde
with his army, abowte twelue myle of, he encamped in the
vylage of an other kynge, which thinhabitantes had forsaken for feare of owre men, yet makynge dyligent search, they
fownde two, by whom they had knowleage that there was
enne kynges with *Maiobanexius* in his palaice of *Capronum*, with
n army of eight thousand Ciguauians. At the Lieutenantes
yrst approche, he durst not gyue them battayle vntyll he had
umwhat better searched the Region: yet did he in the meane
yme skyrmysshe with them twyse. The nexte nyght abowte
mydnyght, he sent furth scoutes, and with them guydes of
he Ilande men which knewe the countrey. Whom the Ciguauians espyenge from the mountaynes, prepared them selues,
o the battayle with a terrible crye or alarome after their ma-
er : but yet durst not coome owte of the wooddes, supposing
hat the Lieutenaunt with his mayne army had byn euen at
ande. The day folowynge, when he brought his army to the
lace where they encamped, leaping owt of the wooddes, they
wyse attempted the fortune of warre, fiercely assaylyng owre
men with a mayne force, and woundinge manye before they
oulde coouer them with theyr targettes. Yet owre men put
hem to flyght, slewe many, and tooke many. The resydewe
ledde to the wooddes, where they kept them styll as in their
moste safe houlde. Of them which were taken, he sent one, &
with hym an other of the Ilande men which was of his parte
o *Maiobanexius* with commaundement in this effect. The Lieue
tenaunt brought not hether his army. (O *Maiobanexius*) to kepe
warre eyther agaynst yowe or yowre people : For he greatly
despyeth yowre frendeshyppe. But his entent is, that *Guario-*
nexius who hath persuaded yowe to bee his ayde agaynste hym
to the greate destruction of yowre people and vndoynge of

J. ii. yowre

Marginal notes:

kynge Maio-
banexius.

An army of
viii. thousand
Ciguauians.

A Larome.

The Ciguaui-
ans put to
flyght ageine

The Lieute-
naunt his am
bassage to
kynge Maio-
banexius.

powre countrey, may haue dewe cozrection aſwell foz his o[...]
obedience towarde him, as alſo foz raysing tumultes among[...]
the people. Wherfoze, he requyzeth powe and exozteth pow[...]

kynge Guari-oneꝛius.

to deliuer *Guarionexius* into his handes. The whic[...] thynge [...]
powe ſhall perfozme, the Admirall his bzother wyll not on[...]
gladly admitte powe to his frendeſhyppe, but alſo enlarge [...]
defende powre dominion. And if herein powe refuſe to acco[...]
plyſhe his requeſte, it wyll folowe, that powe ſhall ſhoztely
repent powe therof. Foz powre kyngedome ſhall be waſte[...]
with ſwoozde and fyer, and powe ſhall abyde the fortune [...]
warre wherof powe haue had experience with fauour, as po[...]
ſhall further know here after to powre payne, yf with ſtobe[...]
nes powe pzouoke hym to ſhewe the vttermoſte of his pou[...]

Maiobanexi-us his an-ſwere.

When the meſſenger had thus doone his errante, *Maiobanexi*[...]
anſwered, that *Guarionexius* was a good man, indued with m[...]
ny vertues as all men knewe: And therfoze he thought hy[...]
woꝛthy his ayde: eſpecially in as muche as he fledde to hy[...]
foz ſuccoure, and that he had made him ſuch pzomeſſe, who[...]
alſo he had pzoued to bee his faithfull frende. Ageyne, th[...]

Naturall ha-tred of vyce.

they were nawghty men, violent and cruell, deſyzinge oth[...]
mens gooddis, and ſuche as ſpared not to ſhede innocente[...]
bludde: In fyne, that he wolde not haue to doo with ſuch[...]
myſcheuous men, noꝛ yet enter into frendeſhippe with the[...]
When theſe thynges came to the Lieutenauntes eare, he co[...]
maunded the vylage to be burnte where he hym ſelfe encan[...]
ped, with many other vylages there abowte. And when [...]
dzewe nere to the place where *Maiobanexius* lay, he ſent meſſe[...]
gers to hym ageyne, to common the matter with hym, and [...]
wyll hym, to ſende ſume one of his moſte feythful frendes [...]
entreate with hym of peace. Where vppon the kynge ſent b[...]

The Lieute-nauntes gen-telneſſetoward maiobanexius

to hym one of his cheefe gentelmen, and with hym two oth[...]
to wayte on hym. When he came to the Lieutenauntes p[...]
ſence, he frendly requyzed hym to perſuade his loꝛd and m[...]
ſter in his name, and erneſtly to admonyſſhe hym, not to ſu[...]
fer his floꝛyſhinge kyngedome to bee ſpoyled, oꝛ hym ſelfe [...]
abyde the haſarde of warre foz *Guarionexius* ſake: And furth[...]
to exhoꝛte hym to deliuer hym, excepte he wolde pzocure t[...]
deſtruction bothe of hym ſelfe, his people, and his countrey[...]
When the meſſenger was returned, *Maiobanexius* aſſembled t[...]
people, declaring vnto them what was doone, but they crie[...]
ow[...]

wote on hym to delyuer Guarionexius : And beganne to curse the
daye that euer they had receaued hym, thus to disturbe theyr
quietnes. Maiobanexius answered them, that Guarionexius was a
good man, and had well deserued of him, giuinge hym many
princely presentes : And had also tawght both his wyfe and
hym to synge and daunce, whiche thynge he dyd not lyttle
esteeme. And was therfore fully resolued in no case to forsake
hym, or ageynste all humanitie to betraye his frende whiche
fledde to hym for succoure: but rather to abyde al extremities
with him, then to minister occasion of obloquye to slaunderes
to reporte that he had betrayed his geste whom he tooke into
his house with warranties. Thus dismissinge the people sigh
inge and with sorowfull hartes, he caulled Guarionexius before
hym, promysinge hym ageyne, that he wolde bee partaker of
his fortune whyle lyfe lasted. In so muche that he thowght
it not beste to sende any further woorde to the Lieuetenaunt:
but appoynted hym whome before he sent to hym, to keepe
the way with a garryson of men, to thintent that if any messengers shulde be sent from the Lieuetenaunt, to sleye them by
the way, and admitte none to communication or further entre
of peace. In the meane tyme, the Lieuetenaunt sent twoo,
wherof the one was a captiue Ciguauian, and the other an I
inde man of them which were frendes to owre men : They
were bothe taken and slayne. The Lieuetenaunt folowed the
anely with ten footemen and foure horsemen. Fyndinge his
messengers deade in the waye, he was further prouoked to
wrathe, and determyned more extremely to deale with Maioba
rexius. And therfore wente forwarde incontinently with his
hole army to his cheefe palaice of Capronum where he yet laye
in campe. At his approche, all the kynges fledde, euery man
his way, and forsooke theyr capitayne Maiobanexius : who also
with all his famelye, fledde to the rowgh mountaynes. Sum
of the Ciguauians, sowght for Guarionexius to sley hym, for
that he was the cause of all these troubles. But his feete saued his lyfe. For he fledde in tyme to the mountaynes where
he lurked in maner alone amonge the desolate rockes.

Whereas nowe the Lieuetenauntes souldiers were toyled
with longe warre, with watchinge, laboure, and hun-
er, (for it was nowe thre moonethes sence the warres beganne) many desyred leaue to departe to the towre of Concep

A rare fayth-
fulnes in a
barbarous
kynge.

The Lieuete-
nauntes mes-
sengers are
slayne.

Al the kinges
are dryuen to
flyght.

tion, where they had graunges and exercised tyllage. He gaue them theyr paxeportes with alowance of vytayles, and soo that only thyrtie remayned with hym. These three moonethes warre, they contynued very paynefull and myserablye : Soo that duryng al that tyme, they had none other meate but only *Cazibi* : that is, suche rootes whereof they make theyr breade, and that but syldome to theyr fyll : Also *Vsias*, that is, lyttle beastes lyke Conyes, if by chaunce now and then, they tooke sume with theyr houndes. Their drinke was none other then water, such as they fownde, sumtyme sweete, and sumtyme muddy saueringe of the marysshes. Emonge these delicates, that lyttle sleepe that they had, was euer for the moste parte abrode vnder the firmamente : And that not without watche men, and in contynual remoouinge as the nature of warre requyreth). With these fewe therfore, the Lieutenaunt determined to searche the mountaynes, dennes, & caues, if he coulde in any place fynde the steppes of *Maiobanexius* or *Guarionexius*. In the meane tyme certeyne of his menne (whom hunger enforced to goo a huntinge to proue if they coulde take any conies) chaunced vppon twoo of *Maiobanexius* familyers, whiche were sent to certeyne vylages of his, to make prouision of breade. These he enforced to declare where theyr lord lay hydde. And vsed the same also for guides to bringe owre men to the place. Twelue of owre men tooke this enterpryse in hand, paintinge them selues after the maner of the Ciguanians. Soo that by this stratageme or policie, they came sodenly vppon *Maiobanexius*, and tooke hym prisoner with his wyfe, children, and familie, and conueighed them to the towre of Conception to the Lieutenaunt. Within a fewe dayes after, hunger compelled *Guarionexius* to coome owte of the dennes : whome, certeine of the people fearinge the Lieutenaunt, bewrayde to owre hunters. The Lieutenaunt beinge certified hereof, sent furthe a bande of foote men, commaunding them to lye in ambushe vntyll suche tyme as *Guarionexius* wente from the playnes to the mountaynes, and then soodenly to intrappe hym. They went as they were commaunded, tooke hym, and browght hym a waye with them. And by this meanes were all the Regions nere abowte, pacified and quyeted. A certeyne noble woman of nere kynred to *Maiobanexius*, and wyfe to an other kynge whose dominion was yet vntouched, folowed hym in al their aduer

The Spanyardes are penful in the warres.

A desperate aduenture with xxii. men

A police,

kynge Maiobanexius is taken.

Guarionexius is taken.

aduerſities. They affirme this woman to bee the fayꝛeſt and moſte bewtifull that euer nature bꝛowght fooꝛthe in the Iſlande. Whom, when the kynge her huſbande who looued her moſte ardently (as her bewtie deſerued) harde ſaye that ſhee was taken pꝛiſoner he wandered vppe and downe the deſertes lyke a man owte of his wytte, not knowinge what to doo oꝛ ſaye. But at the lengthe, he came to the Lieutenaunte, pꝛomyſinge moſte faythfully that he wold ſubmitte hym ſelfe and all that he coulde make, vnder his poure, ſoo that he wolde reſtoꝛe hym his wyfe. The Lieutenaunt accepꝛed the cōdition & reſtoꝛed him his wife, with certeyne other rulers and gentelmen which he had taken pꝛiſoners befoꝛe: Charginge hem, and byndinge them with an othe, to bee euer redye at his commaundement. Shoꝛtly after, this kynge, of his owne ſree motion, came ageyne to the Lieutenaunt, bꝛingyng with hym ſyue thouſande men without weapons, ſayinge onely ſuche inſtrumentes as they vſe in tyllage of theyꝛ growande. He bꝛought with hym alſo, ſeedes to ſowe: wherwith at his owne charge, he cauſed ſuche plentie of theyꝛ coꝛne and fruites to growe in ſundꝛy places of the large vale wherof wee ſpake befoꝛe, that ſhoꝛtely after, were ſeene manye fayꝛe and ſruiteſull fieldes that came therof. And foꝛ his gentſines beinge rewarded of the Lieutenaunte with certeyne of owre thynges, he departed ioyfully. When the repoꝛt hereof came to the Ciguauians, it mooued the myndes of the kynges to hope of clemencie. Where vppon they came togyther to the Lieutenaunt with humble ſubmiſſion and faythful pꝛomeſſe euer after to bee vnder his obedience: deſyꝛing hym to reſtoꝛe vnto them theyꝛ kynge, with his famylie. At theyꝛ requeſte, the kynges wyfe and his houſeholde was ſette at Libertie, but he kepte ſtill as a pꝛiſoner. Theſe thynges dyd the Lieutenaunt in the Ilande, not yet knowinge what his aſuerſaries and accaſers had layde to his charge befoꝛe the kynge of Spayne: who beinge diſquieted with theyꝛ querelinges and accuſacions, and eſpecially foꝛ that by reaſon of theyꝛ diſcencion, of too greate abundaunce of golde and other thynges, there was as yet but lyttle bꝛowght into Spayne, appointed a newe gouernour which ſhuld ſee a redꝛeſſe in theſe thinges: and eyther to punyſhe ſuche as were fautie, oꝛ elles to ſende them to hym. What was fownde ageynſte the Admirall and

Ꝑ. ooo

An vnwoorthy rewarde for soo greate paynes.

his brother, or ageynst his aduersaries whiche accused hym
I doo not wel knowe. But this I am sure of, that both ꝫ
brethrene are taken, browght, and cast in prison, with tha
goodes confiscate. But as soone as the kynge vnderstoo
that they were browght bounde to Cales, he sent messenge
in poste, with commaundemente that they shulde bee loos
and coome freely to his presence : wherby he declared that
tooke theyr troubles greeuouslye. It is also sayde, that t
newe gouernoure sent letters to the kynge, wrytten with t
Admiralles hande in straunge and vnknowen sypheringes,
his brother the Lieutenaunt beinge absente, wyllynge hy
to bee in a redynes with a poure of armed men to coome a
ayde hym if the Gouernoure shulde profer hym any violen
Wherof the gouernour hauinge knowleage (as he saythe)
inge also aduertised that the Leauetenaunt was gonne to
brother before the men whic he had prepared were in a re
nes, apprehended them bothe vnwares, before the multitu
came togyther. What wyl folowe, tyme, the moste trewe a
prudent Iudge, wyll declare. Thus fare ye well.

❡ The eyghth booke of the fyrste Decade, to Cardinall Lodouike.

The Ocean sea heretofore vnknowen.

He greate ryche, and plentifull Ocean f
heretofore vnknowen, and nowe fownde
Christophorus Colonus the Admyrall, by thaut
tic and furtherance of the Catholyke kyng
I haue presented vnto yowre honoure (ryg
noble Prince) lyke a golden cheyne vnwoo
manly wrought.   But yowe shall nowe

Shipmasters vnder the Admiral.

ceaue a precious iewell to bee appendaunt therto. Therfore
monge suche as were pylottes or gouernoures vnder the A
myrall, and had dylygently marked the courses and differe
ces of the wyndes, many had licences graunted them of ꝫ
kynge to seeke further of theyr owne charges, vppon cond
on to pay hym faithfully his portion, which is the fyrst pa

The fifte portion dewe to the kynge.

But bycause emonge all other, one *Petrus* Alphonsus calned N
nus by his surname) sayled towarde the South: with m
prosperous fortune then any of the other, I thinke it best f
to speake sumwhat of his vyage. He therfore, with only o

The nauigation of Petrus Alphonsus.

ship

...ippe, well furnyſhed at his owne charges, after that he had
...s paſſeporte with commaundement in no caſe to caſte anker
...aſſe fyftie leaques diſtante from any place where the Admy:
...ll hadde touched, ſayled fyrſte to Paris where the Admyrall
...ownde bothe the men and women ſoo laden with cheynes,
...arlandes, and braſelettes of pearles, as wee haue ſayde be:
...re. Coaſtynge therfore alonge by the ſame ſhore accordinge
...o the kynges commaundement, (yet leauinge behynde hym
...e Regions of Cumani and Manacapana) he came to the Region
...hich thinhabitantes thereof, caule Curiana : where he fownd
...hauen (as he ſaythe) muche lyke the porte of Gades or Cales,
...n to the which enteringe, he ſawe a farre of certeyne how:
...s on the ſhore, and perceaued when he drewe nere, that it
...as a vylage of onely eyght howſes. Proceadynge yet fur:
...er for the ſpace of three myles, he eſpyed an other vylage
...ell replenyſhed with people, where there met hym fyftie na:
...d men on a coompany hauinge with them a certeyne ruler,
...ho deſyred Alphōſus to coome to theyr coaſtes. He browght
...ith hym at this tyme, many haukes belles, pynnes, nedels,
...aſelettes, cheynes, garlandes, and ryngcs with counterfet
...nes and glaſſes, and ſuch other tryfelles, the which with:
...the momente of an houre, he hadde erchaunged for. rb.
...ces of theyr pearles which they wore abowte theyr neckes
...d armes. Then they yet more erneſtly deſyred him to ſayle
...theyr coaſtes : Promyſynge hym that he ſhulde there haue
...many pearles as he wolde deſyre. He condecended to their
...queſte : And the daye folowynge, came to the place where
...ey appoynted hym : Lyinge there at anker, a great multy:
...de of people reſorted to hym, inſtantely requyringe hym to
...ome alande. But when he conſydered the innumerable mul:
...rude of people which was there aſſembled, and that he had
...ly. rrriii. men in his coompany, he durſte not commyt hym
...lfe to theyr handes, but gaue them to vnderſtand by ſignes
...d tokens that they ſhulde coome to the ſhyppe with theyr
...noas. For theyr boates (which the men of the Iland caule
...roas) are made only of one hole pecce of woodde as in the I
...ndes : yet more rude, and not ſoo artificially as theyrs are.
...heſe they caule Gallitas : They ſwarmed therefore to the ſhyp
...faſte as they myght, brynginge with them great plentie of
...arles (which they caule Tenoras) erchaunginge the ſame for
                        K.i.   owre

Paris.

Cumana.
Manacapana.
Curiana.

Perles for try fels.

Great plentie of pearles.

Humayne people.

owre marchaunties. He fownde this people to bee of genty
nature, ſimple and innocente, beinge conuerſant with them i
theyr houſes, for the ſpace of .xx. dayes.   Theyr houſes ar
made of woodde, coouered with the leaues of date trees

Shelfyʃhes
in which per-
les are engen-
dred.
Beaſtes and
foules.

Theyr meate for the moſte parte, is the ſhelfyſhes in the wh
the pearles are engendred, wherof theyr ſea coaſtes are ful
They haue alſo greate plentie of wylde beaſtes, as hartes
wylde bores, and coonys lyke vnto hares, both in colour an
byggenes. Stocke doues alſo, and turtle doues. Lykewyſ
geeſe and duckes which they nooryſhe in theyr houſes as we
doo. Peacockes flye abowte in maner in euerye woodde an
groue: but they are not diſtinct with ſundry coloures as our
are: for the cockes are lyke vnto the hennes. Theſe people

Hunters and
archers.

Curiana, are craftie hunters and exceding cunning archers, ſo
that they wyll not lyghtly myſſe any beaſt or byrde that the
ſhoote at. Owre men conſumed certeyne dayes here very pl
ſauntely. Durynge which tyme, who ſoo euer brought the
a peacocke, had for the ſame, foure pynnes. He that brough

Theyr maner
of bargening

a pheaſaunt, had twoo: And for a ſtocke doue or turtle dou
one: And for a gooſe, a ſmaul lookyng glaſſe or a lyttle ſto
of glaſſe. Thus they bought and ſoulde with proferynge an
byddynge, denyinge and refuſinge as it had byn in a grea

The Vſe of
pynnes.

market. When pynnes were profered them, they aſked wh
they ſhulde doo with them, beinge naked. But owre men ſ
tiſfied them with a craftie anſwere, declaring by tokens tha
they were very neceſſary to picke theyr teeth and to pul tho
nes owte of theyr fleſhe. But aboue al thynges haukes be

Haukes bels
in great eſti-
mation.

les were moſt eſteemed amonge them, for theyr ſounde & fai
coloure: And woulde therfore gyue much for one of thē. Ow
men lodginge in theyr houſes, harde in the nyght ſeaſon h

Roringe of
wyld beaſtes

ryble noyſes and roryngs of wylde beaſtes in the woodde
which are full of exceadinge greate and hygh trees of ſundr
kyndes. But the beaſtes of theſe wooddes, are not noyſom
to men. For the people of the countrey goo dayly a huntin
naked, with theyr bowes and arrowes: yet hath it not b
harde of, that any man hath byn ſlayne of any wylde beaſt

Hartes and
wyld bores.

As many hartes or wylde bores as owre men woolde deſy
them to brynge, they woolde kyll in the wooddes with the
bowes and arrowes, and not fayle to brynge theim.   Th
lacke kyne, goates, & ſheepe. Theyr breade is made of roote

is theyr of the Ilandes. This nation, hath blacke heare,
offe and sumwhat curlde, yet longe also. They keepe theyr
th very whyte: And for that purpose vse to cary a certeine
rbe betwene theyr lyppes for the most parte of the day, and
wasshe theyr mouthes when they cast it away. The women
o all theyr busynes at home in theyr howses, and haue al=
the cure of tyllage of the grounde. But the men apply them
lues to the warres and huntynge, to playe, singynge and
unsing. They haue sundry kyndes of water pottes, iugges,
d drinckinge cuppes made of earthe in other places abowt
eym and brought thether for erchaunge of other thynges:
or they vse fayres and markettes for the same purpose: and
e gretly desyrous of such thynges, as are not brought forth
made in theyr countrey, as nature hath gyuen a dispositi=
to al men to desyre and bee delyted with newe and strange
ynges. Many of them, had hangynge at theyr pearles, the
mages of certeine beastes and birdes very artificiously made
golde, but not pure. These also are brought them from o=
er places for exchange of other thynges. The golde wher=
they are made, is natiue, and of much lyke finenes to that
herof the florenes are coyned. The men of this countrey, in
ose theyr priuie members in a gourde, cutte after the fashion
a coddepiece: or els, coouer the same with the shelle of a tor=
yse, tyed abowte theyr loynes with laces of gossampine cot=
n. In other places of that tract, they thrust the synew with
the sheethe therof, and bynde the skinne fast with a stringe.
he greate wylde beastes wherof wee spake before, and many
her thynges whiche are not founde in any of the Ilandes,
ssifie that this regiõ is part of the cõtinẽt or firme land. But
e chiefest cõiecture wherby they argue the same, is, that by
e coastes of that lande, from *Paris* towarde the weste, they
yled abowte three thousande myles, fyndynge no signe or
ken of any ende. These people of *Curiana* (whiche sum caule
rtana) beinge demaunded where they hadde suche plentie of
olde, signified that it was brought them from a Region cau
d *Cauchieta* or *Cauchieta*, being distant from them syre soonnes,
at is, syre dayes iourney westwarde: And that theyr Ima=
es of goulde, were made in the same Region. Where vppon
re men directed theyr vyage thyther immediatly: and arry
d there at the calendes of Nouember, in the yeare of Christ

Blacke and curlde heare. White teethe.

Earthen vessels.

Conninge artificers.

Base golde.

A strange maner of coueringe theyr priuities.

Tokens of the continent or firme lande.

The golden Regiõ of Cauchieta.

a thoufande and fyue hundꝛeth. The people of the countre
reſoꝛted to them withoute feare, bꝛyngynge with them of th
golde which we ſayde to bee natyue in that Region. This pe
ple had alſo collers of pearles abowte theyꝛ neckes, which
were bꝛought them frome *Curiani* foꝛ exchange of theyꝛ ma
chandies. None of them wolde exchaunge any of thoſe thin
ges which they had owte of other countreys : as nother th
Curians golde, noꝛ the Canchietans pearles. yet amonge th
Canchietans, they fownde but little gold redy gathered. The
toke with thē frō thenſe, certen very fayꝛe marmaſets oꝛ mu
keys, ⁊ many popingayes of ſundꝛy coloures. In the moneth
of Nouember, the ayer was there moſt temperate, ⁊ nothyn
coulde. The gardens of the noꝛth pole, were owte of ſyght
bothe theſe people, they are ſoo nere to the Equinoctiall. A
the degrees of the pole, they can gyue none other accownpt
Theſe people, are wel diſpoſed men, of honeſt condicions, an
nothinge ſuſpicious. Foꝛ all moſt all the nyght longe, they r
ſoꝛted to the ſhippe with theyꝛ boates, and went aboozde ſh
withowte feare, as dyd the Curians. They caule pearles, c
rixas. They are ſumwhat ielyous. Foꝛ, when any ſtraunger
coome emonge them, they euer place theyꝛ women behynd th
In this Region of *Canchieta*, the goſſampine trees growe
them ſelues commonly in many places, as doo with vs elmes
wyllowes, and ſalowes. And therfoꝛe they vſe to make bꝛe
ches of cotton, wherwith they coouer theyꝛ pꝛyuie partes
many other Regions there aboute. When they had yet ſayle
on foꝛwarde by the ſame coaſtes, there came fooꝛth ageynſt
them abowte twoo thouſande men, armed after theyꝛ maner
foꝛbydding them to coome aland. Theſe people were ſoo rud
and ſaluage, that owre men coulde by no meanes allure the
to familiaritie. Owre men therfoꝛe, contented only with the
pearles, returned backe the ſame way they came : where the
remayned with the Curians continually foꝛ the ſpace of twe
tie dayes, and fylled theyꝛ bellyes wel with good meate. An
here it ſeemeth to me, not farre from my purpoſe, to declar
what chaunced vnto theim in theyꝛ returne, when they cam
nowe within the ſyght of the coaſte of *Paria*. They happene
therfoꝛe in the way, at *Os Draconis* and the goulfes of *Paria*
(wherof wee ſpake befoꝛe) to meete with a nauie of.xviii. C
noas of Canibales which went a rouyng to hunt foꝛ mē. Wh
as ſoon

Temperate
ayer in No
uember.
The Equinoc
tial lyne.

humane peo
ple.

Goſſampine
trees.

Choꝛlyſhe
people

Alphōſus re
turneth to
Paria.

Canibales in
the goulfes
of Paria.

oone as they had espyed owr men, assailed theyr shippe fierce
ly and without feare enclosed the same, disturbing owre men
in euery syde with theyr arrowes. But owre men so feared
hem with theyr gunnes, that they fledde immediatly, whom
owre menne folowinge with the shippe boate, tooke one of
theyr Canoas, and in it, only one Canibal (for the other had
escaped) and with hym, an other man bownde : Who, with
teares runninge downe his cheekes, and with gesture of his
handes, eyes, and heade, signified that syxe of his coompanyons had byn cruelly cutte in pieces and eaten of that mys-
chenous nation : and that he shulde haue byn lykewyse hande
led the day folowynge. Wherfore they gaue hym poure ouer
the Canyball, to doo with hym what he wolde. Then with
the Canibales owne clubbe, he layde on hym al that he might
dryue with hande and foote, grinninge and freting as it had
byn a wylde bore: Thinkynge that he had not yet sufficiently
reuenged the death of his companyons, when he had beaten
owte his braynes and guttes. When he was demaunded after what sorte the Canibales were woont to inuade other con
treys, he answered that they euer vsed to carye with them in
theyr Canoas, a greate multitude of clubbes : The whiche,
where soo euer they lande, they pitche in the grownde, and
encampe them selues within the coompasse of the same, to lye
the more safely in the nyght season. In *Curiana*, they fownde
the head of a capitaine of the Canibales, nailed ouer the doore
of a certeyne gouernoure, for a token of victorie, as it hadde
byn the standerde or helmette taken from the enemye in battayle. In these coastes of *Paria*, is a Region cauled *Haraia*, in
the whiche, greate plentie of salte is gathered after a strange
sorte. For the sea beinge there tossed with the poure of the
wyndes, dryueth the salte waters into a large playne by the
sea syde: where : afterward when the sea wareth caulme, and
the soonne begynnethe to shyne, the water is congeled into
moste pure and whyte salte, wherewith innumerable shyppes
might bee laden, if men doo resorte thether for the same beefore there faule any rayne. For the rayne meltethe it, and cau
seth it to synke into the sande, and soo by the pores of the
earthe, to returne to the place from whense it was dryuen.
Other say, that the playne is not fylled from the sea, but of
certeine sprynges whose water is more sharpe and salt then the

B.iii. water

Death for
death.

howe the ca-
nibales forti-
fie their cápe

Haraia.
Salte engen-
dred of the
water of the
sea.

Sprynges of
of salt water.

water of the fea. Thinhabitantes doo greatlye efteeme thi
bay of falte. Which they vfe, not only foz theyz owne comm
ditie, but alfo woozkinge the fame into a fquare fozme lyk
vnto bzickes, they fell it to ftrangers foz exchaunge of othe
thynges whiche they lacke. In this Region, they ftretch

The bodies of prynces dzyed & referued

and dzye the deade bodies of theyz kinges and noble men, la
inge the fame vpon a certeyne frame of woodde much lyke b
to a hurdle oz grediren, with a gentell fyze vnder the fame
thus by lyttle and lyttle confuminge the flefhe and keeping
the fkynne hole with the bones inclofed therein. Thefe dzye
carcafes, they haue in greate reuerence, and honour them fo
theyz houfeholde and famplier goddes. They fay that in thi
place they fawe a man, and in an other place a woman, thu
dzyed and referued. When they departed from *Curians*, the. vi

Threefcore & xvi. poundes weight of perles foz. v. fhillynges.

The courfe of the fea toward the wefte.

day of the Ides of February to returne to Spayne, they ha
thzee fcoze and.xvi. poundes weight (after.viii. vnces to th
pownde) of perles, which they bought foz exchange of owr
thynges, amountinge to the value of fyue fhyllinges. Depar
tinge therfoze, they confumed thzee fcoze dayes in theyz iou
ney (althowgh it were fhozter then frome *Hifpaniola*) by reafo
of the contynuall courfe of the fea into the wefte, whiche dy
not only greatly ftey the fhippe, but alfo fumtymes dzyue
backe. But at the length they came home foo laden with per

perles as comon as chaffe petrus Alphonfus in prifon.

les, that they were with euery marygner, in maner as commo
as chaffe. But the mafter of the fhyppe, *Petrus Alphonfus*, being
accufed of his coompanyons that he had ftowlen a great mul
titude of precious perles, and defrauded the kynge of his poz
tion which was the fyueth parte , was taken of *Fernando de V
ga*, a man of greate lerninge and experience and gouernour o
Gallecia, where they arryued, and was there kepte in pzyfon
longe tyme. But he ftyll denyeth that euer he deteyned any

Orient perles as bygge as hafel nuttes.

parte of the perles. Many of thefe perles were as bygge a
hafell nuttes, and oriente, (as we caule it) that is, lyke vnt
them of the Eafte partes. yet not of foo greate pzice, by rea
fon that the holes therof are not foo perfecte. When I m
felfe was prefente with the ryght honozable Duke of *Methyn*
and was bidden to dyner with hym, in the citie of Ciuile, the
bowght to hym aboue a hundzeth and twentie vnces of per
les to be foilde: which furely did greatly delyte me with thei
faypzenes and bzightnes, Sum faye, that *Alphonfus* hadde n
thei

heſe perles in *Curiana* being diſtante from *Os Draconis* moꝛe thē hundꝛeth and twentie leagues, but that he had them in the regions of *Cumana* and *Manacapana*, nere vnto *Os Draconis* and the Jlande of *Margarita*. Foꝛ they deny that there is any perles fownde in *Curiana*. But ſithe the matter is yet in controuerſie, we wyll paſſe to other matters. Thus muche yowe haue whereby yowe maye coniecture what commoditie in tyme to coome may bee looked foꝛ from theſe newe landes of the weſt Ocean, wheras at the fyꝛſte diſcoueringe, they ſhewe ſuch tokens of greate ryches. Thus fare ye well.

Curiana
Os Draconis.
Cumana.
Manacapana.
The Jland of
Margarita.

❡ The .ix. booke of the fyꝛſt Decade to Cardynall Lodouike.

Incentiagnes *Pinzonus*, and alſo *Aries Pinzonus*, his neuie, by his bꝛothers ſyde, which accompanyed the Admiral *Colonus* in his fyꝛſte vyage, and were by him appoynted to bee maſters of twoo of the ſmaule ſhippes which the Spaniardes caule *Carauelas*, beinge mooued by the greate ryches and amplytude of the new landes, furnyſhed of theyꝛ owne charges, foure carauels in the hauen of theyꝛ owne countrey which the Spanyardes caule *...dos*, boꝛtheringe on the weſte Ocean. Hauynge therfoꝛe the kynges licence and paſſepoꝛt to departe, they looſed frō the hauen, aboute the Calendes of December, in the yeare +99. This hauen of *Palos* is thꝛee ſcoꝛe and twelue myles diſtant from *Cades*, commonly cauled *Cales*: and thꝛee ſcoꝛe and foure myles from Ciuile. All thinhabitantes of this towne, not one excepted, are greatly gyuen to ſearchinge of the ſea, and continually exercyſed in ſayling. They alſo directed their vyage fyꝛſt to the Jlandes of Canarie by the Jlandes of *Heſperides*, nowe cauled *Cabouerde*, which ſum caule *Gorgodes Meducias*. Saylinge therfoꝛe directly towarde the ſouthe frome that Jland of the *Heſperides* which the Poꝛtugales (being poſſeſſers of the ſame) caule *Sancti Iacobi*, and departinge frome thenſe at the Ides of January, they folowed the ſouthweſt wynde, beinge in the myddeſt betwene the ſouth and the weſte. When they ſuppoſed that they had ſayled aboute thꝛee hundꝛethe leaques by the ſame wynde, they ſay that they loſte the ſyght of

The nauigati
on of Vincenti
us and Aries
Pinzonus.

Licence and
paſſepoꝛte.

Cales. Ciuile.

The Jlandes
of Canarie
Cabouerde.

ſ. James J:
lande.

The South pole owte of syght.

habitable Regions vnder the Equinoctiall lyne.

An other order of starres

A thicke mist

A rysinge in the myddest of the earth.

of the Northe starre : and were shortelye after, tossed with erceedinge tempestes bothe of wynde and sea, and vexed with intollerable heate. yet sayled they on further (not withoute greate daunger) for the space of twoo hundrethe and fortie leaques, folowing yet the same wynde by the lost pole. Wherfore, whether habitable Regions bee vnder the Equinoctiall lyne or not, let these men and the owlde wryters, aswel Philosophers as poetes and cosmographers discusse. For these men, affirme it to bee habitable, and maruelously replenished with people: and they, that it is vnhabitable by reason of the soone beames dependinge perpendicularly or directlye ouer the same. yet were there many of the oulde wryters, whiche attempted to proue it habitable. These marynters beinge demaunded, if they sawe the south pole, they answered that they knewe no starre there lyke vnto this pole, that myght be decerned aboute the poynte. But that they sawe an other order of starres, and a certeyne thicke myst rysynge from the horizontall lyne, which greatly hyndered theyr syght. They contende also, that there is a great heape or rysynge in the myddest of the earth, which taketh away the syght of the southe pole, vntyll they haue vtterly passed ouer the same. But they verely beleue that they sawe other images of starres, muche differinge from the situation of the starres of owre hemisphærie or halfe circle of heauen. Howe soo euer the matter bee, as they informe vs, wee certifie yowe. At the lengthe, the seuenth day of the calendes of Februarye, they espied lande a farre of. And seinge the water of the sea to bee troubelous, soundinge with theyr plummet, they founde it to bee .xvi. fathames deepe. Goinge a lande, and tarienge there for the space of twoo dayes, they departed bycause they saw no people steringe, althowghe they fownde certeyne steppes of men by the sea syde. Thus grauinge on the trees and the stones nere vnto the shore, the kynges name and theyrs, and the tyme of theyr comming thether, they departed. Not farre frō this station, folowynge the fyers on the lande by nyght, they founde a nation lyinge vnder the open fyrmamente after the maner of warre. Owre men thought it not beste to trowble them vntyll the morninge. Therefore, at the rysinge of the soonne, fortie of owre men well armed, wente toward them: ageynst whom came furth, xxxii. of them, with bowes, slinges and

nd dartes, euen redy to the feyght. The other coompanye
olowed them, armed after the same maner. Owr men affirme
hat they were of hygher ſtature then eyther the Almaynes oʒ
ʒannonians. They behelde owre men with frownynge and
hʒeatenynge countenaunce. But owre men thought it not
ood to faule to bickeringe with them, vncerteyne whether it
oere foʒ feare, oʒ bycauſe they wolde not dʒyue thē to flight.
vherfoʒe they went aboute to allure them by faire meanes &
ewardes. But they refuſed all kynde of gentelnes, & ſtoode
uer in a redines to feight, declaringe the same by ſignes and
okens. Thus owr men reſoʒted to theyʒ ſhippes, and they to
he place from whence they came, without any further buſy-
es. The ſame nyght abowte mydnyght, they ſtedde, and left
he place voyde where they lay in campe. Owre men ſuppoſe
hem to bee a vagabunde and wanderinge nacion lyke vnto
he Scythians, witholwte houſes oʒ certeyne dwellinge pla-
es, lyuinge onely with the fruites of the earth, hauing theyʒ
oynes and chyldʒen folowinge them. Such as meaſured their
ooteſteppes in the ſande, affirme with greate othes, that one
f theyʒ feete is almoſt as longe as twoo feete of owre men of
he meane ſoʒte. Saylinge on yet further, they founde an o-
her ʒyuer, but not of deapth ſufficient to beare the carauels.
They ſent therfoʒe the foure ſhippe boates to lande, ful of ar-
ued men to ſearch the countrey. They eſpyed vppon a hyghe
yll nere vnto the ſea ſyde, a greate multitude of people, to
ohom owre coompany ſent furthe one man with certeyne of
wre thynges to allure them to exchaunge. And when he had
aſt a haukes bell towarde them, they caſt downe a wedge of
olde a cubette longe. The which as he ſtouped to take vppe,
hey ſoodenly incloſed hym, and caryed hym awaye. But he
oas ſhoʒtly after reſcued by his coompanyons, to ſum of their
aynes: foʒ they ſlewe eyght of owre men, and wounded ma-
y a farre of, with theyʒ arrowes, and dartes made of wood
ardened at the endes with fyʒe. After this, they encoompa-
ed owre ſhippe boates within the ʒyuer, and came raſhelye
oithin the reache of owre men, layinge houlde on the boates
ydes, where they were thʒuſt thʒowgh and hewen in peeces
as it had byn ſheepe, by reaſon they were naked. Yet wolde
hey not foʒ al this, gyue ouer: but tooke from owre men one
f their boates, hauing noo men in it. Foʒ the gouernour ther

L.i.

of

people of
hygh ſtature.

A vagabunde
kynde of men

Giantes.

Deſperate
bouldenes.

of being ſlayne with an arrowe, the other ſledde and eſcape
And thus they lefte this fierce and warlyke people, ſayling
towarde the northweſte alonge by the ſame coaſtes, with ſ
rowfull hartes for the death of theyr coompanyons. Whe
they had ſayled abowte .xl. leagues, they chaunced into a ſe
of ſuche freſſhe water, that they fylled theyr barelles and ho
ges heades therwith. Searchyng the cauſe hereof, they vnde
ſtoode that a vehement courſe of ryuers diſcended with grea
violence from the toppes of certeyne greate hylles. They ſa
also that there lyeth within the ſea, many fortunate and fru
full Jlandes, and well inhabyted: And that thinhabitante
of this tracte are men of mecke nature and ſuche as doo no
refuſe ſtrangers: yet lyttle profytable to them, bycauſe the
had noo marchandyes for their purpoſe, as golde or precyou
ſtones. For lacke whereof, they brought frome thenſe thyrt
captiues to ſell for ſlaues. Thinhabitantes caule this Regio
Mariatambal. The Region of the eaſte parte of that ryuer, is ca
led _Camomorus_: And that of the weſte parte, _Paricora_: in the mi
lande whereof, thinhabitantes ſignified that there is great
plentie of golde. For, folowynge this ryuer directly towar
the Northe (as the bendynge of the ſhore requyred) they rec
uered ageyne the ſyght of the north pole. All the coaſte of thi
tracte, perteyneth to _Paria_, the which (as we ſayd before) wa
fyrſt founde by _Colonus_ hym ſelfe, and hath in maner in euer
place, greate abundaunce of pearles. They ſaye that the
coaſtes are adioynynge vnto, and all one with Os _Draconis_, an
also bortherynge vppon the Regions of _Cumana_, _Minacapani_, _Cu
rians_, _Cauchieta_, and _Cuchibachoa_. Wherfore they thought it to b
parte of the firme lande of India beyonge the ryuer of _Ganges_
For the greate and large coompaſſe therof, dothe not perm
that it ſhulde bee an Jlande. Albeit, the hole earth vncouere
with water, largely taken, may bee cauled an Jlande. Fro
the poynte of that land where they loſt the ſight of the nort
pole, ſaylynge by a continuall tracke abowte three hundret
leagues towarde the weſte ſyde of _Paria_, they ſay that almoſt
in the mydde way, they chaunced into a ryuer cauled _Maragno
num_, which they affirme to bee of ſuch exceedinge breadth, tha
it myght ſeeme incredible, if the antiquitie dyd not make me
tion of the lyke. Beinge demaunded of me if it were not ſalt
water where it diuided the lande, they anſwered, that the wa

A ſea of freſ-
ſhe water.

many fruite-
full Jlandes.

humane
people.

Mariataball.
Camomorus.
Paricora.

Regions of
Paria.

Golde and
perles.

Os Draconis.

Cumana.
Minacapana.
Curiana.

The hole
earth largely
taken, maye
bee cauled
an Jlande.
Maragnonue
a ryuer of ex-
cead nge
breadth and
full of Jlands
looke decade
ii. liber.ix.

er therof was very fresshe and sweete : And that the further
ranne, to bee soo muche the fressher : Also full of Ilandes &
somsome fythe. They dare auouche the breadth therof, to bee
more then thirtie leaques. yet if wee well weighe and consy-
er the largenes and wydenes of *Boriostomea* and *Spiriostomea*, the
mouthes of the famous ryuer of *Ister* (nowe cauled *Danubius*) &
nowe farre they violate or corrupte the salte water with their
resshenes, wee shall cease to marueile, althowgh this other ryer bee greater. For, who can diminysshe the poure of nature,
ut that it may make this bigger then the other, and an other
ygger then this. And I suppose this to bee the ryuer wher-
Colonus the Admirall made mention in the discription of his
yage in these coastes. But wee shall hereafter haue further
nowleage herof. Let vs nowe therfore returne to the com-
odities of these Regions. They fownde in many Ilandes a
owte *Paria*, great wooddes of brasile trees : And brought a-
aye with them, three thousande poundes weight therof.
hey say that the brasile of *Hispaniola*, is muche better then
is, to dye clothe with a more fayre and durable colour. Frõ
ense, folowynge the wynde (whiche the Spanyardes caule
orduest, and the Italians *Græco*) they passed by many Ilandes
ery frutefull, yet lefte desolate and wasted by reason of the
ueltie of the Canibales. For they went alande in many pla-
s, and fownde the ruines of many destroyed howses. yet in
m places, they founde men, but those exceadinge fearefull,
ynge to the mountaynes, rockes, and wooddes at the sight
f euery straunger or shippe, and wanderinge without houses
certeyne abydinge places, for feare of the Caniballes lay-
ge wayte and huntinge after them. Here they founde those
reat trees which of thē selues in dyuers places bringe furth
e fruite or spice whiche the Apothecaries caule *Cassia fistula* :
nd that of noo lesse goodnes then that which the phisitians
inister to such as bee diseased with the ague. But it was not
pe at theyr beinge there. They affirme that there are trees of
che byggenes, that xvi. men ioyninge handes togyther and
andinge in coompasse, can scarsely embrase sum of them. E-
onge these trees is fownde that monstrous beaste with a
owte lyke a foxe, a tayle lyke a marmasette, eares lyke a
atte, handes lyke a man, and feete lyke an ape, bearing her
helpes abowte with her in an owtwarde bellye muche lyke

Boriostomea, and Spirio-stomea, mouthes of the ryuer of Danubius,

The commodities of the Regions and Ilandes about paria. Brasile.

Mani fruitful Ilandes lefte desolate.

Canibales.

Trees of Cassia fistula.

Trees of maruelous byggenes. A monstrous beaste.

vnto a greate bagge or purse. The deade carkas of this beaſt
you ſawe with me, and turned it ouer and ouer with your
owne handes, marueylynge at that newe belly and wonder
full prouiſion of nature. They ſay it is knowen by experience
that ſhee neuer letteth her whelpes goo owte of that purse, o
ercept it bee eyther to play, or to ſucke, vntyl ſuche tyme tha
they bee able to gette theyr lyuing by them ſelues. They took
this beaſte with her whelpes: But the whelpes dyed ſhortel
after in the ſhyppes. yet the damme liued certeyne mooneth

Alteracion of ayer τ chãge of meate

But at the length, not beinge able to abyde ſoo greate altera
tion of ayer, and chaunge of meate, ſhee dyed alſo in the way
But of this beaſte, wee haue ſayde enowgh. Let vs now ther
fore returne to the autoures of theſe thynges. Theſe twoo P.
zoni, the vncle and the newe, ſuſteyned manye great trowble
and horrible tempeſtes and perilles in this nauigation. Fo
when they had nowe ſayled by the coaſtes of Paria abowte. b
hundreth leagues, and (as they ſuppoſed) beyonde the cit

Cathay In India beyonde the ryuer of Ganges
A ſhipwrake by tempeſt.

of Cathay and the coaſtes of Eaſte India beyonde the ryuer
Ganges, there roſe ſoodenly ſoo fierce a tempeſte in the mo
neth of July, that, of the foure carauels which they had wit
them, twoo were drowned euen befoze theyr eyes: and th
thyrde lyenge at anker, with lyke ſoodennes caryed owte o
theyr ſyght throwgh the violence of the tempeſte: The four
alſo lyinge at anker, was ſoo ſhaken and brooſed, that al th
ſeame s therof were almoſt looſed. yet came they to lande ow
of this laſte ſhyppe, but vtterlye deſpayrynge of the ſhyppe

Extreme remedie in a deſperat caſe

Wherfore conſultynge with them ſelues what was beſt to be
doone in ſoo extreeme a caſe, and how to prouide them a ſa
dwellinge place in thoſe Regions beinge owt of al hope hou
to departe from thenſe, they determined to ſley all the inhal
tantes of the countrey nere abowte them, leaſte they with th
other ſhulde conſpire togyther to kyl them, but theyr fortun
was better. For the carauell which the tempeſte had caryed
way, was coome to them ageyne. This had in it. xviii. men
And the other that remayned, was ſaued and repayred. Wit
theſe twoo therfore, they tooke theyr vyage directely to Spain
And thus beinge toſſed with tempeſtes and vered with aduer
ſities, they returned to theyr natiue contrey of Palos, to they
wyues and children, the day befoze the Calendes of October
with the loſſe of many of theyr dere frendes and neighbours
The

they browght with them Cinamome and gynger: but not very good, bycause they were not there fully seasoned with the heate of the soone before they brought them frō thense. They browght also, certeyne precious stones, whiche *Baptista Elyssus.* that excellent philosopher and yowre lordeshippes phisitian, affirmeth to bee trewe Topases. After these mens returne, other of theyr neighbours beinge moued thereto by a certeyne emulation, to proue yf theyr fortune wolde bee anye better, lyke men of good corage, beinge nothing discomforted by the harde fortune of theyr neighboures, knowinge that it often tymes chaunceth that that which is one mans vndoinge is another mans makynge, attempted a newe vyage towarde the sowthe by the coastes of *Paria,* folowynge the steppes of *Colonus* the Admiral, who had fyrst discouered the same. They also browght with them greate plentie of *Cassia fistula:* And fownde that precious medecine caulel of the Spanyardes, *Animæ album,* whose perfume is of most excellent effect to heale the reumes, murres, and heauines of the heade. As touchinge this vyage, as yet I knowe noo other newes that I thought worthy to certifie yowe of. Wherfore, I wyl nowe make an ende of this booke, bycause yow put me so often in rememberance of your departure. Yet to accomplysshe the Decade, I wyll declare sumwhae of the superstitions of *Hispaniola.* Yowe shall nowe therfore vnderstand the illusions wherwith the people of the Ilande haue byn seduced after the errours of the owlde gentilitie, and wandered in the ignorance and blyndenes of humane nature corrupted by the disobedience of owr fyrst parentes, which hath remayned in all nations vpon the face of the earth, except where it hath pleased god by the lyght of his spirite by his woorde, to poure vppon his electe the grace of renouation, by the lyght wherof the naturall darkenes receaueth sume clearenes as in a glasse, vntyll imperfection shalbe abolysshed. Owre men therfore, were longe in the Ilande of *Hispaniola,* before they knewe that the people thereof honorede any other thynge thē the lyghtes of heauen, or had any other Religion. But when theye had byne nowe longe conuersante with them, and by vnderstandyng their language, drewe to a farther familiaritie, they had knowleage that they vsed dyuers rytes and superstitions. I haue therfore gathered these fewe thynges folowynge, owte of a booke wrytten by one
Ramos

Cinamome and gynger

Topases.

men of noble corage.

A nother vyage

Animæ album.

The superstitions of Hispaniola.
The errours of the owlde gentilitie.

The grace of renouation.

Ramonus an heremyte, whom *Colonus* had lefte with certeyn
kynges of the Ilande to inſtruct them in the Chriſtian fayth.
And bycauſe in maner their hole religion is none other thin
then Idolatry, I wyll begynne at theyr Idoles. It
therfore apparente by the Images which they honour open
ly and commonly, that there appere vnto them in the nyght
ſeaſons certeyne phantaſies and illuſions of euyll ſpirites
ſeducinge them into many fonde and folyſhe errours. For the
make certeyne Images of goſſampine cotton foulded or wre
thed after theyr maner, and harde ſtopped within. Theſe I
mages they make ſyttinge, much lyke vnto the pictures of ſp
tes and deuylles which owr paynters are accuſtomed to pain
vppon waules. But foraſmuch as I my ſelfe ſent yowe foure
of theſe Images, yowe may better preſently ſignifie vnto th
kynge yowre vncle, what maner of thynges they are, & how
lyke vnto paynted deuelles, then I can expreſſe the ſame b
wrytynge. Theſe Images, th'inhabitantes caule *Zemes* : whe
of the leaſte, made to the lykenes of younge deuls, they bin
to theyr forheades when they goo to the warres ageynſt ther
enemies : And for that purpoſe haue they thoſe ſtrynges han
gynge at them which yowe ſee. Of theſe, they beleue to ob
teyne rayne if rayne be lackyng, and lykewyſe fayre wether
For they thinke that theſe *Zemes* are the mediatours and me
ſengers of the greate god, whom they acknowleage to be on
ly one, eternall, withowte ende, omnipotent and inuiſible.
Thus euery kynge hath his particuler *Zemes* which he honou
reth. They caule the eternall god, by theſe twoo names, *Ioca*
na, and *Guamaſonocon*, as theyr prediceſſours tawght them. Affi
minge that he hath a father cauled by theſe fyue names : tha
is, *Attabeira*, *Mamona*, *Guacarapita*, *Liella*, *Guimazoa*. Nowe ſhall yow
heare what they fable on the earth as touchinge the originall
of man. There is in the Ilande a Region cauled *Caunana*, whe
they fayne that mankynde came fyrſt owte of twoo caues of
mountayne : and that the byggeſt ſorte of men, came furth o
the mouth of the byggeſt caue, and the leaſt ſorte owte of th
leaſte caue. The rocke in the which theſe caues are, they caul
Cauta. The greateſt denne, they name *Cazibaxagua*, and the leſt
Amaiauna. They ſay, that before it was lawful for men to come
foorth of the caue, the mouth of the caue was kepte and wa
ched nyghtly by a man whoſe name was *Machochael*. This *Ma*
chocha

Marginal notes

Ramonus an heremyte.

Idolatry and Idoles.

Illuſions of euyl ſpirites.

Images of goſſampine cotton.

zemies. younge deuyls.

Mediatours.

Only one god eternall. The names of god.

The father of god.

The originall of man kynde

Fables much lyke Ouide his transfor: mations.

bochael, departinge sumwhat farre from the caue to thintente
to fee what thynges were abrode, was foodenly taken of the
foonne (whofe fight he was forbydden) and was turned into
a ftone. They fayne the lyke of dyuers other, that whereas
they went foorthe in the nyghte feafon a fyffhynge, fo farre
from the caue that they coulde not returne befoze the ryfynge
of the foonne (the which it was not lawful foz them to behold)
they were transfozmed into myzobalane trees, which of them
felues growe plentifully in the Ilande. They fay further=
moze, that a certeyne ruler cauled _Vagoniona_, fent one furth of
the caue to goo a fyffhynge, who by lyke chaunce was turned
into a nyghtyngale bycaufe the foonne was ryfen beefoze he
came agayne to the caue: And that yearelye abowte the fame
tyme that he was turned into a byzde, he dothe in the nyght
with a moozinynge fonge bewayle his myffoztune, and caule
foz the helpe of his maifter _Vagoniona_. And this they thynke to
be the caufe why that byzde fingeth in the night feafon. But
Vagoniona, beinge foze troubled in his mynd foz the loffe of his
familier frende whom he loued foo intierly, leauinge the men
in the caue, bzought foozth onely the women with theyz fuc=
kynge chyldzen, leauinge the women in one of the Ilandes of
that tracte, cauled _Mathinino_, and caryed the chyldzen awaye
with hym: which pooze wzetches oppzeffed with famine, fain
ted and remained on the banke of a certeine ryuer where they
were turned into frogges, and cryed _toa, toa,_ that is, _mama, ma=
a_, as chyldzen are wont to crye foz the mothers pappe. And
hereof they fay it commeth that frogges vfe to cry fo pytiful=
ly in the fpzynge tyme of the yeare: And that men were featte=
red abzode in the caues of _Hifpaniola_ withowte the companye
of women. They fay alfo, that whereas _Vagoniona_ hym felfe,
was accuftomed to wander in dyuers places, and yet by a fpe
ciall grace, neuer transfozmed, defcended to a certeyne fayze
woman whom he fawe in the bottome of the fea, and reccaz=
ued of her certeyne pibple ftones of marble (whiche they caule
ibas) and alfo certeine yelowe and bzight plates of laton, whi
che they caule _Guaninos_: Thefe thynges to this day are had in
greate eftimation amonge the kynges, as goodly iewels and
moft holy reliques. Thefe men whiche we fayde befoze were
lefte in the caues withowte women, went furth in the nyght
(as they fay) to waffhe them felues in a ponde of raine water
and fawe

The original of myzoba=lane trees.

The nightin=gale.

The Iland of Mathinino.

Children tur=ned into frog ges.

A speciall grace.

holy reliques

and ſawe a farre of by the way a greate multitude of certein beaſtes in ſhape ſumwhat lyke vnto women, creping as thick as antes aboute the myrobalane trees : And that as they attempted to take theſe beaſtes, they ſlypped owte of their handes as they had byn yeles. Where vppon they conſulted, and determyned bythaduice of the elders, that al ſuche ſhulde be ſowght foorthe amonge them, as were ſcabbyd and leprous to thintente that with theyr rowghe and harde handes, they myght theſelyer take holde of them. Theſe men, they caul *Caracaracoles* : And ſente them foorthe a huntinge to take theſe beaſtes. But of many which they tooke, they coulde keepe bur only foure : The whiche as they wolde haue vſed for women they fownde that they lacked womans priuities. Wherefor caulinge thelders ageyne to counſayle, to conſult what wer beſte to bee done in this caſe, theyr aduice was that the byrd which wee caule the Pye, ſhuld bee admitted with his byll t open a place for that purpoſe, whyle in the meane tyme theſe men cauled *Caracaracoles*, ſhulde hould faſt the womens thighes abrode with theyr rowgh handes. Full wyſely therfore was the pye put to this office, and opened the womens priuities and hereof the women of the Ilande haue theyr original an offſpringe. But nowe doo I ceaſe to maruayle that the owld Grekes dyd fable and wryte ſo manye bookes of the peopl cauled *Myrmidones*, which they fayned to bee engendred of an tes or piſſemeres. Theſe and ſuche lyke, the ſageſt and wyſel of the people, preache continually to the ſimple ſorte, and re hearſe the ſame as moſte holy oracles. But it is yet more chyl dyſſhe that they fable as touchinge thoriginall of the ſea. For they ſaye that there was once in the Ilande, a man of greate power, whoſe name was *Iaia* : whoſe only ſoonne being dead, he buryed hym within a greate gourde. This *Iaia*, greuouſly takyng the death of his ſoonne, after a fewe moonthes, came ageyne to the gourde : The which when he had opened, ther iſſhewed foorth many great whales and other monſters of th ſea : where vppon he declared to ſuche as dwelt abowte hym, that the ſea was encloſed in that gourde. By which report foure brethren (borne of one woman who dyed in her trauail beinge moued, came to the gourde in hope ito haue many fyſ ſhes. The whiche when they had taken in theyr handes, and eſpied *Iaia* comming, (who oftentymes reſorted to the gourd

to

women are ſlippery cat: tayle. Al wiſedome goeth not by age.

here nedeth ſum tropolo: gicall inter: pretour.

Myrmidones

preachers for the deuyl.

A vengeable greate gourd.

The originall of the ſea.

o biset the boones of his soonne, fearing least he shulde sus=
pecte them of thefte and sacrileage, sodaynely let the gourde
aule owte of theyr handes: which beinge broken in the saule
he sea furthwith brake owte at the ryftes therof, and so fyl=
ed the vales, & ouerflowed the playnes, that only the moun=
aynes were vncouered, whiche nowe conteyne the Ilandes The originall of Ilandes.
which are seene in those coastes. And this is the oppinion of
theyr wyse men as concernynge thoriginall of the sea. But
nowe (most noble prince) you shall heare a more pleasaunt fa=
le. There is a certeyne caue cauled Iouanaboina, in the territo
ye of a certeyne kynge whose name is Machinnech. This caue A holy caue.
hey honour more religiously then dyd the Grekes in tyme
aste, Corinth, Cyrrha, or Nysa: And haue adourned it with
ictures of a thousand fasshions. In thenterance of this caue
hey haue twoo grauen Zemes, wherof the one is cauled Bin= Images.
aitel, and the other Marohu. Beinge demaunded why they had
his caue in soo greate reuerence, they answered ernestly, by=
ause the Soonne and the Moone came fyrst owt of the same The originall of the soone and moone. pylgramage.
o gyue lyght to the worlde. They haue religious concourse to
hese caues, as wee are accustomed to goo on Pylgramage to
Rome or Uaticane, Compostele, or Hierusalem, and most ho=
ye and heade places of owre Religion. They are also subiect
o an other kynde of superstition. For they thinke that deade walkynge sprytes.
olkes walke in the nyght, and eate of the fruite cauled Guan=
aba, vnknowen vnto vs, and sumwhat lyke vnto a quynse.
Affirmynge also that they are conuersant with lyuing people, Incubi.
euen in theyr beddes, and to deceaue women in takynge vp=
pon them the shape of men, shewynge them selues as thowgh
they wolde haue to doo with them: But when the matter cō=
meth to actual deede, soodenly to vanysshe away. If any doo A remedye a= geynst wal= kyng spirtes.
suspecte that a deade body lyeth by hym when he feeleth anye
straunge thynge in the bedde, they say hee shalbe owt of dout
by feelynge of the belly therof: affirmyng that the spirites of
deade men may take vppon them al the members of mans bo=
dy, sauinge only the nauell. If therfore by lacke of the na=
uell he doo perceaue that a deade body lyeth by hym, the fee=
lynge is immediatly resolued. They beleue verely, that in the
nyght, and often tymes in theyr iourneys, and especially in
common and hygh wayes, deade men doo meete with the ly=
uynge. Ageynste whome, if any man bee stoute and owte of
M,i, feare

phantasies
proceadynge
of feare.

**Al is notgood
that is owlde**

Syngynge ⁊
playinge

piestes and
diuines.
phisitians.

Jgnorance is
noryshed
with super=
stition.

Fastynge and
outward clen
lynes.

A pouder of
maruelous
effecte.

Juggelynge.

A strange ma
ner of curing

feare, the phantasye banyssheth incontinentely. But yf any
feare, the phantasy or vysion doth soo assaute hym and stryke
hym with further feare, that manye are thereby astonysshe
and haue the lymmes of theyr bodyes taken. Thinhabi
tantes beinge demaunded of whom they had those vayne su
perstitions, they answered that they were lefte them of theyr
forefathers as by discent of inheritance: And that they had
had the same (before the memory of man) composed in certein
rymes and songes, which it was lawful for none to lerne bu
onely the kynges soonnes, who commytted the same to me
morye, bycause they hadde neuer any knoweleage of letters
These they synge beefore the people on certeyne solemne an
festiuall dayes, as moste religious ceremonies: whyle in th
meane tyme they play on a certeyne instrumente made of on
hole peece of woodde sumwhat holowe lyke a tymbrell.The
piestes and diuines (whom they caule Boitios) instructe them
in these superstitions. These piestes, are also phisitians, de
uisinge a thousande craftes and subtylties howe to deceau
the simple people which haue them in greate reuerence. For
they persuade them that the Zemes vse to speake with them
familierlye, and tel them of thynges to come. And if any hau
bin sicke ⁊ are recouered, they make them beleue that they ob
teyned theyr healthe of the Zemes. These Boitii, bynde them
selues to muche fastinge and owtewarde clenlynes and pour
geinges: Especially when they take vppon them the cure of
any Prince. For then they drynke the pouder of a certeyn
herbe, by whose qualitie they are dryuen into a furye: At wh
che tyme (as they say) they lerne many thynges by reuelation
of the Zemes. Then, puttinge secreatly in theyr mouthes, ey
ther a stone, or a bone, or a piece of flesshe, they coomme to th
sicke person, commaundinge al to departe owte of that place
excepte one or twoo, whom it shall please the sicke man to ap
poynt. This doone,they goo about hym thrice or foure tymes
greatly deforminge theyr faces, lyppes, and nosethrils with
sundry fylthy giestures: blowynge, breathinge, and suckyn
the forheade, temples, and necke of the pacient, wherby (they
saye) they drawe the euyll ayer from hym, and sucke the di
sease owt of his veynes. Then rubbinge hym about the shoul
ders, thyghes, and legges, and drawynge downe theyr han
des close by his feete, holdinge them yet faste togyther, they
runn

runne to the doze beinge open, where they vnclose and shake theyz handes, affirminge that they haue dzyuen away the disease, and that the pacient shall shoztely bee perfectly restozed to health. After this, commynge behynde hym, he conueygheth the piece of fleshe owte of his owne mouth like a iuggeler, and sheweth it to the sicke man, sayinge, beholde what you haue eaten to muche: you shall nowe bee hole, bycause I haue taken this from you. But if he intende yet further to deceaue the pacient, he persuadeth hym that his *Zemes* is angry, eyther bycause he hath not buylded hym a chapell, oz not honozed hym religiously, oz not dedicated vnto him a groue oz garden. And if it soo chaunce that the sicke person dye, his kinsfolkes by wytchecrafte enfozce the deade to confesse whether he dyed by naturall destenye, oz by the neglygence of the *Boitius*, in that he had not fasted as he shulde haue doone, oz not mynistred a conuenient medicine foz the disease. Soo that yf this phisitian bee founde fautie, they take reuenge of hym. Of the stones oz bones which these *Boini* carye in theyz mouthes, yf the women can coome by them, they keepe them religiously beleauinge them to bee greatly effectuall to helpe women whiche trauayle with chylde: And therfoze honoure them as they doo theyz *Zemes*. Foz dyuers of thinhabitantes, honour *Zemes* of dyuers fasshions. Sume make them of woodde, as they were admonyshed by certeyne visions apperinge vnto them in the wooddes. Other, whiche haue receaued answere of them amonge the rockes, make thē of stone and marble. Sum they make of rootes to the similitude of suche as appeare to them when they are gathering the rootes cauled *Ages*, wherof they make theyz bzeade, as we haue sayde befoze. These *Zemes*, they beleue to send plentie and frutefulnes of those rootes, as the antiquitie beleued suche fayzies oz spirites as they cauled *Dryades*, *Hamadryades*, *Satyros*, *Panes*, and *Nereides*, to haue the cure and pzouidence of the sea, wooddes, spzynges and fountaynes, assigninge to euery thynge, theyz peculier goddes. Euen soo doo thinhabitantes of this Jlande attribute a *Zemes* to euery thynge, supposinge the same to gyue eare to theyz inuocations. Wherfoze, as often as the kynges aske counsaile of their *Zemes* as concerning their warres, increase of fruites oz scarsnes, oz health and sickenes, they enter into the house dedicate to theyz *Zemes*, where, snuffinge vp into theyz nosethzyls the

M.ii, pouder

Marginal notes

Angery gods

They make the deade to speake.

Diuers Jdols of sundzy shape.

Fayzies oz spirites of the gentyles.

peculier goddes.

They aske cō saile of Jdols

The pouder of the herbe Cohobba.

pouder of the herbe cauled Cohobba (wherwith the Boitii are dryuen into a furye) they say that immediatly they see the houses turne topsy turuye, and men to walke with theyr heeles vpwarde : of suche force is this pouder vtterly to take away all sense. As soone as this maddenes ceaseth, he embraseth his knees with his armes, holdynge downe his heade. And whē he hath remayned thus a whyle astonyshed, he lyfteth vp his heade as one that came newe owt of sleepe : And thus loking vp towarde heauen, Fyrst he fumbeleth certeyne confounded woordes with hym selfe. Then certeyne of the nobilitie or

Secreate misteries.

chiefe gentelmen that are about him (for none of the common people are admytted to these mysteries) with lowde voyces gyue tokens of reioysing that he is returned to them from the speache of the Zemes, demaundynge of hym what he hathe seene. Then hee openinge his mouthe, doateth that the Zemes

Reuelations.

spake to hym durynge the tyme of his traunce : declaring that he had reuelations eyther concerninge victorye or destruction: famyne or plentie : health or syckenes, or what soo euer happeneth fyrst on his toonge. Nowe (moste noble Prince) what

The spirite of Apollo.
The Sibilles

neede you hereafter to marueyle of the spirite of Apollo soo thakynge his Sibylles with extreme furie ? Yowe had thowght that the superstitious antiquitie hadde peryshed. But nowe wheras I haue declared thus much of the Zemes in generall, I thowght it not good to lette passe what is sayde of them in particuler. They saye therefore, that a certeyne kynge cauled

I haue harde the lyke of eyther in Englande.

Guamaretus, had a Zemes whose name was Corochotum : who (they say) was often tymes woonte to descende frome the hyghesse place of the house where Guamaretus kepte hym faste bounde. They affirme, that the cause of this his breakynge of his bandes and departure, was eyther to hyde hym selfe, or to goo

hungery and lecherous gods.

seeke for meate, or els for the acte of generation : And that sumtymes beinge offended, that the kynge Guamaretus had byn negligent and slacke in honouringe hym, he was woonte to lye hyd for certeyne dayes. They say also that in the kynges vyllage there are sumtyme chyldren borne hauing twoo crownes

Childrē with two crownes

which they suppose to bee the children of Corochotum the Zemes. They sayne lykewyse, that Guamaretus beinge ouercome of his enemyes in the battayle, and his vyllage with the palaice consumed with fyer, Corochotus brake his bandes and was afterwarde founde a furlonge of, safe and withowte hurte. He
hath

hath alſo an other Zemes cauled Epileguanita, made of woodde, in ſhape lyke a foure footed beaſte: who alſo is ſayde, often tymes to haue gonne from the place where he is honoured, in to the wooddes. As ſoone as they perceaue him to bee gonne, a great multitude of them gather togyther to ſeeke hym with deuoute prayers: And when they haue fownde hym, brynge hym home religiouſly on theyr ſhulders to the chapell dedica= ted vnto hym. But they coomplayne that ſence the commynge of the Chriſtian men into the Ilande, he fledde for all togy= ther, and coulde neuer ſence bee founde, wherby they diuined the deſtruction of theyr countrey. They honoured an other Ze= mes in the lykenes of a woman, on whom wayted twoo other lyke men, as they were miniſters to her. One of theſe, execu= ted thoffice of a mediatour to the other Zemes which are vnder the power and commaundement of this woman, to rayſe wyn des, cloudes, and rayne. The other is alſo at her commaunde mente a meſſenger to the other Zemes whiche are ioyned with her in gouernaunce, to gather togyther the waters whiche faule from the hygh hylles to the valleys, that beinge looſed, they may with force bruſt owte into greate fluddes and ouer= flowe the countrey if the people doo not gyue due honoure to her Image. There remayneth yet one thynge woorthy to bee noted, wherwith we wyll make an ende of this booke. It is a thynge well knowen, and yet freſſhe in memory amonge the inhabitantes of the Ilande, that there was ſumetyme twoo kynges (of the which one was the father of Guarionexius of whō we made mention before) which were woont to abſteyne fyue dayes togyther continually from meate and drinke, to knowe ſumwhat of theyr Zemes of thynges to coome: And that for this faſtynge beinge acceptable to theyr Zemes, they receaued anſwere of them, that within fewe yeares, there ſhuld coome to the Ilande a nation of men couered with apparell, which ſhulde deſtroye al the cuſtomes and cerymonyes of the Iland. and eyther ſley all theyr chyldren, or brynge them into ſerui= tude. The common ſort of the people, vnderſtoode this oracle to bee mente of the Canibales. And therefore when they had any knowleage of theyr commyng, they euer fledde, and were fully determyned neuer more thaduenture the battayle with them. But when they ſawe that the Spanyardes had entered into the Ilande, conſultinge amonge them ſelues of the mat=

(marginal notes)

wanderinge Images.

Mediatours.

A woman ze= mes of great poure.

Fyue dayes faſtinge.

A maruelous illuſion of the deuyll.

The deuyll ſumtyme tel= leth truth.

The Idols abolyshed.

ter, they concluded that this was the nation which was ment by thoracle. Wherin, theyr opinion deceaued them not. For they are nowe all subiecte to the Christians, all suche beinge slayne as stoobernely resisted. Nor yet remayneth there anye memory of theyr Zemes: for they are al brought into Spayne, that we myght bee certified of theyr illusions of euyl spirites and Idoles, the which yow yowre selfe (most noble Prince) haue seene and felte when I was present with yowe. I let passe many thynges bycause yow put me in remembrance that to morowe yowe take yowre iorney towarde yowre countrey, to brynge home the queene yowre aunte, whom yowe accoompanyed hether at the commaundemente of kynge Frederyke yowre vncle. Wherfore I byd yowe farewel for this tyme, desyrynge yowe to remember yowre Martyr, whome yowe haue compelled in the name of the kynge yowre vncle, to gather these fewe thynges owte of a large feelde of hystoryes.

¶ The tenth and laste booke of the fyrst decade, as a conclusion of the former bookes: Wrytten to Inacus Iopez Mendocius, countie of Tendilla, and viceroye of Granats.

T the fyrst begynnynge and newe attempte, when Colonus had taken vppon hym thenterpryse to search the Ocean sea, I was ernestly moued and requyred by the letters of certeyne of my frendes and noble men of Rome to wryte suche thynges as shoulde happen. For they whyspered with greate admiraci-

The Lawe of nature.

on, that where as there were many newe landes founde, and nations which liued naked and after the lawe of nature, they coulde here noo certentie therof, beinge greately desyrous of the same. In this meane tyme had fortune overthrowne Ascanius

Slayne in the hands of the frenchmē

(hisbrother Lodouike beinge cast owt of Mylayne by the frenchmen) whose autoritie wold not suffer me to bee idle, but euer to haue my pen in hande. To hym I wryte the twoo fyrst bookes of this decade, besyde many other of my hyd commentaries whiche yowe shall see shortely. Fortune dyd noo lesse withdrawe my mynde frome wrytynge, then disturbe Ascanius from power, As he was tossed with contrary stormes and cea-

sed

sed to perſuade me, euen ſoo ſlacked my feruentnes to enquyre
any further, vntyl the yeare of Chriſte. 1500. When the court
remayned at *Granata* where yowe are viceroye : At which time
Lodouike the Cardinall of Aragonie, neuie to kynge Frederike by his brothers ſyde (beinge at *Granata* with the queene
Parthenopea the ſyſter of owre catholike kynge) browght me
kynge Frederikes letters, wherby he exhorted me to fynyſhe
the other bookes whiche folowed the twoo eppiſtell bookes,
which I wryte to *Aſcanius*. For they both acknowleaged that   **Epiſtel bookes**
they hadde the copie of all that I wryte to cardinall *Aſcanius*.
And albeit that euen then I was ſicke (as yowe knowe) yet
tooke I the burden vppon me, and applyed my ſelfe to wrytynge. I haue therfore choſen theſe fewe thynges, owte of a
greate heape of ſuche as ſeemed to me moſt woorthy to bee no
ted amonge the large wrytynges of the autoures and ſearchers of the ſame. Wherfore, foraſmuch as yowe haue endeuoured to wreſte owt of my handes the hole exemple of al my
woorkes, to adde the ſame to the innumerable volumes of
yowre librarie, I thowght it good nowe to make a briefe re-   **The hiſtorye
folowing, con
teyneth the
actes of ten
yeare.**
herſall of thoſe thynges which were done from that yeare of
a thowſande and fyue hundreth, euen vnto this yeare which
is the tenth from that. For I entende to wryte more largelye
of theſe thynges hereafter, if god graunte me lyfe. I hadde
wrytten a hole booke by it ſelfe of the ſuperſtitions of the peo
ple of the Ilande, ſuppoſinge therwith to haue accomplyſhed
the hole Decade conſiſtynge of tenne bookes. But I haue ad
ded this to the tenthe as a perpendiculer lyne, and as it were
a backe guyde or rerewarde to the other : So that yowe may
knytte the fyrſt tenthe, to the nynthe, and impute this to occupie the place of the tenthe to fyll vp the Decade. This order haue I appoynted, leſt I ſhulde bee compelled often times
to wryte ouer the hole woorke, or ſende yowe the ſame defaced with blottes and interlynynge. But nowe let vs coome to
owre purpoſe. The ſhippe maſters and maryners ranne ouer
many coaſtes durynge theſe tenne yeares : But euer folowed
ſuche as were fyrſte fownde by *Colonus*. For raſinge continual   **Paria, part of
the firme lãd
of Eaſt India**
ly alonge by the tracte of *Paria*, which they beleue to bee parte
of the firme lande or continent of eaſte India, ſume of theym
chaunced vppon certeyne newe landes towarde the eaſte, and
ſume towarde the weſte, in which they fownde bothe goulde
                                                              and

Golde & franken-
sence.

and frankensence. For they brought from thense many iewels and ouches of golde, and greate plentie of frankensence.
whiche they had of the people of those countreys, partely for
exchange of sume of owre thynges, and partely by force, ouer
commynge them by warre. Yet in sume places, althowgh they
bee naked, they ouercame owre men, and slewe hole armyes.
For they are exceedinge fierce, and vse venemous arrowes, and
longe staues lyke iauelens, made harde at the ende with fyer
They fownde many beastes, both creepinge and foure footed,
muche differinge from owres, variable and of sundrye shapes,
innumerable: yet not hurtflul, excepte Lyons, Tygers, and
Crocodiles. This I meane in sundry Regions of that great
lande of Paris: but not in the Ilandes: No not soo much as
one. For all the beastes of the Ilandes, are meeke and with
owre hurte, except men which (as wee haue sayde) are in many Ilandes deuourers of mans flesshe. There are also dyuers
kyndes of foules. And in many places battes of such bygnes,
that they are equall with turtle doues. These battes, haue
often tymes assauted men in the nyght in theyr sleepe, and so
bytten them with theyr venemous teethe, that they haue byn
therby almoste dryuen to madnes, in soo much that they haue
byn compelled to flye from such places, as from rauenous har-
pies. In an other place, where certeyne of them slepte in the
nyght season on the sandes by the sea syde, a monster commynge owte of the sea, came vppon one of them secreatly and
caryed hym away by the myddeste owte of the sight of his felowes to whome he cryed in vayne for helpe vntyll the beaste
lepte into the sea with her praye. It was the kynges pleasure
that they shulde remayne in these landes, and buylde townes
and fortresses. Where vnto they were soo wel wyllynge, that
dyuers profered them selues to take vppon them the subduing
of the lande, makyng great sute to the kynge that they might
bee appoynted therto. The coaste of this tracte is exceadynge
greate and large: and the Regions and landes therof extende
maruelous farre: Soo that they affirme the continent of these
Regions with the Ilandes abowte the same, to bee thryse as
bygge as al Europe, besyde those landes that the Portugales
haue fownde southwarde, whiche are also exceadynge large.
Therfore doubtlesse Spayne hathe deserued greate prayse in
these owre dayes, in that it hath made knowen vnto vs soo
many

The fierce-
nes of the na-
ked people.

Innumerable
beastes vn-
lyke vnto
owres.

Nothing hurt
full in the I-
landes.

Battes as
bygge as tur-
tle doues.

A man deuou-
red of a mon-
ster of the sea

The Spany-
ardes profer
them selues
to subdue the
newe landes.

Note the lar-
genes of the
newe landes.

Commendaci-
on of the
Spaniardes

many thowſandes of Antipodes which leye hyd befoze and vn=
knowen to owre fozefathers: And hath thereby mynyſtred ſo
large matter to wzyte of, to ſuche lerned wyttes as are deſy=
rous to ſette furthe knowleage to the commoditie of men : to
whom J opened away when J gathered theſe thynges rudely
to gyther as powe ſee: The which, neuertheleſſe J truſt powe
wyll take in good parte, aſwell foz that J can not adourne
my rudeneſ with better veſture, as alſo that J neuer tooke
penne in hande to wzyte lyke an hiſtoziographer, but only by
epiſtels ſcribeled in haſte, to ſatiſfie theym, from whoſe com=
maundementes J myght not dzawe backe my foote. But now
J haue digreſſed enowghe. Let vs nowe therefoze returne to
Hiſpaniola.   Owre men haue founde by experience, that the
bzeade of the Jland is of ſmaule ſtrength to ſuch as haue byn
vſed to owr bzeade made of wheate: And that theyz ſtrenthes
were much decayed by vſynge of the ſame. Wherfoze the king
hath of late commaunded that wheate ſhulde bee ſowen there
in diuers places and at ſundzy tymes of the yeare. Jt groweth
into holowe reedes, with fewe eares, but thoſe verye bygge
and frutefull. They fynde the lyke ſoftenes oz delicatenes to
bee in herbes, which growe there to the height of cozne. Meat
oz cattall, bzcoome of bygger ſtature and exceadynge fat, but
theyz fleſſhe is moze vnſauery, and theyz bones (as they ſay)
eyther withowte marye, oz the ſame to bee verye waterylſhe.
But of hogges and ſwyne, they affirme the contrarye, that
they are moze holſoome and of better taſte, by reaſon of cer=
teyne wylde frutes whiche they eate, beinge of muche better
noozyſhement then maſte. There is almoſt none other kynd of
fleſſhe commonly ſoulde in the market. The multitude of hog=
ges, are exceedingly encreaſed, , and becoome wylde as ſoone
as they are owte of the ſwyncheardes keepynge. They haue
ſuche plentie of beaſtes and foules, that they ſhall heareafter
haue noo neede, to haue any bzought from other places. Thin=
creaſe of all beaſtes, growe bygger then the bzoode they came
of, by reaſon of the rankenes of the paſture, althowgh theyz
feadynge bee only of graſſe, withowte eyther barley oz other
grayne. But wee haue ſayde enowgh of Hiſpaniola. They haue
nowe fownde that Cuba, (which of longe tyme they thowght
to haue byn firme lande foz the greate length therof) is an J=
lande, yet is it noo maruell that thinhabitantes them ſelues
M.i.   towlde

The autours excuſſe.

Hiſpaniola.

The nature of the place, al=
tereth the foz
mes and qua=
lities of
thynges.
wheate.
herbes.
Catayle,

hogges.

Plentie of
beaſtes and
foule.

Cuba, is an
Jlande.

towlde owre men when they searched the length therof, that
it was withowte ende. For this nacion being naked and contente with a lyttle, and with the limittes of theyr owne contrey, is not greatly curyous to know what theyr neyghbours
doo, or the largenes of theyr dominion. Nor yet knewe they
if there were any other thinge vnder heauen, besyde that whi-

The descrip-
tion of Cuba.

che they walked on with theyr feete. Cuba, is frome the Easte
into the Weste, muche longer then Hispaniola: And in breadthe
from the Northe to the Southe, much lesse then they supposed at the fyrst: for it is very narowe in respecte to the length:
And is for the moste parte, very frutefull and pleasaunt. Eastwarde not farre from Hispaniola, there lyethe an Ilande, lesse

The Iland of
Burichena or
S. Iohannis.
Golde mynes

then Hispaniola more then by the halfe, which owre men cauled
Sancti Iohannis, beinge in maner square. In this they founde excedynge ryche golde mynes. But beinge nowe occupied in the
golde mynes of Hispaniola, they haue not yet sent labourers in
to that Iland. But the plentie and reuenewe of golde of al o-
ther Regions, gyue place to Hispaniola, where they gyue theim

The order of
woorkynge in
the golde
mynes.

selues in maner to none other thynge then to gather golde, of
which woorke this order is appoynted. To euery such wyttie
and skylfull man as is put in truste to bee a suruoier or ouer-
seer of these woorkes, there is assigned one or more kynges
of the Ilande with theyr subiectes. These kynges accordyng

The kynges
brynge theyr
subiectes to
woorke in the
golde mynes.

to theyr league, coome with theyr people at cerreyne tymes of
the yeare, and resorte euery of them to the golde myne to the
which he is assigned: where they haue all maner of dyggynge
or mynynge tooles deliuered them: And euery kynge with his
men, haue a certeyne rewarde alowed them for theyr labour.
For when they departe from the mynes to sowynge of corne,
and other tyllage (wherunto they are addict at certeyne other
tymes, leaste theyr foode shulde fayle them) they receaue for

Tyllage.

theyr laboure, one a ierken, or a dublet, an other a sherte, an
other a cloke or a cappe. For they nowe take pleasure in these
thynges, and goo no more naked as they were wont too doo.
And thus they vse the helpe and laboure of the inhabitantes
both for the tyllage of theyr ground, and in theyr gold mines
as thowghe they were theyr seruauntes or bondemen. They
beare this yoke of seruitude with an euyll wyll: but yet they
beare it. They caule these hyred labourers, Anaborias. yet the
kynge doth not suffer that they shulde bee vsed as bondemen:
And

And onely at His pleasure they are sette at libertie or appoynted to woozke. At suche tyme as they are cauled together of theyr kynges to woozke (as souldiers oz pioners are assembled of theyr centurians) many of them stele away to the mountaynes and wooddes, where they lye lurkynge, beinge content foz that tyme to lyue with wyld frutes, rather then take the paynes to laboure. They are docible and apte to lerne, and haue nowe vtterly fozgotten theyr owlde superstitions. They beleue godly, and beare wel in memozy suche thynges as they haue lerned of owre faith. Theyr kynges childzen are bzought vp with the chiefest of owre men, and are instructed in letters and good maners. When they are growen to mans age, they sende them home to theyr countreys to bee exemple to other, and especially to gouerne the people if theyr fathers bee dead that they maye the better set foozthe the Chzistian Religion, and keepe theyr subiectes in loue and obedience. By reason wherof, they coome nowe by fayre meanes and gentell persuasions to the mynes which lye in twoo Regions of the Ilande aboute thirtie myles distante frome the citie of Dominica: wherof the one is cauled Sancti Christophori: And the other being distante aboute foure scoze and tenne myles, is cauled Cibaua, not farre from the cheefe hauen cauled Portus Regalis. These regions are very large: In the which in many places here and there, are fownd sumtyme euen in the vpper crust of the earth and sumtyme amonge the stones, certeyne rounde pieces oz plates of golde, sumtyme of smaule quantitie, and in sum places of great weyght: In so muche that there hath byn found rounde pieces of thzee hundzeth pounde weyght, and one of thzee thousande, thzee hundzeth and tenne pounde weyght: The whiche (as yowe harde) was sente hole to the kynge in that shyppe in the which the gouernour Boadilla was comming home into Spayne, the shyppe with all the men beinge dzowned by the way, by reason it was ouer laden with the weight of golde and multytude of men. Albeit, there were moo then a thowesande persons whiche sawe and handeled the piece of golde. And wheras here I speake of a pounde, I doo not meane the common pounde, but the summe of the ducate of golde, with the coyne cauled Triens, which is the thyzde parte of a pounde, whiche they caule Pesus. The sum of the weyght hereof, the Spanyardes caule Castellanum Aureum. Al the golde that

N.ii.

Marginal notes:
They abhoure laboure
They are docible.
The kynges chyldren.
The two chiefe golde myres of Hispaniola.
Golde founde in the vpper part of the earth.
A piece of golde weighinge three thousande thzee hundzeth z ten pounds. A coastly ship wzake.
Pesus.

The fynynge and distributi on of golde.

that is dygged in the mountaynes of *Cibaua* and Porte Re gale, is caryed to the towre of Conception, where shoppes with al thynges apperteyninge are redy furnysshed to fyne it melte it, and caste it into wedges. That doone, they take th kynges portion therof, whiche is the fyfte parte, and soo re store to euery man his owne whiche he gotte with his labour But the golde whiche is fownde in saynt Christophers myn and the Region there aboute, is caryed to the shippes which

Three hun dreth thousād weyght of gold molten verely in his paniola.
Controuerses

are in the bylage cauled *Bonauentura*. In these twoo shippes, i molten yerely, aboute three hundreth thousand pounde weigh of golde. If any man bee knowen deceatefully to keepe back any portion of golde, wherof he hathe not made the kynge officers pryuie, he forfiteth the same for a fyne. There chaunc amonge them often tymes many contentions and controuer sies, the whiche onlesse the magistrates of the Ilande doo fy nysshe, the case is remoued by applelation to the hyghe coun sayle of the courte, from whose sentence it is not lawfull t appele in all the dominions of Castyle. But lette vs nowe re

The newe landes.

The Spany ardes noble enterpryses. are not inferi our to the actes of her cules or Sa turnus. &c.

Enlarging of the Christian Religion
The originall of trewe nobi litie.

turne to the newe landes frome whense wee haue digressed They are innumerable, dyuers, and exceadynge fortunat Wherfore the Spanyardes in these owre dayes, and theyr n ble enterpryses, doo not gyue place eyther to the factes of *s. turnus*, or *Hercules*, or any other of the ancient princes of famou memorie which were canonized amonge the goddes cauled H *roes* for theyr searchinge of newe landes and regions, & brin ginge the same to better culture and ciuilitie. Oh God: how large and farre shal owre posteritie see the Christian Religio extended? Howe large a campe haue they nowe to wander in whiche by the trewe nobilitie that is in theym, or mooued b vertue, wyll attempte eyther to deserue lyke prayse among men, or reputacion of well doinge before god. What I con ceaue in my mynde of these thynges, I am not able to expres with penne or tonge. I wyll nowe therfore soo make an end of this perpendiculer conclusion of the hole Decade, as myn dinge hereafter to searche and gather euery thynge particule lye, that I maye at further leasure wryte the same more a large. For *Colonus* the Admiral with foure shyppes, and a hu dreth threescore and tenne men appoynted by the kynge, di couered in the yeare of Christe. 1520. the lande ouer ageynst the weste corner of *Cuba*, distant from the same aboute a hun

dret

dreth and thyrtie leaques: In the myddeſt of which tracte, ly: The Ilande. of Guanaſſa eth an Ilande cauled *Guanaſſa*. From henſe he directed his vy: age backewarde towarde the Eaſte by the ſhore of that coaſt, ſuppoſinge that he ſhulde haue founde the coaſtes of *Paria*: byt it chaunced otherwyſe. It is ſayd alſo that *Vincentius Agnes* (of whom we haue ſpoken before) and one *Iohannes Diaz* The vyage of Iohannes Diaz. (with dyuers other of whoſe vyages I haue as yet no certeyne knowleage) haue ouer runne thoſe coaſtes. But if God graunt me life, I truſt to know the truthe hereof and to aduertiſe yowe of the ſame. Thus fare ye well.

C The ſeconde Decade foloweth.

¶THE FYRST BOOKE OF THE SECONDE Decade, to *Leo* byſſhop of Rome, the tenthe of that name, of the ſuppoſed Con: tinent or firme lande.

 ENSE the tyme that *Galeatius Butrigarius* of Bo: nonie, and *Iohannes Curſius*. of Florence (moſte holye father) came to the catholyke kynge of Spayne, the one, of yowre holynes ambaſage, and thother for thaffaires of his cōmon welth, I was euer for the moſte parte in theyr coom: panie, and for theyr vertues and wyſedoome, had theym in greate reuerence. And wheras they were greatly gyuen to ſtu: dye, and continuall reuoluinge of dyuers autours, they chaun: ced vppon certeyne bookes negligently let ſlyppe owte of my handes, entreatinge of the large landes and Regions hether: weſt Antipo: des. to lyinge hyd, and almoſt weſt *Antipodes*, fownde of late by the Spanyardes. yet beinge allured and delited with the newe: nes and ſtrangenes of the matter althowgh rudely adourned, they commended the ſame: Therwith erneſtly deſyringe me

in theyr owne names, and requyring me in the name of yowr
holynes, to adde here vnto all suche thynges as were fownde
after that tyme, and to gyue them a copie thereof to sende to
yowre holynes, that yowe myght therby vnderstande, both
howe greate commoditie is chaunced to the progenye of man
kynde, as also increase of the militante congregation in these
owre dayes, by the fortunate enterpryses of the kynges of
Spayne. For lyke as rased or vnpaynted tables, are apte to
receaue what formes soo euer are fyrst drawen theron by the
hande of the paynter, euen soo these naked and simple people, doo soone receaue the customes of owre Religion, and by
conuersation with owre men, shake of theyr fierce and natiue
barbarousnes. I haue thowght it good therefore to satisfie
the request of these wyse men, especially vsinge thautoritie of
yowre name, wherunto not to haue obeyed, I shulde esteeme
my selfe to haue commytted a heynous offence. Wherefore I
wyl nowe brefely reherse in order, what hyd coastes the Spanyardes ouerranne, who were the autours therof, where they
rested, what further hope they browght, and fynallye what
great thynges those tractes of landes doo promesse in tyme to
coome. In the declaration of my decade of the Ocean, which
is nowe prynted and dispersed throwghowte Christendome
vnwares to me, I described howe *Christophorus Colonus* fownd
those Ilandes wherof we haue spoken, and that turnyng
from thense towarde the lefte hande southwarde, he chaunced into greate regions of landes, and large seas, distant from
the Equinoctial lyne, onely from fyue degrees to tenne: where
he founde brode ryuers and exceadinge hygh mountaynes couered with snowe and harde by the sea bankes, where were
many commodious and quyet hauens. But *Colonus* being now
departed owte of this lyfe, the kynge beganne to take care
howe those landes myght be inhabited with Christian men to
thincrease of owre fayth: Where vppon he gaue licence by his
letters patentes to al such as wolde take the matter in hand,
and especially to twoo, wherof *Diego Nicuesa* was one, and the
other was *Alphonsus Fogeda*. Wherfore aboute the Ides of December, *Alphonsus* departinge fyrst with three hundreth sould-
ers from the Ilande of *Hispaniola* (in the which wee sayde the
Spanyardes had builded a citie, and planted theyr habitacion) and saylynge in maner full southe, he came to one of the
hauens

The increase
of the Christi-
an congrega-
tion.

Christophorus
Colonus.

Of landes di-
stante from the
Equinoctiall
from fyue de-
grees to ten.
The death of
Colonus.

A generall
lycence.

The nauigati-
on of Alphon-
sus Fogeda.

Iauens founde before whiche Colonus named Portus Carthaginis, bothe bycause of the Ilande standynge ageynste the courſe of he ſtreame, & alſo that by reaſon of the largenes of the place nd bendynge ſydes, it is muche lyke to the hauen of Spaine auled Carthago. Thinhabitantes caule the Ilande Codego, as he Spanyardes caule the Ilande of theyr hauen, Scombria. This Region is cauled of the inhabitantes Caramairi: In the whiche they affirme bothe the men and women to bee of goodly ſtature, but naked. The men haue theyr heare cutte rownde y theyr eares, but the women weare it longe. Bothe the men nd women are very good archers. Owre men fownde certen rees in this prouince, whiche bore greate plentie of ſweete ap les, but hurteful, for they turne into wormes when they ate aten. Eſpecially the ſhadowe of the tree, is contagious, for uche as ſleepe vnder it any tyme, haue theyr headdes ſwolne nd loſe theyr ſight. But if they ſleepe but a whyle, theyr ꝺght commeth ageyne after a fewe dayes. This porte is dy ꞇant foure hundreth fyftie and ſyxe myles from that parte of iſpaniola whiche the Spanyardes caule Beata, in the which alſo hey furnyſſhe them ſelues when they prepare anye vyage to eeke other newe landes. When Fogeda had entered into the auen, he inuaded, ſlewe, and ſpoyled the people, whome he ounde naked and ſcattered. For they were gyuen hym for a raye, by the kynges letters patentes bycauſe they hadde bin efore tyme cruel ageynſt the Chriſtians, and coulde neuer bee lured to permytte them quietly to coome within theyr domi ꞇions. Here they founde gold, but in no greate quantitie, nor ꞇt that pure. They make of it, certeyne breſt plates and broo hes, which they weare for coomelynes. But Fogeda not con ent with theſe ſpoyles, vſinge certeyne captiues whiche he ad taken before, for guydes, entered into a vylage twelue wples diſtante frome the ſea ſyde further into the lande, into he whiche they were fledde whom he fyrſt inuaded. Here he ounde a naked people, but apte to warre. For they were ar ꞇed with targettes, ſhieldes, longe ſwoordes made of wood, nd bowes with arrowes typte with bone, or hardened with ꝑꞇꞇ. As ſoone as they had eſpyed owre men, they with their ſꞇꞇes whom they had receaued, aſſayled them with deſperate ꝛꝑndes, beinge thertto more erneſtly prouoked, beholdinge the alamitie of theſe whiche fledde vnto theym, by the violence
doone

Portus Cartha ginis.

The Region of Caramairi.

people of goodly ſtature

Apples whi che turne in to woormes. A tree whoſe ſhadowe is hurtfull.

Fogeda his autoritie con firmed by the kynges let ters patents.

warlyke people.

doone to theyr women and chyldren, in the spoyle and slaugh

The Spany
ardes haue
the ouer
throwe.

Arrowes in
fected with
poyson.

The nauigati
on of Diego
Nicuesa.

The regions
of vraba and
Leragua.

The Spany
ardes reuenge
the death of
theyr compa
nyons.

A greate
slawghter.

Canibales.

The hunger
of golde.

ter. In this conflicte owre men had the otherthrowe: In the
which, one Iohannes de Lacossa (beinge in autoritie nexte vnto Fo
geda the capitayne, and also the fyrste that gathered golde in
the sandes of Vraba) was slayne with fyftie souldiers. For
these people infecte theyr arrowes with the deadly poyson of
a certeyne herbe. The other with theyr capitayne Fogeda be
inge discoomfited, fledde to the shyppes. Whyle they remayned
thus in the hauen of Carthago sorowfull and pensyue for the
losse of their companions, the other capitayne Diego Nicuesa,
(whom they lefte in Hispaniola, preparyng hym selfe towarde
the vyage in the hauen Beata) came to them with fyue ship
pes and seuen hundrethe foure score and fyftecne menne.
For the greater number of souldyers, folowed Nicuesa,
both bycause free libertie was gyuen them to choose which of
the capptaynes them lyst, and also that by reason of his age,
he was of greater autoritie : But especially bycause the tu
moure was that Beragua beinge by the kynges commission ap
poynted to Nicuesa, was rycher in golde then Vraba assigned to
Alphonsius Fogeda. Therfore, at the arryuall of Nicuesa, they con
sulted what was beste to bee doone: And determyned fyrste to
reuenge the deathe of their felowes. Where vppon, settynge
theyr battayle in arraye, they marched in the nyght towarde
them whiche slewe Cossa with his coompanyons. Thus stea
lynge on them vnwares in the last watche of the nyght, and
encoompasinge the vyllage where they laye, consistynge of a
hundreth howses and more, hauynge also in it thryse as ma
ny of theyr neyghbours as of them selues, they set it on fyer
with diligent watche that none myght escape. And thus in
shorte tyme they browght theym and theyr howses to asshes
and made them pay the raunsome of bludde with bludde. For
of a greate multitude of men and women, they spared one
ly fyxe chyldren, al other being destroyed with fyer or swor
except fewe which escaped pryuily. They lerned by the reser
ued chyldren, that Cossa and his felowes were cutte in piece
and eaten of them that slewe them. By reason wherof, the
suppose that these people of Caramairi tooke theyr originall o
the Caribes otherwyse cauled Canibales. Here they founde sun
golde amonge the asshes. For the hunger of golde, dyd no
lesse encorage owr men to aduenture these perels and labour
the

then dyd the possessynge of the landes. These thynges thus
fynysshed, and the death of *Cossa* and his felowes reuenged,
they returned to the hauen. After this, *Fogeda* whiche came
fyrst, fyrst lykewyse departinge with his army to seeke *Vraba*,
commytted to his gouernaunce, sayled by an Ilande cauled　The Ilande
Fortis, lyinge in the mydwaye betwene *Vraba* and the hauen of　Fortis.
Carthago. In to the which descendinge, he fownde it to bee an
Ilande of the Canybales, bryuginge with hym frome thense
two men and seuen women : for the residue escaped. Here he
fownde in the cotages of them that fledde, a hundrethe foure　wrought gold
score and tenne drammes of golde, caste and wrought in dy=
uers formes. Saylynge forwarde from hense, he came to the
Easte coastes of *Vraba*, whiche thinhabitantes caule *Caribana*,　Caribana.
from whense the Caribes or Canibales of the Ilandes are
sayde to haue theyr name and originall. Here he beganne to
buylde a fortresse, and a vyllage nere vnto the same, therein
intendynge to place theyr fyrst habitacion. Shortly after, be=
inge instructed by certeyne captyues that there was aboute
twelue myles further within the lande, a certeyne vyllage cau
led *Tirufi*, hauinge in it a ryche golde myne, he determyned to　A gold myne.
destroye the vylage. To the which when he came, he fownde
thinhabitantes redye to defende theyr ryght : And that soo　The Spany=
stoutly, that encounterynge with them, he was repulsed with　ardes are re=
shame and domage. For these people also, vse bowes and ve=　pulsed.
nemous arrowes. within a fewe dayes after, beinge enfor=
sed for lacke of vytales to inuade another vyllage, he hym
selfe was stryken in the thyghe with an arrowe. Sume of his　Fogeda is
felowes say, that he was thus wounded of one of thinhaby=　wounded.
tantes whose wyfe he had ledde awaye captiue before. They
say also that he had first frendly comoned with *Fogeda* for re
demynge of his wyfe, & had appoynted a day to brynge a por
tion of golde for her raunsome : And that he came at the daye　Ransome.
assigned, not laden with golde, but armed with bowes and
arrowes, with eyght other confethcrate with hym, whiche
had bin before parretakers of the iniuries doone to them first
at the hauen of *Carthago*, and afterward at the burnyng of the
vyllage. In reuenge wherof they had desperatly consecrated
hem selues to death. But the matter beinge knowen, the cap
ayne of this conspiracie was slayne of *Fogeda* his coompany=
ns, and his wyfe deteyned in captiuitie, *Fogeda* also throwgh
　　　　　　　　　D.i.　　　　　the

Fogeda consumeth by force of the Beragua and Uraba.

Nicuesa.

The goulfe Coiba.

Dyuers languages.

Bergantines or brigātines.

Barnardino de Sibsuera.

Ancisus.

the malicioulnes of the veneme, consumed and was dryed vp by lyttle & lyttle. Whyle these thynges chaunced thus, they elpyed Nicuesa the other capitayne to whom Baragus the region of the weste syde of Vraba, was assigned to inhabite. He gaue wynde to his sayles to take his vyage towarde Beragua, the day after that Fogeda departed owte of the hauen of Carthago. He with his army which he browght with hym, coasted euer alonge by the shore vntyll he came to the goulfe Coiba, whose kynges name is Careta. Here he founde theyr language to bee in maner nothynge lyke vnto that of Hispaniola or of the hauen of Carthago : wherby he perceaued that in this tracte there are many languages differinge from theyr owne borderers. Nicuesa departinge frome Coiba, wente to the prouince or Lieutenauntshippe of Fogeda his companion. Within a fewe dayes after he hym selfe enteringe into one of those marchaunt shippes whiche the Spanyardes caule Carauelas, commaunded that the bygger vessels, shulde folowe farre behynde.   He tooke with hym twoo smaule shyppes commenly cauled bergantines or brygantynes. I haue thowght it good in all the discourse of these bookes, to vse the common names of thinges, bicause I had rather bee playne then curious : especially forasmuch as there doo dayly aryse manye newe thynges vnknowen to the antiquitie, wherof they haue lefte noo trewe names. After the departure of Nicuesa, there came a shippe from Hispaniola to Fogeda, the capitayne wherof, was one Barnardino de Calauera, who had stoulne the same from Hispaniola with thre scoremen, withowte leaue or aduice of the Admirall and the other gouernours. With the vytayles whiche this shippe browght they refresshed theym selues and sumewhat recouered theyr strengthes muche weakened for lacke of meate, Fogeda his companyons whyspered and muttered ageynste hym dayly more and more, that he fedde them furthe with vayne hope. For he had towlde them that he left Ancisus in Hispaniola (whom he chose by the kynges commission to bee a Iudge in causes, bycause he was lerned in the lawe) to coome shortly after him with a shippe laden with vytayles : And that he marueyled that he was not coome many dayes sense. And herein he sayd nothinge but trewth. For when he departed, he lefte Ancisus halfe redy to folowe hym. But his felowes supposinge that all that he sayde of Ancisus had byn fayned, sume of them determined termyned priuilie to steale away the twoo brigantynes frome Fogeda, and to returne to Hispaniola. But Fogeda hauing knowleage hereof, preuented theyr diuise. For leauynge the custodie of the fortresse with a certeyne noble gentelman cauled Francisco Pizarro, he hym selfe thus wounded, with a fewe other in his companie, entered into the shyppe wherof we spake before, and sayled directly to Hispaniola, both to heale the wound of his thygh if any remedy myght bee found, & also to knowe what was the cause of Ancisus taryinge: Leauing hope with his felowes (which were nowe browght from three hundreth to three scroe, partly by famyne and partly by warre) that he wolde returne within the space of. xv. dayes: prescribyng also a condition to Pizarro and his companions, that it shulde not bee imputed to them for treason to departe from thense if he came not ageyne at the day appoynted with vytayles and a newe supply of men. These. xv. dayes beinge nowe paste, whereas they coulde yet heare nothynge of Fogeda, and were dayly more and more oppressed with sharpe hunger, they entered into the twoo brigantynes which were lefte, and departed from that land. And as they were nowe saylynge on the mayne sea towarde Hispaniola, a tempeste soodeynly arysynge, swalowed one of the brygantynes with all that were therein. Sum of theyr felowes affirme that they playnely sawe a fyshe of houge greatenes swymmyng abowte the brygantyne (for those seas brynge furthe greate monsters) and that with a stroke of her tayle, shee broke the rudder of the shyppe in peeces: which saylynge, the brigantine beinge dryuen abowt by force of the tempest, was drowned not farre from the Ilande cauled Fortis, lyinge betwene the coastes of the hauen Carthago and Vraba. As they of the other brygantyne wolde haue landed in the Ilande, they were dryuen backe with the bowes and arrowes of the fierce barbarians. Proceadynge therfore on theyr vyage, they mette by chaunce with Ancisus betweene the hauen of Carthago, and the Region of Cuchibacoa in the mouthe of the ryuer whiche the Spanyardes cauled Boiú gatti, that is, the house of the catte, bycause they sawe a catte first in that place: and Boium, in the toonge of Hispaniola, is a house. Ancisus came with a shyppe laden with all thynges necessarye, bothe for meate and drynke, and apparell, bryngynge also with hym an other brigantine. This is he for whose comming

D.ii.　　the

Marginal notes:

Fogeda returneth to Hispaniola.

Famyne

A brigantine drowned with the stroke of a fyshe.

The Ilande Fortis.

Ancisus. The Region of Cuchibacoa. Boiú gatti.

the capitayne Fogeda looked for soo longe.   He loosed anker from Hispaniola in the Ides of September: And the fourth day after his departure, he espyed certeyne hyghe mountaynes, the whiche for the abundaunce of snowe which lyeth continually in the toppes therof, the Spanyardes cauled Serra Neuata, when Colonus the fyrst fynder of those Regions passed by the same. The fyfte daye, he sayled by Os Draconis. They whiche were in the brygantyne, towlde Ancisus that Fogeda was returned to Hispaniola. But Ancisus supposing that they had fayned that tale, commaunded them by thautoritie of his commission to turne backe ageyne. The brigantiners obeyed and folowed hym: yet made they humble sute vnto hym that he woolde graunte them that with his fauour they myght eyther goo ageyne to Hispaniola, or that he hym selfe woolde brynge theim to Nicuesa: And that they woolde for his genteines declared towarde them in this behalfe, rewarde hym with twoo thousande drammes of golde. For they were ryche in golde, but poore in breade. But Ancisus assented to neyther of theyr requestes: affirmynge that they myght by no meanes goo anye other way then to Vraba the prouince assigned to Fogeda. Whereuppon, by theyr conduct, he tooke his vyage directly toward Vraba. But nowe let it not seme tedious to yowre holynes to heare of one thyng worthy to bee remembred, whiche chaunced to this Lieuetenaunt Ancisus as he came thether. For he also cast anker in the coastes of the region of Caramairi whiche were sayde to bee famous by reason of the hauen of Carthago: and of the goodly stature, strength, and beawty of both men and women beinge in the same. Here he sent certeyne to goo alande on the shore, both to fetche fresshe water, and also to repaire the shippe boate which was sore broosed. In this meane tyme A greate multitude of the people of the countrey armed after theyr maner, came aboute owre men as they were occupied a bowte theyr busynes, and stoode in a redynes to feight, for the space of three dayes contynually: durynge whiche tyme, neyther durst they set vppon owre men, nor owre men assayle them. Thus bothe parties keepynge theyr arraye, stoode styl three hole dayes the one gasynge on the other.   Yet all this tyme owre men applyed theyr woorke, placinge the shippewrightes in the myddeste of theyr armye. As they stoode thus amased, twoo of owre coompanye wente to fyll theyr water pottes

(marginal notes, left column)

Mountaynes couered with snowe.

Serra Neuata.

Os Draconis.

Riche in gold and poore in breade.

The Region of Caramairi

Feare on both partes.

Ship wryghtes.

pottes at the mouthe of the ryuer nere vnto them both, where soodenly there came furthe ageynste them a capitayne of the barbarians with ten armed men which inclosed them, & with terrible countenaunce bent theyr arrowes ageynste them, but shotte theym not of. One of owre men fledde: but the other remayned, caulynge his felowe ageyne and rebukynge hym for his fearefulnes. Then he spake to the barbarians in their owne language which he had lerned beinge conuersant with the captiues that were caryed from thense longe before. They marueylynge to here a straunger speake in their natiue tonge, put of theyr fiercenes and fell to frendly communication, demaundinge who were the capitaynes of that coompanie whiche were arryued in theyr lande. He answered that they were strangers passyng by: And that he marueyled why they wold attempte to dryue them from theyr coastes and disturbe theyr shyppes: arguinge them of follye and crueltie, and further threatinge their ruine and destruction, except they woold vse them selues more frendely towarde them. For hee aduertised them that there wolde shortly coome into theyr lande armed men, in nomber lyke to the sandes of the sea: And that to theyr ter destruction, not only if they resysted them not, but also except they receaued them and enterteyned them honorably. In the meane tyme *Ancisus* was enformed that his men were deteyned. Wherefore suspectinge sume deceate, he browght forth al his target men for feare of theyr venemous arrowes: And settinge them in battell arraye, he marched forwarde towarde them which steyed his men. But he which communed with the barbarians, gyuinge him a signe with his hande to procede noo further, he steyed. And cauling to hym the other, he knewe that all was safe. For the barbarians profered him peace, bycause they were not they whom they suspected them to haue byn: meanynge by *Fogeda* and *Nicuesa*, who had spoyled the vyllage standinge there by the sea syde, and caryed away many captiues, and also burnte an other vyllage further within the lande. And therefore (as they sayde) the cause of theyr comminge thether, was to reuenge those iniuries, if by any meanes they coulde. Yet that they woolde not exercyse theyr weapons ageynste the innocente. For they sayde it was vngodly to fyght ageynst any, not beinge prouoked. Layinge a parte therefore theyr bowes and arrowes, they enter-

The vse of targettes agenst venemous arrowes.

The barbarians haue respect to iustice

entertepned owre men gentelly, and gaue them greate plentie of salted fyshe and breade of theyr contrey: And fylled theyr vessels with syder made of theyr contrey frutes and seedes, not inferiour to wyne in goodnes. Thus *Ancisus* hauinge entered into frendshyp and made a league of peace with thinhabitantes of *Caramairi* whiche were before sore prouoked by other capitaynes, he lanched from that lande, and directed his course to *Vraba* by the Jlande *Fortis*, hauinge in his shippe a hundreth and fyftie fresshe men whiche were substitute in the place of suche as were deade. Also twelue mares, and manye swine, and other beastes both males and females for increase. Lykewyse, fyftie pieces of ordinaunce, with a greate multytude of targettes, swoordes, iauelyns, and suche other weapons for the warres. But all this with euyl speede and in an euyll houre. For as they were euen nowe enteringe into the hauen, the gouernour of the shippe which satte at the helme, stroke the shyppe vppon the sandes, where it was soo fast enclosed, and beaten with the waues of the sea, that it opened in the myddeste, and al lost that was therin. A thynge surely miserable to beholde. For of all the vytaples that they had, they saued onely twelue barels of meale, with a fewe chieses, and a lyttle byskket breade. For al the beastes were drowned: And they them selues scaped hardly and halfe naked by helpe of the brigantine *&*ship boate, caryeng with them only a fewe weapons. Thus they fell from one calamitie into an other, beinge nowe more carefull for theyr lyues then for golde. yet beinge browght alyue and in health to that land which they soo greatly desyred, they coulde doo noo lesse then to prouide for the susteynynge of theyr bodyes, bycause they coulde not lyue onely by ayer. And wheras theyr owne fayled, they must needes lyue by other mens. yet amonge these soo many aduersities, one good chaunce offered it selfe vnto them. For they founde, not farre from the sea syde, a groue of date trees, amonge the which, *&* also amonge the reke or weedes of the maryshes, they espyed a multitude of wylde bores, with whose flesshe they fed the selues wel certeine dayes. These they say to bee lesse then owres: And with soo shorte tayles, that they thought they had byn cutte of. They dyffer also from owres in theyr feete: for theyr hynder feete are hole vndiuided, and also withowte any howfe. But they affirme that they haue
proued

Salted fisshe.

wyne of fruites and seedes.

Vraba.

Artillerie.

Ancisus ship wracke.

Meale, cheeses, & byskket.

A groue of date trees.

Wylde bores.

proued by experience theyr fleſſhe to bee of better taſte & moze holſoome then owres. Durynge this tyme, they fedde alſo of dates and the rotes of younge date trees, which they eate like wyſe in Ciuile and *Granata* where they caule them *Palmitos*, of the leaues wherof they make bieſomes in Rome. Sumetymes alſo, they eate of the appels of that Region, whiche haue the taſte of pzunes, and haue alſo ſtones in them, and are but lyt-tle and of redde coloure. J ſuppoſe them to bee of that kynde wherof J eate in the citie of *Alexandria* in Egypt in the moneth of Apzell : The trees wherof, the Jewes that dwel there, be-inge lerned in the lawe of Moyſes, affirme to bee the Ceders of Libane, which beare owlde fruites and newe all the yeare as dothe the ozange tree. Theſe apples are good to bee eaten, and haue a certeyne ſweetnes myrte with a gentell ſharpnes, as haue the frutes cauled *Sorbes*. Thinhabitantes plant theſe trees in theyr ozchyardes and garedens, and noozyſhe theym with greate diligence as wee doo cheries, peaches, and quyn-ces. This tree in leaues, heyght, and trunke, is verye lyke vnto the tree that beareth the frute cauled *Zizipha*, which the Apothecaries caule *Iuiuba*. But wheras now the wylde bozes beganne to faile them, they were ageyne enfozced to conſulte and pzoupde foz the tyme to coome. Where vppon with theyr hole army, they entered further into the land. The Canibales of this pzouince, are moſte experte archers. *Ancifus* had in his coompany, a hundzeth men. They mette by the way with only thzee men of thinhabitantes, naked, and armed with bowes and benemous arrowes, who without al feare, aſſayled owr men fiercely, wounded manye, and ſlewe manye : And when they had emptied theyr quyuers, fledde as ſwyftely as the wynde : foz (as we haue ſayde) they are excedynge ſwyfte of foote by reaſon of theyr looſe goinge frome theyr chyldes age They affirme that they lette ſlyppe no arrowe owte of theyr bowes in vayne. Owre men therfoze returned the ſame waye that they came, much moze infoztunate then they were befoze and conſulted amonge them ſelues to leaue that laude : eſpe-cyally becauſe thinhabitantes had ouerthzowne the foztreſſe which *Fogeda* buylded, and had burnte thirtie houſes of the vyllage, as ſoone as *Pizarrus* and his company lefte of *Fogeda*, had fozſaken the lande. By this occaſion therfoze, beinge dzyuen to ſeeke further, they had intelligence that the weſte

ſyde

Apples of a ſtrange kynd

Ceders of Libane.

Sorbes are cauled in french Cozmi-er they grow not in Eng-lande.

The frute cauled zizi-pha oz Juuba Canibales.

Men of deſ-perat bold-nes.

The seconde decade.

The goulfe of Vraba.

fyde of that goulfe of *Vraba*, was more frutefull and better to inhabite. Wherfore, they sent the one halfe of theyr men thither with the brigantine, and lefte the other nere to the sea syde on the easte part. This goulfe, is .xxiiii. myles in bredth: And howe muche the further it entereth into the firme lande, it is soo muche the narower. Into the goulfe of *Vraba*, there

The great ryuer of Darié, faulleth into the goulfe of Vraba.

faule many ryuers : but one (as they say) more fortunate then the ryuer of *Nilus* in Egypte. This ryuer is caulled *Darien*, vppon the bankes whereof, beinge verye frutefull of trees and grasse, they entended to playnte their newe colonie or habitacion. But thinhabitantes maruelynge at the brigantine beinge bygger then theyr canoas, and specially at the sayles therof, fyrst sente away theyr chyldren and weakesse sorte of theyr people with theyr baggage and housholde stuffe, and assembled all suche togyther bothe men and women, as were meete for the warres: Thus beinge armed with weapons and desperate myndes, they stoode in a redynes to feight, and taryed the comminge of owre men vppon a lyttle hyl, as it were to take thaduantage of the grounde. Owre men iudged them to bee aboute fyue hundreth in number. Then *Ancisus* the capitayne of owre men, and Lieutenaunt in the steede of *Fogeda*, settinge his men in order of battayle array, and with his hole

prayer and vowes.

coompany kneelinge on his knees, they al made humble prayers to god for the victorie, and a vowe to the Image of the blessed virgin whiche is honoured in Ciuile, by the name of *Sancta Maria Antiqua*, promysinge to sende her manye golden gyftes and a straunger of that contrey : also to name the vyllage *Sancta Maria Antiqua* after her name : lykewyse to erecte a temple caulled by the same name : or at the leaste to dedicate the king of that prouince his palaice to that vse, if it shulde please her to assiste them in this daungerous enterpryse. This doone, al

The souldiers make an othe.

the souldiers tooke an othe, that noo man shulde turne his backe to his enemies. Then the capptayne commaundinge them to bee in a redines with theyr targets and iauelens, and the trumpyter to blowe the battayle, they fiercely assayled

The barbarians are dryuen to flight.

theyr enemyes with a larome. But the naked barbarians, not longe able to abyde the force of owre men, were putte to flyght, with theyr kynge and capitayne *Cemaccus*. Owre men entered into the vyllage, where they fownde plentie of meate suche as the people of the contrey vse, sufficiente to assuage they theyr prefent hunger, as bꝛeade made of rootes, with certeine fruites vnlyke vnto oures, whiche they referue foꝛ ſtoꝛe as wee doo cheſnuttes. Of theſe people, the men are vtterly naked: but the women from the nauell downewarde, are couerd with a fyne clothe made of goſſampine cotton. This Region is vtterly withowte any ſharpenes of wynter. Foꝛ the mouthe of this ryuer of *Darien*, is onlye eyght degrees diſtante from the *Equinoctiall* lyne: So that the commone ſoꝛte of owre men, ſcarſely perceaue anye difference in lengthe betwene the day and nyght all the hole yeare. But bycauſe they are ignorant in aſtronomie, they can perceaue noo ſmaule difference. Therfoꝛe wee neede not much paſſe if the degree do differ ſumwhat from theyr opinion, foꝛ aſmuche as the difference can not bee greate. The day after that they arryued at the lande, they ſayled alonge by the ryuer, where they founde a greate thicket of reedes continuinge foꝛ the ſpace of a myle in length ſuppoſing (as it chaunced in deede) that the boꝛtherers there aboute which had ſledde, had eyther lyne lurkynge there, oꝛ els to haue hyd theyr ſtuffe amonge thoſe reedes: Where vppon, armynge them ſelues with theyr targettes, foꝛ feare of the people lyinge in ambuſhe, they ſearched the thicket dilygently, and founde it withowte men, but replenyſhed with houſeholde ſtuffe and golde. They fownde alſo a great multitude of ſheetes, made of the ſylke oꝛ cotton of the goſſampine tree. Lykewyſe dyuers kyndes of veſſels and tooles made of woodde, and many of earth: Alſo many bꝛeſt plates of gold and ouches wꝛought after theyr maner, to the ſum of a hundꝛeth and twoo pounde weight. Foꝛ they alſo take pleaſure in the bewtie of gold, and woꝛke it very artificially, although it bee not the pꝛice of thynges amonge them as with vs. They haue it owte of other Regions foꝛ exchannge of ſuch thynges as theyr contrey bꝛingeth furthe. Foꝛ ſuche Regions as haue plentie of bꝛeade and goſſampine, lacke golde: And ſuche as bꝛynge furth golde, are foꝛ the moſt parte rowght with montaynes and reckes, and therfoꝛe baren. And thus they exerciſe marchandies withowte the vſe of money. Reiopſing therfoꝛe with double gladdenes, aſwell in that they ſawe greate lꝛkenes of golde, as alſo that foꝛtune hadde offered them ſoo ſayꝛe and frutefull a contrey, they ſent foꝛ theyr felowes whō they hadde lefte befoꝛe in the caſte ſyde of the goulfe of *Vraba.*

P.i.   Ytt

Cheſnuttes.

The ryuer of Darien, but vIII. degrees from the Equinoctial.

Golde founde in a thicket of reedes.

Sheetes of goſſampine.

Breſte plates of golde.

The golden Regions are foꝛ the moſte parte baren.

yet fume faye that the ayer is there vnholſome, bycauſe that parte of the Region lyethe in a lowe valley enuironed with mountaynes and maryſſhes.

¶ The ſeconde booke of the ſeconde decade, of the ſuppoſed continente.

Fogeda, the Lieuetenaunt of Vraba. Nicueſa the Lieutenaunt of Beragua.

I Haue deſcribed to yowre holynes where Fogeda with his coompany (to whome the large tractes of Vraba was aſſigned to inhabite) intended to faſten there foote. Lette vs nowe therfore leaue them of Vraba for a whyle, and returne ageyne to Nicueſa to whom the gouernaunce and Lieutenauntſhippe of the moſte large prouince of Beragua (beinge the weſte ſyde of the goulfe of Vraba) was appoynted. We haue declared howe Nicueſa departinge with one carauell and twoo brigantines frome Vraba the iuriſdiction of his frende and companyon Fogeda, directed his courſe weſtwarde to Beragua, leauinge the bygger ſhippes

Nicueſa loſte his felowes in the night.

ſumewhat behynde hym, to folowe hym a farre of. But he tooke this diuiſe in an euyll howre. For he bothe loſte his felowes in the nyght, and went paſt the mouth of the ryuer of

Lupus Olanus

Beragua, which he chiefely ſowght. One Lupus Olanus a Cantabrian, and gouernoure of one of the greate ſhippes, had the conducte of one of the brigantines. He commynge behynde, lerned of thinhabitantes which was the waye Eaſtewarde to the goulfe of Beragua ouer paſſed and lefte behynde of Nicueſa. Olanus therfore directinge his courſe towarde the Eaſte, mette with the other brigantine which had alſo wandered owte of

Petrus de vmbria

the way by reaſon of the darkenes of the nyght. The gouernour of this brigantine, was one Petrus de Vmbria. Thus bothe beinge gladde of theyr meetinge, they conſulted what was beſt to bee doone, and which way they coulde coniecture their

The capitay-nes conſulte where to find theyr loſt gouernour.

gouernour had taken his vyage. After deliberation, they iudged that Nicueſa could no more lacke ſum to put him in remembraunce of Beragua, then they them ſelues were myndful therof, hoppynge alſo to fynde hym there. They ſayled therfore towarde Beragua: where they founde within .xvi. myles dyſtant, a ryuer which Colonus named Lagartos, bycauſe it noryſhethe greate lyſardes whiche in the Spanyſſhe toonge are

cauled

cauled Lagartos. These lysertes are hurtfull bothe to man and beaste, and in shape muche lyke vnto the Crocodiles of the ryuer of Nilus in Egypte. In this ryuer, they founde theyr companyons and felowes of theyr erroure lyinge at anker with the greate shippes which folowed behynde by the gouernours commaundement. Here the hole assemble beinge carefull and disquieted by reason of the gouernours erroure, after consultacion, by thaduise of the capitaynes of the brigantines, who had rased nere vnto the coastes of Beragua, they sayled directly thether. Beragua, in the language of thinhabitantes of the same prouince, is as much to saye, as the golden ryuer. The region it selfe is also cauled by the same name, takynge name of the ryuer. In the mouth of this ryuer, the greatest vessels cast anker, and conueighed al theyr vytailes and other necessaries to lande with theyr shippe boates: and elected Lupus Olanus to bee theyr gouernour in the steede of Nicuesa whom they had losse. By thaduice therfore of Olanus and the other vnder capitaynes, that all hope of departure myght bee taken from the souldiers which they had nowe browght thether, and to make them the more wyllinge to inhabite that land, they vtterly forsooke and caste of those shyppes beinge nowe rotten for age, and suffered them to bee shaken and broosed of the surges of the sea. Yet of theyr soundest plankes, with other newe, made of the trees of that Region (which they say to be exceedinge bygge and hygh) they framed a newe carauel shortly after, whiche they myght vse to serue for theyr necessitie. But Beragua was founde by the vnfortunate destenie of Petrus de Vmbria. For he, beinge a man of prompt wytte and apt for wardenes to attempte thynges (in whiche sumetyme fortune wyll beare a stroke notwithstandinge owre prouidence) tooke vpon hym thaduenture to searche the shore to thintent to find a waye for his felowes where they myght beste coome alande. For this purpose, he chose hym twelue maryners, and wente aboorde the shippe boate whiche serued the greatest shyppes. The dowinge of the sea, raged and rored there, with a horrible whurlinge as wee reede of the daungerous place of Scylla in the sea of Sicilie, by reason of the houge and ragged rockes reachyng into the sea, from which the waues rebounding with violence, make a greate noyse and rowghnes on the wa..., whiche rowghnes or redowinge, the Spanyardes cauled

P.ii. Resacca

The ryuer Lagartos.

The golden ryuer of Beragua.

The enterprise & death of Petrus de Vmbria.

The daungerous place of Scilla in the sea of Cicilie.

Refucos. In these daungers wretched Vmbria wrestled a while. But in shorte space, a waue of the sea almost as bygge as a mountayne, reboundinge from the rockes, ouerwhelmed the boate and deuoured the same with the men, euen in the sight of theyr felowes: So that of them all, onely one escaped by

Swymminge

reason he was experte in swymmynge. For gettinge holde of the corner of a rocke, and susteynynge the rage of the sea vntyll the nexte daye when it wexed caulme, and the shore was drye by the faule of the water, he escaped and resorted to his coompanye. But Vmbria with the other eleuen, were vtterlye caste away. The resydue of the coompany, durst not committe them selues to the shippe boates, but went alande with theyr brigantines. Where remaynynge a fewe dayes, and saylinge alonge by the ryuer, they founde certeyne vyllages of thinhabitantes, which they caule Mumu. Here they beganne to build a fortresse, and to sowe seedes after the maner of theyr countrey, in a certeyne vale of frutefull grownde, bicause in other places the region is baren. As these thynges were thus dooinge in Beragua, one of their coompanye standynge vppon the toppe of a hyghe rocke of especiall, and lyftynge his eyes towarde the Weste, beganne to crye, Lynnyn sayles, lynnyn sayles. And the nerer it drewe towarde hym, he perceaued it to

The fysher boate of Nicuesa his caruele.

bee a shyppe boate comminge with a lyttle sayle. yet receaued they it with muche reioysinge: for it was the fysher boate of Nicuesa his caruele, and of capacitie to carye onely fyue men, and had nowe but three in it, which had stoulne it from Nicuesa bycause he refused to gyue credit to theim that he had passed Beragua, and lefte it behynde hym Eastwarde. For they seinge Nicuesa and his felowes to consume dayely by famynne, thought they woolde proue fortune with that boate, if their chaunce myght bee to fynde Beragua, as in deede it was. Debatinge therefore with theyr felowes, of these matters, they

The miserable case of Nicuesa.

declared howe Nicuesa erred and loste the caruele by tempest, and that he was nowe wanderinge amonge the maryshes of vnknowen coastes, full of myserie and in extreeme penurie of all thynges, hauinge nowe lyued for the space of three score and tenne dayes, only with herbes and rootes, and syldoome with frutes of the countrey, contented to drinke water, and yet that often tymes faylynge, bycause he was instant to trauayle westwarde by foote, supposing by that meanes to come

io

to Beragua. Colonus the fyrste fynder of this mayne lande, had coasted alonge by this tracte, and named it Gratia Dei : but the inhabitantes caule it Cerabaro. Throwghe this Region, there runneth a ryuer which owre men named Sancti Matthei, distante from the weste syde of Beragua aboute a hundreth and thirtie myles. Here I lette passe the name of this ryuer, and of manye other places by the names which thinhabitantes vse, bycause owre men are ignorant thereof. Thus Lupus Olanus the conductor of one of the shippes of Nicuesa, and nowe also vice Leautenaunt in his steede, after that he hadde receaued this information of the maryners, sente thether a brigantine vnder theyr guydynge, these maryners therfore, which came in the fyrster boate, founde Nicuesa, and browght hym to the place where Olanus laye, whome at his commynge he caste in pryson, and accused hym of treason bycause he vsurped thautoritie of the Lieutenauntshippe, and that for the despyte he had to beare rule and bee in autoritie, he tooke no care of his errours : also that he behaued hym selfe negligently : demaundinge further more of hym, what was the cause of his soo longe delay. Lykewyse he spake to al the vnder officers sharply and with a troubled mynde : And withyn fewe dayes after commaunded them to trusse vp theyr packes, and make them redye to departe. They desyred hym to quyet hym selfe, and to forbeare them a while vntyl they had reaped the corne that they had sowne, which wolde shortly bee rype. For all kynd of corne wareth rype there euery fourth moonethe after it is sowne. But he vtterly denyed to tarye any whytte : but that he woolde foorthwith departe from that vnfortunate lande : And plucked vp by the rootes al that euer was browght into the goulfe of Beragua, and commaunded them to directe theyr course towarde the Easte. After they had sayled aboute the space of .xvi. myles, a certeyne younge man whose name was Gregorie, a Genues borne, and of a chylde browght vp with Colonus, caused to rememberance that there was a hauen not farre frome thense : And to proue his sayinge trewe, he gaue his felowes these tokens : that is, that they shulde fynde vppon the shore, an anker of a loste shyppe halfe couered with sande : And vnder a tree nexte vnto the hauen, a sprynge of cleere water. They came to the lande : founde the anker and the sprynge, and commended the wytte and memorye of the

The Region of Gratia Dei: Cerabaro.
The ryuer of Sancti Matthei.

The rigorousnes of Nicuesa.

Corne wareth rype euery fourth month

The commendation of a younge man browght vp with Colonus

younge man, that he only amonge many of the marynes whiche had searched those coastes with Colonus, bore the thynge
soo well in mynde. This hauen, Colonus cauled Portus Bellus.
Wheras in this vyage for lacke of vytayles they were sumetymes enforced to goo alande, they were cruel entreated of the
inhabitantes. By reason wherof, theyr strengthes were soo
wekened with hunger, that they were not able to keepe warre
agaynst naked men, or scarsely to beare theyr harnes on their
backes. And therfore owre men loste twentie of theyr coompanie, which were slayne with venemous arrowes. They consulted to leaue the one halfe of theyr felowes in the hauen of
Portus Bellus: And the other parte Nicuesa tooke with hym towarde the Easte: where abowte twentie and eyght myles fro
Portus Bellus, he intended to buylde a fortresse harde by the sea
syde vppon the poynte or cape which in tyme paste Colonus named Marmor. But they were soo feeble by reason of longe hunger, that theyr strength serued them not to susteyne suche laboure. Yet he erected a lyttle towre able to resyst the fyrst assaute of the inhabitantes. This towre he cauled Nomen Dei.
From the tyme that he left Beragua, what in the iorney amonge
the sandie playnes, then also for hunger whyle he buylded
the towre, of the fewe which remayned a lyue, he loste twoo
hundreth. And thus by lyttle and lyttle, the multitude of seuen hundreth foure score and fyue men, was nowe browght
to scarsely one hundreth. Whyle Nicuesa lyued with these few
miserable men, there arose a contention amonge them of Vraba,
as concerninge the Lieutenantshippe. For one Vaschus Nunnez,
by the iudgemente of all men, trustynge more to his strengthe
then wytte, stoured vp certeyne lyght felowes agaynst Ancisus,
sayinge that Ancisus had not the kynges letters patentes for
that office: And that it was not sufficient that he was autorised by Fogeda, And therfore forbodde that he shulde execute
the office of the Lieutenauntershippe: And wylled theym to
chuse certeyne of theyr owne coompanye, by whose counsayle and authoritie they myght bee gouerned.
Thus beinge diuided into factions by reason that Fogeda, their
capitayne came not agayne, whom they supposed to bee nowe
deade of his venemous wounde, they contended whether it
were beste to substitute Nicuesa in his place. The wyseste sorte
suche as were famylier with Nicuesa, and coulde not beare thin-
solence

Marginal notes:

Portus Bellus.

weakenes of hunger.

Cap, Marmor.

Nomen Dei.

Nicuesa his men consumed

Contencion a bout the lieu-tenauntship of Uraba.

Uaschus Nun-nez moueth sedition.

Ancisus lieu-tenaunt for Fogeda.

folencie of *Vafchus Nunnez*, thowght it good that Nicuefa ſhuld bee, Nicueſa.
ſowght owt throwgh owr all thoſe coaſtes. Foz they had
knowledge that he departed from Beragua bycauſe of the ba=
rennes of the grounde: And that by therexample of Ancifus, and
ſuche other as had made ſhippewzacke, it were poſſible that
he might wander in ſume ſecreate place: And that they coulde
not be quiete in theire myndes vntyll they knewe the certetie,
whether he with his felowes were alyue oz deade. But Vaſchus Nunnez, fearinge leaſſe at the commyng of Nicueſa he ſhulde
not bee had in autozitie emonge his felowes, ſayde they were
mad men to thinke that Nicueſa lyued: And althowgh he were
alyue, yet that they hadde noo neade of his helpe. Foz he
auouched that there was none of his felowes, that were not
as meete to rule as Nicueſa. While they were thus reaſonynge Rodericus Col=
too and froo, one Rodericus Colmenaris arryued in thoſe coaſtes menaris.
with two greate ſhippes hauinge in theym thzee ſcoze freſſhe The nauiga=
men, with greate plentie of bitailes and apparel. Of the na= tion of Rode=
bigation of this Colmenaris, I intende to ſpeake ſumewhat ricus Colme=
moze. He therfoze departed from the hauen of Hiſpaniola cauled naris.
Beata (where they pzepare and furnyſſhe theym ſelues whiche
make any biage into theſe landes) aboute the Ides of Oc=
tober in the yeare. 1510: And landed the.ix.of Nouember in a
Region in the large pzouince of Paria founde by Colonus betwene
the hauen Carthago and the Region of Cuchibachoa. In this biage Cuchibacoa.
what by the rowghnes of the ſea & fiercenes of the barbariās,
he ſuffered many incommodities. Foz when his freſſhe water
ſayled, he ſayled to the mouthe of a certeyne riuer which thin
habitantes caule Gaira, beinge apte to receaue ſhippes. This The ryuer
ryuer had his courſe from the toppe of an exceadinge hyghe Gaira.
mountayne couered with ſnowe, hygher then the which, all An exceding
the coompanyons of this capitayne Rodericus, ſaye that they ne= hygh moun=
uer ſawe. And that by good reaſon, yf it were couered wyth tayne coue=
ſnowe in that Region which is not paſt ten degrees diſtante red with
from the Equinoctial lyne. As they beganne to dzawe water owt ſnowe.
ſf their ſhippeboate, a certeyne Kynge made towarde theym
apparteled with beſtures of goſſampine cotton, hauinge twen= Apparteled
tie noble men in his coompanye appareled alſo: Whyche men.
thinge ſeemed ſtraunge to owre men, and not ſeene befoze in
thoſe parties. The Kinges apparell, hunge looſe from his
ſhoulders to his elbowes: And from the gerdle downewarde,

it was muche like a womans kettle, reachinge euen to his heeles. As he drewe neere towarde owre men, he seemed frendly to admonyshe theym to take none of the water of that ryuer, affirminge it to bee vnholsome for men: And shewed theym that not farre from thense, there was a ryuer of good water. They came to the ryuer. And endeuouringe to coome nere the shore, they were dryuen backe by tempeste. Also the burbulinge of the sande, declared the sea to bee but shalowe there. They were therefore enforced to returne to the fyrste ryuer where they myght safely caste anker. This Kinge layde wayte for owre men. For as they were fyllinge theire barrelles, he set on theym with abowt seuen hundreth men (as owre men iudged) armed after theire maner, althowgh they were naked. For only the kynge and his noble men were appareled. They

Seuen and forty Spanyardes are slaine with venemous arrowes.

Ierxa.
A remedy agenste venemous arrowes

tooke away the shippeboate, and brooke it in maner to chips: soo fiercely assaylinge owre menne with theyr venemous arrowes, that they slewe of them fortie and seuen beefore they coulde couer them selues with theyr targettes. For that poyson is of such force, that albeit the woundes were not great, yet they dyed therof immediatly. For they yet knewe noo remedie agaynste this kynde of poyson, as they after lerned of thinhabitantes of Hispaniola. For this Ilande bringeth foorth an herbe which quencheth and mortifieth the violent poyson of the herbe wherewith theyr arrowes are infected, soo that it bee ministred in tyme. Yet of owre coompany whiche went

Seuen men left behynde.

for water, seuen escaped that conflicte, and hyd them selues in a hollowe tree, lurkynge there vntyll nyght. Yet escaped they not the handes of theyr enemyes. For the shippe departed from thense in the nyght season and lefte them there, supposinge that they had byn slayne. Thus by manye suche perels and daungers (which I lyghtly ouerpasse bicause I wyl

The hauen of Vraba.

not bee tedious to powre holynes) he arryued at the length at the hauen of Vraba, and cast anker at the easte syde therof, fro whense not longe before, owre men departed to the west syde by reason of the barennes of that soyle. When he had continued a whyle in the hauen, and sawe noo man stourynge, marueylinge at the silence of the places (for he supposed there to haue fownde his felowes) he coulde not coniecture what this shulde meane: and there vppon beganne to suspecte that eyther they were deade, or that they had chaunged the place

of

of theyr habitacion. To knowe the certentie hereof, he commaunded all the greate ordinaunce and other smaule gunnes which he had in his shippes, to bee charged: And fyers to bee made in the nyght vppon the toppes of the rockes. Thus the fyers beinge kyndeled, he commaunded all the gunnes to bee shotte of at one instante: by the horrible noyse whereof, the goulfe of *Vraba* was shaken, althowghe it were xxiiii. myles distante: for soo brode is the goulfe. This noyse was harde of theyr felowes in *Dariena*. And they aunswered them agryne with mutual fyers. Wherfore, by the folowynge of theise fyers, *Colmenaris* broughte his shippes to the Weste syde. Here those wretched and miserable men of *Dariena* which nowe tho rowgh famen and feeblenes holde theyr wery sowles in theyr teethe redy to departe from theyr bodies by reason of the calamities which befell vnto them after *Ancisus* shippewracke, lyftinge vp theyr handes to heauen, with the teares runnynge downe theyr cheekes bothe for ioye and sorowe, embraced *Rodericus* and his felowes with such kynde of reioysinge as their presente necessitie seemed to requyre. For whereas they were before his comminge, withowte vytayles and almoste naked, he brought them abundance of meates, drynke, and apparelh. It resteth nowe (moste holy father) to declare what came of the dissention amonge them of *Vraba*, as concernynge the gouernaunce after the losse of theyr capitaynes.

The goulfe of Uraba.

Dariena.

Famen.

what became of the conten cion of Uraba

☞ The thyrde booke of the seconde Decade of the supposed continent.

LL the chiefe officers in *Beragua*, and such as were moste politike in counsayle, determyned that *Nicuesa* shulde bee sowght owte if by any meanes he coulde bee founde. Where vppon they tooke from *Ancisus* the gouernoure refusinge the comminge of *Nicuesa*, a brygantyne whiche he made of his owne charges: And agreed, agaynst bothe the wyll of *Ancisus*, and the master of fence *Vaschus Nunnez*, that *Nicuesa* shulde bee sowght foorthe to take away the stryfe as touchinge the gouernement. They elected therfore *Colmenaris* (of whom we spake before) to take this matter in hande: wyllynge hym to make diligent search

Beragua.

Nicuesa is sought foorth

Q.i.   for

for Nicuesa in those coastes where they supposed he erred. For they harde that he had forsaken Beragua, the region of an vnfrutefull grounde. They gaue hym therfore commaundement to brynge Nicuesa with hym, and further to declare vnto hym that he shulde doo ryght good seruice to coome thether, in takyng away thoccasion of theyr seditions. Colmenaris tooke the thynge vppon hym the more gladly bycause Nicuesa was his very frende : Supposinge that his commynge with vytayles shulde bee noo lesse thankefull to Nicuesa and his coompanie, then it was to them of Vraba. Furnysshynge therefore one of his owne shippes whiche he browght with hym and also the brigantyne taken frome Ancisus, he frayghted the same with part of the vytayles and other necessaries which he browght with hym before from Hispaniola to Vraba. Thus coursynge alonge by all the coastes and goulfes nere there abowte, at the length at the poynte cauled Marmor, he founde Nicuesa, of all lyuynge men most infortunate, in maner dryed vppe with extreeme hunger, fylthye and horrible to beholde, with onely three score men in his company, lefte alyue of seuen hundreth. They al seemed to hym soo miserable, that he noo lesse lamented theyr case, then yf he had founde them deade. But Colmenaris conforted his frende Nicuesa : and embrasinge hym with teares and cherefull woordes, relyued his spirites, and further encoraged hym with greate hope of better fortune : declarynge also that his commynge was looked for and greatelye desyred of al the good men of Vraba, for that they hoped that by his autoritie, theyr discorde and contention shulde bee fynysshed. Nicuesa thanked his frende Colmenaris after such sorte as his calamitie requyred. Thus they tooke shyppe to gyther, and sayled directly to Vraba. But so variable and vnconstant is the nature of man, that he soone groweth owte of vse, becommeth insolente and vnmyndful of benefites after to much felicitie. For Nicuesa, after thus many teares and weepynges after dyuers bewaylinges of his infortunate desteny, after so many thankes geuynge, ye after that he had faulen downe to the grounde and kyssed the feete of Colmenaris his sauioure, he begann to quarel with hym before he came yet at Vraba, reprouinge hym and them all for thalteracion of the state of thynges in Vraba, and for the gatheringe of golde : Affirming that none of them owght to haue layde hande of any golde with
owte

Nicuesa is founde in a miserable case.

Insolencie of to much felicitie.

owte the aduice of hym oz of Fogeda his coompanion. When thefe fayinges and fuche lyke, came to the eares of thepm of Vrabs, they foo ftoured vp the myndes of Ancifus Lieutenaunte foz Fogeda, and alfo of Vafchus Nunnex, of the conttrary parte, ageinfte Nicuefa, that fhoztely after his arryuall with his thzee fcoze men, they commaunded hym with thzeatenynge to departe frō thenfe. But this pleafed not the better fozt. yet feaxynge leaft tumult fhulde bee amonge the people whom Vafchus Nunnex had ftered to factions, the beft parte was fayne to giue place to the greateft. This wzetched man therfoze Nicuefa thus dzowned in miferies, was thzuſte into the brigantyne whiche he hym felfe bzowght: and with hym only feuentene men, of his thzee fcoze which remayned alyue. He tooke fhyppe in the Calendes of Marche in the yeare .1511. intendynge to goo to Hifpaniola to coomplayne of the raſfhynes of Vafchus Nunnex, and of the violence doone to hym by Ancifus. But he entered into the brigantine in an vnfoztunate houre : foz he was neuer feene after. They fuppofe that the brigantine was dzowned with all the men therin. And thus vnhappie Nicuefa faulynge headlonge owte of one miferye into an other, ended his lyfe moze myſerablye then he lyued. Nicuefa beinge thus vylely reiected, & al theyz vytaples confumed which Colmenaris bzowght them, faulynge in maner madde foz hunger, they were enfozced lyke raueninge wooluesſeakynge theyz pzaye, to inuade fuche as dwelte abowte theyz confynes. Vafchus Nunnex therefoze, theyz newe capitayne of theyz owne election, aſſembling togpther a hundzeth and thirtie men, and fettinge them in ozder of battell after his fwoozdeplayers faſſhion, puffed vppe with pzyde, placed his fouldiers as pleafed hym in the foze= warde and rerewarde, and ſume as petrifens abowt his owne perfon. Thus aſſociatinge with hym Colmenaris, he wente to fpoyle the kynges which were bozderers there abowte, and came fyzſt to a Region abowte that coaſte, cauled Coiba, (wher of we made mencion befoze) imperiouſly and with cruel coun= tenaunce commaundinge the kynge of the region whofe name was Careta, (of whome they were neuer troubled as often as they paffed by his dominions) to gyue them vytaples. But Careta denyed that he coulde gyue them any at that tyme : al= leagyng that he had oftentymes apded the Chziſtians as they paſſed by thofe coaſtes : by reafon wherof his ſtoze was nowe

confumed

Nicuefa faulleth from one miſerie inⱦo an other.

The greateſt part ouercom meth the beſt

The death of Nicuefa.

Famen enfoz= ſeth them to faule to ſpoy= lynge.

Vafchus vſur peth thautozi= tie of the Lieuⱦenant= ſhippe.

Careta, kinge of Coiba.

consumed : Also that by the meanes of the contynuall warr which he kepte euer from his chyldes age with a kyng whose name is *Poncha*, borthering vppon his dominion, he and his famelie were in greate scarsenes of all thynges. But *Vaschus* woolde admytte none of these excuses : And thervppon tooke *Careta* prisoner, spoyled his vyllage, and browght hym bownd with his twoo wyues and chyldren and all his famelie to *Dariens*. With this kynge *Careta*, they founde three of the felowes of *Nicuesa*, the whiche when *Nicuesa* passed by those coastes to seeke *Beragua*, fearynge punyshement for theyr euyll deservinge, stoole away from the shyppes lyinge at anker : And when theyr nauie departed, committed them selues to the mercie of *Careta* who entertuyned them very frendely. They had nowe byn there .xviii. moonethes, and were therefore as vtterly naked as the people of the contrey. Duringe this tyme, the meate of thinhabitances seemed vnto them delicate dishes and princely fare : especially bycause they enioyed the same withowte any stryfe for myne and thyne, which twoo thynges moue and enforce men to such harde shyftes and miseries, that in lyuing they seeme not to lyue. Yet desyred they to returne to theyr owlde cares, of suche force is education and natural affection towarde them with whom we haue byn browght vp. The vitayles whiche *Vaschus* browght frome the vyllage of *Careta* to his felowes lefte in *Dariens*, was rather sumwhat to aswage theyr present hunger, and vtterly to take away theyr necessitie. But as touchinge *Ancisus* beinge Lieutenaunt for *Fogeda*, whether it were before these thynges or after, I knowe not. But this I am sure of, that after the retirynge of *Nicuesa*, many occations were sought agenst *Ancisus* by *Vaschus* and his factionaries. Howe soo euer it was, *Ancisus* was taken, and cast in pryson, and his goodes confiscate. The cause hereof was (as *Vaschus* alleaged) that *Ancisus* hadde his commission of the Lieutenauntshippe, of *Fogeda* onely whome they sayde to be nowe deade, and not of the kynge. Sayinge that he woolde not obey any man that was not put in office by the kyng hym selfe by his letters patentes. Yet at the request of the grauest sorte, he was sumwhat pacified, and delt more gentelly with hym, hauinge sum compassion of his calamities. And therby pon commaunded hym to bee loosed. *Ancisus* beinge at libertie tooke shyppe to departe from thense to *Hispaniola*. But befor

kynge Careta is taken and spoyled.

vunger is the best sauce.

Myne & thine the seedes of al mischefe.

Ancisus Lieutenaunt for Fogeda is cast in prison.

Ancisus taketh his Vyage to Hispaniola.

had hoyſed vppe his ſayle, all the wyſeſt ſorte reſorted to
om, humbly deſyzinge hym to returne ageyne: promyſynge
at they wolde doo theyz diligence, that *Vaſchus* beinge recon
led, he myght bee reſtozed to his full autozitie of the Lieue=
nauntſhippe. But *Ancisus* refuſed to conſent to theyz requeſt
d ſoo departed. yet ſume there were that murmured that
d and his angels ſhewed this reuenge vpon *Ancisus*, bycauſe
cuſa was reiected thzowgh his counſayle. Howe ſoo euer
bee, the ſearchers of the newe landes, faule headlonge in=
rune by theyz owne follye, conſuminge them ſelues with
uile diſcozde, not weighinge ſoo greate a matter, noz em=
ployinge theyz beſte endeuoure aboute the ſame as the wooz=
ynes of the thynge requyzeth. In this meane tyme, they de
empned all with one agreemente, to ſende meſſenjers into
paniola to the younge Admirall and viceroy, ſonne and heyze
Chriſtophorus Colonus the fynder of theſe landes, and to the o=
er gouernoures of the Ilande (from whom the newe landes
ceaue theyz ayde and lawes) to ſignifie vnto the what ſtate
ey ſtoode in, and in what neceſſitie they lyued: alſo what
ey had founde, and in what hope they were of greater thin
s if they were furnyſhed with plentie of vytayles and other
eceſſaries. Foz this purpoſe they elected at the aſſignement
Vaſcus, one *Valdiuia*, beinge one of his faction, and inſtruc=
d by hym agenſt *Ancisus*. And to bee aſſiſtant with hym, they
ppoynted one *Zamudius* a Cantabzian: So that commaunde=
nt was gyuen to *Valdiuia* to returne from *Hiſpaniola* with vy=
ayles: And *Zamudius* was appoynted to take his vyage into
payne to the kynge. They tooke ſhippe both togyther with
ncisus, hauinge in mynde to certifie the kynge howe thynges
ere handeled there, vnche otherwyſe then *Zamudius* infozma
on. I my ſelfe ſpake with both *Ancisus* and *Zamudius* at their
ommynge to the courte. Whyle they were occupied aboute
eſe matters, thoſe wretched men of *Dariena* looſed *Careta* the
ynge of *Coiba* vppon condition that he ſhulde ayde theym in
eyz warres agenſt his enemy and theyz, kynge *Poncha* boz
deringe vppon his dominions. *Careta* made a league with the,
complynge that as they paſſed by his kyngedome, he woolde
yue them all thynges neceſſarie, and meete them with an ar=
ue of men, to goo fozwazde with them to the battaile agenſt
oncha. Theyz weapons are nother bowes noz venimed ar=

rowes

The reuenge
of God.

The inconue
niences of
diſcozde.

The ſonne ꝛ
heyze of Colo
nus, is Admi
rall and vice=
roy of Hiſpa=
niola.

Valdiuia.

Zamudius ꝛ
Ancisus, take
their vyage
to Spayne.

kinge Poncha.

rowes, as we sayde thinhabitantes to haue which dwel east=
warde beyonde the goulfe. They feight therefore at hande,
with longe swordes (which they caule Macanas) made of wood

Swoordes of woodde.

bycause they haue noo Jren. They vse also longe staues lyke
iauelens hardened at the endes with fyer, oz typte with bone.
Also certeyne slynges and dartes. Thus after the league made
with Careta, bothe he and owre men had certeyne dayes ap=
poynted theym to tyll theyr grounde and sowe theyr seedes.

kynge Careta conspireth with the Spa nyardes a= genst kynge Poncha.

This doone, by the ayde of Careta and by his conduction, they
marched towarde the palaice of Poncha, who fledde at theyr cō
mynge. They spoyled his vyllage and mytigated theyr hun=
ger with such vytayles as they founde there. yet coulde they
not helpe their felowes therwith by reasō of the farre distance
of the place, althowghe they had greate plentie. For the vyl=
lage of Poncha was moze then a hundzeth myles distant from
Dariena : wheras was also none other remedy but that the same

wrought gold

shulde haue byn caryed on mens backes to the sea syde beinge
farre of, where they left theyz shyppes in the which they came
to the vyllage of Careta. Here they founde certeyne powndes
weyght of gold, grauen & wrought into sundzye ouches. Af=
ter the sacking of this vyllage they resozted toward the shyps
intendyng to leaue the kinges of the inland vntouched at this
tyme, & to inuade onely them which dwelt by the sea coastes.
Not farre from Coiba, in the same tracte, there is a Region na=
med Comogra, and the kinge therof, cauled Comogrus after the

The region of Comogra, distant frome Dariena. xxx. leaques.

same name. To this kinge they came fyzst next after the sub=
vertion of Poncha: And founde his palaice situate in a frutefull
playne of tweluc leaques in bzedthe, at the rootes of the fur=
ther syde of the nexte mountaynes. Comogrus had in his courte
a certeyne noble man of nere consanguinitie to kynge Careta,
whiche had fledde to Comogrus by reason of certeyne dissensiō
whiche was betwene Careta and hym. These noble men, they

kynge Come= grus.

caule Iura. This Iura therfoze of Coiba, mette owre men by th=
way, and conciled Comogrus to them, bycause he was well kno=
wen to owre mē from the tyme that Nicuesa passed fyzst by those
coastes. Owre men therefore went quietlye to the palaice of
Comogrus beinge distante from Dariens thirtie leaques by a plaine
waye abowte the mountaynes. This kynge Comogrus, had se=
uen sonnes, younge men of comelye forme and stature, whiche

The kynges palaice.

he had by sundzy wyues. His palaice was framed of postes

proppes made of trees fastened togepther after a straunge
sorte,and of soo stronge bylding,that it is of no lesse strength
then waules of stone. They which measured the length of the
doure thereof, founde it to bee a hundreth and fyftie pases,
and in breadthe, foure score foote: beinge roofed and paued
with maruelous arte. They founde his store house,furnysshed
with abundance of delicate bitailes after the maner of theyr
countrey:And his wyne celler replenished with great bessetles
of earth and also of woodde fylled with theyr kynde of wyne
and syder. For they haue noo grapes. But lyke as they make
theyr breade of those three kyndes of rootes cauled Iucca, agis,
and Naixium, (whereof we spake in the fyrste decade) Soo
make they theyr wyne of the frutes of date trees, and syder
of other frutes and seedes, as doo the Almaynes,Flemynges
Englysshe men, and owre Spanyardes whych inhabite the
mountaynes,as the Bascons and Asturians: likewise in the
mountaynes of the Alpes,the Moricians, Sueuians, and Hel:
uians,make certeyne drynkes of barley,wheat,hoppes,and
apples. They say also that with Comogrus,they droonk wynes
of sundry tastes,both whyte and blacke. But nowe yow shall
heare of a thynge more monstrous too behoulde. Enteryinge
therfor ito the inner partes of the palaice,they were browght
into a chamber hanged aboute with the carkeses of men,tyed
with ropes of gossampine cotton. Beinge demaunded what
they ment by that superstition,they answered that those were
the carkeses of the father,graundfather,and great graund:
father with the other auncestours of theyr Kyng Comogrus. De
claringe that they had the same in greate reuerence, and that
they tooke it for a godly thynge to honoure them religiously:
And therfore appareled euery of the same sumptuouslye with
golde and precious stones accordynge vnto theyr estate. After
this sorte dyd the antiquitie honoure theyr Penates, whyche
they thowght had the gouernaunce of their lyues. Howe they
kepe these carkeses vppon certeine instrumetes made of wood,
lke vnto hurdels,with a softe fyer vnder the same, so that
onely the skynne remayneth to houlde the bones together, we
haue described in the former decade. Of Comogrus his seuen
sonnes,the eldest had an excelente naturall wytte. He ther:
fore thowght it good to flatter and please thys wandrynge
kynde of men(owr men I meane)lyuynge onely by shiftes and
spoyle

wyne & syder

Blacke wine.

The bodyes
of deade kyn
ges,religiou-
ly honoured.

Penatos.

The carcases
of men dryed

The kynges
sonne a yonge
man of excel-
lent wytte.

spoyle, leaſt beinge offended and ſeekynge occaſions ageynſte hym and his familie, they ſhuld handle hym as they dyd other whiche ſowght noo meanes howe to gratifie thepm.

Foure thou ſande vnces of wrought golde.

Wherefore, he gaue Vaſchus and Colmenaris foure thouſande ounces of golde artificially wrought, and alſo fyftie ſlaues whyche he had taken in the warres. For ſuche, eyther they ſell for exchaunce of other thinges, or otherwiſe vſe them as theym lyſteth. For they haue not the vſe of money. This golde with as muche more which they had in an other place, owre men wayed in the porche of Comogrus his palaice to ſeparate the fyſte parte thereof, whiche portion is due to the kynges eſcheker.

The diſtribu tion of golde.

For it is decreed that the fyft parte of both golde, perles, and precious ſtones, ſhalde be aſſigned to the kinges treaſourers: And the reſydue, to bee diuided emonge theym ſelues by compoſition. Here as brabblynge and contention aroſe emonge owr men abowt the diuidinge of gold, this eldeſt ſoonne of kynge Comogrus beinge preſente, whome we prayſed for his wyſedome, commynge ſume what wyth an angery countenaunce towarde hym whiche helde the balences, he ſtrooke theym wyth his fyſte, and ſcatered all the golde that was therein, abowte the porche, ſharpely rebukynge theym with woordes in this effecte.

young Como grus his ora tiou.

What is the matter yowe Chriſtian men, that yow ſoo greatly eſteme ſoo litle a portiou of golde more then yowr owne quietnes, whiche neuertheleſſe yow entend to deface from theſe fayre ouches and to melte the ſame into a rude maſſe. If yowre hunger of goulde bee ſoo inſatiable that onely for the deſyre yowe haue therto, yowe diſquiete ſoo many nations, and yow yowre ſelues alſo ſuſteyne ſo many calamites and incommodities, lyuing like baniſhed men owte of yowre owne countrey, I wyll ſhewe yowe a Regiou

The hunger of golde.

A regiou flo winge wyth golde.

floweinge with goulde, where yowe may ſatiſfie yowr rauen inge appetites. But yowe muſte attempte the thynge with greater powre: For it ſtandeth yow in hande by force of armes to ouercome kynges of greate puiſſaunce, and rigorous defenders of theyr dominions. For bycyde other, the greate king

kynge Tuma nama.

Tumanama wyll coome foorthe ageynſte yowe, whoſe kengdom is moſte ryche with golde, and diſtante from hence onely ſyx ſoonnes: that is, ſyx dayes: for they number the dayes by the ſonne. Furthermore, or euer yowe canne coome thether, yow muſt paſſe ouer the mountaynes inhabited of the cruell Canibal

Canibales.

ales a fierce kynde of men, deuourers of mans fleſſhe, lyuing
without lawes, wanderinge, and withowte empire. For
they alſo, beinge deſyrous of golde, haue ſubdewed them vn
er theyr dominion whiche before inhabited the golde mynes
f the mountaynes, and vſe them lyke bondemen, vſyng their
laboure in dygginge and workynge theyr golde in plates and
ſundry Images lyke vnto theſe whiche powe ſee here. For
oce doo no more eſteeme rude golde vnwrought, then we doo
cloddes of earthe, before it bee formed by the hande of the
workeman to the ſimilitude eyther of ſume veſſell neceſſarie
or owre vſe, or ſume ouche bewetifull to be worne. Theſe
thynges doo wee receaue of theim for exchaunge of other of
owre thynges, as of priſoners taken in warre, whiche they
ype to eate, or for ſheetes and other thynges perteynynge to
the furnyture of houſeholde, ſuche as they lacke which inha
te the mountaynes : And eſpecially for vitayles wherof they
ſtande in greate neede by reaſon of the barrennes of the moun
aynes. This iorney therfore, muſt bee made open by force of
men. And when powe are paſſinge ouer theſe mountaynes
poyntinge with his fynger towarde the ſouthe mountaynes,
owe ſhal ſee an other ſea, where they ſayle with ſhyppes as
ygge as powres (meanynge the caraucles) vſinge both ſay-
es and ores as powe doo, althowghe the men bee naked as
oee are . All the waye that the water runneth frome the
mountaynes, and all that ſyde lyinge towarde the Southe,
bryngeth foorth golde abundantly. As he ſayde theſe woor-
es, he poynted to the veſſelles in whiche they vſe to ſerue
heyr meate, affirmynge that kynge _Tumanama_, and all the o-
her kynges beyonde the mountaynes, had ſuche and al their
ther houſeholde ſtuffe of golde: And that there was noo leſſe
lentie of golde amonge thoſe people of the Southe, then of
ren with vs. For he knewe by relation of owre men, wher-
f owre ſwoordes and other weapons were made. Owre ca-
taynes maruelyng at the oration of the naked younge man
for they had for interpretours thoſe three men whiche had
yn before a yere and a halfe conuerſant in the court of kynge
areta) pondered in theyr myndes, & erneſtly conſidered his ſay-
nges. Soo that his raſſhenes in ſcatteringe the golde owte
f the balances, they turned to myrth and vrbanitie, commen
ynge his dooinge and ſayinge therin. Then they aſked hym

R . i . frendely

The golde
mynes of the
mountaynes .

Unwrought
golde not eſte
med.

Exchaunge .

Abundance
of golde.

houſeholde
ſtuffe of gold

frendely, vppon what certeyne knowleage he fpake thof
thynges : Or what he thowght beſte herein to bee doone, y
they ſhulde brynge a greater ſupplye of men. To this, poang
Comogrus, ſtayinge a whyle with hym ſelfe as it were an ora
tour preparinge him ſelfe to ſpeake of ſume graue matter, an
diſpoſynge his bodye to a gieſture meete to perſuade, ſpak
thus in his mother tonge. Gyue eare vnto me o yowe Chry
ſtians. Albeit that the gredie hunger of golde hathe not ye
uered vs naked men, yet doo we deſtroy one an other by rea
ſon of ambition and deſyre to rule. Hereof ſpringeth mortal
hatred amonge vs, and hereof commethe owre deſtruction.
Owre prediceſſours kepte warres, and ſoo dyd *Comogrus* m
father with princes beinge bortherers abowte hym. In th
which warres, as wee haue ouercoome, ſo haue wee byn ouer
coome, as dothe appere by the number of bondemen among
vs, which we tooke by the ouerthrowe of owre enemyes, o
the whiche I haue gyuen yowe fiftie. Lykewyſe at an othe
tyme, owre aduerſaries hauinge thupper hande agenſte vs
ledde away manye of vs captiue. For ſuche is the chaunce o
warre. Alſo, amonge owre familiers (wherof a great numbe
haue byn captiues with them) beholde here is one whiche o
longe tyme ledde a paynefull lyfe in bondage vnder the yok
of that kynge beyonde the mountaynes, in whoſe kyngdom
is ſuche abundance of golde. Of hym, and ſuche other innu
merable, and lykewyſe by the reſort of free men on theyr ſyd
cominuge to vs, and ageyne of owre men reſortinge to them
by ſafe conduct, theſe thynges haue byn euer as well knowen
vnto vs, as owre owne poſſeſſions. But that yowe maye be
the better aſſured hereof, and bee owte of all ſuſpection tha
yowe ſhal not bee deceaued, make me the guyde of this viage
bynbynge me faſt and keepyng me in ſafe cuſtodie to bee han
ged on the nert tree, yf yowe fynde my ſayinges in any poin
vntrewe. Folowe my counſayle therfore, and ſend for a tho
ſande Chriſtian men apte for the warres, by whoſe power w
may with alſo the men of warre of *Comogrus* my father armed
after owre maner, inuade the dominions of owre enemyes
where, bothe yowe may bee ſatiſfyed with golde, and we fo
owre conductinge and aydynge yowe in this enterpryſe, ſhal
thynke owre ſelues abundantly rewarded, in that yowe ſhal
helpe to delyuer vs from the iniuries and perpetuall feare o
owr

owre enemies. After these woordes, this prudente younge Comogrus helde his peace. And owre men moued with greate hope and hunger of golde, beganne ageine to swalowe downe theyr spettle,

The fourth booke of the seconde Decade, of the supposed Continent.

AFter that they had taryed here a fewe dayes and baptised Comogrus with all his famelie, and named hym by the name of Charles after the kynge of Spayne, they returned to theyr felowes in Dariena leauinge with hym the hope of the thousande souldyers, which his sonne requyred to passe ouer those mountaynes towarde the South sea. Thus enteringe into the vyllage which they had chosen to inhabite, they had knowleage that Valdiuia was returned, within syxe moonethes after his departure: but with noo great plentie of vytayles, bycause he browght but a smaule shippe: yet with hope that shortely after, there shalde bee sent them abundaunce of vytayles with newe supply of men. For younge Colonus, the Admiral and viceroy of Hispaniola, and the other gouernours of the Ilande, acknowleaged that hetherto they had noo respecte to theym of Dariena, bycause they supposed that Ancisus the Licuetenant had safely arryued there with his shippe laden with vatayles: wyllynge them from hensefoorth to bee of good cheere, and that they shulde lacke nothynge hereafter: But that at this present tyme, they had noo bygger shippe wherby they myght sende them greater plentie of necessaries by Valdiuia. The vytayles therfore which he browght, serued rather sumwhat to mytigate theyr present necessitie, then to satisfye theyr lacke. Wherfore within a fewe dayes after Valdiuia his returne, they fel ageine into lyke scarsnes: especially for asmuch as a great storme and tempest whiche came from the hyghe mountaynes with horrible thunder and lyghtnynge in the mooneth of Nouember, browght with it suche a sudde, that it partely caryed away and partly drowned all the corne and seedes whiche they had sowne in the moonethe of September in a fruytefull grounde before they went to kyng Comogrus. The seedes which

R,ii, they

Bread of Maizius & hobba

they of *Hispaniola* caule *Maizium*, and they of *Vraba* caule Hobb
Wherof they make theyr breade, which also wee sayde to b
rype thryse euery yeare, bycause those Regions are not bytt
with the sharpnes of wynter by reason of theyr nerenes to t
Equinoctial lyne. It is also agreeable to the principles of n
turall philosophie, that this breade made of *Maizius* or Hobb
shulde bee more holsome for thynhabitantes of those contre
then breade made of wheate, by reason that it is of easyer d

Digestion strengthened by outwarde colde.

gestion. For wheras coulde is wantinge, the naturall hea
is not dryuen frome the outewarde partes into the inwar
partes and precordials, whereby digestion is much strength
ned. Beinge therfore thus frustrate of the increase of the
seedes, and the kynges nere aboute them spoyled of both
tayles and golde, they were enforced to seeke theyr meate f

hunger.

ther of: And therwith to signifie to the gouernours of *Hisp
ola* with what great necessitie they were oppressed: And wh
they had lerned of *Comogrus* as concernynge the Regions t
warde the Southe: wyllynge them in consideration therof

A newe supply of a thousande souldyers.

aduertyse the kynge to sende them a thousande souldiers,
whose helpe they myght by force make waye throwghe t
mountaynes diuidynge the sea on bothe sydes, if they coul
not brynge the same to passe quyetly. The same *Valdiuia* w
also sent on this message, caryinge with hym to the kyng
treasourers (hauinge theyr office of recepte in *Hispaniola*) th
hundreth poundes weyght of golde after eyght ounces to t
pounde, for the fyfte portion dewe to the kynges eschek

Marcha.

This pounde of. viii. vnces, the Spanyardes caule Marc
whiche in weyght amounteth to fyftie pieces of golde caul

Pesus.

Castellani. But the Castilians, caule a pound *Pesum*. We conclu
therfore, that the same hereof, was .xb. thousande of tho
peeces of golde cauled *Castellani.* And thus is it apparente

A thousande and fyue hundreth pounde weyght of wrought geld

this accompte, that they receaued of the barbarous kynges
thousande and fyue hundreth poundes of eyght ounces to
pounde. All the whiche they founde redy wrought in sund
kyndes of ouches, as cheynes, braselets, tablets, and plate
bothe to hange before theyr brestes, and also at theyr eare
and noserhryls. *Valdiuia* therefore tooke shyppinge in the sa
carauell in the whiche he came last, and returned also beefo
the thyrde day of the Ides of January, in the yeare of Chri
M. D. XI. What chaunced to hym in this vyage, wee wi
Decla

clare in place conuenient. But let vs nowe returne to them
hich remayned in Vraba. After the dismissinge of Valdiuia, be=
ge pricked forwarde with owtragious hunger, they deter=
ned to searche the inner partes of that goulfe in sundry pla
. The extreme angle or poynt of the same goulfe is distant
m the enterance therof, aboute foure score myles. This an
or corner, the Spanyardes caule Culata. Vaschus hym selfe
me to this poynte with a hundreth men, coastynge alonge
the goulfe with one brygantine and certeyne of the
ates of those regions, which the Vrabians caule Vru, lyke
to them whiche thinhabitantes of Hispaniola caule Canoas.
om this poynt, there faulteth a ryuer from the East into the
ulfe, ten tymes bygger then the ryuer of Dariena which al=
faulteth into the same. Saylyng alonge by the ryuer about
space of thirtie myles (for they caule it nyne leagues) and
mwhat inclynynge towarde the ryght hande southwarde,
ey founde certeyne vyllages of thinhabitantes, the kynge
herof, was cauled Dabaiba. Owre men also were certifyed
ore, that Cemacchus the kynge of Dariena whom they put to
ght in the battayle, fledde to this Dabaiba. But at the com=
nge of owre men, Dabaiba also fledde. It is thowght that
was admonyshed by Cemacchus, that he shulde not abyde
brunte of owre men. He folowed his counsayle: forsooke
s vyllages, and lefte all thynges desolate. yet owre men
unde heapes of bowes and arrowes: Also much houshold
ffe and many fysshyng boates. But those marysshe groundes
re neyther apte for sowinge of seedes or planting of trees.
y reason wherof, they founde there fewe suche thynges as
ey desyred: that is, plentie of vytayles. For thinhabitantes
this Region, haue noo breade but such as they get in other
ntreys nere abowte them by exchaunge for theyr fysshe, on=
to serue theyr owne necessitie. yet founde they in the hau=
s of them that fledde, golde wrought and grauen, amoun=
nge to the sume of seuen thousande of those pieces whiche
lapde to bee cauled Castellani: Also certeyne canoas: of the
ich they brought away twoo with them, and great plentie
theyr houholde stuffe, with certeyne bundels of bowes and
owes. They saye, that from the marysshes of that ryuer,
ere coome certeyne battes in the nyght season, as bygge as
tle dooues, inuadyng men and bytinge them with a deadly
B. iii wounde

The goulfe of Vraba.
Culata.

Vaschus sear cheth the goulfe of Vra ba.

A maruelous great ryuer, faulyng into the gulfe of Vraba.

kynge Dabaiba and Cemacchus, are dryuen to flyght.

Marysshe grounde

wrought gold wherebynge vii. thousand Castellanes.

Battes as bygge as turtle doues.

wounde, as sume of them testifie whiche haue byn bytten
the same. J mp selfe communing with Ancisus the Lieutena
whom thep reiecced, and amonge other thynges askynge h
of the benemous bytinge of these battes, he toulde me that
hym selfe was bytten by one of them on the heele, his foote
inge vncouered in the npght by reason of the heate in somm
seasom: But that it hurt hym noo more, then yf he hadde by
bytten by any other beaste not venemous. Other sape, th
the bytynge of sume of them is venemous: pet that the sam
is healed incontinently, if it be wasshed with water of th
sea. Ancisus toulde me also, that the benemous woundes ma
by the Canibales arrowes infected with popson, are heale
by wasshynge with water of the sea, and also by cauterisin
with hotte Jrens: And that he had experience thereof in t
region of Caribana, where many of his men were so wounde
They departed therfore, from the poynte of the goulfe of Vra
not well contented bycause thep were not laden with vitaile
Jn this their returne, there arose soo greate a tempest in th
wyde goulfe, that thep were enforced to caste into the sea, a
the householde stuffe whiche they tooke from the poore wre
ches whiche iyued onely by fisshinge. The sea also swalowe
vpp the two boates that they tooke from theym, wherewyt
the men were likewise drowned. The same tyme that Vasch
Nunnez attempted to searche the poynte of the goulfe towar
the southe, euen then by agreemente, dyd Rodericus Colmenaris tab
his viage towarde the mountaynes by the caste, with threesc
men, by the ryuer of the other goulfe. Aboute fortie miles di
tante from the mouthe of the ryuer, (for they caule it twelu
leaques)he founde certeyne vilages situate vppon the bank
of the ryuer, whose Chiui,(that is,) kinge, thep caule Turui. Wit
this kinge dyd Colmenaris pet remapne when Vaschus after his r
turne to Dariena, saplmg by the same ryuer, came to hym. Her
refresshinge thepr hole coompany with the vitailes of this Tu
ui, they departed from thense togpther. Other fortie myle
from hence, the ryuer encoompaseth an Jland inhabited wit
fysscher men. Jn this, bycause they sawe greate plentie of th
trees whiche beare Cassia fistula, thep named the Jland Cannassstula
Thep found in it, three score villages of tenne cotages apiece
On the right syde of the Jland there runneth an other ryuer
whose chanell is of depth suffient to beare brigantines. Th
ryuc

ner they cauled *Riuum Nigrum*: from the mouthe wherof about
..myles distante they founde a towne of fyue hundreth hou:
s seuered: whose *Chebi*, (that is,) kinge, was cauled *Abenama:*
.. They all forsooke theyr houses as soone as they harde
owre mennes commyng. But when they sawe that owre
en pursued them, they turned ageyne and ranne vppon them
ith desperate mindes, as men driuen from their owne posse.ss
..s. Theyr wepons, are swordes of wod, and long staues like
uelens, hardened at the ende with fyer: But they vse ney:
er bowes nor arrowes: nor any other of thinhabitantes of
.. weste syde of the goulse. The pore naked wretches were
sely dryuen to flight with owre weapons. As owre men fo:
wed theym in the chase, they tooke the kinge *Abenamachei* and
rteine of his noble men. A common souldier of owres whom
e kynge had wounded, coonminge to hym when he was ta:
n, cutte of his arme at one stroke with his swoorde. But
is was doone vnwares to the capitaynes. The number of
e Christian men which were here, was aboute a hundrethe
d fiftie: the one halfe whereof, the capptaynes lefte here,
d they with the resydue, rowed vpp the ryuer ageyne with
clue of the boates of those Regions, whiche they caul. *Vru*,
they of *Hispaniola* caule them *Canoas*, as we haue sayde. From
e ryuer of *Riuus Niger* and the Iland of *Cannafistula*, for the space
threescore and ten myles, leauing both on the right hande &
the lefte many riuers faulinge into it bigger then it selfe,
ey entred into one by the conductynge of one of the naked
habitantes, beinge appoynted a guyde for that purpose.
ppon the banke of this ryuer next vnto the mouthe of the
ne, there was a kynge cauled *Abibeiba*: who, bycause the
gion was full of marysshes, had his palaice buylded in the
ppe of a highe tree, a newe kynde of byldynge and seldome
ne. But that lande beareth trees of suche exceding heigth,
.r emonge theyr branches, a man may frame large houses:
s haue reede the like in diuers autoures howe in many Regi:
s where the ocean sea ryseth and ouerfloweth the lande,
e people were accustomed to flye to the high trees, and after
e faule of the water, to take the fysshe lefte on the lande.
.is maner of buyldinge, is to laye beames crosse ouer the
.unches of the trees, faste bownde togyther, and there vp:
n to rayse theyr frame, strangly made agaynste wynde and

trees

She ryuer of *Riuus Niger*.

A towne of v. hundreth houses.

Th'inhabitantes of the west syde of the goulse.

kynge Abenamachei, is taken and his arme cut of.

Many other ryuers faulling into *Riuus Niger*.

kyng abibeiba dwelleth in a tree.

Abundance of moyster & heat is cause of byggenes.

The rysinge of the Ocean sea.

wether. Owre men suppose that they buylde theyr house[s]
trees, by reason of the greate fluddes and ouerflowinge o[f]
uers whiche often tymes chaunce in those Regions.   Th[e]
trees are of suche heighth, that the strength of no manes a[rme]
is able to hurle a stone to the houses buylded therein . A[nd]
therfore doo I gyue the better credit to Plinie and other
tours whiche wryote that the trees in same places in India
soo high by reason of the frutefulnes of the grounde, ab[un]
daunce of water, and heate of the Region, that noo man is a[ble]
to shute ouer theym with an arrowe.   And by iudgement[of]
all men, it is thowght that there is noo frutfuller ground[e vn]
der the soonne, then this is whereof wee nowe entreate. O[wre]
men measuringe manye of these trees, founde theym to be [of]
suche biggues, that seuen men, ye sumetymes eight, holdi[ng]
hande in hande with theyr armes streached furthe, were s[carce]
sely able too fathyme them aboute.   Yet haue they theyr [cel]
lers in the grounde, weil replenysshed with such wynes w[herof]
of wee haue spoken beefore.   For albeit that the vehemen[cie]
of the wynde, is not of poure to caste downe those houses [or]
to breeke the branches of the trees, yet are they tossed th[er]
with, and swaye sumwhat from syde to syde, by reason wh[er]
of, the wyne shulde bee muche troubeled with moouinge. [With]
other necessarye thinges, they haue with theym in the tree[s.]
When the kynge or any other of the noble men, dyne or su[p]
in these trees, theyr wynes are browght theym from the ce[l]
leres by theyr seruauntes, whyche by meanes of exercise, [&]
accustomed with noo lesse celeritie to runne vppe and do[wne]
the steaues adherente to the tree, then doo owre waytynge [lac]
kyes vppon the playne grounde, fetche vs what wee caule [wine]
from the cobbarde bysyde owr dyninge table. Owre men t[here]
fore, came to the tree of kinge Abibeiba, and by thinterpretou[rs]
cauled hym foorthe to communication, gyuinge hym signe[s of]
peace, and there vppon willinge hym to coomme downe. [But]
he denyed that he woolde coomme owte of his house: D[esi]
ringe them to suffer hym to lyue after his faschion. But o[wre]
men fell from fayre woordes to threateninge, that excepte [he]
wolde descende with all his familie, they wolde eyther o[uer]
throwe the tree, or elles set it on fyer.   When he had der[ided]
them ageyne, they fell to hewinge the tree with theyr ar[mes.]
Abibeiba feeinge the chyppes faule from the tree on euery sy[de,]
                                                          cha[unged]

aunged his purpose, a nd came downe with only two of his
ones. Thus after they had entreated of peace, they commu=
d of gatheringe of golde. *Abibeiba* answered that he had noo
lde, and that he neuer had any neede therof, nor yet regar=
d it any more then stones, layd But when they were instante
pon hym, he sayde vnto them. If gowe soo greatly desyre
lde, I will seeke for sume in the nexte mountaynes, and
inge it vnto gowe. For it is plentifully engendred in those
untaynes. Then he appoynted a day when he wold bringe
is golde. But *Abibeiba* came neyther at the day, nor after the
pe appoynted. They departed therfore from thense well re
shed with his vitailes and wyne, but not with goulde as
ey hoped. Yet were they enformed the like by *Abibeiba* and
s ditionaries as concerninge the golde mynes and the Cani
les, as they harde before of kinge *Comogrus*. Saylinge yet
ther aboute thirtie myles, they chaunced vppon certeyne
ages of the Canibales: But vtterly voyde with owte men
stuffe. For when they had knowleage that owre men wan
red in the prouinces nere aboute theym they resorted to the
untaynes, carpinge al theyr goodes and stuffe wyth them.

**GOLD NO MORE
ESTEMED THEY
STONES.**

CANIBALES.

❡ The fyfte booke of the seconde Decade of the supposed continent.

IN the meane tyme whyle these thynges were
doone alonge by the shores or bankes of the
ryuer, a certeyne Decurian, that is a capp=
tayne ouer tenne, of the coompanye of those
which *Vascus* and *Colmenaris* had lefte for a gar
ryson in *Riuo Nigro* in the dominion of kynge
Abinamachei, whether it were that he was com
lled through hunger, or that his fataule dayes was nowe
ome, he attempted with his souldiers to searche the coun=
ys nere there about, and entered into the vyllage of a king
lled *Abraiba*. This capitaynes name was *Rais*: whom *Abra=
lnewe, with two of his felowes: but the resydue fledde.
ithin a fewe dayes after, *Abraiba* hauinge compassion of the
amitie of his kynseman and neyghbour *Abenamacheius* being
uen from his owne possessians (whose arme also we sayd
ore that one of the souldiers cut of at the riuer of *Riuo Nigro*

kyng Abraiba

S. i.   and

and nowe remaynynge with Abraiba to whome he fledde
stelth after he was taken, went to Abibeiba thinhabitour of t
tree, who had nowe lykewyse forsaken his contrey for fea
of owre men, and wandered hyghe desolate mountaynes a
wooddes. When he had therfore spyrde him, he spake to hi
in this effecte. What thynge is this Oh vnfortunate Abibeib
or what nation is this that soo tormenteth vs that wee ca
not enioye owre quyet lybertie? Howe longe, howe longe
say shall wee suffer theyr crueltie? were it not much better f
vs to die, then to abide such iniuries and oppressions as yow
as Abinamicheius owre kynseman, as Cemicchus, as Careta, as Po
iba, as I and other prynces of owr older doo susteyne? Can
any thynge bee more intollerable then to see owre inyue
owre chyldren, and owre subiectes, to bee ledde awaye ca
tiues, and owre goodes to be spoyled euen before owre face

I take the goddes to wytnes, that I speake not soo mu
for myne owne part as I doo for yowe whose case I lamen
for albeit they haue not yet touched me, neuerthelesse, by t
example of other, I owght to thynke that my destruction
not farre of. Let vs therfore (yf wee bee men) trye owre stre
gthe and proue owre fortune ageynst them whiche haue del
thus cruelly with Abenamicheius, and dryuen hym owre of h
contrey. Let vs set on them with all owre poure, and vtte
destroy them And yf wee can not stepe them al, yet shall w
make them afrayde eyther to a Tayle vs ageyne, or at the le
diminyny the theyr poure. For what soo euer shall befaule, n
thynge can chaunce woorse vnto vs then that which we no
suffer. When Abibeiba harde these woordes and such other li
he condecended to doo in al thinges as Abraiba wolde requyr
Whervppon they appoynted a day to brynge theyr conspira
cie to passe. But the thynge chaunced not accordynge to the
despre. For of those whiche wee sayde to haue passed to t
Canibales, there returned by chaunce to Riuus Niger the nygt
before the day appoynted to woorke theyr feate, thirtie m
to the ayde of theym whiche were lefte there yf anye seditio
shulde ryse as they suspected. Therfore at the dawnyng of t
day, the confetherate kynges with fyue hundreth of theyr
tionaries armed after theyr maner, beseaged the vyllage wi
a terrible alarome, knowynge nothynge of the newe men
whiche came thether the same nyght, Here owre target m

Marginal notes:

Abraiba causeth the kynges to rebell.

Men good enowgh yf they had iren

The kynges are dryuen to flyght.

me foorth ageynſt them, and fyrſt aſſayled them a farre of
ith theyr arrowes, then with theyr pykes, and laſte with
eyr ſwoordes: But the naked ſeely ſowles, perceauinge a
reater number of theyr aduerſaries then they looked for, were
ſone dryuen to flyght, and ſlayne for the moſt parte lyke ſca=
rynge ſheepe. The kynges eſcaped, they ſlewe manye, and
oke many captiues whiche they ſente to *Dariena* where they
ſe them for labourers to tyll and ſowe theyr grounde. Theſe
ynges thus happely atchyued, and that prouince quyeted,
ey returned by the ryuer to *Dariens,* leauinge theyr thyrtie
en for a garryſon vnder the gouernaūce of one *Furatado* a ca=
itayne. This *Furatado* therfore, ſente from *Riuo Nigro* where
e was appoynted gouernoure, twentie of his felowes & one
oman, with .xviii. captiues to *Vaſchus* and his company, in
ne of the byggeſt *Canoas* of that prouince.　As they rowed
owne by the ryuer, there came foorth ſoodenly ouerthwarte
e ryuer ageynſt them, foure greate *Canoas,* which ouerthrew
eyr boate and ſlewe as many of them as they coulde coome
r, bycauſe they were vnprepared ſuſpecting noo ſuch thinge.
heſe men were all drowned and ſlayne excepte twoo, which
d them ſelues amonge certeyne fagottes that ſwamme on
e water, in the whiche they laye lurkynge, and ſoo eſcaped
theyr felowes in *Dariens*: who by them bringe aduertyſed
erof, beganne to caſte theyr wyttes what this thyng might
eane: beinge no leſſe ſolicitate for them ſelues, then medita=
nge in what daunger theyr felowes had byn in *Riuo Nigro,*
ccepte by good fortune, thoſe thirtie newe men which were
nte to them, had coome to the vyllage the nyght before the
nſpiracie ſhulde haue byn wrought. Conſulting therfore
hat was beſt to bee doone herein, at the lengthe with dyly=
ent ſearchynge they had intelligence that fyue kynges, that
 to wytte, *Abibeiba* the inhabitoure of the tree, and *Cemacchus*
ryuen from his vyllage, whiche owre menne nowe poſſeſſed,
braibs alſo and *Abenamacheius,* kynſemen, with *Dabaiba* the king
f the fyſher men inhabytinge the corner of the goulfe whiche
e cauled *Culata,* were all aſſembled to conſpire the Chriſtian
ens deſtruction at a day aſſigned. Which thynge had ſurely
oome to paſſe, if it had not byn otherwyſe hyndered by gods
rouidence. It is therfore aſcrybed to a myracle: And trewly
ot vnwoorthely if wee weye howe chaunce deteeted and be=

wrayed

Marginal notes (right column):

Captyues.

A garyſon of xxx. men.

xviii. Spany=
ardes ſlayne
and drowned

The kinges
which conſpi
red the death
of the Chriſti=
ans.

A ſtrange
chaunce.

wrayed the counsayle of these kynges. And bycause it is wo-
thy to bee harde, I wyll declare it in fewe woordes. *Vaschu*
Nunnez therfore, who rather by poure then by election, vsurped the gouernaunce in *Dariena*, beinge a master of fence, and
rather a rasshe royster then politike capitayne (althowgh fortune sumtyme fauoureth fooles) amonge many women which
in dyuers of these regions he had taken captyue, had one whyche in fauoure and bewtie excelled all other. To this woma
her owne brother often tymes resorted, who was also dryuen
owte of his contrey with kynge *Cemacchus*, with whom he was
very familier and one of his chiefe gentelmen. Amonge other
communication which he had with his syster whom he loued
entierly, he vttered these woordes. My deare and welbeloued
syster, gyue eare to my sayinges, and keepe moste secreately
that whiche I wyll declare vnto yowe, yf yowe desyre yowr
owne wealth and myne, and the prosperitie of owre contrey
and kynsefolkes. The insolencie and crueltie of these menn
whiche haue dryuen vs owte of owre possessions, is soo into-
lerable, that the princes of the lande are determyned noo longer to susteyne theyr oppressions.

By the conductinge therfore of fyue kinges (which he named
in order) they haue prepared a hundreth greate *Canoas*, with
fyue thousande men of warre by lande and by sea, with vita-
les also in the village of *Tichiri*, sufficient to maintayne such a
army. Declaringe further, that the kinges by agremente, haue
diuided emonge theym the goodes and headdes of owre menn
And therfore admonysshed her, at the daye appoynted by sum
occasion to conueigh her selfe owte of the way, leste shee shul
bee slayne in the confusion of the bataile. For the souldie
victourer, is not woonte to spare any that commethe in his
rase. And thus shewinge his syster the daye assigned to th
slawghter, he departed. But the younge woman (for it is th
swoord that women feare and obserue more then the grauiti
of *Cato*,) whether it were for the loue or feare that shee had t
Vaschus, forgettinge her parentes, her kynsfolkes, her countre
and all her frendes, ye and all the kinges into whose throte
Vaschus, had thruste his swoorde shee opened all the matter vn
to hym, and conceled none of those thinges whiche her vndis
crete broother had declared to her. When *Vaschus* therfore ha
hard the matter, he caused *Fuluia*, (for soo had they named her

Vaschus.

women can
keepe no
counsayle.

An army of C
canoas and
fyue.M. men.

Tryumphe
before victory

Effection cor-
rupteth trew
iudgement.

o sende for her brother, who came to her immediatly, was ta
ken, and enforced to tell the hole circunstances of the matter.
Where vppon, he playnely confessed that kinge Cemacchus hys
lorde and master, sente those foure canoas to the destruction
of owre men, and that these newe conspiraces were attempted
by his consaile. Likewise that Gemacchus sowght the destructi: on of Vaschus hym selfe when he sent hym fortie men vnder pre sence of frendshippe to tyll and sowe his grownd after the ma ner of the contrey, gyuinge them in commaundement to slaye Vaschus at Marris, whyther he resorted to comforte his laboures as the maner is of all good husbandes. yet durste they at noo tyme execute theyr lordes commaundemente vppon hym, by: cause Vaschus came neuer emonge them afoote or vnarmed, but was accustomed to ryde to theym in harnes with a iauelen in his hande and a swoorde by his syde. Wherfore Cemacchus be: inge frustrate of his particuler consaile, tooke this laste thing in hande to his owne destruction and his neighbours. For he conspiracie beinge detected, Vaschus cauled threescore and enne souldiers, commaundinge them to folow him, but decla: red nothing vnto them whether hee wente or what hee enten ded to do. He wente forwarde therfore fyrste towarde Cemac: chus which ley from hym, onely tenne myles. But he had know leage that he was fledde to Dababa the kinge of the marishes of Culata. yet searchinge his village, he founde a noble man a ruler vnder hym and also his kinsleman, whome he tooke pri: soner with many other of his familiers and frendes both men and women. The same houre that he sette forwarde to secke or Cemacchus, Rodericus Colmenaris rowed vp the ryuer with foure of theyr biggeste canoas and threescore men by the conduction of the maydes brother who browght hym to the village of Ti: biri, in the which we sayd all their vitailes to remayne whiche were prepared for theyr armye. Colmenaris therfore, sacked the village, and possessed all their vitayles and wyne of sundry colours: likewise tooke the gouernoure thereof prisoner, and hanged hym on the tree in whiche he dwelte hym selfe, com: maundinge hym too bee shotte throwgh with arrowes in the sight of thinhabitantes, and with hym foure other rulers to bee hanged on iebbettes to the exemple of other rebelles. This punyshmente thus executed vppon the conspiratours, strooke the hartes of all thinhabitantes of the prouince wyth suche

S. iii. feare

The con'spi
r tie of the
kynges is de:
tected.

kyng Cemac:
chus, conspy
reth the deth
of Vaschus.

Vaschus pur
seweth the
kynges with
threescore &
ten men.

Colmenaris
sacketh the
Vyllage of Ti
chiri.

Fyue rulers
hanged and
shot throwgh
with arrows.

feare, that there is not nowe a man that dare ftooze his fing
ageynft the wzathe of owre men.   They lyue nowe therefo
quietly: And the other kinges by theyz exemple doo the gla
lyer liue in fubiection, with leffe offence bearinge the po
whyche they can by noo meanes fhake of.

The fyrte booke of the feconde decade
of the fuppofed continente.

Hefe thinges, thus fynyfhed, affemblinge
their company togither they determined w
one confente, that a meffynger fhulde foo
with bee fente to *Hifpaniola* (from whenfe th
haue their lawes and ayde) to declare t
hole ozder of all thefe affayzes, fyzfte to t
admirall and gouernoure of the Jlande, a
afterwarde to the Kinge of Spayne, and to perfuade hym

The golden
regions on
the fouthfide
the moun:
taynes.

fenfe thofe thoufand men which younge *Comogrus* faid to b
expediente to paffe ouer the mountaynes lying betwene th
and the golden regions towarde the Southe. *Vafchus* him fel
dyd greatly affecte this embafage: But neyther woolde t
refpdewe of his felowes electe hym therto, noz his faction
ries fuffer hym to departe: Afwell foz that therby they tho
ght they fhulde bee left defolate, as alfo that they murmur
that if *Vafchus* fhulde once goo from theym, he wolde neuer

The death of
Ualdiuia and
Zamudius.

diuis and *zamudius*, who had byn now abfente fence the moone
of January, in foo muche that they thowght they woolde n
uer coomme ageine. But the matter was otherwife then th
tooke it, as J wyl fhewe in his place. Foz they were perifh.
At the length after many fcrutinies, they elected one Jo

Johannes
Quiced is is
fent to Spain

Quicedus, a graue man well in yeares, & treafourer of the kin
efcheker in thofe pzouinces. They had conceaued a good o
nion of this *Quicedus* that all thynges fhulde bee well bzow
to paffe by his meanes, afwell foz his wyfdome, as alfo t
they were in good hop of his returne, bycaufe he had bzoug
his wiffe with hym to thofe regions, whome he lefte with
felowes foz a pledge of his comminge ageyne. When they
thus elected *Quicedus*, they were ageyne of diuers opinio
whome they might ioyne with hym foz affiftance: Affirmin
th

nat it were a daungerous thinge to committe soo weightye a matter to one mans handes. Not that they mistrusted Quicedus. but bycause the life of man is frayle, and the chaunge of the ayer perelous, especially to theym hauynge nowe of longe time byn accustomed to the temperature nere bnto the Equinoctiall, if they shulde be: compelled to returne to the Northe with alteratiõ of ayer & dyet. They thowght it therfoze good to appoynt a cõpaniõ to Quicedus, that if by chance the one shuld fayl the other might remayne: And that if they both escaped, the king shuld gyue the better credit to the relation of both. After longe consultatiõ therfoze, they chose Rodericus Colmenaris a man of good experience, of who we haue often tymes made mẽcion. For from his youth, he had trauayled ouer al Europe by land and by sea, and was present at the doinges of all thynges in Italy ageynst the Frenchemen : Of whose returne also, they had noo smaule hope bycause he had many fermes and hadde tilled and sowne much grounde in Dariena, by th'increase wher of he might get much gold by sellyng the same to his felows. He lefte therfoze the charge of al his affayres in Dariena, with his partener Alphonsus Nunnex, a Judge of the lawe, who also was lyke to haue byn chosen procuratoure of this byage be fore Colmenaris if one had not put them in remembraunce that he had a wyfe at Matritis : fearyng least beinge ouercoome with her teares, he woolde no moze returne. Colmenaris therfoze, a free man and at libertie being associate assistant with Quicedus they tooke shyppyng togyther in a brigantine, the fourth day of the Calendes of Nouember, in the yeare of Chzist. 1512. In this byage, beinge tossed with sundzy tempestes, they were by the violence of the wynde, cast vppon the Weste coastes of that large Ilande whiche in the fyzste Decade we cau led Cuba, supposed to haue byn fyzme lande. They were soze oppressed with hunger. For it was nowe three moonethes since they departed from theyz felowes. By reason whereof, they were enfozced to take lande to pzoue what ayde they woulde gette amonge the inhabitantes. Theyz chaunce therefore, was to arryue in that part of the Ilande, where Valdiuia was yyuen alande by tempest. But o h yowe wretched men of Dariena? Tary foz Valdiuia whom yowe sent to pzouide to helpe yowre necessities? Pzouyde foz yowre selues rather and trust not to them whose fortune yowe knowe not, For when he ar ryued

Chaunge of the ayer is daungerous.

Rodericus Colmenaris, assistant with Quicedus.

A wyfe is a hynderance

Cuba.

Three mooneths from Dariena to Cuba, by reason of tepest.

The death of Valdiuia.

rpued in Cubs, thinhabitantes flewe him with al his felowes
and lefte the carauell wherin they were caried, tozne in piece
and halfe coucred with fande on the fhoze: where Quicedus an
Colmenaris fyndyng the fragmentes therof, bewayled their fe
lowes mysfoztune. But they founde none of theyz carkefes
fuppofinge that they were eyther dzowned, oz deuoured o
the Canibals, which oftentymes make incurfions into that z
lande to hunte foz men. But at the length, by twoo of the z
lande men which they had taken, they had knowleage of v.
diuis his deftruction: And that thinhabitantes the moze gree
hurt of la-
uyfhence of
the tonge.
dely attempted the fame, foz that they had harde by the bab
lynge of one of his felowes that he had great plentie of gold
Foz they alfo take pleafure in the belotie of gold, which the
forme artificially into fundzy ouches. Thus owre men firp
ken with penfyuenes foz the cruell deftenie of theyz felowes
and in vayne feekynge reuenge foz theyz iniuries, determyne
to forfake that unfoztunate lande, departynge from thofe co
ueteous naked barbarians with moze fozowe and neceffiti
then they were in befoze. Oz euer they had paffed the South
The calami-
tie z death of
Fogeda.
fyde of Cubs, they fel into a thoufande mysfoztunes: and ha
intellygence that Fogeda arryued thereaboute, leadynge a my
ferable lyfe, toffed and turmoyled with tempeftes and vere
with a thoufand perplexities: Soo that departyng from thenfe
maladies z
famen.
almoft alone, his felowes beinge foz the moft parte all confu
med with maladies and famyn, he came with much difficulti
to Hispaniola, where he dyed by force of the poyfon of his vene.
The profpe-
rous vyage
of Ancifus.
mous wound which he had receaued in Vraba as we haue faid
befoze. But Ancisus elected Lieuetenaunt, fayled by all thofe
coaftes with much better foztune. Foz as he hym felfe toulde
me, he founde profperous wyndes in thofe parties, and was
well enterteyned of thinhabitantes of Cuba. But this fpecial-
ly in the dominion of a certeyne kynge whofe name was Commendator. Foz wheras he defyzed of the Chziftian men whiche
A kyng of Cu-
ba baptifed
by the name
of Commen-
dator.
paffed by, to bee baptifed, demaundynge the name of the goz
uernour of the Ilande next unto Hispaniola, beinge a noble man
and a knyght of thozder of Calatrsua of which ozder al are cau
led Commendatores, this kynges defyze was to bee named after
hym. Kynge Commendator therfoze, frendely receaued Ancisus,
and gaue hym greate abundance of al thynges neceffarie. But
Ancifus
what Ancisus lerned of theyz religion durynge the tyme of his
remaynynge

emaynynge there, J haue thowght good to aduertyse yowre
olynes. yowe shall therefore vnderstande, that certeyne of
wre men saylinge by the coastes of Cuba, lefte with kynge
ommendator a certeyne poore maryner beinge diseased. Whoin
orte space recoueringe his health, and hauynge nowe sum-
that lerned theyr language, beganne to growe into great estimation with the kynge and his subiectes, in soo muche that
e was oftentymes the kynges Lieutenaunt in his warres a
eynst other princes his borderers. This mans fortune was
oo good, that all thynges prospered well that he tooke in
ande. And albeit that he were not lernd, yet was he a ver-
tous and well meanynge man accordynge to his knowleage,
nd dyd religiously honoure the blessed virgin, bearynge euer
bout with hym her picture fayre paynted vpon paper glowd
n his apparell nere vnto his breste : Signifyinge vnto the
yng, that this holynes was the cause of al his victories: per-
uadynge hym to doo the lyke, and to cast away all his Zemes
hich were none other then the symilitudes of euyll spirites,
noste cruell enemyes and deuourers of mens soules : And to
ake vnto hym the holy virgin and moother of god to bee his
atronesse if he despysed all his affayres asswell in warre as in
eace to succede prosperously. Also that the blessed virgin
oolde at noo tyme fayle hym, but bee euer redye to helpe hym
nd his, if they woolde with deuoute hartes calle vppon her
ame. The maryner had soone persuaded the naked nation:
Ind there vppon gaue the kynge (who demaunded the same)
is pycture of the virgin, to whom he buylded and dedicate a
hapell and an altare, euer after contemnynge and reiectynge
is Zemes. Of these Zemes made of gossampine cotton to the
imilitudes of spirytes walkynge in the nyght which they of-
entymes see, and speake with them familierly, wee haue spo-
en sufficiently in the nynth booke of the fyrst Decade. Fur-
hermore, accordynge to the institution of this maryner, when
he soonne draweth towarde the faule, this kynge Comnends-
r with all his family bothe men and women, resorte daylye
o the sayde chapell of the virgin Marie, where kneelyng on
heyr knees and reuerently bowyng downe theyr heades, hol-
oynge theyr handes ioyned togyther, they salute thimage of
he virgin with these woordes : Aue Maria, Aue Maria. For fewe
of them can rehearse any more woordes of this prayer. At
Ancisus

A maruelous
historie howe
God wrought
miracles by
the simple
fayth of a
maryner.

Be not rashe
in iudgement

Zemes.

A chapel buil-
ded to the pic-
ture of the
virgin Mary

God respec-
teth the infan-
cie of fa.the
for zeles sake

Ancisus his beinge there, they tooke hym and his felowes b
the handes, and ledde them to this chapell with reioysinge
sayinge that they woolde shewe theym maruelous thynges.

One Religion turned into an other, holdeth styl many thynges of the fyrst.

When they were entered, they poynted with theyr fyngers t
the Image of the virgin altobeset and hanged abowte wit
ouches and iewels and many earthen pottes, fylled sum wit
sundry meates, and sume with water, rownde aboute all th
tabernacle. For these thynges they offer to the image in th
steede of sacrifice, accordynge to theyr owlde superstition t
warde theyr Zemes. Beinge demaunded why they dyd thus
they answered, leaste the image shulde lacke meate if perhap
it shuld be a hungerd. For they most certenly beleue that ima
ges may hunger, and that they doo eate and drynke.

A strange fantasie.

But what ayde and helpe they confesse that they haue had o
the godly poure of this image, that is of the blessed virgin,
is a thynge woorthy to be harde, and most assuredly to bee t
ken for a wunder. For by the report of owre men, there is suc
seruet godly loue & zeale in these simple men toward the hol
virgin, that to them beinge in the daungers of warre agaynt
theyr enemies, they doo in maner (yf I may soo terme it) con

The effect of godly zeale.

pel her to descende from heauen to helpe them in theyr nece
sities. For such is the goodnes of god, that he hath lefte bi
to men in maner a pyece wherby wee may purchase hym wit
his holy angels and sayntes, that is to wytte, burnyng loue
charitie & zeale. Howe therfore can the blessed virgin at an
time be absent fro the which call for her helpe with pure fait
& feruent loue? Commendator him selfe, with al his noble men an
gentlemen, doo testifie with one voyce, that in a fought bat

A miracle in the tyme of the battayle

tayle in the which this maryner was capitayne, bearyng wit
hym this picture of the virgin Marie, the Zemes of theyr ene
mies turned their backes and trembeled in the presence of th
virgins Image and in the syght of them all. For euery of th
brynge theyr Zemes to the battayle, hopynge by theyr help
to obteyne the victorie. ye they say furt her, that duryng th
tyme of the battayle, they sawe not only an Image, but a littl
ly woman clothed in fayre and whyte apparel, aydynge them

The virgin Mary, is present at the battayle.

agaynst theyr enemies: whiche thynge also the enemyes them
selues acknowleaged, confessynge that on the contrary part
shee appeared to them, shakynge a septer in her hande wit
threatenynge countenaunce, whiche caused theyr hartes t

shak

ake and faynt for feare. But after that this maryner depar=
d from them, beinge taken into a shyppe of certeyne Christi=
as passynge by those coastes, Commendator declared that he
ith all his subiectes, continually obserued his institucions:
n soo muche that beinge at contention with an other prince,
hich of theyr Zemes were moste holy and of greateste poure,
e matter growe to suche extremitie that they tryed it with
ande strokes: And that in all these attemptes, the blessed
rgin neuer fayled hym, but was euer presente in the brunte
the battayle, and gaue hym easye victorie with a smaule
ure of men, ageynst a mayne armye of his enemies. Beinge
maunded with what woordes they cryed vppon the birgin
ary when they asayled theyr enemies, they answered that
ey had lerned noo other woordes of the mariners doctrine,
at Sancta Maria adiuua nos, Sancta Maria adiuua nos : That is, holy Ma
helpe vs, holy Marye helpe vs: And this also in the Spa=
nishe tonge. For he had lefte these woordes in the mouthes
all men. Whyle they murthered and destroyed them selues
us on bothe sydes, they fell to entreatie of peace and agre=
to trye the matter, not hande to hande by combatte of cer=
yne chosen for bothe parties as the maner was amonge the
omaynes and dyuers other nations in the owlde tyme, or by
y flyght or policie, but that twoo younge men shulde bee
osen, for eche partie one, with theyr handes bounde fast be=
ynde them in the playne fielde, bothe parties beinge sworne
acknowleage that Zemes to bee the better, which fyrst loo=
d the bandes of the younge man whiche stoode bounde for
e tryall of his religion. Thus diuidinge them selues, and
aceinge the sayde younge men before them in the syght of
em al, with theyr handes fast bounde by theyr enemyes, the
ntrary parte cauled fyrst on theyr Zemes (that is, the deuyll
whose similitude theyr Images are made) who immediatly
opered in his lykenes aboute the younge man that stoode
ounde in the defence of Sathans kyngedome.
ut as soone as Commendator with his coompanye cryed Sancta
nis adiuua nos, Sancta Maria adiuua nos, forthwith there appeared
fayre birgin clothed in whyte, at whose presence the deuell
anquished immediatly. But the birgin hauinge a longe rod
her hande, & putting the same on the bandes of the younge
an that stoode for Commendator, his handes were loosed imme

A maruelus
experience of
fayth

muche lyke
vnto this, is
redde in Reg.
19.
The deuil ap
peareth in
his lykenes

An other miracle.

diatly in the syght of them all, and his bandes founde abou
the handes of hym that stoode for the other partie, in somuc
that they them selues fownde hym dowble bounde. But fo
all this, were not the enemies satisfyed: querelinge that th
thynge was doone by sum slyght or diuise of man, and not b
the poure of the better Zemes. And there vppon requyred fo
thaduoydynge of all suspection, that there myght bee eygh
graue and sage men appoynted, for eche syde foure, which
shulde bynde the men in the syght of them all, and also gy
iudgemente whether the thynge were doone withowte craf
or gyle. Oh pure simplicitie and constant fayth: Oh golde
and blessed confidence. Commendator and his familiers, doubt

Math. 14.

not to graunte theyr enemies theyr requeste with lyke fayth
wherwith the diseased woman obteyned healthe of the flu
of her bludde, and wherby Peter feared not to walke on th
sea at the syght of his master Christe. These younge men th
fore were bounde in the presence of these eight graue men, an
were placed within theyr lystes in the syght of bothe partie
Thus vppon a signe gyuen, when they cauled vppon they

The deuyl appereth agein.

Zemes, there appered in the syght of them all, a deuyll with
longe tayle, a wyde mouthe, greate teeth, and hornes, resen
blynge the similitude of the Image which the kyng being en
mye to Commendator, honoured for his Zemes. As this deuyl a
tempted to loose the bandes of his cliente, the blessed virgi

The virgin Mary ouercommeth the deuyll.

was immediatly presente as before at the cause of Commendat
and his subiectes, and with her todde loased the bandes o
her suppliant, which were agayne lykewyse founde fast tye
aboute the handes of hym that stoode for the contrarye part
The enemies therefore of Commendator, beinge stryken wi
greate feare and amased by reason of this greate miracle, co
fessed that the Zemes of the virgin was better then their Zem
for the better profe wherof, these pagans beinge borthervr

Infidels conuerted by miracle, and baptised.

to Commendator, which had euer before byn at continuall warr
and enmitie with hym, when they had knowleage that Ancis
was arryued in those coastes, they sente ambasadoures vnt
hym, to desyre hym to send them preestes of whom they migh
bee baptised: Where vppon he sent them twoo which hee ha
with hym there at that present. They baptised in one day
hundreth and thirtie of thinhabitantes, sumtyme enemyes t
Commendator, but now his frendes & ioyned with him in aliaunc
a

All suche as came to bee baptised, gaue the preestes of theyr owne liberalitie, eyther a cocke or a henne. But no capons: for they can not yet skyl how to carue theyr cocke chykes to make them capons. Also certeyne salted fysshes, and newe fyne cakes made of theyr breade: likewise certeyne foules franked and made fatte. When the preestes resorted to the shippes, pte of these newe baptysed men accompanied theym laden with vitailes, wherwith they ledde a ioyfull Easter. For on the Sunday two dayes before saynte _Lazarus_ day, they depar= ted from _Dariena_, and touched at that tyme, onely to the cape or angle of _Cuba_ nere vnto the Easte syde of _Hispaniola_. At the requeste of _Commendator_, _Ancisus_ lefte with hym one of his coom= panie, to thintente too teache hym and his subiectes wyth o= ther his bortherers, the salutacion of the angell whiche we caule the _Aue Maria_. For they thinke them selues to be soo much

the more beloued of the blessed virgin, as they can reherse the more wooldes of that prayer. Thus _Ancisus_ takinge his

caue of kynge _Commendator_, directed his course to _Hispaniola_, from whiche he was not farre. Shortely after, he tooke his viage to Spayne, and came to _Valladoleto_ to the kynge, to whom he

made greuous complaint of the insolencie of _Vaschus Nunnes_, in so muche that by his procuremente, the Kynge gaue sentence a= geynste hym. Thus muche haue I thowght good (moste holy father) wherof to aduertyse yowr holynes as concernyng the religiõ of these nations, not only as I haue byn instructed of _Ancisus_ (wyth whom I was dayly couersante in the court and vsed hym familiarlye) but also as I was enformed of dyuers other men of greate autoritie, to thintente that yowre excel= lencie may vnderstande howe docible this kynde of men is, and wyth what facilitie they may bee allured to embrase owr religion. But this can not bee doone soodenlye, yet we haue greate cause to hope that in shorte tyme they wilbe all drawen by litle and litle to the euan gelicall lawe of Chriise, to the great en= crease of his flocke. But let vs nowe returne to the messengers or pro curatours as concernynge the affayres of _Dariena._

The

¶ The seuenth booke of the seconde decade of the supposed continente.

From Dariena to Hispaniola viii. dayes saylyng.

ROM Dariena to Hispaniola is eyghte dayes fa= linge and fumtymes leffe with a profpero wynde. yet Quicedus and Colmenaris the proc ratoursof Dariena, by reafon of tempeftes a: contrary wyndes, coulde fcarfely faile it in hundrethe dayes. When they had taryed fewe dayes in Hispaniola, and had declared t caufe of the comminge to the admirall and the other gouer nours, they tooke shippinge in two marchante shippes beinge redye furnyfshed, which were alfo accuftomed to faile too an froo betwene Spayne and the Ilande of Hispaniola. Th departed from Dariena(as we fayde before)the fourthe day the calendes of nouember in the yeare of Chrift.1512, and cam not to the courte before the calendes of May in the yeare f lowinge beinge the yeare of Chrifte. 1513. At thyr commyng to the courte, Iohannes Fonseca (to whom at the begynnynge t charge of thefe affayres was committed, whom alfo for hy faithful feruice towarde the kinge, ye were holpnes created g nerall commiffarie in the warres agaynfte the moores) recei ued them honorably, as men comminge from the newe worl from naked nations, and landes vnknowen to other menn

The procura= tours of Dari ena, are hono rably recea= ued at the courte.

¶ By the prefermente therefore of the byfshope of Burge Quicedus and Colmenaris were brought before the king, and dec red theyr legacie in his prefence. Suche newes and prefent as they brought, were delectable to the kinge and his nob men, for the newnes and ftraungnes thereof. They alfo fu ned with me often tymes. Theyr countenaunces doo decla the intemperatenes of the ayer and region of Dariena. For th are yelowe lyke vnto them that haue the yelowe gaundice And alfo fwolne. But they afcrybe the caufe hereof, to t hunger which they fufteyned in tyme paft. J haue byn adue tifed of tha fayres of this newe wooldde, not onely by the procuratours of Dariena, and Ancifus, and Zamudius, but alfo t conference with Bacois the lawier, who ranne ouer a grea parte of thofe coaftes. Likewyfe by relation of Vincentius An the patrone of the shippes, and Alfonsus Nignus, both being me of greate experience and wel trauayled in thofe parties, befi ma

Their copler tion is altered

Of whomthe autour had information

any other, of whom wee haue made mention in other places
or there came neuer any from thense to the court, but tooke
great pleasure to certifie mee of al thynges eyther by woozde
of mouth oz by wzytynge. Of many thynges therfoze which
lerned of them, I haue gathered suche as to my Iudgemēt
seme moste woorthy to satiffie them that take delyte in hyffo=
ries. But let vs nowe declare what folowed after the com=
inge of the pzocuratours of Dariena. Therfoze, befoze theyz
tyuall there was a rumoure spzeade in the courte, that the
iefe gouernoures and Lieuctenauntes Nicuefa and Fogeda, al=
Iohannes De la Cofſa (a man of such reputacion that by the kyn=
s letters patentes he was named the greate maffer of the
nges ſhippes) were all peryſhed by mifchaunce: And that
oſe fewe which yet remayned alyue in Dariena, were at con=
ncion and difcozde amonge them ſelues: So that they ney=
er endeuoured theyz diligence to allure thofe ſimple natiōs
owre faythe, noz yet had regarde to fearche the natures of
oſe Regions. In confideracion wherof, the kynge was de=
rmyned to ſende a newe capitayne thyther whiche ſhulde re=
c and ſet all thynges in good ozder, and put them owte of
toritie whiche hadde vfurped thempire of thofe pzouinces
thowte the kynges fpeciall commaundement. To this of=
e, was one Petrus Arias afligned, a man of greate prowes
d a citifen of Segouia. But when the pzocuratours of Dariena
d publiſhed in the courte howe greate a matter it was, and
what moment, many laboured ernefſly to the kyng, to take
e office owte of his handes. But the byſſhop of Burges be=
ge the kynges chiefe chaplayne, and one of the commiffio=
rs appoynted by hym in thefe matters, beinge aduertifed
reof, came immediatly to the kynge, and fpake to hym in
is effect. May it pleaſe powre hyghnes to vnderfſand (moſt
tholyke pzince) that wheras Petrus Arias a man of valiente
age and greate feruice, hath offered hym felfe to aduenture
s lyfe in powre maiefties affayzes, vnder vncerteyne hope of
yne and moſte certeyne perels, yet that notwithfſandynge
m other haue ambitiouſly maliced his felicitie and pzefermēt
bouringe foz thoffice wherto he is elected: It maye pleafe
wre grace herein foo to ſhewe hym powr fauour and permit
m to enioye his fayde office, as powre maieftie doo knowe
m to bee a woorthy and meete man foz the fame, hauyng in
tyme

The greate
maſter of the
kynges ſhips

Petrus arias
is elected go=
uernour of
Dariena.

Thoracion of
the byſhop.
of Burges in
the defence
of petrus ari
as.

tyme paste had greate experience of his prowesse and valian
nesse, aswell in behauinge hym selfe as orderinge his sould
ers, as yowr hyghnes may the better consyder if it shal pleas
yowe to caule to remembrance his doinges in the warres of A
phrica, where he shewed hym selfe bothe a wyse Capitayne
and valient souldier. As concerninge his maners and vsage
other wayes, they are not vnknowen to yowre maiestie, vn
der whose wynge he hath of a chylde byn browght vp in th
courte, and euer founde faythfull towarde yowre hyghnesse
Wherfore, to declare my opinion vnder yowre graces fauou
(whom it hath pleased to appoynt me a commissioner in thes
affayres) I thinke it were vngodly that he shuld bee put fron
his office at the sute of any other, especially beinge there
moued by ambition and couetousnes: who perchaunce wool
proue them selues to be the same men in the office if they sha
obteyne it, as they nowe shewe them selues in the ambitiou
desirynge of the same. When the byshoppe had sayde thes
woordes, the kynge confirmed the election of Petrus Arias i
more ample maner then before: wyllynge the byshoppe to ap
poynt hym a thousande and twoo hundreth souldiers at hi
charges, makynge hym a warrante to thofficers of his esche
ker to delyuer hym money in preste for the same purpose. Pe
trus Arias therfore beinge thus put in office and authorysed b
the kynges letters patentes vnder his brode seale, chose
greate number of his souldiers in the court, and soo departe
frome Valladoleto aboute the calendes of October in the year
1513: And sayled fyrst to Ciuile beinge a verye ryche citie an
well replenyshed with people: where by the kynges magistra
tes he was furnyshed with men and vytayles and other nece
saries perteynynge to soo greate a matter. For the king hat
in this citie erected a house seruinge only for thaffayres of th
Occean, to the which al they that goo or coome from the new
landes and Ilandes, resorte to gyue accomptes aswell wha
they cary thyther as what they brynge from thense, that th
kynge may bee truly answered of his custome of the fyfte par
bothe of golde and other thynges as wee haue sayde before
This house, they caule the house of the Contractes of Indi
Petrus Arias founde in Ciuile aboute twoo thousand younge me
which made great sute to goo with hym: lykewyse noo smal
number of couetous owlde men: of the whiche, many offere
the

The warres of Aphrica.

Petrus Arias Lieuetenante of Dariena.

Petrus Arias hath a thousand & twoo hundreth men appoynted at the kynges charges.

A house in Ciuile appoynted to the affayres of India.

Perularia.

hem selues to goo with him of theyr owne charges withowt
he kynges stipende. But leste the shippes shulde bee pestered
oith to great a multitude, oz leaft bytayles shulde fayle them,
he libertie of free passage was restraynt. It was also decre=
o that noo stranger might passe withowt the kynges licence.
oherfoze J doo not a lyttle maruaile at Aloisius Cadamustus a be
etian and wzyter of the Poztugales byages, that he was
ot ashamed to wzyte thus of the Spanyardes nauigations :
oe went : we sawe : we dyd. Wheras he neuer went, not any
Jenetian sawe. But he stoule certeyne annotacions owte of
he thzee first bookes of my fyzst Decade wzytten to Cardinal
scanius and Arcimboldus, supposinge that J woolde neuer haue
ublysshed the same. It myght also happen that he came by
ye copie therof at the hande of sum ambasadoure of Uenice.
foz J haue graunted the copie to many of them, and was not
aungerous to fozbyd them to comunicate the same to other.
Jowe so euer it bee, this honeste man Aloisius Cadamustus feared
ot to chalenge vnto hym the frute of an other mans laboure.
Of the inuentions of the Poztugales (which surely are woon
erfull) whether he haue wzytten that whiche he hath seene
as he sayth) oz lykewise bereaued other men of the iuste com=
nendacions of theyr trauayles, J wyll not iudge, but am con
ent to let hym lyue after his maner. Emonge the company of
hese souldiers, there were none embarked but suche as were
icenced by the kynge, except a fewe Italians, Genues, who
y frendshippe and sute were admitted foz the Admirals sake
ounge Colonus, sonne and heyze to Christopherus Colonus the fyzst
ynder of those landes. Petrus Ariss therfoze tooke shippyng in
he ryuer Betis (nowe cauled Guadalqueuir) runnyng by the citie of
Siuile, aboute the beginnynge of the yeare of Chziste. 1514.
But he loosed anker in an euyll houre. Foz suche a tempeste
olowed shoztly after his departure, that it rent in pieces two
f his shippes, and soo tossed the other that they were enfoz=
ced to heaue ouer boozde parte of theyr bytayles to lyghten
hem. All such as escaped, sayled backe ageyne to the coastes
of Spayne : where, beinge newely furnysshed and refreshed, by
he kynges officers, they went fozwarde on theyr viage. The
naster pylot of the gouernoures shyppe, was Johannes Vesputius a
Floentine, the neuie of Americus Vesputius, who lefthym as it
were by discente of inheritance, thexperience of the mariners
　　　　　　　　U.i.　　　　　　facul

Many profe them selues to go of they owne char= ges.

Aloisius Ca= damustus is reproued.

The poztu gales inuen tions.

The nauiga= tio of Petrus Arias.

A shipwracke

Americus Vespu tius.

facultie, and knowleage of the sea, carde and compasse. B
wee were aduertised of late by certeyne which came from H
pæniolæ, that they had paſſed the Ocean with moꝛe pꝛoſpero
wynde. Foꝛ this marchaunt ſhyppe commynge from *Hiſpanic*
founde them landinge at certeyne Jlandes nere there about
But in the meane tyme whyle my impoꝛtunate caulers on, G
leſceus Butrigarius and *Iohannes Curſius*, men ſtudious by al meane
to gratifie yowꝛe holynes, ceaſed not to put me in rememb
rance that they had one in a redines to depart into Jtaly, an
caryed onely to cary with hym vnto yowꝛe holynes theſe n
fayꝛe *Nereides* althowgh rudely decked, leaſteJ ſhulde beſto
muche tyme in vayne, J haue let paſſe many thynges, & wy
reherſe onely ſuch as ſeeme in my iudgement moſte wooꝛth
memoꝛy, althowgh ſumwhat diſoꝛdered as occaſion hath ſ

A notable ex:
emple of a va
lient woman. ued. So it is therfoꝛe that this *Petrus Ariâs* hath a wyfe name
Heliſabeth à Boadillâ, beinge niefe by the bꝛoothers ſyde to th
marques of *Boadillâ*, which rendered the citie of *ſegouis* to F
nando and Heliſabeth pꝛinces of Spayne at ſuch tyme as t
Poꝛtugales inuaded the kingdome of Caſtile: by reaſon wh
of they were encoꝛaged fyꝛſte to reſyſte, and then with ope

kynge Henry. warre to aſſayle and expulſe the Poꝛtugales foꝛ the great tr
ſure which kynge Henry bꝛother to queene Heliſabeth hadd
gathered togyther there. This marqueſſe whyle ſhe lyued
dyd euer ſhewe a manly and ſtoute mynde, bothe in peace an
warre, ſo that by her counſayle manye noble thynges wer
bꝛowght to good effecte in Caſtile: vnto this noble woman
the wyfe of *Petrus Ariâs* was niefe by her bꝛothers ſyde. Sh
folowyng the magnanimitie of her aunt, perceauinge her hu
bande nowe furnyſhyng hym ſelfe to depart to the vnknowe
coaſtes of the newe wooꝛlde, and thoſe large tractes of land

The wyfe of
Petrus Ariâs and ſea, ſpake theſe woꝛdes vnto hym. My moſte deare an
welbeloued huſbande, we owght not nowe to foꝛget that fr
owꝛe younge yeares we haue byn ioyned togyther with th
yoke of holy matrimonie to thintente that wee ſhulde ſoo lyu
togyther and not a ſunder durynge the tyme of owꝛe natura
lyfe. Wherefoꝛe foꝛ my parte to declare my affection herein
yowe ſhall vnderſtande, that whyther ſo euer yowꝛe fatal de
ſtenye ſhall dꝛyue yowe, cyther by the furious waues of th
greate Ocean, oꝛ by the manyfoulde and hoꝛrible daungers o
the lande, J wyll ſurely beare yowe coompany, There can n
per

perell chaunce to me so terrible, noz any kynde of death so cru
ell, that shal not bee much easyer foz me to abyde, then to liue
so farre seperate from powe. It were muche better foz me to
dye, and eyther to bee cast into the sea to bee deuoured of the
syshes, oz on the lande to the Canibales, then with continuall mournynge and bewaylinge, to lyue in deathe and dye lyuinge, whyle I consume in lookyng rather foz my husbandes
letters then foz hym selfe. This is my full determinacion, not
rashely noz presentely excogitate, noz conceaued by the lyght
phantasie of womans bzayne, but with longe deliberatiō and
good aduisement. Nowe therfoze choose to whether of these
twoo powe wyll assente : Eyther to thzuste powre swoozde in
my thzote, oz to graunte me my requeste. As foz the chyldzen
which god hath giuen vs as pledges of owr inseperable loue,
(foz they had foure sonnes and as many dowghters) shal not
stay me a moment. Let vs leaue vnto them suche gooddes and
possessions as haue byn left vs by owre parentes and frendes
wherby they may lyue amonge the woozshipful of theyz ozder.
Foz other thynges I take no care. When this noble matrone
of manly vertue had fynisshed these woozdes, her husbande
seinge the constant mynde of his wyfe, and her in a redynes to
doo accozdynge to her woozdes, had no hart to denye her lo-
uinge peticion : but embzasinge her in his armes, commended
her intente and consented to her requeste. Shee folowed hym
therfoze as dyd *Ipsicratea* her *Mithridates* with her heare hange-
inge loose aboute her shulders. Foz shee loueth her husbande
as dyd *Halicarnassea* of *Caria*, hers beinge deade, and as dyd *Ar-
temisia* her *Mausolus*: We haue also had aduertisemēt sence their
departure that she (being bzowght vp as it were amonge soft
fethers) hath with noo lesse stoute cozage susteyned the rozin-
ges and rages of the Ocean, then dyd eyther her husband oz
any of the maryners bzought vp euen amonge the surges of
the sea. But to haue sayde thus much hercof, this shal suffice.
Let vs nowe speake of other thynges no lesse woozthy memo
rie.   Therfoze, whereas in the fyzst Decade we haue made
mencion of *Vincentius Annex Pinxonus*, ye shal vnderstande that he
accoompanyed *Christophorus Colonus* the Admirall in his fyzst vyage, and afterwarde made an other vyage of his owne charges with onely one shyppe. Ageyne, the fyzste yeare after the
departinge of the Capitaynes *Nicuesa* and *Fogeda*, he ran ouer

The thyrde nauigation of Vincentius Pinzonus.

those coastes from Hispaniola, and searched all the southe syde of Cuba from the Easte to the weste, and sayled rownde about that Ilande which to that day for the greate length thereof, was thowght to haue bin parte of the continent or firme land, althowgh sume other say that they dyd the lyke. Vincentius An=nex therfore, knowyng nowe by experience that Cuba was an Ilande, sayled on further, and found other landes westward from Cuba, but such as the Admirall had fyrst touched. Wherfore, beinge in maner encompased with this newe lande, turninge his course towarde the leftehande, and rasing the coastes of that lande by the East, ouerpassinge also the mouthes of the goulfes of Beragua, Vraba, and Cuchibachos, he arryued at the Region which in the fyrst Decade we cauled Paria and Os Draconis: And entered into the greate goulfe of freshe water, which Colonus discouered, beinge replenished with great abundance of fysshe, and famous by reason of the multitude of Ilandes lyinge in the same, beinge distant Eastwarde from Cu=riana aboute a hundreth and thirtie myles, in the which tract are the Regions of Cumana and Manacapana, whiche also in the syxte booke of the fyrst Decade we sayde to bee Regions of the large prouince of Paria, where many affirme to bee the greateste plentie of the beste pearles, and not in Curiana.

Cuba.

Beragua. Vraba. Cuchibachos. Paria. Os Draconis

Curiana, Cumana. Manacapana,

Plentie of Pearles.

The kinges of these regions (whom they caul Chiscones, as they of Hispaniola caule theym Cacici) beinge certified of the comminge of owre men, sente certeyne spyes to enquire what newe nation was arryued in theyr coastes, what they browght, and what they woolde haue: and in the meane tyme furnysshed a number of theyr Canoas (whiche they caule Chichos) with men armed after their maner. For they were not a lytle astonisshed to beholde owre shippes with the sayles spreade, wheras they vse no sayles, nor can vse but smaule ons if they woolde, by reason of the narowones of theyr canoas. Swarmynge therfore aboute the shippe with theyr canoas (which we may well caule Monoxyla, bycause they are made of one hole tree,) they feared not to shute at owr men beinge yet within their ships and keepinge theym selues vnder the hatches as safely as yf they had byn defended with stone waulles. But when owre men had shotte of certeyne pieces of ordinance ageynst theym they were soo discomfited with the noyse and slawghter therof that they droue them selues to flight. Beinge thus dispat=cled

Monoxyla. The Barbarians a sayle owre men beinge in theyr shyppes.

The vse of gunnes.

eled, oure men chased them with the ſhippe bote, tooke many, and ſlewe many. When the kynges harde the noyſe of the gunnes, and were certyfied of the loſſe of their men, they ſent ambaſadours to *Vincentius Agnes* to entreate of peace, fearinge the ſpoyle of theyr goodes and deſtruction of theyr people, if oure men ſhulde coomme alande in theyr wrathe and furye. They deſyred peace therfore, as could bee coniectured by their ſignes and poyntinges: For oure men vnderſtoode not one woorde of theyr language. And for the better prooffe that they deſired peace, they preſented oure men with thre thouſand of thoſe weights of gold that the Spanyardes caule *Caſtellanum Aureum*, which they commonly caule *Peſum*. Also a greate barell of woodde full of moſte excellente maſculine frankenſence, weighing about two thouſande and ſyxe hundreth poundes weight after eight ounces to the pounde : Whereby they knewe that that lande browght furthe greate plentie of frankenſence. For there is noo entercourſe of marchaundies betwene thinhabitantes of *Paria* and the Sabeans beinge ſoo farre diſtante, wheras alſo the of *Paria* kñowe nothynge with oure theyr owne coaſtes. With the golde and frankenſence whiche the preſented to oure men, they gaue them alſo a greate multitude of theyr peacockes, bothe cockes and hennes, deade and alyue, aſwell to ſatiſfie theyr preſent neceſſitie, as alſo to cary with theym into Spayne for encreaſe. Lykewyſe certeyne carpettes, coouerlettes, table clothes and hanginges made of goſſampine ſilke fynelye wrought after a ſtraunge diuiſe with pleſante & variable coloures, hauing golden belles & ſuche other ſpangles and pendauntes as the Italians caule *Sonaglios*, and the Spanyardes *Caſcaueles*, hanging at the purſes therof. They gaue theym furthermore ſpeakinge popingiais of ſundry colours as many as they woolde aſke. For in *Paria*, there is no leſſe plentie of popingiais, then with vs of Doues or ſparous. Thinhabitantes of theſe Regions both men and women are appareled with veſtures made of goſſampine cotten, the men to the knees, and the women too the calfe of the legge. The faſhion of theyr apparell, is ſymple and playne muche like vnto the Turkes. But the mens, is double and quilted like that whiche the Turkes vſe in the warres. The princes of *Paria*, are rulers but for one yeare: But their autoritie is noo leſſe emonge the people both in peace and warre, then

Great abundance of gold and frankenſence.

Olibanum,

Sabea, is a contrey in Arabie, which bringethfouth frankenſence *Paria.*

peacockes which, wee caule Turkye cockes.

Carpets and couerlettes fynely wrought.

popyngayes.

Thapparell of the inhabitantes of paria

Rulers for one yeare.

The greate goulfe of paria.

is thautoritie of other kynges in those Regions. Theyr villages are buylded in coompasse, along by the bankes of all that greate goulfe. Fyue of theyr princes came to owre men wyth theyr presentes, whose names I thowght worthy to bee put in this historie in remembrance of soo notable a thinge Chiscco⸗nus Chisuaccha, (that is the prince of Chiauccha, for they caule prin⸗ces or kinges Chiaconos) Chiaconus Pintiguanus, Chiaconus Chamailaba, Chiaconus Polomus, and Chiaconus Potto. The goulfe beinge fyrste founde of the admirall Colonus, they caule Baia Natiuitatis, bycause

Baia Natiuitatis the gret goulfe of paria.

he entered into the same in the day of the natiuitie of Christe: But at that tyme he only passed by it withowte anye further searching, and Baia in the Spanysshe tong, signifieth a goulfe. When Vincentius had thus made a league with these Princes,

Uincentius maketh a league with v. princes. of paria.

folowinge his appoynted course, he founde many regions to⸗warde the East, desolate by reason of diuers fluddes and ouer flowynges of waters: also many standynge pooles in dyuers places, and those of excedynge largenes. He ceased not to fo⸗lowe this tracte vntyll he came to the poynte or cape of that

Mount Atlas in aphrike.

moste longe lande. This poynte semethe as though it woolde inuade the monte Atlas in Aphrica. For it prospectethe towarde that parte of Aphrike, whiche the portugales caule Caput Bonæ Sperantiæ. The poyntes or capes of the mount Atlas, are rough and saluage nere vnto the sea. The cape of Bona Speranza, ga⸗therethe thirtie and foure degrees of the Southe pole, cauled the pole antartike: But that poynte, onely seuen degrees. I suppose this lande to bee that, whiche I fynde in owlde wry⸗

The great I⸗land atlantike

ters of Cosmographie to bee cauled the greate Iland Atlan⸗tike, withowt any further declaringe eyther of the sytuation, or of the nature therof.

❡ The eight booke of the seconde decade of the supposed continente.

Contention betwene the Castilians & Portugales for the newe landes

Hen Johan the king of portugale lyued which was predicessoure to hym that nowe reigneth, there arose a great contention betwene the Cas⸗tilians and Portugales as concerninge the do⸗minion of these newe founde landes. The Por⸗tugales, bycause they were the firste that durst atte............Ocean sea sence the memorie of man, affirmed

affirmed that all the nauigations of the Ocean, ought to pertepne to theym onely. The Caftilians argued on the contrarie parte, that what fo euer god by the miniftratió of nature hath created on the earth, was at the begynnynge common emong men: And that it is therfore lawfull to euery man to poffeffe fuche landes as are voyd of Chriftian inhabitours. Whyle the matter was thus vncertepnly debated, bothe parttes agreed that the controuerfie fhulde bee decerned by the byffhope of Rome, and plighted faithe to ftande to his arbitrimente. The kyngedome of Caftile was at that tyme gouerned by that great Queene Helifabeth with her hufbande: for the roialme of Caftile was her dowerye. Shee alfo and the kynge of Portugale, were cofyn germaynes of two fyfters: by reafon wher of the diffention was more eafely pacified. By thaffent therfore of both parties, Alexander the byffhop Rome, the .vi. of that name, by thautorite of his leaden bull, drewe a right line from the North to the South a hundreth leaques weftwarde withowte the paralelles of thofe Ilandes whiche are cauled Caput Viride or Cabouerde, Within the compafe of this lyne (although foomme denye it) faulethe the poynte of this ilande wherof we haue fpoken, which they caule Caput Sancti Auguftini, otherwyfe cauled Promontorium Sancti Auguftini, that is, faynt Auguftines cape or poynte. And therfore it is not lawful for the Caftilians to faften foote in the beginnynge of that lande. Vincentius Annex therfore, departed from thenfe, beinge aduertifed of thinhabitantes, that on the other fyde of the hyghe mountaynes towarde the South, lyinge before his eyes, there was a Region cauled Ciamba, which browght foorth greate plentie of golde. Of certeyne captiues whiche he tooke in the goulfe of Paria (which certenly perteyneth to the dominion of Caftile) he browght fume with hym to Hifpaniola, and lefte them with the younge Admirall to lerne owre languáge. But he hym felfe, repayzed to the courte to make erneft fute to the kynge that by his fauoure, he myght bee gouernour of the Iland of Sancti Iohannis (otherwyfe cauled Burichena, beinge diftante from Hifpaniola onely .xxv. leaques) bycaufe he was the fyrft fynder of golde in that Ilande. Before Vincentius made fute for this office, one Don Chriftopher a Portugale, the foonne of the countie of Camigna, was gouernoure of the Ilande: whom the Canibales of the other Ilandes flewe, with all the Chriftian men

The byffhop of Rome diuideth the land

Cabouerde loke decade i. lib. iii

The golden region of Ciamba.

The Iland of S. Iohannes

men that were in the same, excepte the byshop and his familiers, which fledde and shyfted for them selues, forsakynge the church and all the ornamentes thereof. For yowre holynes hath consecrated fyue byshoppes in these Ilandes at the request of the most catholyke kynge. In *Sancto Dominico* being the chiefe citie of *Hispaniola*, *Garsia de Padilla*, a reguler fryer of the order of saynt Fraunces, is byshop. In the towne of Conception, Doctor *Petrus Xuarex* of *Deza*: And in the Ilande of saynte John or *Burichena*, *Alfonsus Mensus* a licenciate, beinge bothe obseruantes of thinstitucion of saynt Peter. The fourth, is fryer Barnarde of *Mesa*, a man of noble parentage, borne in *Toledo*, a preacher, and byshop of the Ilande of *Cuba*. The fyfte is *Iohannes Cabedus*, a fryer preacher, whom yowre holynes annoynted mynister of Christ, to teache the Christian faithe amonge the inhabitantes of *Dariena*. The Canibales shall shortely repent them, and the bludde of owre men shalbe reuenged: And that the sooner, bycause that shortly after they had committed this abhominable slaughter of owre men, they came ageyne from theyr owne Ilande of *Sancta Crux* (otherwyse called *AyAy*) to the Ilande of *Sancti Iohannis*. and slewe a kynge whiche was a frende to owre men, and eate hym and all his famely, vtterly subuertinge his vyllage, vppon this occasion that violatinge the lawe of hostage, he had slayne seuen Canibales whiche were lefte with hym by composicion to make certeyne canoas, bicause the Ilande of *Sancti Iohannis* beareth greater trees and apter for that purpose, then doth the Ilande of *Sancti Crux* the chiefe habitacion of the Canibales. These Canibales yet remaynynge in the Ilande, certeine of owre men saylinge from *Hispaniola*, chaunced vppon them. The thynge being vnderstode by thinterpretoures, owre men quarelynge with theym and caulynge them to accompte for that mischeuous drede, they immediatly directed theyr bowes and venemous arrowes agaynst them, and with cruell countenaunces threatened the to bee quyet, least it shulde repent them of theyr commyng thyther. Owre men fearynge theyr venemous arrowes (for they were not prepared to fyght) gaue them signes of peace. Being demaunded why they destroyed the vyllage, and where the kynge was with his famelye, they answered that they rased the vyllage and cutte the kynge with his famelie in peeces & eate them in the reuenge of theyr seuen woorkemen: And that

they

Fyue byshoppes of the Iland made by the byshop of Rome.

The Canibales of the Iland of Sancta Crux.

they had made faggottes of theyr bones to cary theim to the
wyues and chyldzen of theyr flayne woozkemen, in wytnesse
that the bodyes of theyr hufbandes and parentes lay not vnre-
reuenged: and therewith shewed the faggottes of bones to
owre men: who beinge aftonyshed at theyr fiercenes and crueltie, were enfozced to diffimble the matter and houlde theyr
peace, quarelynge noo further with them at that tyme. Thefe
and fuche other thynges doo dayly chaunce, the which I doo
let passe leaft I shulde offende the eares of yowr holynes with
fuche bluddy narrations. Thus haue wee fufficiently digreffed from the regions of *Beragua* and *Vraba* beinge the chiefeffe
foundations of owre purpose. Wee wyll nowe therefore entreate fumewhat of the largenes and depthe of the ryuers of
Vraba: Alfo declare bothe what they and the landes whiche
they runne thzough doo bzynge foozth: lykewife of the greatnes of the lande from the Eafte to the Weft, and of the bzedth
therof from the Southe to the Nozth, and what theyr opinion and hope is of thynges yet vnknowen in the fame. Wee
wyll therfoze beginne at the newe names wherwith the Spanyardes haue named thefe prouinces fence they were vnder
the dominions of the Chziftians.

❧ The nynth booke of the feconde Decade, of the fuppofed Continent.

Eragua therfoze, they cauled *Caftella Aurea*, that
is golden Caftile: And *Vraba* they named *An-
daluzia Noua*, that is, newe Andalufia. And
lyke as of many Ilandes which they fubdu-
ed, they choofe *Hifpaniola* foz the chiefe place
of theyr habitacion, foo in the large tract of
Paria, they appoynted theyr coloine oz bydyng
place in the twoo regions of *Vraba* and *Beragua*, that all fuche
as attempte any vyages in thofe coaftes, may refozte to them
as to fafe poztes to bee refreshed when they are wery oz dzyuen to neceffitie. All owre feedes, and plantes, do nowe maruelously encreafe in *Vraba*. Lykewyfe blades, fettes, flippes,
graffes, fuger canes, and fuche other as are bzought from o-
ther places to thofe regions, as also beaftes and foules as we
haue fayde befoze. O maruelous frutefulnes. Twentie dayes

The frutful nes of Dariena.

after the feede is fowne, they gather rype cucumers, and fuch lyke, But colwortes, beetes, Letufe, Borage are rype within the fpace of ten dayes. Gourdes, melones, and pompones, within the fpace of .xxviii. dayes. *Dariena* hathe many natiue trees and frutes of dyuers kyndes with fundry taftes, & holfome for the vfe of mē: of the which I haue thowght it good to defcrybe certeyne of the beft. They noozyThe a tree which

Dyuers holfomy frutes of trees.

Guaiana,

they caule *Guaiana*, that beareth a frute much refemblynge the kynde of citrons which are commonly cauled limones, of tafte fumwhat fharpe myxt with fwetenes. They haue alfo abundance of nuttes of pynetrees, and great plentie of date trees,

pine trees.

Date trees.

whiche beare frutes bygger then the dates that are knowen to vs : but they are not apte to bee eaten for theyr to much forwetnes. Wylde and haven date trees, growe of them felues in fundry places, the branches wherof they vfe for biefommes, and eate alfo the buddes of the fame. *Guarauana*, being big ice

Guarauana

and bygger then the orange tree, bringeth furth a great frute as bygge as pome citrons.

Ther is an other tree much lyke to a cheftnut tree whofe frute is lyke to the bygger fort of fyge, beinge holfome & of plefant tafte. *Mameis*, is an other tree that bringeth foorthe frute as

Mameis,

bygge as an orange, in tafte nothynge inferioure to the beft kyndes of melones. *Guananala*, beareth a frute leffe then any of

Guananala.

the other, but of fweete fauoure lyke fpice, and of delectable tafte. *Houos*, is an other tree whofe frute bothe in fhape and

Houos.

tafte, is much lyke to prunes, but fumwhat bygger. They are furely perfuaded that this is the *Myrobalane* tree. Thefe growe

Mirobalani, hogges fed with mirobalanes

foo abundantely in *Hifpaniola*, that the hogges are fedde with the frute therof as with mafte amonge vs. The hogges lyke this kynde of feadynge foo well, that when thefe frutes war rype, the fwyneherdes can by no meanes keepe them owte of the wooddes of thefe trees : by reafon wherof, a greate multytude of them are become wylde. They alfo affirme, that in

Swynes fleffhe of better taft and more holfum then mutton.

Hifpaniola, fwynes fleffhe is of much better tafte and more holfome then mutton. For it is not to bee doubted, but that dyuers kyndes of meates do engender fundry taftes and qualities in fuche as are norysfhed therwith. The mofte puiffaunte prince *Ferdinandus*, declared that he had eaten of an other frute browght from thofe landes, beinge full of fcales with keyes much lyke a pine apple in forme and colour, but in tendernes equal to melopepones, and in tafte exceedyng al garden frutes.

foz it is noo tre, but an herbe much lyke vnto an archichoke, oz Acantho. The kynge hym selfe, gaue the cheefest commenda tion to this. J haue eaten none of these frutes. foz of a great number which they bzowght from thense, only one remayned bncozrupted, the other being putrified by reason of the longe byage. All suche as haue eaten of theym newely gathered in theyz natyue soyle, doo maruelously commende theyz swete nes and pleasaunt taste. They dygge also owte of the ground certeyne rootes growynge of them selues, whiche they caule Betatas, much lyke vnto the nauie rootes of Mylayne, oz the greate puffes oz musherons of the earth. Howe soo euer they bee dzessed, eyther fryed oz sodde, they gyue place to noo such kynde of meate in pleasaunt tendernes. The skyn is sumwhat towgher then eyther of nauies oz mushero:ms, and of earthy coloure: But the inner meate therof, is verye whyte. These are noozysshed in gardens, as we sayde of Iucca in the fyzste Decade. They are also eaten rawe, and haue the taste of rawe chestnuttes, but are sumwhat sweeter. Wee haue spoken suf ficiently of trees, herbes, and frutes. Wee wyll nowe there foze entreate of thynges sencitiue. The laundes and desolate pastures of these regions, are inhabited and deuoured of wild and terrible beastes, as Lions, Tygers, and such other mon sters as we nowe knowe, and haue byn descrybed of owlde au toures in tyme past. But there is especially one beast engende red here, in which nature hath endeuoured to shewe her cun nyng. This beaste is as bygge as an oxe, armed with a longe snoute lyke an Elephant, and yet no Elephant. Of the colour of an oxe and yet noo oxe. With the howse of a hozse, and yet noo hozse. With eares also much lyke vnto an Elephant, but not soo open noz soo much hangyng downe: yet much wyder the the eares of any other beaste. Of the beast which beareth her whelpes about with her in her seconde belly as in a purse (beinge knowen to none of the owlde wzyters) J haue spoke in the fyzst Decade which J doubte not to haue coome to the handes of powre holynes. Let vs nowe therfoze declare what resteth of the fluddes and ryuers of Vraba. The ryuer of Dariena fawleth into the goulfe of Vraba with a narowe chanel, scarsly able to beare the canoas oz lyghters of that prouince, and run neth by the vyllage where they chose theyz dwellynge place. But the ryuer in the cozner of the goulfe which we sayde that

X, ii, Gratyus

(marginal notes)

Frutes putri fyed on the sea.

Betatas.

Lions and Tygers.

A straunge beast.

The ryuers of Uraba.

The ryuer of Dariena fau leth into the goulfe of Uraba.

A league is
xxiiii furlõges

Vaschus passed by, they found to bee. xxiiii. furlonges in bꝛedth (which they caule a league) and of exceadynge depthe, as of twoo hundꝛeth cubettes, faulynge into the goulfe by dyuers mouthes. They say that this ryuer fauleth into the goulfe of

Danubius.

Vraba, lyke as the ryuer *Ister* (otherwyse cauled *Danubius,* and Danowe) fauleth into the sea Pontike, and *Nilus* into the sea of Egypte: wherfoꝛe they named it *Grandis,* that is great: whi

Grandis oꝛ
Rio grandis
A crocodile is
much lyke an
eute, but of
exceadyng big
nes.
The autoure
of this booke
was in Egipt
The riuer Ni
lus in Egypte
Montes,
Lunæ.

che also they affirme to nooꝛyphe many and great Crocodyles, as the owld wꝛyters testifie of *Nilus,* and especially as I haue lerned by experience, hauinge sayled vp and downe the ryuer of *Nilus* when I was sent ambasadoure to the Soldane of Al cayꝛ at the commaundement of the moste cath'olyke kynge. What I may therfoꝛe gather owte of the wꝛytynges of so ma ny lerned autours as concerninge the ryuer of *Nilus,* I knowe not. Foꝛ they say that nature hath gyuen two riuers of that name to water the lande, whether they wyll them to spꝛynge owte of the mountaynes of the moone oꝛ the soonne, oꝛ owte of the toppes of the rowgh mountaines of *Ethiopia:* Affirming one of the same to faule into the goulfe of Egypte towarde the Noꝛthe, and the other into the South Ocean sea. What shall wee saye in this place? Of that *Nilus* in Egypte, there is noo doubte. The Poꝛtugales also which'e sayle by the coastes of

The portuga
les nauigaci:
ons.

the Ethiopians cauled *Nigritæ,* and by the kyngedome of *Me lindæ* passinge vnder the Equinoctiall lyne, amonge theyꝛ mir uclous inuentions haue founde an other towarde the South, and ernestly affirme the same to bee also deriued frõ the moun taynes of the moone: And that it is an other chanell of *Nilus,* bycause it bꝛyngeth fooꝛth Crocodyles, whereas it hathe not

The ryuer
Senega, an o
ther chañell
of the ryuer
of Nilus.

byn reade befoꝛe tyme that any other ryuer nooꝛysshed Croco dyles sauinge onely *Nilus.* This ryuer, the Poꝛtugales caule *Senega.* It runneth thꝛowgh the Region of the *Nigritas,* beinge very frutefull towarde the noꝛth shoꝛe: but on the southe syde

Crocodiles.
The thyꝛde ꝛ
fourth Nilus.
Delagattos.

sandie and rowghe. Crocodiles are also engendꝛed herein. What shall wee then say of this thyꝛde: ye I may wel say the fourth. Foꝛ I suppose them also to bee Crocodiles which *Co lonus* with his coompany founde armed with scales as harde as shelles in the ryuer cauled *Delagartos* wherof wee haue made mention befoꝛe. Shall wee say that these ryuers also of *Darien* and *Vraba,* haue theyꝛ oꝛiginall frome the mountaynes of the moone, wheras they spꝛynge owte of the nexte mountaynes, and

and can by noo meanes haue the same originall with Nilus in
Egypte, or that in Nigrita, or els that in the kyngedome of Me
landa, from whense soo euer they are deryued. Whereas these
other (as we haue sayde) springe owt of the next mountaines
whiche deuyde an other southe sea with noo greate distaunce
from the North Ocean. Wherfore it appeareth by experience
of such as haue trauayled the worlde in owre time, that other
waters besyde the ryuer of Nilus in Egypte, maye lykewyse
brynge foorth Crocodiles. In the maryshes also and fennes
of the Regions of Dariena, are founde greate plentie of Phe
sauntes and peacockes, (but not of variable coloures) with
many other kyndes of byrdes and foules vnlyke vnto owres,
as well apte to bee eaten, as also to delite the eares of menne
with pleasaunt noyse. But owre Spanyardes, bycause they
are ignorant in foulynge, take but fewe. Also innumerable po
pyngayes of sundry kindes are found chattering in the groues
of those fenny places. Of these there are sume equall to Ca
pons in byggenes, and sume as lyttle as sparowes. But of
the diuersitie of popingayes, we haue spoken sufficientely in
the fyrst Decade. For in the case of this large lande, Colonus
hym selfe browght and sent to the courte a greate number of
euery kynde, the which it was lawfull for all the people to be
holde, and are yet dayly browght in lyke maner.   There re
mayneth yet one thynge moste woorthy to bee put in hystorye:
The which I had rather to haue chaunced into the handes of
Cicero or Liuie, then into myne. For the thynge is soo maruey
lous in my estimation, that I fynde my wytte more entange
led in the description hereof, then is sayde of the henne when
shee seeth her younge chykyn inwrapped in towe or dare. The
breadth of that lande from the North Ocean to the south sea
is only syxe dayes iourney by relation of thinhabitantes. The
multitude therfore and greatnes of the ryuers on the one side
and on the other syde the narowenes of the lande, brynge me
into suche doubte howe it can coome to passe, that in soo little
a space of three dayes iourney, measurynge from the hygh top
pes of those mountaynes,   I doo not vnderstande howe soo
many and soo great ryuers, may haue recourse into this north
sea. For it is to bee thought that as many doo flowe towarde
thinhabitantes of the southe, These ryuers of Vraba are but
smaule, in comparison of many other in those coastes. For the

Spanyardes say, that in th: tyme of Colonus, they founde and passed by an other ryuer after this, whose goulfe faulynge in to the sea, they affirme to bee lyttle lesse then a hundreth myles in the fyrste coastes of Paria, as wee haue sayde elsewhere. For they saye that it faulieth from the toppes of hyghe mountaynes with soo swyfte and furious a course, that by the violence and greatnes therof, it dryueth backe the sea althowgh it bee rowghe and enforced with a contrary wynde. They all affirme lykewyse, that in all the large tracte therof, they felt noo sower or salte water, but that all the water was fresshe, sweete, and apte to bee droonke. Thinhabitantes caule this ryuer Maragnonum: And the regions adiacent to the same, Maristambal, Camamorus, and Paricora. Besyde those ryuers whiche I haue named before, as Darien, Grandis, Dabaiba, Beragua, Sancti Mathei, Boius gati, Delagartos, & Gaira, they which of late haue searched those coastes, haue founde many other. Deliberatinge therefore with my selfe, from whence these mountaynes beinge soo narowe and nere vnto the sea on bothe sydes, haue such great holowe caues or dennes of suche capacitie, and from whense they are fylled to cast foorth such abundance of water, hereof also askynge them the opinions of the inhabitantes, they affirme them to bee of dyuers iudgementes herein: Alleagynge syrst the greatnes of the mountaynes to bee the cause, whiche they say to bee very hygh, which thynge also Colonus the first fynder therof affirmeth to bee trewe: Adding there vnto that the Paradise of pleasure is in the toppes of those mountaines whiche appeare from the goulfe of Paria and Os Draconis, as he is fully perswaded. They agree therfore that there is greate caues within these mountaynes: but it resteth to consyder from whense they are fylled. If therfore all the ryuers of fresshe waters by thoppinion of manye, do soo flowe owte of the sea as dryuen and compelled throwghe the passages or pores of the earth by the ponderous weyght of the sea it selfe, as wee see them breake furth of the spryinges and directe their course to the sea agepne, then the thynge is lesse to bee marueyled at here then in other places. For wee haue not redde that in any other place twoo such seas haue enuironed any lande with soo narowe lymittes. For it hath on the right syde, the great Ocean where the sonne goeth downe on the lefte hande: And an other on the other syde where the sonne ryseth, nothynge

inferioure

A ryuer of maruelous byggenes loke the first decade the ix.boke.

The great ryuer Maragnonus.liber.i. decade.i. Mariatambal. Camamorus. Paricora.

Paradice. Loke.vi.loke fyrst decade.

The sea.

The land enclosed with two seas.

inferioure to the fyrſt in greatenes, foꝛ they ſuppoſe it to bee myꝛte and ioyned as all one with the ſea of Eaſt India.

This lande therefoꝛe being burdened with ſo great a weight on the one ſyde and on the other (yf this opinion bee of anye value) is enfoꝛced to ſwalowe vp ſuch deuoured waters, and ageyne to caſt fooꝛth the ſame in open ſpꝛinges and ſtreames. But if wee ſhall denye that the earth dꝛaweth humours of the ſea, and agree that all fountaynes oꝛ ſpꝛynges are engendered of the conuerſion oꝛ turnynge of ayer into water diſtilling within the holowe places of the montaynes (as the moſt part thinke) we wyll gyue place rather to thautoꝛitie of them whiche ſpeke to thoſe reaſons, then that owre ſenſe is ſatiſfyed of the full truth therof. Yet doo I not repugne that in ſume caues of mountaynes, water is turned into ayer.

Conuerſion of ayer into water in the caues of mountaynes.

Foꝛ I my ſelfe haue ſeene, howe in the caues of manye mountaynes in Spayne, in maner ſhowers of rayne doo faule continually: And that the water gathered by this meanes, doth ſend furth certeyne ryuers by the ſydes of the mountaynes, wherwith al ſuche trees as are planted on the ſtiepe oꝛ foote of the mountaynes, as vines, Oliue trees, and ſuche other, are watered. And this eſpecially in one place: As the ryght honoꝛable Loꝛdouike the Cardinall of Aragonie moſte obſequious to yowre holynes, and twoo other vpſhoppes of Italy, wherof the one is _Siluius Pandonus_, and the other an Archebyſhop (whoſe name and tytle I doo not remember) can beare me wytnes. Foꝛ whē wee were togyther at Granata, lately delyuered from the dominion of the Mooꝛes, and walked foꝛ owre paſtyme to certeine pleaſaunte hylles (by the whiche there ranne a fayꝛe ryuer) Whyle Cardinall Loꝛdouike occupied hym ſelfe in ſhuꝛynge at byꝛdes whiche were in the buſhes nere vnto the ryuer, I and the other twoo byſhops determined to clime the mountaynes to ſearche thoꝛiginall and ſpꝛinge of the ryuer: foꝛ wee were not farre from the toppes therof. Folowynge therefoꝛe the courſe of the ryuer, wee founde a greate caue in which was a continuall faule of water as it had byn a houre of rayne: the water wherof, faulyng into a trenche made with mans hand, encreaſeth to a ryuer, and runneth downe by the ſydes of the mountaynes. The lyke is alſo ſeene in this famous towne of Valdolero (where we nowe ſuioꝛne) in a certeyne greene cloſe, not paſt a furlonge diſtant from the waules of the towne. I

Showers of rayne in the caues of mountaynes

graunt

graunte therfoze that in certeyne places by conuerſion of the ayzic dewe into water within the caues of ſuche mountaynes, many ſpzynges and ryuers are engendzed. But I ſuppoſe that nature was not ſollicitate to bzynge furthe ſuche greate fludes by this ſo ſmaule induſtry. Twoo reaſons therfoze, do ſounde beſte to my iudgement: whereof the one is, the often faule of rayne: The other, the continuall autumne oz ſpzynge tyme, which is in thoſe regions beinge ſoo nere vnto the Equinoctial that the common people can perceaue no difference betwene the length of the day and the night thzowgh owt al the yeare whereas theſe two ſeaſons are moze apte to engender abundance of rayne then eyther extreme wynter oz feruent ſummer An other reaſon in effect much lyke vnto the fyzſt, is this: If the ſea bee full of pozes, and that by the pozes therof beinge opened by the Southe windes, wee ſhal conſent that vapours are lyfted vp wherof the watery cleudes are engendzed, this lande muſt needes bee moyſted with moo ſhoures then anye other, yf it bee as narowe as they ſaye, and enuironed with twoo mayne ſeas collaterally beatinge on the ſame. Howe ſo euer it be: I can not but gyue credit to the repozt of ſuch woz thy men as haue recourſe to thoſe regions: And can noo leſſe then declare the ſame albeit it may ſeeme incredible to ſume ignozant perſons not knowynge the poure of nature to whom Plinie was perſuaded that nothynge was impoſſible. We haue therfoze thought it good to make this diſcourſe by the way of argument, leaſt on the one ſyde, men of good lernyng and iudgement, and on the other ſyde, ſuche as are ſtudiouſ to fynde occaſions of quarelynge in other mens wzytynges, ſhulde iudge vs to bee ſo vndeſcreete lyghtly to gyue credit to euery tale not beinge conſonant to reaſon. But of the foz and greate violence of thoſe freſhe waters, which repulſing the ſea make ſo greate a goulfe (as wee haue ſayde) I thinke the cauſe therof to bee the greate multitude of fluddes and ryuers, which beinge gathered togither, make ſo great a poole and not one ryuer as they ſuppoſe. And for as muche as the mountaynes are excedynge hyghe and ſtiepe, I thinke the violence of the faule of the waters to be of ſuch foze, that the conflicte betwene the waters, is cauſed by thimpulſion of the poole that the ſalte water can not enter into the goulfe. But here perhappes ſume wyll marueyle at me why I ſhulde main teyne

Side notes (left margin):

The often fal of rayne and continuall ſpzynge time.

The Equinoctiall.

The pozes of the ſea & the South wynde.

Nothinge impoſſible to the poure of nature.

The cauſe of the greatnes and foze of the goulfe.

Hygh and ſtiepe hylles.

ueple soo muche hereat, speakynge vnto me scornefully after this maner. Why dothe he soo marueyle at the greate ryuers of these Regions? Hathe not Italye his *Eridanus*, named the kynge of ryuers of the owlde wryters? Haue not other regions also the lyke? as wee reede of *Tanais*, *Ganges*, and *Danubius*, which are sayde soo to ouercoome the sea, that freshe water may bee drawne fortie myles within the same. These menne I woolde satisfie with this answere. The famous ryuer of *...adus* in Italye (whiche they nowe caule *Po*, and was of the Greekes cauled *Eridanus*) hath the greate mountaynes cauled *...lpes* diuidinge Fraunce, Germanie, and Pannonie from I*...*alpe, lyinge at the backe therof as it were bulwarges agger, ull of moysture: And with a longe tracte receauinge *Ticinum* with innumerable other great ryuers, faulleth into the sea A*...*riatike. The lyke is also to bee vnderstode of the other. But hese ryuers (as owre men were enformed by the kynges) faul nto the Ocean sea with larger and fuller chanels nere hand. And sume there are which affirme this lande to bee very large n other places althowgh it bee but narowe here. There com*...*meth also to my remembrance an other cause: the whiche al*...*howgh it bee of no greate force, yet doo I entende to wryte *...*t. Perhappes therfore the length of the lande reachyng far rom the Easte to the weste, if it bee narowe, may bee a helpe *...*ereunto. For as wee reade that the ryuer *Alpheus* passethe hrough the holowe places vnder the sea from the citie of *Elis* n *Peloponeso*, and breaketh foorth at the fountayne or sprynge *Arethusa* in the Ilande of *Sicilia*, so is it possible that these moun*...*aynes may haue suche longe caues perteynynge vnto theim, hat they may be the receptacles of the water passing throwgh he landes beinge farre distante : And that the same waters ommynge by soo longe a tracte, may in the way bee greatly ncreased by the conuersion of ayer into water, as wee haue ayde. Thus muche haue I spoken freely, permittinge bothe o them whiche doo frendely enterprete other mens doinges, nd also to the malicious scorners, to take the thynge euen s them lysteth. For hetherto I can make no further declara*...*ion hereof. But when the truth shalbe better knowen, I wyl do ny diligence to commit the same to wrytinge. Nowe therfore, orasmuche as we haue spoken thus muche of the breadth of his land, we entend to descrybe the length & forme of thesame.

P. i. The

The fludde Eridanus.

Tanais.
Ganges.
Danubius.
Padus.

Alpes.

Ticinum.

The sea Adriatike, sume caule the goulfe of Uenes.

An other reason

The ryuer Alpheus.

Arethusa
Longe caues in the mountaynes.

ℂ The tenth booke of the seconde Decade, of the supposed Continent.

The length and fourme of the Jland. Cap. S. Augusti.

Eyght tymes bygger then Italy befyde that part whiche the Portugales possesse. Italy is in length a thousand and two hundreth myles, and in breadth foure hundreth and ten.

Cardes of the sea.

The carde of Americus Uesputius.

The carde of Colonus.

The carde of Johannes de la Cossa.

That lande reacheth foorth into the sea euen as doth Italy, althowgh not like the legge of a man as it doth. But I nowe compare a Pigmean or a dwarfe to a giant. For that part therof which the Spaniardes haue ouer runne from the sayde Easte poynt which reacheth towarde the sea Atlantike (the ende not beinge yet founde towarde the Weste) is more then eyght tymes longer then Italye. And by what reason I am moued to say eyght tymes, yowre holynes shall vnderstande. From the tyme therefore that I fyrste determined to obeye their requestes who wylled me fyrste in yowre name to wryte these thynges in the laten tonge, I dyd my endeuoure that all thinges myght coome foorth with dewe tryall and experience. Wherupon I repayred to the byshoppe of Burges beinge the chiefe refuge of this nauigation. As wee were therfore secretly togyther in one chamber, we had many instrumentes perteynynge to these affayres as globes and manye of those mappes which are commonly cauled the shipmans cardes, or cardes of the sea. Of the which, one was drawen by the Portugales, wherunto Americus Vesputius is sayde to haue put to his hande, beinge a man moste experte in this facultie and a Florentyne borne: who also vnder the stipende of the Portugales, hadde sayled towarde the south pole many degrees beyond the Equinoctiall. In this carde we founde the fyrst front of this land to bee brooder then the kynges of Vraba had persuaded owre men of theyr mountaynes. To an other, Colonus the Admirall whyle he yet lyued and searched those places had gyuen the beginnynge with his owne handes: Wherunto Bartholomeus Colonus his brother and Lieuetenaunt had addid his iudgement, for he also, had sayled aboute those coastes. Of the Spanyardes lykewyse, as many as thought them selues to haue any knowleage what perteyned to measure the lande and the sea, drewe certeyne cardes in parchement as concernyng these nauigations. Of all other, they moste esteeme them which Iohannes de la Cossa the coompanion of Fogeda (whom wee sayde to bee slayne of the people of Caramairi in the hauen Carthago,) and an other

other expert pylot cauled *Andreas Moralis*, had set foorth. And this aswell for the greate experience which they bothe hadde (to whom these tractes were as wel knowen as the chambers of theyr owne houses) as also that they were thought to bee cunninger in that parte of Cosmographie which teacheth the description and measuringe of the sea. Conferringe therefore all these cardes togyther, in euery of the whiche was drawen a lyne expressinge, not the myles, but leagues after the maner of the Spanyardes, we tooke owre compases and beganne to measure the sea coastes after this order. From that poynt of foonte which we sayde to bee included within the lyne pertey-nynge to the Portugales iurisdiction, beinge drawen by the paralelles of the Ilandes of *Cabouerde*, but a hundreth leagues further towarde the weste. (which they haue nowe also sear-ched on euery syde) we founde three hundreth leagues to the vtterance of the ryuer *Maragnonum*: And from thense to *Os Dra-conis*, seuen hundreth leagues: but sumwhat lesse in the descrip-tion of sume: For they doo not agree in al poyntes exquisite-ly. The Spanyardes wyll that a league conteyne foure myles by sea and but three by lande. From *Os Draconis*, to the cape or poynt of *Cuchibacoa*, which beinge passed, there is a goulfe on the lefte hande, we measured three hundreth leagues in one carde, and much thereabout in an other. From this poynt of *Cuchibacoa*, to the region of *Caramairi* in which is the hauen *Car-thago* (which sum caule *Carthagena*) we found about a hundreth and seuentie leagues. From *Caramairi* to the Ilande *Fortis*, fif-tie leagues. From thense to the goulfes of *Vraba* amonge the which is the byllage cauled *Sancta Maria Antiqua* where the Spa-nyardes haue apoynted theyr habitacion, only. xxxiii. leagues. From the ryuer of *Vraba* in the prouince of *Dariena* to the ry-uer of *Beragua* where *Nicuesa* hadde intended to haue fastened his foote if god hadde not otherwyse decreed, we measured a hundreth and thirtie leagues. Frome *Beragua* to that ryuer whiche wee sayde of *Colonus* to bee cauled *Sancti Matthei*, in the which also *Nicuesa* loosinge his carauell, wandered in greate calamities, we founde in owre cardes, onely a hundreth and fortie leagues: yet many other which of late tyme haue coome from these partes, haue descrybed many moo leagues in this tracte frō the ryuer of *Sancti Matthei*: In which also, they place dyuers ryuers, as *Aburema* with the Ilande cauled *Scutum Cateba*

lyinge

The carde of *Andreas mo-ralis*.

The maner of measuring the cardes.

Loke decade i. liber. iii.

The Iland of *Cabouerde*.

Maragnonum

Os Draconis

A league.

Cuchibacoa.

Caramairi.

Carthago.

The Iland *Fortis*.

Vraba.

Beragua.

R. *Sancti Mat-thei*.i

R. *Aburema*

Scutum Cateba

R. Zobroba.
Vrida.
Duraba,
Cerabaro,
Hiebra.

Note.

R. d. los perdidos.

The nauigati
on of Io. an
nee Dias.

The eleuatiõ
of the pole.

The iurisdic:
tion of the
portugales.

Parix,

Darleña,

Beragua,

Hercules pyl
lers.

lyinge before it, whose kynges name is *Facies combusta*. Lyke
wise an other ryuer cauled Zobraba: after that, Vrida: and thē
Duraba in the which gold is founde. Furthermore, many good
ly hauens, as Cerabaro and Hiebra, soo cauled of thinhabitan:
tes. And thus if youre holynes wyll conferre these numbers
togyther, yowe shall fynde in this accompte, a thousand fiue
hundreth twentie and fyue leagues, whiche amounte to fiue
thousande and seuen hundreth myles from the poynt of Sanct
Matthei, which they caule Sinum perditorum: that is, the goulfe of
the losse men. But we may not leaue here. For after this, one
Ashur Oyetensis, otherwyse named Iohannes Dias de Solis, borne in Ne
brissa (which bringeth foorth many lerned men) saylinge frome
this ryuer towarde the weste, ouer ranne manye coastes & lea:
gues: But the myddesse of that shore, bendethe towarde the
North: And is not therfore directly placed in order with the
other. Yet may we gather by a diameter or ryght lyne, aboue
three hundreth leagues. Hereby maye yowe gather what is
the length of this lande. But of the breadth, perhappes wee
shall hereafter haue further knowleage. Let vs nowe speake
sumwhat of the varietie of the degrees of the eleuation of the
pole starres. This lande therfore, althowgh it reache foorth
from the East into the Weste, yet is it crooked and hathe the
poynt bendynge soo toward the south, that it loseth the sight
of the North pole, and is extendend beyonde the Æquinoctiall
lyne seuen degrees towarde the South pole. But the poynt
herof, perteyneth to the iurisdiction of the Portugales as we
haue sayde. Leauinge this poynt and saylinge toward Paria
the north starre is seene ageyne, and is so much the more lyf:
ted vp, in howe much the region enclyueth more towarde the
Weste. The Spanyardes therfore, haue dyuers degrees of ele:
uations, vntyl they come to Dariena beinge their chiefe station
and dwellynge place in those landes. For they haue forsaken
Beragua, where they found the North pole eleuate .viii. degrees
But from hense the lande doth soo muche bende towarde the
North, that it is there in maner equall with the degrees of
the strayghtes of Hercules pyllers: especially yf wee measure
certeyne landes founde by them towarde the Northe syde of
Hispaniola. Emonge the which, there is an Ilande, about three
hundreth and .xxv. leagues from Hispaniola, as they say which
haue searched the same, named Boinca or Agnaneo, in the which

is a continual spynge of runnynge water of such maruelous
vertue, that the water therof beinge dronk, perhappes with
sume dyete, maketh owld men younge ageyne. And here must
I make protestacion to yowre holynes, not to thynke this to
bee sayde lyghtly, or rashely. For they haue soo spredde this
rumour for a truth throwghowt all the courte, that not onely
all the people, but also many of them whom wisedome or fortune hath diuided from the common sort, thinke it to be true.
But if yowe shal aske my opinion herein, I wyl answere that
I wyll not attribute so greate poure to nature : but that god
hath noo lesse reserued this prerogatiue to hym selfe, then to
searche the hartes of men, or to gyue substance to priuation,
(that is) beinge to noo beinge : Excepte we shall beleue the fable of *Colchis* of *Eson* renouate, to bee as trewe as the wrytin-
ges of *Sibylla Erythrea*. Albeit perhappes the scoles of phisitians
and naturall philosophers wyll not muche stycke to affirme
that by thuse of certeyne secreate medecines and dyete, the ac-
cidentes of age (as they caule them) may be longe hydden and
deferred, which they wyll to bee vnderstoode, by the renoua-
cion of age. And to haue sayde thus much of the length and
breadthe of these Regions, and of the rowghe and hugious
mountaynes with theyr watery caues, also of the dyuers degrees of that lande, I thinke it sufficient. But I thowght it
not good to let passe what chaunced to these miserable men a
monge theyr generall calamities. I remember that when I
was a chylde, mee thowght my bowelles grated and that my
spirites were maruelouslye troubeled for verye pitie, when I
readde in the poet Uirgyl howe *Achemenides* was lefte of *Vlysses*
vpon the sea bankes amonge the giantes cauled *Cyclopes*. where
for the space of many dayes from the departinge of *Vlysses* vntyll the commynge of *Eneas* he eate none other meate but only
berryes and hawes. But owre vnfortunate Spanyardes whiche folowed *Nicuesa* to inhabite *Beragua*, woolde haue estemed
hawes and berryes for greate delicates. What shulde I heare
speake of the heade of an asse bowght for a greate price, and
of such other extremities as men haue suffered in townes beseaged ? After that *Nicuesa* hadde determyned to leaue *Beragua*
for the barrennes of the soyle, he attempted to searche *Portum
Bellum*, and then the coastes of the poynt cauled *Marmor*, if he
myght there fynde a place more fortunate to inhabite, In this
meane

The Ilande
Boiuca or
Agnaneo.

A water of
maruelous
vertue.

The renoua-
tion of age.

The acciden-
tes of age
may bee hyd-
den.

*Achemenides,
Vlysses.
Eneas.*

Extreme hun-
ger.

This was at
the siege of
Hierusalem.
*Portus Bellus
Marmor.*

Mangy dogs eaten.

meane tyme, so greuous famen oppꝛeſſed his ſouldiers, that they neyther abſteyned from eatinge of mangie dogges which they had with them aſwell foꝛ theyꝛ defence as foꝛ huntyng (foꝛ in the warre ageynſt the naked peaple, dogges ſtoode them in greate ſteade) noꝛ yet ſumtymes from the ſlayne inhabitantes. Foꝛ they founde not there any frutefull trees oꝛ plentie of foules as in Dariena, but a barren grounde and not meete to bee inhabited. Here certeyne of the ſouldiers made a bargein with one of theyꝛ felowes foꝛ the pꝛice of a leane dogge, who

A mangy dog bere ſold.

alſo was almoſte deade foꝛ hunger: They gaue the owner of the dogge many of thoſe pieces of golde which they caule Peſo oꝛ golden Caſtellans. Thus agreinge of the pꝛice, they fleä the dogge to bee eaten, and caſte his mangie ſkynne with the bones of the heade hangynge therto, amonge the buſhes. The day folowynge, a certeyne footeman of theyꝛ company, chaun ced to fynde the ſkynne beinge nowe full of maggottes and

Broth of a mangy dogs ſkynne.

ſtynkynge. He bꝛought it home with hym, ſodde it, and eate it. Many reſoꝛted to hym with theyꝛ dyſſhes foꝛ the bꝛoth of the ſodde ſkynne, pꝛoferinge hym foꝛ euerye dyſſhefull a piece of golde. An other founde twoo toades and ſodde them

Toades eatē

which a ſicke man bought of hym foꝛ twoo fyne ſhertes curi ouſly wꝛought of lynen intermyxt with golde. Certeyn other wanderinge abowte to ſeeke foꝛ vytayles, founde in a pathe way in the myddeſt of a fyelde, a deade man of thinhabitan tes whiche had byn ſlayne of his owne coompanye and was

A deade man eaten.

nowe rotten and ſtynkynge. They dꝛewe hym aſyde, diſmem berde hym ſecreatly, roſted hym and eate hym, therewith aſ ſwagynge theyꝛ hunger as yf they had byn fedde with pheaſauntes. One alſo, which departinge from his companions in the nyght ſeaſon, went a fyſhyng amonge the reedes of the maryſſhes, lyued only with ſlyme oꝛ mudde foꝛ the ſpace of certeyne dayes, vntyll at the lengthe creepinge and almoſte deade, he founde the way to his felowes. And thus theſe mi ſerable men of Beragua vered with theſe and ſuche other afflic tions, were bꝛowghe from the number of ſeuen hundꝛeth thꝛee ſcoꝛe & ten ſouldiers, ſcarſely to foꝛtie, beinge nowe alſo ad ded to the coompany of them in Dariena. Fewe were ſlayne of thinhabitantes. But the reſydewe conſumed by famen, bꝛea thed owt theyꝛ wery ſowles, openynge a waye to the newe landes foꝛ ſuch as ſhal coome after them, appeaſinge the fury

Q

of the barbarous nations, with the price of theyr bloode. Con
syderinge therfore after these stormes, with what eale other
men shall ouerrunne and inhabite these landes, in respecte to
the calamities that these men haue suffered, they shall seeme
to goo to bryde feastes where all thynges are redy prepared a
geynst their commynge. But where *Petrus Arias* arryued with
the kynges nauie and newe supply of men, to this houre
I knowe no certentie. What shall chaunce herafter
I wyll make diligente inquisition if I shall vnderstande this to bee acceptable to youre holynes.
Thus I byd youe hartely farewell: from the
courte of the mooste Catholyke kynge,
the daye beefore the nones of
December, in the yeare of
Christe, M. D.
XIIII.

The fyrst booke of the thyrde Decade, to the byshoppe of Rome Leo the tenth.

Was determyned (moste holye father) to haue
closed vp the gates to this newe worlde, supposinge that I had wandered farre enowgh
in the coastes therof, while in the meane time
newe letters were brought me frome thence,
which caused me ageyne to take my penne in
hande. For I receaued letters not only from
certeyne of myne acquaintaunce there, but also frome *Vaschus*
Nunnez whome we sayde by the confidence of his owne poure
with his confetherates, to haue vsurped the gouernaunce of
Dariena after the reiecting of *Nicuesa* and *Aneisus*, Lieutenantes.
By his letter wrytten after his warlyke maner, wee vnderstand that he hath passed ouer the mountaynes, diuidyng the
Ocean knowen to vs, from the other mayne sea on the south
syde of this lande hetherto vnknowen. His epistell is greater
then that cauled *Capreensis de Seiano.* But wee haue gathered out
of that and other, onely suche thynges as we thowght moste
woorthy to bee noted. *Vaschus* soo behaued hym selfe in these
affayres, that he dyd not onely pacifie the kynges displeasure
conceaued

conceaued ageynst hym, but also made hym so fauozable and
gracious good lozde towarde hym, that he rewarded him and
his coompanions with many honozable gyftes and priuileges
foz theyz attemptes. Wherfoze I despze powre holynes to in
clyne powre attentiue eares, and to confyder with a ioyfull
mynde what they haue bzowght to passe in these great enter
pzyses. Foz this valiante nation (the Spanyardes I meane)
haue not onely with greate paynes and innumerable dangers
subdued to the Chzistian empire, infinite hundzedes and legi
ons, but also myziades of men. Vaschus Nunnez therfoze, whe
ther it were that he was impacient of Idlenes (foz a valiente
mynde can not rest in one place oz bee vnoccupyed) oz leaste a
ny other shulde pzeuent hym in soo great a matter (suspecting
the newe gouernour *Petrus Arias*) oz being moued by both these
causes, and especially foz that the kynge had taken displea
sure with hym foz such thynges as he had doone befoze, toke
thaduenture vppon hym with a fewe men to bzynge that to
passe which the sonne of kynge *Comogrus* thought could hard
ly haue byn doone with the ayde of a thousande men, wherof
Petrus Arias was appoynted capitayne foz the same purpose. As
semblynge therfoze certeyne of the owlde souldiers of *Dariens*,
and many of those whiche came lately from *Hispaniola*, allured
by the fame of greater plentie of golde, he gathered an armye
of a hundzeth fourescore and tenne men. Thus beinge furi
nysshed and redie to take his vyage by sea, whyle the wynde
serued hym, he departed frome *Dariena* with one bzygantine
and tenne of theyz boates whiche they caule Canoas as wee
haue sayde. Fyzst therfoze arryuynge in the dominion of *Care
ta* kynge of *Coiba* and frende to the Chzistians, and leauynge
his shyppe and boates there, he made his deuout pzayers to al
myghtie god, and therwith went fozwarde on his iourney by
lande toward the mountaynes. Here he fyzst entered into the
region of kynge *Poncha*, who fledde at his commyng as he had
doone befoze. But Vaschus sent messengers to hym by the con
duct of certeyne of *Careta* his men, pzomysinge hym frendshyp
and defence ageynst his enemies, with many other benefites.
Poncha thus entysed with the fayze speache and frendely pzof
fers bothe of owre men and of the Caretans, came to owr men
gladly and wyllyngely makynge a league of frendshippe with
them. Vaschus enterteyned hym very frendely, and persuaded
hym

Commendati
on of the Spa
nyardes.

A valient
mynd can not
bee ydle.

A desperate
aduenture

Vaschus his
viage toward
the golden
mountaynes.

Careta kynge
of Coiba

kyng Poncha

hym neuer therafter eo ftande in feare.   Thus they ioyned
handes, embzafed, and gaue greate gyftes the one to the o=
ther to knytte vp the knotte of continuall amitie. *Poncha* gaue
Vaschus a hundzeth and ten poundes weyght of golde, of that
pounde which the Spanyardes caule *Pefum*. He had no grea=
ter plentie of golde at this tyme, by reafon he was fpoyled
the yeare befoze as we haue fayde. *Vaschus* to recompence one
benefyte with an other, gaue hym certeyne of owre thynges,
as conuerfet rynges, Chziftal ftones, copper cheynes & bzafe
lettes, haukes belles, lokynge glaffes, and fuche other fyne
ftuffe. Thefe thynges they fet much by and greately efteeme.
foz fuche thynges as are ftraunge, are euery where counted
pzecious. He gaue alfo to *Poncha* certeyne axes to fell trees :
which he accepted as a pzincely gyfte, bycaufe they lacke J=
ren and all other metals except golde : by reafon wherof they
are enfozced with greate laboure to cut theyz trees to buylde
theyz houfes,   and efpecially to make theyz boates holowe
withowte inftrumentes of Jren, with certeyne fharpe ftones
whiche they fynde in the ryuers. Thus *Vaschus* leaupnge all
thynges in fafetie behynde hym, marched fozwarde with his
armye towarde the mountaynes, by the conducte of certeyne
guydes and labourers which *Poncha* had gyuen hym, as well
to leade hym the way, as alfo to cary his baggages and open
the ftraightes thzough the defolate places and craggy rockes
full of the dennes of wylde beaftes. foz there is feldoome en=
tercourfe oz byinge and fellynge betwene thefe naked people,
bycaufe they ftand in neede of fewe thynges and haue not the
vfe of money. But yf at any tyme they exercife any bartering
they doo it but nere hande, exchangynge golde foz houfholde
ftuffe with theyz confines whiche fumewhat efteeme the fame
foz oznamente when it is wzought. Other fuperfluities they
vtterly contemne, as hynderances of theyz fweete libertie, foz
afmuch as they are gyuen only to play and Jdelnes. And foz
this caufe, the high wayes which lye betwene theyz regions
are not much wozne with many iozneys. yet haue theyz fcou
tes certeyne pziuie markes whereby they knowe the waye the
one to inuade the others dominions, and fpoyle and infefte
them felues on bothe fydes with mutual incurfions pziuilie in
the nyght feafon. By the helpe therfoze of theyz guydes and
labourers, with owre carpenters, he paffed ouer the hozrible

Z , i ,   mountaynes

A hundzeth τ
r. poundes
weyght of
golde.

Strange thin
ges are coun=
ted pzecious.

Lacke of Iren

A ftone in the
fteede of Jrē.

Superfluti=
ties hynder
libertie.

Carpenters.

mountaynes and many greate ryuers lyinge in the way, ouer
the which he made brydges eyther with pyles oz trunkes o_
trees. And here doo I let palTe manye thynges whiche they
fuffered foz lacke of necelTaries, beinge alfo in maner ouer
come with extreme laboure, lealTe I fhulde bee tedious in re_
herfinge thynges of fmaule balue. But I haue thought i_
good not to omitte fuche doinges as he had with the kynges
by the waye. Therefoze oz euer he came to the toppes of th_
hygh mountaynes, he entered into a Region cauled *Quarequa*
and mette with the kynge thereof cauled by the fame name
with a greate bande of men armed after theyz maner, as with
bowes and arrowes, longe and bzode two handed fwozdes
made of wodde, longe ffaues hardened at the endes with fy_
er, dartes alfo and flynges. He came pzoudely and cruelly a_
geynff owre men, and fent melTengers to them to byd theyn
ffande and pzocede no further: demaundynge whyther they
went and what they hadde to doo there. Herewith he cam_
foozth and fhewed hym felfe beinge appareled with al his no_
bilitie: but the other were all naked. Then appzochinge to_
warde owre men, he thzetened the with a lions countenanc_
to depart from thenfe except they woolde bee flayne euery mo_
thers fonne. When owre men denyed that they woolde, goo_
backe, he alTayled them fiercely. But the battayle was fone_
fynyfhed. Foz as foone as they harde the noyfe of the har_
gabufies, they beleued that owre menne caryed thunder and
lyghtenynge about with them. Many alfo beinge flayne and
foze wounded with quarels of croffebowes, they turned thei_
backes and fledde. Owre men folowynge them in the chafe,
hewed them in piefes as the butchers doo flefhe in the fham_
welles, from one an arme, from an other a legge, from hym_
a buttocke, from an other a fhulder, and from fume the necke
from the bodye at one ffroke. Thus, fyre hundzeth of them
with theyz kynge, were flayne lyke bzute beaftes. *Vafchu_*
founde the houfe of this kynge infected with moff abhomina_
ble and vnnaturall lechery. Foz he founde the kynges bzo_
ther and many other younge men in womens apparell, fmoth_
& effeminately decked, which by the report of fuch as dwelt_
abowte hym, he abufed with pzepofterous venus. Of thefe_
abowte the number of foztie, he commaunded to bee gyué foz_
a pzay to his dogges. Foz (as we haue fayd) the Spaniardes_
vfe_

Brydges.

The region of Quarequa.

kinge Quare-
qua is dzyuen
to flyght.

hargabufies.

Croffebowes

VI.C. Barbari
ans areflaine

vnnaturall le-
chery.

bſt he helpe of dogges in their warres agaynſt the naked people whom they inuade as fiercely and rauenyngely as yf they
were wylde boares oʒ hartes. In ſoo muche that owre Spanyardes haue founde theyʒ dogges noo leſſe faythful to them
in all daungiours and enterpʒiſes, then dyd the Colophoni-
ans oʒ Caſtabalenſes which inſtituted hole armies of dogges
ſoo made to ſerue in the warres, that beinge accuſtomed to
place them in the foʒe froonte of the battayles, they neuer
ſhrunke oʒ gaue backe. When the people had harde of the ſeuere punyſſhement which owr men had exrecuted vppon that
fylthy kynde of men, they reſoʒted to theim as it had byn to
Hercules foʒ refuge, by violence bʒyngyng with them al ſuch
as they knewe to bee infected with that peſtilence, ſpettynge
in theyʒ faces and cryinge owte to owre men to take reuenge
of them and rydde them owte of the woʒlde from amonge mē
as contagious beaſtes. This ſtinkynge abhomination hadde
not yet entered amonge the people, but was exerciſed onely
by the noble men and gentelmen. But the people lyftinge vp
theyʒ handes and eyes toward heauen, gaue tokens that god
was greuouſly offended with ſuch vyle deedes. Affirmynge
this to bee the cauſe of theyʒ ſoo many thunderinges, lyghtnynge, and tempeſtes wherwith they are ſoo often troubeled:
And of the ouerflowinge of waters which dʒowne theyʒ ſets
and frutes, wherof famenne and dyuers diſeaſes inſue,
as they ſimplye and faythfully beleue, although they knowe
none other god then the ſoonne, whom onely they honoure,
thinkynge that it dooth bothe gyue and take awaye as it is
pleaſed oʒ offended. Yet are they very docible, and eaſye to
bee allured to owre cuſtomes and religion, if they had any tea-
chers. In theyʒ language there is nothynge vnpleaſaunte
to the eare oʒ harde to bee pʒonounced, but that all theyʒ
wooʒdes may bee wʒytten with latin letters as wee ſayde of
thinhabitantes of *Hiſpaniola*. It is a warlyke nation, & hath
byn euer hetherto moleſtous to theyʒ boʒtherers. But the region is not foʒtunate with frutful grounde oʒ plentie of gold.
Yet is it full of greate barren moun-aynes beinge ſumewhat
colde by reaſon of theyʒ heyght. And therfoʒe the noble men
and gentelmen are apparelled. But the common people lyue
content onely with the benefytes of nature. There is a region not paſt two dayes iourney diſtant from *Quarequa*, in which

---

The vſe of
dogges inth
warre agenſt
the naked
Barbarians.

Naturaul ha-
tred of vnna-
tural ſinne.

Palatini.

I wolde all
men were of
this opinion.

The harueſt
is great & the
woorkemen
but fewe.

warrelyke
people.

The hygher
the cou.der.

they founde only blacke Moores: and thofe exceedynge fierce
and cruell.   They fuppofe that in tyme paft certeyne
blacke mores fayled thether owt of *Aethiopia* to robbe: & that
by fhippewracke or fume other chaunce, they were dryuen to
thofe mountaynes. Thinhabitantes of Quaregua lyue in continuall warre and debate with thefe blacke men. Here vafchus

leauinge in Quarequa many of his fouldiers (which by reafon
they were not yet accuftomed to fuch trauayles and hunger,
fell into dyuers difeafes) tooke with hym certeyne guydes of
the Quarequatans to conduct hym to the toppes of the moun-

taynes. From the palaice of kynge Poncha, to the profpect of
the other fouth fea, is only fyre dayes iorney: the which ne
uertheleffe by reafd of many hynderances and chaunces, and
efpecially for lacke of vptayles, he coulde accomplyhe in noo

Va'chus is
coome to the
fyght of the
newe fouth
fea.

leffe then .xxv. dayes. But at'the length, the feuenth daye of
the calendes of October, he behelde with woonderinge eyes
the toppes of the hygh mountaynes fhewed vnto hym by the
guydes of Quarequa, from the whiche he myght fee the other
fea foo longe looked for, and neuer feene befoze of any man
commynge owte of owre worlde. Approchinge therefore to
the toppes of the mountaynes, he commaunded his armye to
ftey, and went him felfe alone to the toppe, as it were to take
the fyrft poffeffion therof. Where, faulynge proftrate vppon

the grounde, and rayfinge hym felfe ageyne vppon his knees
as is the maner of the Chriftians to pray, lyftynge vppe his
eyes and handes towarde heauen, and directinge his face to
warde the newe founde fouth fea, he pooned foorth his hum

ble and deuout prayers befoze almyghtie God as a fpirituall
facrifice with thankes gyuing, that it had pleafed his diuine
maieftie to referue vnto that day the victorie and praife of fo
greate a thynge vnto hym, beinge a man but of fmaule witte
and knowleage, of lyttle experience and bafe parentage.
When he had thus made his prayers after his warlike maner
he beckened with his hande to his coompanions to coome to
hym, fhewynge them the greate mayne fea heretofore vnknowen to thinhabitantes of Europe, Aphrike, and Afia. Here
ageyne he fell to his prayers as befoze: defyringe almyghtie
God and the bleffed birgin to fauour his beginninges, and to
gyue hym good fucceffe to fubdue thofe landes to the glorie
of his holy name and encreafe of his trewe religion. All his
                                                    companions

coompanions dyd lykewyse, and prayſed god with loude voyces foz ioye. Then Vaſchus, with no leſſe manlye cozage then Hanniball of Carthage ſhewed his ſouldiers Italye and the promontozies of the Alpes, exhozted his men to lyft vp their hartes, and to behoulde the lande euen nowe vnder theyz feete, and the ſea befoze theyz eyes, whiche ſhulde bee vnto them a full and iuſt rewarde of theyz great laboures and trauayles nowe ouerpaſſed. When he had ſayde theſe woozdes, he commaunded them to raiſe certeine heapes of ſtones in the ſtede of alters foz a token of poſſeſſion. Then deſcendynge from the toppes of the mountaynes, leaſt ſuch as might come after hym ſhulde argue hym of lyinge oz falſhod, he wrote the kynge of Caſtelles name here and there on the barkes of the trees bothe on the ryght hande and on the lefte: and rayſed heapes of ſtones all the way that he went, vntyll he came to the region of the nexte kynge towarde the ſouth whoſe name was Chiapes. This kynge came foozthe ageynſte hym with a greate multitude of men: thzeateninge and fozbyddynge him not onely to paſſe through his dominions, but alſo to goo no further. Hereuppon, Vaſchus ſet his battayle in array, and exhozted his men (beinge nowe but fewe) fiercely to aſſayle theyz enemies, and to eſteeme theym noo better then dogges meate as they ſhulde bee ſhoztly. Placeinge therfoze the hargabuſiers and maſties in the fozefroonte, they ſaluted kynge Chiapes and his men with ſuch a larome, that when they hard the noyſe of the gunnes, ſawe the flames of fyer, and ſmelte the ſauour of bzymſtone (foz the wynde blewe towarde them) they dzoue them ſelues to flyght with ſuche feare leaſt thunderboultes and lyghtnynges folowed them, that manye fell downe to the grounde: whom owre men purſuinge, fyzſt keepinge theyz ozder, and after bzeakyng theyz array, ſlewe but fewe and tooke many captiue. Foz they determined to vſe no extremitie, but to pacifie thoſe Regions as quietlye as they myght. Enteringe therfoze into the epalaice of kynge Chiapes, Vaſchus commaunded many of the captiues to bee looſed: wyllynge them to ſearch owte theyz kynge, and to exhozte hym to coome thyther: And that in ſoo doinge, he woolde bee his frende and pzofer hym peace, beſyde many other benefites. But if he refuſed to coome, it ſhulde turne to the deſtruction of hym and his, and vtter ſubuerſion of his contrey, And that

that they myght the moze affuredly do this meſſage to Chiapes he ſent with them certeyne of the guydes whiche came with hym from Qnnrequs.

Thus Chiapes beinge perſuaded aſwel by the Quareqans who coulde coniecture to what ende the matter woolde coome by therperience whiche they had ſcene in them ſelues and theyz kynge, as alſo by the reaſons of his owne men to whome Vaſchus hadde made ſoo frendely promples in his behalfe, came foozthe of the caues in the whiche he lurked, and ſubmytted hym ſelfe to Vaſchus, who accepted hym frendelye. They ioyned handes, embzaſed the one the other, made a perpetuall league of frendeſhippe, and gaue greate rewardes on bothe ſydes. Chiapes gaue Vaſchus foure hundzeth poundes weyght of wzought goulde of thoſe poundes whiche they caule Peſos: And Vaſchus recompenſed hym ageyne with certeyne of owre thynges. Thus beinge made freendes, they remayned togyther a fewe dayes vntyll Vaſchus ſouldiers were coome which he lefte behynde hym in Quarequs. Then caulinge vnto hym the guydes and labourers which came with hym from thenſe he rewarded them liberallye and diſmiſſed theym with thankes. Shortly after, by the conduct of Chiapes hym ſelfe, and certeyne of his men, departinge from the toppes of the mountaynes, he came in the ſpace of foure dayes to the bankes of the newe ſea: where aſſemblynge al his men togyther with the kynges ſcribes and notaries, they addicted al that maine ſea with all the landes adiacent there vnto to the dominion and Empire of Caſtile. Here he left part of his ſouldiers with Chiapes ſt, that he myght theſelier ſearche thoſe coaſtes. And takyng with hym nyne of theyz lyghters made of one hole tree (which they caule Culchas as thinhabitantes of Hiſpaniola caul them Canoas) and alſo a bande of foureſcoze men with certeine of Chiapes men, he paſſed ouer a greate ryuer and came to the region of a certeyne kynge whoſe name was Coquera. He attempted to reſyſte owre men as dyd the other, and with lyke ſucceſſe: for he was ouercoome and put to flyght. But Vaſchus who entended to wynne hym with gentelnes, ſente certeyne Chiapeans to him to declare the greate poure of owre menne: howe inuincible they were: howe mercifull to ſuch as ſubmit them ſelues, alſo cruell and ſeuere to ſuch as obſtinatly withſtande them, Promyſinge hym furthermoze, that by the fred hym

Chiapes ſubmitteth hym ſelfe to Vaſchus.

iiii. C. poundes weyght of wzought gold

Vaſchus addicteth the newe land & ſea, to the dominion of Caſtile.

kynge Coquera is dzyuen to flyght.

Vaſchus vſeth both gentelnes and rigour.

ſhippe of owre men, he myght bee well aſſured by theꝛemple
of other, not onely to lyue in peace and quietnes hym ſelfe,
but alſo to bee reuenged of thiniuries of his enemies. Wyllinge
hym in concluſion ſoo to weigh the matter, that if he refuſed
this gentelnes pꝛofered vnto hym by ſoo greate a victourer,
he ſhalde oꝛ it were longe, lerne by feelynge to repent him to
late of that perel which he myght haue auoyded by hearing.
Coquera with theſe wooꝛdes and eꝛemples, ſhaken with great
feare, came gladly with the meſſengers, bꝛyngyng with him
ſyxe hundꝛeth ꝯ.l. Peſos of wꝛought gold, which he gaue vnto
owre men. Vaſchus rewarded hym lykewiſe as we ſayd befoꝛe
of Poncha, Coquera beinge thus pacified, they returned to the
palaice of Chiapes. Where, viſitinge theyꝛ companions, and re
ſtynge there a whyle, Vaſchus determyned to ſearch the nexte
greate goulfe, the which, from the furtheſt reachynge therof
into the lande of theyꝛ countreys, from the enteraunce of the
mayne ſea, they ſaye to bee thꝛeeſcoꝛe myles. This they na:
med ſaynt Mychaeld goulfe, which they ſay to bee full of in:
habited Ilandes ans hugious rockes. Enteringe therefoꝛe
into the nyne boates oꝛ Culchas wherwith he paſſed ouer the
ryuer befoꝛe, hauinge alſo with hym the ſame coompanye of
foureſcoꝛe hole men, he wente foꝛwarde on his purpoſe, al:
though he were greatly diſſuaded by Chiapes, who erneſtly de
ſyred hym not to attempt that vyage at that tyme, affirming
the goulfe to be ſoo tempeſtious and ſtoꝛmy thꝛee moonethes
in the yeare, that the ſea was there by noo meanes nauigable:
And that he had ſeene many Culchas deuoured of whirlepoles
euen beefoꝛe his eyes. But inuincible Vaſchus, impacient of
idlenes, and voyde of all feare in goddes cauſe, aunſwered
that god and his holy ſayntes woolde pꝛoſper his enterpꝛy:
ſes in this caſe, foꝛaſmuche as the matter touched God and
the defence of the Chꝛiſtian religion, foꝛ the mayntenaunce
wherof it ſhulde bee neceſſarie to haue great abundance of ry:
ches ꝯ treaſure as the ſynewes of war ageynſte the enemies
of the faythe. Thus vſinge alſo thoffice both of an oꝛatoure
and pꝛeacher, and hauinge perſuaded his coompanyons, he
lanched from the lande. But Chiapes, leaſt Vaſchus ſhulde any
thynge doubt of his faythfulnes towarde hym, pꝛofered him
ſelfe to goo with hym whither ſoo euer he went : And wolde
by noo meanes aſſent that Vaſchus ſhulde depart from his pa:
aroſe

Vi.C. and.l.
poundes
weyght of
wꝛouȝht gold

A goulfe of
thꝛeeſcoꝛe
myles.

Saynt Micha
els goulfe

The manly
corage and
godly zeale of
Vaſchus

Rychesare
the ſynewes
of warre

The faythful
nes of kynge
Chiapes.

A tempeſt
on the ſea.

laice, but that he woolde bzynge hym on the waye and take part of his foztune. Therfoze as soone as they were nowe entered into the maine sea, such sourges and conslictes of water arose ageynst them that they were at theyz wyttes endes whither to turne them oz where to reste. Thus beinge tossed and amased with feare, the one loked on the other with pale and bucherefull countenaunces. But especially *Chiapes* and his coompany, who had befoze tyme with theyz eyes seene therperience of those ieoperdies, were greatly discomfozted. Yet (as god woolde) they escaped all, and landed at the nexte Ilande: Where makynge faste theyz boates, they rested there that nyghte. Here the water soo encreased, that it almost ouerflowed the Iland. They say also that that south sea doth soo in maner boyle and swelle, that when it is at the hyghest it doth couer many greate rockes, which at the faule therof, are seene farre aboue the water. But on the contrary parte, all suche as inhabite the Nozth sea, affirme with one voyce, that hit scarsely riseth at any tyme a cubet aboue the bankes as they also confesse which inhabite the Ilande of Hispaniola and other Ilandes situate in the same. The Ilande therfoze beinge nowe dzye by the faule of the water, they resozted to theyz boates which they founde all ouerwhelmed and full of sande, and sume soze bzused, with great ryftes, and almost lost by reason theyz cables were bzoken. Such as were bzused, they tyed fast with theyz gyzdels, with slippes of the barkes of trees, and with tough and longe stalkes of certein herbes of the sea, stopping the ryftes oz chynkes with grasse accozdynge to the pzesente necessitie. Thus were they enfozced to returne backe ageyne lyke vnto men that came frome shippewzacke, beinge almost consumed with hunger, bycause theyz vytaples were vtterly destroyed by tempeste. Thinhabitantes declared that there is harde all the yeare hozrible rozynge of the sea amonge those Ilandes as often as it ryseth oz fauleth. But this most especially in those thzee monethes in the which it is moste boystious as *Chiapes* towlde *Vaschus* befoze: Meanynge (as they coulde coniecture by his woozdes) October, Nouember, and December: foz he signified the pzesent moone and the twoo moones folowynge, countynge the moonethes by the moones, whereas it was nowe October. Here therefoze refresshynge hym selfe and his souldiers a
whyle

The increasing of the South sea.

The Nozthe Ocean.

Hard shyft in necessitie.

whyle, and paſſynge by one bnpꝛofitable kynge, he came to
an other whoſe name was Tumaccus, after the name of the re:　
came fooꝛth ageynſte owꝛe men as dyd the other, and wirh
lyke foꝛtune. Foꝛ he was ouercoome, dꝛyuen to flyght, and　kynge Tus
many of his men flayne. He hym ſelfe was alſo ſoꝛe woun:　maccus is dꝛ
ded, but yet eſcaped. Vaſchus ſent certeyne meſſengers of the　uen to flyght.
Chiapeans to hym to returne, and not to bee afrayde. But he
could be nothyng moued nether by pꝛompſſes noꝛ thꝛeatenin
ges. yet when the meſſengers were inſtant, ⁊ ceaſſed not to
thꝛeaten death to him and his famely, with the btter deſola:
cion of his kyngedome if he perſiſted in that obſtinacie, at the
lcngth he ſent his ſoonne with them: whom Vaſchus honoꝛ
rably enterteyninge, apparelinge hym goꝛgiouſly and gyuing
hym many gyftes, ſent hym to his father, wyllynge hym to
perſuade hym of the puiſſaunce, munificence, liberalitie, hu
manitie, and clemencie of owꝛe men. Tumaccus beinge mooued
by this gentelnes declared towaꝛd his ſonne, came with hym
the thyꝛde day, bꝛyngynge nothynge with hym at that tyme.
But after that he knewe that owꝛe men deſyꝛed goulde and　
and two hundꝛeth and foꝛtie of the biggeſt and fayꝛeſt perles
beſyde a great number of the ſmauleſt ſoꝛte. Owꝛe men mar:
ueyled at the byggenes and fayꝛencs of theſe perles although
they were not perfectely whyte bycauſe they take theym not
owꝛe of the ſea muſculs except they fyꝛſt roſt them, that they　
haue the better taſte, whiche they eſteeme foꝛ a delicate and
pꝛincely dyſſhe, and ſet moꝛe thereby then by the perles them
ſelues. Of theſe thynges I was enfoꝛmed of one Arbolantius
beinge one of Vaſchus coompanions whom he ſent to the kyng
with manye perles and certeyne of thoſe ſea muſculs. But
when Tumaccus ſawe that owꝛe men ſoo greatly regaꝛded the　Fyſſhyng foꝛ
bꝛutie of the perles, he commaunded certeyne of his men to　perles.
pꝛepare them ſelues to goo a fyſſhynge foꝛ perles. Who de:　xii pounde
partinge, came ageyne within foure dayes, bꝛingynge with　weyght of
them twelue pounde weight of oꝛient perles after eight oun:　perles.
tes to the pounde. Thus reioyſinge on bothe parties, they
embꝛaſed and made a league of continual frendeſhippe. Tumac:
us thought him ſelfe happie that he had pꝛeſented owꝛe men

with such thankeful gyftes and was admitted to theyr frend
shippe : and owre men thinkynge them selues happie and bles
sed that they had founde suche tokens of great ryches, swalowed downe theyr spettle for thyrste. At all these doinges,
kynge Chiapes was present as a wytnes and coompanion. He
also reioysed not a lyttle, aswell that by his conductinge he
sawe that owre men shulde bee satisfied of theyr desyre, as al
so that by this meanes he had declared to the next kynge his
bortherer and enemie, what frendes he had of owre men, by
whose ayde he myght lyue in quyetnes and bee reuenged of
his aduersarie if neede shulde soo requyre. For (as wee haue
sayde) these naked kynges infeste theim selues with greuous
warres onely for ambition and desyre to rule. Vaschus bosteth
in his epistell, that he lerned certeyne maruelous secreates of
Tumaecus him selfe as concernynge the greate ryches of this
lande : wherof (as he sayth) he woold vtter nothyng at this
presente, for asmuche as Tumaecus toulde it him in his eare.
But he was enformed of bothe the kynges, that there is an
Ilande in that goulfe, greater then any of the other, hauing
in it but onely one kynge, and hym of soo great poure, that at
suche tymes of the peare as the sea is caulme, he inuadeth
theyr dominions with a greate nauie of Culchas, spoyling and
carying away for a praye, all that he meeteth. This Iland
is distant from these coastes, onely twentie myles : Soo that
the promontories or poyntes therof rechyng into the sea, may
bee seene from the hylles of this Continent. In the sea nere
about this Ilande, sea musculs are engendred of such quanti
tie, that many of them are as brode as buckelers, In these
are perles founde (beinge the hartes of those shell fysshes)of-
ten tymes as bygge as beanes, sumtymes bygger then olyues
and such as sumptuous Cleopatra myght haue desyred. Al
thoughe this Ilande bee soo nere to the shore of this firme
lande, yet is the begynnyng therof in the mayne sea without
the mouth of the goulfe. Vaschus beinge ioyfull and mery with
this rych communication, fantasinge nowe in maner nothing
but princes treasures, beganne to speake fierce and cruell
woordes ageynst the tyranne of that Ilande, meanyng hereby too woonne the myndes of the other kynges, and bynde
them to hym with a nearer bonde of frendeship. yet therfore
raylynge further on hym with spyteful and opprobrious
woordes

Marginal notes:

The thyrst of golde.

Ambition a-monge naked men.

This Ilande is cauled margarites Diues, or Dites.
A kynge of greate poure.

Biggeperles.

Cleopatra, queene of E-gypt resolued a pearle in vineger and drunke it, price v. thousande pounde of owr mony. thesecreenes of Vaschus.

woordes, he swoze great othes that he woolde furthwith in uade the Jlande, spoylynge, destroyinge, burnynge, dzow: nynge, and hangynge, sparinge neyther swoozde noz fyze, bntyll he hadde reuenged theyz iniuries: And therwith com: maunded his Culchus to bee in a redynes. But the twoo kyn: ges Chiapes and Tumaccus, exhozted hym frendly to deferre this enterpzise bntyll a moze quiete season, bycause that sea was not nauigable withowte greate daunger, beinge nowe the be gynnynge of Nouember. Wherin the kynges seemed to saye trewe. Foz as Vaschus hym selfe wzyteth, great rozyng of the sea was harde amonge the Jlandes of the goulfe by reaso of the raginge and conflicte of the water. Great ryuers also des cending from the toppes of the mountaynes the same time of the peace, & ouerflowyng theyz bankes, dzpuyng downe with theyz byolence greate rockes and trees, make a marueylous noyse. Lykewise the furie of the South and Nozthcast wyn des, associate with thunder and lyghtnynge at the same sea: son, dyd greatly moleste them. Whyle the wether was fayze they were bexed in the night with could: and in the day time the heate of the sonne troubled them: wherof it is noo mar: uaile, fozasmuche as they were neare bnto the Equinoctiall lyne, although they make noo mention of the eleuation of the pole. Foz in such regions, in the nyght, the mone and other coulde planettes: but in the daye, the soone and other hotte planettes, doo chiefely exercise theyz influence: Althowghe the antiquitie were of an other opinion, supposinge th Equi noctiall circle to bee bnhabitable and desolate by reason of the heate of the soonne hauinge his course perpendiculerly oz directely ouer the same: except a fewe of the contrary opinion, whose assertions the Poztugales haue at these dayes by ex: perience pzoued to bee trewe. Foz they saile yearely to thinha: bitantes of the south pole, being in maner Antipodes to the peo ple cauled Hyperborei bnder the Nozth pole, and exercise mar: chaundies with them. And here haue J named Antipodes, fozas much as J am not ignozant that there hath byn men of singu lar witte and great lernyng, which haue denyed that there is Antipodes: that is, such as walke feete to feete. But it is most certeyne, that it is not gyuen to anye one man to knowe all thynges. Foz euen they lso were men: whose pzopertie is to erre and bee deceaued in many thynges. Neuertheleke, the

Poztugales

Greate ryuers faulyng from mountaynes.

Thunder and lyghtnynge in Nouember.

Colde in the nyght nere the Equinoc: tial.

habitable re: gions bnder the Equinocti all lyne.

The natiuita: tions of the poztingales towarde the southe pole. Antipodes. he meaneth S. Augustine and Lectau: tius.

Portugales of owre tyme, haue sayled to the fyue and fyftie degree of the south pole: Where, coompasinge abowte the poynt thereof, they myght see throughowte al the heauen abour the same, certeyne shynynge whyte cloudes here & there amonge the starres, lyke vnto theym whiche are seene in the tracte of heauen cauled *Lactea via*, that is, the mylke whyte waye. They say, there is noo notable starre neare about that pole lyke vnto this of owres which the common people thynke to bee the pole it selfe (cauled of the Italians *Tramontana*, and of the Spanyardes *Nortes*) but that the same fauleth benethe the Ocean. When the sonne descendeth from the myddeste of the axiltree of the woozlde frome vs, it ryseth to them, as a payre of balances whose weyght inclynynge from the equall poyse in the myddest towarde eyther of the sydes, causeth the one ende to ryse as much as the other fauleth. When therefore it is autumne with vs, it is spzynge tyme with thē: And summer with vs when it is wynter with them. But it suffiseth to haue sayde thus much of strange matters. Let vs now therfoze returne to the histozie and to owre men.

❡ The seconde booke of the thyzde Decade.

Aschus by thaduice of kynge *Chiapes* and *Tumaccus*, determyned to deferre his vyage to the sayde Ilande vntyll the nexte spzynge oz summer, at which tyme *Chiapes* offered hym selfe to accoompany owre men and ayde them therin all that he myght. In this meane tyme *Vaschus* had knowleage that these kynges had nettes and fysshynge places in certeyne stations of that sea nere vnto the shoze, where they were accustomed to fysshe foz sea muscules in the which perles are engendzed: And that foz this purpose they had certeyne dyuers oz fysshers exercised frome theyz youthe in swymmynge vnder the water. But they doo this onely at certeyne tymes when the sea is calme, that they may theselues coome to the place where these shell fysshes are woonte to lye. Foz the bygger that they are, soo much lye they the deaper and neuer to the bottome. But the lesser, as it were dowghters to the other, are neuer the bzyme of of the water. Lykewyse the leaste of all, as it were their nieses, are yet nearer to the superficiall parte therof. Too them of the byggesse sorte whiche lye lowesse, the fysshers descende the depthe of three mens heyght, and sumtyme foure. But to the doughters or nieses as their succession, they descend onelye to the mydde thygh. Sumtymes also, after that the sea hathe byn disquyeted with vehemente tempestes, they fynde a greate multytude of these fysshes on the sandes, beyng dryuen to the shore by the vyolence of the water. The perles of these whiche are founde on the sande, are but lytle. The fisshe it selfe, is more pleasaunte in catynge then are owre oysters as owre men report. But perhappes hunger the sweete cause of all meates, caused owre men soo too thynke. Whether perles bee the hartes of sea musculs (as Aristotell supposed) or the byrthe or spaune of there intrals (as *Plinye* thought) Or whether they cleaue contynually to the rockes, or wander by coompanies in the sea by the guydinge of theldesse: Whether euerye fysshe bryngeforth the one perle or more, at one byrthe or at dyuers: Also whether theye bee fyled frome the rockes wherunto theye cleaue, or maye bee easylye pulled awaye, or otherwyse faule of by them selues when theye are coomme to there full grouth: Lykewyse whether perles bee harde within the shelle or softe, owre men haue as yet noo certayne experyence. But I trusse or it bee longe, too knowe the truth hereof. For owre men are euen nowe in hande with the matter. Also, as soone as I shall bee aduertysed of the arryuall of *Petrus Arias* the cappytayne of owre men, I wyll desyre hym by my letters to make diligent searche for these thynges, and certifye me therof in all poyntes. I knowe that he wyll not bee slacke or omytte any thynge herein. For he is my verye frende: and one that taketh greate pleasure in consyderynge the woorkes of nature. And surelye it seeme h vnto me vndecente, that wee shoulde with sylence ouerslyppe so greate a thynge whiche aswell in the owlde tyme as in owre dayes, hathe, & yet doothe, drawe bothe men and women to emmoderate desyre of superfluous pleasure. Spayne therefore shal be able hereafter with perles to satisfie the greedye appetite of suche as in wanton pleasures are lyke vnto *Cleopatra* & *Asopus* So that frome hensforth we shal neyther enuye nor reuerence the nyse frucefulnes of *Stoidum*, or *Taprobana*, or the redde sea.

Dyuers questios as cócernynge perles

Petrus arias

wanton and superfluous pleasures. Cleopatra. Asopus. Stoidum. Taprobana.

The thyrde decade.

But lette vs nowe returne to owre purpose. Vaschus therfore determined with the fyſſhers of Chiapes to proue what myght bee doone in his fyſhe pooles oꝛ ſtations of ſea muſcules. Chiapes to ſhewe hym ſelfe obediente to Vaschus his requeſte, although the ſea were bꝏyſtꝛous, cꝏmmaunded thirtye of his fyſſhers to pꝛepare them ſelfes and to reſoꝛte to the fyſſhinge places. Vaschus ſente onelye ſyxe of his men with them to bee holde them frome the ſea bankes, but not to cꝏmmitte them ſelues to the daunger of the ſea. The fyſſhynge place was diſtante frome the palayce of Chiapes aboute tenne myles. They durſte not aduenture to dyue to the bottome by reaſon of the ſurpe of the ſea. yet of the muſcules whiche lye hyghcſt, and of ſuche as were dꝛyuen to the ſhoꝛe by the vyolence of the water, theye bꝛoughte ſyxe greate farthels in the ſpace of a fewe dayes. The perles of theſe were but lyttle, aboute the bygnes of ſmaule fytches: yet verye fayꝛe and bewtyfull, by reaſon theye were taken newely owte of the fyſſhe, beinge yet rawe. And that they ſhulde not bee repꝛoued of lyinge as concerninge the bignes of theſe ſea muſculs, they ſente many of them into Spayne to the kynge with the perles, the fyſſhe beynge taken owte. Wee thinke verily that there maye in noo place bygger bee founde. Theſe ſhelle fyſſhes therfoꝛe beynge thus founde here in ſoo manye places in that ſea, and gold in maner in euerye houſe, dꝏ argue the ryche treaſurye of nature too bee hyd in thoſe coaſtes, foꝛaſmuche as ſuche greate ryches haue byn founde as it were in the lytle fynger of a gyantes hande. What then maye wee thynke of the hole hande of the gyante (foꝛ hetherto theye haue onely bynne in hande with the confynes of Vraba) when theye ſhall haue thoꝛowly ſearched all the coaſtes and ſecreates of the inner partes of all that large lande. But Vaschus contented with theſe ſygnes & ioyfull of his good ſucceſſe in theſe enterpꝛiſes, determined by an other waye to returne to his felowes in Dariena, where alſo, they haue golde mynes aboute tenne myles from the village. He gaue therfoꝛe kyng Chiapes leaue to depart, and to folowe hym nꝏ further. Conſailyng hym to continue faythfull to the chꝛiſtian kynge his loꝛde & maiſter. Thus embꝛaſinge the one the other, & ioyninge handes, Chiapes departed, with teares declaring the good mynde which he boꝛe to owre men. Vaschus leaning his ſicke men with Chiapes, went foꝛward on his
ioꝛneye

The fyſſhing place of king Chiapes.

Golde in maner in euery houſe.
The ryche treaſurye of nature.

The golde mynes of Dariena.

iourney with the resydue, hauinge also with him for guydes three of Chiapes maryners. He conueyghed his armye ouer a greate ryuer into the dominion of a certeine kynge cauled Teaocha: who beinge aduertised of the coommyng of owre men, of whose famous actes he had harde muche before, was verye gladde therof and entertepned them honozably: So that for a token of his frendely affection towarde them, he gaue Vaschus twentie poundes weyght of wrought golde after eyght ounces to the pounde: Also twoo hundzeth bigge perles: but not fayze, by reason they were taken owt of the musculs after they had byn sodden. After they had ioyned handes, Vaschus recompensed hym with certeyne of owre thynges. Lykewise rewardynge his guydes the seruantes of Chiapes, he dismissed them with commendations to theyr lord. Kyng Teaocha at the departure of owr men from his palaice, dyd not onely appoint them guydes to conduct them in the way, but also gaue them certeyne slaues in the steede of beastes to cary thryr bytayles, bycause they shulde passe thorowgh many desertes, baren and rowgh mountaynes and terrible wooddes full of tygers and Lions. He sent also one of his sonnes with these slaues, ladynge them with salted and dyzed fysshe, and bzeade of those regions, made of the rootes of Maizium and Iucca. He also commaunded his sonne not to depart from owr men untyl he were licenced by Vaschus. By theyr conductinge therfore, Vaschus came to the dominion of an other kyng whose name was Pacra, a cruell tyranne, fearefull to the other kynges his boztherers, and of greater peure then any of them. This tyran, whether it were that his giltie conscience for his mischeuous actes, put him in feare that owre menne woolde reuenge the same, oz that he thought hym selfe inferioz to resist them, fled at theyr commynge. Vaschus wzyteth that in these regions in the mooneth of Nouember he was sore afflicted with greate heate and intollerable thirst, by reason that syde of the mountaynes hath lyttle water: In soo muche that they were in daunger to haue perished but that certeyne of thinhabitantes showed them of a spzynge which was in the secreate place of a woodde, whither Vaschus with all speade sent twoo quycke and strange younge men of his coompanions with theyr goutdes and suche water be Telles as Teaocha his men bzowghte with them, Of thinhabitantes, there durst none depart from thyzre

Kynge Teaocha enterteyneth Vaschus frendelye.

Twentye pounde weight of wroughte golde.

Desertes full of wylde beastes.

Dzyed fysshe

Kynge Pacra a tyranne.

Greate heate in the monethe of Nouember.

there coompany bycause the wylde beastes doo soone inuade naked men. For in those moūntaynes, and especially in th wooddes neare vnto the springe, they saye that they are sum tymes taken owte of there houses in the nyght, excepte they take good heede that the doores bee well sparde. It shall no bee frome my purpose, hereto declare a particular chaūce be fore I enter any further in this matter. Theye saye therfor that the laste yeare the regyon of *Dariena* was noolese infested and trowbeled with a fierse tyger, then was *Calidonia* in tym paste with a wylde bore, and *Nemea* with a horrible lyon. For they affyrme that for the space of syre hole moonethes ther passed not one nyghte withowte summe hurte doone : so that it kylled nyghtlye eyther a bullocke, a mare, a dogge or a hogge, sumtimes euen in the highe wayes of the village For owre men haue nowe greatheardes of cattayle in those regions. They say also that when this tyger had whelpes noo man myght safelye goo furthe of his doores, bycause she spared not men if shee mette fyrste with them. But at the len geth, necessitye enforced them to inuente a policye howe they myght bee reuenged of suche bludshed. Searchynge therfor dilygently her footesteppes, and folowynge the pathe wher bye shee was accustomed in the nyght season to wander owte of her denne to seeke her praye, theye made a greate trench or pytte in her walke, coueringe the same with hurdels wher vppon theye caste parte of the earthe and dispersed the resy due. The dogge tyger chaunced fyrste into this pitfaul, and fe vppon the poyntes of sharpe stakes and suche other ingeni as were of purpose fyxed in the bottome of the trenche. Be ynge thus wounded, he rored soo terrybly, that it grated th bowels of suche as harde hym, and the wooddes and mon taynes neare aboute, rebounded the noyse of the horryble crye. When they perceaued that he was layde faste, they re sorted to the trenche and slewe hym with stones, dartes, and pykes. With his teethe and clawes, he broke the dartes in to a thousande clyppes. Beynge yet deade, he was fearefull to all suche as behelde hym: what then thinke you he woolde haue doone beynge alyue and loose. One *Iohannes Ledismi* of Ciuile, a nere frynde to *Vaschus* and one of the coompanyons of his trauayles, toulde me that he hym selfe dyd eate of the fleshe of that tiger: and that it was nothinge inferyor to bief

in

Marginal notes:

Hurte by wylde bea stes.
A tyger.
Calydonia is a foreste in Scotlande.
Nemea is a wodde in Greece.

Tigers whel pes.

Thus the E gyptians take Crocodiles.

The dogge tyger taken.
The roryng of the tyger.

Tigers flesh eaten.

in goodnes. Kynge demaunded howe they knewe hit to bee a tyger forasmuche as none of them had euer seene a tyger, they answered that they knewe hit by the spottes, fiercenes, agilitye, and suche other markes and token wherby the anciente wryters haue described the tiger. For sum of them, had fore tyme seene other spotted wilde beastes, as lybardes & panthers. The dogge tiger beynge thus kylled, theye folowynge the trase of his steppes towarde the mountaines, came to the denne where the bytche remayned with her twoo younge suckynge whelpes. But shee was not in the denne at there coommynge. Theye fyrste caryed awaye the whelpes with them. But afterwarde fearynge leaste they shulde dye cause theye were very younge, entendynge when they were bygger to sende them into Spayne, they put cheynes of yren boute there neckes, and caryed them agayne to there denne: whither returnynge within a fewe dayes after, theye founde the denne emptye and the cheynes not remoued frome there place. Theye suppose that the damme in her furye tore them in pyeces and caryed them awaye, leste anye shulde haue the truition of them. For theye playnely affirme that it was not possible that they shulde bee loosed frome the chaynes alyue. The skynne of the deade tyger stuffed with drye herbes and strawe, theye sente to *Hispaniola* to the admyrall and other of the chiefe rulers frome whome the newe landes receyue there lawes and succoure. It shall at this tyme suffyce to haue wryten thus much of the tygers, as I haue lerned by the reporte of them whiche bothe susteyned domage by there rauenynge, and also handeled the skynne of that whiche was slayne. Let vs nowe therfore returne to kynge *Pacra* frome whome wee haue disgressed. When *Vaschus* had entred into the houses forsaken of *Pacra*, he sente messengiers to reconcyle hym as he had doone the other kinges. At the first he refused to coomme. But after threatenynges, he came with three other kynges in his coompanye. *Vaschus* wryteth that he neuer sawe a more monstrous and deformed creature: And that nature hath onely gyuen hym humane shape, and otherwyse to bee worse the a brute beaste, with maners accordynge to the lynyamentes of his bodye. He abused with moste abhominable lechery the doughters of foure kynges his brotherers frome whome hee had taken them by vyolence. Of the fylthye behauoure of

The bitche tyger.

Tigers whelpes.

A straunge thynge.

kynge pacra.

Bb   Pacra

Naturall hatred of vyce.

Pæra, of his crueltye and iniuryes doone by hym, many of the other kynges made greuous coomplayntes to Vasebus as vnto a hygh Judge and iuste reuenger: Moste humblye besechyng hym to see suche thynges punysshed, forasmuche as theye tooke hym for a man sente of god for that purpose. Herevppon Vasebus aswell to wynne their good wylles, as also too shewe an example of terroure to suche as vsed lyke faschions,

Foure kinges deuoured of dogges.

commaunded that this monstrous beaste with the other three kynges whiche were subiecte to hym and of lyke condicions, shulde bee geuen for a praye to his feyghtinge dogges, and their torne carkeses to bee burned. Of these dogges whiche theye vse in the warres, theye tell maruelous thynges.

The vse of dogges in warre ageinst naked men.

For theye saye that theye runne vppon thinhabitantes armed after there maner, with noo lesse fiercenes then if theye were hartes or wylde boxes, if the Spaniardes doo but onely poynte towarde them with their fyngers: In soo muche that oftentymes they haue had no neede too dryue their enemyes too fyght with swoordes or arrowes: But haue doone the same onely with dogges placed in the forefronte of their battayle, and lettynge them slyppe with their watche woorde and pryuye token. Wherevppon the barbaryans stryken with feare by reason of the cruell countenaunces of the masties, with their desperate bouldenes and vnaccustomed houlynge and backynge, haue disparcled at the fyrste onsette and broke their arraye. yet it chaunseth otherwyse when theye haue anye conflicte agaynst the Canibales and the people of

The Canybales are experte archers.

Caramairi. For these are fyerser, and more warrelyke men: Also so experte archers, that theye can moste certenlye dyrect their venemous arrowes against the dogges with suche celeritye as if theye were thunderboltes. By reason wherof, they sumtymes kyl many of thē. Thinhabytantes of these

Swoordes of woodde.

montaynes, doo not keepe warre with bowes and arrowes: But vse onelye Machanis, that is certayne longe and broude swoordes made of woodde: Also slynges, longe pykes and dartes hardened at the endes with fyere. Whyle kynge Pæra yet lyued, noo man coulde knowe of hym neyther by fayre meanes nor by foule, where he had the golde whiche was

Fiftie pounde weyght of golde.

founde in his house. For owre men founde in his iewel house fyftye poundes weyght of golde. Beynge therfore demaunded where he had it, he answered that they whiche gathered
the

the ſame in thoſe montaynes in his fathers dayes, were all deade: And that ſenſe he was a chylde, he neuer eſteemed golde moze then ſtones. More then this, thiye coulde not gette of hym. By this ſeuere punyſhment executed vppon, Paʒ era, Vaſchus coueyled vnto hym the myndes of all the other kynges of that prouynce. And by this meanes it came too paſſe, that when he ſente for the ſpoke men, whiche he lefte behynde hym with kynge Chiapes an other kynge whiche was in the myddle waye (whoſe name was Bononiama) entertʒ teyned them gentellye, and gaue them vij. pounde weyghts of pure wrought golde, beſyde great plentye of vyttayles. And not this onely, but alſo accompanyed them hym ſelfe vntyll he had brought them ſafely frome his palaice into th dominyon of Chiapes. Where takynge eche of them by the ryghte handes, he delyuered them to Vaſchus hym ſelfe, as a faythefull pledge committed too his charge, and there with ſpake to Vaſchus in this effecte. Moaſte myghtye and valyaunte vyctourer, beholde I here delyuer vnto powe, powre coompanions in ſuche plight as I receaued them wiſſhynge that I had byn aſwell able to gyue them healthe, as they were hertely welcoome to ſuche poze enterteynement as I was able to ſhewe them. For the fauoure and gentelneſſe whiche I haue founde bothe in powe and them, he ſhall re warde powe whiche ſendeth thunderynge and lyghtelyng to the deſtruction of myſcheuous men, and of his clemencye gi ueth vnto good men plentie of Iucca and Maizium in dewe ſea ſon. As he ſpake theſe woordes, he lyfted vppe his handes and eyes towarde the ſoonne whome they honoure for god. Then he ſpake further to Vaſchus, ſayinge: In that powe haue deſtroyed and ſlaine owre vyolent and proude euemics, powe haue brought peace and quyetneſſe to vs and owre ſa melues, and bounde vs for euer to loue and obeye powe. powe haue ſoo euercoome and tamed wylde monſters, that wee thynke powe to bee ſente from heauen for the puny ſhe ment of euell men and defence of innocentes, that vnder the protection of powre myghtye ſwoorde, wee maye hereafter leade owre lyues withowte feare, and with moze quietneſſe gyue thankes to the giuer of all good thinges for hʒs mercie beowed vnto vs in this behalfe. When thinterpretoure had toulde Vaſchus that kyng Bononiama had ſayde theſe woordes,

kynge Bono nima; frende to the chriſti ans.

wroughte golde.

The oration of kynge Bononiama

The ſparke of the lawe of nature, is the lawe written in the hartes of men.

and suche lyke, _Vaschus_ rendered hym lyke thankes for his
humanitye declared towarde owre men, and rewarded hym
as he had doone other in whome he founde lyke gentilnesse.
Vaschus wryteth that he lerned manye thynges of this kyng
as concernynge the greate rychesse of these regions: But
that he woolde at this present speake nothynge therof: And
reherseth the same as thynges lyke to haue good successe.
What this implicate _Hiperbole_, or aduauncement meaneth, I
doo not well vnderstande. But he playnely seemeth hereby to
prompte many greate thynges. And surely it is to be thought
that accordynge to his hope, greate riches maye bee looked
for. For they came in maner into none of thinhabytauntes
houses, but that they found in them, eyther brestplates or
cuirettes of golde, or elles golden ouches, iewels, or garlandes to weare aboute there heades, neckes, or armes. I
coniecture therfore thus by a symilitude of owre houses: If
amonge vs any man of great powre were moued with the desyre to haue great plentye of Iron, and woolde enter into I-
talye with a mayne force as dyd the Gothes in tyme paste,
what abundaunce of Iron shoulde he haue in their houses,
where as he shulde fynde in one place a fryingpan, in an o-
ther a chauldron, here a truet, and there a spytte, and these
in maner in euery pore mannes house, with suche other innumerable: Wherby any man maye coniecture that Iren is
plentifully engendred in suche regions where they haue soo
greate vse therof. Owre men also perceaued that thinhabytantes of these regions do no more esteeme golde then we do
Iren: nor yet soo muche after they sawe to what vse Iren
serued vs. Thus muche haue I thought good to write to-
powre holynesse of suche thynges as I haue gathered owt
of the letters of _Vaschus Nunnez_, and learned by woorde of
mouthe of such as were his companyons in these affayres. As
wee receyue them, so wee gyue them vnto powe. Tyme which
reueleth all secretes, shall hereafter mynyster larger argument of wrytynge. Theye coulde at this tyme doo no greate
thynge in searchynge the golde mynes, forasmuche as of one
hundreth fourescore and tenne men which _Vaschus_ brought
with hym from _Dariena_, there remayned onely threescore and
ten, or at the most fourescore, whose ayde he nowe vsed in
these daungerous aduentures, leauynge euer the crased men
behynde

Hiperbole.

Great plentye
of golde.

A symilitude
for the profe
of plentye of
golde.

Iren more
esteemed then
golde.

elped hym to the kynges howses all the waye that he went
but they woulde especte ... allo feisandye diseases, whiche
came lately from Hispaniola. For they were not able to abyde
the calamities as to lyue onely contented with the breade
of those regions, and wylde herbes without salte, drinkinge
none other then pure water, and that oftentimes eyther lac=
ynge or unwholsome, where asbefore their stomakes had byn
fed to good meates. But the owlde souldiours of Dariena,
were hardened to abyde all sorowes, and exceadynge tolle=
able of labour, heate, hunger and watchynge. In so muche
that merilye they make their booste that they haue obserued
longer and sharper lent then euer powre holinesse inioyned.
For they saye that for the space of foure hole yeares, they
are none other then herbes and frutes, excepte nowe and
then perhappes fyshe, and verye seldoome fleshe. Yea, and
that sumtime for lacke of al these, they haue not abhorred fro=
maungye dogges and filthye toades as wee haue layde be=
fore. The owlde souldiers of Dariena, Iraule those whiche
erste folowed the cappraynes Nicuefa and Fogeda to inhabyte
the lande, of the whiche nowe fewe were lyuynge. But lette
vs nowe omytte these thynges, and retourne to Vaschus the
fearcher of the montaynes.

The thyrde booke of the thyrde Decade.

Hen Vaschus had remained thirtye dayes in the
palayce of kynge Pacra, concilynge vnto hym
the myndes of thinhabitantes and prouidinge
thynges necessarye for his coompanions, he
departed frome thenke by the conducte of cer=
tayne of kynge Tesoeba his men, and came too
the banke of the ryuer Comogrus, wherof the region and king
herof, are named by the same name. He founde the spdes of
thefe montaynes fo rude and baren, that there was nothinge
apte to bee eaten, but wilde roores and certayne vnplesante
rutes of trees. Two kynges beinge neare of blidde, inhabyt=
ed this infortunate region, whiche Vaschus ouerpalTed with
all fpeede for feare of hunger. One of these poore kinges was
named Coterbus, and the other Ciuriza. He tooke them bothe

B b,iii   with

Marginal notes:
- Chaunge of dyet is daungerous.
- Owlde soul=diers.
- A longe lent.
- Comogrus.
- Two poore kynges,

Desertes.

with hym to gyyde hym in the waye, and dismyssed Tedoch his men with vytayles and rewardes. Thus for the space of three dayes, he wandered throughe many deserte wooddes, craggye mountaynes, & muddy marystes full of suche quamyres that men are oftentymes swalowed vp in them if they looke not the more warelye to their fiete. Also through places not frequented with resorte of men, and suche as nature had not yet opened to their vse, forasmuche as thinhabitantes haue seldoome entercourse betwene them, but onely by sundrye incurtions, the one to spoyle and destroye the other. Beynge otherwise contented to lyue onely after the lawe of nature, withowte worldly toyle for superfluous pleasures.

kynge Bechebuca submytteth hym selfe

Thus enteringe at the lengthe into the territorye of another kynge whose name was Bechebuca, they founde all thynges voyde and in silence : For the kynge and his subiectes, were all fledde to the wooddes. When Vaschus sente messengers to fetche hym, he dyd not onely at the fyrste submytte hym selfe, but also promysse his ayde with all that he mygyte make : Protestynge furthermore, that he fledde not for feare that owre men woolde doo hym any iniurie, but that he hyd hym selfe for verye shame and griefe of mynde, for that he was not able to receyue them honorablye accordynge vnto their dignitye, bycause his store of vytayles was consumed.

Vessels of golde.

Yet in a token of obedience and frendeshyppe, he sente owre men many vesselles of golde, desyringe them to accepte them as the gifte of a friud whose good will wanted not in greater thynges if his abilytye were greater. By whiche woordes the poore man seemed to insinuate that he had byn robbed and otherwise cruelly handled of his bortherers. By reason wherof, owre men were enforced to departe from thense more hungerly then theye came. As theye wente forwarde therfore, they espyed certeine naked men coomminge downe from a hylle towarde them. Vaschus coommaunded his armye to staye, and sente his interpretours to them to knowe what they wold haue. Then one of the to whom the other seemed to gyue reuerence, spake in this effect. Owre lorde & kinge

kynge Chiorisus sendeth Vaschus certeyne vessels of pure golde.

Chiorisus, greeteth yowe well : Wyllynge vs to declare that he hath harde of yowre puissaunce and vertue wherby yowe haue subdued euell men and reuenged the wronges doone to innocentes, For the whiche yowe noble factes and impre,

aa

as he dooth honour powre fame, soo woolde he thinke him
selfe moste happye if he myght receiue powe into his palaice.
But, forasmuche as his fortune hath byn so euell (as he im=
uteth it) that beynge owte of powre waye, powe haue o=
erpassed hym, he hath sent powe this golde in token of his
good wyll and fryndshyppe towarde powe. And with these
woordes he deliuered to *Vaschus* thirty dishes of pure golde.
Addynge hereunto, that when so euer it shulde please him to
ake the paynes to coomme to their kynge, he shulde receyue
greater gyftes. He declared further, that a kynge whyche
was their bortherer and mortall enemye, was very ryche in
golde : And that in subduynge of hym they shulde bothe ob=
cine greate rychesse, and also delyuer them from daylye ver=
tions : whiche thinge myght easilye be doone by their helpe
ycause they knewe the countrey. *Vaschus* put them in good
coomforte, and gaue them for rewarde certayne Iren axes
whiche they more esteemed then greate heapes of golde. For
hey haue lyttell neede of golde, hauynge not thuse of pesti=
crous money. But he that maye get but one axe or hatchet,
thynketh hym selfe rycher then euer was *Crassus*. For euen
hese naked men doo perceyue that an axe is necessarye for a
housande vses : And confesse that gold: is desyred onely
or certayne vaine and effeminate pleasures, as a thyng whi=
he the lyfe of man maye lacke withowte any inconuenience.
For owre glutteny and superfluous sumptuousnesse hath not
et corrupted them : By reason wherof they take it for noo
hame to lacke coobardes of plate, where as the pride and wan=
onnes of owre tyme dooeth in maner impute it to vs for ig=
comnye to bee withowte that, wherof by nature we haue no
eede. But their contentation with the benefytes of nature
doothe playnly declare that men may leade a free and happy
fe withowt tables, table clothes, carpettes, napkyns, and
owels, with suche other innumerable wherof they haue no
se, excepte perhappes the kynges furnishe their tables with
a fewe golden vessels. But the common people dryue away
unger with a pyece of their breade in the one hande, and a
uece of broylde fyshe or summe kynde of fruite in the other
ande. For they eate fleshe but seldome. When their fingers
are imbrued with any ounctuous meates, they wype them
ether on the soules of their feete, or on their thyghes, ye &
sumtymes

Axes of Iren
more esteemed
then any golde

Superfluous
and effemy=
nate plesures

An exemple
of the lyfe of
owre fyrst pa=
rentes.

‡Plentye of gold & scarcenesse of meate

knig Pecchorosa submytteth hym selfe.

xv. pounde weyghte of wroughte gode.

kyng Tumanama, looke decad. ii. lib. iiii

A good policye.

sumtymes on the skynnes of their priuye members in the stede of a nappekynne. And for this cause doo they ofte tymes washe them selues in the ryuers. Owre men therfo wente forwarde laden with golde, but sore afflicted wit hunger. Thus they came at the length to the dominion o kynge Pocchorosa who fledde at their coommynge. Here fo the space of thirtye dayes they fylled their emptye bellie with breade of the rootes of Maizium. In the meane tyme Vaschus sente for Pocchorosa: who beynge allured with pro misses and fayre woordes, came and submytted hym self bryngynge with hym for a present. xv. poundes weighte o wrought golde, and a fewe slaues. Vaschus rewarded hym a he had doone other before. When he was mynded to depar he was aduertised that he shulde passe through the domini of a certayne kynge whose name was Tumanama. This is h whome the soonne of kynge Comogrus declared to bee of s great poure and fearefull to all his borderers, & with who many of Comogrus familyers had byn captyue. But owre me nowe perceiued that they measured his poure by their own For their kinges are but gnattes compared to elephante in respecte to the poure and pollicye of owre men. Ow men were also enformed by suche as dwelte neare aboute manama, that his region was not beyonde the montaynes they supposed: Nor yet so ryche in golde as younge Com grus had declared. yet consulted they of his subduyng: wh che they thoughte they myght thealyer brynge to passe b cause Pocchorosa was his mortall enemye, who moste glad prompsed them his aduice and ayde herein. Vaschus therfo leauynge his sycke men in the vyllage of Pocchorosa, too with hym threscore of his moste valiante souldiers, and d clared vnto them howe kynge Tumanama had oftentymes sp ken prowde and threatnyng woordes ageynste them: Lyk wise that it nowe stoode them in hande of necessitye to pa through his dominion: And that he thought it beste to set vppon hym vnwares. The souldiers consented to his aduic and exhorted him to gyue thaduenture, promisinge that th woolde folowe hym whether so euer he wente. They dete mined therfore to go two dayes iorney in one daye, that manama not knowynge of their sooden commyng, myght ha no leasure to assemble an armye. The thynge came to pa

cii.

men as they had deuyſed. For in the fyrſte watche of the
nyght, oure men with the Poccharroſiais, inuaded the vyllage
and palaice of Tumanama, where they tooke hym priſoner ſuſ-
peccynge nothinge leſſe. He had with hym two younge men
whiche he abuſed vnnaturally: Alſo fourſcore women which
he had taken vyolently from dyuers kynges. Lykewiſe a
greate number of his gentelmen and ſubiectes were taken
ragelynge in other vyllages neare aboute his palaice. For
their houſes are not adherent togither as oures bee, bycauſe
they are oftentimes troubeled with vehement whirlewyndes
by reaſon of the ſudden chaunges and motions of the ayre
cauſed by the induence of the planetes in the equalitie of the
aye and nyght beynge there in maner bothe of one lengthe
throughowte all the yeare, foraſmuche as they are neare vnto the Equinoctiall lyne as we haue ſayde before. Their houſes are made of trees, couered and after their maner thetched
with the ſtalkes of certayne towghe herbes. To the palayce
of Tumanama, was onely one houſe adherent, and that euen
ſo bygge as the palayce it ſelfe. Eyther of theſe houſes were
in length a hundreth and twentie pales, and in bredth fyftie
pales as oure men meaſured them. In theſe two houſes the
kynge was accuſtomed to muſter his men as often as he
repared an armye. When Tumanama therfore, was thus taken captyue with all his Sardanapantcall familye, the Poc-
corroſians bragged and threatened hym beynge nowe baunde,
that he ſhulde ſhortly bee hanged. The other kynges alſo his
bortherers, reioyſed at his mysfortune. Wherby oure men
perceaued that Tumanama was noleſſe troubleſome to his neighbours, then was Pacra to the kinges of the ſouthe ſyde of the
montaynes. Vaſchus alſo the better to pleaſe them, threatned
hym greuouſly: But in deede entended no euell toward him.
He ſpake therfore ſharpely vnto hym with theſe woordes:
Thou ſhalte nowe ſuffer punyſhment thou cruell tyranne, for
thy pryde and abhominations. Thou ſhalte knowe of what
poure the chriſtians are whom thou haſte ſoo contemned and
threated to drawe by the heare of their heades to the nexte
ryuer and there to drowne them as thou haſte often tymes
made thy baunte emonge thy naked ſlaues. But thou thy
ſelfe ſhalte fyrſte feele that whiche thou haſte prepared for o-
ther. And herewith commaunded hym to bee taken vppe.

Marginal notes:

ky
nama is take
priſoner.

The cauſe of
vehemente
wyndes nere
the Equinoc-
tial.

kynge Tuma
nama his
palaice.

vaſchus his
woordes to
kynge Tuma
nama.

Neuertheleſſe gyuynge a priuye tooken of pardon to them
whiche layde haudes on him. Thus vnhappye *Tumanams*, fearynge and beleuynge that *Vaſchus* had mente in ernefte as he
commaunded, fell proftrate at his feete and with teares defyred pardon: Proteffynge that he neuer ſpake any ſuch
woordes. But that perhappes his noble men in their droon-
kenneſſe had ſo abuſed their toonges whiche he coulde no
rule. For their wynes although they bee not made of grape
yet are they of force to make men droonken. He declared furthermore that the other kynges his bortherers had of malice ſurmyſed ſuche lyes of hym enuyinge his fortune bycauſe
he was of greater poure then they. Mofte humbly deſyring
Vaſchus that as he tooke hym to bee a iufte vyctoruer, ſo to
gyue no credyte vnto their vniufte and malycious complain-
tes. Addynge herevnto that if it woolde pleaſe hym to pardon hym not hauinge offended, he woolde bringe him greate
plentie of gold. Thus layinge his ryght hande on his breaft
he ſwore by the ſonne, that he euer loued and feared the
chriſtians ſence he fyrfte harde of their fame and vyctorye.
Specially when he harde ſaye that they had *Machaus*, that
is, ſwoordes ſharper then theariſe, and ſuch as cutte in pieces al thynges that coomme in their waye. Then directyng
his eyes towarde *Vaſchus* who had his ſwoorde in his hande
he ſpake thus.   Who (excepte he were owte of his wytte)
dare lyfte vppe his hande ageynfte this ſwoorde of powers
wherwith powe are able with one ſtrooke to cleaue a man
from the heade to the nauell. Lette no man therfore perſwade
powe (o mofte myghtye vyctoruer) that euer ſuche woorde
proceded owte of my mouthe. As *Tumanams* with tremblyng
ſpake theſe woordes, therwith ſwalowynge downe the kare
of deathe, *Vaſchus* ſeemed by his teares to bee moued to compaſſion: And ſpeakyng to hym with chearefull countenance
commaunded hym to bee looſed. This doone, he ſente immediatly to his palaice for. xxx. poundes weyght of pure gold
artifycially wrought into ſundry ouches whiche his wyues
and concubynes vſed to weare. Alſo the thyrde daye fol-
wynge, his noble men and gentylmen ſent threſcore poundes weight of golde for their fyne and raunſumme. *Tumanam*
beyng demaũded wher they had that gold, anſwered that it
was not gathered in his dominiõs But that it was brought

O derunt quem metuunt.

kyng Tuma-nams his woordes.

Tumanams is pardoned.

xxx. poynde weyghte of wroughte golde.

lx poundes weyght of golde.

ly

his auncestours from the ryuer Comogrus towarde the southe,
But the Pocchorrosians & other his enemies, sayd that he lyed:
Affirmynge that his kyngdome was ryche in golde. Tumanama
on the contrary part, instantely protested that he neuer knewe
any golde myne in all his dominions. yet denyed not but
that there hath sumtimes byn founde certaine smaule graines
of golde, to the gatherynge wherof, he neuer had any regarde, bycause they coulde not gette it without great & longe
labour. Whyle these thynges were dooinge, the speke men
whiche Vaschus had lefte in the village of Pocchorrosa, came to
hym the. viii. day of the Calendes of January in the yeare
of Chryste. M. D. XIII. bryngyng with them certayne labourers from the kynges of the southe with sundrye instrumentes to dygge the grounde and gather golde. Thus passynge ouer the day of the natiuitye of Chryst without bodely
labour, vppon sainte Steuens daye he brought certeyne myners to the syde of a hyll not farre dystaunte from the palaice
of Tumanama, where (as he saith) he perceaued by the coloure
of the earth that it was lykely to brynge furthe golde. When
they had dygged a pytte not past a hand breadth and a halfe,
and syfted the earthe therof, they founde certayne smaule
graynes of golde no bygger then lintell seedes, amountynge
to the weyght of twelue graynes as they proued with their
balances of assaye before a notarie and wytnesse that the better credytte myghte bee gyuen therto. Wherby they argued
that the rychenesse of that lande was agreable to the reporte
of the borderers, although Vaschus coulde by noo meanes
cause Tumanama to confesse the same. They suppose that he nothynge esteemed so smaule a portion. But other saye that he
denyed his countrey to bee frutefull of golde, leaste by reason
therof the desyre of golde, myght intyse owre men to inhabyte his kyngdome, as in deede the seely kynge was a prophet in soo thinkynge. For they chose that and the region of
Pocchorrosa to inhabyte, and determyned to buylde townes in
them bothe, if it shulde so please the kynge of Castyle: Aswell
that they myght bee baytinge places and vytaylynge houses
for suche as shulde iorney towarde the southe, as also that
both the regions were frutefull and of good grounde to beare
frutes and trees. Intendynge nowe therfore to departe from

They ab-
horre labour.

The coloure
of the golden
earthe and a
tryall of the
same.

thenfe, he tried the earth by chaunce in an other place, where
the colour of the grounde with certayne fhyninge ftones, feemed to bee a tooken of golde. where canfynge a fmaule pitte
to bee dygged lyttell beneath thupper crufte of the earthe, he
founde fomuche golde as weyghed that pyece of golde whiche the Spaniardes caule *Caftellanum aureum*, and is commonly
cauled *Pefus*, but not in one grayne. Reioyfynge at thefe tookens in hope of great riches, he badde *Tumanama* to be of good
coomforte, promyfynge hym that he woolde bee his frende
and defender, foo that he troubeled not any of the kynges
whiche were frendes to the Chriftians. He alfo perfwaded
hym to gather plentye of golde. Summe faye that he ledde a-
waye all *Tumanama* his women, and fpoyled him leafte he fhuld
rebell. yet he delyuered his foonne to *Vafchus* to bee broughte
vppe with owre men, to learne their languiage and relygyon,
that he myght therafter the better vfe his helpe afwell in all
thynges that he fhulde haue to doo with owre men, as alfo
more polytykelye rule, and obtayne the loue of his owne fubiectes. *Vafchus* at this tyme fell into a vehement feuer by reafon of exceffe of labour, immoderate watchyng, and hunger:
In fomuche that departynge from thenfe, he was fayne too
bee borne vppon mennes backes in fheetes of goffampyne cotton. Lykewyfe alfo many of his fouldiers whiche were foo
weake that they coulde nother go nor ftonde. To this purpofe they vfed the helpe of thinhabytantes, who fhewed them
felues in althynges wyllynge and obedyente. Alfo fumme of
them whiche were fumwhat feeble and not able to trauayle,
although not greuoufly fycke, were ledde by the armes vntyll they came to the domynion of kynge *Commogrus* a greate
frende to the Chriftians, of whom wee haue largely made
mention before. At *Vafchus* commynge thether, he founde that
the owlde kynge was deade, and his foonne (whome we fo
prayfed for his wifedome) to raygne in his fteade: And that
he was baptifed by the name of Charles. The palayce of this
Comogrus, is fituate at the foote of a fteepe hyll well cultured.
Dauynge towarde the fouthe a playne of twelue leages in
breadth and veary frutefull. This playne, they caule *Zauana*.
Beyonde this, are the great and hyghe montaynes whiche
denyde the two feas wherof we haue fpoken before. Owte of
the fteepe hylles, fpryngeth the ryuer *Comogrus*, whiche runneth

Tokens of great plentie of golde.

Vafchus fauleth ficke.

Feeblenes of hunger and watchynge.

kynge Comogrus frendes to the Chriftians.

The large & fruteful plaine of Iauana.

Tho ryuer Comogrus.

neth through the sayde playne to the hyghe montaynes, receauynge into his chanell by their valleys, all the other ryuers, & so fauleth into the south sea. It is distante from Dariena, aboute threescore and tenne leages towarde the weste. As owre men therfore came to these parties, kynge Comogrus (otherwyse cauled Charles by his christian name) mette the company and entertayned them honorably, gyuynge them their fyll of pleasaunte meates and drynkes. He gaue also to Vaschus, twenty pounde weyght of wrought golde. Vaschus recompensed him with thinges which he esteemed muche more: As axes and sundry kyndes of carpenters tooles. Also a souldiours cloke, and a faire sherte wrought with needle woorke. By these gyftes, Comogrus thought hym selfe to bee halfe a god amonge his borderers. Vaschus at his departynge from hense, ernestly charged Comogrus and the other kynges to remayne faithfull and obedient to the christian king of Castile, if they desyred to lyue in peace and quietnesse: And that they shulde hereafter more diligently applye them selues to the gatheringe of golde to bee sente to the great christian Tiba (that is) kyng. Declaryng further, that by this meanes they shuld bothe gette them and their posterity a patrone and defender agaynst their enemyes, and also obtayne great abundaunce of owre thinges. These assayes thus happely achiued, he wente forwarde on his vyage to the palaice of kyng Poncha, where he founde foure younge men whiche were come from Dariena to certify hym that there were certayne shyppes coomme from Hispaniola laden with vyttayles and other necessaries. Wherfore takyng with him twentie of his moste lusty souldiers, he made haste to Dariena with longe iorneys: leauinge the resydue behynd him to folow at their leasure. He writeth that he came to Dariena the. xiiii. Cal. of Fe. An. 1514. The date of his letter is: From Dariena, the. iiii. day of march. He writeth in the same letter, that he had many fore conflictes, & that he was yet neyther wounded, or loste any of his men in the bataile. And therfore in al his large letter, there is not one leafe without thankes geuynge to almyghty god for his delyuery and preseruation from so many imminent perels. He attempted no enterprise or tooke in hande any viage withowt thinuocation of god and his holy faintes. Thus was Vaschus Balboa of a vyolente Goliath, tourned into Heliseus: And from

Co. v.   Amicus

xx. pounde weyght of wrought gold

Uaschus returneth to Dariena.

The good fortune of Uaschus.

Uaschus was turned from Goliath to Eliseus.

Anteus too *Hercules* the conquerour of monsters.   Beyng
therefore thus tourned from a rasshe royster to a polytyke
and discreate capitayne, he was iudged woorthy to bee a
uaunced to greate honoure. By reason whereof, he wa
bothe receaued into the kynges fauour, and therevppon cre
ted the generall or Lieuetenaunt of the kynges army in thos
Regions. Thus much haue I gathered bothe by the letter
of certeyne my faythefull frendes beinge in *Dariena*, and a
so by woorde of mouth of suche as came lately frome thens
It youre holynes desyre to knowe what I thynke herein
Suerly as by suche thynges as I haue seene, I beleue the
thynges to bee trewe, euen so thorder and agreinge of *Vasch
and his coompanions warrelyke letters, seeme to confirm
the same. The Spanyarde therfore shall not neede hereafte
with vndermynynge the earth with intollerable laboure t
breake the bones of owre mother, and enter many myles in
her bowels, and with innumerable daungers cut in sunde
hole mountaynes to make a waye to the courte of infernal
Pluto, to brynge from thense wycked golde the seede of innu
merable mischeues, withowte the whiche notwithstandyng
we may nowe scarsely leade a happy lyfe sithe iniquitie hat
so preuayled and made vs slaues to that wherof we are lord
by nature : The Spanyarde (I say) shall not neede with suc
trauayles & difficultie to dygge farre into the earth for gold
but shal fynde it plentifully in maner in the vpper crust of th
earth, or in the sandes of ryuers dryed vppe by the heate o
sommer, onely wasshynge the earth softely frome the same
And shall with lyke facilite gather plentie of pearles.   Cer
tenly the reuerent antiquitie (by al the Cosmographers aTen
obteyned not soo greate a benefyte of nature, nor yet aspire
to the knowleage hereof, bycause there came neuer man be
fore owte of owre knowen worlde to these vnknowen nat
ons: At the leaste, with a poure of men, by force of armes,
maner of conquest : wheras otherwise nothyng can be gotte
here, forasmuch as these nations are for the most part seuer
defenders of theyr patrimonies, and cruell to straungers, i
no condition admittinge them otherwyse then by conquest :
specially the fierce Canibales or Caribes. For these wyly
hunters of men, gyue them selues to none other kynde of e
ercyse but onely to manhuntynge and tyllage after theyr ma
ne

O flaterynge
fortune, looke
his death in
the booke of
the Ilande
latelyfounde.

The earth is
owre general
mother.

The courte
of infernall
Pluto.

There is a
better waye
then this.

The Spani
ardes con
questes.

Manhunters

ner. At the commynge therfore of owre men into theyr regi=
ons, they loke as suerly to haue them faule into their snares
as if they were hartes or wylde bores : and with no lesse con=
fidence licke their lippes secreately in hope of their praye . If
hey gette the vpper hande, they eate them greedely : If they
mystruste them selues to bee the weaker parte, they truste to
heyr feete, and flye swyfter then the wynde. Ageyne, yf the
matter bee tryed on the water, aswell the women as men can
dyue and swymme, as though they had byn euer brought vp
and fedde in the water. It is noo maruayle therfore yf the
large tracte of these regions haue byn hytherto vnknowen.
But nowe sithe it hath pleased God to discouer the same in
owre tyme, it shall becoome vs to shewe owre naturall loue to
mankynde and dewtie to God, to endeuoure owre selues to
brynge them to ciuilitie and trewe religion, to thincrease of
Christes flocke, to the confusion of Infidels and the Deuyll
heyr father who delyteth in owre destruction as he hathe
doone frome the begynnynge. By the good successe of these
first frutes, owre hope is, that the Christian regilion shall
breathe foorth her armes very farre. Which thyng shulde the
sooner coome to passe yf all menne to theyr poure (especially
Christian Princes to whom it chiefely perteyneth) wolde put
theyr handes to the plowe of the lordes vineyarde. The har=
uest suerly is greate, but the woorkemen are but fewe. As we
haue sayde at the begynnynge, powre holpnes shall hereafter
noorysshe many myriades of broodes of chekins vnder powre
wynges. But let vs nowe returne to speake of *Beragus* beinge
the weste syde of *Vraba*, and fyrst founde by *Colonus* the Admi
rall, then vnfortunately gouerned by *Diego Nicuesa*, and nowe
lefte in maner desolate : with the other large regions of those
prouinces brought from theyr wylde and beastly rudenes to
ciuilitie and trewe religion.

The fierse=
nesse of the
Canibales.

Owre duty to
god, and na=
turall loue to
mankynde.

Thoffice of
Christian
prynces.
The haruest
is great, &c.

Beragua.

Nicuesa.

❡ The fourth booke of the thyrde Decade.

I Was determyned (moste holy father) to haue
proceded no further herein, but that one fierye
sparke yet remaynynge in my mynde, woolde
not suffer me to cease. Wheras I haue therfore
declared howe *Beragua* was fyrste fownde by
Colonus

The fourth nauigation of Colonus the Admirall.

Colonus, my thincke I ſhulde commytte a heynous cryme if I ſhuld defraude the man of the due commendations of his tra-uayles, of his cares and troubles, and fynally of the daun-geours and perels, whiche he ſuſteyned in that nauigation. Therfore in the yeare of Chriſte. 1502. in the. vi. daye of the Ides of Maye, he hoyſed vppe his ſayles and departed from the Ilandes of Gades with. iiii. ſhyppes of fyftie or. iii. ſcore tunne a piece, with a hundreth thieſcore and tenne mē, and came with proſperous wynde to the Ilandes of Canaris within fiue daies folowinge, from thenſe arryuinge the.xvi. day at the Ilande of Dominica beinge the chiefe habitation of the Canibales, he ſayled from Dominica to Hiſpaniola in fyue o-ther daies. Thus within the ſpace of. xxvi. daies, with proſ-perous wynde and by the ſwyfte faule of the Ocean from the Eaſte to the weſt, he ſayled from Spaine to Hiſpaniola : Which

From Spaine to Hiſpaniola a thouſande and two hun-dreth leagues

courſe is counted of the mariners to bee no leſſe then a thou-ſande and twoo hundreth leaques. He taryed but a whyle in Hiſpaniola, whether it were wyllingly, or that he were ſo ad-moniſhed of the viceroye. Directing therfore his vyage from thenſe towarde the weſte, leauyng the Ilandes of Cuba and Iamaica on his ryght hande towarde the northe, he wryteth that he chaunſed vppon an Ilande more ſouthewarde then

The flory-ſhyng Ilande of Guanaſſa.

Iamaica, whiche thinhabitantes caule Guanaſſa, ſo floryſhinge and frutefull that it myghte ſeeme an earthlye Paradyſe. Coaſtynge alonge by the ſhores of this Ilande, he mette two of the Canoas or boates of thoſe prouinces, whiche were drawne with two naked ſlaues ageynſt the ſtreame. In theſe boates, was caryed a ruler of the Ilande with his wyfe and chyldren, all naked. The ſlanes ſeeynge owre men a lande, made ſignes to them with proude countenaunce in their maiſters name, to ſtande owte of the waye, and threatned them

Simple people.

if they woolde not gyue place. Their ſympelnes is ſuche that they nother feared the multitude or poure of owre men, or the greatnes and ſtraungenes of owre ſhippes. They thought that owre men woolde haue honoured their maiſter with like reuerence as they did. Owre men had intelligēce at the length

A greate marchaunt.

that this ruler was a greate marchaunte whiche came to the marte from other coaſtes of the Ilande. For they exerciſe bying and ſellynge by exchaunge with their confines. He had alſo with him good ſtore of ſuche ware as they made

iii

In neede of oz take pleasure in : as laton belles, rasers, knyues, and hatchettes made of a certeyne sharpe yelowe bzyght stone, with handles of a stronge kynd of woodde. Also many other necessary instrumentes with kychen stuffe and vesselles for all necessary vses. Lykewise sheetes of gossampine cotton bzought of sundzye coloures. Owze men tooke hym pzysoner with all his famely. But *Colonus* commaunded hym to bee losed shoztely after, and the greatest parte of his goodes to bee restozed to wynne his fryndeshippe. Beinge here instructed of a lande lyinge further towarde the southe, he tooke his vyage thether. Therfoze lytle moze then tenne myles distant frō hense, he founde a large lande whiche thinhabitantes cauled *Quiriquetana*: But he named it *Ciamba*. When he wente a lande and commaunded his chaplaine to saye masse on the sea bankes, a great confluence of the naked inhabitantes flockȝd thither symplye and without feare, bzinkynge with them plentey of meate and freshe water, maruelpynge at owze men as they had vpn summe straunge miracle. When they had pzesentȝed their giftes, they went sumwhat backeware and made lowe curtesy after their maner bowinge their heades and bodyes reuerently. He recompensed their gentylnes rewardinge them with other of owze thynges, as counters, bzasettes and garlandes of glasse and counterfecte stoones, lookynge glasses, nedelles, and pynnes, with suche other trashe, whiche seemed vnto them pzecious marchaundies. In this great tracte there are two regions wherof the one is cauled *Taia* and the other *Maia*. He wziteth that all that lande is very fayze and holsome by reason of the excellent temperacnesse of the ayer: And that it is inferiour to no lande in frutefull ground beinge partely full of montaines, and partely large playnes: Also replenyshed with many goodly trees, holsome herbes, and frutes, continupnge greene and flozyshynge all the hole yeare. It beareth also verye many holy trees and pyne aple trees. Also .vii. kyndes of date trees wherof summe are frutefull and summe baren. It bzingeth furth lykewyse of it selfe *Pelyoras* and wilde vynes laden with grapes euen in the wooddes emonge other trees. He saythe furthermoze that there is suche abundaunce of other pleasaunte and pzofitable frutes, that they passe not of vynes. Of one of those kyndes of date trees, they make certeyne longe and bzode swoozdes and dartes,

D d

The region of Queriquetana oz Ciamba.

Gentle people.

The regyons of Taia and Maia.

Seuen kyndes of date trees. Wylde vines.

les.　Thele regyons beare also goſſampyne trees here and
there commonly in the woodds. Lykewiſe *Mirobalanes* of ſun=
dry kyndes, as thoſe which the phyſitians calle *Emblicos* and
Chebulos. *Mirzium* alſo, *Iucces*, *Ages*, and *Battatas*, lyke vnto thoſe
whiche we haue ſayde before to bee founde in other regions
in theſe coaſtes. The ſame noryſſheth alſo lyons, Tygers,
Hartes, Roes, Goates, and dyuers other beaſtes. Lyke=
wyſe ſundry kyndes of byrdes and foules: Enonge the
whiche they keepe onely them to franke and feede, whiche
are in colour, bygnes, and taſte, muche lyke vnto owre pe=
hennes. He ſaith that thinhabitantes are of high and good=
ly ſtature, well lymned and proportioned both men and wo=
men: Coueryinge their pryuye partes with fyne breeches of
goſſampine cotton wrought with dyuers colours. And that
they may ſeeme the more cumlye and bewtifull (as they take
it) they paynte their bodyes redde and blacke with the iuce
of certeyne apples whiche they plante in their gardens for
the ſame purpoſe. Summe of them paynte their hole bodies:
ſumme but parte: and other ſumme drawe the portitures,
of herbes, floures, and knottes, euery one as ſeemeth beſt
to his owne phantaſye. Their language differeth vtterly
from theirs of the Ilandes nere aboute them.　From theſe
regions, the waters of the ſea ranne with as full courſe to=
warde the weſte, as if it had byn the faule of a ſwyfte riuer.
Neuertheleſſe he determined to ſearche the Eaſte partes of
this lande, reuoluynge in his mynde that the regions of *Pa=*
ria and *Os Draconis* with other coaſtes founde before toward
the Eaſte, ſhalde bee neare therabouts as in deede they were.
Departyng therfore from the large region of *Quiriquetana* the
riii. daye of the calendes of September, when he had ſailed
thirtie leaques, he founde a ryuer, without the mouth wher=
of he drewe freſhe water in the ſea. Where alſo the ſhore
was ſo cleane withowte rockes, that he founde grounde e=
uery where, where he myght aptely caſt anker. He wryteth
that the ſwifte courſe of the *Ocean* was ſo behement and con=
trarye, that in the ſpace of fortye dayes he coulde ſcarcelye
ſayle threeſcore and tenne leaques, and that with muche dif=
fycultie with many fetches and coompaſynges, fyndyng him=
ſelfe to bee ſumtimes repulſed and dryuen farre backe by the
vyolente courſe of the ſea when he woolde haue taken lande
　　　　　　　　　　　　　　　　　　　　　　　　towarde

Margin notes:
Mirobalanes
Byrdes and foules.
people of goodlyſtature
They paynt theyr bodyes
The ſwyfte courſe of the ſea from the Eaſt to the weſt. Paria.
Freſhe water in the ſea.
Fetches and compaſinges

towarde the euenynge, leaste perhappes wanderynge in vn= knowen coastes in the darckenesse of the nyght, he myght bee in daunger of shyppwracke: He wryteth that in the space of eyght leaques, he found thre great and fayre ryuers vp= pon the banckes wherof, there grewe reedes bygger then a mannes thygh, In these ryuers was also greate plentye of fyshe and great tortoyses: Lykewise in many places, multi= tudes of Crocodiles lyinge in the sande, and panyng to take the heate of the soonne: Besyde dyuers other kyndes of beastes wherunto he gaue no names. He sayth also that the people of that lande is very diuers and variable: beyng sum= where stonye and full of rough and craggie promontories of roppnes reachynge into the sea. And in other places as frut= full as maye bee. They haue also diuers kynges and rulers. In summe places they caule a kynge *Cacicus*: in other places they caule hym *Quebi*, and sumwhere *Tiba*. Suche as haue behaued them selues valiantly in the warres ageynste their enemies, and haue their faces full of scarres, they caule *Cu= pra*, and honour them as the antiquitie dyd the goddes whi= che they cauled *Heroes*, supposed to bee the soules of suche men as in their lyfe tyme excelled in vertue aud noble actes. The common people, they caule *Chiui*: and a man, they caule *Homem*. When they saye in their language, take man, they say *Hoppa home*. After this, he came to an other ryuer apte to beare great shyppes: Before the mouthe wherof, lye foure smaule Ilandes full of florishyng and frutfull trees. These Ilandes he named *Quatuor tempora*, from hense saylynge towarde the Easte for the space of. viii. leaques styll ageinste the vyolent course of the water, he founde twelue other smaule Ilandes. In the whiche bycause he founde a newe kynde of frutes muche like vnto owre lemondes, he cauled them *Limonares*. Wanderynge yet further the same waye for the space of. vii. leaques, he founde a great hauen enteryng into the land af= ter the maner of a goulfe the space of thre leaques, and in maner as brode, into the whiche fell a great ryuer. Here was *Nicuesa* loste afterwarde when he soughte *Beragua*: By reason wherof they cauled it *Rio de los perdidos*: that is, the ryuer of the loste men. Thus Colonus the Admirall yet further contynu= ynge his course ageynste the furye of the sea, founde manye hyghe mountaynes and horrible valleys, with dyuers ryuers

D D.ii.   and

Faire ryuers.
Great reedes

Great tortoy= ses.

Dyuers lan= guages.

Heroes.

Quatuor tem= pora.

Twelue I= landes named Limonares.

Rio de los per= didos.

and hauens, from all the whiche (as he faythe) proceeded
fweete fauers greatly recreatynge and conforrynge nature,
In fo muche that in all this longe tracte there was not one
of his men defcafed vntyll he came to a region whiche thin=
habitantes caule Quicuri, in the whiche is the hauen cauled
Cariai, named Mirobalanus by the admirall bycaufe the Mirobal=
lane trees are natiue in the regions therabout. In this hauen
of Cariai, there came about two hunderth of thinhabitantes
to the fea fyde with euerye of them three or foure dartes in
their handes : yet of condition gentell enoughe, and not re=
fufyng ftraungers. Their commyng was for none other pur=
pofe then to knowe what this newe nation mente, or what
they broughte with them. When owre men had gyuen then
fygnes of peace, they came fwymmynge to the fhyppes and
defyred to barter with them by exchaunge. The admirall to
allure them to frendfhippe, gaue them many of owre thinges:
But they refufed them, fufpectynge fumme difceate thereby
bycaufe he woolde not receyue theirs. They wroughte all by
fygnes : for one vnderftoode not a woorde of the others lan=
guage. Suche gyftes as were fente them, they lefte on the
fhore and woolde take no part therof. They are of fuche ciui=
litye and humanytie, that they efteeme it more honorable, to
gyue then to take. They fente owre men two younge women
beinge vyrgines, of cómendable fauour and goodly ftature,
fygnifyinge vnto them that they myghte take them awaye
with them if it were their pleafure. Thefe women after the
maner of their countrey, were couered from their ancles fum=
what aboue their priuye partes with a certeyne clothe made
of goffampine cotton. But the men are al naked. The women
vfe to cutte their heare : But the men lette it growe on the
hynder partes of their heades, and cutte it on the fore
parte. Their longe heare, they bynde vppe with fyllettes, ¢
winde it in fundry rowles as owre maydes are accuftomed to
do. The virgins which were fente to the Admirall he decked
in fayre apparell, ¢ gaue them many gyftes, and fent theym
home ageyne. But lykewife all thefe rewardes and apparell
they left vppon the fhore bycaufe owre men had refufed their
gyftes. Yet tooke he two men away with him (and thofe ve=
ry wyllyngly) that by lernyng the Spanyfhe tonge, he might
afterwarde vfe them for interpretours. He confidered that
the

The region
of Quicuri.

The hauen
of Cariai or
Mirobalanus

Ciuile and hu
mane people

the tractes of these coastes were not greately troubled with
vehement motions or ouerflowynges of the sea, forasmuche
as trees growe in the sea not farre frome the shore, euen as
they doo vppon the bankes of ryuers. The whiche thynge as
so other doo affirme whiche haue latelyer searched those coastes, declaring that the sea riseth and falleth but lyttle there
aboute. He sayth furthermore, that in the prospecte of this
lande, there are trees engendred euen in the sea, whiche after
that they are growen to any height, bende downe the toppes
of theyr braunches into the grounde: which embrasing them
causeth other braunches to sprynge owt of the earth, and take
roote in the earth, bryngynge foorth trees in theyr kynde suc-
cessiuely as dyd the fyrst roote from whense they had theyr o-
riginall, as do also the settes of vines when onely the the
endes therof are put into the grounde. Plinie in the twelfth
booke of his natural historie maketh mention of suche trees,
describynge them to bee on the lande, but not in the sea. The
admirall wryteth also that the lyke beastes are engendred
in the coastes of Caria, as in other prouinces of these regions,
and such as we haue spoken of before. Yet that there is one
founde here in nature much differinge from the other. This
beaste is of the byggenes of a greate moonkeye, but with a
tayle muche longer and bygger. It lyueth in the wooddes,
and remoueth from tree to tree in this maner. Hangynge by
the tayle vppon the braunche of a tree, & gatheryng strength
by swayinge her body twyse or thryse too and fro, she casteth
her selfe from braunche to braunche and so from tree to tree as
though she flewe. An archer of owres hurt one of them. Who
perceauinge her selfe to be wounded, leapte downe from the
tree, and fiercely set on hym which gaue her the wounde, in
so muche that he was fayne to defende hymselfe with his
sworde. And thus by chaunce cuttyng of one of her armes,
he toke her, and with muche a doo brought her to the shyps
where within a whyle, shee waxed tame.   Whyle she was
thus kepte and bownde with cheynes, certeyne other of owre
men hidde chased a wylde bore owt of the maryshes nere
with the sea syde. For hunger and desyre of fleshe, caused the
to take double pleasure in huntynge. In this meane tyme or
they which remayned in the shippes, goinge a lande to recre-
ate them selues, tooke this moonkey with them,   Who as

D D, iii,   soone

(margin: Trees gro-
wynge in the
sea after a
straunge sort.

Plinie.

A straunge
kynde of
moonkeys.

A moonkeye
feyghteth
with a man)

A conflict be-twene a mon-key and a wylde boze.

soone as ſhee had eſpied the boze, ſet vp her briſtels & mad towarde her. The boze lykewyſe ſhooke his briſtels & whett his teethe. The moonkey furiouſly inuaded the boze, wrap-pynge her tayle about his body, and with her arme reſerued of her victourer, helde hym ſo faſt aboute the throte, that he

The bodyes of kynges dry-ed & reſerued

was ſuffocate. Theſe people of Cariai, vſe to drye the dead bodyes of their princes vppon hurdels, and ſo reſerue them inuolued in the leaues of trees. As he went forwarde about twentie leagues from Cariai, he founde a goulfe of ſuch larg-nes that it contayned .xii. leagues in compaſſe. In the mouth of this goulfe were foure lyttle Jlandes ſo nere togyther that they made a ſafe hauen to enter into the goulfe. This goulfe is the hauen which we ſayde before to be cauled Cera-

Cerabaro.

baro of thinhabitantes. But they haue nowe lerned that only the lande of the one ſyde therof, lyinge on the ryght hand

Aburema.

at the enterynge of the goulfe, is cauled by that name. But that on the lefte ſyde, is cauled Aburema. He ſayth that al this goulfe is ful of fruteful Jlandes wel replenyſſhed with goodly trees: And the grounde of the ſea to bee verye cleane withowt rockes, and commodious to caſt anker: Lykewyſe the ſea of the goulfe to haue greate abundance of fyſſhe: and the landes of both the ſydes to bee inferior to none in frutful-nes. At his fyrſt arryuynge, he eſpyed two of thinhabitantes hauynge cheynes about their neckes, made of ouches (which

Cheynes of golde.

they caule Cuſuines.) of baſe golde artificially wrought in the formes of Eagles, and lions, with dyuers other beaſtes and foules. Of the two Cariaians whiche he brought with hym from Cariai, he was enformed that the regions of Cerabaro and Aburema were rych in golde: And that the people of Cariai haue

Plentie of golde.

all their golde frome thenſe for exchaunge of other of their thynges. They towlde hym alſo, that in the ſame regions there are fyue byllages not farre from the ſea ſyde, whoſe in-

Fiue villages rych in gold.

habitantes apply them ſelues onely to the gatherynge of gold. The names of theſe byllages are theſe: Chirara, Puren, Chitaza, Iureche, Atames. All the men of the prouince of Cerabaro, go na-ked, and are paynted with dyuers coloures. They take great pleaſure in wearynge garlandes of floures, and crownes made of the clawes of Lions and Tygers. The women couer

Crownes of beaſts clawes

only their priuie partes with a fyllet of goſſampine cotton. Departinge from henſe and coaſtynge ſtyll by the ſame ſhore

for

o: the space of .xviii. leagues, he came to another ryuer, where he espyed abaute three hundreth naked men in a company. When they sawe the shippes drawe neare the lande, they cryed owte aloude, with cruell countenaunces shakynge vp woodden swoordes and hurlynge dartes, takynge also oare in theyr mouthes and spoutyng the same ageynst our men: wherby they seemed to insinuate that they woolde receaue no condition of peace or haue owght to doo with them. Here he commaunded certeyne pieces of ordinaunce to be shot of toward them: yet so to ouershute them, that none myght be hurt therby. For he euer determyned to deale quietly and peaccably with these newe nations. At the noyse therfore of the gunnes and syght of the fyer, they fell downe to the grounde, and desyred peace. Thus enteringe into further frendshippe, they exchaunged theyr cheynes and ouches of golde for glasses and haukes belles and such other marchandises. They vse drummes or tymbrels made of the shelles of certeyne sea fysshes, wherewith they encorage thepm selues in the warres. In this tract are these seuen ryuers, *Acatebs, Quirebs, Zobroba, Aiaquitin, Vrida, Duribba, Beragua,* in all the whiche, golde is founde. They defende them selues ageynste rayne and heate with certeyne great leaues of trees in the steade of clokes. Departinge from hense, he searched the coastes of *hetere,* and *Embigar,* into the which faule the goodly ryuers of *Zohoran* and *Cubigar:* And here ceaseth the plentie and frutefulnes of golde, in the tracte of fiftie leagues or there about. From hense onely three leagues distant, is the rocke whiche in the vnfortunate discourse of *Nicuesa* we sayde was cauled of owre men *Pignonem.* But of thinhabitantes the Region is cauled *Vibba.* In this tracte also aboute syxe leagues frome hense, is the hauen which *Colonus* cauled *Portus Bellus* (wherof we haue spoken before) in the region whiche thinhabitantes caule *Xaguaguara.* This region is very peopulous: but they go all naked. The kyng is paynted with blacke colours, but all the people with redde. The kynge and seuen of his noble men, had euery of them a lyttle plate of golde hangynge at theyr nosethrylles downe vnto theyr lyppes. And this they take for a cumly ornamente. The menne inclose theyr priuie members in a shell: And the women couer theyrs with a syket of gossampine cotton tyed about theyr loynes. In theyr gardens

[marginal notes:]
Spytefull people.

Gunns make peace.

Seuen golde ryuers

Note where the plentie of golde endeth

Pignonem.
Vibba.
Portus Bellus

Paynted people.
A strange syght.
A shel in the steede of a codpiece.

gardens they noozyſſhe a frute muche lyke the nutte of a pyne tree : the, whiche (as we haue ſayde in an other place) groweth on a ſhrubbe muche lyke vnto an Artichocke : But the frute is muche ſofter, and meate for a kynge. Alſo. certeyne trees whiche beare gourdes, wherof we haue ſpoken before. This tree, they caule *Hibuero*. In theſe coaſtes they mette ſumtymes with Crocodiles lyinge on the landes, the whiche when they fled, or tooke the water, they lefte a very ſweete ſauour behynde them ſweeter then muſke or *Caſtoreum*. When I was ſente amba Taſadour for the catholike king of Caſtile to the Soltane of Babilon oz Alcayer in Egipte, the inhabitantes nere vnto the ryuer of *Nilus* toulde me the like of their female Crocodiles. Affyrmyng furthermore that the fatte oz ſewette of them is eqnall in ſweetnes with the pleaſaunte gummes of Arabie. But the Admirall was nowe at the length enforced of neceſſytie to departe from henſe, aſwell for that he was no longer able to abyde the contrarye and vyolente courſe of the water, as alſo that his ſhyppes were daily moze and moze putrified and eaten thzowgh with certeyne wormes which are engendzed of the warmenes of the water in all thoſe tractes nere vnto the Equinoctial line. The Venetians caule theſe woozmes *Biſſas*. The ſame are alſo engendzed in two hauens of the citie of *Alexandria* in Egipt and deſtroye the ſhyppes if they lye longe at anker. They are a cuber in length, and ſumwhat moze : not paſſyng the quantitie of a fynger in bygneſſe. The Spanyſhe mariner cauleth this peſtilence *Broma*. *Colonus* therfore whom before the great monſters of the ſea coulde not feare, nowe fearyng this *broma*, beynge alſo ſoore vexed with the contrary faule of the ſea, directed his courſe with the *Ocean* towarde the weſt, and came firſt to the ryuer *Hiebra*, diſtant onely two leaques from the ryuer of *Beragua*, bycauſe that was commodious to harbozowe great ſhippes. This region is named after the riuer, and is cauled *Beragua* the leſſe : Bycauſe bothe the ryuers are in the dominion of the kyng which inhabiteth the region of *Beragua*. But what chaunſed vnto hym in this vyage on the ryghte hande and on the lefte, lette vs nowe declare. Whyle therfore *Colonus* the Admirall remayned yet in the ryuer *Hiebra*, he ſent *Bertholomeus Colonus* his brother and Lieutenaunte of *Hiſpaniola*, with the ſhyppe boates and thzeeſcore and. viii. men

Crocodiles of sweete ſa-uour.

Alcayr oz Ba-bilon in Egipt

Shippes ea-ten with wormes.

Alexandria in Egypte.

Broma.

Hiebra,

Beragua.

men to the ryuer of Beragua, where the king of the region be=
inge naked and painted after the maner of the countrey, came
towarde them with a great multitude of men waytynge on
hym, but all vnarmed and without weapons, gyuinge also
sygnes of peace. When he approched nerer, and entered com=
munication with owre men, certeyne of his gentelmen nea=
reste aboute his person, remembringe the maiestie of a king,
and that it stoode not with his honour to bargen stondynge,
tooke a greate stoone owte of the ryuer, wasshynge an? rub=
bynge it very decently, & so put it vnder hym with humble
reuerence. The kyng thus syttyng, seemed with sygnes & to=
kens to insinuate that it shuld be lawfull for owre men t? sear
che & viewe al the ryuers within h?s dominion. Wherfore, the
vi. day of the Ides of February, leauing his boates with cer=
teyne of his coempany, he wente by lande a foote from the
bankes of Beragua vntyl he cam e to the ryuer of Duraba, whi=
che he affirmeth to be richer in gold then eyther Hiebra or Bera=
gus. For gold is engendred in al the riuers of that land. In so
muche that emonge the rootes of the trees growynge by the
bankes of the ryuers, & amonge the stones left of the water, &
also where so euer they dygged a hole or pyt in the grounde
not paste the deapehe of a handfull and a halfe, they founde
the earthe taken owte therof, myxte with golde: Where vp=
pon he determyned to fasten his foote there and to inhabyte.
Whiche thynge the people of the countrey perceauynge, and
smellynge what inconuenyence and myschiefe myght therof
enswe to their countrey if they shulde permitte straungers to
plante their habitation there, assembled a great army, and
with horrible owte crye assayled owre men (who had nowe
begoonne to buylde houses) soo desperately that they were
scarcely able to abyde the fyrste brunte. These naked barba=
rians at their fyrst approche, vsed onely slynges and dartes:
But when they came nearer to hande strookes, they foughte
with their woodden swoordes which they caule Machanas, as
wee haue sayd before. A man woolde not thinke what great
malice and wrath was kyndeled in their hartes ageinst owre
men: And with what desperate myndes they fought for the
defence of their lybertie whiche they more esteeme then lyfe
or ryches. For they were nowe so voyde of all feare, and
contemnynge deathe, that they neyther feared longe bowes

Ee   or cros=

how the king
of Beragua
enterteyned
the lyeutes
naunte.

Their reue=
rence to ther
kynge.

Golde in the
ry'er of Dus=
raba.

Great plenty
of golde.

Slynges and
dartes.

Lyberty more
esteemed thē
ryches.

oʒ croſſebowes, noʒ yet (whiche is mooʒe to be marueyled) were any thynge diſcouraged at the terryble noyſe of the gunnes ſhotte of from the ſhyppes. They retyʒed once. But ſhoʒtly after encreaſynge their noumber, they retuſned moʒe fiercely then at the fyʒſte. They woolde haue byn contented to haue receyued owʒe men frendly as ſtraungers, but not as inhabitours. The moʒe inſtance that owʒe men were to cermaine, ſo muche the greater multitude of boʒtherers flocked togytheʒ dayly, diſturbyng thẽ both nyght & daye ſumtymes on the one ſyde & ſumtymes on the other. The ſhyps lyeng at anker neare bnto the ſhoʒe, warded them on the backe halfe. But at the length they were fayne to foʒſake this lande, and retourne backe the ſame way by the which they came. Thus with much diffyculty and danger, they came to the Iland of *Iamaica* lyenge on the ſouth ſyde of *Hiſpaniola* and *Cuba*, with their ſhyppes as full of holes as ſieues, and ſo eaten with wooʒmes, as though they had byn boʒed through with wimbles. The water entered ſo faſte at the ryftes and holes, that if they had not with the paynefull laboʒe of their handes empted the ſame as faſte, they were lyke to haue peryſſhed. Where as yet by this meanes they arryued at *Iamaica*, althoughe in maner halfe deade. But their calamitie ceaſed noʒ here. Foʒ as faſt as their ſhyppes leaked, their ſtrengthe dimyniſſhed ſo that they were no longer able to keepe them from ſynkynge. By reaſon wherof, faylynge into the handes of the barbarians, and incloſed withowte hope of departure, they led their lyues foʒ the ſpace of tenne monthes among the naked people moʒe myſerably then euer dyd *Achemenides* emonge the gyantes cauled *Ciclopes*: rather lyuing thẽ beinge eyther contented oʒ ſatiſfied with the ſtrange meates of that Ilande: and that onely at ſuch tymes as pleaſed the barbarians to gine them part of theirs. The deadly enmity and malice whiche theſe barbarous kinges beare one ageinſt an other, made greatly with owʒe men. Foʒ at ſuche tymes as they attempted warre ageinſt their boʒtherers they woold ſumtymes gyue owʒe men parte of their breade to ayde them. But howe myſerable and wretched a thyng it is to lyue onely with breade gotten by beggynge, yowʒe holyneſſe maye eaſylye coniecture: Eſpecially where all other accuſtomed foode is lackynge, as wyne, oyle, fleſſhe, butter, cheſe, and mylke

The Spanyardes are dryuen to flight.

The Ilande of Jamaica.

A myſerable caſe.

milke, wherwith the ſtomakes of owr people of Europe haue
euer byn nooriſſhed euen from their cradelles. Therfore as
neceſſyty is ſubiecte to no lawe, ſo doothe it enforce men to
attempte deſperate aduentures. And thoſe the ſoner, which
by a certeyne noblylytie of nature do no further eſteeme lyfe
then it is ioyned with ſumme felicity. Bertholomeus Colonus therfore, intendynge rather to proue what god woolde do with
hym and his companyons in theſe extremities, then any longer to abide the ſame, commaunded Diegus Mendex his ſteward
with two guydes of that Ilande whome he had hyred with
promyſſes of great rewardes at their retournie, to enter into one of their canoas and take their wage to Hiſpaniola.
Beynge thus toſſed on the ſea two and fro from rocke too
rocke by reaſon of the ſhorteneſſe and narowines of the canoa, they arryued at the length at the laſte corner of Hiſpaniola, beynge diſtante from Iamaica fortie leagues. Here his
guydes departynge from hym, returned ageine to Colonus for
the rewardes which he had promyſed them. But Diegus Mendex wente on forward a foote vntyll he came to the citie cay-
led Sanctus Dominicus beynge the chiefe and heade citye of the
Ilande. The offycers and rulers of Hiſpaniola, beynge enformed of the matter, appoynted hym two ſhyppes wherwith
he retourned to his maiſter and coompanions. As he founde
them, ſoo came they to Hiſpaniola, verye feeble and in maner
naked. What chaunced of them afterwarde, I knowe not
as yet. Lette vs nowe therfore leaue theſe particulers, and
ſpeake ſumwhat more of generals. In al thoſe tractes whiche we ſayde here befoꝛe to haue bynne found by Colonus the
Admyrall, bothe he, hym ſelfe wryteth, and all his coompanyons of that vyage confeſſe, that the trees, herbes, and frutes, are florꝰhing and greene all the hole yeare, and the ayer
ſo temperate and holeſome, that of all his coompanye there
neuer fell one man ſycke, noꝛ yet were vered eyther with extreme coulde oꝛ heate for the ſpace of fyftie leagues, from the
great hauen of Cerebaro to the ryuers of Hiebra and Beragua.
Thinhabitantes of Cerebaro, and the nations whiche are be-
twyxte that and the ſayde ryuers, applye not them ſelues to
the gatherynge of golde but onely at certeyne tymes of the
yeare: And are very experte & cunnyng herein, as are owre
myners of ſyluer and Iren. They knowe by longe experience
Ee.ii. in what

Neceſſytie hath no lawe howe farre lyfe is to bee eſteemed.

A daungerous enterpryſe.

Sanctus Dominicus.

Landes foūd by Colonus.

Temperate regions and holſome aier

Cerebaro. Hiebra. Beragua.

Experte myners.

In what places golde is mooste abundantly engendzed : as by the colour of the water of the ryuers, and suche as faule frō the mountaynes : And also by the colour of the earthe and stones . They beleue a certeyne godly nature to be in golde, for asmuche as they neuer gather it excepte they vse certeyne religyons expiations oz pollcyynge, as th abstlyn from women, and all kyndes of pleasures and delicate meates and dzinkes, during all the tyme that their golden haruest lasteth. They suppose that men do naturally lyue and dye as other beastes do, and therfore honour none other thynge as god. yet doo they praye to the sunne, and honour it when it ryseth. But lette vs nowe speake of the mountaines and situation of these landes. From all the sea bankes of these regyons, exceding great and hyghe mountaynes are seene towarde the Southe, yet reachynge by a continuall tracte from the Easte into the weste. By reason wherof I suppose that the two greate seas (wherof I haue spoken largly befoze) are deuided with these mountaynes as it were with bulwarkes, leaste they shoulde ioyne and repugne, as Italye deuideth the sea cauled *Tirrhenum*, from the sea Adriatyke, which is nowe commonly cauled the goulfe of Uenes.

For whiche waye soo euer they sayled from the poynte cauled *Promontorium, S. Augustini* (whiche perteyneth to the Poztugales & prospecteth ageynste the sea Atlantike) euen vnto *Vraba* and the hauen *Cerabaro*, and to the furthest landes found hytherto westwarde, they had euer greate mountaynes in syghte bothe nere hande and farre of, in all that longe race. These mountaynes were in sume place, smooth, pleasaunt and frutfull, full of goodly trees and herbes : And sumwhere, hygh, rowgh, ful of rockes, and barein, as chaunseth in the famus mountayne of *Taurus* in *Asia*, and also in dyuers coastes of our mountaynes of *Apennini*, and suche other of lyke byggenesse. The rydgies also of these mountaynes are diuided with goodly and fayre ualleis. That part of the mountaynes which includeth the springes of *Beragua*, is thought to be hygher then the cloudes, in so much that (as they saye) the tops of them can seldome bee seene for the multitude of thicke cloudes which are beneath the same. *Colonus* the Admirall the fyrst fynder of these regions, affirmeth that the toppes of the mountaynes of *Beragua* are moze then fiftie myles in heyghth. De

sayh

fayth further, noze that in the fame region at the rotes of the montaynes the way is open to the fouth fea, and compareth it as it were betwene Uenice and *Genua*, oz *Ianus* as the Genues wyll haue it cauled, whiche fable that theyz citie was buylded of *Ianus*. He affirmeth alfo that this lande reacheth foorth towarde the fouth: And that from henfe it taketh the begynnynge of breadth, lyke as from the Alpes owte of the narowe thygh of Italy, we fee the large and mayne landes of Fraunce, Germanye, and Pannonye, to the Sarmatians and Scythyans, euen ynto the mountaynes and rockes of Riphea and the frofen fea, and embrafe therwith as with a continuall bonde, all Tracia, and Grecia, with all that is included within the promontorie oz poynte of *Malea* and *Hellespontus* fouthwarde, and the fea *Euxinus* and the mary Ihes of *Meotis* in *Scythia* northwarde. The Admirall fuppofeth, that on the lefte hande in faylynge towarde the wefte, this lande is ioyned to *India* beyonde the ryuer of *Ganges*: And that on the ryght hande towarde the Nouth, it bee extended to the frofen fea, beyonde the Hyperboreans and the Nouth pole: So that both the feas (that is to meane that fouth fea which we fayde to bee founde by *Vafchus*, and owter Ocean) fhulde ioyne and meete in the cozners of that land: And that the waters of thefe feas doo not onely inclofe and compaffe the fame withowt diuifion as Europe is inclofed with the feas of *Hellefpontus* and *Tanais*, with the frofen Ocean, & owte fea of *Tyrrhenum* with the Spanyfhe feas. But in my opinion, the behement courfe of the Ocean towarde the wefte, doth fignifie and lette that the fayde two feas fhulde not fo ioyne togyther: But rather that that land is adherent to the firme landes towarde the Nozthe, as we haue fayde befoze. It fhall fuffice to haue fayde thus muche of the length hereof. Let vs nowe therfoze fpeake fumwhat of the breadth of the fame. We haue made mention befoze howe the fouth fea is diuided by narowe lymittes from owre Ocean, as it was pzoued by thexperience of *Vafchus Nunnez* and his coompanions which fyzft made open the way thyther. But as dyuerfly as the mountaynes of owre Alpes in Europe are fumwhere narowe and in fume place bzode, euen fo by the lyke pzouidéce of nature, this lande in fume parte therof reacheth faure in bzeadth, and is in other places coarcted with narowe limet: tes from

Ianus otherwyfe cauled Iaphet, the fon of Noe.

Italy is lyke vnto a legge in the fea, & the mountaynes of the alpes, are in the thyghe therof. Colonus his opinion of the fuppofed Continent. By this coniecture, the way fhuld te open to Cathay by the hyperboreans

Looke the inuigation of Cabote. deca. iii lib. vi.

The breadth of the lande.

res from sea to sea, with valleys also in sume places, wherby men may passe from the one syde to the other. Where we haue descrybed the regions of *Vraba* and *Beragua* to bee situate, these seas are diuided by smaule distaunce. Yet owght we to thynke the region which the great ryuer of *Maragnonus* runneth through, to bee very large if we shall graunt *Maragnonium* to bee a ryuer and no sea, as the freshe waters of the same owght to persuade vs. For in suche narowe canes of the earth, there can bee no swalowinge goulfes of such bygnesse as to receaue or vndorpght so great abundance of water. The lyke is also to bee supposed of the great ryuer of *Dabaiba* which we sayde to bee from the corner of the goulfe of *Vraba* in sume place of fortie fathomes depth, and sumwhere fiftie: Also three myles in breadth, and so to faule into the sea. We must needes graunt that the earth is brode there, by the whiche the ryuer passeth from the hyghe mountaynes of *Dabaiba* from the East and not from the west. They say that this ryuer consisteth and taketh his encrease of foure other ryuers faulynge from the mountaynes of *Dabaiba*. Owre men caule this ryuer *Flumen S. Iohannis*. They say also that from hense it faulleth into the goulfe of *Vraba* by seuen mouthes as dooth the ryuer of *Nilus* into the sea of Egypte. Lykewyse that in the same region of *Vraba* there are in sume places narowe strayghtes not passynge fyftene leaques: and the same to bee saluage and withowt any passage by reason of dyuers marysshes and desolate wayes, which the Latines caule *Lamus*: But the Spanyardes accordynge to theyr varietie, caule the *Tremodales, Trampales, Cenegales, Sumideros*, and *Zabondaderos*. But before we passe any further, it shall not bee greatly from owr purpose to declare from whence these mountaynes of *Dabaiba* haue theyr name accordynge vnto thantiquities of thinhabitantes. They saye therefore that *Dabaiba* was a woman of greate magnanimitie and wysedome emonge theyr predicessours in owlde tyme: whom in her lyfe, all thinhabitantes of those prouinces did greatly reuerence, and beinge deade gaue her diuine honour and named the region after her name, beleupnge that shee sendeth thunder and lyghtnynge to destroy the fruites of the earth yf shee bee angered, and to send plentie if shee bee well pleased. This superstition hathe byn persuaded them by a craftie kynde of men vnder pretense of religion

religion to thintent that they might enioye suche gyftes and
offerynges as were brought to the place where shee was ho=
noured. This is sufficient for this purpose. They saye fur=
thermore that the maryshes of the narowe lande wherof we
haue spoken, brynge foorth great plentie of Crocodiles, dra=
gous, battes, and gnattes beinge very hurtfull. Therefore
when so euer they take any iorney towarde the south, they
go owte of the way towarde the mountaynes, and eschewe
the regions neare vnto those perelous fennes or maryshes.
Sume thinke that there is a valley lyinge that way that the
ryuer runneth which owre men caule *Rio de los perdidos*, that is,
the ryuer of the lost men (so named by the missfortune whiche
there befell to *Nicuesa* and his coompany) and not far distant
from the hauen *Cerabaro* whiche diuideth those mountaynes
towarde the south. But let vs nowe fynishe this booke with
a fewe other thynges woorthy to bee noted. They say there=
fore that on the ryght hande and lefte hande frome *Dariena*,
there are twentie ryuers in all the whiche, greate plentie of
golde is founde. Being demaunded what was the cause why
they brought no greater abundance of gold from thence, they
answered that they lacked myners: And that the men which
they tooke with them from Spayne thyther, were not accu=
stomed to laboure, but for the moste parte brought vp in the
warres. This lande seemeth also to promesse many precious
stones. For besyde those which I sayde to bee founde neare
vnto *Curia* and *Sancta Martha*, one *Andreas Moralis* a pylot (who
had trauayled those coastes with *Iohannes de la Cosa* whyle he
yet lyued) had a precious diamonde which he bought of a na=
ked younge man in the region of *Oramni* in the prouince of
Paria. This stone was as longe as two ioyntes of a mans mid=
dell fynger, and as bygge as the fyrst ioynte of the thumbe :
beinge also paynted on euery syde, consistynge of eyght squa=
res perfectly formed by nature. They say that with this they
made scarres in anuylles and hammers, and brake the teethe
of fyles, the stone remayning vnperyshed. The younge man
of *Cumana*, wore this stone aboute his necke emonge other ou=
ches, and coulde it to *Andreas Moralis* for fyue of our coonterfect
stones made of glasse of dyuers colours wherwith the igno=
rant younge man was greatly delyted. They founde also cer=
teyne topases on the shore. But thestimation of golde was so
farre

Dragons and
crocodiles in
the marishes

The hauen
Cerabaro.

Twentie gol=
den ryuers.

Precious
stones.

a precious di=
emonde of
exceedynge
bygnes.

Topases.

**The Spany=
erdes con=
temne effemi
nate pleſures**

farre entered into the heades of owre men, that they had no
regarde to ſtones. Alſo the moſt part of the Spanyardes, do
laugh them to ſcorne which vſe to weare many ſtones: ſpeci
ally ſuch as are common: Iudginge it to bee an eſſeminate
thynge, and more meete for women then men. The noble mē
onely when they celebrate ſolenn mariages, or ſet forth any
triumphes, weare chepnes of gold byſet with precious ſtones,
and vſe fayre apparell of ſylke embrothered with golde inter
mixt with pearles and precious ſtones: And not at other ty=
mes. They thynke it no leſſe eſſeminate for men to ſmell of

**Sweete ſa=
uours.**

the ſweete ſauours of Arabie: And iudge hym to bee infected
with ſum kynde of fylthy lechery, in whom they ſmell the ſa=
uour of muſke or Caſtoreum. But lyke as by one apple taken
from a tree, we may perceyue the tree to bee fruitfull, and by
one fyſhe taken in a ryuer, we may knowe that fyſhe is ingen=
dered in the ſame, euen ſo, by a lyttel gold, and by one ſtone,

**A ſimilitude
prouing great
plentie of
golde & preci=
ous ſtones.
The chauen of
Sancta Mar=
tha.
Carisi.**

we owght to conſyder that this lande bringeth forthe great
plentie of golde and precious ſtones. What they haue found
in the porte of Sancti Marthi in the region of Carisi when the
hole naupe paſſed therby vnder the gouernaunce of Petrus Ar=
rias and his toompany with certeine other of the kynges of=
fycers, I haue ſuffyciently declared in his place. To be ſhorte
therefore, all thynges do ſo floryſhe, growe, encreaſe, and
proſper, that the laſte are euer better then the fyrſte. And

**The heroical
factes of the
Spaniardes.**

ſurely to declare my opinion herin, what ſo euer hath hereto
fore byn diſcouered by the famous trauayles of Saturnus and
Hercules, with ſuch other whō the antiquitie for their heroical
factes honoured as goddes, ſeemeth but lyttell and obſcure
if it be compared to the Spanyardes victorious labowres.
This I byd powre holpues fare well, deſyringe yowe to cer=
tifye me howe yowe lyke theſe fyrſte frutes of the Ocean,
that beyng encoraged with yowre exhortations,
I maye the gladlyer and with leſſe
tediouſneſſe wryte ſuche
thynges as ſhal
chaunce
heraf
ter.

The fyst booke of the thirde decade.

A L suche lyuynge creatures as vnder the cer-
cle of the moone bzinge fozthe any thynge,
are accustomed by thinstincte of nature as
soone as they are delyuered of their byzthe,
eyther to close vppe the matrice, oz at the
leaste to bee quyete foz a space. But owre
mooste frutefull Ocean and newe woozlde,
engendereth and bzingeth furthe dayly newe byzthes wherby men of great wytte, and especially suche as are studyous
of newe and meruelous thinges, may haue sumwhat at hand
wherwith to feede their myndes. If yowze holpnesse do a ke
to what purpose is al this, ye shal vnderstand, that I had
scarcely fynysshed the histozye of suche thynges as chaunced
to *Vaschus Nunnez* and his coompanye in their vyaze to the
southe sea, when soodenly there came newe letters from *Petrus Arias* the newe gouernour whom the kyng had appoynted
the yeare befoze with an army of men and a nauye of shippes
to sayle to these newe landes. He sygnifyeth by his letters,
that he with his nauye and coompany, arryued all safelye.
Furthermoze, *Iohannes Cabedus* (whome yowze holpnes at the
requeste of the moste catholyke kynge had created byshoppe
of that prouynce of *Dariena*) and thzee other of the chiefe offycers ioined in comission to be his assystance, as *Alfonsus de Ponte,
Diequs Marques*, and *Iohannes de Tauira*, confyzmed the same letters and subscribed them with their names. The nauygation therfoze of *Petrus Arias*, was in this maner. The daye before the Ides of Apzyll, in the yeare of Chziste. 15I4. he hoysed vppe his sayles in the towne of saincte *Lucar de Barrameda*,
sytuate in the mouthe of the ryuer *Betis*, whiche the Spaniardes nowe caule *Guadalchebir*. The seuen Ilandes of *Canarie*
are about foure hundzeth myles distant from the place where
this riuer fauleth into the sea. Summe thinke that these are
the Ilandes which the owlde wziters did caule the Fortunate
Ilandes. But other thynke the contrary. The name of these
Ilandes, are these. The two whiche appere fyzste in syght,
are named *Lanzelota* and *Fortisuentura*. On the backehalfe of
these, lyeth *Magna Canaria* oz *Grancanaria*. Beyonde that is Te-
nerif and *Gomera* sumwhat towarde the nozthe frome that.

The bysshop
of Dariena.

The nauigati-
on of Petrus
Arias.

Saint Lucar.

The Iland of
Canarie.

Palma and *Ferrea*, lye behynde as it were a bulwarke to all the other. *Petrus Arias* therfore, arriued at *Gomera* the eyghte daye after his departure, with a nauye of. xvii. shippes and a. M. and fyue hundreth men, althoughe there were onely a thousande and two hundreth assygned hym by the kynges letters. It is sayde furthermore that he lefte behynd hym more then two thousande verye pensyue and syghynge that they also myght not be receaued, proferynge them selues to go at their owne chyrges. He taried. xvi. dayes in *Gomera* to thintente

prouifion of fresshe water and fuell. to make prouifion of fuell and fresshe water: But chiefely to repayre his shyppes beynge fore brosed with tempestes, and especially the gouernours shippe whiche had loste the rudder. For these Ilandes are a commodious restynge place for all suche as intende to attempte any nauygations in that mayne sea. Departynge from hense in the nones of Maye, he sawe

The Iland of Dominica. no more lande vntyll the thirde daye of June, at the whiche he arriued at *Dominica* an Ilande of the *Canibales*, being distant from *Gomera* aboute eyght hundreth leaques. Here he remayned foure dayes, makinge newe prouifion of freshe water and fuell, durynge whiche tyme he sawe no man nor yet any steppes of men: But founde plentie of sea crabbes and greate lysartes.

Guadalupea, otherwyfe cauled Caruteura, or Que raquiera. From hense he sayled by the Ilandes of *Matininu* (or otherwyfe cauled *Madanino*) *Guadalupea*, and *Galanta* (otherwyse cauled *Galana*) of all whiche, we haue spoken in the fyrste decade. He passed also throughe the sea of herbes or weedes, continuyng a long tracte. yet nother he, nor *Colonus* the Admyrall (who fyrste founde these Ilandes and sayled through this sea of weedes) haue declared any reason howe these

The sea of herbes. weedes shoulde coome. Summe thynke the sea too be verye muddye there, and that these weedes are engendred in the bottome therof, and so beynge loosed, to ascende to the vppermooste parte of the water, as wee see oftentymes chaunce in certeyne stondynge pooles, and sumtymes also in greate ryuers. Other suppose that they are not engendred there, but to bee beaten from certeyne rockes by the vyolence of the water in tempestes. And thus they leaue the matter in dowte: Neyther haue they yet any certeyne experyence whether they stycke faste and gyue place to the shyppes, or wander loose vppon the water. But it is to bee thought that they are engendred there, For otherwyse they shulde bee dryuen togyther

togyther on heapes by thympulſyon of the ſhyppes euen as a beaſome gathereth the ſweepynges of a houſe, and ſhulde alſo lette the courſe of the ſhyppes. The fourth day after that he departed frome Dominica, the hyghe mountaynes couered with ſnowe (wherof we haue ſpoken in the ſeconde Decade) appered vnto hym. They ſaye that there the ſeas runne as ſwyftely towarde the weſte, as it were a ryuer faulyng from the toppes of hyghe montaynes: Although they ſayled not directly toward the weſt, but inclined ſumwhat to the ſouth. From theſe montaynes faulyth the ryuer of Gaira, famous by the ſlaughter of owre men at ſuch tyme as Rodericus Colmenares paſſed by thoſe coaſtes as we haue ſayde befoze. Lykewyſe many other fayre ryuers haue their ozigynall from the ſame montaynes. This prouynce (in the whiche is alſo the regyon of Caramairi) hath in it two notable hauens, of the which owre men named the one Carthago oz Carthagena, and the other ſancta Martha, the region wherof, thinhabitantes caule Saturma. The pozte of Sancta Martha, is nearer to the montaines to uered with ſnowe cauled Montes Niuales: foz it is at the rootes of the ſame montaines. But the hauen of Carthago, is moze weſtewarde aboute fyftie leaques. He wziteth marueylous thynges of the hauen of Sancta Martha, whiche they alſo con firme that came lately frō theſe: Of the which younge Veſputius is one to whō Americus Veſputius his vncle (being a Flozētine bozne) left the eract knowlege of the mariners facultie, as it were by inheritance after his death foz he was a very expert maiſter in the knowledge, of his carde, his compaſſe, and the eleuation of the pole ſtarre with all that perteineth ther to. This younge Veſputius was aſſygned by the kyng to bee one of the maiſters of the gouernours ſhyppe, bicauſe he was cunninge in iudgyng the degrees of the eleuation of the pole ſtarre by the quadzante. Foz the charge of gouernynge the rudder, was chiefely coommytted to one Iohannes Serranus a Spaniarde, who had oftentymes ouer runne thoſe coaſtes. Veſputius is my verye familyar frende, and a wyttie younge man in whoſe coompany I take great pleaſure, and there foze vſe hym oftentymes foz my geſte. He hath alſo made many vyages into theſe coaſtes, and diligently noted ſuche thinges as he hath ſeene. Petrus Arias therfoze wziteth), and he confyzmeth the ſame, that thinhabitantes of theſe regy ons tooke

Theſe moun taynes are cauled Mon tes Niuales oz Serra Ne uata, dec ide ii. liber.t x.ii.
The ſwyfte courſe of the ſea towarde the weſt.
The ryuer Gaira.
Caramairi
Carthago.
Saturma.

Mountaynes couered with ſnowe.

Americus Veſpu tius.

ons tooke their originall of the Caribes or Canibales, as ap
peared by the desperate fiercenes and crueltie which they o
tentymes shewed to owre men when they passed by their co
stes. Suche stoutenes and fortitude of mynde is naturall
engendered in these naked Barbarians, that they feared n
to assayle owre hole nauy & to forbyd them to coome a lan
They feygh: with venimous arrowes as we haue sayde b
fore. Perceiuynge that owre men contempned their threa
nynges, they came furiously into the sea, euen vppe to t
breastes, nothynge fearinge eyther the bygnes or multitu
of owre shyppes, but ceased not continually beinge thus
the water, to cast dartes and shute their venemous arrow
as thicke as hayle: In so muche that owre men had byn
in great daunger if they had not byn defended by the cag
or pauisses of the shyppes and their targettes. yet were th
of them wounded whiche died shortely after. But this co
flycte continued so sharpe, that at the length owre men we
enforced to shute of their byggest pieces of ordinaunce wi
hayle hotte: At the slaughter and terrible noyse wherof t
barbarians beynge sore discomfited and shaken with fear
thynkynge the same to be thunder and lyghtnynge, tourne
their backes and fledde amayne. They greatly feare thu
der bycause these regyons are oftentymes vexed with tha
der and lyghtnynge by reason of the hyghe montaynes a
nearenesse of the same to the region of the ayer wherin su
fierie tempestes are engendered which the philosophers ca
Meteora. And all be it that owre men had nowe dryuen the
enemyes to flyght, and sawe them disparcled and owte of o
der, yet dowted they and were of dyuers opinions whetl
they shulde pursue them or not On the one partie, shame p
ked them forwarde, and on the other syde feare caused the
to caste many perelles, especially consyderynge the venemo
arrowes whiche these barbarians canne direct so certeynel
To departe from theym with a drye foote (as saithe the p
uerbe) with so great a nauye and suche an armye, they rep
ted it as a thynge greatly soundynge to their reproche a
dishonour. At the length therfore shame ouercommyng fear
they pursued them and came to land with their shippe boate
The gouernoure of the nauie, and also *Vesputius* doo wry
that the hauen is no lesse then three leagues in compasse, b

iii.

...ge alfo fafe withowt rockes, and the water therof fo clere, ...it a man may fee pybble ftones in the bottome twentie cu...ettes deape. They faye lykewyfe that there fauleth twoo ...yꝛe ryuers of freffhe water into the hauen : but the fame to ...e meeter to beare the canoas of thefe ꝓuincees then anye ...ygger veffels. It is a delectable thynge to heare what they ...l of the plentie and varietie, and alfo of the pleafaunt taft ...f the fpffhes afwel of thefe riuers as of the fea there about. ...y reafon wherof they founde here many fyffher boates and ...ettes woonderfully wꝛought of the ftalkes of certeyne her...es oꝛ weedes dyped and tawed and wꝛethed with coꝛdes of ...unne goffampine cotton. Foꝛ the people of *Caramairi, Gaira,* ...d *Saturma,* are very cunnynge in fyffhynge, and vfe to fell ...offhe to theyꝛ boꝛtherers foꝛ exchaunge of fuche thynges as ...ey lacke. When owre men had thus chafed the Barbary...ns from the fea coaftes, and hadde nowe entered into theyꝛ ...oufes, they affayled them with newe fkyꝛmuffhes, efpecial...I when they fawe them faule to fackyngeand fpoylyng, and ...eyꝛ wyues and chyldꝛen taken captiue. Theyꝛ houfchꝛlde ...fe was made of great reedes which growe on the fea ban...es, and the ftalkes of certeyne herbes beaten and afterward ...ade harde. The ftoures therof were ftrewed with herbes of ...ndꝛy coloures : And the waules hanged with a kynde of ...apꝛy artificially made of goffampine cotton, and wꝛought ...ith pictures of Lions, Tygers, and Eagles. The dooꝛes of ...heyꝛ houfes and chambers were full of dyuers kyndes of ...elles hangynge loofe by fmaule coꝛdes, that beinge fhaken ...y the wynde they myght make a certeyne rattelynge and al...o a whyftelynge noyfe by gatherynge the wynde in theyꝛ ho...lowe places. Foꝛ herein they haue greate delyte, and impute ...his foꝛ a goodly oꝛnamente. Dyuers haue fhewed me many ...woonderfull thynges of thefe regions : Efpecially one *Gonxa...liernandus Ouiedus* beinge one of the maieftrates appointed in ...hat office which the Spanyardes caule *Veedor,* who hath al...o herherto entered further into the lande then any other. He ...firmeth that he chaunced vppon the fragmente of a faphyre ...ygger then the egge of a goofe. And that in certeyne hylles ...here he trauayled with thirtie men, he founde many of the ...ecious ftones cauled Smaragdes, calcidones, and Jafpers, ...yde greaꝛ pieces of amber of the montaines. He alfo with

Ff. iii.

Diuers

Sidenotes (right margin):

Plentie of fyffhe.

Cunnynge fyffhers.

Theyꝛ houfe-holde ftuffe.

Tapftry.

A ftrainge phantafy.

This is he whom Cerda-nus praifeth.

Pꝛecious ftones The Smaragde is the trewe emerode

Another kind of amber is founde in whales.

Golde & brasile.

Marchasites are flowers of metals, by the colours wherof, the kyndes of me tals are knowen.

These locustes burne the corne with toching and deuoure the residewe they are in India of .iiii. foote length. The fayre region of Cara-mairi.

dyuers other do affirme that in the houses of sume of the Ca-nibales of these regions, they found the lyke precious stones set in golde and inclosed in the tapstry or arras (if it may soo bee cauled) wherewith they hange theyr houses. The same lande bryngeth foorth also many wooddes of brasile trees & great plentie of golde: In so much that in maner in al places they founde on the sea bankes and on the shoores, certeyne marchasites in token of golde. *Fernandus Ouiedus* declareth fur-thermore that in a certeyne region cauled *Zenu*, lyinge foure score and tenne myles from *Dariena* Eastwarde, they exercyse a straunge kynde of marchaundies. For in the houses of the inhabitantes, they founde greate chestes and baskets made of the twigges and leaues of certeyne trees apte for that pur-pose, beinge all full of gresshoppers, grylles, crabbes, or crefysshes: snayles also, and locustes whiche destrowe the fieldes of corne, all well dryed and salted. Beinge demaun-ded why they reserued such a multitude of these beastes, they answered that they kepte them to bee soulde to theyr borthe-rers which dwell further within the lande: And that for the exchange of these precious byrdes and salted fysshes, they re-ceaued of them certeyne strange thynges wherin partely they take pleasure, and partely vse them for theyr necessary affay-ers. These people dwel not togyther, but scattered here and there. Thinhabitantes of *Caramairi*, seeme to dwel in an earth-ly paradise, theyr region is so fayre and frutefull, withowt owtragious heate or sharpe coulde, with lyttle difference of the length of day and nyght throwghowt all the yeare. Af-ter that owre men had thus dryuen the barbarians to flyght, they entered into a valley of two leagues in breadth & three in length, extendynge to certeyne frutful mountaynes ful of

Fruteful mon taynes.

grasse, herbes, and trees, at the rootes wherof, lye twoo o-ther valleys towarde the ryght hande and the left, throwgh epther of the which runneth a fayre ryuer, wherof the ryuer of *Gaira* is one, but vnto the other they haue yet gyuen noo name. In these valleys they founde manye fayre gardeyns and pleasaunte fyeldes watered with trenches distrybuted in maruelous order, with no lesse arte then owre Insubrians and Hetrurians vse to water theyr fyeldes. Theyr common meate, is *Ages, Iucca, Maizium, Battate,* with suche other rootes and frutes of trees, and also suche fysshe as they vse in the

Gardens.
Insubres are nowe cauled Lumbardes, and Hetruscr, Tuscans.

Ilandes

Jlandes and other regions of these prouinces. They eate
mans flesh: but seldome, bycause they meete not oftentymes
with straungiers, except they goo foorth of theyr owne domi=
nions with a mayne army of purpose to hunt for men, when
theyr rauenynge appetite pricketh them forwarde. For they
absteyne from them selues, and eate none but suche as they
take in the warres or otherwyse by chaunce. But suerly it
is a miserable thynge to heare howe many myriades of men
these fylthy and vnnaturall deuourers of mans flesshe haue
consumed, and lefte thousandes of moste fayre and frutfull
Jlandes and regions desolate withowte menne. By reason
wherof owre men founde so many Jlandes whiche for theyr
fayrenes and frutefulnesse myght seeme to bee certeyne earth
ly Paradyses, and yet were vtterly voyde of men. Hereby
yowre holynesse may consider howe pernitious a kynde of
men this is. We haue sayde before that the Jlande named
Sancti Iohannis (which thinhabitantes caule *Burichena*) is nexte to
Hispaniola. It is sayde that onely the Canibales which dwell
in the other Jlandes nere about this, as in the Jlande cau=
led *Hayhty* or *Sancti Crucis*, and in *Guadalupea* (otherwise cauled
Querqueiera, or *Carucuiera*) haue in owre tyme vyolentely taken
owte of the sayde Jlande of *Sancti Iohannis*, more then fyue
thousande men to bee eaten. But let it suffice thus much to
haue wandered by these monstrous bludsuckers. We wyll
nowe therfore speake sumewhat of the rootes whereof they
make theyr breade, forasmuch as the same shall hereafter bee
foode to Christian men in steede of breade made of wheate,
and in the steade of radyshe with such other rootes as they
haue byn accustomed to eate in Europe. We haue oftentymes
sayde before that *Iucca* is a roote whereof the beste and moste
delicate breade is made bothe in the firme landes of these regi=
ons, and also in the Jlandes. But howe it is tylled or husz=
banded, howe it groweth, and of howe dyuers kyndes it is,
I haue not yet declared. Therfore, when they intende to
plante this *Iucca*, they make a hole in the earth knee deape,
and rayse a heape of the earth taken owte of the same, fashio=
nynge it lyke a square bedde of nyne foote breadth on euerye
syde, settynge twelue trunkes of these rootes (beinge about
a foote and a halfe longe a piece) in euery of the sayd beddes
conteynynge three rootes of a syde, so layde a slope, that the
endes

Many coun=
treys lefte de
solate by the
fiercenes of
the Canibas=
les.
One myriade
is ten thous
sande.

A miserable
hearynge.

Breade of
rootes.

The maner
of plantinge
the roote Iuc
ca.

endes of them ioyne in maner togyther in the center or myddell of the bedde within the grounde. Owt of the ioyntes of the rootes and spaces betwene the same, spryngeth the toppes and blades of newe rootes, which by lyttle and lyttle encreasynge, growe to the byggenes and length of a mans arme in the brawne, and ofteutymes as bygge as the thygh: So that

by the tyme of theyr full rypenes, in maner all the earthe of the heape, is conuerted into rootes. But they say that these rootes are not rype in lesse tyme then a yeare & a halfe: And that the longer they are suffered to growe euen vntyll thoo yeares complete, they are so muche the better and more per-

fecte to make breade therof. When they are taken foorth of the earth, they scrape them and dyse the with certeyne sharpe stones seruynge for the same purpose: And thus lapinge the betwene two great stones, or puttynge them in a sacke made of the stalkes of certeyne rowgh herbes and smaule reedes,

they presse them (as we do cheese or crabbes to drawe owte the iuse therof) and so let them drye a daye before they eate them. The iuse or lyquoure, they cast away: for (as we haue sayde) it is deadly poyson in the Ilandes. yet is the iuse of suche as growe in the firme lande, holsome if it bee sodde, as is the whey of owre mylke. They saye that there are manye kyndes of this Iucca, wherof sume are more pleasaunte and delycate then the other, and are therefore reserued as it were to make fine manch t for the kynges owne tables. But the gentelmen eate of the meaner sorte, and the common people

of the basest. The fynest they caule Cazabbi, which they make rounde lyke cakes in certeyne presses before they seeth it or bake it. They saye furthermore that there are lykewyse dy-

uers kyndes of the rootes of Ages and Battata. But they vse these rather as frutes and dysshes of seruice, then to make breade therof, as we vse rapes, radysshes, mushromis, naues, persneppes, and such lyke. In this case, they moost especially esteeme the best kynde of Battatas, which in pleasant tast and tendernes farre exceadeth owre mushromes. It sha suffice to haue sayde thus muche of rootes. We wyll now

therefore speake of an other kynde of theyr breade. We declared before that they haue a kynde of grayne or pulse much lyke vnto Panicum, but with sumwhat bygger graines, which they beate into meale vppon certeyne greate hollowe stone

wil

ith the labour of their handes when they lacke *Iucca*: And
this is made the more vulgar oꝛ common bꝛeade. It is
wen thꝛise a yeare, so that the frutfulnesse of the grounde
ap beate it by reason of the equalitie of the tyme, whereof
ce haue spoken suffycyently befoꝛe. In these regyons they
unde also the graine of *Maizium*, and sundꝛy kyndes of fru=
s of trees diligentely planted and well husbanded. The
ape betwene the regyons of *Caramairi* and *Saturma*, is fayre,
ode, and ryghte foorther. They founde here also sundꝛye
ndes of waterpottes made of earthe of dyuers colours, in
e whiche they bothe fetche and keepe freshe water. Lyke=
se sundꝛy kyndes of iugges, godderdes, dꝛynkyng cuppes,
ttes, pannes, dysshes, and platters artifycially made.

hen the gouernour had gyuen commaundement by pꝛocla=
tion, that thinhabitantes shulde eyther obey the Chꝛistian
nge and embꝛase owꝛe relygion, oꝛ elles to depart owte of
eir countrey, they answered with venemous arrowes. In
is skyꝛmysshe, owꝛe men tooke summe of theym: whereof
othynge the moste parte in faire apparell, they sente them
eyne to their owne coompany: But leadyng the resydue to
e shyppes to thintent to shewe them the poure and magny=
cence of the chꝛistians that they myght declare the same to
eir coompanions, therby to wynne their fauour, they ap=
teled them lykewyse and sente them after their felowes.
hese affyrme that in all the ryuers of those toūkes, theye
we great argumentes and tokens of goldꝛ. They founde
re and there in their houses good stoꝛe of hartes flesshe and
es flesshe, wherwith they fedde them selues dylycately.
hey also, haue greate plentie of sundꝛy kyndes of byꝛdes
d foules, wherof they bꝛynge vppe many in their houses,
mme foꝛ nere tayre foode, and other foꝛ dayntye dysshes as
e do hennes and partriches. Owꝛe men hereby coniecture
at the ayer of these regions is veary holsome, foꝛ as muche
s sleapynge all nyghte vnder the fyꝛmament on the bankes
the ryuers, none of them were at any tyme offended with
umes oꝛ heade ache by reason of any noysome humoure oꝛ
apoure pꝛoceadynge from the earthe, ayer, oꝛ water. Owꝛe
n furthermoꝛe, founde there many great bothomes of gos=
mpyne cotton reaby spunne, and fardelles of dyuers kyn=
s of fethers wherof they make them selues cresses and plu=
　　　B g　　　　　　　mes after

he meanethe
the equall
length of day
and nyght
which is con=
tinually in re=
gions vnder
the Equinoc=
tiall lyne.
Maizium.
Earth of dy=
uers colours.

Golde in
ryuers.
hartes and
bores.
Foules.

Volsome ayer

Gossampine
cotton.
Fethers.

Bowes and arrowes.

mes after the maner of owre men of armes : also certeine clokes whiche they esteeme as moste cumly ornamentes. The founde lykewyse an innumerable multitude of bowes and arrowes. Thinhabitantes also of these regiōs, in summe place vse to burne the carkeses of their prynces when theye are deade, and to reserue their bones buryed with spyces in certeyne hylles. In other places, they onely drye theym and

Deade bodies reserued.

imbaume them with spyces and sweete gummes, and soo reserue them in sepulchers in their owne houses. Sumwher also, they drye them, spyce them, adourne them with precyous iewells and ouches, and so reuerently place them in certeyne tabernacles made for the same purpose in their owne

Ouches of laton.

Gonzalus Ouiedus, sayth that they gilt maruelously with the iuse of a certeyne herbe.
Whyte marble.

palayces. When owre men had many of their tabellets, bracelettes, collers, and suche other ouches (whiche they cau Guanines) they founde them rather to bee made of laton then of golde: wherby they suppose that they haue bied to exchaunge their ware with summe craftie straungers whiche broughte thē those counterfect ouches to defraude them of their golde. For euen owre menne perceaued not the deceate vntyll they came to the meltynge. Furthermore, certayne of owre buylders wanderynge a lyttell way from the sea coastes, chaunced to fynde certayne pyeces of white marble. Wherby they

The great ryuer Maragnonus. This ioyneth with the myghty ryuer called Flumen Amazonum, found of late.

thynke that in tyme paste summe straungers haue coome to those landes, whiche haue dygged marble owte of the mountaines, and lefte those fragmentes on the plaine. There owre men learned that the ryuer Maragnonus descendeth frome the montaynes couered with snowe cauled Montes Niuales or Sierra Neuata : And the same to bee encreased by many other ryuers whiche faule into it throughowte all the lowe and watery regions by the whiche it runneth with so longe a tracte from the sayde montaynes into the sea : And this to bee the cause of the greatnesse therof. These thynges beyng thus broughte to passe, the gouernour cōmaunded the trumpit our to blowe a retraite : Whervppon they whiche were sente to lande (beynge fyue hundreth in nournber) makynge a great boute for ioye of their victory, sette them selues in order of batrayle and so keping their array, returned to the shippes laden with spoyle of those prouinces, and bryngynge in souldiers cloke

Clokes of fethers.

of fethers, with faire plumes and crestes of variable colours In this meane tyme hauynge repaired their shyppes and fur
nyshe

nyſſhed the ſame with all neceſſaries, they looſed anker the
xvi. daye of the Calendes of July, directynge their courſe to
the hauen of *Carthagena*, in the whiche viage they deſtroyed
and waſted certayne Ilandes of the Canibales lyinge in the
waye, accordynge as they were commaunded by the kynge.
But the ſwifte courſe of the water deceaued bothe *Iohannes*
Soranus the chiefe Pilet of the gouernours ſhyppe, and all the
other, althoughe they made their boſte that they perfectly
knewe the nature therof. For they affyrme that in one night
they were caried forty leaques beyonde their eſtimation.

The ſwyfte
courſe of the
water.
xl. leaques in
one nyght.

The fyrſt booke of the thirde Decade.

Ere muſte we ſumwhat digreſſe from coſmography, and make a philoſophicall diſcours
to ſearche the ſecreate cauſes of nature. For
wheras they al affyrme with on cõſent, that
the ſea runneth there from the Eaſte to the
weſte as ſwyftly as it were a ryuer faulinge
from hyghe mountaynes, I thoughte it not
good to lette ſo great a matter ſlyppe vntouched. The whiche while I conſyder, I am drawen into no
ſmaule ambyguitie and doute, whether thoſe waters haue
their courſe whiche flowe with ſo contynuall a tracte in circuite from the Eaſte, as thowghe they ſtedde to the weſt neuer to retourne, and yet neyther the weſte therby any whitte
the more fylled, nor the Eaſte emptied. If we ſhall ſaye that
they faule to their centre (as is the nature of heuye thynges)
and aſſigne the Equinoctiall lyne to be the centre (as ſumme
affyrme) what centre ſhall we appointe to bee able to receaue
ſo great aboundaunce of water? Or what circumference ſhal
be founde weate? They whiche haue ſearched thoſe coaſtes,
haue yet founde no lykely reaſon to be trewe. Many thynke
that there ſhoulde bee certeyne large ſtraightes or enteraunces
in the corner of that great lande whiche we deſcribed to bee
eyght tymes bygger then Italye, and the corner therof to be
full of goulfes, wherby they ſuppoſe that ſumme ſtrayghtes
ſhoulde paſſe through the ſame lyinge on the weſte ſyde of the
Ilande of *Cuba*: And that the ſayde ſtraightes ſhoulde ſwalowe vp thoſe waters, and ſo conuey the ſame into the weſte

Sundry opini-
ons why the
ſea runneth
with ſo ſwyft
courſe from
the Eaſt into
the weſt.

The quinocti-
all lyne.
Why all wa-
ters moue to-
warde the
ſouth or Equi-
noctial, reade
Cardanus de ſub
tilit.liber.ii.
Elementis.
Strayghtes.

B g,ii.　　　　　and

As by the strayght of Magellanus. The north landes.

and from thenſe ageyn into owre Eaſte Ocean, or north ſeas as ſumme thynke. Other wyll, that the goulfe of that great lande bee cloſed vppe: and the land to reache farre towarde the northe on the backe ſyde of *Cuba*: ſo that it embrace the northe landes whiche the froſen ſea encompaſeth vnder the northe pole: And that all the lande of thoſe coaſtes, ſhulde ioyne togyther as one firme lande. Wherby they coniecture that thoſe waters ſhulde bee turned aboute by the obiecte or reſyſtaunce of that lande ſo bendynge towarde the north, as we ſee the waters tourned aboute in the crooked bankes of certeyne ryuers. But this agreeth not in all poyntes. For they

The froſen ſea.

alſo whiche haue ſearched the froſen ſea, and ſayled frome thenſe into the weſte, do lykewyſe affyrme that thoſe northe ſeas flowe contynually towarde the weſte, although nothing ſo ſwiftely. Theſe northe ſeas haue byn ſearched by one Se-

Sebaſtian. Cabot.

baſtian Cabot a Venetian borne, whom beinge yet but in maner an infante, his parentes caryed with them into Englande

The Venetians. The viage of Sebaſtian Cabot from England to the froſen ſea. Froſt in the month of July.

hauyng occaſion to reſorte thether for trade of marchandies, as is the maner of the Venetians too leaue no parte of the worlde vnſearched to obteyne riche &c. He therfore furniſ- ſhed two ſhippes in England at his owne charges: And fyrſt with three hundreth men, directed his courſe ſo farre toward the northe pole, that euen in the moonethe of July he founde monſtrous heapes of Iſe ſwimming on the ſea, and in maner continuall day lyght. Yet ſawe he the lande in that tracte, free from Iſe, whiche had byn molten by heate of the ſunne. Thus ſeyng ſuche heapes of Iſe before hym he was enforced to tourne his ſayles and folowe the weſte, ſo coaſtynge ſtyll by the ſhore, that he was thereby broughte ſo farre into the ſouthe by reaſon of the lande bendynge ſo muche ſouthward that it was there almoſte equall in latitude with the ſea cau-

Fretum her- culeum, diui- deth Spayne frome the worlde and is nowe called the ſtrayghtes of Marrok. Bacallaos, or Terra Bacallas, &c.

led *Fretum Herculeum*, hauynge the north pole eleuate in maner in the ſame degree. He ſayled lykewiſe in this tracte ſo farre towarde the weſte, that he had the Ilande of *Cuba* his lefte hande in maner in the ſame degree of langitude. As he tra- ueyled by the coaſtes of this greate lande (whiche he named *Baccallaos*) he ſayth that he found the like courſe of the waters towrd the weſt, but the ſame to runne more ſoftely and gen- telly then the ſwifte waters whiche the Spanyardes found in their nauigations ſouthewarde,

Wherfore

Wherefore, it is not onely more lyke to bee trewe, but ought also of neceſſitie to bee concluded, that betwene both the landes hetherto vnknowen, there ſhulde bee certeyne great open places wherby the waters ſhulde thus continually paſſe from the Eaſt into the weſte: which waters I ſuppoſe to bee dryuen about the globe of the earth by the vnceſſaunt mouynge and impulſion of the heauens: and not to bee ſwalowed vp and caſt owt ageyne by the breathynge of Demogorgon as ſume haue imagined bycauſe they ſee the ſeas by increaſe and decreaſe, to flowe and reflowe. Sebaſtian Cabot him ſelfe, named thoſe landes Baccallaos, bycauſe that in the ſeas therabout he founde ſo great multitudes of certeyne bigge fyſhes much lyke vnto tunies (which thinhabitantes caule Baccallaos) that they ſumtymes ſtayed his ſhippes. He founde alſo the people of thoſe regions couered with beaſtes ſkynnes: yet not without thuſe of reaſon.

He ſaythe alſo that there is greate plentie of beares in thoſe regions, whiche vſe to eate fyſſhe. For plungeinge theym ſelues into the water where they perceue a multitude of theſe fyſhes to lye, they faſten theyr clawes in theyr ſcales, and ſo drawe them to lande and eate them. So that (as he ſaith) the beares beinge thus ſatiſfied with fyſſhe, are not noyſom to men. He declareth further, that in many places of theſe regions, he ſawe great plentie of laton amonge thinhabitantes. Cabot is my very frende, whom I vſe famliierly, and deſyre to haue hym ſumtymes keepe mee company in myne owne houſe. For beinge cauled owte of England by the commaundement of the catholyke kynge of Caſtile after the deathe of Henry kynge of Englande the ſeuenth of that name, he was made one of owre counſayle and aſſyſtance as touchynge the aſayres of the newe Indies, lookynge dayely for ſhippes to bee furnyſhed for hym to diſcouer this hyd ſecreate of nature. This vyage is appoynted to bee begunne in March in the yeare next folowynge, beinge the yeare of Chriſt M. D. XVI. Whate ſhall ſucceade, yowre holynes ſhalbe aduertiſed by my letters if god graunte me lyfe. Sume of the Spanyardes dnye that Cabot was the fyrſt fynder of the lande of Baccallaos: And affirme that he went not ſo farre weſtewarde. But it ſhall ſuffice to haue ſayde thus much of the goulfes & ſtrayghtes, and of Sebaſtian Cabot. Let vs nowe therefore returne

The mouyng of heuen cauſeth the ſea to moue.
Demogorgon is the ſpirite of the earth.

People couered with beaſtes ſkins howe beares take and eate fyſſhes of the ſea.

Perhappes this laton is copper which holdeth gold. For lato hath no myne, and is an artificiall metal and not natural. Cabot cauled owt of Englande into Spayne. The ſecond viage of Cabot.

returne to the Spanyardes. At this tyme, they let passe t
hauen of Carthago vntouched, with all the Ilandes of the C
nibales there aboute, whiche they named Insulas sancti Bernard
Leauynge also behynde theyr backes, all the region of Car
mairi. Heare by reason of a sooden tempeste, they were cal
vppon the Ilande Fortis, beinge about fyftie leagues distan
from the enteraunce of the goulfe of vraba. In this Ilande
they founde in the houses of thinhabitantes, many basket
made of certeyne greate sea reedes, ful of salte. For this J
lande hath in it many goodly salte bayes: by reason wherec
they haue greate plentie of salte which they sell to other na
tions for such thynges as they stande in neede of. Not far
from hense, a great curlewe as bygge as a storke came flyin
to the gouernours shippe, and suffered her selfe to bee leasil
taken: which beinge caryed about amonge all the shippes o
the nauie, dyed shortly after. They sawe also a great mult
tude of the same kynde of foules on the shore a farre of.
The gouernour his shyppe which we sayde to haue lose th
rudder beinge nowe sore broosed and in maner bnprofytable
they lefte behynde to folowe at leasure. The nauie arriued a
Dariena the twelfth day of the Calendes of July, and the go
uernour his shippe (beinge voyde of men) was dryuen a land
in the same coastes within foure dayes after. The Spany
ardes whiche nowe inhabited Dariens, with theyr Capitayn
and Lieuetenant Vaschus Nunnez Balboa (of whom we haue larg
ly made mention before) beinge certified of thartyual of Petri
Arias and his coompanye, wente foorthe three myles to meet
him, & receaued him honorably & regiliously with the psalm
Te deum Laudamus, giuing thankes to god by whose safe conduct
they were brought so prosperously thether to al theyr confor
tes. They receaued them gladly into theyr houses builded a
ter the maner of those prouinces. I may well cause these re
gions, Prouinces, a Procul victis, (that is) such as are ouercom
farre of, forasmuch as owre men doo nowe inhabite the same
all the barbarous kynges and Idolatours beinge electee.
They enterteyned them with such chere as they were able t
make them: as with the frutes of those regions, and newe
breade bothe made of rootes and the grayne Maizium. Othe
delicates to make vp the feast, were of theyr owne store whi
che they brought with theym in theyr shyppes, as poudered
fle be

The Ilandes of the Canybales.

The Ilande Fortis. Salte

A straunge thynge.

howe Petrus Arias with the kynges nauy arriued at Dariena.

howe Vaschus receaued the new gouernour.

whye these regions are caulled prouynces.

de.The, falted fyſſhe, and bꝛeade made of wheate. Foꝛ they bꝛought with them many barrelles of wheate meale foꝛ the fame purpofe. Here maye yowꝛe holynes nꝛt withowt iuſte caufe of admiracion beholde a kynges nauie and great multitude of Chꝛiſtians, inhabytinge nꝛt onely the regions ſituate ynder the circle of heauen cauled *Tropicus Cancri*, but alfo in maner ynder the Equinoctiall lyne, contrary to thopinion of the owlde wꝛyters, a fewe excepted. But after that they are nowe metre togꝛther, let vs further declare what they determyned to doo. Therefoꝛe, the daye after that the nauie arriued, there aſſembled a coompany of the Spanyardes thinhabitoures of *Dariena*, to the number of foure hundꝛeth and fyſtie men. *Petrus Arias* the gouernour of the nauie and his coompany, conferred with them bothe pꝛiuilie and openlye of certeyne articles wherof it was the kynges pleaſure he ſhulde enquire: And moſt eſpecially as concernyng ſuch thynges wher of *Vaſchus* the fyꝛſte fynder and Admirall of the Southe fea, made mentió in his large letter fent frõ *Dariena* to Spayn. In this inquiſition they founde all thynges to bee trewew, herof *Vaſchus* had certifyed the kynge by his letters : And there vpon concluded that in the dominions of *Comogra, Pocchorrofa,* & *Cumanana*, at thaſſignement of *Vaſchus*, certeine foꝛtreſſes ſhuld bee erected fooꝛthwith to thintente there to plant theyꝛ colonie oꝛ habitacion. To the better accomplyſhemente hereof, they fent immediatly one *Iohannes Aiora* a noble younge gentelman of *Corduba* and ynder Lieutenant, with foure hundꝛeth men and foure carauelles and one other lyttle ſhippe.Thus departinge, he fayled fyꝛſt directly to the hauen of *Comogrus*, by dant from *Dariena* aboute twentie and fyue leagues, as they wꝛyte in theyꝛ laſt letters. Fromehenfe, he is appoynted to fende a hundꝛeth and fyftie of his foure hundꝛeth, towarde the South by a newe and ryghter way founde of late, by the which (as they fay) it is not paſſe.xxvi. leagues from the palaice of kynge *Comogrus* to the enteraunce of the goulfe of *Sancti Michaelis*. The reſidewe of the foure hundꝛeth, ſhall remayne there to bee an ayde and fuccour to all fuch as ſhall ioꝛney to and fro. Thofe hundꝛeth and fiftie which are aſſigned to go fourthwarde, take with them foꝛ interpretours certeine of owre men which had lerned the footherne language of the bonde men which were gyuen to *Vaſchus* when he ouerranne thofe

Barrelles of meale.

habitable regions ynder the Equinoctiall lyne.

where the newe gouernour planted his habitatió

The viage of Iohannes Aiora
The hauen of Comogrus

Sainte Mychaels goulfe

those regions, and also certeyne of the bondemen them felues which had nowe lerned the Spanyſhe tonge. They fay that the hauen of Pocchorrofa, is onely feuen leaques diſtante frome the hauen of Comogrus. In Pocchorrofa, he is aſſigned to leaue

fyftie men with the lyghteſt ſhyp which maye bee a paſſinger betwene them: that lyke as we vſe poſte horſes by lande, fo may they by this currant ſhippe, in ſhorte ſpace certifie the Lieuetenaunt and thinhabitours of Dariens of fuche thynges as ſhall chaunce. They entende alfo to buylde houſes in the

regiou of Tumanama. The palaice of kynge Tumanama, is diſtant from Pocchorrofa about twentie leaques. Of theſe foure hundreth men, beinge of the owlde fouldiers of Dariens and men of good experience, fyftie weare appoynted to bee as it were Decurians, to guide and conducte the newe men from place to place to do their affaires. When they had thus fette all thynges in order, they thought it good to aduertife the king

hereof, and therwith to certifye hym that in thoſe prouinces there is a kynge named Dabaiba whoſe dominion is very riche in golde: But the fame to be yet vntouched by reaſon of his

great power. His kingedome ioyneth to the feconde greate ryuer named Dabaiba after his name, whiche faulteth into the fea owt of the corner of the goulfe of Vraba as we haue large ly declared before. The common reporte is, that all the lande

of his dominions is ryche in golde. The palayce of kynge Dabaiba is fyfty leaques diſtante from Dariens. Thinhabitantes fape that from the palaice, the golde mynes reache to the

borthers on euery fyde. Albeit, owre men haue alfo golde mynes not to bee contempned, euen within thjee leaques of Dariens, in the which they gather golde in many places at this prefente: yet do theye affyrme greater plentie to bee in the mynes of Dabaiba. In the bookes of owre fyrſte frutes wrytten to powre holpneſſe, we made mention of this Dabaiba, wherin owre men were deceaued and myſtooke the mat-

ter. For where they founde the fyſher men of kyng Dabaiba in the marpſhes, they thought his region had byn there alfo. They determyned therfore to fende to kynge Dabaiba,

three hundreth choyfe younge men to be chofen owte of the hole army as moſte apte to the warres, and well furnyſhed with all kyndes of armoure and artillery, to thintent to go vnto hym and wyl hym, eyther frendly and peaceably to per-

mytte

mytte them to inhabyte parte of his kingdome with the fruition of the golde mynes, oʒ elles to bydde him battayle and dʒyue hym owte of his countrey. In their letters, they often tymes repete this foʒ an argument of great rychesse to coome, that they in maner dygged the grounde in noo place, but founde the earthe myʒte with sparkes and smaule graynes of golde. They haue also aduertised the kynge that it shalbe commodious to place inhabitours in the hauen of *Sancta Martha* in the region of *Saturma*, that it maye bee a place of refuge foʒ them that saple from the Ilande of *Dominica* from the whiche(as they saye) it is but foure oʒ fyue dayes saplyng to that hauen of the regyon of *Saturma*: And from the hauen, but thʒe dayes saplyng to *Dariena*. But this is to bee vnderstode in goȝpnge and not in retournynge. Foʒ the returnyng from thense is so laboʒious and difficulte by reason of the contrary course of the water, that they seeme as it were to ascende hyghe montaynes and stryue ageynste the poure of *Neptunus*. This swyfte course of the sea towarde the Weste, is not so violente to theym whiche retourne to Spayne frome the Ilandes of *Hispaniola* and *Cuba*: Althoughe they also do laboure ageynste the faule of the Ocean: The cause wherof is, that the sea is here verye large, so that the waters haue their full scoope. But in the tracte of *Paria*, the waters are constrayned together by the bendynge sydes of that great lande, and by the multytude of Ilandes lyinge ageynste it, as the lyke is seene in the straightes oʒ narowe seas of Sicilie where the violent course of the waters cause the daungerous places of *Scylla* and *Charybdis*, by reason of those narowe seas whiche conteine *Ionium, Libicum,* and *Tirrhexum. Colonus* the fyʒst fynder of these regyons, hath lefte in wʒytynge, that saplynge from the Ilande of *Guanassa,* and the pʒouynces of *Iaia, Maia,* and *Cerabaro,* beyng regyons of the west marches of *Beragua,* he founde the course of the water so vehemente and furious ageynste the fore-parte of his shippe whyle he sailed from those coastes towarde the Easte, that he coulde at no tyme touche the grounde with his soundynge plummet, but that the contraʒy vyolence of the water woolde beare it vppe from the bottome. He affyʒmeth also, that he coulde neuer in one hole daye with a meately good wynde, wynne one myle of the course of the water. And this is the cause why they are oftentimes

D h.i.

The regyon of Saturma
The Ilande of Dominica,

Dariena.

Difficulte saylyng ageynst the course of the sea,

The daungerous straightes of Scylla ʒ Charybdis,

Guanassa.
Iaia,
Maia.
Cerabaro.
Beragua.
The vehement course of the sea fro the east to the west.

Great plentie of golde,

tentymes enforced to fayle fyrste by the Jlandes of Cuba and Hispaniola, and so into the mayne sea toward the North wher they returne to Spaine, that the Northe wyndes maye further their vyage whiche they can not brynge to passe by a directe course. But of the motions of the Ocean sea to and fro, this shal suffyce. Let vs now therfore reherse what they wryte of Dariena, & of their habitation there, which they caule Sancta Maria Antiqua, planted on the sea bankes of Dariena. The situation of the place, hath no natural munition or defense: And the ayer is more pestiferous then in Sardus. The Spanyshe inhabitours, are all pale & yelowe, lyke vnto them that haue the yelowe giaundyes. Whiche neuerthelesse commeth not of the nature of the region as it is situate vnder the heauen. For in many regyons beyng vnder the selfe same degree of latitude, hauyng the pole of the same eleuation, they fynd holsome & temperate ayer, in such places where as the earth bryngeth forth fayre sprynges of water, or where holsome ryuers runne by bankes of pure earthe without mudde: but moste especyally where they inhabyte the sydes of the hylles and not the valeyes. But that habytation whiche is on the bankes of the ryuer of Dariena, is sytuate in a deepe valley, and enuironed on euery syde with hyghe hylles: By reason wherof, it receaueth the soonne beames at noonetyde directly perpendicular ouer their heades, and are therfore sore vexed by reflection of the beames bothe before, behynde, and from the sydes. For it is the reflection of the soonne beames whiche causeth feruente heate, and not their accesse or nerenesse to the earth. Forasmuche as they are not passyble in them selues as dothe manyfestly appeare by the snowe lyinge contynually vnmolten vpon certeyne hygh montaynes, as powre holynesse knoweth ryghte well. The soonne beames therfore faulyng on the montaynes, are reflected downewarde into the valley by reason of thobiecte of the declynynge sydes of the hylles, as it were the faule of a greate rounde stoone rowled frome the toppe of a montayne. The valley therfore receaueth, both those beames whiche faule directly theron, and also those whiche are reflected downwarde from euery syde of the montaynes. Their habitation therfore in Dariena, is pernicious and vnholsome onely of the particular nature of the place, & not by the sytuation of the regyon as it is placed vnder the heauen

The northe wynde.

Sancta maria Antiqua, the fyrst habitation of the spaniardes in the fyrme lande. Sardus the Jlande of Sardinia, The variety of regions lyynge vnder one paralel,

By what meanes the sonne beames are caused of feruent heate.

The pernicious ayer of Dariena.

heauen oz ffeare to the ſoonne. The place is alſo contagious
by the nature of the ſoyle, by reaſon it is coompaſed aboute
with muddy and ſtynkynge maryſſhes, thinfection wherof
is not a lyttle encreaſed by the heate. The vyllage it ſelfe,
is in a maryſſhe, and in maner a ſtandynge puddle, where, of
the dzoppes faulyng from the handes of the bond men whyle
they water the pauementes of their houſes, toades are en=
gendered immediately, as J my ſelfe ſawe in an other place
the dzoppes of that water turne into ſlees in the ſoomer ſea=
ſon. Furthermoze, where ſo euer they dygge the grounde
the deapthe of a handefull and a halfe, there ſpringeth owre
vnholſome and cozrupte water of the nature of the ryuer
which runneth through the deepe & muddy chanel of the val=
ley, and ſo fauleth into the ſea. Now therfoze they conſulte
of remouyng their habytation. Neceſſytie cauſed them fyzſt
to faſten their foote heare, bycauſe that they whiche fyzſt ar=
ryued in thoſe landes, were oppzeſſed with ſuche vrgente
hunger, that they had no reſpecte to chaunge the place al=
thoughe they were thus vexed by the contagion of the ſoyle
and heate of the ſoonne, beſyde the cozrupte water and in=
fectious ayer by reaſon of venemous vapours and exhalati=
ons rpſynge from the ſame. An other great incommoditie
was, that the place was deſtitute of a commodious hauen,
beynge thzee leaques diſtante from the mouthe of the goulfe.
The waye is alſo roughe and diffyculte to bzynge vyttaples
and other neceſſaries from the ſea. But lette vs nowe ſpeake
ſumwhat of other particular thynges whiche chaunſed.
Therfoze ſhoztly after that they weare arryued, there happe=
ned many thynges wherof they had no knowledge befoze.
A certayne well learned phiſytion of Ciuile, whome partely
thauctozytie of the byſſhoppe of Dariena, and partely the de=
ſyre of golde had allured to thoſe landes, was ſo ſcarred
with lyghtnynge in the nyghte ſeaſon lyinge in bedde with
his wyfe, that the houſe and all the ſtuffe therin beynge ſette
on fyer and barnte, he and his wyfe beynge bothe ſooze
ſcoched, ranne foozthe crpinge and almoſte naked, hardely
eſcappynge the daunger of deathe. At an other tyme, as cer=
tayne of them ſtoode on the ſhooze, a great Crocodyle ſoden=
ly caryed awaye a maſty of a yeare and a halfe owlde, as a
kyte ſhulde haue ſnatched vppe a chicken: And this euen in

H h. ii.   the

Toades and
ſlees engen=
dered of dzop=
pes of water,

Neceſſytie
hath no lawe

A houſe ſette
on fyer with
lyghtnynge,

A dogge de=
uoured of a
crocodyle,
Tanquam canis
e Nilo.

the presence of theym all, where the myserable **dogge** cryed
in vayne for the helpe of his mayster. In the nighte season
they were tormented with the bytynge of battes whiche are
there soo noysome that if they byte any man in his sleape,
they putte hym in daunger of lyfe, onely with drawynge
of bludde: In so muche that summe haue dyed therof, faul-
lynge as it were into a consumption through the malycious-
nesse of the venemous wounde. If these battes chaunce to
fynde a cocke or a henne abrode in the nyght season, they
byte them by the combes and so kyll them. They also whiche wente laste into these regions, do wryte, that the lande
is troubeled with Crocodyles, Lyons, and Tigers: But that
they haue nowe deuised artes and ingens howe to take them.
Lykewyse that in the houses of their felowes, they founde
the hydes and cases of suche Lyons and Tygers as they had
kylled. They wryte furthermore, that by reason of the ranke
nesse and frutefulnesse of the grounde, kyne, swyne, and horses, doo maruelously increase in these regions, and growe to
a muche bygger quantitie then they whiche weare of the first
broode. Of the excedynge hyghnesse of the trees with their
fruites, of the garden herbes, fruites, plantes, and seedes
whiche owre men broughte from Spayne and sowed and set
the same in these regions, lykewyse of the hertes and other
foure footed beastes bothe tame and wylde, also of dyuers
kyndes of foules, byrdes, and fysshes, they wryte euen as
we haue declared in the decades before. *Careta* the kynge of
the region of *Ciobs*, was with them for the space of three
dayes: whome when they had frendly enterteyned and shewed hym the secreate places of their shyppes, their horses also with their trappars, bardes, and other furnimentes, besyde many other thinges whiche seemed straunge to hym,
and had further delited his mynd with the harmony of their
musycall instrumentes, and gyuen hym many rewardes, they
dysmyssed hym halfe amased with to muche admyration.
He sygnifyed vnto them, that their trees in that prouynce,
of the planckes wherof, if shyppes were made, they shoulde
bee safe from the woormes of the sea whiche they caule *Bro-*
mai. Howe these woormes knawe and corrode the shyppes,
wee haue declared before. Owre shyppes are greatly trouble-
led with this plage if they lye longe in the hauens of these
regyons

The byting
of battes.

Lyons and
tygers,

Beastes wer
bygger in
their kynde,

how the go-
uernour en-
terteyned
kyng Careta,

Note.

Bromis or
Bissa, are
woimes whi-
che destroy
shyppes,

regyone. But they affyrme, that the woodde of this tree is soo bytter, that the woormes wyll not taste therof. There is also an other tree peculyar to these landes: whose leaues if they onely touche the bare in any place of a mannes body, they cause greate blysters, and those soo malycious that except the same bee foorthwith healed with salte water or fastynge spyttle, they doo incontynently engender deadely paynes. They saye lykewyse, that the sauour of the woodde is presente poyson: And that it can noo whither bee caryed without daunger of lyfe. When thinhabitauntes of the Ilande of *Hispaniola* had oftentymes attempted to shake of the yoke of seruytude, and coulde neuer brynge the same to passe neyther by open warre nor yet by priuye conspiracees, they were determyned in the nyghte season to haue kylled owre men in their sleepe with the smoke of this woodde. But when the Christian men had knowledge hereof, they compelled the poore wretches to confesse their intents, and punysshed the chiefe autours of the deuyse. They haue also a certayne herbe with the sauour wherof they are preserued from the hurte of this venemous woodde so that they maye beare it safely. Of these smaule thynges it shall suffyce too haue sayde thus muche. They looke dayly for many greater thynges to certyfye vs of from the Ilandes of the south sea, for at suche tyme as the messenger whiche broughte owre letters departed from thense, *Petrus Arias* prepared an expedition to that ryche Ilande whiche lyeth in the mouthe of the goulfe caulled *Sinus S. Michaelis*, and reacheth into the southe sea, beyng also lefte vntouched of *Vaschus* by reason that the sea was at that tyme of the yeare sore troubeled with tempestes, as wee haue further declared in *Vaschus* his vyage to the southe. Wee looke therfore dayly for greater thynges then are hetherto paste. For they haue nowe taken in hand to subdue manye other prouynces, whiche wee suppose too bee eyther verye ryche, or to brynge furthe summe straunge woorkes of nature. *Iohannes Diaz Solisius* of *Nebrissa* (of whome we haue made mention before) is sente by the froonte of the cape or poynte of *Sancti Augustini* (whiche reacheth seuen degrees beyonde the Equinoctiall lyne, and perteyneth to the dominion of the Portugales) to thintent to ouer runne the southe syde from the backehalfe of *Paria*, *Cumana*, *Cuquibacoa*,

D ij, iij. with

A venemous tree.

perhappes they: venemous arrows are made of this woodde: &c.

A preseruatiue agaynst poyson,

The Ilandes of the south sea,

The ryche Ilande caulled Dites,

Cab, sancti Augustini, Of the euyll successe of these viages, reade decade iij, Liber, ix.

with the hauens of *Carthago* and *Sancta Martha*, of *Dariena* also and *Beragua*, that moze perfecte and certeyne knowledge may bee had of those tractes. Furthermoze, one *Iohannes Poncius* was sente foozthe with thzee shyppes to destroye the Canibales bothe in the lande and Ilandes there aboute: aswell that the nations of the moze humane and innocente people maye at the length lyue without feare of that pestiferous generation, as also the better and moze safely to searche the secreates and rychesse of those regions. Many other lykewise were sente dyuers and sundzy wayes: as *Gasper Baddiocius* too searche the Weast partes: *Franciscus Bezerra*, to sayle by the corner of the goulfe: And *Valleius*, to passe by the mouthe oz enteraunce therof to the Easte coastes of the goulfe to searche the secreates of that lande, in the whiche *Fogeda* with his coompanye had of late begunne to plante their habitation, and had buylded a foztresse and a byllage. *Baddiocius* departed fyzste frome *Dariens* with fourescoze souldiours well appoynted: Whome *Lodouicus Mercado* folowed with fyftye: To *Bezerra* were also fourescoze assygned, and thzee scoze and tenne to *Valleius*. Whether they shall arryue at safe and commodious hauens, oz faule into vnfoztunate stations, he onely knoweth whose pzoudyence ruleth all: Foz as foz vs men wee are included within the knowledge of thinges after they haue chaunced. Lette vs nowe therfoze coome to other matters.

An expedition to destroy the Canibales,

Fogeda.

Looke. decad. iii. Lib. ix.

The seuenthe booke of the thirde decade.

The nauigations of Andreas Mozalis.

Petrus Arias the gouernour of the supposed continente, was scarsly entred into the mayne sea with his nauye onwarde on his vyage to *Dariena*. But I was aduertised that one *Andreas Mozalis* a pilot who had oftentymes ouer runne the coastes of these new seas and the Ilandes of the same, was coome to the courte to sell suche marchaundies as he bzoughte with hym frome thense. This man had dyligently searched the tracte of the supposed continente, and especyally thynner regyons of the Ilande of *Hispaniola*, wherunto he was appoynted by his

his brother Nicolaus Ouandus (the gouernour of the Jland and chiefe Commendatory of the order of the knyghtes of Alcantara) bycause he was a wytty man and more apte to searche suche thynges then any other: So that with his owne handes he drewe faire cardes and tables of suche regyons as hee discouered. Wherin as he hath bynne founde faythfull of suche as haue sense had better tryall herof, so is he in most credyt emongest the best sorte. He therfore resorted to me as all they are accustomed to doo, whiche retourne from the Ocean. What I learned of hym and dyuers other of thynges heretofore vnknowen, I wyll nowe declare. The begynnynge of this narration, shalbe the particular description of the Jlande of Hispaniola, forasmuche as it is the heade and as it weare the principall marte of all the lyberality of the Ocean, and hath a thousande and againe a thousande fayre, pleasaunt, bewtifull, and ryche Nereides whiche lye aboute it on euery syde, adownynge this their ladye and moother, as it were an other Tethis the wyfe of Neptunus, enuyronynge her aboute, and attendynge vppon her as their queene and patronesse. But of these Nereiades (that is to saye, the Jlandes placed aboute her) we wyll speake more hereafter. Lette vs in the meane tyme declare sumwhat of the Jlande whiche olure men named Margarites Diues (whiche the Spanyardes caule Delas perlas) beyng nowe well knowen, and lyinge in the southe sea in the goulfe cauled Sinus Sancti Michaelis (that is sainte Michaels goulfe. This Jland hath presently brought to owre knowledge many straunge and woonderfull thynges and promysseth no smaule hope of greater thynges in tyme to coome. In this is founde great plentie of pearles so fayre a great, that the sumptuous queene Cleopatra myght haue seemed to weare them in her crownes, chaynes, and braselettes. Of the shelfyshes wherin these are engendered, wee wyll speake sumwhat more in thende of this narration. But let vs nowe retourne to Hispaniola moste lyke vnto the earthly paradyse. In the description hereof, we wyll begynne of the imposytion of dyuerse names: Then of the forme of the Jlande, temperate ayer and benefyciall heauen: And fynally of the deuisyon of the regyons. Therfore for the ryghter pronunciation of the names, yowre holynesse muste vnderstande that they are pronounced with thaccent, as yowe may know by the

A particular description of the Jlande of Hispaniola

Nereides are nymphes of the sea, he meaneth Jlandes,

Tethis the wyfe of Neptunus and goddesse of the sea,

The Jlande of Margaritea Diues, Sainte Michaels goulfe

Great perles

Hispaniola lyke vnto the earthly paradyse,

by the verge sette ouer the heddes of the bowels, as in the
name of the Jlande Matinino, where the accente is in the laſt
bowell, and the lyke to be vnderſtoode in all other names.

**The fyrſt in-
habitours of
Hiſpaniola**

They ſaye therfoze, that the fyrſte inhabitours of the Jland
were tranſpozted in their Canoas (that is boates made of one
hole pyece of woodde) from the Jlande of Matinino, beynge
lyke banyſſhed men dzyuen from thenſe by reaſon of certaine
contrary faccions and diuiſyons emonge them ſelues, lyke as
wee reade howe

**Dardanus.
Teucrus.
Troianum.
Tirians,
Sidonians:**

Dardanus came from Corytho, and Teucrus from
Creta into Aſia, and that the regyon where they placed their
habitation, was afterwarde cauled Troianum. The lyke wee
reade howe the Tirians and Sidonians arryued with their
naupe in Libya by the fabulous conduction of Dido. Theſe
Matininans in like maner beynge banyſſhed from their owne
countrey, planted their fyrſte habytation in that parte of the
Jland of Hiſpaniola whiche they caule Cahonao, vpon the banke

**Eneas.
Latium.**

of the ryuer named Bahaboni: As is redde in the begynnynge
of the Romaynes that Eneas of Troye aryued in the region
of Jtaly cauled Latium vppon the bankes of the ryuer of Tiber. Within the mouthe of the ryuer of Bahaboni, lyeth an J-
lande where it is ſayde that thinhabitauntes buylded their
fyrſte howſe whiche they named Camoteia. This howſe they
conſecrated ſhoztely after, and honoured the ſame reuerently
with continual gyftes and monumientes, euen vntyl the com-

Hieruſalem

mynge of owre men, lyke as the Chriſtians haue euer relygy-
ouſly honoured Jeruſalem the fountayne and oryginall of
owre faythe: As alſo the Turkes attribute the lyke to the

**Mecha.
The Jlandes
of Conarie,**

cytie of Mecha in Araby, and thinhabytantes of the foztunate
Jlandes (cauled the Jlandes of Canarye) to Tyrma buylded
vppon a hyghe rocke from the whiche many were wounte
with ioyfull myndes and ſonges to caſte them ſelues downe
headlonge, beyng perſuaded by their prieſtes that the ſoules
of all ſuche as ſo dyd foz the loue of Tyrma, ſhulde therby enioye eternall felycity. The conquerours of the Jlandes of
Canarie, founde them yet remaynyng in that ſuperſtition, e-
uen vntyll owre tyme: Moz yet is the memozy of their ſacri-
fyces vtterly wozne awaye: The rocke alſo reſerueth the
owlde name vnto this daye. J haue alſo learned of late,
that there yet remayneth in the Jlande ſumme of the faction

**Betanchoz,a
frenchman,**

of Betanchoz the frenſhe man and fyrſte that bzoughte the J-
landes

landes to good culture and ciuilitie beyng therto lycenced by
the kynge of Caſtile as I haue ſayde befoze. Theſe doo yet
(foz the moſte parte) obſerue bothe the language and maners
of the Frenchemen, although the eyres and ſucceſſours of Betanchor, had ſoulde the two ſubdued Ilandes to certeyne men
of Caſtile. yet thinhabitours whiche ſucceded Betanchor, and
buylded them houſes and encreaſed their families there, do
contynue to this daye: And lyue quietly and pleaſauntly
with the Spanyardes, not greued with the ſharpe coulde of
Fraunce. But lette vs nowe returne to thinhabitauntes of
Matinino and Hiſpaniola. The Ilande of Hiſpaniola was fyzſte

The fyzſt na-
mes of Hiſ-
paniola.

named by the fyzſte inhabitours, Quizqueia, and then Haiti.
And this not by chaunce, oz at the pleaſure of ſuche as diuiſed theſe names, but of credulitie and belefe of ſumme great
effecte. For Quizqueia, is as muche to ſaye as a great thinge:
And that ſo great that none maye bee greater. They interprete alſo, that Quizqueia ſygnifyeth, large, vniuerſall, oz al,
in like ſignification as the Greekes named their god cauled
Pan: Bycauſe that foz the greatnes therof, theſe ſymple ſoules ſuppoſed it to bee the hole woзlde: And that the ſoonne
beames gaue lyghte to none other woзlde but onely to this
Iland with the other adiacente aboute the ſame: And
thervppon thoughte it moſt wooзthy to bee cauled great, as
the greateſt of all other knowen to them. Haiti is as muche to
ſaye by interpretation, as roughe, ſharpe, oz craggie. But
by a fyguratiue ſpeache cauled denomination (wherby the
hole is named by part) they named the hole Iland Haiti (that
is) roughe: For as muche as in many places the face of this
Iland is rough by reaſon of the craggie montaynes, hoзrible

The roughe-
neſſe of Hiſ-
paniola.

thicke wooddes, and terrible darke and diepe valleys enuy-
roned with great and highe montaynes, althoughe it bee in
manye other places exceadynge bewtifull and floзyſſhynge.
Here muſte wee ſumwhat digreſſe from thoзder we are entered into. Perhappes your holpneſſe wyll maruell by what
meanes theſe ſymple men ſhoulde of ſoo longe contynuance
beare in minde ſuche principles, where as they haue no know
ledge of letters. So it is therfoзe, that from the beginninge,
their princes haue euer byn accuſtomed to committe their chil-

The maner
of lernynge.

dзen to the gouernaunce of their wiſe men whiche they cauſe
Boitios, to bee inſtructed in knowledge, and to beare in me-
moзie

Ii

moꝛe ſuche thynges as they lerne. They gyue them ſelues chieflye to two thynges: As generally to lerne thoꝛiginall and ſucceſſe of thynges: And particularlye to reherſe the noble factes of their graundefathers great graundefathers and aunceſtours aſwell in peace as in warre. Theſe two thynges they haue of owlde tyme compoſed in certeyne myters and ballettes in their language. Theſe rhymes oꝛ ballettes, they caule Arcitos. And as owre mynſtrelles are accuſtomed too ſynge to the harpe oꝛ lute, ſo doo they in lyke maner ſynge theſe ſonges and daunce to the ſame, playenge on tymbꝛelles made of ſhels of certen fyſſhes. Theſe tymbꝛels they caule Maguei. They haue alſo ſonges and ballettes of loue: And other of lamentations and mooꝛnyng: Summe alſo to encorage them to the warres, with euery of them their townes agreable to the matter. They exercyſe theym ſelues muche in daunceinge, wherin they are verye actyue and of greater agilitie then owre men, by reaſon they gyue them ſelues to nothyng ſo muche, and are not hyndered with apparell whiche is alſo the cauſe of their ſwiftneſſe of foote. In their ballettes lefte them of their aunceſtours, they haue pꝛophecies of the comminge of owre men into their countrey. Theſe they ſynge with mooꝛnyng and as it were with gronyng, bewayle the loſſe of their lybertie and ſeruitude. Foꝛ theſe pꝛophecies make mention that there ſhoulde coonne into the Ilande Maguacochios, that is, men clothed in apparell, and armed with ſuche ſwooꝛdes as ſhulde cutte a man in ſunder at one ſtroke: vnder whoſe yoke their poſteritie ſhulde bee ſubdued. And here I do not maruell that their pꝛediceſſours coulde pꝛophecye of the ſeruitude and bondage of their ſucceſſyon, if it bee trewe that is ſayd of the familiaritie they haue with ſpirites whiche appeare to them in the night, wherof we haue largely made mention in the nynth booke of the firſt decade, where alſo wee haue entreated of their zemes(that is) their Idoles and Images of diuelles whiche they honoured. But they ſaye that ſence theſe zemes were taken awaye by the Chꝛiſtians, the ſpirites haue no moꝛe appeared. Owre men aſcribe this to the ſygne of the croſſe wherwith they defende theym ſelues from ſuche ſpirites. Foꝛ they are nowe all clenſed and ſanctifyed by the water of baptime wherby they haue renounced the deuel and are conſecrated the holy members of Chꝛiſt. They

Ballets and rhymes.

Singing and daunceing. Soonges of loue and mooꝛnynge.

Pꝛophefies.

Note

They: familiaritie with ſpirites

The deuyl is dꝛyuen awaye by baptiſme

They are vniuerſally ſtudyous to knowe the boundes and lymettes of their regions and kingdomes: And eſpecially their
Mitaini (that is) noble men, So that euen they are not vtterlye
ignozante in the ſuruepinge of their landes. The common
people haue none other care then of ſettynge, ſowynge, and
plantynge. They are mooſte experte fyſſhers, by reaſon that
throughowte the hole yeare, they are accuſtomed daylye to
plounge them ſelues in the ryuers, ſo that in maner they lyue
no leſſe in the water then on the lande. They are alſo giuen
to huntynge. Foz (as J haue ſayde befoze) they haue twoo
kyndes of foure footed beaſtes, wherof the one is lyttle cuu-
nes cauled Vtias, and the other Serpentes named Iuannas,
muche lyke vnto Crocodiles, of eyght foote length, of mooſte
pleaſaunte taſte, and lyuynge on the lande. All the Jlandes
noozyſhe innumerable byzdes and foules. As ſtocke doues,
duckes, geeſe, hearons, byſyde noleſſe number of popingiais
then ſparowes with vs. Euery kynge hath his ſubiectes diuided to ſundzye affaires: As ſumme to huntynge, other to
fyſſhynge, and other ſumme to huſbandzye. But let vs now
returne to ſpeake further of the names. We haue ſayde that
Quizqueia and Haiti, were the oulde names of this Jlande.
The hole Jlande was alſo cauled Cipanga of the region of the
montaynes aboundynge with golde: Lyke as owrs anciente
poetes cauled all Jtalye Latium of parte therof. Therfore as
they cauled Auſonia and Heſperia, Jtalie, euen ſoo by the names of Quizqueia, Haiti, and Cipanga, they vnderſtode the hole
Jlande of Hiſpaniola. Owre men dyd fyzſte name it Iſabella of
queene Heliſabeth whiche in the Spanyſhe tongue is cauled
Iſabella: And ſo named iy of the fyzſt Colonie where they planted their habitation vpon the banke nere vnto the ſea on the
Nozthe ſyde of the Jlande, as wee haue further declared in
the fyzſte decade. But of the names, this ſhall ſuffyce. Lette
vs nowe therfoze ſpeake of the fozme of the Jlande. They
whiche fyzſte ouer ranne it, deſcribed it vnto me to bee lyke
the leafe of a cheſtnutte tree, with a goulfe towarde the weſt
ſyde, lyinge open ageynſt the Jlande of Cuba. But the experte
ſhyppe mapſter Andreas Moralis, bzoughte me the fozme therof
ſumwhat differynge from that. Foz from bothe the cozners,
as from the Eaſt angle and the Weſt, he deſcribed it to be indented and eaten with many great goulfes, and the cozners

---

Marginal notes:

Surueyers

They lyue as much in the water as on the lande

Serpentes
A Crocodile is much lyke to owr ewte oz Lyſerte
Byzdes and foules
popingayes

Cipanga.

Jtaly cauled Latium

Jſabella

The fozme of the Jlande of Hiſpaniola

to reache foorthe verye farre: and placeth manye large an[d]
safe hauens in the great goulfe on the East syde. But I tru[st]
shortely sno to trauayle further herein; that a perfecte card[e]
of the particular description of Hispaniola maye bee sente vnt[o]
yowre holynesse. For they haue nowe drawne the Geogra[-]
phicall description therof in cardes, euen as yowre holynes[se]
hath seene the forme and sytuation of Spayne and Italy
with their mountaines, valleyes, ryuers, cities, and colonies

Lette vs therfore without shamfastnesse compare the Ilande
of Hispaniola to Italie, sumtyme the heade and queene of th[e]
hole worlde. For if wee consyder the quantitie, it shalbe
founde lyttle lesse, and muche more fruitefull. It reacheth
from the Easte into the Weste, fyue hundreth and fortye my[-]
les accordynge to the computation of the later searchers:
Althoughe the Admyrall sumwhat inueased this number a[s]
wee haue sayde in the fyrste decade. It is in breadth summe
where, almoste three hundreth myles: And in summe place[s]
narower where the corners are eyrended. But it is suerly

muche more blessed and fortunate then Italie: Beynge fo[r]
the moost parte therof so temperate and frupschynge, tha[t]
it is neyther vexed with sharpe coulde, nor afflycted wit[h]
immoderate heate. It hath bothe the beyinges or conuersy[-]

ons of the soonne (cauled solstitia) in maner equall with th[e]
Equinoctiall, with lyttle difference betwene the length o[f]
the daye and nyghte throughout all the yeare. For on the
the south syde, the day ascendeth scarcely an houre in length
aboue the nyghte, or contrary wyse. But the dyfference is

more on the northe syde. yet are there summe regions in the
Ilande in the whiche the coulde is of sum force. But yowre
holynesse muste vnderstonde this to bee incident by reason o[f]
the obiecte or neareneste of the mountaines, as wee wyl more
largely declare hereafter. yet is not this coulde so pearcynge
or sharpe, that thinhabitantes are molested with snowe o[r]

byrynge froste. In other places, the Ilande enioyeth perpe[-]
tuall spryngetyme, and is fortunate with contynuall soomer
and harueste. The trees floryshe there all the hole yeare: And
the medowes contynue alway greene. All thynges are ercea[-]
dynge fortunate, and growe to great perfection. How won[-]

derfully all garden herbes and frutes doo encrease, soo that
within the space of syrtene dayes after the seede is sowne, al[l]
herbes

erbes of smaule steames, as lettesse, borage, radyshe, and suche other, coome to their full ryppenesse: And also howe erbes of the bygger sorte, as gourdes, melones, cucumers, pompons, citrons, and suche other, coome to their perfection in the space of thirtie dayes, wee haue sufficiently declared elles where. Of the beastes transported out of Spaine thether, wee haue sayde howe they growe too a muche greater kynde: In so muche that when they faule into communication of the oxen or kyne, they compare them in bignesse to eliphantes, and swyne to mules: But this summewhat by an excesyue kynde of speache. Wee haue also made mention how their swynes flesshe is most sauourye, and of farre better and more pleasaunte taste and more holsome then others, by reason they are fedde with the frutes of Myrobalane trees, and other pleasaunte and nuryshynge fruites of that contrey, whiche growe there of them selues, as do with vs beeches, hollye, & okes. Vynes woolde also prosper there with maruelous encrease, if they had any regard to the plantinge therof. The lyke encrease commeth of wheate if it be sowen vppon the mountaynes where the colde is of sume strength: but not in the playnes, by reason of to much fatnes and rankenes of the growndе. It is in maner incredible to heare, that an eare of wheate shuld bee bygger then a mans arme in the brawne, and more then a spanne in length, bearynge also more then a thousande graynes, as they all confesse with one voyce, and ernestly affirme the same with others. Yet they say the bread of the Ilande (cauled Cazabbi made of the roote of Iucca, to bee more holsome, because it is of easyer digestion, and is cultured with lesse labour and greater increase. The residue of the tyme which they spende not en settynge and plantynge, they bestowe in gatheringe of golde. They haue nowe suche plentie of foure footed beasts, that horses and oxe hydes with shepe skynnes and goate skyns and such other, are brought from thense into Spayne: So that nowe the doughter in many thynges helpeth and succurreth her mother. Of the trees of brasile, spices, the graine which coloureth scarlet in bright shynynge redde, mastix, gossampine cotton, the precious metall cauled Electrum, and such other commodities of this Ilande, we haue spoken sufficiently before. What therfore can chaunce more happy vnto man vpon the earth, then there

Ii, iiii. to lyue

Beastes

Oxen and swyne of exceadyng bygnesse,

Swyne fed with myrobalanes

Vines

wheate

An eare of wheate as byg as a mans arme in the brawne

The bread of the Ilande.

Golde,

Great plentie of cattayle,

Brasile, Mastix, Gossampine Electrum.

Incommodi-
ties of intem
perat regions

to lyue where he neede not to bee dryuen to close chaumbers
with sharpe coulde oz faynynge heate? Noz yet in wynter
eyther to bee laden with heauy apparell, oz to burne the shin
nes with continual syttyng at the fyer, which thynges make

holsome ayer
and water

men oulde in short tyme by resoluinge the natural heate, wher
of a thousande diseases insue. They also affirme the ayer to
bee very healthfull: and the waters of the ryuers to bee no

Golde, euery
where

lesse holsome, as they whiche haue theyz continuall course
through the earth of the golden mynes. Foz there is in maner no ryuer, no mountaynes, and but fewe playnes that are
vtterly without golde. But let vs nowe at the length coome

The descripti
on of the ma-
ner partes of
the Jlande,

to the particular description of the inner partes of this blessed Jlande. We haue befoze declared howe it is in maner e-
qually diuided with foure greate ryuers descendynge frome
hygh mountaynes: wherof that which runneth towarde the
East, is cauled Iunna, as that towarde the West is named A-
tibunicus: The thyrde is Naiba oz Haina which runneth Southwarde: The fourth is cauled Iacba, and fauleth towarde the
Nozth. But this shippe master, hath brought an other description obserued of thinhabitantes from the begynnynge.
Let vs therfoze diuide the hole Jlande into fiue partes, caulynge the regions of euery prouince by theyz owlde names:
and fynally make mention of suche thynges as are woozthye
memozy in euery of them. The begynninge of the Jlande on
the East syde, is conteyned in the prouince named Caizcimu.
so named foz that in theyz language cimu, signifieth the front
oz begynnynge of any thynge. After this, foloweth the prouince of Huhabo, and then Caihabo. The fourth is Bainoa, Guacca
iarima conteyneth the west cozner. But the last saue one, Bainoa
is of larger boundes then the three other. Caizcimu reachethe
from the fyzst fronte of the Jlande to the ryuer Hozama, whiche runneth by the citie of saynt Dominicke. But towarde
the Noeth syde, it is ended at the rough mountaynes of Haiti. Huhabo, is included within the mountaynes Haiti and the
ryuer Iaciga. Caiabo the thyzde prouince, conteyneth all that
lyeth betwene Cubabo and Dahatio, euen vnto the mouth of the
ryuer of Iacba oz Iaebo (one of the foure which diuide the J-
lande equally) and ascendethe to the mountaynes of Cibaus,
where the greateste plentie of golde is founde: Oute of the
which also the ryuer Demahus spzingeth: and ioynynge with
the

The citie of s
Dominicke

The moun
taynes of
Haiti

The moun-
taynes of Ci-
baua

the fpringes of the ryuer of Naiba, (being an other of the foure
which diuideth the Jlande towarde the fouth fea) fauleth to
an other banke of the ryuer of faynt Dominicke. Balnoa, begynneth at the confines of Caiabi, and reacheth euen vnto the
Jlande of Cahini which lieth neare vnto the fea bankes of the
north fyde of the Jlande where wee fayde that they erected
the fyrft colonie or habitacion. The prouince of Guaccaiarima,
occupieth the remanent towarde the weft. This they named
Guaccaiarima, bycaufe it is the extreme or vttermoft parte of the
Jlande. For Iarima in theyr language fignifieth the tayle or
ende of any thynge: And Gua, is an article whiche they vfe
often tymes in the names of thynges: And efpecially in the
names of theyr kynges : as Guarionexius, and Guaccanarillus. In
the prouince of Caiximu, are thefe regions : Higuei, Guanama, Reyzn,
Xagua, Aramana, Arabo, Hazoa. Macorix, Caiacoa, Guaiagua, Baguanimabo
and the rough mountaynes of Haiti. Here let vs fpeake fume
what of theyr afpirations which they vfe otherwyfe then the
Latins doo. It is to bee noted that there is no afpiration in
theyr vowels, which hath not theffecte of a confonant. So
that they pronounce theyr afpirations more vehemently then
wee do the confonant .f. ye, all fuche woordes as in their
tonge are afpirate, are pronounced with lyke breath and fpi-
ritc as is .f. fauing that herein the neather lyppe is not moued to thuppermoft teethe. With open mouthes and fhakynge
theyr breftes, they breath out thefe afpirations, ha, he, hi, ho, hu,
as the Hebrewes and Arabians are accuftomed to pronounce
theyrs. I fynde alfo that the Spanyardes vfe the lyke vehe-
mence in the afpirations of thofe woordes whiche they haue
receaued of the Moores & Arabians which poffeffed Spaine,
and continued there many yeares: As in thefe woordes :Almo
hada, whiche fignifieth a pyllowe or bolfter: Alfo Almohaza,
that is, a horfe combe: with dyuers fuch other woordes whi
che they fpeake in matter with panting breftes and vehement
fpirite. I haue thought it good to reherfe thefe thynges, by
caufe amonge the Latines it often tymes foo chaunceth that
onely the accent or afpiration, chaungeth the fignification of
the woorde : as hora, for an houre, and ora for the plurale
number of this woorde os, which fignifieth the mouth : Alfo
ora, which fignifieth regions or coaftes. The lyke alfo chaun
ceth in the diuerfitie of the accente, as occido I kyll, and occi
do I

The Jlande of Cahini

Of prouinces diuided into regions

Of theyr afpi-rations

The pronunci-ation of the Hebrewes & Arabians, The Moores and Arabians poffeffed Spayne

howe the af-piration chan-geth the fig-nification of woordes

to J faule. Euen so in the language of these simple men, ther
are many thynges to bee obserued. But let vs nowe returne
to the description. In the prouince of Hububo, are these regions: Xamana, Canabacoa, Cubabo, with many other, the name
wherof J haue not yet learned. The prouince of Caibabo, conteyneth these regions: Maguas, and Cacacubana. Thinhabitantes of this region, haue a peculiar language much differing
from the common language of the Jland, and are cauled Ma-
coryxes. There is also an other region cauled Cubana, whose
language differeth from the other. Lykewyse the region o
Baiobaigua, hath a dyuers toonge. There are also other regions, as Dahabon, Cybabo, and Manabaho. Cotoy is in the mydd
of the Jlande. By this runneth the ryuer Nizaus: And th
montaynes cauled Mehatin, Hizua, and Neibaynao, confine wit
the same. In the prouince of Bainoa, are the regions of Maguana, Iagohaincho, Biuruco, Dahaiagua, and Attibuni, so named of th
ryuer: Also Cainoa, Buaaici, Dahabonici, Maiaguarida, Arici, Macaxin-
Guahabba, Anniuici, Marien, Guaricco, Amaguei, Xaragua, Yaguana, Axxue
Iacchi, Honorucco, Disguo, Camaie, and Neibaimao. In Guaccaierima th
last prouince, these regions are conteyned: Mauicaruo, Guahagua
Taquensaabo, Nimaea, Bainoa the lesse, Cabaymi, Iamuixi, Manabaxao, Zu
na, Habacoa, and Ayqueroa. But let vs entreate sumwhat of th
particulars of the regions. In the prouince of Caixcinu, with
in the great goulfe of the beginnynge, there is a greate cau
in a hollowe rocke vnder the roote of a hygh mountayne, a
bout twoo furlonges from the sea. The enterie of this cau
is not much vnlyke the doores of a great temple, beinge ver
large and turnynge many wayes. Andreas Morales the shyp ma
ster, at the commaundement of the gouernoure, tempted t
searche the caue with the smaullest vessels. He sayth that b
certeyne priuie wayes, manye ryuers haue concourse to th
caue as it were to a sinke or chanell. After therperience her
of, they ceased to maruaile whither other ryuers ranne wh
the commynge fourescore and tenne myles, were swalowe
vp, so that they appeared no more, nor yet fell into the se
by any knowen wayes. Nowe therfore they suppose that r
uers swalowed vp by the holowe places of that stony moun
tayne, faule into this caue. As the shypmaster entered into th
caue his shippe was almost swalowed. For he sayth that thei
are many whyrlepooles and rysinges or boylinges of the wa
ter

Dyuers lan
guages in
the Jlande

A greate caue
in the rocke
of a moun-
tayne,

A daungerus
enterpryse

Riuers deuou
red of caues,

er, which make a violent conflicte and horrible rorynge one
encounterynge the other. Also many huge holes & holowe pla:
es: So that what on the one syde with the whirle pooles, &
n the other side with the boyling of the water, his shyp was
ong in maner tossed vp and downe lyke a baule. It greatly
epented hym that he had entered, yet knewe he no way how
o come forth. He now wandered in darkenesse, aswel for the
bscurenesse of the caue into the which he was farre entered,
s also that in it were thicke cloudes engendered of the moist
apours proceading of the conflicte of the waters whiche cō:
nually faule with great violence into the caue on euery side.
He compareth the noyse of these waters, to the faule of the
amous ryuer of Nilus from the montaines of Ethyope. They
ere al so deafe, that one could not here what an other sayd.
But at the length with great daunger & feare, he came foorth
of the caue as it had byn owte of hel. Aboute three score mi:
es distante from the chiefe citie of sainte Dominicke, there
re certeyne hyghe montaynes vppon the toppes wherof is a
ake or standynge poole inaccessible, neuer yet seene of them
hiche came latelye to the Ilande, bothe by reason of the
oughnesse of the montaines, and also for that there is noo
athe or open waye to the toppes of the same. But at the
ength the shyppe maister beinge conducted thether by one of
ynges, ascended to the toppes of the montaines and came
o the poole. Hee saith that the coulde is there of sum force.
And in token of wynter, hee founde ferne and bramble bus:
hes, whiche two, growe only in coulde regions. These mon:
aynes, they caule Ymizui Hibabaino. This poole is of freshe
water three myles in compasse, and wel replenyshed with di:
uerse kindes of fyshes. Many smaule riuers or brookes faule
into it. It hath no passage owte, bycause it is on euery
syde enclosed with the toppes of montaynes. But
lette vs nowe speake of an other poole whiche
maye well bee cauled a sea in the mydlande,
and bee coompared to the Caspian or
Hircanian sea in the fyrme lande of
Asia: with certeyne other la:
kes and pooles of
freshe water.

R s   The

Marginal notes:

whirlepooles and conflicte of waters,

Clowdes in the caue.

The Cataractes of Nilus

A standynge poole in the toppe of a hygh moun- tayne.

Ferne and bramble bus- shes, growe only in coulde regions.

The Caspian and hircani- an sea.

¶The eyghte booke of the thirde decade.

A great lake
of soure and
salte water.
Swalowinge
goulfes.

Sea fysshes
n lakes of
the midlande

The deuou-
rynge fysshe
cauled Tibu-
ronus.

The ryuers
that faue in-
to the lake
Caspium,

CCC spzynges
within the
space of a
furlonge.

A myracle.

The Indian
language.

¶He prouynce of Bainoa beynge thrise as bygge as the three fyrst, that is, Caizcimu, Vhabo, and Caihabo, includeth a valley named Caiouani, in the whiche there is a lake of salte, soure, and bytter water, as wee reade of the sea cauled Caspium, lyinge in the firme lande betwene Sarmatia and Hircania. Wee haue therfore named it Caspium, although it bee not in the region of Hircania. It hath manye swalowinge goulfes, by the whiche, bothe the water of the sea spzingeth into it, and also suche as faule into it from the montaines, are swalowed vppe. They thyncke that the caues therof, are so large and deepe, that great fysshes of the sea passe by the same into the lake. Emonge these fysshes, there is one cauled Tiburonus whiche cutteth a man in sunder by the myddest at one snappe with his teethe, and deuoureth hym. In the ryuer Hozama, runnynge by the chiefe citie of sayncte Dominicke, these Tiburoni do sumtymes coome from the sea and deuoure manye of thinhabitauntes: Especially suche as do dayly ploonge themselues in the water to thintent to keepe their bodyes verye cleane. The ryuers whiche faule into the lake, are these. From the Mozthe syde, Guanicabon: From the Southe, Xaccoei: from the Easte, Guannabo And from the West, Occoa. They saye that these ryuers are great and continuall: And that besyde these, there are xx. other smaule ryuers whiche faule into this Caspium. Also on the Mozthe syde within a furlonge of the lake, there are aboue twoo hundzeth spzinges, occupyinge lykewise aboute a furlonge in circuite, the water wherof is coulde in soomer, fresshe also, and holsome to bee dzoonke. These spzynges make a ryuer that can not bee waded ouer, whiche neare at hande ioynynge with the other, fauleth into the lake. Here muste wee staye a whyle. The kynge of this region founde his wyfe pzayinge in a chapel builded by the Chzistians with in the pzecincte of his dominion, and required her coompanie to satisfye his flesshely luste. His wyfe repzoued hym, and put hym in remembzaunce to haue respecte to the holye place. The woozdes whiche shee spake to hym, were these: Teitoca, Teitoca, citoca : Whiche is as muche to saye, as, bee quyet, bee quyet? Techeta cynato guamechyna : That is, god wyl bee greatly angerie. Guamechyna, sygnifyeth god, Techeta greatly, Cynato angrie. But the husbande halpynge her by the arme , sayde : Guaibba, that is, go : Cynato macabuca guamechyna : That is : what is that to me if god be angerye? And with these woordes as he pro‐ fered her violence, soodenlye he became dumme and lame. yet by this myracle beynge striken with repentaunce, he euer after ledde a relygious lyfe : In soo muche that from thense foorthe hee woolde neuer suffer the chapell to bee swepte, or decked with any other mannes hande. By the same myracle, manye of thinhabitauntes and all the Christians beyng mo‐ ued, resorted deuoutly to the chappell. They take it in good parte that the kynge suffered the reuenge of that reproche. Lette vs nowe retourne to Caspium. That salte lake is tossed with stormes and tempestes : And oftentymes drowneth smaule shyppes or fyssher boates, and swaloweth them vppe with the maryners. In so muche that it hath not byn harde of, that any man drowned by shyppewracke, euer plonged vppe ageyne, or was cast on the shore, as commonly chaun‐ ceth of the deade bodyes of suche as are drowned in the sea. These tempestes, are the deintie banquetes of the Tiburones. This Caspium, is cauled Hagueigabon. In the myddest hereof, lyeth an Ilande named Guarizacca, to the whiche they resorte when they go a fysshynge. But it is not cultured. There is in the same playne, an other lake nexte vnto this, whose wa‐ ter is myxte of salte and freshe : And is therfore nother apte to bee droonke, not yet to bee refused in vrgente necessytie. This conteineth in length .xxv. miles, and in breadth eighe myles : In summe places also nyne or ten. It receaueth ma‐ nye ryuers whiche haue no passage owte of the same, but are swalowed vppe as in the other. Water springeth out of the sea into this also : but in no great quantitie, whiche is the cause that it is so commyxte. In the same prouynce to‐ warde the Weste syde, there is an other lake of freshe water, not farre distance from Caspius. This thinhabitauntes caule Iainagua. The same salte lake, hath on the North syde therof, an other named Guaccca. This is but lyttle : as not past three or foure myles in breadth, and one in length. The water of this, maye well bee droonke. On the Southe syde of the salte

K k. ii.　　　　lake,

A kyng stric‐ ken dumme and lame by myracle.

Such as are drowned in the lake are not cast vp ageyne.

The Ilande Guarizacca in the myddest of the poole, A lake of salt and freshe water.

A lake of freshe water

lake, there lyeth an other named Babbareo, of thre myles
length and in maner rounde. The water of this is freshe a
of the two other. This lake bycause it hath no passage ow
nor yet any swalowynge goulfes, conueyeth the superfluou
waters to the sea if it be encreased with the streames which
faule sumtimes more abondantly frô the montaines. This
in the region of Xamana in the prouince of Bainoa. There is a
other caulled Guaniba, lyeng betwene the East & the South ne

A lake of ten myles in length

vnto the syde of Caspius. This is ten myles in length and a
moste rounde. There are furthermore many other smaule sta
dyng pooles or lakes disparsed here and there in the Iland
whiche I wyll lette passe leste I shulde bee tedious in rema
nynge to longe in one thynge. I wyll therfore make an en
with this addition, that in all these, great plentie of fyshe an
faule is nourysshed. All these lakes lye in a large playne, th

A playne of a hundreth and twentie miles

whiche from the East reacheth into the West a hundreth an
twentie myles: beyng of breadth, xviii. myles where it is na
rowest, and xxv. where it is largest. Lookyng toward th
West, it hath collaterally on the lefte hande the montaines o
Daigunni: And on the ryght hande, the montaines of Caigua
so caulled of the name of the vale it selfe. At the rootes of th
montaines of Caigua toward the Northe syde, there lyeth an

A playne of two hundreth myles in length.

ther vale much longer & larger then that before named. Fo
it conteineth in length, almoste two hundreth myles: And i
breadth xxx. wher it is largest, & about, xx. wher it is narowe
This vale in summe parte therof, is caulled Maguana: In a
other place, Iguamue, & elles where, Hathathiei. And forasmuch
as wee haue here made mention of this parte of the vale na
med Hathathiei, wee wyll sumwhat digresse from the discour
of this description, and entreate of a thinge so straunge an
maruelous, that the lyke hath not byn hard of. So it is ther
fore, that the kyng of this region named Caramatexius, taket
great pleasure in fysshinge. Into his nettes chanced a younge
fyshe of the kynde of those huge monsters of the sea which

The maruelous fyshe the Manati.

thinhabitours caule Manati, not founde I suppose in ow
seas nor knowen to other men before this tyme. This fyshe
foure footed, and in shape lyke vnto a tortoyse: althoughe sh
be not couered with a shel, but with scales: And those of such
hardnesse & couched in suche order, that no arrowe can hitt
her. Her scales are byset & defend with a thousand knobbes
De

er backe is playne, and her heade vtterly lyke the heade of
n ore. She lyueth both in the water and on the lande : She
flowe of mouynge : of condition meeke, gentell, aſſocpable
nd louing to mankind and of a maruelous ſenſe oʒ memoʒie
s are the elephant and the delphyn. The king noʒiſſhed this
ſhe certeine daies at home with the bʒeade of the countrey,
ade of the roote of *Iucca* and *Panyeke* with ſuche other rootes
s men are accuſtomed to eate. Foʒ when ſhee was yet but
ounge, he caſt her into a poole oʒ lake neare vnto his palaice
ere to bee fedde with hande. This lake alſo receaueth wars and caſteth not the ſame foozth ageine. It was in tyme
aſte cauled *Guaurabo* : But is nowe cauled the lake of *Manati*
ter the name of this fyſhe whiche wandered ſafelye in the
me foʒ the ſpace of .xxv. yeares, and grewe exceDyng byg.
hat ſo euer is wʒitten of the Delphines of Baian oʒ Art-
, are muche inferioʒ to the doninges of this fyſh which foʒ
r gentle nature they named *Matum*, that is gentle oʒ noble.
herefoʒe when ſo euer any of the kynges famylyers, eſpeci-
ly ſuche as are knowen to her, reſoʒte to the bankes of the
ke and caule *Matum, Matum*, then ſhe (as myndefull of ſuche
neſites as ſhe hath receaued of men) lyfteth vp her heade
d commeth to the place whither ſhe is cauled, and there re-
aueth meate at the handes of ſuche as feede her. If any
ſrous to paſſe ouer the lake, make ſignes and tokens of
eyʒ intente, ſhe boweth her ſelfe to them, therewith as it
ere gentelly inuitynge them to amount vppon her, and con-
yth them ſafely ouer. It hath byn ſeene that this mon-
cous fyſhe hath at one tyme ſafely caryed ouer tenne men
nginge and playinge. But if by chaunce when ſhe lyfted
p her heade ſhe eſpyed any of the Chziſtian men, ſhe woolde
mediatly ploonge downe ageyne into the water and refuſe
o obey, bycauſe ſhe had once receaued iniury at the handes
f a certeyne wanton younge man amonge the Chziſtians,
he hadde caſte a ſharpe darte at her, although ſhe were not
urte by reaſon of the hardenes of her ſkynne beinge roughe
nd ſul of ſkales and knobbes as we haue ſayde. yet dyd ſhe
eare in memoʒie thiniurie ſhe ſuſteyned, with ſo gentell a re-
enge requitynge thingratitude of hym which had delte with
r ſo vngentelly. From that day when ſo euer ſhe was cau-
d by any of her familiers, ſhe woolde fyſt looke circumſpect

*A monſter of
the ſea fedde
with mans
hande.*

Matum.

*A fyſhe car-
eth men ouer
the lake.*

*A maruelous
thynge.*

ly about her, leaſt any were preſent apparelled after the manner of the Chriſtians. She woolde oftentymes play and wreſtle vppon the banke with the kynges chamberlens: And eſpecially with a younge man whom the kynge fauoured well, beinge alſo accuſtomed to feede her. Shee woolde bee ſumetymes as pleaſaunt and full of play as it had byn a moonkey or marmaſet: And was of longe tyme a great comfort and ſolace to the hole Ilande. For no ſmaule confluence aſwell of the Chriſtians as of thinhabitantes, had dayly concourſe to beholde ſo ſtraunge a myracle of nature, the contemplation wherof was no leſſe pleaſaunt then woonderfull. They ſay that the meate of this kynde of fyſhe, is of good taſte: And that many of them are engendered in the ſeas therabout. But at the length, this pleaſaunt playfelowe was loſte, and caried into the ſea by the great ryuer *Attibunicus*, one of the foure which diuide the Ilande. For at that tyme there chaunced ſo terrible a tempeſt of wind, & rayne, with ſuch fluds enſewing that the like hath not lightly byn hard of. By reaſon of this tempeſt, the ryuer *Attibunicus* ſo ouerflowed the bankes, that it fylled the hole vale & myxt it ſelfe with all the other lakes. At which tyme alſo, this gentell *Matum* and pleaſaunte companyon, folowynge the vehemente courſe and faule of the ſuddes, was therby reſtored to his oulde moother and natyue waters, and ſence that tyme neuer ſeene ageyne. Thus hauynge digreſſed ſufficiently, let vs nowe coome to the ſituation of the vale. It hathe collaterally the mountaynes of *Cibaus* and *Caiguam* which brynge it to the South ſea. There is an other vale beyonde the mountaynes of *Cibaua* towarde the North. This is cauled the vale of *Guarionexius*, bycauſe that before the memorie of man, the prediceſſours and aunceſtours of kyng *Guarionexius* to whom it is deſcended by right of inheritaunce, were euer the lordes of the hole vale. Of this kynge, we haue ſpoken largely in the fyrſt narration of the Ilande in the fyrſt Decade. This vale is of length from the Eaſt to the Weſt, a hundreth and foureſcore myples: And of breadth from the South to the North, thirtie myles where it is narowoeſt, and fiftie where it is brodeſte. It begynneth from the region *Canobocoa* by the prouinces of *Huhabo* and *Caibo*: And eudeth in the prouince of *Bainoa* and the region of *Maciens*. It lyeth in the myddeſt betwene the mountaynes of *Cibau*

The ryuer Attibunicus.

The ſituation of the great vale.

The mountaynes of Cibaua and Caiguam.

The greate Vale of Guarionexius.

haus, and the mountaynes of *Cabonai* and *Caxdcubuna*. There is no prouince noz any region, which is not notable by the maiestie of mountaynes, frutefulnes of vales, pleasauntnesse of hylles, and delectablenes of playnes, with abundaunce of fayze ryuers runnynge through the same. There are no sides of mountaynes oz hylles, no ryuers, which abound not with golde and delycate fysshes, except only one ryuer which from thoziginall therof, with the spzynges of the same bzeakynge foorth of the mountaynes, commeth owt salte and so contynueth vntyll it peryshe. This ryuer is cauled *Bahuan* : and runneth through the myddle of the region *Maguana* in the prouince of *Bainoa*. They suppose that this ryuer hathe made it selfe awaye vnder the grounde by sume passages of playster oz salte earthe. For there are in the Ilande many notable salte bayes, wherof we wyl speake moze hereafter. We haue declared howe the Ilande is diuided by foure ryuers & fyue prouinces. There is also an other particion, whiche is this. The hole Ilande consysteth of the tops of foure mountaines which diuide it by the myddest from the East to the weste. In all these is abundance of noozysshynge moysture and greate plentie of golde : of the caues also of the whiche, the waters of al the riuers (into the which the caues emptie them selues) haue theyz oziginall and increase. There are lykewyse in the hozryble dennes, obscure and darke vales, and myghtie rockes of stone. There was neuer any noysome beaste founde in it : Noz yet any rauenynge foure footed beaste. No lyon, no beare no fierce tygers, no craftie foxes, noz deuouring woolkes. Al thynges are blessed and foztunate : And nowe moze foztunate, foz that so many thousandes of men are receaued to bee the sheepe of Chzistes flocke, all theyz zemes and Images of deuylles being reiectted and vtterly out of memozie. If I chaunce nowe and then in the discourse of this narration to repeate one thynge dyuers tymes oz otherwise to make digression, I must desyze yowre holynes therwith not to bee offended. Foz whyle I see, heare, and wzyte these thinges, mee seemeth that I am herewith so affected, that foz verye ioy I feele my mynde stirred as it were with the spirite of Apollo as were the Sibylles, whereby I am enfozced to repeate the same ageyne : Especially when I consyder howe farre the amplitude of owre religion spzeadeth her wynges

Pe

mountaynes, vales. hylles. playnes. Ryuers.

Golde in all mountaynes, and golde and fysshe in all ryuers.

Salte bayes.

howe the Ilande is diuided with mountaynes Golde.

The ryuers haue theyz increase from the caues of the mountaynes

No hurtful oz raueninge beast in the Ilande.

The autours excuse.

Yet amonge these so many blessed and fortunate thynge
this one greeueth me not a lyttle: That these simple poo
men neuer brought vp in labour, do dayly peryshe with inte
lerable trauayle in the golde mynes: And are therby broug
to suche desperation, that many of them kyll them selues,
vpynge no regarde to the procreation of chyldren. In so mu
that women with chylde, perceauynge that they shall bryn
foorth such as shalbe slaues to the Christians, vse medecin
to destroy theyr conception. And albeit that by the kyng
letters patentes it was decreed that they shulde bee set at l
bertie, yet are they constrayned to serue more then seeme
conuenient for free men. The number of the poore wretch
is woonderfully extenuate. They were once rekened to b
aboue twelue hundreth thousande heades: But what th
are nowe, I abhorre to rehearse. We wyll therefore let th
passe: and returne to the pleasures of Hispaniola. In the mo
taynes of Cibaua, which are in maner in the myddest of the
lande in the prouince of Caiabo (where we sayd to bee the gr
test plentie of natyue golde) there is a region named Cotohi
tuate in the clowdes, enuironed with the toppes of hyg
mountaynes, and well inhabited. It consisteth of a play
of xxv. myles in length, and. xv. in breadth. This playne
hygher then the toppes of other mountaynes: So that the
mountaynes, maye seeme to bee the chiefe and progenitou
of the other. This playne suffereth alterations of the fou
tymes of the yeare: as the Sprynge, Soomer, Autumne, a
wynter. Here the herbes waxe wythered, the trees loo
theyr leaues, and the medowes become hoare: The whicl
thynges (as we haue sayde) chaunce not in other places
the Ilande, where they haue only the Spring and Autumn
The soyle of this playne bryngeth foorth ferne and bramb
busshes bearynge blacke berries or wylde raspes, which th
are tokens of coulde regions. Yet is it a fayre region: for tl
coulde therof is not very sharpe: neyther dooth it afflicte th
habitantes with frost or snowe. They argue the fruetfulne
of the region by the ferne, whose stalkes or steames are by
ger then a spere or iauelen. The sydes of those mountayne
are ryche in golde. Yet is there none appoynted to dygge f
the same, bycause it shalbe needefull to haue apparelled m
ners, and such as are vsed to labour. For thinhabitantes l
nyn

By what mea
nes the peo-
ple of the I-
land are gret
ly consumed.

The plesures
of hispaniola.

The region
of Cotohi, si-
tuate in the
Clowdes.
A playne in
the toppes of
mountaynes

The hygher,
the coulder.

Moderate
coulde in the
mountaynes.

Ferne of mar-
uelousbignes

Golde.

nge contented with lyttle, are but tender: And can not ther=
se away with labour oz abyde any coulde. There are two
uers which runne through this region, and faule from the
oppes of the present mountaynes. One of these is named Co
ityx, whose course is towarde the West, and fauleth into
e chanell of Naiba. The other is cauled Tirecotus: which ran=
nge towarde the East, ioyneth with the ryuer of Iunna. In
e Ilande of Creta (nowe cauled Candie) as I passed by in
legacie to the Soldane of Alcayz oz Babylon in Egypte,
e Uenetians toulde me that there laye suche a region in the
ppes of the mountaynes of Ida, whiche they affirme to bee
ze frutefull of wheate cozne then any other region of the
land. But forasmuch as once the Cretenses rebelled agenst
e Uenetians, and by reason of the streight and narowe way
the toppes therof, longe defended the region with armies
ainst thauctozitie of the Senate, and at the length beinge
werped with warres, rendered the same, the Senate com=
aunded that it shulde bee lefte deserte, and the streightes of
enteraunces to bee stopped, lest any shulde ascende to the
gion without their permissyon. yet in the yeare of Christe
. D. ii. lycence was graunted to the husband men to tyll
d manure the region, on suche condition that no suche as
re apte to the warres, myght enter into the same. There
also an other region in Hispaniola named Cotohy after the
me name. This diuideth the boundes of the prouinces of
bo and Caiabo. It hath mountaynes, vales, and plaines.
ut bycause it is baren, it is not muche inhabited. yet is it
hest in golde: Foz the ozginall of the abundaunce of gold,
gunneth here: In so muche that it is not gathered in smaule
aines and sparkes as in other places: but is founde hole,
assie, and pure, emonge certaine softe stones and in the vai=
s of rockes, by breakynge the stones wherof, they folowe
e vaynes of golde. They haue founde by experience, that
e vayne of golde is a lyuinge tree: And that the same by
snapes that it spreadeth & springeth from the roote by the
te pozes and passages of the yearth, putteth foozth bzan=
es euen vnto the vppermost part of the earth, & ceaseth not
ypl it discouer it selfe vnto the open ayer: At whiche time,
sheweth foozth certaine bewtifull colours in the steede of
ures, rounde stones of golden earth in the steede of frutes,

Ll   and

Thinhabi=
tantes of His=
paniola can
abyde no la=
bou: noz
coulde.

The Iland of
Creta oz Can=
die, vnder the
domini on of
the Ueneti=
ans.

Pure and
massie golde
in the region
of Cotoy.
The vaine of
golde, is a ly=
uynge tree.

These colers
oz floures are
cauled Mar=
chasites,
pyrites.

and thynne plates in steede of leaues. These are they which are disparcled throughout the hole Ilande by the course o the ryuers, eruptions of the spr̄nges owte of the montaines and violent faules of the fluddes. For they thincke that suc

The roote of the golden tree,

graines are not engendered where they are gathered: especia ly on the dry land: but otherwise in the riuers. They say tha the roote of the golde tree extendeth to the center of the eart & there taketh noꝛishement of increase. For the deaper that the

The braun= ches of the golden tree.

dygge, they fynd the trunkes therof to be so muche the grea ter as farre as they maye folowe it foꝛ abundaunce of wate spꝛinging in the montaines. Of the braunches of this tree they fynde summe as smaule as a threde, and other as bygg as a mannes fynger accoꝛdynge to the largenesse oꝛ straight

Caues sustey ned with pyl= lers of golde.

nesse of the ryftes and clyftes. They haue sumetimes chaun ced vpon hole caues susteyned and boꝛne vp as it were wit golden pyllars: And this in the wayes by the whiche th braunches ascende: The whiche beynge fylled with the sub

The stones of the golde mynes.

staunce of the truncke creapynge from beneath, the branch maketh it selfe waye by whiche it maye passe owte. It is of tentymes diuided by encounterynge with sum kynde of hard stone. Yet is it in other clyftes nooꝛisshed by the exhalation and vertue of the roote. But now perhappes yowe will ask me what plentie of golde is bꝛought from thense. Yowe shal

what gold is bꝛought yere= ly from His= paniola into Spayne.

therfoꝛe vnderstande that onely owte of _Hispaniola_, the sum o foure hundꝛeth and sumtymes fyue hundꝛeth thousande du cates of gold is bꝛought yearely into Spayne: as may be ga thered by the fyfthe poꝛtion dewe to the kynges Excheker which amounteth to the sum of a hundꝛeth and fourscoꝛe, o fourescoꝛe and ten thousande Castellanes of golde, and sum tymes moꝛe. What is to bee thought of the Ilande of _Cub_ and _Sancti Iohannis_ (otherwise caulec _Burichena_) beyng both ve ry ryche in golde, we wyll declare further hereafter. To hau

Salte of the mountaynes, very hard and cleare.

sayde thus muche of golde, it shall suffyce. Wee wyll now therfoꝛe speake sumwhat of salte wherwith wee may season and reserue suche thynges as are bought with golde. In region of the pꝛouince of _Bainoa_, in the montaynes of _Daiagu_ about twelue myles distant from the salte lake caulec _Caspiu_ there are salte bayes in the montaynes in a maner as hard a stoones, also clearer and whiter then cristall. There are lyke wyse suche salte baies whiche growe woonderfully in _Lalet_

Thu

ꝭ (now cauled Cataloma) in the territorie of the duke of Cadona
he chiefe ruler in that region. But suche as knowe theym
othe, affyrme that thefe of Bainoa are moste notable. They
aye alfo that this can not be clefte without wedges and bea
clles of Iron. But that of Laletana, maye eafyly bee broken
as I my felfe haue proued. They therfore compare this to fu:
he ftoones as may eafely bee broken : And the other to mar:
ble. In the prouince of Caximu, in the regions of Iguanama, Ca-
cos, and Guariagua, there are fprynges whofe waters are of
maruelous nature, beynge in the fuperfytial or vppermooste
parte, frefhe : In the myddest, myrte of falte and frefhe :
and in the loweft parte, falte and fower. They thincke that
he falte water of the fea, iffheweth owte foftely, and the
refhe, to fprinke owte of the mountaines. The one fauleth
owne and the other ryfeth : ⁊ are not therfore fo vniuerfal:
o myxt wherby the one may vtterly corrupt thother. If any
nan laye his eare to the grounde neare to any of thefe fprin:
es, he fhal perceaue the ground there to bee fo hollowe, that
he reboundyng noyfe of a horfeman comminge may be harde
or the fpace of three myles, and a foote man one myle. In
he laste region towarde the fouthe named Guaccaiarima, in the
lordfhyp of Zauana, they fay there are certeyne wyld men whi
he lyue in the caues ⁊ dennes of the montaynes, contented
nely with wilde fruites. Thefe men neuer vfed the compa:
ye of any other : nor wyll by any meanes becoome tame.
They lyue without any certaine dwellynge places, and with
owte tyllage or culturynge of the grounde, as wee reade of
hem whiche in oulde tyme lyued in the golden age. They fay
alfo that thefe men are withowte any certaine language.
They are fumtymes feene. But owre men haue yet layde
handes on none of them. If at any tyme they coome to the
fyght of men, and perceyue any makynge toward them, they
flye fwifter then a harte. ye they affyrme them to bee fwifter
then grehowndes. What one of thefe folytarie wanderers
oyd, it is worth the hearyng. So it is that owr men hauyng
granges adioynyng nere vnto the thicke wods, certen of the
repaired thither in the mooneth of September in the yeare.M.
D. xiiii. In the meane tyme, one of thefe wylde men came
trappynge owte of the woodde. And approchynge fumwhat
toward them with fmyling countenaunce, foodenly fnatched

Marginal notes:
- Salt as hard as ftones.
- Sprynges of falt, freffhe and fower water.
- holowe caues in the grounde
- Certeyne wyld men lyuing in caues and dennes
- Men without a certeyne language
- Men as fwift as greihoûds
- A wyld man runneth a: way with a chylde

Ll. ii.   vppe

vppe a childe of therse beynge the soonne of the owner of the graunge, whiche he begotte of a woman of the Ilande. He ranne awaye with the childe, and made sygnes to owre men to folowe hym. Many folowed aswel of owre men as of the naked inhabytantes, but all in vayne. Thus when the pleasaunt wanderer perceaued that the Christians ceased to pursue hym, he lefte the childe in a crosse waye by the whiche the swyneheardes were accustomed to dryue the swyne to the pasture. Shortly after, a swynehearde founde the chyld and brought hym home to his father yet tormentynge hym self for sorowe, supposynge that wylde man to haue byn one of the kynde of the Canibales, and that his soonne was now deuowred. In the same Ilande they gather pytche which sweateth owte of the rockes, beynge muche harder and forcer then the pitche of the tree : and is therfore more commodious to calke or defende shyppes ageynste the woormes called Bromas, wherof wee haue spoken largely before. This Ilande also bryngeth foorth pitche in two kyndes of trees, as in the Pyne tree and another named Copeia. I neede not speake of the pyne tree, bycause it is engendered and knowen in maner euery where. Lette vs therfore speake sumwhat of the other tree cauled Copeia : Pitche is lykewyse gathered of it as of the pyne tree : although summe saye that it is gathered by distyllyng or droppyng of the woode when it is burnt. It is a straunge thynge to here of the leafe therof : and how necessary prouision of nature is shewed in the same. It is to be thought that this is the tree in the leaues wherof the Chaldeans (beynge the fyrste fynders of letters) expressed their myndes before the vse of paper was knowen. This leafe is a spanne in breadth and almost round. Owre men write in them with pynnes or nedles or any suche instrumentes made of metall or woodde, in maner as well as on paper. It is to be laughed at what owre men haue perswaded the people of the Ilande as towchynge this leafe. The symple soules beleue that at the commandement of owre men, leaues do speake and disclose secreates. They were brought to this credulitie by this meanes. One of owre men dwellynge in the citie of Dominica the chiefe of the Ilande, delyuered to his seruaunt (beyng a man borne in the Ilande) certayne rosted connies (whiche they caule Vtias beynge no bygger then myse) wyllynge

Pitche of the rocke.

Pitche of two kyndes of trees.
The pyne tree.
The tree Copeia.

The leafe of a tree in the steede of paper.

They beleue that leaues do speake.
A pretie stone.

ynge hym to carie the same to his frende whiche dwelte fur=
ther within the Ilande. This messenger, whether it were
that he was therto constrayned through hunger, or enticed
by appetite, deuoured three of the connies by the waye.
¶e to whome they were sente, wrtt to his frynde in a leafe
howe manye he receaued. When the mayster had looked a
whyle on the leafe in the presence of the seruaunt, he sayde
thus vnto hym. Ah soonne, where is thy faythe? Coulde
thy gredye appetyte pxeuayle so muche with the as to cause
the to eate the connies commytted to thy fydelytie? The
poore wretche trembelynge and greatlye amased, confessed
his faute: And therwith desyred his mayster to tell hym
howe he knewe the treweth therof. This leafe (quod he)
whiche thou browghtest me, hath toulde me all. Then hee
further rehearsed vnto hym the houre of his coommynge to
his frende, and lykewyse of his departynge when hee re=
tourned. And thus they merylye deceaue these seely soules
and keepe theym vnder obedyence: In so muche that they
take owre men for goddes, at whose coommaundement lea=
ues doo disclose suche thynges as they thyncke mooste hyd
and secreate. Bothe the sydes of the leafe receaueth the for=
mes of letters euen as dooeth owre paper. It is thycker
then double parchemente, and meruelous toughe. While it
is yet florysshynge and newe, it sheweth the letters whyte
in greene. And when it is drye, it becommeth whyte and
harde lyke a table of woodde: but the letters were yelowe.
It dooeth not corrupte or putrifye: nor yet looseth the let=
ters thoughe it bee wette: nor by any other meanes excepte
it bee burnte. There is an other tree named Xagua: the iuise
of whose soure apple beynge of a darke redde coloure, stay=
neth and coloureth what soo euer is touched therwith: And
that soo fyrmely, that noo wasshynge canne take it awaye
for the space of twentie dayes. When the apple is full ripe,
the iuise looseth that strength. The apple is eaten, and of
good tast. There is also an herbe whose smoke (as we haue
rehersed the like before of a certen woodde) is deadly poison.
On a tyme when the kynges assembled together and conspi=
red the destruction of owre men, where as they durste not at=
tempte thenterprise by open warre, theyr duuise was, pryui=
lye to lay many bundels of thyse herbes in a certeyne house,

II. iiii.   which

Ignorance
causeth ad=
miration.

The leafe
wherin they
wryte.

A stronge co=
lour of the
iuise of an
apple.

An herbe
whose smoke
is poyson.

whiche fhoztly after they intended to fet on fyer, to thinte
that owre men makynge hafte to quenfhe the fame, myg
take theyz death with the fmoke therof. But theyz purpofe
pzactyfe beinge bewzayed, thautours of the diuife were p
nyfhed accozdyngly. Nowe (mofte holy father) foz as mu
as yowre holpneffe wzyteth that what fo'euer we haue wz
ten of the newe wozlde, dooth pleafe yowe ryght well, w
wyll reherfe certeyne thynges owte of ozder, but not great
from owre purpofe. Of the fettynge the rootes of *Maixiu*
Agis, *Iucca*, *Battatas*, and fuch other beinge theyz common food
and of thufe of the fame, we haue fpoken fufficiently befoz
But by what meanes they were fyzfte applyed to the comm
ditie of men, we haue not yet declared. We nowe therefo
entende to entreate fumwhat hereof.

⊂ The nynth booke of the thyzde Decade.

The kyndes
of fruites
wherwith
thinhabitan-
tes lyued
fyzft.

HEY faye that the fyzfte inhabitours lyue
contented with the rootes of dates, and M
gucans, which is an herbe muche lyke vn
that which is commonly cauled Sengrene
Dzpin. Alfo the rootes of Guaiegans, wh
che are rounde and greate muche lyke vn
puffes of the earth oz muftheromes. The
did lykewife eate *Guaieros*, lyke vnto perfeneppes: *Cibaios* lyk
nuttes, *Cabaioes* and Macoanes, lyke vnto onions, with d
uers other fuche rootes. They fay that after many yeares,
certeyne *Boition*, that is, a wyfe oulde man, fawe vppon tl
bankes fyde, a bufhe lyke vnto fenel : and tranfplantyng tl
roote therof, bzought it from wyldenes to a better kynde, b
noozyfhynge it in gardens. This was the begynnynge c

Neceffitie
the moother
of all artes.

Iucca, which at the fyzfte was deadely poyfon to all fuche a
dyd eate therof rawe. But foz as muche as they perceaued
to bee of pleafaunte tafte, they determyned many wayes
pzoue the vfe therof : And at the length founde by experien
that beinge fodde oz fryed, it was leffe hurtefull : by whicl
meanes alfo, they came to the knowledge of the veneme ly
inge hyd in the iufe of the roote. Thus by dzyinge, faltynge
feafonynge, and otherwyfe temperynge it, they bzought

o theyr fine breade which they caule. Cazabbi, more delectable nd holsome to the stomacke of manne then breade made of wheate, bycause it is of easyer digestion. The same is to bee nderstoode of other rootes and the grayne of Maizium whiche they haue chosen for their chiefe meate amonge the seedes f nature, as we reade howe Ceres the doughter of Saturnus, athered wheate and barley (with suche other corne as are owe most in vse amonge men) in Egypte of certeyne graynes aken owt of the mudde dryuen from the mountaynes of Ethiopia by thincrease of the ryuer Nilus, and lefte in the plaine t such tyme as Nilus resorted ageyne to his chanell. For the which facte, we reade that the antiquitie gaue diuine honour o Ceres, who fyrst norished and increased such chosen seedes. There are innumerable kyndes of Ages: the varietie wherof, s knowen by theyr leaues and floures. One kynde of these, o caulled Guanaguax. This is whyte boothe within & without in other named Guaraguei is of vyolet colour without & white within. The other kyndes of Ages, they caul Zazaueios. These re redde without and whyte within. Squiueies, are whyte within and without. Tunna, is all together of vyolet coloure. okos is yelowe boothe of skynne and inner substance. There s an other named Atibunieix: The skynne of this is of violet colour, and the substance whyte. Aniguamar, hath his skynne lso of vyolet coloure, and is whyte within. Guaccaracca, hath whyte skynne, and the substance of vyolet colour. There re many other which are not yet brought to vs. But I feare ne least in the rehearsall of these, I shal prouoke the spurres f malicious persons ageynst me which wyll scorne these owr doinges for that we haue wrytten of many such smaule thinges to a prince occupyed in suche weyghty affayres, as vnto yowre holynes vppon whose shulders resteth the burthen of the hole Christian worlde. But I wolde aske of these malycious enuyers of other mens trauayles, whether Plinie and suche other famous wryters, when they dyrected and dedicated suche thinges to kynges and princes, entended only to prouoke them to whom they consecrated the frute of theyr knowleage. They sumtymes intermyxte famous thynges with obscure thynges, lyght with heauie, and greate with smaule, that by the foortheraunce of princes, theyr vniuersall posteritie myght enioye the fruition of the knowleage of thynges.
and

The fine breade Cazabbi, made of the rootes of Zucca.

Howe Ceres fyrst founde wheate and barly in Egypte.

The rootes of ages.

The autoure ercuse.

plinie.

At other tymes also, beinge intent about particular thynges
and desyrous of newe thynges, they occupyed them selues i
the searchinge of pacticular tractes and coastes, with suc[?]
thynges as nature brought foorth in the same: by this mea
nes to coome the better to more absolute and vniuersal knov[?]
leage. Let theym therefore contemne owre doinge: And we
wyll laugh to scorne, not theyr ignoraunce and slothfulnes
but pernicious curiousnes: And therewith hauynge pitie o
theyr frowarde dispositions, wyll commit them to the vene
mous serpentes of whom enuie tooke his fyrst originall. J
shall in the meane tyme abundantly contente vs that thes
thynges do please yowre holynes: And that yowe doo no
dispise owre simple vestures wherwith we haue only weauec
togyther and not adourned, gathered and not described suc[?]
maruelous thynges in the garnyshynge wherof, nature hat[?]
sufficiently shewed her cunnynge. Owre desyre is none othe[?]
but herein for yowre sake to doo owre endeuoure that thes
thynges maye not peryshe. Let euery man take hereof wha[?]
lyketh hym best. Of the sheepe or bullocke soulde in the mar
ket, nothynge remayneth in the euenynge, bycause the shul
der pleaseth one, the legge an other, and the necke an other,
ye, same haue most phantasie to the bowels, and sume to th[?]
feete. Thus hauynge enough wandered, lette vs returne to
owre purpose and declare with what woordes they salute the
kynges chyldren when they are fyrst borne: or howe they ap
ply the begynnyng of theyr lyues to the end: And why thei[?]
kynges are caulde by many names. Therfore when the kynge
hath a sonne borne, such as dwel neare about his pallaice or
vyllage, repayre to the queenes chamber, where one saluteth
the newe borne chylde with one name, and an other with an
other name. God saue the thowe shyninge lampe sayth one:
An other cauleth him bryght and cleare. Sume name him the
victouer of his enemies: and other sume, the puissaunt con
querour descended of bludde royall, and bryghter then gold,
with dyuers other suche vayne names. Therfore lyke as euc
ry of the Romane emperours was caulde Adiabenicus, Parthicus, Ar
menicus, Dacicus, Gothicus, and Germanicus, accordynge to the titles
of theyr parentes and auncestours, euen so by thimposition of
names inuented by other kynges, Beuchicus Anacaoba the lord
of the region of Xaragua (of whome and of the wyse woman
Ana[?]

By what na-
mes they sa-
lute the kyn-
ges chyldren
when they
are borne.
The names
and tytles of
the Romane
Emperours.

Anachiona his fyſter, we haue ſpoken largely in the fyrſt Deade) was cauled by all theſe names folowynge: Tureigua Ho-
in: whiche is as muche to ſaye, as, a kynge ſhynynge as
ryght as laton. Starei, that is, bryghte: Huiho, hyghneſſe:
uibeynequen, a ryche fludde. With all theſe names and more
hen fortye other ſuche, doeth kynge Beuchius magnifye hym
elfe as often as he commaundeth any thynge to bee doone or
auſeth any proclamation to bee made in his name. If the
ryer by neglygence leaue owte any of theſe names, the king
hynketh it to ſounde greatly to his contumely and reproche.
The lyke is alſo of other. Howe fondely they vſe them ſel-
es in makynge their teſtamentes, wee wyll nowe declare.
They leaue thinheritaunce of their kyngedomes to theldeſt
oonnes of their eldeſt ſyſters. If ſhee fayle, to theldeſt of
he ſeconde ſyſter and ſo of the thirde if the ſecond alſo faile.
For they are owte of doubte that thoſe children coome of
heir bludde. But the children of their owne wyues, they
ounte to bee not legitimate. If there remayne none of their
yſters children, they leaue thinheritaunce to their brothers.
And if they faile, it deſcendeth to their owne ſoonnes. Laſte
f all, if al theſe faile, they aſſygne it to the woorthieſt, as to
ym that is of greateſt power in all the Ilande, that he may
efende their ſubiectes from their auncient enemyes. They
ake as many wyues as them lyſteth. They ſuffer the beſt be-
oued of the kynges wyues, and concubynes to bee buryed
with hym. Anachaona the ſyſter of Beuchius the kyng of Xaragua,
being a woman of ſuche wiſedome and cunnynge that in makynge of rhymes and balettes ſhee was counted a propheteſſe
emonge the beſte, commaunded, that emonge all the wyues
and concubynes of the kinge her brother, the fayreſt (whoſe
name was Guanahattabenechina) ſhulde be buryed alyue with him,
and two of her waytyng maydes with her. Shee woolde alſo
haue appointed dyuers other to that offyce, if ſhe had not
byn otherwiſe perſwaded by the prayers of certeyne fryers
of ſaincte Fraunces order whiche chaunced then to bee preſente. They ſaye that this Guanahattabenechina had none in all
the Iland comparable to her in bewtie. She buried with her
all her iewelles and twentie of her beſt ornamentes. Their
cuſtome is, to place beſyde euery of them in their ſepultures,
a cuppe full of water and a portion of the fyne breade of Ca-
ſabbi.

howe they
make their
teſtamentes

So byrd greē
Alexander

The kynge ꝰ
wyues and
concubines
are buryed
with hym.

They burie
theyr iewels
with them.
A dreame of
an other lyfe
after this.

W iij

where it ray=
neth but fel=
dome.

xabbi. In *Xaragua*, the regyon of this kynge *Beuchius*, and i
Haxua, parte of the regyon of *Caiabo*, also in the fayre vale o
falte and freſhe lakes, and lykewiſe in the region of *Yaquin*
in the prouynce of *Balnos*, it rayneth but feldome. In al theſ
regyons are foſſes or trenches made of oulde tyme, wherb
they conueye the waters in order to water their fpeldes, wit
no leſſe arte then doo thinhabitours of newe Carthage, an
of the kyngedome of *Murcien* in *Spartaria* for the feldoome faul
of rayne. The region of *Maguana*, deuydeth the prouynce o

where it ray=
neth much.

Balnos from *Caiabo*, and *Zauana* from *Guaccaiarima*. In the deep
vales, they are troubled with raine more often then nedeth
Alfo the confynes of the chiefe citie named fainct Dominik

variable mo=
tions of the
elementes.

are moifter then is neceſſary. In other places, it rayneth mo
derately. There are therfore in the Jlande of *Hiſpaniola*, dy
uers & variable motions of the elementes, as we reade th
lyke of manye other regions.   Of their colonies o

The colonies
and vyllages
which the
Spanyardes
haue buylded

mantions which the Spaniardes haue erected in this Jland
we haue fpoken fuſſycientelye beefore.   They haue fenc
that tyme buylded theſe vyllages: *Portus Plate*, *Portus Regalis*, La
res, *Villanoua*, *Azuam*, and *Saluaterra*. Hauynge fayde thus much
of the Jlande of *Hiſpaniola* the moother and ladye of the othe

The other J=
landes about
hiſpaniola.

Jlandes, and as it were *Tethys* the moſte bewtifull wyfe o
Neptunus the god of the fea, let vs nowe entreate fumwhat o
her Nymphes and faire *Nereides* whiche waite vppon her an

The Jlande
Arethuſa.

adourne her on euery fyde. Wee wyll therfore begynne at the
neareſt cauled the newe *Arethuſa*, foo named of the fontayne
Arethuſa in the Jlande of Sicilie. This is famous by reaſon
of a fprynge: but otherwyfe vnprofytable. Owre men na
med it of late, *Duas Arbores*, bycaufe it hath onely twoo tree

A fprynge run
nyng vnder
the fea frome
hiſpan.ola to
Arethuſa.

groynge in it: nere vnto the whiche is a fountaine that com
meth from the Jlande of *Hiſpaniola* throughe the fecreate paſ
fages of the earth vnder the fea, and breaketh foorth in this
Jlande, as the ryuer *Alpheus* in *Achaia* runneth vnder the fea
from the citie of *Elide*, and breaketh foorth in the Jlande of
Sicilie in the fonntayne *Arethuſa*. That the fontayne of this
newe *Arethuſa* hathh s original from the Jlande of *Hiſpaniola*,
it is manifeſt hereby, that the water iſſhewynge owre of the
fonntayne, bryngeth with it the leaues of many trees whiche
growe in *Hiſpaniola*, and not in this Jlande. They faye that
the fonntayne hath his originall from the ryuer *Viamiros* in
the region of *Guaccaiarima* confynynge with the land of *Zauana*

This Jlande is not paste a myle in circuite, and commodi=
ous for fyscher men. Directly towarde the Easte (as it were
he porter kepynge the enterie to Tethys) lyeth the Jlande of
ancti Iohannis (otherwyse cauled Burichena) wherof wee haue
poken largely before. This aboundeth with golde: and in
truitefull soile, is equall with her moother Hispaniola. In this
are many colonies or mansions of Spaniardes, whiche ap=
lye them selues to gatherynge of golde. Towarde the west
on the Northe syde, great Cuba (for the longenesse therof,
onge supposed to be the continent or fyrme lande) wardeth
owre Tethys on the backe halfe. This is muche longer then
Hispaniola: And from the Easte to the Weste, is diuyded in the
myddest with the circle cauled Tropicus Cancri. Hispaniola and the
other lyinge on the South syde of this, are included almost
in the mydde space betwene the sayde Troppke and the Equi=
noctiall lyne, whiche many of the oulde wryters supposed to
bee vnhabitable & desert by reason of the feruent heate of the
soonne in that clyme as they coniectured. But they were
deceaued in their opinion. They affyrme that rycher golde
mynes are founde in Cuba then in Hispaniola. They saye also
that euen nowe while I wryte these thynges, there is golde
gathered together ready to the meltyng, amountynge to the
quantitie of a hundreth and fourescore thousande Castellans
of gold, an argument surely of great rychesse. Iamaica is more
towarde the Southe then these: And is a pleasaunte and
fruitefull Jlande, of soyle apte for corne, graffes, and settes,
it consysteth of onely one mountayne. Thinhabitauntes are
warrelyke men and of good wytte. Colonus compared it to
Sicilie in bygnesse. They whiche of late searched it more ex=
actely, saye that it is sumwhat lesse: but not muche. It is
thought to be without gold and precious stoones, as the like
was supposed of Cuba at the begynnynge. The Jlande of
Guadalupea (fyrste named Caraqueira) lyinge on the Southe syde
of Hispaniola, is foure degrees nearer the Equinoctiall. It is
eaten and indented with two goulfes (as wee reade of great
Bretanye nowe cauled Englande, and Calidonia nowe cau=
led Scotlande) beinge in maner two Jlandes. It hath fa=
mous portes. In this they founde that gumme whiche the
Apothecaries caule Animæ Album, whose fume is holesome a=
gainst reumes and heauynesse of the heade. The tree whiche

M m. ii.   engendereth

The Jland of
Sancti Iohan
nis.

The Jlande
of Cuba.

habitable re=
gions vnder
the Equinoc=
tiall.

The ryche
golde mynes
of Cuba.

The Jland of
Iamaica.

The Jland of
Guadalupea.

England and
Scotlande

The gumme
cauled Anime
album.

Dates,

engendereth this gumme, beareth a fruite muche lyke to
Date, beinge a spanne in length. When it is opened, it se
meth to conteyne a certayne sweete meale. As owre husband
men are accustomed to reserue chestenuttes and suche oth
harde fruites all the wynter, soo do they the dates of th

Pine trees.

tree, beynge muche lyke vnto a fygge tree. They founde a
so in this Ilande, Pyne trees of the beste kynde, and such
other deyntie dysshes of nature, wherof wee haue spoke
largely before. ye, they thyncke that thinhabitauntes of o

**The Cani-
bales.**

ther Ilandes, had their seedes of soo many pleasaunt frute
from hense. For the Canibales beinge a wylde and wand
rynge people, and ouer runnynge all the countreys abou
them to hunte for mannes flesshe, were accustomed to bryng
home with them what so euer they founde straunge or prof
table in any place. They are intractable, and wyll admyt
no straungiers. It shall therfore bee nedefull to ouercoom

**wherby it
was thought
that there
were Ilandes
of women.**

them with great poure. For as well the women as men, ar
experte archiers, and vse to inueneme their arrowes. Whe
the men go foorthe of the lande a man huntynge, the wome
manfully defende their coastes ageynst suche as attempte t
inuade the same. And hereby I suppose it was thought tha
there were Ilandes in the Ocean, inhabited onely with wo
men, as *Colonus* the admirall hym selfe perswaded me, as I
haue sayde in the fyrste decade. This Ilande hath also frute

**Hony in trees
and rockes.**

full mountaynes and playnes, and notable ryuers. It nou
rysseth honye in trees, and in the caues of rockes, as in
Palma one of the Ilandea of *Canarie*, honye is gathered emon
the briers and bramble busshes. Aboute. xviii. myles East
ward from this Iland, lieth an Iland which owr men name

**The Ilande
desiderata.
The Ilande
Galanea.
The Ilandes
of Todos
Sanctos or
Barbata.**

Desiderata, beynge. xx. myles in circuite and verye fayre. Als
aboute ten myles from *Guadalupes* towarde the Southe, lyet
the Ilande of *Galantis*, beynge thirtie myles in circuite an
playne. It was so named for the neatenesse and bewtifulnes
therof. Nyne myles distant from *Guadalupes* toward the East
there are syxe smaule Ilandes named *Todos Sanctos* or *Barbata*.
These are full of rockes and barren: yet necessarye to be
knowen to suche as vse to trauayle the seas of these coastes.

**The Ilander
monserratus**

Ageyne, from *Guadalupes*. xxxv. myles towarde the Northe
there is an Ilande named *Monserratus*, conteynynge in circuit
fortye myl es, hauynge also in it a mountayne of notabl
heyght

heyght. The Jlande named *Antiqua*, diſtante from *Guadalupea*
thirtie myles, is aboute foztye myles in circuite. *Diegus Colo-*
nus the ſoonne and heyre of *Chriſtophorus Colonus*, toulde me that
his wyfe (whome he lefte in the Jlande of *Hiſpaniola* at his
comming into Spaine to the courte) did write vnto hym, that
of late emonge the Jlandes of the Canibales, there is one
founde whiche aboundeth with golde. On the lefte ſyde of
Hiſpaniola towarde the Southe, neare vnto the hauen *Beata*,
there lyeth an Jlande named *Portus Bellus*. They tell maruelous thynges of the monſters of the ſea aboute this Jlande,
and eſpecially of the toztoyſes. For they ſaye that they are
bygger then greate rounde targettes. At ſuche tyme as the
heate of nature moueth theym too generation, they coome
foozthe of the ſea : And makynge a deepe pytte in the ſande,
they laye thzee oz foure hundzeth egges therin. When they
haue thus emptied their bagge of conception, they putte as
muche of the ſande ageyne into the pytte, as maye ſuffyce
to couer the egges : And ſoo reſorte ageyne to the ſea, nothynge carefull of their ſucceſſyon. At the daye appoynted
of nature to the pzocreation of theſe beaſtes, there creapeth
owte a multitude of toztoyſes, as it were pyſſemares : ſwar-
mynge owte of an ante hyll : And this onely by the heate
of the ſoonne withowte any helpe of their parentes. They
ſaye that their egges are in maner as bygge as geeſe egges.
They alſo coompare the fleſhe of theſe toztoyſes, to be equall
with veale in taſte. There are beſyde theſe, innumerable J-
landes the whiche they haue not yet ſearched : noz yet is it
greatly neceſſarye to ſyfte this meale ſo fynely. It maye
ſuffyce to vnderſtond that there are large landes & many regyons whiche ſhal hereafter receaue owre nations, tounges,
and maners : and therwith embzaſe owre relygion. The
Tropans dydde not ſoodenly replenyſhe Aſia, the Tyrians
Libia, noz the Greekes and Phoenices Spayne.
As touchynge the Jlandes which lye on the nozth ſyde of *Hiſ-*
paniola, I haue let paſſe to ſpeake. For albeit they are commo
dious foz tyllage and fyſſhynge, yet are they lefte of the Spa
nyardes as poore and of ſmaule value. We wyll nowe therefore take owre leaue of this owlde *Tethis* with her moyſt and
watery Nymphes : And receaue to owre newe acquaintance
the bewetifull ladye of the South ſea rychely crowned with

Mm, iii,　　　great

great pearles, the Jlande of Dites beinge ryche both in nam
and in treaſure. In my epiſtell booke whiche I ſente vnt
powre holynes this laſt yeare, I declared howe Vaſchus Nunne
Balboa the capitayne of them whiche paſſed ouer the daunge
rous mountaynes towarde the South ſea, learned by repo
that in the proſpect of thoſe coaſtes there laye an Jlande
boundynge with pearles of the greateſt ſorte: And that th
kynge therof was ryche and of great power, infeſtynge wit
warres the other kynges his borderers, and eſpecially Chi
apes and Tumacchus. We declared further howe at that tyme
was lefte vntouched by reaſon of the raggynge tempeſtes wh
che troubled that South ſea three moonethes in the yeare.
But it is nowe better knowen to owre men, who haue now
alſo brought that fierce kynge to humanitie: and conuerte
hym from a cruell tyger to one of the meeke ſheepe of Chriſt
flocke ſanctifyed with the water of baptiſme with all his fa
melie and kyngedome. It ſhall not therefore bee from owr
purpoſe to declare by the gouernaunce of what capitaines o
by what meanes theſe thynges were ſo happely atchyued.

The Jland of
pearles.

wylde beaſts
muſt be tamed
with the rod.

The tenth booke of the
thyrde Decade.

T the arryuall of Petrus Arias the newe goue
nour of Dariena, he gaue commaundment tha
one Gaſpar Moralis ſhuld take in hande therp
dition to the Jlande of Dites. He therefo
tooke his vyage fyrſt to Chiapes and Tumacchu
kynges of the South, whom Vaſchus befor
had conciled and left fryndes to the Chriſti
ans. They frendely and magnifycally enterteyned owr me
who prepared them a nauie of the kynges boates to paſſe o
uer into this Jlande, whiche they caule Dites and not Margarit
or Margarites, although it abounde with pearles whiche in th
latin tonge are cauled Margarite. For they fyrſt cauled an othe
by this name, whiche lyeth nexte to the mouth of Os Draconis i
the region of Paris, in the whiche alſo is founde greate plenti
of pearles. Gaſpar brought with hym onely threeſcore armed
men to the Jlande, for that he coulde conuey ouer no greate
number by reaſon of the ſmaulnes and narownes of they
boates

An expeditiō
to the Jlande
of Dites in
the ſouth ſea

The Jland of
Margarites.

Os Draconis.
Paris.

oates oʒ barkes which they caule Culchas, made of one hole
iece of tymber as we haue sayde bⁱfoʒe. The kynge of the I
nde came foozth ageinſt them fiercely with cruell and thʒead
eunage countenaunce, and with a great bande of armed men
rpinge in maner of a larome and in token of the battayle,
uazzauara, Guazzauara, which is as much to saye as, battayle a:
ꝛepnſt the enemie: And is as it weare a watch woʒde to giue
honſet, wherwith alſo they thʒewe theyʒ dartes. Foʒ they
aue not thuſe of bowes. They were ſo obſtinate and deſpe:
ate that they aſſayled owre men with foure Guazzauaras. that
s, battrayles. At the length owre men with certeyne of Chi:
r and Tumaccbus men (beinge oulde enemies to this kynge of
he Ilande, gotte the vpper hande by reaſon they aſſayled
he kynge ſoodenly and vnwares. yet was he determyned to
ſſemble a greater power, and once ageyne to attempt the foʒ
une of warre, but that he was otherwyſe perſuaded by the
nges his boʒtherers which counceled him to gyue ouer and
ubmyt hym ſelfe: ſumtyme by theremple of them ſelues and
ther thʒeatenynge the deſtruction of his ſtoozyſhynge kynge:
ome: And otherwhyles declarynge vnto hym the humani:
ie and gentelnes of owre men, by whoſe frendſhip he might
breyne honoure and quyetnes to hym and his: wyllyng hym
urthermoʒe to conſider what chaunced vnto them which the
care befoʒe reſyſted and aduentured the haſarde of the bat:
aple as dyd theſe kynges, Poncba, Poccborrofa, Quarequa, Chiapeſ
nd Tumaccbus with ſuch other. By theſe perſuaſions, the king
ſubmytted hym ſelfe and came freendely to owre men whom
e conducted to his palaice which they ſay to be maruelouſly
adoʒned and pʒincelyke. As ſoone as they entered into the
palaice, he bʒought foozth a baſket of curious woozkemanſ
hyp and full of pearles which he gaue them. The ſumme of
heſe pearles amounted to the weyght of a handreth and ten
ꝑundes after, viii. vnces to the pounde. Beinge ageyne re:
warded of owre men with ſuch tryfles as they bʒought with
hem of purpoſe, as garlandes of Chʒiſtall and glaſe and o:
ther counterfet ſtones of dyuers coloures, with lookyng glaſ
ſes alſo and laton belles, and eſpecially two oʒ thʒee Iren
hatchets (which they moʒe eſteme then great heapes of gold)
he thaughyt hym ſelfe abundantly recompenſed. They laughe
owre men to ſcoʒne that they wyll departe with ſo great and
necceſſaʒye

A conflict.

The kynge of
the Ilande of
Dites ſubmit
teth him
ſelfe.
The kynges
palaice.
A handreth ꝛ
ten pounde
weyght of
pearles.

ares and hat:
chets moʒe
eſteemed thē
golde.

neceſſarie a thynge for any ſumme of golde : aſſyrmynge a...
are or hatchet to bee profytable for manye uſes of men : an...
that golde ſerueth onely for wanton pleaſures, and not to b...
greatly neceſſary. Beynge therfore ioyfull and gladde of th...
frendeſhyppe of owre men, he tooke the capitaine by the han...
and brought him with certeine of his familiars to the highe...
towre of his palaice, from whenſe they myght proſpecte th...
mayne ſea. Then caſtyng his eyes about hym on euery ſide...
and lookynge towarde the Eaſte, he ſayde unto them. Be...
holde here lyeth open before yowe the infynite ſea extende...
beyond the ſoonne beames. Then tournyng hym toward th...
Southe and Weſte, he ſygnyfied unto them that the land...
which laye before their eyes, the toppes of whoſe great mou...
taynes they myght ſee, was exceadynge large. Then coom...
mynge ſumwhat nearer, he ſayde : Beholde theſe Ilande...
on the ryght hande and on the lefte, whiche all obeye un...
owre emppre, and are ryche, happye, and bleſſed, if yow...
caule thoſe landes bleſſed whiche abounde with golde and...
perle. Wee haue in this Ilande lyttle plentie of golde : Bu...
the deepe places of all the ſeas aboute theſe Ilandes, are ful...
of perles : wherof yowe ſhall receaue of me as many as yow...
wyll requyre, ſo that ye perſyſte in the bonde of frendeſhyppe...
whiche yowe haue begunne. I greatly deſyre yowre frende...
ſhyppe, and woolde gladlye haue the fruition of yowre thyn...
ges, whiche I ſette muche more by then myllyons of perles...
yowe ſhall therfore haue no cauſe to doubte of any unfayth...
fulneſſe or breache of frendeſhyppe on my behalfe. Owre men...
gaue hym lyke frendly woordes : and encouraged hym with...
many fayre promyſſes to doo as he had ſayde. When owre...
men were nowe in a redyneſſe to departe, they couenaunted...
with hym to paye yearely to the greate kynge of Caſtyle a...
hundreth pounde weyghte of perles. He gladlye agreed to...
their requeſt, and tooke it for no great thyng : nor yet thought...
hym ſelfe any whitte the more to becoome tributarie. With...
this kynge they founde ſuche plentie of hartes and connies,...
that owre men ſtondynge in their houſes myght kyll as ma...
nye as them lyſte with their arrowes. They lyue heare very...
pleaſauntly, hauynge greate plentie of al thynges neceſſary...
This Ilande is ſcarſely ſyre degrees diſtant from the Equi...
noctiall lyne. They haue the ſame maner of breade made of...

rootts

The kynges
woordes.

Ilandes rych
in golde and
pearles.

C. pounde
weyght of
perles yerely
for a tribute.

plentie of
hartes and
cunnies.

ootes and the graine of Maizium, and wyne made of seedes
nd fruites, euen as they haue in the region of Comogra and ‖ wyne of frui-
n other places alwell in the Ilandes as in the firme lande. ‖ tes and sedes

This kynge is nowe baptiſed with all his familye and ſub: ‖ The kynge is
ectes. His deſyre was at his baptiſme, to bee named Petrus ‖ baptiſed.
arias after the name of the gouernour. When owre men de-
arted, he accompanied them to the ſea ſyde and furnyſhed ‖ The fyft part
hem with boates to retourne to the continent. Owre men ‖ of perles due
inided the perles emonge them, reſeruyng the fyfte portion ‖ to the kynge.
o be delyuered to thoffycers of the kynges Excheker in thoſe
artes. They ſaye that theſe perles were maruelous precious, ‖ Bys perles.
aire, oriente, and exceadynge bygge: In ſo muche that they
roughte manye with theym bygger then haſell nuttes. Of
ohat pryce and value they myghte bee, I conſyder by one ‖ A perle for a
erle the which Paulus prediceſſour to yowre holines, bowght ‖ pope.
t the ſecond hand of a marchant of Uenece for foure & forty
houſande ducates. yet emonge thoſe whiche were brought
rom this Ilande, there was one bought euen in Dariena for a
houſande and two hundreth Caſtelans of golde. This was ‖ An other
lmoſt as bygge as a meane walnutte: And came at the length ‖ perle of great
o the handes of Petrus Arias the gouernoure, who gaue it to ‖ price.
hat noble and faithefull woman his wyfe, of whoſe maner
f departure with her huſbande, wee haue made mention be-
ore. Wee muſte then needes thinke that this was verye pre-
ious which was bowght ſo deare emonge ſuche a multitude
of perles where they were not bought by one at once, but by
poundes and at the leaſt by ounces. It is alſo to be thought
hat the Uenecian marchaunte boughte his for no great ſum ‖ Nice and ſu-
of mony in the Eaſt parts. But he ſould it the dearer for that ‖ perfluous
he chaunced to lyue in thoſe laſciuious and wanton dayes ‖ pleaſures.
when men were gyuen to ſuche vyſe and ſuperfluous pleaſu-
res, and mette with a marchaunt for his purpoſe. But lette ‖ Dyuers opini-
vs nowe ſpeake ſumwhat of the ſhelfyſhes in the whiche ‖ ons of the
perles are engendered. It is not vnknowen to yowre holy- ‖ generation
neſſe, that Ariſtotell, and Plinie his folower, were of ‖ of pearles.
dyuers opinions as concernynge the generation of perles.
But theſe Indians and owre men, reſt onely in one aſſertion,
not aſſentyng to them in any other : as eyther that they wander in the ſea, or that they moue at anye tyme after they
are borne. They wyll therfore that there bee certayne greene

N n　　　　places

Herbes in the bottome of the sea,

places as it were medowes in the bottome of the sea, bryngynge foorthe an herbe muche lyke vnto thyme, and affyrme that they haue seene the same: And that they are engendered, norysshed, and growe therin, as wee see thincreare and succession of oysters to growe aboute them selues. Also that these fysshes delyteth not in the conuersation or coompany of the sea dogges: Nor yet to bee contented with onely one, twoo, or thre, or at the moste foure pearles: Affyrmyng that in the fysshynge places of the kynge of this Ilande, there was founde a hundreth pearles in one fyshe, the whiche Gaspar Moralis the capitayne hym selfe, and his coompanions diligently numbered. For it pleased the kynge at their beynge there & in their presence, to commaund his diuers to go a fysshynge for those kynde of fysshes. They compare the matrices of these fysshes, to the places of conception in hennes, in the whiche their egges are engendered in great multitudes and clusters: And beleue that these fysshes bryngefoorth their byrth in lyke maner. For the better profe wherof, they saye that they founde certaine pearles coommynge foorthe of their matreces, as beynge nowe coome to the tyme of their full rypenesse, and moued by nature to coome owte of their moothers wombe openynge it selfe in tyme conuenient. Lykewise that within a while after, they sawe other succede in lyke maner. So that to conclude, they sawe sum coommynge foorthe, and other summe yet abydinge the tyme of their perfection: whiche beyng complete, they also became loose and opened the matrice. They perceaued the pearles to bee inclosed in the myddest of their bellies, there to bee norysshed and increase as an infante suckynge his moothers pappes within her wombe, before hee moue to coome foorthe of her priuye places. And if it chaunce any of these shelfysshes to be founde scatered in the sande of the sea (as I my selfe haue seene oysters disparcled on the shores in diuers places of the Ocean) they affyrme that they haue byn violently dryuen thither from the bottome of the sea by force of tempestes, and not to haue wandered thither of them selues. But, that they becoome white by the cleareness of the mornynge dewe, or waxe yelowe in troubled wether, or otherwyse that they seeme to reioyse in faire weather and cleare ayer, or contrary wyse to bee as it were astonisshed and dymme in thunder and tempestes

A hundreth perles in one shell fysshe.

The matrke of the perle fysshe.

The byrth of perles,

tempestes, with suche other, the perfecte knowledge hereof
is not to bee looked for at the handes of these vnlearned men
whiche handell the matter but grossely, and enquire no further then occasyon serueth. yet do they affyrme by thexperi-
ence and industrie of the dyuers, that the greatest pearles where the byggest, meane, and least pearles are engedred
lye in the deepest places, they of the meane sorte hygher, and
the least hyghest of all and nearer to the brymme of the water. And saye therfore that the greatest do not wander: but
that they are created, nouryshed, and increase in the deepest places of the sea, whether fewe, dyuers, and that but
seeldome dare aduenture to diue so deepe to gather them, aswel for feare of the sea crabbes whiche wander emonge these Sea crabbes
perle fyshes to feede of them, and for feare of other monsters
of the sea, as also leste their brethe shuld fayle them into long
remaynynge in the water. And this they saye to bee the cause
why the owldest and therfore byggest sea muscles, inhabyte The sea mus-cles wherin perles are engendied.
the deepest places from whense they are not lyghtly moued
by tempestes. Furthermore, howe muche the bygger and oul-
der these fyshes are, they say that in their larger matrices, the
greater number and bygger pearles are founde: And that for
this cause, there are fewer founde of the byggest sorte. They
thyncke also, that when they fyrste faule from their fylshes
in the deepe places, they are deuoured of other fylshes, bycause they are not yet harde. Ageyne, the smaulest differ from
the byggest in a certayne swellynge or impostumation whiche
the Spaniardes caule a tympane. For they denye that to be
a pearle whiche in oulde muscles cleaueth fast to the shel: But
that it is a warte, whiche beynge rased from the shell with a
fyle, is rounde and bryght but onely of one syde, and not pre-
cions, beynge rather of the nature of the fyshe it selfe, then
of a pearle. They confesse that they haue seene certayne of
these muscles cleauynge on rockes: yet these but fewe, and
nothynge woorthe. It is also to bee thought that the pearle
fylshes or sea muscles whiche are founde in India, Arabie,
the redde sea, or Taprobana, are ruled in suche order as the
afore named famous autours haue written. For their opinion herein is not vtterly to bee reiected, forasmuche as they
were learned men and trauayled longe in the serchynge of
these thynges. But wee haue nowe spoken suffyciently of
these sea fylshes and of their egges whiche the fonde nysenes

and wantonnesse of men haue made dearer then the egges of
hennes oz geese. Lette vs therfoze entreate sumwhat of o=
ther particular thynges whiche are coome to owre know=
ledge of late. We haue elles where largely deſcribed the mou
thes of the goulfe of Vraba, with ſundzye and variable regi=
ons diuided with the manyfolde goulfes of that ſea. But as=
concernynge the Weſt coaſtes in the whiche owre men haue
buylded houſes and planted their habitations on the bankes

The regions of the Eaſt ſyde of the goulfe of Vraba.

of Dariens, I haue no newe matter to wzite. Yet as touching
the Eaſt partes of the goulfe, I haue learned as foloweth.
They ſaye that the vniuerſal lande of the Eaſt region of the
goulfe from the cozner therof farre reachynge into the ſea,
and from the extreame oz vtter moſte mouthe of the ſame re=
ceauynge the waters of the ſea whiche faule into it, euen vn=

The region of Caribana.

to Os Draconis and Paria, is by one generall name cauled Cari=
bana, of the Caribes oz Canibales whiche are founde in euery
regyon in this tracte. But from whenſe they had their par=
ticular originall, and howe leauynge their natiue ſoyle, they

The original of the Cani=bales.

haue ſpzedde their generation ſo farre lyke a peſtiferous con=
tagion, wee wyll nowe declare. Therfoze from the fyzſte
fronte reachynge foozth into the ſea (in whoſe tracte we ſaid
that Fogeda faſtened his foote) toward the cozner, about nyne

The vylages of Caribana.

myles diſtant, there lyeth a vyllage of Caribana named Futeraca.
Thzee myles diſtant from this, is the vyllage of Vraba, of the
whiche it is thoughte that the hole goulfe tooke his name,
becauſe this vyllage was once the heade of the kyngeddome.
Aboute ſyxe myles from this, is Feti. Nyne myles from Feti,

Manhunters.

is Zerema: And about tweluc myles from this, Sorache. Owre
men founde all theſe vyllages full of people, all the whiche
gyue them ſelues onely to manhuntynge. In ſo muche that
if they lacke enemyes ageynſt whom they maye keepe warre,
they exerciſe crueltie ageynſt them ſelues, and eyther ſleye the
one the other, oz elles dzyue the vanquyſſhed to flyghte.
Whereby it is apparante that by theſe their continuall war=
res, and dzyuynge the one the other owre of their countreis,
this infection hath gonne ſo farre not onelye on the fyzme
lande, but alſo into the Ilandes. I was alſo aduertiſed of an
other thynge the whiche to my iudgement, ſeemeth woo2=
thye to bee putte in memozye.
One Cozrales a iudge in cauſes of lawe amonge the Spany=
ardes

ardes of Dariena, ſayth that on a tyme walkyng abrode with his booke in his hande, he met by the waye with a fugityue which had fledde from the great landes lyinge farre toward the weſte, and remayned here wyth a Kynge wyth whom he was entertepned. When this man perceaued the lawier lookynge on his booke, marueylynge thereat, he came runninge vnto him, and by interpretours of the kynge whom he ſerued, ſpake thus vnto him: Haue yowe alſo bookes wherin yowe may reſerue thynges in perpetual memorye? And letters wherby yowe may declare yowre mynde to ſuche as are abſent? And herewith deſyred that the booke might bee opened vnto hym, ſuppoſyng that he ſhulde therein haue founde the letters of his owne countrey. But when he ſawe theim vnlyke, he ſayde further that in his countrey there were cities foztified with waules and gouerned by lawes: and that the people alſo vſed apparell. But of what religion they were, I dyd not learne. yet had owre men knowleage both by the woozdes and ſignes of this fugitiue, that they were circumciſed. What nowe thinke yowe hereby (moſt holy father) Oz what do yowe diuine may come hereof when tyme ſhall ſubdue al theſe vnder yowre thzone? Let vs nowe entermyngle certeyne ſmaule thynges amonge theſe great matters. I haue not thought good to pzetermitte that which chaunced to Iohannes Solſius, who, to ſearche the South ſyde of the ſuppoſed continent, departed with thzee ſhippes from pozte Ioppa (not farre diſtante from the Ilandes of Gades oz Cales in the Ocean) the fourth day of the Ides of September in the yeare. M D.rb. Oz what ſucceſſe Iohannes Pontius had, whom the newe gouernour Petrus Arias appoynted to vanquiſhe and deſtroy the Caribes oz Canibales, deuourers of mans fleſhe. Alſo to what ende the vpages of the other capitaynes came, whiche were ſent foozth dyuers wayes at the ſame tyme: As Gonzalus Badaiocus, Franciſcus Bezerra, and Valleius, Iohannes Solicius tooke the matter in hande in an euyll houre. He ſayled beyonde the poynt of ſaynt Auguſtine, (which they caule Cabo. S. Auguſtini) toward the South ſyde of the ſuppoſed continent beyonde the Equinoctiall lyne. Foz (as we haue ſayde befoze) that poynt reacheth Southwarde to the ſeuenth degree of the South poole cauled the pole Antartike. He pzoceaded in that viage ſyre hundzeth leagues: And founde the lande from the poynte to extende

Bookes Loke in the begynnyng of the booke of the landes lately founde.

Circumciſed people.

What chaunced to the Capitaines whiche the gouernour ſent dyuers wayes.

Looke decade iii. liber. vi.

The vyage of Iohannes Soliſius. Cap. S. Auguſtini.

extende so farre towarde the South beyonde the Eguinocti-
all, that he came to the thirtie degree of the South pole. As
he sayled thus forwarde, hauynge nowe on his backe halfe
the starres named *Csput Draconis*, (that is, the dragons heade)
and the regions of *Paris* lyinge northwarde frome hym, and
prospectynge towarde the pole Artyke, he chaunced to faule
into the handes of the fylthye Canibales. For these craftie
foxes seemed to make signes of peace, when in theyr mindes
they conceaued a hope of a daintie banquet: And espying their
enemies a farre of, beganne to swalowe theyr spettle as their
mouthes watered for greedines of theyr pray. As vnhappye
Solysius descended with as many of his coompanie as coulde en
ter into the boate of the byggest shippe, soodenly a great mul-
typtude of thinhabitantes brust foorth vppon them, and slew
them euery man with clubbes, euen in the syght of theyr felowes. They caried away the boate, and in a moment broke
it all to fytters. Not one man escaped. Theyr furie not thus
satisfied, they cutte the slayne men in pieces euen vppon the
shore where theyr felowes might beholde this horrible specta
cle from the sea. But they being stryken with feare through
this exemple, durst not coome foorth of theyr shyppes, or diuise howe to reuenge the death of theyr Capitaine and coompanyons. They departed therefore from these vnfortunate
coastes: And by the waye ladynge theyr shippes with brasell
returned home agayne with losse and heauie chere. Of these
thynges I was aduertysed of late by theyr owne letters.
What they haue els doone, I shal haue more particular knowleage hereafter. *Iohannes Pontius* was also repulsed by the Canibales in the Ilande of *Gusdalupes* beinge one of the chiefe I-
landes of theyr habitacion. For when they sawe owre men
a farre of on the sea, they ley in ambushe soodenly to inuade
them when they shulde coome alande. Owre men sent foorth
a fewe foote men and with them theyr laundresses to wasshe
theyr shertes and sheetes. For from the Ilande of *Ferres* beinge one of the Ilandes of Canarie (euen vnto this Ilande,
for the space of foure thousande and twoo hundreth myles)
they had seene no lande where they myght fynde any fresshe
water: for as muche as in all this large space, the Ocean is
without Ilandes. At theyr commynge therfore to lande, the
Canibales assayled them, caried awaye the women, and put
the

John Solysi-
us is slaine of
the Caniba-
les.
The fierce-
nes of the Ca
nibales.

Brasell.

Johannes Pō-
tius is repul-
sed by the Ca
nibales.

the men to fuche diftreffe that fewe of them efcaped. By reafon whereof, Pontius being greately difcomfited, durfte not inuade the Canibales, fearynge theyr venemed arrowes which
thefe naked manhunters can direct moft certenly. Thus good
Pontius faylyng of his purpofe, was fayne to gyue ouer the Canibales, whome (beinge fafe and vnder the houfe roufe) he
threatened to vanquyfhe and deftroy. Whether he went from
thenfe, or what newe thynges he founde, I haue as yet no
further knowleage. By thefe myffortunes, Solyfius loffe his
lyfe, and Pontius his honour. Let vs nowe fpeake of an other
whofe enterpryfe came to lyke purpofe the fame yeare. Iohannes Aiora boʒne in the citie of Corduba, a man of noble parentage,
fent in fteade of the Lieutenaunt (as we haue fayde) more co
uetous of golde then carefull of his charge oꝛ defyrous of
prayfe foꝛ well deferuynge, fought occafions of querelynge
agaynft the kynges and fpoyled many, violently extoꝛtynge
golde of them agaynft ryght and equitie : And further handeled them fo extremely, that of frendes they became moft cruel
enemies: In fo much that they ceafed not with defperat myndes by all meanes they coulde to fley owre men openly oꝛ pꝛi-
uilye. By reafon whereof it is coome to paffe, that where before they bartered quyetly exchanginge ware foꝛ ware, they
are nowe fayne to doo all thynges by foꝛce of armes. When
he had thus exacted a great quantitie of golde of them (as it
is fayd) he fledde pꝛiuilie and tooke away a fhyppe with him
by ftelth as the common rumoure goeth : Noꝛ yet hetherto
haue we hard whyther he went oꝛ where he is arryued. Sum
fufpect that Petrus Arias the gouernour fhulde confente to his
departure bycaufe this Iohannes Aiora is bꝛother to Gonfalus Aiora
the kynges hiftoꝛiographer, a man booth lerned, and expert
in the difcipline of warre: and fo much the gouernours frend,
that thefe two amonge a fewe, may be counted exemples of
rare amitie. I my felfe alfo am greately bounde vnto theym
bothe and haue longe enioyed theyr frendefhippe. yet fhall
I defyre them bothe to pardone me in declarynge my phan-
tafie herein, that in all the turmoyles and tragicall affayres
of the Ocean, nothynge hath fo muche difpleafed me as the
couetoufnes of this man who hath fo difturbed the pacified
myndes of the kynges. Nowe emonge thefe troubelous chaunces, let vs rehearfe the variable foꝛtune of Gonfalus Badaioctus,
and

The vyage of
Johannes
Aiora.
Locke decade
iii. liber, vi.

The lewde
behauour of
John Aiora.

The variable
fortune of Hō
salus Badaio-
cius.

Cerabaro. De
cade.iii.li.iiii

This felowes, whose prosperous begynnynges, ended with
vnfortunate successe. Gonsalus therfore in the moneth of May
in the yeare of Chryste M. D. xv. departed from Dariens with
fourescoze armed men, directynge his vyage towarde the
Southe, and restynge in no place vntyll he came to the region of Cerabaro which owre men named Gratia Dei, distant from
Dariens about a hundzeth and fourescoze myles: foz they caule
it thzescoze leaques. He spente certeyne dayes here in Idel-
nesse: foz he coulde neyther by fayze meanes noz by foule, allure the kynge of the regyon to coome to hym. While he laye
thus idelly, there came to hym other fyftie men sente frome
Dariens vnder the gouernaunce of capytayne Lodouicus Mercado
who departed from Dariens in the calendes of Maye, to thintent to searche thinner partes of those regyons. When they
mette together, they determyned after consultation, to passe
ouer the mountaynes lyinge towarde the Southe, euen vnto
the Southe sea latelye founde. Beholde nowe a wonderfull
thynge: That in a lande of suche maruelous longitude in
other places, they founde it here to bee onely aboute fyftie

The South
sea.
A leaque con-
teyneth foure
myles by sea
and but three
by lande.

myles distant to the Southe sea: foz they counte it. xvii.lea-
ques, as the maner of the Spanyardes is to reken, and not
by myles. Yet saye they that a leaque consysteth of thzee myles by lande and foure by sea as wee haue noted befoze. In
the toppes of the mountaynes and turnynge of the waters,
they founde a kynge named Iuana, whose kyngedome is also
named Coiba as is the regyon of kynge Careta, of whome we

The golden
region of Coi-
ba Dytes.

haue made mention elles where. But foz as muche as the regyon of this Iuana, is rycher in golde, they named it Coiba Dites, that is, Coiba the rych. Foz, whersoeuer they dygged the
grounde, whether it were on the dzie lande oz in the weaxe
chanelles of the ryuers, they founde the sande whiche they
caste foozthe, myxte with golde. Iuana fledde at the coommynge of owre men, and coulde neuer bee bzought ageyne.

Sande myxte
with golde.
howe theyr
slaues are
markedin the
face.

They spoyled all the countrey neare aboute his palayce. Yet
had they but lyttle golde: foz hee had caryed all his stuffe
with hym. Here they founde certeyne slaues marked in the
faces after a straunge sozte. Foz with a sharpe pzycke made
eyther of bone, oz elles with a thozne, they make holes in
theirfaces: and foozthwith spzinkelynge a pouder theron,
they moiste the pounced place with a certeyne blacke oz redde
iuise,

iuile, whose substaunce is of suche tenacitie and clamminesse, that it wyll neuer weare awaye. They brought these slaues away with them. They saye that this iuile is of such sharpnesse and putteth them to suche payne, that for extreeme dolourc they haue no stomacke to their meate certaine dayes after. The kynges whiche take these slaues in their warres, vse their helpe in seekynge for golde and in tyllage of the grounde, euen as do owre men. From the pallaice of Iusna folowynge the course of the water aboute tenne myles towarde the Southe, they entered into the dominion of an other kynge, whome owre men named the oulde man, bycause hee was oulde, not passynge of his other name. In the region of this kynge also, they founde golde in all places bothe on the lande and in the ryuers. This region is verye fayre and frutefull: and hath in it many famous ryuers. Departynge from hense, in fyue dayes iorneye they came to a lande lefte desolate. They suppose that this was destroyed by ciuile discorde for as muche as it is for the mooste parte fruiteful, and yet not inhabited. The fyfth daye, they sawe two men commynge a farre of. These were laden with breade of Maixium, whiche they caryed on their shulders in sackes. Owre men tooke them: and vnderstoode by them that there were twoo kynges in that tracte: The one was named Periquete, whoe dwelte neare vnto the sea. The others name was Totonoga. This Totonoga, was blynde and dwelte in the continent. The twoo men whiche they mette, were the fysshers of Totonoga, whome he had sente with certayne fardelles of fyshe to Periquete, and had agepne receaued breade of hym for exchaunge. For thus do they communicate their commodities one with an other by exchaunge, without thuse of wycked money. By the conductinge of these twoo men, they came to kynge Totonoga dwellynge on the Weste syde of sayncte Michaelles goulfe in the Southe sea. They had of this kynge, the sum of sixe thousande Castellans of golde bothe rude and artificially wrought. Emonge those groumes of rude or natyue golde, there was one founde of the weyghte of two Castellans, whiche argued the plentifull rychenesse of the ground. Folowing the same coastes by the sea syde toward the West, they came to a kynge whose name was Taracuru, of whome they had golde amountynge to the weyght of eight thousand

D o   Pesos.

Golde.

A fruteful region left desolate by ciuile discorde.

kynge Periquete.

S. Michael, kynge Totonoga.

Six thousand Castellans of golde.

kyng Taracuru.

viii. thousand pesos of gold

kynge Pananome.

kyng Tabor. kynge Cheru.

iiii. thousande pesos of gold Salte.

kyng Anata. rv. thousande pesos of gold

Theyr maner of warre.

Fourescore thousand Castellans of golde.

kyng Scoria. kyng Pariza.

Gasalus Badaiocius hath the ouerthrow and is spoyled of great ryches of golde.

Pesos. Wee haue sayde befoze that Pesus is the weyghte of a Castelane not coyned. From hense they wente to the dominion of this kynges bzoother named Pananome, who fledde at their commynge, and appered no moze afterwarde. They saye that his kyngdome is ryche in golde. They spoyled his pallaice in his absence. Syre leaques from hense, they came to an other kyng named Tabor. From thense they came to the kyng of Cheru. He frendly entertepned owre men, and gaue them foure thousande Pesos of golde. He hathe in his dominion many goodly salte bayes: the region also aboundeth with golde. About twelue myles from hense, they came to an other kyng cauled Anata, of whome they had, rv. thousande Pesos of golde whiche he had gotten of the kinges his bozthe rers whom he had vanquisshed by warre. A great part of this golde was in rude fozme bycause it was molten when he set the kynges houses on fyer whom he spoyled. For they robbe and stey the one the other, sackynge and fyzyng their villages, and wastinge their countreys. They keepe warre barbarously and to vtter destruction, executing extreme crueltie ageinst them that haue the ouerthzowe. Gonsalus Baddaiocius with his felowes, wandered at lybertie vntyll they came to this kyng: And had gathered great heapes of gold of other kinges. For, what in bzasletres, collers, earinges, bzesse plates, helmettes, and certeine barres wherwith women beare vppe their bzestes, they had gathered together in gold the sum of fourescoze thousande Castellans, whiche they had obteyned partly by exchaunge foz owre thinges where they founde the kinges their frendes, & otherwise by forceible meanes where they founde the contrary. They had gotten also fozty slaues whose helpe they vsed both foz cariage of their vitailes and bagagies in the steade of moiles oz other beastes of burden, and also to relieue suche as were sycke and forweried by reason of their longe fozneys and hunger. After these pzospe rous viages, they came by the dominion of kynge Scoria, to the palaice of a kynge named Pariza: where (fearyng no such thing) Pariza enclosed them with a great armye, and assayled them stragglyng and vnwares, in suche sorte that they had no leasure to put on their armure. He slewe and wounded about fyftie, and put the residue to flyghte. They made suche hast, that they had no respect eyther to the gold they had ga thered,

thered, oz to their ſlaues: but lefte all behynde them. Thoſe
fewe that eſcaped, came to Dariena. The opinion of all wyſe
men as concernynge the varyable and inconſtant chaunces
of foztune in humane thinges, were falſe, if al thinges ſhuld
haue happened vnto them proſperouſly. Foz ſuch is the na=
ture of this blynde goddeſſe, that ſhe oftentimes delyteth in
the ouerthzowe of them whom ſhe hath exalted: and taketh
pleſure in confounding hygh thinges with lowe, and the con=
trary. Wee ſee this ozder to bee impermutable, that who ſoo
wyll applye hym ſelfe to gather rootes, ſhall ſumtymes meete
with ſweete lyquereſſe, and other whiles with ſoure cockle.
yet wo vnto Parixa: foz he ſhall not longe ſleape in reſt. The
gouernour him ſelfe was of late determined with thzee hun=
dzeth and fyftie choiſe ſouldiers to reuenge the death of owr
men: But where as he by chaunce fell ſycke, his poure went
fozward vnder the conducting of his Lieutenant Gaſpar Spino=
ſa, a Judge in caſes of lawe in Dariena At the ſame time other
were ſent foozth to the Jlande of Dites to exacte the poztion
of pearles lymited to the king foz his tribute. What ſhal ſuc=
cede, tyme will bzing to owr knowleage. The other two, at=
tempted thinhabitantes beyond the goulfe Franciſcus Bexerra paſ=
ſyng ouer by the cozner of the goulfe and the mouthes of the
ryuer of Dabaiba, with two other capitaines and a hundzeth
and fyftie ſouldiers well appointed, went to make warre vp=
pon the Canibales euen in Caribana their owne chiefeſt domini=
on, toward the vyllage of Turuſy, wherof we haue made men=
tion befoze in the comming of Fogeda. They bzought alſo with
them diuers engens of warre: as thzee pieces of ozdinanunce
whoſe ſhot were bygger then egges: Likewiſe fozty archers,
and, xxv. hagbutters to thintent to reache the Caniballes a
farre of, and to pzeuent their venemed arrowes. But what
became of hym and his company, oz where they arriued, we
haue yet no parfecte knowleage. Certaine which came of late
from Dariena to Spaine, repozted that at their departure, they
of Dariena ſtode in great feare leaſt they alſo were toſſed with
ſum miſfoztune. The other capitaine Valleius, obteyned the
fore parte of the goulfe. But he paſſed ouer by an other waye
then dyd Bexerra. Foz he tooke the beginning of Caribana, and
Bexerra the ende. Valleius returned ageine. But of the thzee
ſcoze and ten men whiche he conueighed ouer with hym, hee

The Jnconſtancie of fortune.

The expediti=on of Fraun=ces Bezarra a=geynſt the Canibales.

Gunnes,

Valeius repul=ſed of the Ca=nibales.

lefte fortye and eyght flaine emonge the Canibales. Thefe are the newes whiche they bringe that came lafte from Dariena. There came to me the day before the Ides of October in this yeare M. D. rvi. Rodericus Colmenares (of whom we haue made mention before) and one Francifcus Delapuente. This Francifcus, was one of the vnder capitaines of this bande, whofe chiefe capitaine was Gonfalus Baddaiocius who hardly efcaped the handes of kyng Pariza. Thefe twoo capitaines therfore, Rodericus and Francifcus who departed from Dariena immediatly after the misfortune whiche befell to Baddaiocius and his companye, do both affirme, the one that he hath harde, and the other that he hath feene, that in the Southe fea there are diuers Ilandes lying weftwarde from the Iland of Dites and fainte Michaels goulfe, in many of the whiche are trees engendred and nourifhed which bring foorth the fame aromaticall fruites, as doth the region of Collocutea. This lande of Collocutea, with the regions of Cochinus and Camemorus, are the chiefe marte-places from whenfe the Portugales haue their fpices. And hereby do they coniecture that the land where the frutefulneffe of fpyce begynneth, fhulde not be farre from thenfe. In fo much that many of them whiche haue ouerrunne thofe coaftes, do onely defyre that leaue may be graunted them to fearche further, and that they wil of their owne charges frame and furnifhe fhippes and aduenture the viage to feeke thofe Ilandes and regions. They thinke it beft that thefe fhippes fhulde bee made and prepared, euen in fainte Michaels goulfe: And not to attempte this vyage by fainte Auguftines point, which waye were both longe and diffyculte, and ful of a thoufande daungers, and is faide to reache beyonde the forty degree of the pole Antartike. The fame Francifcus, being partener of the trauailes and daungiers of Gonfalus, faithe that in ouer running thofe landes, he founde great heardes of hartes and wylde bores: and that he toke many of them by an arte which thinhabitauntes taught him: whiche was to make pittes or treches in their walkes, and to couer the fame with bowues. By this meanes alfo they deceaue al other kindes of wild and foure footed beaftes. But they take foules after the fame maner that we do: As ftocke doues with an other tame ftocke doue brought vp in their houfes. Thefe they tye by a ftrynge, and fuffer them to flye a little emong the trees. To the which as other

The Ilandes of the fouth f.a.

In this fea ly the Ilandes of Molucca, moft frutefull of fpices.

Collocutea. Cochinus and Camemorus, from whenfe the Portugales haue their fpyces.

he meaneth bythe ftreight of Magellanus.

howe they take hartes and wylde bores.

Stocke doues

as other birdes of their kind resort, they kil thē with their arrowes. Otherwyse they take thē with nettes in a bare place pourged from trees & busshes : and scaterynge certeyne seedes rounde about that place, in the myddeste whereof they tye a tame foule or byrde of the kynde of them whiche they desyre to take. In lyke maner do they take popingiayes and other foules. But they say that popingiayes are so simple, that a great multitude of them wyll flye euen into the tree in whose boumes the fouler sytteth: & swarme about the tame chatterynge popingiaye, sufferynge them selues to bee easely taken. for they are so without feare of the syght of the fouler, that they tary whyle he cast the snare about theyr neckes, the other beinge nothynge feared hereby, thoughe they see hym drawe them to him with the snare, and put them in the bagge which he hath about hym for the same purpose. There is an other kynde of foulynge, heretofore neuer harde of, and pleasaunt to consyder. We haue declared before howe that in certeyne of the Jlandes, and especially in *Hispaniola*, there are dyuers lakes or standynge pooles. In sume of these (beinge no deaper then men may wade ouer them) are seene great multytudes of water foules: as wel for that in the bottome of these lakes, there growe many herbes and weedes, as also that by reason of the heate of the sonne pearceinge to the naturall place of generation and corruption, where beinge doubled in force by reflection and preserued by moyster, there are engendered of the slymines of the earth and water, and by the prouidence of the vniuersall creator, innumerable lyttle fysshes, with a thousande sundry kyndes of frogges, wormes, knattes, flyes and such other. The foules which vse these lakes, are of dyuers kyndes: As duckes, geese, swannes, seemewes, gulles, and such other. We haue sayde also that in theyr orchardes they noryshe a tree which beareth a kynde of greate gourdes. Of these gourdes therefore well stopped leaste any water shulde enter in at theyr ryftes and cause them to sinke, they cast many in the shalowe pooles : where, by theyr continuall wanderynge and wauerynge with the motions of the wynde and water, they put the foules owt of suspection and feare. The fouler in the meane tyme, disguysinge hym selfe as it were with a visour, putteth a great gourde on his head much lyke to a helmet, with two holes neare about his eyes,

hys

Theyr maner of foulynge.

Popingiayes are easely taken.

A straunge kynde of foulynge.

Fysshes and wormes engendered of slime

Foules.

Gourdes of the tree.

The thyrde decade.

his face and hole heade belyde beinge couered therwith. And thus entereth he into the poole euen vnto the chynne. For beinge from theyr infancie exercised in swymmynge and accustomed to the waters, they refuse not to continue therein a longe space. The foules thynkynge this gourde to be one of the other that swymme vppon the water, the fouler goeth softely to the place wher he seeth the greatest flocke of foules: And with waggynge his heade, counterfectinge the mouing of the wauerynge gourdes, drawethe neare to the foules: where softely puttynge foorth his ryght hande, he soodenly snatcheth one by the legges and plungeth her into the water where he putteth her into a bagge whiche he hath with hym of purpose The other foules supposinge that this dyued into the water of her owne motion to seke for foode(as is their maner) are nothyng moued hereby, but go forwarde on their waye as before, vntyll they also faule into the same snare. I haue here for this cause entered into the declaration of theyr maner of huntynge and foulynge, that by these more pleasaunt narrations I may sumwhat mytigate and asswage the horrour conceaued in yowre stomake by the former rehersall of theyr bluddy actes and cruell maners. Lette vs nowe therfore speake sumwhat ageyne of the newe and later opinions as concernynge the swyfte course of the sea towarde the

Later opinions of the swift course of the Ocean cowarde the west.

west about the coastes of *Paria*: also of the maner of gathering of golde in the golde myne of *Dariena*, as I was aduertised of late. And with these two quyet and peaceable thynges, we wyl make an ende of the tragical affayres of the Ocean: and therwith byd yowre holynes fare wel. So it is therfore, that *Andreas Moralis* the pylot, and *Ouiedus* (of whom we haue made mention before) repayred to me, at my house in the towne of Matrite, As we met thus togyther, there arose a contention betwene them two, as concernynge this course of the Ocean.

The continet of firme land.

They both agree that these landes and regions perteynynge to the dominion of Castile, doo with one continuall tract and perpetuall bonde, embrase as one hole firme lande or continent al the mayne lande lyinge on the north syde of *Cuba* and the other Ilandes, beinge also northwest both from *Cuba* and *Hispaniola*. yet as touchynge the course of the water, they varie in opinion. For *Andreas*, wyll that this vyolent course of water bee receaued in the lappe of the supposed continente whiche

which bendeth so much and extendeth so farre towarde the
North, as we haue said: And that by the obiect or resistance
of the lande so bendynge and crookynge, the water shulde as
it were rebounde in coompasse, and by force therof be dryuen
about the north syde of Cuba and the other Ilandes excluded
without the circle cauled Tropicus Cancri, where the largenes of
the sea maye receaue the waters faulynge frome the narowe
streames, and therby represse that inordinate course, by reason that the sea is there very large and great. I can compare
his meanynge to nothynge more aptely then to the swyfte
streame commyng foorth of a mylle and faulyng into the myl
poole. For in al suche places where waters runne with a vyolent faule through narowe chanels, and are then receaued in
large pooles, they are soodenly disparcled and theyr violence
broken: So that wheras before they seemed of such force as
to ouerthrowe all thynges beinge in theyr waye, it can not
then be perceaued which way they runne. The Admiral him
selfe Diegus Colonus, sonne and heyre to Christophorus Colonus the
fyrst fynder of these landes (who had nowe in commyng and
goinge, foure tymes passed throughe these seas) beinge demaunded of me what he founde or perceaued in saylynge too
and fro, answered that there was muche difficultie in returnynge the same way by the which they go. But wheras they
fyrst take the waye by the mayne sea towarde the North before they directe theyr course to Spayne, he saythe that in
that tract, he felt the shippe sumtymes a lyttle dryuen backe
by the contrary course of the water. yet supposeth that this
chaunceth onely by the ordinarie flowynge and reflowynge
of the sea: And the same not to be enforced by the circumflec
tion or course of the water reboundynge in compasse as we
haue sayde. But thinketh rather, that this mayne lande or
supposed continent, shulde sumwhere bee open: And that the
sayde open place, shoulde bee as it were a gate, enterie, or
streyght, diuydyng the North partes of that lande from the
South: by the which also, the Ocean runnynge towarde the
West, may by the rotation or impulsion of the heauens, bee
dryuen about the hole earth. Ouiedus agreeth with Andreas Mo
ris as touchynge the continuall adherence and closenes of
the sayde continente. yet neyther that the waters shulde so
brate ageynst the bendynge backe of the West lande, or bee in
suche

The Vyages
of Diegus
Colonus.

The Vyage
from the new
landes to
Spayne.

ſuch ſorte repulſed and dryuen into the mayne ſea. But ſaith
that he hath diligently conſydered, that the waters runne
from the deepeſt and myddeſt of the maine ſea, towarde the
Weſt. Alſo that ſaylinge nere vnto the ſhore with ſmaule veſ
ſelles, he founde the ſame waters to returne ageine toward
the Eaſt. So that in the ſame place, they runne together with
contrary courſe, as we oftentimes ſee the lyke to chaunce in
riuers wherby the obiecte of the bankes, diuers whirlepooles
and turnynges aryſe in the water. By reaſon wherof, if any
chaffe, ſtrawe, woodde, or any other thyng of lyght ſubſtaunc
be caſte in any ſuche places in ryuers, it foloweth that al ſuch
as runne with the water in the myddeſt of the chanell, pro
cede well forwarde: But ſuche as faule into the bendyng
goulfes and indented margentes of the crooked bankes, ar
caryed ouerthwarte the chanell, and ſo wander about vntyl
they meete with the ful and directe courſe of the ryuer. Thus
haue we made powe partener of ſuche thinges as they hau
gyuen vs, and written their dyuers opinions. We wyll ther
gyue more certeyne reaſon, when more certeyne truth ſhalbe
knowen. We muſt in the meane tyme, leane to opinions vnti
the day coome appointed of god to reueale this ſecreate of na
ture, with the perfecte knowleage of the pointe of the pole
ſtarre. Hauyng ſayd thus muche of the courſe of the Ocean
a briefe declaration of the golde mynes of Dariena, ſhall cloſ
vppe owre Decades and make an ende of owre trauayles.
Wee haue ſayde, that nyne myles diſtante from Dariens, at
the ſydes of the hylles and the drye playnes in the which
golde is gathered bothe on the drye lande, and alſo on th
bankes and in the chanelles of ryuers. Therfore to al ſuch
as are wyllynge to gather golde, there is of ordinarie cuſtom
appointed to euery man by the ſuruoiers of the mynes, a
ſquare plotte of grounde conteyning twelue paſes, at the ar
bitriment of the chooſer, ſo that it bee not grounde alreada
occupied, or lefte of other. The portion of grounde being
thus choſen (as it were aſſygned of the augures to buylde a
temple) they incloſe their ſlaues within the ſame, whoſe
helpe the Chriſtians vſe in tyllynge of their grounde and ga
therynge of golde, as we haue ſaide. Theſe places appointed
vnto them, they keepe as long as them lyſte. And if they per
ceaue tookens of lyttle golde, they requyre an other plotte of
groun

Marginal notes:

The contrary courſe of waters.

The poynt of the pole ſtar.

The golde mynes of Dariena, and the maner of gatherynge golde.

grounde of twelue pases to be assigned them, leauyng the first
in commen. And this is thorder which the Spaniardes inha=
bitinge *Dariena* obserue in gatherynge of golde. I suppose al=
so that they vse the lyke order in other places: How be it, I
haue not yet enquired so farre. It hath byn proued that these
twelue pases of grounde, haue yelded to their choosers, the
summe of fourescore Castellans of golde. And thus leade they
theyr lyues in fulfyllynge the holy hunger of golde. But the
more they fyll their handes with fyndynge, the more increa=
seth their couetous despre. The more woodde is layde to the
fyer, the more furiously rageth the flame. Unsaciable couet=
couslnesse is no more diminisshed with increase of rychesse,
then is the dtinesse of the dropsye satisfyed with drinke. I
lette passe manye thynges wherof I intende to write more
largely in tyme conuenient, if I shall in the meane season vn=
derstande these to be acceptable vnto yowre holynesse: my
dewtie and obseruaunce to whose autoritie, hath caused me
the gladlier to take this labour in hande. The prouidence of
the eternall creatour of all thynges, graunt yowre holynesse
many prosperous yeares.

❧The laste booke of Peter Martyr of Angle=
ria, of the Landes and Ilandes lately
founde: and of the maners of the
inhabitauntes of the same.

 I Haue partli declared before in mi decades how
certeine fugit ues which came owt of the large
West landes arriued in the confynes of *Dariena*:
And howe that marueylinge at the bookes of
owre men, they declared that they sumtyme
dwelte in regions whose inhabitauntes vsed
instrumentes and were ruled by politike lawes. Also
that they had cities fortified with waules, and faire pallaces
with streates well paued, and common places whyther mat=
chauntes resort as to the burse or streate. These landes, owre
men haue nowe founde. Therfore who were thauthours here=
of, or what successe they had herein, who so desireth to know
with the conditions of straunge regions and the maners of

P p   the

the people. let hym giue diligent attendance to such thynge
as folowe. Of the Jland of Cuba (nowe cauled Fernandina, ly
ynge nexte vnto Hispaniola on the west syde, and yet sumwha
so bendynge towarde the Northe that the circle cauled Tropi
cus Cancri deuideth it in the myddeste, wher as Hispaniola is dis
tante from the Tropike and declinynge certen degrees to
ward the Equinoctial line)we haue spoken sumwhat before
In this Jland of Fernandina, there are nowe syxe townes erec
ted. Wherof, the chiefe is named Sanctiago of saynt James th
patrone of the Spanyardes. In this, there is natiue golde
found both in the mountaynes and ryuers: By reason wher
of they are daylye occupied in gathering & digging the same
But shortely after that I had finished my sayde bookes, th
Spanyardes that were the most auncient citizens of Cuba, a
Franciscus Fernandes of Corduba Lupus Ocho, & Christophorus Morantes, d
termined to seeke newe landes, as the myndes of the Spa
nyardes are euer vnquiet and geuen to attempte great enter
prises. They furnyshed at their owne charges, three of thos
shyppes whiche they caule Carauels. And hauynge fyrste ly
cence of Diegus Velasquen the gouernour of the Jlande, they de
parted with a hundreth and ten men from the West angle o
Cuba. For this angle is moste commodious to relieue shyppe
and to make prouision for freshe water and fuell. Thus the
sayled continually syxe dayes and a halfe, betwene the We
and the South, contented onely with the syght of the heaue
and the water : durynge whiche tyme, they suppose that the
sayled not past threescore and syxe myles. For they ley at an
ker all nyght where so euer the faulynge of the sonne took
the day light from them, leaste by wanderynge in vnknowe
seas, they myght chaunce to be cast vppon rockes or sandes
But at the length they chaunced vppon a great Jlande na
med Iucatana, whose beginnyng thinhabitauntes caule Ecca
pi. Owre men went to the citie stondynge on the sea syde, th
whiche for the bygnes therof, they named Cayrus or Alcair
Thinhabitauntes enterteined them very frendly. When the
were entered into the citie, they marueyled to behold the hou
ses buylded lyke towres, magnifycall temples, streates we
paued, and great exercise of bying and sellyng by exchaung
of ware for ware. Their houses are eyther bylte of stone, o
of bricke and lyme, and artifycially wrought. To the fyrs
porche

**The Jland of
Cuba or Fer:
nandina.**

**The Spani:
ardes of Cuba
attempt new
vyages.**

**The west an:
gle of Cuba.**

Note.

**The Jland of
Jucatana.**

**A great citie
well buylded.**

Temples.

**Humane peo:
ple.**

porches of their houses and fyrst habitations, they ascend by ten or twelue steates. They are couered eyther with tyles, slates, reades, or stalkes of certeyne herbes. They gratified the one the other with mutuall gyftes. The barbarians gaue owre men many brooches and iewelles of golde, verye fayre and of cunnyng woorkmanshyppe. Owre men recompensed them with vestures of sylke and woolle, counterfecte stones, of coloured glasse and chrisstall, haukes belles of laton, and suche other rewardes whiche they greatly esteemed for the straungenes of the same. They sette nowght by lookynge glasses, bycause they haue certeyne stoones muche brighter. This nation is appareled after a thousande fasshyons with vestures made of gossampyne cotten or bombage of dyuers coloures. The women are couered from the girdle to the heele hauynge dyuers fasshions of veles aboute their heades and brestes, with great cautele least any parte of their legges or feete bee seene. They resorte muche to their temples: vnto the which the chiefe rulers haue the wayes paued from their owne houses. They are Idolatours and circumcised. They occupie their maner of exchaunginge, with muche fydelitie. They vse to adourne the heares of their heades, being deman ded by thinterpretours of whom they receaued their circum cisyon, they answered that there once passed an exceadynge fayre man by their costes, who lefte them that in tooken to remember hym. Other saye that a manne brighter then the soone, went emonge them and executed that offyce. But there is no certentie hereof. When owre men had remayned there certeyne dayes, they seemed to bee molestous to thinhabitan tes accordynge to the common sayinge. The longer a geste ta rieth, the woorse is his enterteynement. The whiche thynge owre men perceauyng, they made the more hast awaye. Be ynge therfore prouided of all thynges necessary, they tooke their vyage directly towarde the west by the prouidence whi che thinhabitauntes caule Comi and Maium. They ouer passed these regions takyng onely freshe water and fuel in the same. The barbarians both men, women, and chyldren flocked to the sea syde, astonyshed greatly to behold the huge bygnesse of the shyppes. Owre men marueyled in maner no lesse to viewe their buyldynges and especially their temples sytuate neare vnto the sea, and erected after the maner of towers.

Cunnyng arti fycers.

Appareled people.

Circumcised Idolaters.

Comi. Maium.

P p. ii,   Thus

Thus at the length hauyng sayled about a hundreth and ten
myles, they thought it good to ley anker in a prouince named
Campechium, whose chiefe towne consysteth of three thousande
houses. Th'inhabitauntes came swymmynge to the shyppes:
maruelyng excedyngly at the maner of saylinge, and at the
sayles and other tackelynges But when they hard the thunder of the gunnes, sawe the smoke, and smelte the sauour of
brimstone and fyer, they supposed that thunderboultes and
lyghtnynges had byn sente from god. The kynge receaued
owre men honorably and broughte them into his pallayce:
where he feasted them well after his maner. They are accustomed to eate fleše, and haue great plentie of beastes and foules : as peacockes, and other whiche they francke and feede
in their houses : Also dyuers kyndes of wylde foules of the
mountaines, wooddes, and waters : Likewise partriches,
quailes, turtle dooues, duckes, and geese. Of beastes, they
haue connies, woolues, lyons, tigers, foxes, wylde boores,
hartes, and hares.   After this banquet, the kyng with his
traine and famylie broughte owre men into a brode crosse way
where many streates do meete. In this, they shewed them as
it were a great and highe aulter buylded foure square of marble compacte together partly with the toughe cleye of Babilon cauled *Bitumem*, and partly with smaule stoones. It had
on euery syde foure steares. Uppon the altare was an Image
of a man made of marble : and fast by it the Images of two
beastes of vnknowen shape, whiche seemed as thoughe they
wolde with yanynge mouthes haue torne in sunder the bealy
of the mannes Image. On the other syde stoode a great serpent compacte of the sayde toughe cleye and smaule stoones.
This serpent beynge in length. xlvii. foote, and of the bygnesse of a large oxe, seemed to deuour a lyon of marble, and
was al by sparcled with freshe bludde.   Harde by the altare,
were thre postes fastned in the ground, the which three other
trauersed and were susteined with stones. In this place offenders were put to death : In token wherof they sawe innumerable arrowes steined with bludde, sum scatered, sum lyinge
on heapes, and sum broken : Also a great number of mennes
bones lying in a court or yarde nere vnto this funestal place.
Their houses are here also builded of lime and stone. They named this king, *Lazarus*, bicause they arriued at this lande on
saincts

Campechium.

A towne of
three thou-
sand howses.

Plentie of
beastes and
foules.

They: Idoles
and Idolatry.

Houses of
lyme & stone.

faint Lazarus day. Departing fró hense & directing theyr course
styl toward the West for the space of .xv. myles, they came to a
prouince named Aquanil, whose chiefe towne is cauled Mosco, &
the kynge thereof, Cupoton. He behelde owre men with a frowarde countenaunce, and sought occasion to doo them sume
priuie mischiefe whyle they sought for fresshe water. For he
made signes vnto them that on the further syde of the nexte
hyll, they shulde fynde spryngcs of water, intendyng to haue
assayled them in that narowe passage. But by the colouryng
of theyr forheades (as they are accustomed in theyr warres)
and by the bearynge of theyr bowes and other weapons, owr
men perceaued theyr wylynes, and refused to go any further.
yet a thousande of the Barbarians assayled theym vnwares
and vnprepared. By reason wherof, they were put to flyght,
and dyuers of them slayne in the chase. Many that sledde to
warde the shippes, were entangeled in the mudde and maryshes nere vnto the shore. Twentie and two, were slayne with
arrowes, and the resydewe for the most parte, wounded. Fran
cisus Fernandes the gouernour of the nauie, receaued in this con
flicte three and thirtie woundes. And in maner none escaped
without hurt. If they had gonne to the hylles whiche were
appoynted them, they had byn slayne euery man. They ther
fore that escaped, returned to the Ilande of Fernardina frome
whense they came, where they were receaued of theyr felows
with heauie chere. But when Diegus Velasquen the gouernoure
of the Ilande, had intelligence hereof, he im mediatly furnyshed a newe nauie of foure Carauelcs with three hundreth
men. Of this nauie he appoynted John Grisalua his neue,
to be the gouernour : And assigned for vnder capitaynes, Al-
phons Auila, Frances Montegio, and Peter Aluarado. For
the pylot he assigned Antonie Alamino who had the regiment
of the fyrst nauie. They attempted the same vyage ageyne,
but declyned sumwhat more towarde the South about threescore and tenne myles. Before they sawe any lande, they espyed a towne a farre of, by the biewe wherof, they came to an
Ilande named Coxumella, from the whiche they smelte sweete
sauours proceadynge with the wynde, before they approched
to the lande by the space of three myles. They founde the I-
lande to be fortie and fiue myles in circuite. It is playne and
of maruelous frutefull soyle. There is also golde in it, but is
　　　　　　　　　　　　　　　　　　　　　　　　is not

The prouince
Aquanail.
Mosco.

The Spany-
ardes are put
to flyght and
many slayne.

An other ex-
pedition.

The Iland of
Cozumella.
Swecte sa-
uours.
A frutefull
Ilande.

is not engendered there, but brought thether from other regi
ons. It aboundeth with hony, fruites, and herbes: And hath
also great plentie of foules and foure footed beastes.   They
**Towres and
temples.**
older and maner of lyuyng, is in al thynges lyke vnto theyr
of *Iucatans.* Lykewyse theyr howses, temples, streates, and ap
parell. In many of theyr houses, are great postes of marble
after the maner of owre buyldynge. They founde there, the
foundations of certeyne owlde towres ruinate: And one especi
ally with .xviii. steares ascendynge to it, after the maner of so
lemne temples. They marueyled greatly at owre shippes and
maner of saylynge. At the fyrst, they wolde admyt no straun
gers: but shortly after, receaued them gentelly. Theyr chiefe
ruler (whom owre men supposed to bee a preeste) led them vp
to the toppe of the towre, where they erected a banner and
**Cozumella na
med Sancta
Cruz.**
addicted the Ilande to the dominion of the kynge of Castyle,
namynge it *Sancta Crux,* bycause they entered into the same in
the nones of Maye beinge then the feaste of the holye crosse.
They saye that it was cauled *Cozumella* of kynge *Cozumellus,*
whose auncestours were the fyrst that inhabited the Ilande.
In the towre, they founde many chambers furnyshed with I
mages, made both of earthe and marble to the similytude of
**Idoles lyke
beares.**
beares. These they caule vppon with a houlynge and lamen
table songe, perfumyng them with sweete odours, and other
wyse honourynge them as theyr domesticall goddes They
Idolatry.
are also circumcised. The kynge was in fayre apparel made
of gossampine cotton curiously wrought. He was lame on
the one foote by reason that as he once exercysed hym selfe in
swymmynge, a deuourynge fyshe cauled *Tuberon,* byt of al the
toes, of one of his fecte. He entreated owre men very frend
**Gentell
people.**
ly and made them great chiere. After they had byn here thre
dayes, they departed. And saylynge styll towarde the Weste,
they espyed great mountaynes a farre of. But as they drewe
neare, they perceaued it to bee the Ilande of *Iucatans* beinge
**Iucatana but
fyue myles
from Cozu
mella.**
distant from *Cozumella* onely fyue myles. Directynge therfore
theyr course towarde the south syde of *Iucatans,* they compa
sed it on that syde which lyeth nearest to the supposed conti
nent: yet coulde they not sayle rounde about it by reason of
the multitude of rockes, shalowe places, and shelfes of saude.
Then Alaminus the pylot turned his sailes to the North side
wherof he had better knowleage. Thus at the length, they
came

came to the towne Campechium and kynge Lazarus with whom they had bin that attempted the fyrſt vyage the yeare befoze. At the fyrſt, they were gentelly receaued, and requyred to reſoze to the towne. But ſhoztly after, they repented that they had bydden them: and there vpon wylled them to ſtay about a ſtones caſt from the towne, and to pzoceade no further. When owre men deſyzed that they myght make pzouiſion foz freſhe water befoze theyz departure, they aſſigned them to a certeyne well which they had lefte behynde them. Declaringe further, that it ſhulde be lawfull foz them to take water there oz els no wheare. Owre men reſted that nyght in the fyelde adioynynge to the well. The which thynge the Barbarians ſuſpectinge, aſſembled an army of thzee thouſande men, and encamped not farre from them. Bothe partes paſſed awaye the nyght without ſleepe. They fearynge leaſte owre menne ſhulde bzeake into the towne: And owre men, leaſt the Barbarians ſhulde inuade them ſoodenly, on the one parte with trumpettes, and on the other ſyde with the noyſe of timbzels kept them ſtyll wakynge that were diſpoſed to ſleape, At the ſpzynge of the day, the Barbarians appzoched to owre mens campe & cauled foz thinterpzetours of Cuba, whoſe language is much agreable vnto theyzs. They had diuiſed to lyght a tozche of frankenſence and to place the ſame betwene bothe tharmies to thintent that if owre men dyd not depart befoze the tozche were conſumed, to ſtande to theyz perell. The tozch was waſted and the matter came to hand ſtrokes. They ſlewe onely one of owre men with an arrowe bycauſe his target fayled hym. But many were wounded. After this confliete, owre men reſozted to theyz ozdinaunce which they had planted neare vnto the well. When they had diſcharged certeyne pecces, the Barbarians fledde backe into the towne. Owre men were of fierce and greedy courage to haue purſued them, but that Griſalua the gouernour wolde not ſuffer the. From thenſe they pzoceaded to the laſt ende of Iucatana, which they founde to reache moze then two hundzeth myles frome the Eaſt to the Weſt. Here they founde a comodious hauen and named it Portus deſideratus. From henſe they ſayled to other landes, and came to the region nexte to Iucatana Weſtwarde, whiche they doubte whether it be an Ilande oz parte of the firme lande: but thinke it rather to be annext to the continent

In

The Barbarians make reſiſtaunce.

A conflicte.

The length of Iucatana.

The thyrde decade.

The region of Caluacam, o: Oloan.

In this there is a goulfe which they suppose to be incoompassed with bothe the landes. But of this, there is no certentie. Thinhabitantes caule this region *Caluacam* o: otherwise *Oloan*. They founde here also a great ryuer whiche by his violente course and faule, driueth freshe water two myles into the sea. This they cauled *Grisalua* after the name of the gouernoure.

The ryuer Grisalua.

The barbarians marueilyng at the huge greatnesse and mouynge of owre shyppes, came swarmyng the bankes on bothe sydes the ryuer, to the number of syre thousande men armed with targettes and brest plates of gold, bowes and arrowes,

Targets and brest plates of golde.

brode swoordes of heauy woodde, and longe iauelens hardened at the endes with fyer: Thus stondynge in battaple raye to defende their coostes, and with proude countenaunces forbyddinge owre men to coome alande. Bothe parties watched al that nyght in armes. In the dawne of the day, owre men espied about a hundreth canoas (whiche we haue saide to be their boates) full of armed men. Here also the language of *Cuba* agreed well enowghe with thers. When they had admitted the peace profered them by thinterpretours, al the canoas staied excepte one whiche approched toward the shyppes. A certeyne ruler that was in this canoa, demaunded of owre men what they sought in other mennes landes. They answered, gold. And that, for permutation of other ware, and not of gift o: vyolently. The canoa returned and the ruler certified the kyng hereof, who came gladlye to the shyppes. When he had saluted the gouernour, he cauled his chamberlen vnto hym, commaundynge him to bringe his armure and other ornamentes of golde wherwith he armed *Grisalua* from the toppe of the heade to the soule of the foote: In so muche that, what so euer any man of armes armed at all partes, is emong vs accustomed to weare of Iren o: steele when he commeth in to the fielde, all suche kynde of furnitures made of golde and wrought with woonderfull arte, the kyng gaue to the gouernour. He recompensed hym with ventures of sylke, clothe, lynen, and other of owre thinges. In the beginning of this *Iucatana*, when they sayled to *Cozumella*, they chaunced vppon a canoa of fyssher men to the number of nyne, fysshyng with hookes of golde. They tooke them all prisoners. One of them was knowen to this kyng, who promysed the daye folowyng to sende the gouernour as muche gold

Armure of golde.

Experte artificers.

Fysshe hookes of golde.

golde for his raunfome as the man hym felfe waſed. But the gouernour denyed that he coulde releaſe hym withowte the conſent of his felowes: And therfore kept hym ſtyll to proue what he could further knowe of hym. Departing from henſe and ſaylynge ſtyll weſtwarde, they founde a great goulfe in the which three ſmaule Ilandes were ſytuate. Of theſe, they went to the byggeſt. But oh abhominable crueltie: oh moſt corrupted myndes of men, and deuelyſche impietie? Let euery godly man cloſe the mouth of his ſtomake leſt he be deſturbed. They offer younge children of bothe kyndes to their Idoles of marble and earth. Emonge their Idoles of marble, there ſtandeth a lyon hauynge a hole throwgh the necke, into the whiche they poure the bludde of the miſerable ſacrifyce, that it maye from thenſe runne downe into a ſyncke of marble. Lette vs nowe declare with what ceremonies they ſacryfyce the bludde of theſe pore wretches. They cutte not their throttes, but open the very breſtes of theſe ſelye ſoules and take owte their hartes yet pantynge, with the hotte bludde wherof, they anoynte the lyppes of their Idoles, and ſuffer the reſydue to faule into the ſynke. This doone, they burne the harte and bowels, ſuppoſynge the ſmoke therof to be acceptable to their goddes. Of their Idoles, one is made to the ſhape of a man, bowynge downe his heade and lookynge toward the ſynke of bludde, as it were acceptyng the offeringe of the ſlayne ſacrifyce. They eate the fleſhe of the armes, thighes, and legges, eſpecially when they ſacrifyce an enemy taken in the warres. They founde a ſtreame of congeled blud as thoughe it had runne from a boucherye. For this myſchieuous purpoſe, they bringe theſe wretches from the nexte Ilandes. They ſawe alſo innumerable heades, and trunkes of bodies thus mangeled, beſyde many other yet remaining hole and couered with certeine mattes. All the trackes of theſe regions abounde with golde and precious ſtones. One of owre men wanderynge in the Ilande, chaunced to fynde two water pottes of alabaſter artifycially wrought and full of lyttle ſtones of dyuers colours. They ſaye alſo that they founde a ſtone of the value of two thouſand Caſtilans of gold, whiche they ſent to the gouernour. This Ilande they named the Iland of ſacrifyce. The inhabitauntes are circumciſed. There are alſo other Ilandes ſytuate about this *Coluacana, or Caluacam,*

M q the

The Ilandes of Sacrifice.

Chyldren ſacrified to Idoles.

Their Idoles of marble.

Gold and precious ſtones.

A ſtone of great price.

the whiche are inhabited onely with women lyuing without the coompanye of men after the maner of the Amazones. But they that ponder the matter more wisely, thinke them rather to be certeyne women whiche haue vowed chastitie and professed a solytarie lyfe as the nunnes doo with vs, or as the virgins caulded Vestales or Bonæ Deæ, were accustomed to do amonge the gentiles in oulde tyme. At certeyne tymes of the yeare, men of the other Ilandes resorte vnto them. But not for thintent of generation, but moued with pitie to helpe them to dresse their gardens and tyll their grounde. The reporte goeth lykewise that there are other Ilandes of corrupte women to whom men resorte for carnall copulation: And that they cutte of one of the pappes of their women children least it shuld hynder their shootyng. Also that they kepe onely the women children and sende awaye the men children. Owr men therfore drewe nere to the shore of Colluacana where they quyetly exercised marchaundies with thinhabitauntes. The kyng gaue them a great potte of gold: Also braslettes, chaynes, brouches, with many other iewelles, and al of gold. Owre men ageyne on the other parte satisfyed him with such stuffe as they had done other before. Here wolde they gladly haue planted a newe colonie or habitation, but that the gouernour wolde not permytte them, wherat they gruged not a lyttle. The houses and other edifyes of this prouynce, are buylded like vnto towres. It hath also. xv. great townes in it. Of these they affirme that they haue seene sum consisting of more then. xx. thousande houses, not ioyning together, but deseuered with courtes and gardens. They haue also certeyne large market places encompased with waulles, and streates well paued. Likewise fornaces and ouens made of lyme and bricke. Furthermore al sortes of handy craftes men & very cunning artificers. This kinges name was Potanchanus: & the region is cauled Palmaria. The towne where the king kepeth his court, coteineth. xv. thousand houses. When they receaue any straungiers and make a leage of frendshyppe with them, they are accustomed with a knife made of a sharpe stone, to let them selues bludde in the toonge, hande, arme, or sum other parte of the body: And this euen in the syght of them whom they admitte to frendshyp, in token that they are ready to shedde their bludde in their fryndes causes. Their priestes professe a vertuous lyfe, and liue vnmaried. What it is to

Ilandes of women.

Golde.

Houses lyke towres. xv. greate townes in the prouince of Colluacana. Townes of xx. thousande houses.

The region of palmaria.

A token of frendship.

Priestes.

haue to do with women, no man knoweth before he be maried. Fornication and adultery (which selde chaunce emonge the) they counte abhomination. The women are of maruelous chastitie. Eurey noble maister that he haue had one wife, may haue as many concubines as hym lysteth. But a maried woman taken in adulterie, is soulde of her husbande. But this onely to the prince : at whose handes it shal be lawfull for her kynsefolkes to redeeme her. It is not lawfull for suche as are not maried, to sytte at the same table with them that are maried, or to eate of the same dyshe or drinke of the same cup. In the moneth of August and September, they absteine .xxv. dayes not onely from flesshe wherof they haue great plentie, but also from fysshe and al other thinges that lyue by bludde: And durynge these daies, lyue onely with herbes and frutes. They reken twentie dayes to the moneth, and twentie monethes to the yeare. Owre men consumed certeyne dayes here verye pleasauntly. When they departed, coastynge styll by the same shore, they came to an other kyng whom they named *Oxandus.* When he had intellygence that owre men desired golde, he brought foorth certeyne plates of molten gold. But whe the gouernour signified vnto him by thinterpretors that he desyred great plentie of that metal, the day folowing he brought him a mannes Image of golde beinge a cubette in length: Also a fanne of golde, and an Idole of one of his domesticall goddes of curious woorkeman hyppe. Likewyse garlandes of stones of sundry coloures, with many breste plates, brooches, and other kyndes of ornamentes, and all of golde. He gaue hym furthermore aboundaunce of delycate meates well salted and poudred with spices. When he had required owre men to coome alande, he commaunded his seruauntes with all speede to prepare a great multitude of braunches of trees and to waite vppon owre men to his pallayce. As they went thus in order, sum behynde and sum before on bothe sydes, they seemed so to shadowe owre men with the bouwes as thoughe they had gonne in a continuall arbour. The kynge hym selfe hauynge a septer in his hand, dyd sette them in their araye, and sumtyme strike suche as were negligent in bearyng their bouwes. They shewed them selues obedient in all thynges, and with graue countenaunce, humbled them selues to receaue his stripes. When he was demaunded

Q q. ii. where

Chastitie.

The punyshment of adulterie.

Mariage is honoured.

Fastynge.

kynge Oxandus.

Idoles. Iewels, and ouches of gold.

Gold in moun
teynes and
ryuers

Theyr maner
of gatheryng
golde.

Sweete sa-
uours.

A stone of
great price.

where he had suche plentie of golde, he pointed with his
fynger to the next mountaynes, and to the ryuers descen-yng
from the same. They are so accustomed to the riuers and exercised in swymming, that it is al one to them to liue in the water and on the lande. When they desyre togather golde, they
plunge theym selues in the ryuers and brynge from the bottome therof, bothe their handes full of sande, whiche syftynge from hande to hande, they gather owte the graynes
of golde. And by this meanes in the space of twoo houres,
they fyll a reede as bygge as a mannes fynger. Of the sweete
sauours of these landes, many thynges myght be spoken, the
whiche bycause they make rather to theffeminatynge of the
myndes of men, then for any necessarye purpose, I haue
thought best to omytte them.   The kynge also gaue the gouernour a younge virgine of twelue yeares of age, adourned
with ryche and fayre iewelles. Of the stones whiche he had
of this kynge, one was valued at twoo thousande Castellans
of golde. Thus at the length they departed from this kyng,
laden with golde and precious stoones. *Crisalua* the gouernour, sente one of the Carauelles to his vncle *Diego Velasquen*
gouernour of the Ilande of *Cuba*, with messengers to delyuer hym the golde, iewelles, and other ornamentes. The
residue in the meane tyme styll folowed the tracte towarde
the West. One of them in the whiche Frauncis Montegius
the vnder gouernour was caryed, sayled harde by the shore:
and the other twoo kept aloofe within prospecte of the land.
Thinhabitauntes of these coastes also, no lesse maruelynge
at the shyppes then dyd the other, came with twelue Canoas
to Montegius, desyringe hym by thinterpretours to coome
alande, promysynge in the name of their kynge, that hee
shoulde be honorably entertayned. But Montegious answered that hee coulde not assente to their request bycause his
coompanions were so farre from hym. Yet dyd he gyue them
certayne of owre thynges straunge vnto them, and thankes
for their gentylnesse. Shortly after espyinge a great towne
they directed their course thither. Thinhabitauntes prohi-
byted them to coome alande, and came foorthe ageynst them
with bowes & quyuers ful of arrowes, brode swoordes made
of heauy woode, and Iauelens hardned at the ende with fier.
They shotte at owre men a farre of : And owre men discharged

ged certeyne pieces of ozdinaunce ageynst them. The Barba=
rians astonysshed at the noyse of the gunnes, fledde amayne,
and desyzed peace. Here owre mens bytayles began to fayle
them, and theyz shyppes were bzoosed with longe byages.
Hauynge therefoze founde and doone these thynges whereof
we haue spoken, Grisalua returned to the Jlande of *Fernandina*
well contented, but so were not his companions. We muste
nowe diuerte sumwhat from this matter, and speake of an o=
ther nauigation. And from thense wyll we returne to these
landes which owre men haue founde. So it is therfoze, that
Diegus Velasquen the gouernour of the Jland of *Fernandina*, about
the same tyme that he had sent foozth this nauie of foure Ca=
raucles, he prepared an other nauigation of onely one Cara=
uell and one bzygantine with foztie and fyue men. These ex=
ercised byolent handes ageinst thinhabitauntes of those regi=
ons where they arryued, thynkynge that they myght foztea=
bly dzawe them to the dyggynge of golde bycause they were
Castranite Jdolaters and circumcised. There are at the sea
syde not farre from the supposed continent, many lyttle Jlan
des of moste foztunate and frutefull soyle, whereof thzee are
thus named : *Guanapan, Guanguan,* and *Quitilla.* Owte of one of
these (which they named *Sancta Marina*) they byolentely caried
away thzee hundzeth men and women which they thzust in=
to the Carauell and returned immediatly to *Fernandina*, lea=
uynge the bzygantine with. xxb. of theyz felowes to thirtene
to hunt foz moze men. The hauen where the Carauell fyzste
arryued, is caaled *Carenas*, beinge distante from the angle of
Cuba and the chiefe citie of *Sanctiago*, two hundzeth and fyftie
myles. Foz this Jlande of *Cuba*, is bery longe, reachyng in
length from the East to the West, and situate directly bnder
the circle caaled *Tropicus Cancri* as we haue sayde befoze. Now
shall you heare how foztune sought the reuenge of these poze
wzetches. Therfore as theyz kepers went aland and few re=
mained in the Carauel, they perceiuing occasio ministred wher
by they myght receaue theyz libertie, soodeynely snatched up
owr mens weapons and flewe fyre of them which yet remay
ned in the Carauel, whyle the residue lepte into the sea. And
by this meanes the Barbarians possessed the Carauell which
they had soone learned to rule, and thus returned to theyz
owne countreys. But they sayled fyzste to the nexte Jlande
where

Other viages
from Cuba oz
Fernandina.

Many Jlands
betwene Cu
ba and the
firme lande.

Sanctiago
the chiefe ci
tie of Cuba.

The Barbar
ans sley the
Spaniardes
with theyr
owne wea=
pons.

where they burnte the Carauel and caried away the weapons with them. From hence they conueyed them selues to theyr owne countreys with the Canoas of this Ilande. Dearein lyke maner they pryuilie aſſayled them that were lefte with the brigantyne, and ſlewe many of them alſo. The reſidue that eſcaped, fledde to the brigantine where they bewayled theyr felowes deathes and counted theyr owne eſcape a victorie. On the hore not farre from the place where they ſuffered this misfortune, there is a tree, in the toppe wherof they ſet vp a croſſe, and graued this inſcription in the barke of the tree : *Vannuis Aldarieci*. There is a ryuer named Darien, on the banke wherof ſtandeth the chiefe citie of the ſuppoſed continent. The gouernour therfore hauing intelligence herof, ſent with all ſpeede two ſhippes of warre well furnyſhed, to the ayde of them that were lefte. But they were wyſe to lare. yet folowynge the viewe of the croſſe, they came to the hore and redde the letters grauen on the tree, but durſte not attempte fortune. Thus with all theyr hardie ſouldiers departinge from hence with deſpayre, they ſayled to the nexte Ilande, out of the which they caryed away by violence fyue hundreth men and women, ſuppoſynge lykewyſe that they myght lawfully ſo doo bycauſe they were Idolaters and circumciſed. But the like chaunce happened vnto them when they landed at Fernandina. For the Barbarians eſpyinge oportunitie, ſette vppon the Spaniardes in one of the ſhippes with theyr owne weapons and ſlewe theyr keepers. The reſidue that eſcaped, caſtynge them ſelues into the ſea, ſwamme to the nexte carauell, and with theyr felowes aſſayled the carauell that was taken from them. This conflicte was ſo ſharpe, that for the ſpace of foure houres, it was doubtfull whether parte ſhulde obteyne the victorie. The Barbarians both men and women fought verye fiercely, aſwell to recouer theyr libertie, as alſo to holde faſte the praye whiche they had gotten. But in fine, the Spanyardes had the vpper hande by reaſon they were more experte in handelynge of theyr weapons and rulyng of theyr Carauell. The Barbarians beinge thus ouercome, lepte into the ſea : but the Spanyardes tooke theym agayne with the ſhippe boates. About a hundreth of the Barbarians peryſhed, beinge partely drowned and partely ſlayne with the ſwoorde : And but fewe of the Spanyardes. Theſe thynges this

The chiefe citle of the ſuppoſed continent.

The Spanyardes are ſlayne ageyne with theyr owne wepōs.

The barbarious are ſlaine and put to flyght.

thus pacified, the refydue of the Barbarians were caryed to
the towne of Sanctiago and condemned to laboure in the golde
mynes. Shortly after they made owte a newe vyage to an o=
ther of the Ilandes, whiche lye there about fo thicke, that
they commonly caule the number of them Archipelagus, as they
in owre fea of Ionicum are cauled Symplegades. Here owre men
were cruelly handeled: and as many of them as came alande
eyther flayne or wounded. This Ilande they named Florida,
bycaufe they arryued there on Eafter day whiche the Spany=
ardes caule the floryftynge day of the refurrection. They fay
alfo that in this tracte they fawe xxvi. Ilandes which Colonus had ouerpaffed: And the fame fo to lye aboute Hifpaniola &
Cuba, as though they warded them from the furie of the Oce=
an. In many of thefe they founde natiue golde of lyke good=
nes to that which is founde in Granatum. Thinhabitantes al=
fo weare many iewels, and haue many Images of theyr do=
mefticall goddes made both of golde artificially wrought and
alfo of woodde gylted. Francis Chericatus browght one of
theyr Idoles with hym, wherby may bee confidered of what
wytte and aptenes they are. It is a marueluous thynge to fee
what maner of rafers they haue, made of certeyne yelowe
ftones cleare & tranfparent lyke vnto Cryftal. With thefe they
fhaue and carue as though they were made of fine fteele. Whē
the edges are blunte with longe exercife, they fharpen them
not with a whetftone, or powder, or any other ftone, but tem
per them onely with water. They haue alfo a thoufande kin
des of inftrumentes or tooles and fuch other thynges of tyne
denife, which were to longe to rehearfe. Let vs therefore re
turne from whenfe we haue digreffed, as to Cozumella, Iucatana,
Cozumana or Olloa, beinge al landes lately founde, and fo rich
frutefull and pleafaunt, that they may in maner be compared
to the earthly Paradyfe. Therfore, after that it was knowe
in to owre men of howe greate momente thefe trattes were,
the Spanyardes which inhabited the Ilande of Cuba Anunc=
tus beinge the gouernour of the Ilande furnyfhed a newe na
uie of ten Carauelles and fyue hundreth menne, with twoo
fmaule brigantines, as it weare in the fteade of lyght horfe=
men or forerunners whofe ayde they myght vfe as fcoutes to
fearche the wayes for daunger of rockes and fhalow fandes
or felfes. They fhipte alfo certeyne horfes, as fyue ftoned

horfes.

An other vy=
age.
Archipelagus.
A multitude
of Ilandes.

xxvi. Ilandes
about Hifpani=
ela & Cuba.

Images of
golde,

Rafers of
ftone.

Inftrumentes
and tooles.

Landes lyke
vnto thee arth
ly Paradyfe.

An other vy=
age of x. Cara
uels and a.
hundreth mē.

horfes and
mares.

horses and. xvi. mares apte for the warres. For their generall gouernour and Admiral of the nauy, they elected Fernando Cortesius who at that tyme was the chiefe ruler of the citie of Sanctiago. For vnder capitaines, they appointed Alfons Portucarerius, Francis Montegius, Alfons Auila, Aluerado Spatense John Velasquen, & Diegus Ordassus. They styll folowed the same wynde from the last angle of Cuba toward the west. As soone as Frauncis Fernandes of Corduba, and then John Grisalua came within prospecte of the Ilande of Sacrifyces (wherof we haue made mention before) soodenly a tempest of contrary wynde prohibited theym to take lande and drowe them backewarde to Coxumella lying on the East syde of Iucatana. This Ilande hath onely one hauen named sainte Johns porte. And hath in it, onely syxe townes. Also none other water then in welles and cesterns, bycause it lacketh riuers and springes by reason it is plaine, conteynynge onely. xlv. myles in circuite. At the coommynge of owre men, thinhabitauntes fledde to the thicke woods, & forsoke their townes for feare. Owre men entered into their houses where they founde plentie of vyttayles and many ornamentes perteynynge to the furnyshynge of their houses, as hanginges and carpettes of dyuers colours, sheetes also of gossampine cotton (whiche they caulle Amaccas) and muche apparell. They haue furthermore innumerable bookes, of the whiche with many other thynges sent to owre newe Emperour, we wyll speake more largely hereafter. The souldiers wandered about the Iland & biewe althynges diligently, kepyng them selues styll in battell raye least they myght be sodenly inuaded. They founde but a fewe of thinhabitauntes and onely one woman in their coompanie. By thinterpretours of Cuba and other whiche the Spaniardes tooke fyrst from Iucatana, they perswaded the woman to caule the kynges that were absente. They came gladly & made a league of frendshyp with owre men, wherby they were restored to their houses and a great parte of their stuffe. They are circumcised Idolatours, and sacrifyce children of bothe kyndes to their Zemes, which are the Images of their familiar and domesticall spirites whiche they honour as goddes. When I enquired of Alaminus the pilote, also of Frances Montegius and Portucarerius, from whense they had the children they offered in sacrifyce, they answered

Fernando Cortesius.

The Iland of Cozumella.

Carpets and sheetes.

Innumerable bokes.

Circumcised Idolaters.

They Sacrifice Chyldren

answered that they bowght them in the Ilandes theraboute
by exchaunge for golde and other of their trafycke. For in al
this so large a space of land, the deuelyshe anxietie for the desyre of wicked money, hath not yet oppressed thinhabitantes.
They saye the same also of the Ilandes lately founde, wherof two are named *Deslam* and *Sestam*, whose inhabitauntes go
naked: and for scarenesse of childʒen, sacrifice dogges whiche they nourishe aswell for that purpose as also to eate as
wee do connies. These dogges are dumme and can not barke,
hauynge snowtes lyke vnto foxes. Suche as they destinate
to eate, they geld while they are whelpes, wherby they waxe
very fat in the space of foure monethes. They reserue al the
bytches for increase, and but fewe dogges. Owre men dis-
swaded them from these superstitions, declarynge how they
were abhominable and detested of god. They were soone perswaded and despʒed a law whiche they myght folowe. Owre
men therfore declared vnto them that there was onely one
god which made heauen & earth, the geuer of al good thynges, beyng of one incompʒehensyble substaunce vnder triplicitie of person. As soone as they harde these woordes, they
bʒoke their *Zemes*, and pared, scraped, and washed the pauementes and waules of their temples. Owre men gaue them
a painted picture of the blessed vyrgine whiche they placed
reuerently in their temple, and aboue it a crosse to be honored in the remembʒaunce of god and man and the saluation
of mankynde. They erected also an other great crosse of wod
in the toppe of the temple, whyther they oftentymes resorte
togither to honour the Image of the vyrgine. Thinhabitantes signified by thinterpʒetours that in the Iland of *Iucatana*
not far from them, there were seue Chʒistians captiues which
in tyme past were dʒiuen thither by tempeste. The Ilande
of *Coxumella*, is onely fyue miles distant from *Iucatana*. The gouernour *Cortesus* being aduertised herof, furnyshed ii. Carauels
with fyftie me, wyllyng the incontinent to direct their viage
thither & to make serch for these me. They toke with the thʒe
interpʒetours of *Coxumella* (whose laguage agreeth with theirs
with letters to the Chʒistians if any myght be found. He further declared vnto theym howe goodly a matter they shoulde
bʒinge to passe if they coulde bʒinge away any of them. For
he no wayes doubted but that by their information, he shuld

The Ilandes
of Deslam &
Sestam.

Sacrifice of
dogges.

They are
soone persua
ded to owre
religion.

The picture
of the bles-
sed virgine

An other Vy-
age

be fully certified of the commodities of all those tractes, and the maners of thinhabitauntes. Thus they departed with commaundement to retourne within the space of syxe dayes. But when they had remayned there now. viii. dayes, and had no woozde of their Cozumellane interpzeteours whome they had sent alande with the message and letters, owre men returned to *Cozumella* without them, suspectyng that they were other slaine oz deteyned. And where as the hole nauye was now determyned to depart from *Cozumella*, but that they were hyndered by contrary wynde, they sodenly espied towarde the weste a Canoa coommynge from *Iucatana*, and in it, one of the Christian captiues (named *Hieronimus Aquillaris*) who had lyued seuen yeares in that Ilande. With what ioye they embzased the one the other, the chance may declare. They were no lesse desyrous to heare, then he to tell of the mysfoztune whiche befell to hym and his coompanions. And here, it shal not bee greatly from my purpose bzeesely to rehearse how the thynge chaunced. In my Decades I haue made mention of a certayne noble man named *Valdiuia*, whome the Spanyardes whiche inhabited *Dariena* in the supposed continente of the goulf of *Vraba*, sent to the Iland of *Hispaniola* to *Colonus* the Admiral and vieroy with the residue of the Senate and counsel there (to whom perteyneth the redzesse and ozderynge of all thinges in these newe landes) to sygnifye vnto them in what extreme necessitie and penurie they lyued. Vnhappy *Valdiuia* therfore, takyn ge this matter in hand in an euell houre, was with a sudden and vyolent whirlewinde, dzyuen vppon certayne quickesandes in the pzospecte of the Ilande of *Iamaica*, lyinge on the South syde of *Hispaniola* and *Cuba*. These blind and swalowyng sandes, the Spaniardes caule vypers: And that by good reason, bycause in them many shyppes are entangled, as the lycertes are implycate in the tayles of the vypers. While the Carauell thus wzestled with the water, it was so bzaste in sunder, that *Valdiuia* with thirtie of his felowes, coulde scarsely with muche difficultie descende into the shyppe boate: where, without oers, and without sayles, they were caried awaye by the vyolence of the water. Foz (as we haue said befoze in owre Decades) the seas do runne there continually with a vyolent course towarde the West. They wandered thus, xiii. dayes not knowyng whyther they went

no)

Aquillaris, vii. yeares captiue in the Iland of Iucatana.

Valdiuia.

The shipwracke of Valdiuia.

The quicke sandes cauled vypers.

The course of the sea towarde the west.

not yet fyndynge any thyng to eate. Famen consumed seuen of them whiche were caste in the sea to feede the fyshes. The respdue lykewise in maner consumed by famen and faulynge from one calamitie into an other, were dʒiuen to *Iucatana* and fell into the handes of a cruell kynge who slewe *Valdiuia* the gouernour with certayne of his felowes. And when hee had fyʒst sacrifyced them to his *Zemes*, shoʒtely after he eate them with his frindes of that conspiracie. Foʒ they eate onely their enempes and straungiers: And doo otherwise absteyne from mannes fleshe. In this meane tyme, while *Hieronimus Aquillaris* with fyre of his felowes were reserued to be sacrifyced the thirde daye, they bʒooke their bandes, escaped the handes of that cruell tyranne, and fledde to an other kynge be= ynge his enempe, who receaued them, yet onely as bonde= men. It is a straunge thinge to heare of the moother of this *Aquillaris*. Foʒ as soone as she harde that her soonne was fau= len into the handes of the nations that eate mannes fleshe, shee fell madde incontinent: So that when so euer after, shee sawe any meate rostyng at the fyer, oʒ onely ready spytted to laye to the fyer, shee ceased not to crye out in this maner. O me moste wʒetched moother: Behold the members of my son. But to returne to owre purpose. When *Aquillaris* had now re= ceaued the gouernours letter sente by the Coʒumellane mes= sengers, hee declared to the kynge his mayster (whose name was *Taxmarus*) what was their erraunt thither, and wherfoʒe they were sent: vsyng in the meane tyme many large discour= ses in expressynge the great poure and magnifycence of their kynge who had of late arriued in those coastes. Also of their humanitie and gentilnesse toward their frindes and suche as submytted them selues to them, and againe their rygour and fiercenesse agepnst suche as stoobernly eyther contemned them oʒ denyed their requestes. With these woordes he bʒoughte *Taxmarus* into suche feare, that the mayster was now fayne to despre his seruaunt so to handell the matter that they myght quyetly enter into his dominion as his freendes and not as his enemies. *Aquillaris* pʒomised in their behalfe that they shuld not onely coome in peace, but also to ayde hym agepnst his enemyes if neede shulde so require. Wheruppon hee dismissed *Aquillaris* and with hym thʒee of his familiers and coompani= ons. Thus they sayled together from *Coʒumella* to *Iucatana* to

Ualdiuia is sacrificed to Idoles.

Howe Aquil= laris escaped

kynge Taxz marus.

the ryuer whiche they had founde before in the fyrste vyage thither by the gouernaunce of Alaminus the pilot. They found the mouthe of the ryuer stopped with sande, as wee reade of the ryuer of Nilus in Egipte when the wyndes (cauled Etesi) blowe in summer and especially in the canicular dayes. Therfore where as they coulde not enter into the ryuer with the biggeste vessells (although it bee otherwise apte to receaue great shyppes) the gouernour caused two hundreth men to be sette alande with the brigantynes and shyppe boates: wyllynge Aquillaris to offer peace to thinhabitauntes. They demaunded what owre men required. Aquillaris answered, vyttayles. There was a longe space of sande by the syde of the

towne, whither they wylled them to resorte, promysynge to brynge them vyttayles thither the daye folowynge. Owre men wente and they came accordynge to their promisse and brought with them eyght of their hennes beynge as bygge as peacockes, of brownyshe coloure, and not inferiour to peacockes in pleasaunte tast. They brought also as muche bread made of Maizium (whiche is a graine not muche vnlyke vnto panyke) as wolde scarcely serue tenne hungry men: And here with desyred them to departe. But when they perceaued that owre men made no hast away, immediately there came a great coompanye of armed men towarde theym demaundyng what they had to do thus to wander in other mennes landes. Owre men made answere by Aquillaris, that they desyred peace, vyttayles, and golde for exchaunge of other thinges. They answered agyene, that they wolde nother peace nor warre with them. But threatned them to auoyde the lande excepte they woolde bee distroyed euery manne. Owre men sayde that they woulde not departe withowte suffyciente vyttayles to mayntayne their souldyers.

They appoynted the day folowynge to brynge them more vyttayles: but they brooke promisse. yet perceauing the second day that owre men were encamped on the sande and had reposed there that nyght, they brought them as much more vyttayles, and commaunded them in the name of theyr kynge to departe. Owre men sayde that they were desyrous to see the towne, and to haue yet more store of vyttayles. The Barbarians denyed theyr request, and therewith departed whispperynge and muttterynge amonge them selues. In the meane tyme

ryme owre men were styll so oppressed with hunger that they
were enforced to seeke for meate. The gouernoure therefore
sent his vnder capitaynes to lande with a hundreth and fyf=
tic men. As they went disperled in dyuers companyes about
the vyllages of the countrey, the Barbarians met with one
of theyr bandes, and put them to great distresse. But when
theyr felowes beinge not farre from them, harde the noyle of
theyr alarome, they came with all possible haste to theyr res=
cue. The gouernour on the other syde, placinge his ordinance
in the brygantines and shippe boates, approched to the
shore with the residue of his souldiers. The Barbarians
lykewise, beinge redy furnyshed to the battayle, came run=
nynge to the sea syde to disturbe theym that they shulde not
coome alande: And with theyr arrowes, wounded manye a
farre of vnprepared. The gouernoure discharged aboute .xx.
pieces of ordinaunce ageynste them: With the slaughter and
terrible thunder, wherof, & with the flame of fyer and smel of
brimstone, they were so astonished and put to such feare, that
they fled and disparcled lyke wylde beastes: whom owre men
perluinge, entred into the towne which thinhabitantes for=
sooke in maner for feare of theyr owne men whom they sawe
so dismayde. On the banke of this ryuer there is a towne of
such portentous byggenes as I dare not speake. But *Alami=
nus* the pylot, sayth that it conteyneth in circuite fyue hun=
dreth myles, and that it consisteth of .xxv. thousande houses.
Sume make it sumwhat lesse: But they all agree that it is
exceadynge great and notable. The houses are diuided with
gardens, and are buylded of lyme and stone verye artificially
and of cunnynge woorkemanshippe. To theyr haules, cham=
bers, parlers, or other places of habitation, they alcende by
tenne or twelue steares: And haue certeyne spaces betwene
euery house: so that it is not lawful for any to lade his neigh
bours waules with rafters or beames. Theyr houses are sepe
rate one from an other by the space of thre houses: And are
for the more parte couered with reede and thetche: And ma=
ny also with slate or other stone. The barbarians them selues
confessed that they were that day fortie thousande men at the
battayle, which were vanquished of a fewe by reason of the
newe and vnknowen kynde of feyght with gunnes and hor=
ses. For the gouernour had vnbarked .xvi. horses which were
at o

A conflicte.

The Barba=
rians are put
to flyght.

The great
towne of Pos
tantxana or
Uictoria.
A towne of
xxv. thousad
houses.

Gunnes and
horses.

also at the battayle, and so fiercely assayled the Barbarians on the backehalfe, that they brake their array and scattered them as it had byn flockes of sheepe, ouerthrowing, woundynge, and kyllynge them on euery syde. Whiche thynge the seely wretches so imputed to a miracle, that they had not the poure to occupie their wepons. For wheras before they had neuer seene any horses, they thought that the man on horse:backe and the horse, had byn all one beaste, as the antiquitie dyd fable of the monster *Centaurus.* Owr men possessed the towne. xxii. dayes where they made good chere vnder couert, whyle the owners of the houses lay vnder the firmament and durst not assayle owre men who had placed them selues in the strongest parte of the towne, where sume kepte continuall watche (least the Barbarians shulde soodenly inuade theim) whyle other gaue them selues to reste and sleepe. Thinhabitantes caule this towne *Potanchana:* But owre men for the victorie which they obteyned here, named it *Victoria.* It is a maruelous thynge to consider the greatenes, magnificence and finenes of the buyldinge of certeyne palaices they haue in the countrey to the which they resorte sumtymes for their solace and pastyme. These are curiously buylded with many pleasaunt diuises, as galeries, solars, turrettes, portals, gutters with chambers boorded after the maner of owre waynscotte and well flowred. Foure of owr Spanyardes went into one of them of such greatnes, that they wandered in the same for the space of foure houres before they coulde fynde the waye owt. At the length by thinterpretours and certeyne captiues owre men sent for the kynge and suche rulers as were nexte vnder hym in autoritie, wyllyng them to submyt them selues and to coome into the towne vnarmed. Gyuinge the messengers further in commaundement to certifie them that in their so doinge, they wolde commen with them as concernynge conditions of peace, and restore them their towne. They came gladly, and entered euery man into his owne house vppon condition that they shulde euer thereafter absteyne from such ceremonies and horrible sacrifices of mans flesshe to deuils the mortal enemies to mankynd, whose Images they honoured. And to directe the eyes of their myndes to Christe owre god the maker of heauen and earth, who was borne into this worlde of a virgin, and suffered death on the crosse for there:demption

The man & the horse, thought to be one beast.

Centaurus.

Palaices of maruelous bygnes and wel buylded.

They receue owre religio.

demption of mankynde. And fynally to profeſſe them ſelues
ſubiectes to the great Chꝛiſtian kynge of Spayne. They pꝛo-
mpſed both, and were inſtructed as farre as the ſhoꝛtenes of
tyme wolde permitte. Beinge thus reſtoꝛed, they recompenſed owre men with many rewardes: Suppoſynge ſuche men
to be ſent from heauen, which being ſo fewe in number, durſt
attempte battayle ageynſt ſo great a multitude. They gaue
owre men alſo certeyne golde and twentie ſlaues. Departing
therefoꝛe from henſe, and coaſtynge ſtyll alonge by the ſame
ſhoꝛe, they came ageyne to the goulſe whiche _Alaminus_ the pylot founde befoꝛe vnder _Griſalua_. This they named _Bian Sancti_
Iohannis, that is, Saynt Johns goulſe: Foꝛ _Bian_ in the Spanyſhe tonge ſignifieth a goulſe. Here thinhabitantes reſoꝛted to them peaceably. Aboute a myle frome the ſhoꝛe, was a
towne of a thouſande and fyue hundꝛeth houſes ſituate vppon a hyll. They pꝛofered owre men halfe the towne if they
wolde dwel with them foꝛ euer. This perhaps they dyd the
rather eyther fearynge the exemꝑle of thinhabitantes of _Potan-_
chana, the fame wherof myght haue coome to theyꝛ eares, oꝛ
els hopynge that vnder the ſhadowe of ſuche valiant menne,
they myght obteyne ayde and ſuccour ageynſt theyꝛ enemies
and boꝛtherers. Foꝛ (as I haue ſayde befoꝛe) they dyſtroye
one an other with continuall warre foꝛ the deſyꝛe to inlarge
theyꝛ dominions. Owre men refuſed perpetuall habitacion,
and accepted theyꝛ frendely pꝛofer foꝛ a tyme. As they came
alande, the people folowed them on euery ſyde with bowwes
in theyꝛ handes which they helde ouer owre mens heades to
defende them from the rayne as though they had walked in a
continual arbour. Here they encamped. And leaſt the reſidue
lefte in the ſhippes, ſhulde in the meane tyme waxe ſlothefull
with Idlenes, the gouernour gaue commaundement to _Alami-_
_us_ the pylot and Francis Montegius to ſearch the weſt partes of that lande, whyle he relieued the weried ſouldiers and
healed ſuche as were wounded. To them that went foꝛward
on this vyage, he aſſigned two bꝛigantines with fiftie men.
Vnto this goulſe, the courſe of the water was gentyl enough
and moderate. But when they had ſayled a lyttle further to
warde the Weſte, they founde the ſea runnynge with ſo ſwift
a courſe as if it were a great ryuer faulynge from the tops of
hygh mountaynes: In ſo much that in a ſhoꝛte ſpace of tyme
it caried

A towne of a
thouſand τ
fyue hundꝛed
houſes.

An other vy-
age of two
bꝛigantines
τ fiftie men.

where the
ſea runneth
ſwyftly from
the Eaſt to
the Weſt.

A conflict be=
twene the wa
ters cominge
fromthe west
and from the
south.

ſt caried them fiftie myles from theyr felowes. When they
were now entered into this violent ſtreame of the water, they
ſawe on their left hand a large playne ſea which mette with
the courſe of the other waters faulynge from the weſte. And
lyke as two great ryuers that runne contrary wayes, make a
vehement conflycte where they meete, ſo ſeemed the waters
commyng from the Southe to reſyſt theſe waters as enemyes
that had entered into the ryght or poſſeſſyon of an other.
On the contrary parte, they ſawe the lande reachynge farre
bothe on the lefte hande and on the ryght. In this ſtrife be=
twene the waters, they were ſo toſſed on bothe ſydes and
entangled with whirlepooles, that they longe wreſtled with=
owte hope of lyfe. At the length with muche difficultie, tur=
nynge the ſtemmes or forpartes of their ſhyppes agaynſt the
ſtreame from whenſe they came, and labourynge al that they
myght with their oers and ſayles, they coulde ſcarſely ouer
codme the rage of the water : In ſo much that where as they
thought that they had in one nyght ſayled twoo myles, they
founde that they were dryuen backe foure myles. yet at the
length with goddes helpe, they ouercame this daungerous
conflycte. They ſpente. xxii. daies in this lyttle ſpace of ſea.
And when they were nowe returned to their felowes, decla=
red vnto them that that ende was the land of Colluacana whi=
che they adiudged to be parte of the ſuppoſed continent. The
lande whiche they ſawe a farre of before their face, they ſup=
poſe eyther to be annexed to owre continent, or to bee ioyned
to the large North regions cauled Baccalsos, wherof we haue
made mention in owr Decades in the vyage of Sebaſtian Ca=
bote. This matter is yet doubtefull. But wee truſte it ſhall
once bee better knowen. While Alaminus and Montegius
ſearched theſe ſecreates, the kynge of the prouince (whoſe
name was Multoxuman) ſent owre men by one of his chiefe of=
fycers (beynge alſo his Lieutenaunt of the ſayde towne) ma=
ny ryche and goodly preſentes of golde, ſyluer, and precious
ſtoones, ſette and wroughte after a marueylous ſtraunge de=
uyſe and with no leſſe cunnynge woorkemanſhyp. Here they
determined to ſende meſſengiers to owre newe Emperour
to knowe his pleaſure that they myght in this prouince plant
a newe colonie or habitation. And this dyd they withowte
thaduiſe of Diegus Vehiſquen the gouernour of the Iland of Cub=

A dangerous
and peinefull
vyage.

The land of
Colluacana.

The land of
Baccallos or
Baccalearum

Rych preſen=
tes of golde
and precious
ſtones.

Fernandina, who fyrſte ſente them foorth with commaundemēt to returne agepne after they had ſearched theſe regions and obtepned plentie of golde. While they conſulted hereof, they were of dyuers opinions. But the moſte part alleaged that in this caſe it was not requiſyte to make the gouernour of their counſaile. Forasmuche as the matter ſhulde be referred to a higher Judge, as to the kyng of Spaine him ſelfe. When they were thus agreed, they receaued byttayles of the gentle kyng of the prouince, and aſſigned the place of their colonie twelue myples from the ſayde towne, in a frutefull and hollome ſoile. For their generall gouernour, they elected *Corteſſus* the gouernour of the nauye, againſt his wyll as ſum ſaye. For other magiſtrates to gouerne the citie which they intended to build he chooſe Portucarerius and Montegius of whome we haue made mention befoze. They choſe alſo certepne meſſengiers to ſende to the kyng by the conduction of *Alaminus* the pylor. Furthermoze, foure of the princes of this prouince offered them ſelues wyllyngly to go with owre men into Spaine to thintent to ſee owre landes and that kynge whoſe poure is ſoo great and whoſe auctozitie reacheth ſo farre. They bzought lykewiſe two women with them, which ſerued & obeied them in all thinges after the maner of theyr countrey. The people of this nation is of bzoune oz yelowyſhe colour. Bothe the men and the women haue pendauntes of gold and pzecious ſtones hanginge at their eares. The men alſo, booze their nether lyppes full of holes from the vppermoſte parte of the lyppe euen vnto the nethermoſte parte of the gumme. At theſe they hange certepne rynges and plates of golde and ſyluer faſtned to a ſmaule and thynne plate lyinge within betwene the lippe and the gumme. At the byggeſt hole in the myddeſt of the lip, there hangeth a rounde plate of ſyluer as bzode as the coyne cauled a Cozolyne, and as thicke as a mannes fynger. I do not remember that euer J ſawe any thinge that ſeemed moze ſylthy in myne eye. Yet do they thynke that there is nothing moze cumly vnder the circle of the moone. Wherby we may ſee howe bainely mankynde wandereth in his owne blyndneſſe. The Ethiopian thinketh the blacke colour to be fayzer then the white: And the white man thinketh otherwiſe. They that are pouled, thinke that moze decent then to weare a buſh and they that weare beardes, iudge it a defozmitie to be ſhauen.

S ſ

A newe colonie.

This Corteſſus hath written a booke of theſe thinges

They weare rynges and plates at theỉ lyppes.

The dyuers phantaſies of men.

yen. As appetite therfore moueth, and not as reason perswadeth, men runne after vanities : And euery prouynce is ruled by their owne sense, as wryteth saint Ierome. From whense they haue their golde, we haue spoken sufficiently before. But as owre men maruepled where they had their syluer, they shewed them certayne high mountaynes whiche are continually couered with snowe sauynge that at certeyne tymes of the yeare, the onely toppes are seene bare bicause the snow is there molten by reason of the thicke and warme cloudes. The playnes therfore, or mylde, softe, and pleasaunt mountaynes seeme to brynge foorth the golde : And the rough craggye mountaynes with their coulde valleyes, are the places where syluer is engendered. They haue also laton, wherof they make such maces and hammers as are vsed in the warres. Dyggynge matiockes also, and spades : for they haue nother Iren nor steele. But lette vs nowe speake of the presentes sent into Spayne to the kyng : and fyrste of the bokes These procuratours therfore of the newe colonie of the prouynce of *Colluacana*, emong other their presentes, brought also a great number of bookes, the leaues wherof are made of the inner ryndes or barkes of trees, thinner then eyther that of the elme or of the salowe. These they smere or annoint with the pytche of molten *Bitumen*, and while they be softe, extend them to what forme them lysteth. When they be coulde and harde, they rubbe them ouer with a certeyne playster. It is to bee thoughte that they beate the playster into fine floure, and so temperynge it with sum byndynge moister, to make a crusse therwith vppon the leaues, wheron they wryte with any sharpe instrument, and blotte the same againe with a spunge or sum suche other thynge, as marchaunt men and noble mens stewardes are accustomed to do with their wrytynge tables made of the woodde of fygge trees. The leaues of their bokes are not set in order after the maner of owres, but are extended many cubettes in length. The matters whiche they wryte, are conteyned in square tables : Not loose, but so bounde togither with the toughe and flexible cley called *Bitumen*, that they seeme lyke woodden tables whiche had byn vnder the handes of cunnyng bokebynders. Which way so euer the booke lyeth open, there are two leaues seene and two sydes wrytten, with as many lyinge hyd vnder them, except the booke be vnfoulded in length. For vnder one leafe there are many leaues ioyned togyther. The formes of their letters are nothynge lyke vnto owres. But are muche more crooked and entangeled, lyke vnto fysshehookes, knottes, snares, starres, dise, fyles, and suche other muche lyke vnto the Egiptian letters, and written in lynes lyke vnto owres. Here and there betwene the lynes, are pictured the shapes of men & dyuers beastes: And especially the Images of kynges and other noble men. Wherby it is to be thought that in suche bookes, the factes of their kynges are conteyned, as wee see the lyke emonge vs howe owre printers expresse the summe of histories in pictures, that men may therby be the more allured to bye suche bookes. The couerynges of their bookes are also artifycially wrought and paynted. When they are outte, they seeme to differre nothynge from owres in forme. In these bookes are furthermore comprehended their lawes, rytes of ceremonies and sacrifyces, annotations of Astronomie, accomptes, computations of tymes, with the maner of graffynge, sowyng, and other thynges perteinyng to husandry. They begynne the yeare from the goynge downe of the seuen starres cauled *Vergiliæ* or *Pleiades*: And counte theyr monethes accordyng to the moones. They name a moneth, *tona*, of the moone. For in theyr language, they caule the moone *Tona*, they reken the dayes by the soonnes. Therfore as many daies as they name, they saye, so many soonnes. The soonne in their tonge, is cauled *Tonatico*. They destribute the yeare (without any reason why) into twentie monethes: And the moneth into as many dayes. The temples whiche they frequent, they adourne with golden hangynges and other ornamentes of golde and syluer with precious stones intermixte. At the spryng of the daye, they perfume their temples with frankensence and make their praiers before they take in hande any other busynesse. But oh horrible crueltie. For thinhabitauntes of all these tractes also, doo sacrifyce children to their Idoles in lyke maner as wee haue sayde before. At suche tyme as the seedes lye in the ground, and when the corne begynneth to shewe foorth the eare, they destinate to their *Zemes* suche bondmen as they haue bought, or suche captiues as they haue taken in the warres, which they sacrifyce after that they haue made them great chiere and decked them in precious apparell. Also before they sacrifyce these

Theyr letters

What is conteyned in theyr bookes.

Temples rychly adourned.

Prayer.

They sacrifyce chyldren & captyues.

A wronge way to heaue

poore wretches, they lead them about the towne whyle al the people salute them humbly and reuerently, affyrmyng that in shorte space, they shalbe receaued into the coompanye of the goddes. They honour their _Zemes_ with an other sharp kind

Bluddy gods

of deuotion: For they lette them selues bludde, eyther in the tonge, lyps, eares legges, thyghes, or brest, which they take in their handes and hurle it vppe towarde heauen, soo that with the faule therof the pauement of the temple is all spar-cled with bludde, wherby they thincke that their goddes are well pleased. From the newe colonie (cauled _Villa Ricca_) nyne

Villa Ricca.

myles distante, there is a towne of. xv. thousande houses. whiche thinhabitauntes caule _Cemobal_, but owre men named

Siuilla Noua.

it _Sybilla_. The kynge of this towne had fyue men whiche he reserued to be sacrifyced. Whom when owre men wold haue delyuered, the kynge made humble request to them, sayinge that if they tooke awaye suche men as he had consecrated to

The force of an owlde errour.

be offered to the goddes, they shulde brynge vtter destruction to hym and all his kyngdome. For if owre sacrifyces (sayth he) do cease, owre _Zemes_ wyll take suche displeasure with vs that they wyll suffer owre corne, graffes, and frutes, to bee consumed of woormes, scortched with drowth, destroyed with fluddes, or blasted with lyghtnynge. Owre men per-ceauynge his ernestnesse herein, thought it beste to chose the leaste euel, perceauynge that it was yet no tyme to disquyet their myndes, and therfore suffered them to exercise their ac-customed ceremonies. And althoughe their priestes prompte theym immortall glorie, eternall felicytie, and perpetuall conuersation with the goddes after the stormye dayes of this

Theyr priestes lyue chaste.

lyfe, yet do they with heauy countenaunces giue eare to theyr promisses, and had rather be sette at lybertie. Their priestes are named _Quines_ in the plurell number, and _Quin_ in the syn-gular. They leade a pure and chaste lyfe: And are honoured

Faggots of bones.

of the people with feare and reuerence. They make fagots of the bones of their enemyes which they haue taken in the war-res, and hange vppe the same at the feete of their _Zemes_, as tokens of the victories obteyned by their fauour. To these they adde certayne titles and superscriptions as testimonies of the same. This is straunge and woorthy to be noted, that when their children are a yeare oulde, the priestes in their temples with deuoute ceremonies and murmurynge woordes,

por

The thyrde decade. 163

oure water in forme of a crosse vpon their heades with a
cruet, wherby they seeme to baptise them. Neyther do they
as the Iewes and Turkes, thinke their temples polluted if
any of a straunge relygion bee present at their sacrifyces and
other solemnities. Wee haue nowe spoken suffycientely of
their bookes, temples, and superstitions. Lette vs nowe
herfore coome to the other presentes which were brought
to the kynge. Emonge these, there were twoo broode and
rounde plates (whiche summe haue named the Images of
the soonne and moone) the one of siluer and the other of gold
in largenesse and roundnesse muche lyke to the stones of hand
mylles: yet but thynne, and in maner bothe of one circumference, that is xxviii spannes in circuite.
That of golde is of the weyght of three thousande and .viii.
hundreth Castellans, where as wee haue sayde before that a
Castellane is a coyne of golde which weyeth more then a Ducate by a trient, that is the thyrde parte of a pounde. In the
center of this, was the Image of a kynge of halfe a cubette
longe, syttinge in a trone and appareled to the knee, lyke vnto a maumette, with such countenaunce as other paynters are
wonte to paynte fayries or sprites. About the Image, were
the shapes of trees and floures, so that it seemed to sytte as
though it had byn in a fielde. The other of syluer, was made
to the same similitude, beinge also in maner of the same
weyght, and both of pure metall. They brought lykewyse
certeyne graynes of rude golde (that is, suche as was neuer
molten) about the byggenes of fytches or the pulse cauled lin-
tels in token of plentie of natiue golde. Also two cheynes of
golde, wherof the one conteyned .viii. lynkes in the whiche
were set two hundreth threescore and twoo fayre and cleare
redde stones, and yet no rubyes: furthermore, a hundrethe
fourescore and three greene stones, and yet no emerodes. Neuerthelesse, these are in lyke estimation with them as the o-
ther are with vs. At the edge of this cheine, there hange xxvii
golden belles, haupnge betwene euery of them, foure iewels
of precious stones inclosed in golde, at euery of the which in
lyke maner hange certeyne spangels of golde. The other
cheyne consisteth onely of foure golden lynkes, beset rounde
about with a hundreth and two redde stones, and a hundreth
threescore and twelue greene stones, with xxvi. golden belles
curiously

A fygure of
baptisme.

The presen-
tes sent into
Spayne to
the kynge.
Two Images
of gold and
syluer.

Two cheines
of gold mar-
ueilously byset
with precious
stones and
iewels.

curiouſly wꝛought and placed in comely oꝛder. In the very
myddeſt of the cheyne, are ten great pꝛecious ſtones incloſed
in golde, at the whiche alſo hange a hundꝛethe golden pen
dauntes of cunnynge woorkeman ſhippe. They bꝛought fur
thermoꝛe twelue paire of lether buſkynnes of diuers colours
ſumme imbꝛothered with gold and ſumme with ſyluer, wit
plates and iewelles of golde and pꝛecious ſtones incloſed
and at euery of them certayne golden belles. Alſo certeyn
myters beſetて with pꝛecious ſtoones of dyuerſe colours
emonge the whiche ſume are blewe like vnto ſaphires. ɔ
creſſes, gerdles, and fannes made of fethers, I wotte no
what I ſhulde ſaye. But ſurely if euer the wyttes and inuen
tions of men haue deſerued honoure oꝛ comendacion in ſuch
artes, theſe ſeeme moſte woorthy to bee had in admiracion.
I do not maruaile at golde and pꝛecious ſtones. But am in
maner aſtonyſhed to ſee the woorkemanſhyppe excell the ſub
ſtance. For I haue with woonderynge eyes behelde a thou
ſande foꝛmes and ſimilitudes, of the which I am not able t
wꝛite. And in my iudgement, I neuer ſawe any thing whoſ
bewtie myght ſo allure the eyes of men. As they maruepled
at the naturall bewtie of the fethers of owre peacockes and
pheaſantes, ſo dyd we no leſſe maruel at the artifycial bewtie
of ſuche thinges as they make of fethers and quilles impaled
with golde. For I ſawe in manye of their woorkes, all ma
ner of natiue colours euen in the quilles wherof they make
ſuche inſtrumentes. They bꝛought alſo two helmettes gar
nyſſhed with pꝛecious ſtones of a whiteſh blewe colour. One
of theſe is edged with belles and plates of golde, and vnder
euery bell two knobbes of golde. The other, beſyde the ſto
nes wherwith it is couered, is lykewyſe edged with. xxv.
golden belles and knobbes: ꝑ hath on the creſt, a greene bird
with the feete, bylle, and eyes, of golde. Alſo foure ſpeares
muche lyke vnto troute ſpeares oꝛ yele ſpeares, the woodde
wherof is all couered with quilles of diuers colours maruai
louſly wrethed with golden wyers and plates intermyptて.
Euery of theſe ſpeares haue thꝛee pikes, whoſe edges oꝛ teeth
are all of pꝛecious ſtones made faſte with wyers of golde. Of
like woorkmanſhip they bꝛought a great ſcepter byſet with pꝛe
cious ſtoones and belles of gold, alſo a bꝛaſlet of gold, and
ſhowes made of a hartes ſkynne, ſowed b imbꝛothered with
wiers,

Marginal notes (left column):

Buſkyns.

wyers.

how can we
then caul the
beaſtly oꝛ
Barbarous.

If they had
chaged their
gold foꝛ owre
Irē, they had
not ſo ſoone
byn ſubdued.
Quylles.

helmets.

A byꝛde.

Speares.

A ſcepter.
A bꝛaſelet.
Shooes.

golde wyers, with a white sole beneth. Furthermore a glasse
of a bright blewe stone, and an other of white, both encloſed
in golde. Likewiſe a precious ſtone of the kynde of them that
are cauled Sphinges, incloſed in golde. Furthermore the heade
of a great lyſarde, two great welles, two duckes, the ſhapes
of diuers other byrdes, foules, and fylſhes, and all of maſſie
golde. Furthermore. xxiiii. rounde and ſquare targettes,
ſheldes, and buckelers of golde, and fyue of ſyluer. Alſo a
triple crowne of plates and wyers of golde marueylouſlye
wreathed with quilles and fethers of diuers colours, hauing
in the fronte a plate of golde on the whiche is grauen the I=
mage of the Idole Zemes. About this Image, hange foure
other plates like croſſes of golde in the whiche are grauen the
heades of diuers beaſtes, as lyons, tigers, woulues, and ſuch
other. They brought alſo the ſymilitudes of certeyne bea=
ſtes made ſumme of roddes or twygges, and ſum of woodde
with the beaſtes owne ſkynnes theron, and garnyſſhed with
collers of laton belles. Lykewiſe diuers ſhirtes weaued of
goſſampyne cotton of ſundry colours, wherof two are ryche=
ly frynged with golde and precious ſtones, and three other
with quilles and fethers intermyxte with goſſampine cotton
of ſundrye colours and chekered lyke the panes of a cheſſe
olde. Sum are on the one ſyde, of blacke, white, and redde
colours : and on the other ſyde, plaine without any varietie.
Other ſum, are wrought in lyke maner with variable colours
with a wheele or circle of blacke in the myddeſt intermyxte
with ſhyning fethers and ſparkes of golde lyke ſtarres. They
brought alſo cloth of Aras or Verdure of marueylous worke=
manſhyppe. Lekewiſe a ſouldiers cloke ſuche as their pryn=
ces weare in the warres, with certeyne pryue coates of fence,
and ſundrye tirementes perteynyng to their heades, with al=
ſo many ſuche other thynges more bewtifull to the eye then
riche or precious, wherof to entreate particularly, it ſhoulde
be more tedious then profytable. I lette paſſe here alſo to
ſpeake of many particular nauigations and of the trauailes
and daungers whiche they ſuſteyned in the ſame, with the
wonders and ſecreates of nature they ſawe: whiche are all
conteyned in the regeſters of owr Senate of chaffayres of
India, owte of the whiche I haue ſelected theſe fewe anno=
tations, ſuche as ſeemed to me moſte meete to bee publiſſhd.

Not

Margin notes:

Glaſſes.

Byrdes, fou=
les, & fyſſhes
of golde.
Targets. &c.
of gold.
A crowne of
golde.

Croſſes.

Images of
beaſts.
Shietes.

Cloth of ar=
ras.
A ſouldyers
clocke.

Regiſters of
chaffayres of
India.

Notwithstandyng these ryche and goodly presentes, yet we
they that brought them, and also *Cortesius* the gouernour
the natiue and autour of errectinge their newe colonie in tho
remiote regions, adiudged by the Senate to haue doen agein
ryght and equitie, in that they attempted the same withow
thaduice of the gouernour of the Ilande of *Cuba* who sen
them foorthe by the kynges auctoritie, where as they d
other thinges besyde their commyssyon, ye althoughe th
wente to the kynge, not fyrst knowynge his pleasure who
the kyng had substitute his Lieuetenaunt in that Ilande. I
so muche that by his procuratour, he accused them before t
Senate as fugitiue theeues and traytours. They on the oth
parte alleaged, that they had doon the kyng better scrup
then he: And that they had shewed suffycient obedience
appealyng to the kyng as the hygher Iudge. But the gou
nour required by the vertue of his commission and the king
letters pattentes that they myght be headed for their disob
dience ageinst hym whom they knewe to be autorised by t
kynge. They ageine replied that they had not offended t
kyng, but rather deserued rewarde for their great dange
and trauasses. Bothe the rewarde and punishment were d
ferred, and a daye appointed when bothe parties shoulde b
hardt. Leete vs nowe therfore coome to the Spaniardes
Dariena, thinhabitours of the goulfe of *Vraba* in the suppos
Continent. We haue sayde before that *Dariena* is a ryuer ru
nynge towarde the Weste syde of the goulfe of *Vraba*. On th
banke of this ryuer, the Spaniardes planted their fyrst col
nie or habitation after they had vanquished kynge *Chemaccu*
This colonie they named *Sancta Maria Antiqua*, by reason of
vowe whiche they made to the virgine Marie in the tyme
the battaile ageynst *Chemsecus*. To these (as wee haue ma
mention in the ende of owre decades) was *Petrus Arias* sen
with a thousande and two hundreth men at the request of V
chus Nunnez Balboa, who was then the gouernour of *Dariena*, a
the fyrst that found and discouered the large South sea her
tofore vnknowen. Wee haue also declared how at the arriu
of *Petrus Arias* the newe gouernour, he deuided his armye in
Centurions, that is, capitaines ouer hundrethes, whom h
sent foorth dyuers waies. What tragedies folowed herec
I wyll absolue in fewe woordes, bycause all are horrible a
vnpleasa

Thautoritie
of the Lieue-
tenaunt.

The Spany-
ardes of Da-
riena.

Sancta Maria
Antiqua.

Petrus Arias
whom the
Spanyardes
name pedra-
rias.
This sea the
spanyardes
caule Mardel
sur.

npleasaunte. For sence we fynyshed owre Decades, there
ath byn none other then kyllynge, fleyinge, murtherynge
nd accusinge. The kynge made Vaschus gouernoure but du:
ynge his pleasure. His courage was such, and his factes so
otozious, that he coulde not longe abyde the hautynes of Pe
us Arias. To bee breefe, theyr faulynge owte and discozd con
ounded al thynges. John Cacedus the pulpitte fryer of the
der of saynt Frances, dyd his vttermoste endeuour to make
hem frendes, promysynge vnto Vaschus the dowghter of Petrus
rias to wyfe. But no meanes coulde be founde howe these
wo whiche boze the chiefe rule, myght bee bzought to agree:
ent. At the length the matter grewe to such extremitie, that
trus Arias fyndynge occasion of querelynge ageynste Vaschus,
ent pzocesse to the maiestrates of the towne, wherby he com
aunded them to strangle Vaschus, and fyue other which were
hiefe capitaynes vnder hym: Alleagynge that they and their
onfetherates conspired to rebel in the South sea: And that
schus hym selfe foz that intente, had buylded and furnished
oure shippes to search the south coastes of the supposed con:
nent: Also that to his three hundzeth souldiers and compa
ions which he had with hym, he shulde speake woozdes of
his effecte as foloweth. My frendes, and felowes of my
onge peynes and trauayles: Howe longe shall we be subiecte
o the commaundement of other, sythe wee haue bydden this
unt and ouercumme thenterprise foz the whiche this newe
ouernour was sent with so great a multitude? Who can any
onger abyde his pzyde and insolentie? Lette vs therefoze fo:
owe these coastes whyther so euer foztune shall dryue vs:
nd amonge these so many pleasaunt and fruteful pzouinces
f this large lande, let vs chose one in the whiche wee maye
oith libertie spende that poztion of owre lyues which yet re:
ayneth. Who can fynde vs, oz shalbe able to pzofer vs vyo:
nce? When these oz the lyke woozdes were declared to Pe
us Arias, he sente to the Southe partes foz Vaschus, wyllynge
ym by the vertue of his commission to repayze to him foozth
ith). Vaschus obeyed, and at his commynge was caste in pzy:
on: yet constantly denyinge that euer he entended any suche
hynge. Wytnesses were bzought ageynst hym, and his woz
es rehearsed from the begynnynge. To conclude, he was
dged woozthy death, and was put to execution. And this

Contention betwene Uaschus and Petrus Arias.

Petrus Arias commandeth that Uaschus be put to death.

Uaschus is accused.

Uaschus is put to death.

is the rewarde wherwith the blynde goddesse oftentymes re
compenseth such as haue susteyned great trauayles and dan
giours to bee hyghly in her fauoure. *Petrus Arias* leauynge h
wyfe in *Dariena*, embarked hym selfe in the shippes left of V
chus, to thintent to searche those coastes. But whether he
returned or not, we haue yet no certeyne knoweleage. H
hath also his fortune. yet is there an other gouernour a
signed, whose name is *Lupus Sosa*, the viceroye of the I
landes of *Canarie*. What stomake *Petrus Arias* may haue yf he
tutue, let good men iudge. There was nothyng doone vnd
hym woorthy glorie. Sume thynke that he was at the b
gynnyng to slacke and negligent in his office, and not seue
in correctynge errours and misorders. But we wyll leaue h
and rehearse sumwhat wherof we haue byn lately inform
as touchynge the great and diepe ryuer of *Dabaiba*, the whic
for the greatnes and largenes therof, owre men named Gr
dis, that is, great, as we haue noted in owre Decades. Th
riuer faulteth into the furthest corner of the goulfe of *Vruba*
seuen portes or mowthes as dooth the ryuer of *Nilus* into t
Egyptian sea, whose large description yowe may also rea
in owre Decades. That the mountaynes on euery syde abo
this ryuer, are rych in golde, we haue learned by thinform
tion of thinhabitauntes, of whom we made diligent inquis
on. *Vaschus*, and besyde hym other gouernoures and Lieu
nauntes, haue fouretymes entered into this ryuer with the
armyes in battayle array, and with dyuers kyndes of shipp
fyrste for the space of fortie myles, then fyftie, and at the la
fourescore, at an other tyme also ouerthwarte the ryuer. O
shamefull chaunce and detestable coulwardenes of owre me
A naked nation encounterynge with them that had appare
the armed ageynste the vnarmed, had the ouerthrowe in m
ner in all conflictes, and were other all slayne or wounded.
They vse inuenemed arrowes, and are suche experte archer
that if they espye any place of theyr enemie bare or vnarmed
they wyll not lyghtly fayle to stryke him there. They vse a
so many dartes, which in the tyme of the battayle they hu
so thicke a farre of, that they take the lyght of the sonne f
they enemies as it were with a clowde. They haue lykewi
brode and longe swoordes made of a heauie and harde kin
of woodde, wherwith they feyght fiercely neare at hand
Vasch

Petrus Arias.

Lupus Sosa.

The great ry
uer of Dabai
ba or Grandis

The goulfe
of Uraba.

The ryche
mountaynes
of Dabaiba.

Fierce & war
lyke people.

Dartes.

Swoordes of
heauie wood.

...ſchus hym ſelfe receaued many woundes in encounterynge
with them. And thus by reaſon of the fierceues of theſe barbarians, the ryuer of Dabaiba is yet lefte vnſearched. We wil
nowe ſpeake ſumwhat moze of the Iland of Hiſpaniola (which
the Spanyardes caule Spagnuola) the moother and chiefe of al
other landes oz Ilandes wherof we entended to wzyte. In it
the Senate is now reſtozed, and fyue Judges aſſigned to giue
lawes to all thinhabitauntes of thoſe tractes. But in ſhozte
tyme, they ſhall ceaſe gatherynge of golde although there bee
greate plentie : by reaſon they ſhall lacke labourers and myners, fozaſmuch as thinhabitauntes whoſe helpe they vſed
therein, are bzought to a ſmaule number, conſumed partly by
warre, and many moze by famen that yeare that they dygged
vp the rootes wherof they made theyz beſte bzeade, and lefte
ſſowynge theyz grayne of Maizium which is theyz common
foode, ſuppoſinge hereby to haue dzyuen owte men owte of
the Ilande, who had vytaples ſente them from Spayne. A
great number of them alſo, dyed of newe and ſtraunge diſeaſes which in the yeare of Chziſte a thouſande fyue hundzeth
and. xviii. conſumed theym lyke rotton ſheepe.

And (to ſaye the truth) owre mens vnſaciable deſyze of golde,
ſo oppzeſſed theſe pooze wzetches with extreme labour and
toyle, where as befoze they lyued pleaſauntly and at lybertie,
gyuen onely to playes and paſtymes as dauuſynge, fyſſhynge,
foulynge, and huntyng of lyttle connies, that many of them
perifhed euen foz verye anguyſhe of mynde, the whiche (with
their vnaccuſtomed labour) are thynges of them ſelues ſuffy-
cient to engender many newe diſeaſes. But the kynge and
the Senate haue nowe determyned that they be reduced to a
couple, and to gyue them ſelues onely to increaſe, and tyllage of the gound : And that onely ſuch as are bought oz taken owte of other regions, bee appoynted to labour in the
golde mynes. But it ſhall ſuffyce to haue ſayde thus muche
of the peſtiferous hunger of golde. Therfoze to ſpeake of o-
ther matters : It is a marueylous thynge to conſyder howe
all thynges increaſe and profper in this Ilande. There are
nowe. xviii ſuger pzeſſes wherwith great plentie of ſuger
is made. The canes oz reedes wherin the ſuger groweth,
are bygger and hygher then in any other place : And are as
bygge as a mans arme in the bzawne, and higher then the

It. ii. nature

Hiſpan old.
Ouiedus wry-
teth that ther
are nowe. v.
monaſteries.

Newe and
ſtrange diſea-
ſes.

The ſuger of
hiſpaniola.

Suger of Has
leuas.

nature of a man, by the halfe. This is more woonderfull, that where as in Valentia in Spaine (where a great quantitye of suger is made yearely) where so euer they applye them selues to the great increase therof, yet doth euery roote bring foorthe not paste fyue, or syxe, or at the moste seuen of those reedes : wheras in *Hispaniola* one roote beareth twentie, and oftentymes thirtie. Foure footed beastes and cattayle, are marueylously increased in this Ilande. And albeit that the rauenynge hunger of golde hath hitherto greatly hyndered owre men from tyllage of the ground, yet is there great plentye of wheate, whiche prospereth so wel that it yealdeth sum tyme a hundreth foulde : And this especially on the hylles or rydges of the mountaynes prospectynge towarde the North. Vines do also increase here with no lesse frutefulnesse. What shuld I speake of the trees that beare *Cassia fistula*, brought first into this Iland from the other Ilandes neare vnto the supposed Continent, as we haue noted in owr Decades? There is nowe suche plentie herof, that after a fewe yeares we shall haue a pounde of the price that wee paye nowe for an ounce. Of the bresyle and mirobalane trees, with other innumerable prerogatiues and benefites whiche nature hath plentifully giuen to this blessed Iland, we haue spoken suffyciently in owr Decades. yet haue I thought good to repeate part of the same, bycause I think that the wittes of many readers haue diuerted from the weyght of great affaires, to the recordation of such pleasaunt thynges. And yet do not suche thynges as are sauery, engender tedyousnesse, soo that a precious matter bee adourned with a precious vesture.

F I N I S.

A token of maruelous frutfulnes.

Cattayle.

wheate.

Vines.

Cassia Fistula.

Breasyle.
Myrobalanes

167

EXEMPLAR BVLLAE SEV
DONATIONIS, AVTORITATE
CVIVS, EPISCOPVS ROMANVS ALEXAN-
der eius nominis sextus, concessit et donauit Castel-
lae regibus & suis successoribus, regiones & Insulas noui orbis in Oceano occidentali
Hispanorum nauigationi-
bus repertas.

LEXANDER EPISCOPVS,
seruus seruorum Dei, Charissimo in
Christo filio Ferdinando Regi, et
Charissimæ in Christo filiæ Eliza-
beth Reginæ Castellæ, Legionis,
Aragonum, Siciliæ, et Granatæ, illustribus, salu-
tem et Apostolicam benedictionem.

Inter cætera Diuinæ maiestati beneplacita opera
et cordis nostri desiderabilia, illud profecto potissi-
mū existit vt fides catholica & Christiana religio no-
stris præsertim temporibus exaltetur ac vbilibet
amplietur ac dilatetur, animarumq̃ salus procure-
tur, ac barbaræ nationes deprimantur et ad fidē
ipsam reducantur. Vnde cum ad hanc sacram Petri sedem Diuina fauente clementia (meritis licet im-
paribus) euocati fueremus, cognoscentes vos tanq̃
veros catholicos reges et principes: quales semper
fuisse nouimus, & a vobis præclare gesta, toti penę

orbi notifsima demonftrant, nedum id exoptare, fe
omni conatu, ftudio, et diligentia, nullis laboribus
nullis impensis, nullisꝗ parcendo periculis, etiar
proprium fanguinem effundendo efficere, ac omnen
animum veftrum, omnesꝗ conatus ad hoc iam du
dum dedicafse, quemadmodum recuperato regn
Granatæ a tyrannis de Sarracenorum hodiernis ter
poribus per vos, cum tanta Diuini nominis glori
facta, teftatur. Digne ducimur non immerito, ᴇ
debemus illa vobis etiam fponte, ac fauorabiliter co
cedere, per quæ huiufmodi fanctum ac laudabile a
immortali deo acceptum propofitum, indies feruen
tiori animo ad ipfius dei honorem et Imperij Chri
ftiani propagationem, profequi valeatis. Sane acce
pimus ꝗ vos qui dudum animum propofueratis a
liquas infulas et terras firmas remotas et incognitas
ac per alios hactenus non repertas, quærere et inue
nire, vt illarum incolas et habitatores ad colendun
redemptorem noftrum et fidem catholicam profi
tendum reduceretis, hactenus in expugnatione et re
cuperatione ipfius regni Granatæ plurimum occu
pati, huiufmodi fanctum et laudabile propofitun
veftrum ad optatum finem perducere nequiuiftis
Sed tamen ficut Domino placuit, regno predicto
recuperato, volentes defiderium veftrum adimplere
dilectum filium Chriftophorum Colonum virun
vtiꝗ

tiꝗ dignum et plurimum commendatum ac tanto
egotio aptum, cum nauigijs et hominibus ꜳ d simi-
la instructis, non sine maximis laboribus, ac peri-
ulis, et expensis destinastis vt terras firmas et Insu-
as remotas et incognitas, huiusmodi per mare vbi
actenus nauigatum non fuerat, diligenter inquire-
et. Qui tandem (Diuino auxilio facta extrema di-
igentia in mari Oceano nauigantes) certas insulas
emotissimas et etiam terras firmas quæ per alios
actenus repertæ non fuerant, inuenerunt. In qui-
us plurimæ gentes pacifice viuentes, et (vt asseri-
ur) nudi incedentes, nec carnibus vescentes, inhabi-
ant: Et vt præfati nuncij vestri possunt opinati, genes ipsæ in Insulis et terris prædictis habitantes, cre-
lunt vnum deum creatorem in Cœlis esse, ac ad fi-
em catholicam amplexandum et bonis moribus
nbuendum, satis apti videntur: Spesꝗ habetur, ꝙ
crudirentur, nomen Saluatoris Domini nostri Ie-
u Christi in terris et insulis prædictis facile induceꝛe
ur. Ac prefatus Christophorus in vna ex principa-
ibus Insulis prædictis, iam vnam turrim satis mu-
nitam, in qua certos Christianos qui secum iuerant,
in custodiam et vt alias Insulas ac terras firmas remotas et incognitas inquirerent posuit, construi et
ædificari fecit. In quibus quidem Insulis et terris
iam repertis, aurum, aromata, et aliæ quamplurimæ
res

res præciofæ diuerfi generis et diuerfæ qualitatis reperiuntur. Vnde omnibus diligenter, et præfertim
fidei catholicæ exaltatione et dilatatione (prout decet Catholicos Reges et Principes) confideratis, more progenitorum veſtrorum claræ memoriæ Regum,
terras firmas et infulas prædictas, illarumcp incolas
et habitatores, vobis diuina fauente clementia fubii-
cere et ad fidem Catholicam reducere propofuiſtis.
 Nos itacp huiufmodi veſtrum fanctum et laudabile propofitum plurimum in domino commendan-
tes, ac cupientes vt illud ad debitum finem perduca-
tur, et ipfum nomen faluatoris noſtri in partibus il-
lis inducatur, hortamus vos quamplurimum in domino, et per facri lauacri fufceptionem, qua manda-
tis Apoſtolicis obligati eſtis, et p vifcera mifericordiæ
Domini noſtri Iefu Chriſti attente requirimus, vt
cum expeditionem huiufmodi omnino profequi et
affumere prona mente orthodoxæ fidei zelo inten-
datis, populos in huiufmodi Infulis et terris degen-
tes, ad Chriſtianam religionē fufcipiendum induce-
re velitis et debeatis, nec pericula nec labores vllo
vnq̃ tempore vos deterreant, firma fpe fiduciacp con-
ceptis cp Deus omnipotens conatus veſtros fœlici-
ter profequetur. Et vt tanti negotij prouintiam A-
poſtolicæ gratiæ largitate donati, liberius et auda-
cius affumatis, motu proprio non ad veſtram vel

alterius pro vobis super hoc nobis oblatæ petitionis
instantiam, sed de nostra mera liberalitate, et ex cer=
ta scientia, ac de Apostolicæ potestatis plenitudine,
omnes Insulas et terras firmas inuentas et inuenien=
das, detectas et detegendas versus Occidentem et
Meridiem, fabricando et construendo vnam lineam
a polo Arctico, scilicet Septemtrione, ad polum
Antarcticum, scilicet Meridiem, siue terræ firmæ et
insulæ inuentæ et inueniendæ sint versus Indiam
aut versus aliam quamcunq; patte quæ linea distet a
qualibet Insularum quæ vulgariter nuncupantur de
los Azores et Cabo verde centum leucis versus Occi=
dentem et Meridiem. Itaq; omnes Insulæ et terræ
firmæ repertæ et reperiendæ, detectæ et detegendæ
a præfata linea versis Occedentem et Meridiem, quæ
per alium Regem aut Principem Christianum non
fuerint actualiter possessæ vsq; ad diem natiuitatis
Domini nostri Iesu Christi proxime præteritum, a
quo incipit annus præsens Millessimus Quadringen
tessimus Nonogessimus tercius, quando fuerunt per
nuncios et capitaneos vestros inuentæ aliquæ præ=
dictarum Insularum, Autoritate omnipotentis Dei
nobis in beato Petro concesa, ac vicariatus Iesu
Christi qua fungimur in terris, cum omnibus illa=
rum dominijs, ciuitatibus, castris, locis, et villis, iu=
ribusq; et iurisdictionibus ac partinentijs vniuersis,

V v .i.

vobis heredibusᵭ et succefforibus veſtris (Caſtellæ
et Legionis regibus) in perpetuum tenore præſenti
um donamus, concedimus, et aſſignamus: Voſᵭ
et hæredes ac ſucceſſores præfatos illarum Domi-
nos, cum plena, libera, et omnimoda poteſtate, au
toritate, et iuriſdictione, facimus, conſtituimus, e
deputamus. Decernentes nihilo minus per huiuſ
modi donationem, conceſsionem, et aſſignationem
noſtram, nullo Chriſtiano Principi qui actualite
præfatas Inſulas et terras firmas poſſederit vſᵭ ac
prædictum diem natiuitatis Domini noſtri Ieſu
Chriſti ius quæſitum, ſublatum intelligi poſſe au
auferri debere.

Et inſuper mandamus vobis in virtutæ ſancta
obedientiæ (vt ſicut pollicemini et non dubitamus
pro veſtra maxima deuotione et regia magnanimitate vos eſſe facturos) ad terras firmas et Inſulas
prædictas, viros probos et Deum timentes, doctos
peritos, et expertos ad inſtruendum incolas et habitatores præfatos in fide Chatholica et bonis moribus imbuendum, deſtinare debeatis, omnem de-
bitam diligentiam in præmiſsis adhibentes. A qui-
buſcumᵭ perſonis, cuiuſcunᵭ dignitatis, etiam im-
perialis et regalis ſtatus, gradus, ordinis vel condi-
tionis, ſub excommunicationis latæ ſententiæ pœna
quam eo ipſo ſi contra fecerint incurrant, diſtrictius
                                                    inhi

nhibemus ne ad Infulas et terras firmas inuentas et
nueniendas,detectas et detegendas verfus Occiden=
em et Meridiem, fabricando et conftruendo lineam
polo Arctico ad polum Antarcticum, fiuæ terræ
irmæ et Infulæ inuentæ et inueniendæ fint verfus
ndiam aut verfus aliam quamcunog partem quæ
inea diftet a qualibet Infularum quæ vulgariter nun
upantur de los Azores et Cabo verde centum leu=
is verfus Occidentem et Meridiem vt præfertur,pro
nercibus habendis vel quauis alia caufa accedere
oræfumat abfog veftra ac hæredum et fuccefsorum
eftrorum prædictorum licentia fpeciali : Non ob=
tantibus conftitutionibus et ordinationibus Apo=
tolicis, cæterifog quibufcunog, in illo in quo impe=
ia et dominationes et bona cuncta procedunt:Con=
identes og dirigente Domino actus veftros, fi hu=
ufmodi fanctum ac laudabile propofitum profe=
quamini, breui tempore cum fœlicitate et gloria to=
ius populi Chriftiani, veftri labores et conatus exi=
tum fœlicifsimum confequentur. Verum quia diffi=
cile foret præfentes literas ad fingula quæog loca in
quibus expediens fuerit deferri, volumus ac motu et
cientia fimilibus decernimus, og illarum tranffump=
tis manu publici notarij inderogati fubfcriptis, et
igillo alicuius perfonæ in ecclefiaftica dignitate con=
litutæ, feu curiæ ecclefiafticæ munitis, ea prorfus

V u. ii.   fides

fides in iudicio et extra ac alias vbilibet adhibeatur
quæ præsentibus adhiberetur si esent adhibitæ ve
ostensæ.

Nulli ergo omnino hominum liceat hanc pagi
nam nostræ commendationis, hortationis, requisi
tionis, donationis, concessionis, assignationis, con
stitutionis, deputationis, decreti, mandati, inhibi
tionis, et voluntatis infringere vel ei ausu te
merario contraire. Si quis autem hoc at
tentare præsumpserit, indignationem
omnipotentis Dei, ac beatorum
Petri et Pauli Apostolorum
eius, se nouerit in
cursurum.

Datum Romæ apud sanctum Pe
trum: Anno incarnationis Do
minicæ. 1593. quarto nonas
Maij: Pontificatus
nostri anno
primo.

171

❡ The coppie of the Bull oɀ donation, by thautoɀitie whee of, Pope Alexander the syxte of that name, gaue and graunted to the kynges of Castyle and theyɀ succes: sours the Regions and Ilandes founde in the Weſt Ocean sea by the nauigations of the Spanyardes.

Alexander byſhoppe, the seruaunte of the ser: uauntes of God: To owre moſte deare belo: ued sonne in Chɀiſt kynge Ferdinande, And to owre deare beloued doughter in Chɀyſt Elyzabeth Queene of Castyle, Legion, Ara: gon, Sicilie, and Granata, moſt noble Pɀin ces, Greetynge and Apoſtolical benediction. Amonge other woozkes acceptable to the diuine maieſtie and accoɀdynge to owre hartes desyɀe, this certeinely is the chiefe, that the Catholyke fayth and Chɀiſtian religion, spe: cially in this owre tyme may in all places bee exalted, ampli: fied, and enlarged, wherby the health of soules may be pɀo: cured, and the Barbarous nations subdued and bɀought to the fayth. And therefoɀe wheras by the fauoure of gods cle: mentie (although not without equall deſertes) we are caused to this holy seate of Peter, and vnderſtandynge you to bee trewe Catholyke Pɀinces as we haue euer knowen you, and as youre noble and woozthy factes haue declared in maner to the hole woɀlde in that with all your ſtudie, diligence, and induſtrye, you haue spared no trauayles, charges, oɀ perils, aduenturynge euen the ſchedynge of your owne bludde, with applyinge yowre hole myndes and endeuours here vnto, as your noble expeditions achyued in recouerynge the kyngdome of Granata from the tyrannie of the Sarracens in these our dayes, doo playnely declare your factes with so great gloɀye of the diuine name. Foɀ the whiche as we thinke you wooɀ: thy, so owght we of owre owne free wyl fauoɀably to graunt you all thynges wherby you maye dayely with moɀe seruent myndes to the honoure of god and enlargynge the Chɀiſtian empire, pɀosecute your deuoute and laudable purpose moſt ac: ceptable to the immoɀtall God. We are credably infoɀmed that wheras of late you were determyned to secke and spnde certeyne Ilandes & firme landes farɀe remote and vnknowen
                                                                and be

(and not heretofore found by any other) to thintent to bringe
thinhabitauntes of the same to honoure owre redemer and t
professe the catholyke fayth, you haue hetherto byn much o
cupied in therpugnation and recouerie of the kyngedome c
Granata, by reason whereof yowe coulde not bzynge yow
sayde laudable purpose to thende desyzed. Neuertheleste a
it hath pleased almyghty god, the forsayde kyngedome b
inge recouered, wyllyng taccomplyshe your sayde desyze, yo
haue, not without great laboure, perelles, and charges, a
poynted owre welbeloued sonne Chzistopher Colonus (a ma
certes wel commended as moste worthy and apte foz so grea
a matter) well furnysthed with men and shippes and other n
cestaries, to seeke (by the sea where hetherto no manne hat
sayled) suche firme landes and Ilandes farre remote and h
therto vnknowen. Who (by gods helpe) makynge diligent
searche in the Ocean sea, haue founde certeyne remote Ilan
des and firme landes whiche were not heretofoze founde b
any other. In the which (as is sayde) many nations inhabit
lyuinge peaceably and goinge naked, not accustomed to ea
flesche.   And as farre as yowre messengers can coniecture
the nations inhabitynge the fozesayde landes and Ilandes
beleue that there is one god creatoure in heauen : and seem
apte to be bzought to thimbzasinge of the catholyke fayth
and to be imbued with good maners : by reason whereof, w
may hope that if they be well instructed, they may easely be
induced to receaue the name of owre sauiour Jesu Chzist. w
are further aduertised that the fozenamed Chzistopher hath
nowe builded and erected a fortresse with good munition i
one of the fozesayde pzincipall Ilandes in the which he hat
placed a garrison of certeine of the Chzistian men that went
thyther with him : aswell to thintent to defende the same, a
also to searche other Ilandes and firme landes farre remot
and yet vnknowen. We also vnderstande, that in these lan
des and Ilandes lately founde, is great plentie of golde and
spices, with dyuers and many other pzecious thynges of sun
dzy kyndes and qualities. Therfoze al thinges diligently o
sidered (especially thamplifyinge and enlargyng of the cath
like fayth, as it behoueth catholike Pzinces folowyng ther
amples of yowre noble pzogenitours of famous' memozie)
wheras yowe are determyned by the fauour of almightie god
                                                        10

subdue and bzynge to the catholyke fayth thinhabitauntes
of the fozesayde landes and Jlandes.

Wee greatly commendynge this yowre godly and laudable
purpose in owr lozde, and desirous to haue the same bzought
to a dewe ende, and the name of owre sauioure to be knowen
in those partes, doo exhozte yowe in owre Lozde and by the
receauynge of yowre holy baptisme wherby yowe are bounde
to Apostolicall obedience, and ernestely require yowe by the
bowels of mercy of owre Lozde Jesu Chzist, that when yowe
intende foz the zeale of the Catholyke faythe to pzosecute the
sayde expedition to reduce the people of the fozesayde landes
and Jlandes to the Chzistian religion, yowe shall spare no la
bours at any tyme, oz bee deterred with any perels, conceaz
uynge firme hope and confidence that the omnipotent godde
wyll gyue good successe to yowre godly attemptes. And that
beinge autozyzed by the pziuilege of the Apostolycall grace,
yowe may the moze freely and bouldly take vpon yowe thenz
terpzyse of so greate a matter, we of owre owne motion, and
not eyther at yowre request oz at the instant peticion of any oz
her person, but of owre owne mere liberalitie and certeyne
science, and by the fulnesse of Apostolycall power, doo gyue,
graunt, and assigne to yowe, yowre heyzes and successours,
all the firme landes & Jlandes found oz to be found discouered
and to be discouered toward the West & South, dzawyng a line
fzō the pole Artike to the pole Antartike (that is) frō the nozth
to the Southe : Conteynynge in this donation, what so euer
firme landes oz Jlandes are founde oz to bee founde towarde
India, oz towarde any other parte what so euer it bee, beinge
distant from, oz without the fozesayd lyne dzawen a hundzeth
leaques towarde the West and South from any of the Jlanz
des which are commonly cauled De los Azores and Cabo Verde.
All the Jlandes therfoze and firme landes, founde and to be
founde, discouered and to be discouered from the sayde lyne
towarde the West and South), such as haue not actually bin
heretofoze possessed by any other Chzistian kynge oz pzynce
vntyll the daye of the natiuitie of owre Lozde Jesu Chzyste
laste paste, from the which begynneth this pzesent yeare bez
inge the yeare of owre Lozde. M. CCCC. lxxxxiii. when so
euer any such shalbe founde by your messingers & capytaines,
Wee by the autozitie of almyghtie God graunted vnto vs
in

in saynt Peter, and by the office which we beare on the earth
in the steede of Jesu Chriſte, doo for euer by the tenoure of
theſe preſentes, gyue, graunte, aſſigne, vnto yowe, yowre
heyres, and ſucceſſoures (the kynges of Castyle and Legion)
all thoſe landes and Jlandes, with theyr dominions, territo-
ries, cities, caſtels, towres, places, and vyllages, with al
the ryght, and iuriſdictions therunto pertepnynge: conſtitu-
tynge, aſſignynge, and deputynge, yowe, yowre heyres, and
ſucceſſours the lordes thereof, with full and free poure, auto-
toritie, and iuriſdiction. Decree nge neuertheleſſe by this
owre donation, graunt, and aſſignation, that from no Chriſtian Prince whiche actually hath poſſeſſed the foreſayde J-
landes and firme landes vnto the day of the natiuitie of owre
lorde beforeſayde theyr ryght obteyned to bee vnderſtoode
hereby to be taken away, or that it owght to be taken away.

Furthermore wee commaunde yowe in the vertue of holy o-
bedience (as yowe haue promyſed, and as wee doubte not you
wyll doo vppon mere deuotion and princely magnanimitie) to
ſende to the ſayde firme landes and Jlandes, honeſte, vertuous, and lerned men, ſuche as feare God, and are able to in-
ſtructe thinhabitauntes in the Catholyke fayth and good maners, applyinge all theyr poſſible diligence in the premiſſes.

We furthermore ſtreightely inhibite all maner of perſons, of
what ſtate, degree, order, or condition ſo euer they bee, although of Imperiall and regall dignitie, vnder the peyne of
the ſentence of excommunication whiche they ſhall incurre yf
they doo to the contrary, that they in no caſe preſume with-
our ſpeciall lycence of yowe, yowre heyres, and ſucceſſours,
to trauayle for marchaundies or for any other cauſe, to the
ſayde landes or Jlandes, founde or to bee found, diſcouered,
or to bee diſcouered, toward the weſt & ſouth, drawing a line
fro the pole Artyke to the pole Antartike, whether the firme
landes & Jlandes found & to be found, be ſituate toward Indie
or towarde any other parte beinge diſtant from the lyne drawen a hundreth leagues towarde the weſt from any of the J-
landes commonly cauled De los Axores and Cabo Verde: Notwithſtandynge conſtitutions, decrees, and Apoſtolycall ordi-
naunces what ſo euer they are to the contrary: In him from
whom Empyres, dominions, and all good thynges doo procede: Truſtynge that almyghtie god directynge yowre enter-
                                                            priſes

niſes, yf yowe folowe yowre godly and laudable attemptes,
yowre laboures and trauayles herein, ſhall in ſhorte tyme ob=
teyne a happy ende with felicitie and glorie of all Chriſtian
people. But foraſmuch as it ſhulde bee a thynge of great dif=
ficultie theſe letters to bee caryed to all ſuche places as ſhuld
bee expedient, we wyll, and of lyke motion and knowleage
doo decree that whyther ſo euer the ſame ſhalbe ſent, or whee
to euer they ſhalbe receaued with the ſubſcription of a com=
mon notarie thereunto requyred, with the ſeale of any perſon
conſtitute in eccleſiaſticall dignitie, or ſuche as are autoryſed
by the eccleſiaſticall courte, the ſame fayth and credite to bee
gyuen thereunto in iudgement or els where, as ſhulde bee ex=
hibyted to theſe preſentes.

It ſhall therefore bee lawefull for no man to infringe or
raſhely to contrarie this letter of owre commendation, exhor=
tacion, requeſte, donation, graunt, aſſignation, conſtitu=
tion, deputation, decree, commaundement, inhibiti=
on, and determination. And yf any ſhall preſume
to attempte the ſame, he owght to knowe that
he ſhall thereby incurre the indignation
of almyghtie God and his holye
Apoſtles Peter and
Paule. (⸭)
(:)(⸭)

¶ Gyuen at Rome at ſaynt Peters: In the
yeare of thincarnation of owre Lord
M. CCCC. LXXXXIII. The fourth
day of the nones of Maye,
the fyrſte yeare of
owre ſeate.
() ()
O

Xx.i.

To the reader.

Lthough amonge dyuers which haue wrytten of the Ocean and Weste Indies, there is non to be compared to Peter Martyr of Angleria in declarynge by philosophical discourses th secreate causes of naturall affectes bothe a touchynge the lande, the sea, the starres, and other straung woorkes of nature, yet forasmuche as of later dayes thos countreys haue byn better knowen and searched, and dyuer suche particular and notable thynges founde as are contey ned in the hystories of later wryters, emonge the number o whom, *Gonzalus Ferdinandus Ouiedus*, (whom lerned *Cardanus* com pareth to the ancient wryters) is doubtles the chiefe, I haue therfore thought good to ioyne to the Decades of Peter Ma tyr certeyne notable thynges which I haue gathered owte o his booke intiteled the Summarie or abbrigement of his ge nerall hystorie of the west Indies wrytten in the firme land of the same in the citie of *Sancta Maria Antiqua* in *Dariena* (wher he dwelte and was gouernoure many yeares) And dedicate to Themperous maiestie, as maye appeare by the epystell fo lowynge.

¶ To the most hygh and myghtie prince Charles the fyfte o that name : Emperour of Rome, Kynge of Spayne, and o the twoo Sicilies, of bothe the sydes of the streyght of Euro Kynge of Hierusalem and Hungarie, Duke of Burgonie and Earle of Flaundres, Lorde and inheritoure of the firme lande and Ilandes of the Weste Ocean. &c. *Gonzalus Ferdinandus Oui- edus* his most humble seruant wysheth health and per- petual felicitie.

He thynges whiche principally preserue and mayntayne the woorkes of nature in the memo ries of men, are hystories and bookes compo sed of the same. Amonge the whiche certes those are esteemed moste trewe and autentyke which haue byn wrytten by wyttie and exper me

men well trauayled in the worlde, as faythfull wytneſſes of
ſuche thynges as they haue partely ſeene and byn partely in=
formed by credible perſons. Of this mynde and opinion was
Plinie, who better then any other autoure hathe wrytten in
xxxvii. bookes al that perteyneth to the naturall hiſtorie, con
teyned al in one volume dedicated to Ueſpaſian Themperour.
Wherein, as a prudente hiſtoriographer, he declareth ſuche
thynges as he had harde: Attributynge the ſeconde autoritie
to ſuche as he had redde in autoures that wrote before hym:
And thyrdely ioyned to the ſame hyſtorie, ſuch thynges as he
hym ſelfe had ſeene as moſte certeyne teſtimonie. Whoſe exem
ple I folowynge, wyl in this my breefe ſummarie reduce and
repreſent to yowr maieſties memorie ſuch thynges as I haue
ſeene in yowre Empyre of the Weſt Indies aſwell in the I=
landes as in the firme lande of the Ocean ſea, where I haue
ſerued nowe more then twelue yeares in the place of ſuruoy=
er of the golde mynes by the commaundemente of the Catho=
lyke kynge Don Fernando the fyfte of that name and graundfa=
ther vnto yowre maieſtie, to whom god gaue great fame and
glorie. Senſe whoſe death alſo I haue lykewiſe ſerued and
truſt whyle the reſt of my lyfe yet remayneth, to ſerue yowre
maieſtie as ſhall pleaſe yowe to commaunde. As touchynge
which thinges and ſuch other lyke, I haue more largely writ
ten in a hyſtorie begunne as ſone as my age was rype to take
ſuche matters in hande. Wherein furthermore I haue made
mention of ſuche thynges as haue chaunced in Spaine, from
the yeare, 1494. vnto this tyme. Addynge alſo thereunto
ſuche thynges woorthy memorie as I haue obſerued in other
realmes and prouinces where I haue trauayled. And haue
likewiſe particulerly wrytten the lyues and woorthy actes of
the catholyke Princes of famous memorie Don Ferdinando and
lady Elizabeth his wyfe to theyr laſt dayes. After whoſe fru
ition of heauenly Paradyſe, I haue noted ſuche thynges as
haue chaunced in yowre moſt fortunate ſucceſſion. Not omit
tynge particularly to wryte a large booke of ſuch thynges as
haue ſeemed moſte woorthy to bee noted as touchynge yowre
maieſties Indies. But for aſmuche as that volume remaineth
in the citie of San. Dominico in the Ilande of Hiſpaniola where I
dwell and am placed in houſholde with wyfe, chyldren,
and famelie, I haue brought no more with me of that my wri

XX, ii.　　　tynge

tynge then I beare in memozie. Determynynge notwithſtandynge foz powze maieſties recreation to make a bzeefe rehear
ſall of certeyne notable thynges wherof I haue moze largely
entreated in my ſayde general hiſtozie, and ſuch as may ſeeme
moſte woozthy to bee redde of powze maieſtie. Of the which,
although a great parte haue byn wzytten by other who haue
alſo ſeene the ſame, yet perhappes they are not ſo exactly and
particularly deſcribed as of me, fozaſmuche as in maner all
that trauayle into theſe Indies haue greater reſpecte to luker
and gaynes then diligently to ſearche the wooꝛkes of nature
wherunto I haue byn euer naturally inclyned, and haue ther
foze with all poſſible endeuour applyed myne eyes and intelligence to fynde the ſame. And this pzeſente Summarie ſhall
not bee contrary oz dyuers from my larger hiſtozie wherin (as
I haue ſayde) I haue moze amplye declared theſe thynges:
but ſhal onely moze bzeefely expzeſſe theffect therof vntyl ſuch
tyme as Godde ſhal reſtoze me to myne owne houſe, where I
may accompliſhe and fyniſhe my ſayd general hyſtozie. Where
vnto to gyue the fyzſt pzinciple, I ſay that Don Chziſtopher
Colonus (as it is well knowen) beinge the fyzſte Admyzall of
this India, diſcouered the ſame in the dayes of the Catholyke kynge Don Ferdinando and the ladye Elyzabeth his
wyfe, graundfather and graundmother vnto powze maieſtie:
In the yeare. 1 4 9 1.   And came to Barzalona in the yeare
1 4 9 2. with the fyzſt Indians and other ſhewes and pzoſes
of the great ryches and notice of this weſt Empire. The whiche gyfte and benefyte was ſuche, that it is vnto this daye,
one of the greateſt that euer any ſubiect oz ſeruant hath done
foz his pzince oz countrey, as is manifeſte to the hole woꝛlde.
And to ſaye the trewth, this ſhall doubtleſſe bee ſo commodious and pzofytable vnto the hole realme of Spayne, that
I repute hym no good Caſtilian oz Spanyarde that doothe
not recogniſe the ſame. And (as I haue ſayde befoze) foꝛaſmuch as in my ſayde generall hiſtozie I haue moze largely in
treated of theſe thynges, I intend at this pzeſent only bzief-
ly to rehearſe certeyne eſpeciall thynges, the whiche ſurely
are verye fewe in reſpecte of the thouſandes that myght bee
ſayde in this behalfe. Fyzſt therfoze I wyl ſpeake ſumwhat
of the nauigation into theſe parties.   Then of the generation of the nations whiche are founde in the ſame, with their
rytes

rytes, cuſtomes, and cerimonies. Alſo of beaſtes, foules,
byrdes, woozmes, fyſſhes, ſeas, ryuers, ſpzyng s, trees,
plantes, herbes, and dyuers other thinges which are engen=
dered boothe on the lande and in the water. And foraſmuche
as I am one of thozder and company of them that are appoin
ted to returne into theſe regions to ſerue yowre maieſtie, yf
therfoze the thynges conteyned in this booke ſhall not bee di
ſtincte in ſuch ozder as I pzomiſed to perfozme in my greateſt
woozke. I deſyze yowre maieſtie to haue no reſpecte herevn
to, but rather to conſyder the noueltie of ſuche ſtraunge thyn=
ges as I haue herein declared, whiche is the chiefe ende that
moued me to wzite. Pzoteſtyng that in this Summarie I
haue wzitten the trewth of ſuche thynges as coome to my re=
membzaunce : wherof not onely I my ſelfe can teſtifye, but
alſo diuers other woozthy and credible men which haue bin
in thoſe regions, and are nowe pzeſente in yowre maieſties
courte. And thus it ſhal ſuffyce to haue ſaide thus much vn=
to yowre maieſtie in maner of a pzoheme vnto this pzeſent
woozke which I moſt humbly deſyze yowre maieſticas thank
fully taccept, as I haue wzitten it faythfully.

❧ Of the ozdinary nauygation from Spayne ſto the Weſte Indies.

He nauygation whiche is commonly made
from Spayne to the Weſte India, is from
Siuile, where yowre maieſtie haue yowre
houſe of contractation for thoſe partes, with
alſo yowre offycers thervnto perteynynge,
of whom the capitaines take their paſſepozte
and lycence. The patrones of ſuche ſhyppes
as are appoynted to theſe vyages, imbarke theym ſelues at
San Luca di Barameda, where the ryuer Guadalchiber entereth into
the Ocean ſea. And from henſe they folowe their courſe to=
ward the Ilandes of Canarie. Of theſe ſeuen Ilandes, they
commonly touche two, that is, eyther Grancanera oz Gomera.
And here the ſhyppes are furnyſſhed with freſhe water, fuell,
cheeſe, biefe, and ſuche other thynges whiche may ſeeme re=
quiſyte to be added to ſuche as they bzynge with them owte
of Spayne. From Spayne to theſe Ilandes, is coomonly
cyght

eyght dayes faylinge, oz lyttle moze oz leffe. And when they
are arryued there, they haue fayled two hundereth and fyftie
leaques, whiche make a thoufande myles, accomptyng foure
myles to a leaque as is their maner to recken by fea. Depar=
tynge from the fayde Jlandes to folowe their courfe, the ship=
pes tary. rrb. dayes, oz a lyttle moze oz leffe, befoze they fee
the fyzfte lande of the Jlandes that lye befoze that whiche
they caule La Spagnuola oz Hifpaniola. And the lande that is com=
monly fyzfte feene, is one of thefe Jlandes whiche they caule
Ogni fancti Marigalante (oz Galanta) La Deffeada (otherwife cauled Defy=
derata) Matanino, Dominica, Guadalupe, San. Chriftoual, oz fumme other of
the Jlandes wherof there are a great multitude lyinge aboute
thefe afozefaide. yet it fumtymes fo chaunceth that the ship=
pes paffe withowte the fyght of any of the fayde Jlandes, oz
any other that are within that courfe vntyll they coome to
the Jland of Sancti Iohannis oz Hipaniola, oz Iamaica, oz Cuba, whi=
che are befoze the other. It may alfo chaunce that they ouer
paffe all thefe likewyfe, vntyll they faule vppon the coaftes
of the fyrme lande. But this chaunceth when the pylote is
not well practifed in this nauigation oz not perfecte in the
trewe carde. But makynge this viage with experte maryners
(wherof there is nowe great plentie) one of the fayde fyzfte
Jlandes fhall euer bee knowen. And from the Jlandes of
Canarie to one of the fyzfte of thefe, the diftaunce is nyne
hundzeth leaques by faylynge, oz moze. And from henfe to
the citie of faynte Dominike which is in the Jlande of Hifpa=
niola, is a hundzeth and fyftie leaques: So that from Spayne
hitherto, is a thoufand and thzee hundzeth leaques. yet foz
afmuche as fumtimes the nauigation pzocedeth not fo direct=
ly, but that it chaunceth to wander euer on the one fyde oz on
the other, wee may well faye that they haue nowe fayled a
thoufande and fyue hundzeth leaques and moze. And if the
nauigation be flowe by reafon of fumme hynderaunce, it com=
monly chaunceth to be fynifhed in. rrrb. oz. rl. dayes. And
this happeneth foz the moffe parte, not accomptynge the ex=
tremes: that is, eyther of them that haue nowe paffage, oz
of them that arryue in verye fhozte tyme. Foz wee owghte to
confyder that which chaunceth moft commonly. The returne
from thofe partes to Spayne, is not fynyffhed without lon=
ger tyme, as in the fpace of. l. dayes, oz a lyttle moze oz leffe.

Neuer.

Neuertheleſſe in this preſent yeare of. 1525. there came foure ſhyps from the Iland of San Dominico to ſaint Luca in Spaine, in. xxb. dayes. But (as I haue ſayd) we ought not to iudge of that whiche chaunceth ſeldome, but of that which happeneth moſt ordinarily. This nauigation is very ſafe and much vſed, euen vnto the ſayd Ilande. And from this to the firme land, the ſhyppes trauerſe diuers wayes for the ſpace of fiue, ſyxe, or ſeuen dayes ſaylynge, or more, accordyng to the partes or coaſtes whither they directe their vyages, foraſmuche as the ſayde fyrme lande is verye great and large, and many nauigations and vyages are directed to dyuers partes of the ſame. Yet to the fyrme land whiche is neareſt to this Iland, and lyeth directly ageynſt San Dominico, the paſſage is fyniſhed in the tyme aforeſayde. But it ſhalbe muche better to remytte all this to the carde of theſe nauigations and the newe Coſmographie, of the whiche no parte was knowen to Ptolomie or any other of the owlde wrytters.

¶ Of twoo notable thynges as touchyng the Weſt Indies: And of the great rycheſſe brought from thence into Spayne.

Fter my vniuerſall deſcription of the hiſtorie of the Indies, there commeth to my remembraunce two thynges chiefely to be noted as touchynge thempire of this Weſt Indies pertepnynge to the dominion of powre maieſtye. And theſe beſyde the other particulars wherof I haue ſuffycientli ſpoken, are to be conſyderd as thynges of great importaunce. Wherof, the one is the ſhortneſſe of the way & with what expedition powr maieſties ſhyppes maye paſſe beyonde the mayne fyrme lande of theſe Indies into the newe Southe ſea cauled Mare del ſur lyvnge beyond the ſame. And this to thintent to coome to the Ilandes where the ſpices growe, beſyde the other innumerable rycheſſe of the kingedomes and ſignories whiche confine with the ſayde ſea where are ſo many people and nations of diuers toonges and maners. The other thinge, is to conſyder howe innumerable treaſures are entered into Spayne by theſe

theſe Jndies, aſwell that whiche commeth dayly from thenſe as alſo that is continually to bee looked fo2, bothe of golde and perle & other marchaunties which are firſt b2ought into this po2re realme of Spaine befo2e they are ſeene of other nations o2 traded into other realmes. Wherby not onely this po2re realme is greatly intiched, but alſo the benefyte ther= of redoundeth to the great p2ofyte of other countreys which are neare thereunto. A teſtimonye of this, are the double du= cades whiche po2re maieſtie haue cauſed to bee copned, and are diſparſed throughowte the hole wo2lde. But after they are once paſſed owt of this po2re realme, they neuer returne agein bycauſe they are the beſt curraunt money of the wo2ld. And therfo2e if after they haue byn in the handes of ſtraun= gers they chaunce to be retourned ageyne into Spaine, they coome diſguiſed in an other habite, and are diminiſſhed of the goodneſſe of their golde, with the ſtampe of po2re maie= ſtye chaunged : So that if it were not fo2 their ſuche defa= cynges in other realmes fo2 the cauſe afo2eſayde, there ſhulde not bee founde ſo great quantitie of fyne golde of the coyne of any p2ynce in the wo2lde as of po2re maieſties. And the cauſe of all this, are po2re Jndies.

¶Of the mynes of golde, and the ma= ner of woo2kynge in theym.

His particular of the mynes of gold, is a thing greatly to bee noted : And J maye muche bet= ter ſpeake hereof then any other man, fo2aſ= muche as there are nowe twelue yeares paſſe ſenſe J ſerued in the place of the ſuruicer of the meltynge ſhoppes perteynynge to the golde mynes of the firme lande, and was the gouernour of the my= nes of the Catholyke kyng Don Ferdinando, after whoſe depar= ture from this lyfe, J ſerued longe in the ſame roome in the name of po2r maieſtie : By reaſon whereof, J haue had great occaſion to knowe howe golde is founde and w2ought owte of the mynes : And do knowe ryght well that this lande is ex= ceadynge ryche : hauynge by my accompte and by the la= bour of my Jndians and ſlaues, gathered and fyned a great po2tion of the ſame : and may therfo2e the better affy2me this

by

by teſtimonie of ſyght. For I am well aſſured that in no part of Caſtilla del oro, that is, golden Caſtile (otherwiſe ſauled Beragua) no man coulde aſke me of the mynes of golde, but that I durſte haue bounde my ſelfe to haue diſcouered them in the ſpace of ten leagues of the countrey where it ſhulde haue byn demaunded me, and the ſame to bee verye ryche. For I was alowed all maner of charges to make ſearche for the ſame. And although golde be founde in maner euery where in theſe regions of golden Caſtile, yet ought wee not in euery place to beſtowe the trauell, and charge to get it owte, becauſe it is of leſſe quantitie and goodneſſe in ſum place then in ſum. And the myne or veyne whiche oughte to be folowed, ought to bee in a place whiche may ſtande to ſaue muche of the charges of the labourers, and for the adminiſtration of other neceſſary thinges that the charges may bee recompenſed with gaynes. For there is no doubte but that golde ſhalbe founde more or leſſe in euery place. And the golde whiche is founde in golden Caſtile, is verye good, and of xxii. caractes or better in fyneſſe. Furthermore, beſyde this great quantitie of golde whiche I haue ſayde to be founde in the mynes, there is alſo from day to day found or otherwiſe gotten, great treaſure of ſuche wrought gold as hath byn in the cuſtodie of the ſubdued Indians and their kynges, aſwell of ſuche as they haue gyuen for their fyne and raunſome, or otherwiſe as frendes to the Chriſtians, beſyde that whiche hath byn vyolently taken from the rebelles. But the greateſt parte of the wrought gold whiche the Indians haue, is baſe and holdeth ſumwhat of copper. Of this they make braſlettes and chaines and in the ſame they cloſe their iewels whiche their women are accuſtomed to weare and eſteeme more then all the richeſſe of the worlde. The maner howe golde is gathered, is this, eyther of ſuche as is founde in Zauana, that is to ſaye in the plaines and riuers of the champian countrey being withowt trees, whether the earth be with graſſe or without. Or of ſuche as is ſumtymes founde on the land without the riuers in places where trees growe, ſo that to coome by the ſame, it ſhalbe requiſite to cutte downe many and great trees. But after whiche ſo euer of theſe two maners it be founde, eyther in the riuers or ruptures or breaches of waters, or elles in the earth, I wyll ſhewe howe it is founde in bothe theſe places,

P y   and

and howe it is seperate and pourged. Therfore when the
mꝑne of beine is discouered, this chaunceth by serchyng and
plouyng in suche places as by certeyne sygnes and token do
appeare to skylfull men apte for the generation of golde and
to holde golde. And when they haue founde it, they folowe
the mꝑne and labour it, whether it be in the ryuer or in the
plaine as I haue sayde. And if it bee founde on the plaine,
fyrst they make the place verye cleane where they intende to
dygge. Then they dygge eyght or ten foote in length and as
muche in breadth: but they goo no deeper then a spanne or
two, or more as shall seeme best to the maister of the mꝑne,
dyggynge equally. Then they washe all the earthe whiche
they haue taken owte of the sayde space. And if herein they
fynde any golde, they folowe it. And if not, they dygge a
spanne deeper, and washe the earth as they dyd before. And
if then also, they fynde nothynge, they continue in dyggyng
and wasshyng the earth as before vntil they come to the hard
rocke or stone. And if in fyne they fynd no gold there, they folowe no further to seeke golde in that place, but go to another parte. And it is to be vnderstode, that when they haue
founde the mꝑne, they folowe it in digginge in the same measure in leuell and deapth vntill they haue made an ende of al
the mꝑne which that place conteyneth, if it appere to be riche.
This mꝑne oughte to consyst of certen feetes or pases in length
or breadth accordynge to certeyne orders determined. And
within that compasse of earth, it is not lawfull for any other
to dygge for golde. And where as endeth the mꝑne of hym
that fyrste founde the gold, immediatly it is lawfull for any
other man that wyl, with a staffe to assygne hym selfe a place
by the syde of the same, inclosynge it with stakes or pales as
his owne. These mꝑnes of Zauana (that is suchas are found
in the playnes) owght euer to bee sought neare to sum ryuer
or brooke or sprynge of water, or dyke, or standyng poole, to
thende that the golde maye bee wasshed, for the whiche purpose they vse the laboure of certeyne Indians as they doo o-
ther in dyggynge of the mꝑnt. And when they haue dygged
owte the mꝑne, they fyl certeine traies with that earth, whiche other Indians haue the charge immediatly to receaue at
their handes, and to carye those treyes of earth to the water
where it maye bee wasshed, yet do not they that brynge it,
wash

washe it, but delyuer it to other, puttynge it owte of their owne trayes into theirs which they haue ready in their handes to receaue it. These washers for the moste parte, are the Indian women, bycause this woorke is of lesse paine and trauayle then any other. These women when they washe, are accustomed to sytte by the waters syde, with their legges in the water euen vppe to the knees or lesse as the place serueth their purpose. And thus holdynge the trayes with earth in their handes by the handles therof, and puttynge the same into the water, they moue them rownde aboute after the maner of syftynge, with a certeyne aptenesse in suche sorte that there entreth no more water into the trais then serueth their turne: And with the selfesame apte mouynge of their trais in the water, they euer auoyd the foule water with the earth owte of the one syde of the vessell, and receaue cleane water on the other side therof. So that by this meanes by litle and lyttle, the water washeth the earth as the lyghter substaunce owte of the trais, and the golde as the heauier matter resteth in the bottome of the same, beyng rounde and holowe in the, myddest lyke vnto a barbars basen. And when all the earth is auoyded, and the golde gathered togyther in the bottome of the traye, they putte it aparte, and returne to take more earth, whiche they washe contiunally as before. And thus they that laboure in this woorke, do gather dayly suche portion of golde as shal please god to graunt to the patrones of these Indians and suche other as trauaile in the same. Furthermore, it is to bee noted that for euery two Indians that washe, it is requisite that two other serue them to brynge earthe from the myne, and other two to breake the same smaule and fylle their trais therwith. Also besyde these labourers, it is necessarye that there bee other people in the place where they woorke and reste in the nyghte. These are suche as make their breade, and prouyde for vyttrayles and other necessaryes. So that to conclude, there are in all, fyue persons ordinarily assigned to euery traye of washers.

There is an other maner of woorkyng the mynes in riuers or brookes of runnynge waters. And this is, that in auoydynge the water of his course, after that the beddes of the riuers are drye and vtterlye emptied, x they fynde golde amonge the breaches, cliftes, and ryftes of stones, and amonge

all that is in the bottome of the chanell, and where naturally
the riuer runneth of greatest force. So that it chaunceth sum
tyme, that when the bedde of the ryuer is good and ryche,
they fynde in it great quantitie of golde. And therfore yowr
maiestie ought to vnderstande for a generall rule, as it appereth in fact, that all golde is engendered in the toppes and
hyghest places of the montaines: And in continuance of time
is by lyttle and lyttle brought downe to the vales and plaines by the raages of rayne, and the faules of sprynges, ryuers,
and brookes hauynge their originall in the mountaynes and
descendynge from the same, notwithstandynge it bee oftentymes founde in the plaines farre from the mountaynes.
But when it chaunceth to be founde in great quantitie, it is
for the moste parte amonge the mountaynes and in the riuers,
or their braunches, more then in any other parte of the plaine.
And in these two maners is it commonly founde moste abundantly. And for the better profe that golde is engendered
on hyghe, and is brought downe into the lowe places, I haue
sum great token therof, whiche causeth me to beleue it for
certeine. And this is to consyder that coles neuer putrifie nor
corrupt vnder the ground, if they be made of stronge wooode.
Whereby it chaunceth that diggyng the earth by the fouldes
or indented places of the mountaynes, or on the sydes, and
bylakynge a myne in the earthe where it hadnot byn broken
before, and hauyng downe dygged one or two or three poles
in measure, the myners founde certeyne coles of wood vnder
the same leuel where they found gold. And this I saye in the
earth whiche was taken for a vyrgine: that is to saye, such
as had not before byn opened for any myne. The whiche coles
coulde not naturally bee engendred there, or enter in by any
meanes. But when the superficiall part of the earth was equal
with the leuel where the coles were founde, it is lyke that the
coles were left there by sum occasion of fyre, and that they fast
ned there in tyme, and that afterwarde in longe continuance
of tyme, they were by lyttle and lyttle couered with the earth
which the often showers of rayne wasshed from the mountaynes, so that by the course of yeares the earth ouergrewe the
coles vnto the sayde leuell and measure whiche had before
tyme byn the superficiall parte of the earthe where the coles
and golde were founde togyther: whereby it maye appeare
that

that the golde was no moze engendered there then were the coles, but bzought thyther from the mountaynes by the fauꝛles of waters as we haue ſayde : foꝛaſmuche as the mountaynes are the matrices and bowels of all ryche metals. Furꝛther and beſyde this, J ſay that in how much moꝛe the gold is gonne farre from the naturall place of his generation to the place where it is founde, it is ſo muche the moꝛe puryfied and ſyned and of a better carꝛacte. And the nearer that it is founde to his proper myne oꝛ baine where it is engendered, it is ſo muche the baſer, fouler, and moꝛe crude, and of a baꝛſer alay and caracte, and dothe waſt ſo much the moꝛe in melꝛtynge, and remayneth moꝛe bꝛickle. Sumetyme there are founde graynes of golde of greate quantitie and of greate weyght aboue the earth and ſumtymes alſo vnder the earth. And the greateſte of all other that was founde to this daye in the Jndies, was that which was loſte in the ſea about the Jlande Beata, whiche weyed thꝛee thouſande and twoo hunꝛdꝛeth Caſtellans of golde, which are in value foure thouſand a hundꝛeth, thirtie and eyght ducades of golde, which wayꝛe one Arroua and ſeuen pounde, oꝛ xxxii. pounde after xii. ounꝛces to the pounde, whiche make thꝛeeſcoꝛe and foure markes of golde. And J ſawe in the yeare . 1 5 1 5 . in the handes of Mychel Paſſamonte treaſurer to powre maieſtie, two graines of the which one wayde ſeuen poundes, which are xiiii. markes, and are in value about thꝛeeſcoꝛe and ſyue ducades of golde euery marke. The other was of x. markes, which are ſyue poundes of lyke value, and of very good golde of xxii. caracces and better. There are alſo founde many other greate graynes, although not equall vnto theſe in byggenes. And foꝛaſmuche as J haue ſpoken of golde, J haue thoughe good to declare ſumewhat howe the Jndians can very excelꝛlently gylte ſuche veſſelles of copper and baſe golde as they make. Foꝛ they can gyue them ſo fayꝛe and ſhoꝛpſhynge a coꝛloure, that all the maſſe whiche they gylte, appeareth as though it were golde of xxii. caracces and better. This coloure they gyue with a certeyne herbe as thoughe it were wꝛought by the arte of any goldeſmyth of Spayne oꝛ Jtalie, and wold of them bee eſteemed as a thynge of greate ryches, and a ſeꝛcreate maner of gyldynge. And foꝛ as muche as J haue ſpoꝛken ſufficiently of the myne of golde, J wyll howe ſpeake
ſumwhat

A marke, is a pounde of vii. ounces ſumma xl i. li. weyghe viii. ounces, after xii. ounces to the li.

ſumwhat of copper bycauſe J haue made mention thereof.
This metall is founde in many of the Jlandes of the Jndies
and alſo in the firme lande : And is founde dayely in greate
quantitie holdynge ſumwhat of golde. But for the deſyre
that owre men haue to golde, they nothynge eſteeme the copper, although there myght great commoditie and profitte be
had therby, and alſo by other metals whiche they nothynge
regarde excepte ſyluer whiche is founde abundantly in that
parte of the firme lande which is cauled newe Spayne. But
of this it ſhall ſuffice to haue ſayde thus muche, bycauſe J
haue more particularly entreated of theſe thynges in my generall hyſtorie of Jndia.

☙ Of the maner of fyſhynge for perles.

He Jndians exerciſe this kynde of fyſſhynge
for the moſte parte in the coaſtes of the North
in *Cubagua* and *Cumana*. And manye of theym
which dwell in the houſes of certeyne particular lordes in the Jlandes of *San Dominico* and
Sancti Iohannis, reſort to the Jlande of *Cubagua* for
this purpoſe. Theyr cuſtome is to go fyue, ſyxe, or ſeuen, or
more in one of theyr *Canoas* or barkes erly in the mornynge to
ſume place in the ſea there about where it appeareth vnto them
that there ſhulde bee greate plentie of thoſe ſhell fyſſhes (which
ſume caule muſcles and ſume oyſters) wherin perles are engendered. And there they plonge them ſelues vnder the water,
euen vnto the bottome, ſauynge one that remaynethe in the
Canoa or boate which he keepeth ſtyll in one place as neare
as he can, lookynge for theyr returne owte of the water. And
when one of them hath byn a good whyle vnder the water, he
ryſeth vp and commeth ſwymmynge to the boate, enterynge
into the ſame, and leauynge there all the oyſters whiche he
hath taken and brought with hym. For in theſe, are the
perles founde. And when he hathe there reſted hym ſelfe a
whyle, and eaten parte of the oyſters, he returneth agepne to
the water, where he remaynethe as longe as he can endure,
and then ryſeth agepne, and ſwimmeth to the boate with his
pray, where he reſtethe hym as befoze, and thus continueth
courſe by courſe, as doo all the other in lyke maner, being all
                                                        moſte

moste experte swymmers and dyuers. And when the nyght draweth neare, they returne to the Ilande to theyr houses, and presente all the oysters to the master or stewarde of the house of theyr lorde who hath the charge of the sayde Indians. And when he hath gyuen them sumwhat to eate, he layeth vp the oysters in safe custodie vntyll he haue a great quantitie therof. Then hee causeth the same fysscher men to open them. And they fynde in euery of theym pearles other great or smaul, two or three or foure, and sumtymes fiue and syxe, and many smaule graines accordyng to the lyberalitie of nature. They saue the pearles bothe smaule and great whiche they haue founde: And eyther eate the oysters if they wyl, or caste them away, hauynge so great quantitie therof that they in maner abhorre them. These oysters are of hard fleshe, and not so plesaunt in eatyng as are olores of Spayne. This Ilande of Cubagua where this maner of fysshing is exercised, is in the Northe coaste, and is no bygger then the Iland of zelande. Oftentymes the sea increaseth greatly, and muche more then the fysshers for pearles wold, bycause where as the place is very depe, a man can not naturally rest at the bottome by reason of the aboundaunce of aery substaunce whiche is in hym, as I haue oftentymes proued. For althoughe he may by vyolence and force descende to the bottome, yet are his feete lyfted vp agayne so that he can continue no tyme there. And therfore where the sea is verye deepe, these Indian fysshers vse to tye two great stoones aboute them with a corde, on euery syde one, by the weyght wherof they descend to the bottome and remayne there vntyl them lysteth to ryse agayne: At which tyme they vnlose the stones, and ryse vppe at their pleasure. But this their apteneffe and agilitie in swimming, is not the thynge that causeth men moste to maruaile: But rather to consyder howe many of them can stande in the bottome of the water for the space of one hole houre, and summe more or lesse, accordynge as one is more apte hereunto then an other. An other thynge there is whiche seemeth to me very straunge. And this is, that where as I haue oftentymes demaunded of summe of these lordes of the Indians, if the place where they are accustomed to fysse for pearles beynge but lyttle and narrowe, wyll not in shorte tyme bee vtterly withowt oysters if they consume them so faste, they al answered me,

red me, that althoughe they bee consumed in one parte, yet if
they go a fysshynge in an other parte oz an other coaste of the
Ilande, oz at an other contrary wynd, and continue fysshing
there also vntyll the oysters be lykewyse consumed, and then
returne ageyne to the fyzste place, oz any other place where
they fysshed befoze and emptied the same in lyke maner, they
find thē ageine as ful of oysters as though they had neuer bin
fysshed. Wherby we may iudge that these oysters eyther remoue from one place to an other as do other fysshers, oz elles
that they are engendered and encrease in certeyne ozdinarie
places. This Iland of Cumana and Cubagua where they fyshe
foz these perles, is in the twelfe degree of the part of the said
coaste which inclineth toward the Nozth. Lykewise pearles
are founde and gathered in the South sea cauled Mare del Sur.
And the pearles of this sea are verye bygge. yet not so bigge
as they of the Ilande of pearles cauled de las perlas, oz Margu-
rites, whiche the Indians caule Terarequi, lyinge in the goulse
of saincte Michael, where greatter pearles are founde and
of greater pzice then in any other coaste of the Nozthe sea,
in Cumana, oz any other parte. I speake this as a trewe testimonie of syght, hauyng byn longe in that South sea, and makynge curious inquisition to bee certenly infozmed of al that
perteyneth to the fysshynge of pearles. From this Ilande of
Tararequi, there was bzought a pearle of the fasshyon of a
peare, wayinge. xxxi. carattes, whiche Petrus Arias had a-
monge a thousande and soo many poundes weight of other
pearles whiche hee had when capitayne Gaspar Mozales
(befoze Petrus Arias) passed to the saide Ilande in the yeare.
1515. whiche pearle was of great pzice. From the saide I-
lande also, came a great and verye rounde pearle, whiche I
bzought owte of that sea. This was as bygge as a smaule
pellet of a stone bowe, and of the weight of. xxvi. carattes.
I bought it in the citie of Panama in the sea of Sur: And payde
foz it syxe hundzeth and fyftie tymes the weyght therof of
good gold, and had it thze yeares in my custodie: and after my
returne into Spaine, soulde it to therle of Nansao Marquesse
of Zenete, great chamberleyne to powre maiestie, who gaue
it to the Marquesse his wyfe, the ladye Mentia of Mendozza.
I thyncke verely that this pearle was the greatest, faytest,
and roundest that hath byn seeue in those partes. Foz powre

Sur.

Of this reade
moze largely
in the Deca-
des.

By the com-
putation of ye
nice. iiii. grai-
nes make a
sarette.

maieſtie otught to vnderſtande that in the coaſte of the ſea of Sur, there are founde a hundꝛeth greate pearles rounde after the faſſhyon of a peare, to one that is perfecrely rounde and greate. This Ilande of Terarequi, which the Chꝛiſtians caule the Ilande of pearles, & other caule it the Ilande of ſloures, is founde in the eyght degree on the ſouthe ſyde of the firme lande in the pꝛouince of golden Caſtyle oꝛ Beragua. And theſe are the coaſtes of the firme lande where pearles are founde euen vnto this day. J vnderſtande alſo that there are perles founde in the pꝛouince and Jlandes of Cartagenia. And ſence yowr maieſtie appoynted me a gouernour and cappytayne, J haue made further ſearche, and am aduertiſed that pearles are founde in dyuers other places as about the Jland of Code go which lyeth ageynſt the mouth of that poꝛte of the Jlande of Cartagenia which the Jndians caul Coro. The which Jland and poꝛte, are on the Noꝛth ſyde in the tenthe degree of the coaſtes of the firme lande.

❧ Of the familiaritie which certeyne of the Jndians
haue with the deuyll, and howe they receaue
anſwere of hym of thynges to coome.

Hen the Jndians begynne theyꝛ battayle, oꝛ go to any combat oꝛ attempte any other greate matter, they haue certeyne electe menne whom they reuerendely eſteme and caule them Tequinas, whiche in theyꝛ tonge is as muche to ſaye as maſters. Notwithſtandynge that they caule euery man that is cunnynge in any ſcience, by the ſame name, as fyſſhers, foulers, hunters, oꝛ makers of nettes. Theſe Tequinas therfoꝛe, they caule the maſters of theyꝛ aunſweres by cauſe they ſpeake with Tuyra, that is the deuyll, and bꝛynge them aunſwere what he ſaythe, eyther as touchynge ſuche thynges as they haue to doo oꝛ ſhall chaunce to them the day folowynge, oꝛ many dayes to coome. Foꝛ the deuyll beinge ſo auncient an Aſtronomer, knowethe the tymes of thynges and ſeeth howe they are naturally directed and inclined. And makethe theym beleue that they come ſo to paſſe by his oꝛdy-naunce, as though he were the loꝛde and mouer of all that is and ſhalbe: And that he gyueth the day lyght and rayne: cau

Z 3. i.   ſeth

seeth tempest and ruleth the stations of tymes, gyuyng lyfe or
takynge awaye lyfe at his pleasure. By reason wherof, the
Indians being deceaued of hym, and seing also such effectes
to coome certeynely to passe as he hath tolde them before, be=
leue hym in all other thynges and honoure hym in many pla=
ces with sacrifyces of the bludde and liues of men and odori=
ferous spices. And when god disposeth the contrary to that
whiche the deuell hath spoken in oracle wherby he is proued
a lyer, he causeth the Tequiʒus to perswade the people that he
hath chaunged his mynde and sentence for summe of their
synnes, or deuiseth summe suche lye as lyketh hym beste, be=
ynge a skylfull maister in suche subtile and craftie deuises to
deceyue the symple and ignorant people whiche hath smaule
defence againste so mighty and craftie an aduersarie. And as
they caule the deuell Tuyra, so doo they in many places caule
the Christians by the same name, thynkyng that they greatly
honoure them therby, as in deede it is a name very feete and
agreable to many of them, hauynge layde aparte all honestie
and vertue, lyuynge more lyke dragons then men amonge
these symple people.
  Before thinhabitauntes of the Ilande of Hispaniols had re=
ceaued the Christian faithe there was amonge them a secte of
men whiche liued solytarily in the desertes and wooddes and
ledde their lyfe in sylence and abstinence more straightly then
euer dyd the phylosophers of Pythagoras secte, absteinyng in
lyke maner from the eatyng of al thynges that liue by bludde
contented onely with suche fruites, herbes, and rootes as the
desertes and wooddes mynistred vnto them to eate. The pro=
fessours of this secte were cauled Piaces. They gaue them sel=
ues to the knowleage of naturall thynges, and vsed certeine
secreate magicall operations and superstitions wherby they
had familiaritie with spirites whiche they allured into theyr
owne bodyes at suche tymes as they wolde take vppon them
to tell of thynges to coome, whiche they dyd in maner as fol=
loweth. When any of the kynges had occasyon to caule any
of them owte of the desertes for this purpose, their custome
was to sende them a portion of their fyne breade of Cazabbi or
Maizium, and with humble requeste and sute to desyre them to
tell them of suche thynges as they woulde demaunde. After
the requeste graunted and the place and daye appoynted, the
Piaces

Piaces coometh with twoo of his diſciples waytynge on hym, wherof the one bꝛyngeth with hym a veſſell of a ſecreate wa⸗ ter, and the other a lyttle ſyluer bell. When he coommeth to the place, he ſytteth downe on a rounde ſeate made foꝛ hym of purpoſe. Where hauynge his diſciples the one ſtandynge on the one hande and the other on the other euen in the pꝛe⸗ ſence of the kyng and certeyne of his nobles (foꝛ the common people are not admytted to theſe myſteries) and turnynge his face toward the deſerte, he begynneth his inchauntment and cauleth the ſpirit with loude voyce by certeyne names which no man vnderſtandeth but he and his diſciples. After he hath dooen thus a while, if the ſpirite yet deferre his coommyng, he dꝛynketh of the ſayde water, and therwith waxeth hotte and furious, and inuerteth and turneth his inchauntement, and letteth hym ſelfe bludde with a thoꝛne, marueilouſly tur⸗ moylyng hym ſelfe as wee reade of the furious Sybilles not ceaſynge vntyl the ſpirite bee coome: who at his coommyng entereth into hym and ouerthꝛoweth hym as it weare a gre⸗ hounde ſhulde ouerturne a ſquerell. Then foꝛ a ſpace, he ſee⸗ meth to lye as thoughe he were in great payne oꝛ in a rapte, wonderfully toꝛmentynge hym ſelfe, durynge whiche agonie, the other diſciple ſhaketh the ſyluer bell contynually. Thus when the agonie is paſſe and he lyeth quietly (yet withowte any ſence oꝛ feelyng) the kynge oꝛ ſumme other in his ſteade, demaundeth of hym what he deſyꝛeth to knowe, and the ſpi⸗ rite anſwereth by the mouth of the rapte _Piaces_ with a directe and perfecte anſwere to all poyntes. In ſo muche that on a tyme certeyne Spanyardes beynge preſente at theſe myſteries with one of the kinges, and in the Spanyſhe tounge demaun⸗ dynge the _Piaces_ of their ſhyppes whiche they looked foꝛ owte of Spayne, the ſpirite anſwered in the Indian toonge, and toulde them what daye and houre the ſhyppes departed from Spayne, how many they were, and what they bꝛought with⸗ owt faylynge in any poynte. If he be alſo demaunded of the eclypſe of the ſoonne oꝛ moone (which they greatly feare and abhoꝛre) he geueth a perfecte anſwere, and the lyke of tem⸗ peſtes, famen, plentie, warre oꝛ peace, and ſuche other thin⸗ ges. When all the demaundes are fynyſhed, his diſciples caule hym aloude, rynging the ſyluer bell at his eare and blo⸗ wynge a certeyne pouder into his noſethꝛilles wherby he is

Z ʒ.ii.　　　　　rayſed

rapsed as it weare from a deade sleape beinge yet sumewhat heauy headed and faynt a good whyle after. Thus beinge ageyne rewarded of the kynge with moꝛe breade, he departeth ageyne to the desertes with his disciples. But sence the Chꝛistian fayth hath byn disparsed thꝛowghe owte the Ilande, these deuyllyshe practises haue ceased, and they of the members of the deuyll, are made the members of Chꝛyste by baptisme, foꝛsakynge the deuyll and his woꝛkes, with the vaine curiositie of despꝛe of knowleage of thynges to coome, wherof foꝛ the most part it is better to be ignoꝛant then with vexation to knowe that which can not be anoyded.

Furthermoꝛe, in many places of the firme lande, when any of the kynges dye, all his housholde seruauntes, aswell women as men which haue continually serued hym, kyl them selues, beleauynge as they are taught by the deuyl Tuyra, that they which kyll them selues when the kynge dyeth, go with hym to heauen and serue hym in the same place and office as they dyd befoꝛe on the earth whyle he lyued. And that all that refuse so to doo, when after they dye by theyꝛ naturall death oꝛ otherwyse, theyꝛ soules to dye with theyꝛ bodyes and to bec dissolued into ayer and become nothynge as do the soules of hogges, byꝛdes, oꝛ fysshes oꝛ other bꝛute beastes. And that only the other may enioy the pꝛiuileage of immoꝛtalitie foꝛ euer to serue the kynge in heauen. And of this false opinion commeth it that they which sowe coꝛne oꝛ set ꝛootes foꝛ the kynges breade, and gather the same, are accustomed to kyll them selues that they may enioy this pꝛiuileage in heauen. And foꝛ the same purpose, cause a poꝛtion of the graine of Maizium and a bundle of Iucca (wherof theyꝛ breade is made) to bee buryed with them in theyꝛ graues that the same maye serue them in heauen if perhappes there should lacke seedes to sowe. And therfoꝛe they take this with them to begyn with all, vntyl Tuyra (who maketh them all these fayꝛe pꝛomisses) pꝛouyde them of greater quantitie. This haue I my selfe sene in the toppe of the mountaynes of Gusturo, where hauynge in pꝛyson the kynge of that pꝛouince (who rebelled from thobedience of yowꝛe maiestie) and demaundynge of hym to whom perteyned those sepultures oꝛ graues whiche I sawe in his house, he answered that they were of certeyne Indians whi che slewe them selues at the death of his father. And bycause

they

they are oftentymes accuſtomed to burye greate quantities of
wrought golde with them, I cauſed twoo graues to bee ope=
ned, wherein was nothynge founde but a veſſell full of the
grayne of *Maizium*, and a bundell of *Iucca*, as I haue ſayde.
And demaundyng the cauſe hereof of the kinge and the other
Jndians, they aunſwered that they that were buryed there,
were the labourers of the groundes, and men ſkylful in ſow=
ynge of ſeedes and makynge of breade, and ſeruauntes to the
kynges father. And to thende that theyr ſoules ſhoulde not
dye with theyr bodyes, they ſlewe them ſelues at the deathe
of the kynge theyr maſter to lyue with hym in heauen. And
to thintent that they myght ſerue him there in the ſame office
they reſerued that *Maizium* and *Iucca* to ſowe in heauen.
Wherunto I aunſwered them in this maner. Beholde howe
your *Tuyra* deceaueth yowe. And howe all that ye teacheth
yow is falſe. yowe ſee how in ſo long a tyme ſence they are
deade, they haue not yet taken awaye this *Maizium* and *Iucca*
which is nowe putrified and woorth nothynge, and not lyke
to bee ſowen in heauen. To this the kynge replyed, ſayinge:
In that they haue not taken it away nor ſowen it in heauen,
the cauſe is that they chaunced to fynde ynough there, by rea
ſon wherof they had no neade of this. To this errour manye
thynges were ſayde which ſeemed of lyttle force to remoue
hym from his falſe opinion, and eſpecially any ſuch as at that
age are occupyed of the deuyll, whom they paynt of the ſelfe
ſame forme and coloure as he appereth vnto thaym in dyuers
ſhapes and formes. They make alſo Images of golde, copper
and woodde, to the ſame ſimilitudes in terrible ſhapes and ſo
variable as the paynters are accuſtomed to paynt them at the
feete of ſaynte Myhaell tharchangell, or in anye other place
where they paynt them of moſt horrible poſiture. Lykewyſe
when the deuyll greatly intendeth to feare thaym, he threte=
neth to ſende them great tempeſtes which they caule *Huracanas*
or *Haurachanas*, and are ſo behemynt that they ouerthrowe ma
ny howſes and great trees. And I haue ſeene in montaynes
full of many and greate trees, that for the ſpace of three quar
ters of a league the mountayne hathe byn ſubuerted, and the
trees ouerthrowen and plucked owte of the earthe with the
rootes: a thynge doubtleſſe ſo fearefull and terryble to be=
hold, that it may verely appere to be doen by the hand of the
deuell

deupll. And in this caſe the Chꝛiſtian men ought to conſider
with good reaſon, that in al places where the holy ſacrament
is reſerued, the ſayd tempeſtes are no moꝛe ſo owtragious, oꝛ
ſo perelous as they were wonte to bee.

¶ Of the temperature of the regions vnder oꝛ neare to the
burnt lyne cauled _Torrida zona_ oꝛ the Equinoctiall:
and of the dyuers ſeaſons of the yeare.

He landes and regions that are neare about the
clymes of the Equinoctiall lyne, are naturally
hotte, althowghe they bee otherwiſe temperate by the diuine pꝛouidence. And therfoꝛe
ſuche fleſſhe oꝛ fyſhe as is taken and kylled in
theſe regions, can not bee pꝛeſerued from putrefaction except it be roſted, ſodden, oꝛ perboylde, the ſame
daye that it is kylde. And wheras J haue ſayde that ſuch regions are naturally hot, and yet temperate by the pꝛouidence
of god, it is ſo in dede. And therfoꝛe not without cauſe the
aunciént autours were of opinion that the burnte lyne oꝛ _Tor-
rida zona_ where paſſeth the lyne of the Equinoctiall, ſhulde be
vnhabitable by reaſon the ſoonne hath greater dominion in
that place then in any other of the ſphere, remaynynge continually betwene the two tropykes of Cancer and Capꝛicoꝛne.
Foꝛ when in theſe regions the earth is opened oꝛ dygged fro
the ſuperficial parte therof to the depth of a mans heyght, it
is founde temperate. And within this ſpace, the trees and
plantes faſten and ſpꝛeade their rootes, and no dieper. Extendynge the ſame as farre in bꝛeadth in the grounꝺ as do their
bꝛaunches in the ayer. And enter no dieper into the grounde
then J haue ſayde, bycauſe that beneth the depth of the ſaid
ſpace of a mans heyght, the earth is verye hotte, the vpper
parte beinge temperate and verye moyſte aſwell by reaſon of
thaboundaunce of water whiche fauleth from heauen vppon
that earth at certeyne oꝛdinarie ſeaſons of the yeare, as alſo
foꝛ the multitude of great ryuers, bꝛokes, ſpꝛynges and maryſhes, wherby the myghtie and ſupꝛeme loꝛde which made
theſe landes, hath moſte pꝛudently pꝛouyded foꝛ the pꝛeſer-
uation of the ſame.

R. E. Js

R. E. As touchynge this poynt whiche was vnknowen to the owlde wryters, and withowt conſideration wherof reaſon can not perfectly conceaue howe temperate regions ſhulde be vnder the Equinoctiall lyne. J haue thought good for the better manifeſtyngs of this ſecreate wooke of nature, to note owte of Cardanus his booke de Elementis, howe all waters haue theyr courſe toward the South as to the loweſt part of the earth. he wryteth therfore as foloweth. The water was made of leſſe quantitie then the earth and only in maner in the ſuperficiall parte therof, that place might bee lefte for the habitation of beaſtes, and that water by his couldneſſe myght temperate and not deſtroy the lyfe of beaſtes. And bicauſe this generation of lyuynge creatures, was only neceſſary en the ſuperficiall partes of the earth in compariſon to the hole, therfore was the water made to occupie onely the ſuperficiall parte, in the which, metals, plantes, beaſtes, and fyſhes ſhulde bee nuryſhed. And bycauſe there was great perell leaſt it ſhulde be ſo much conſumed by the ayer and heate of the ſoonne, continuall mouinge was ioyned to it, wherby it gathereth courdenes and is preſerued from ſodeyne reſolution. For ſuche waters as doo not moue. doo ſoone putrifie, and are eaſely reſolued into ayer. By reaſon wherof nature prouyded for the generation of water in courde places, as vnder the poles and mountaynes. And whereas the earth vnder the Equinoctiall ſhulde otherwiſe for lacke of moyſter haue bin to much burned and ſcorched. nature alſo prouyded that that parte of the earth ſhulde bee loweſt, by reaſon whereof all waters haue theyr courſe towarde the South to mitigate with moyſter the extremitie of heate which otherwiſe ſhulde haue byn intollerable in that clyme. And by this reaſon, the famous ryuer of Nilus in Egypte, albeit it haue his originall and ſprynge, owt of the mountaynes of the mone called Montes Lunae nere vnto the cyrcle of Capricorne, yet runnynge with all his braunches vnder and beyonde the Equinoctiall cyrcle, it or parſeth throwgh owt the burnt line of Torrida zona, and by the ſame vyolent courſe fauleth into owre ſea nere vnto the citie of Alexandria. Jt was neceſſary therfore that the greateſt parte of the coulde and moyſt element ſhulde haue recourſe hyther and conſiſt there, wheras was the greateſt neceſſitie therof to temper the heate of the ſoonne by moyſtynge and coolynge the earth and the ayer, as vnder the Equinoctiall. And herewith alſo hath moſt prudent nature prouyded for the ſecuritie and preſeruation of the places lyinge betwene bothe the extremities of heate and colde, as betwene the poles and the Equinoctiall. For the waters flowynge eyther one wayes and kyſynge one courſe, no regions can be drowned by fluddes: which thynge they well obſerue that delyuer fieldes from inundations or ouerflowynges, and that take in hande to drye vp maryſhes. Jf therfore waters had not theyr courſe and faul towarde places lowe or declynynge, the hole earth ſhulde bee ouerflowne as a marryſhe. And that the moſt declynynge parte ſhulde bee towarde the South, and ſumwhat hygher about the poles, the cauſe is aſwell the conſumynge heate of the ſoonne in the Southe partes, as the preſeruynge coulde of the hygh mountaynes nere to the poles. For we haue els where proued that heate conſumeth and

waſteth

waſteth as coulde gathereth and preſerueth. And for this cauſe
that parte of the earthe that is neareſt the poles, is, was, and e-
uer ſhalbe higheſt, and likewiſe loweſt in the middeſt furtheſt from
the poles. And therfore it was not conuenient that the ſonne ſhuld
haue his courſe on euery ſyde, neither to the poles. For if it weare
caryed alyke to euery parte throughowt the worlde, it is neceſſary
that the earth bee equall: and by that reaſon ſhulde it eyther bee
altogether dryed, or elles all ouerflowed with water. But where as
this coulde not ſuffyce to the free courſe of ryuers for the often
intercourſe of higher places lyinge in the waye, whereby ouerflowynges and ſtayes of waters and their corruption myght enſue,
the ſame prouydent nature hath gyuen this priuileage to water that it
maye ſo muche aſcende as it hath diſcended: that by this meanes
paſſynge ouer mountaynes and hylles it maye at the length bee caryed into the ſea. &c. hytherto Cardanus, lette vs nowe returne
to the hiſtorie.

There are alſo many roughe and hyghe mountaynes with
temperate ayer and pleaſaunt, cleare, and moderate nightes.
Of the whiche particularitie the auncient writers hauyng no
certeyne knowleage, affyrmed the ſaid burnte lyne or Torrida
zona, or Equinoctiall to be naturally vnhabitable. As touchinge
which thing I am able to witneſſe the contrary, by teſtimonie
of ſyght and feelyng as by moſt certeine ſenſes, hauyng liued
many yeares in this regions, by reaſon wherof better credit
ought to be giuen to me then to ſuche as haue grounded their
opinion onely vpon coniectures. And to ſpeake further of the
ſytuation of theſe regyons, yowe ſhall vnderſtande that the
coaſte of the Northe ſea beynge in the goulfe of Vraba and in
the porte of Darien, where the ſhyppes arryue whiche coome
owte of Spayne, is in the ſyxte degree and a halfe, and in
the ſeuenth, and from ſyxe and a halfe vnto eyght, excepte a
ſmaule pointe which entereth into the ſea toward the North
That pointe which of this land and new parte of the worlde
lieth moſte towarde the Eaſt, is the cape of ſaincte Auguſtine
which is in the eight degree. So that the ſaid goulfe of Vraba
is diſtant from the Equinoctiall lyne, from a hundreth and
twentie to a hundreth and thirtie leaques and three quarters
of a leaque after thaccompte of. xvii. leaques and a halfe for
euerye degree from pole to pole. And thus for a lyttle more or
leſſe, goeth all the coaſte. By reaſon wherof, in the citie of
Sancta Maria Antiqua in Darien, and in all that courſe of the for-
ſayde goulfe of Vraba, at all tymes of the yeare the dayes and
nyghtes are in maner of equall length. And if there bee any
                                                        differenc

Dyfference betwene theym by reaſon of this ſmaule diſtance
from the Equinoctial, it is ſo lyttle, that in.xxiiii. houres ma
kynge a naturall daye, it canne not bee perceaued but by the
iudgement of ſpeculatiue men and ſuche as vnderſtande the
ſphere. From henſe the Noꝛth ſtarre is ſeene very lowe And
when the ſtarres which are cauled the wardens of the noꝛth
ſtarre, are vnder the charriotte, it can not bee ſeene, bycauſe it
is vnder the hoꝛiſontal. And whereas I haue ſayde beefoꝛe
that it rayneth in theſe regions at certeyne oꝛdinarie tymes,
it is ſo in deede. Foꝛ it is wynter and ſummer there at contrary tymes to that whiche is in Spayne, where the greateſt
coulde of froſte and rayne is in December and Ianuary: And
the greateſt heate of ſommer aboute ſaynt Iohannes daye at
mydſommer oꝛ in the moneth of Iuly. But in golden Caſtile
oꝛ *Beragua,* it is contrary. Foꝛ the ſommer and tyme of greateſt dꝛowght and withowt rayne, is at Chꝛiſtmas and a moneth befoꝛe and a moneth after. And the tyme when it rayneth moſt, is about midſommer and a moneth befoꝛe and a mo
neth after. And this ſeaſon whiche they caule wynter, is not
foꝛ that it is any coulder then, then at any other tyme of the
yeare, oꝛ hotter at Chꝛiſtmas then at other ſeaſons, the tyme
in theſe regions being euer after one maner, but foꝛ that that
in this tyme which they caule wynter, the ſoonne is hyd from
theyꝛ ſyghtes by reaſon of cloudes and rayne moꝛe then at o-
ther tymes. Yet foꝛaſmuch as foꝛ the moſte parte of the yeare
they lyue in a cleare, open, and temperate ayer, they ſumwhat
thꝛynke and feele a lyttle coulde durynge the tyme of the ſaid
moiſt and cloudy ayer, althowgh it bee not coulde in deede, oꝛ
at the leaſt ſuche coulde as hath any ſenſible ſharpenes.

⸿ Of dyuers particular thynges, as wooꝛmes, ſerpentes, beaſtes, foules, trees, &c.

Any other thynges myght be ſayde, & much
differyng from theſe wherof I haue ſpoken.
But to lette paſſe the multitude of thynges
whiche are as variable as the power of nature is infinite, and to ſpeake of ſuche thynges as coome chiefely to my rememberaunce
as mooſte wooꝛthy to be noted, I wyll fyꝛſte

speake of certeyne lyttle and troubelous beastes whiche maye seeme to bee engendered of nature to molest and vere menne, to shewe them and gyue them to vnderstand howe smaul and vyle a thynge may offende and disquiete them, to thende that they maye remember the pryncipall ende for the whiche they were created, that is, to knowe theyr maker and procurer of theyr saluation by the waye whiche is open to all Christian men and all other whiche wyll open the eyes of theyr vnder: standynge. An) although the thynges whereof wee entende nowe to speake may seeme vyle and lyttle to bee esteemed, yet are they woorthy to bee noted and consydered to vnderstand the difference and variable woorkes of nature. So it is ther: fore, that whereas in many partes of the firme lande by the which aswell the Christians as Indians don trauel, there are such marysshes and waters in the way that they are fayne to go withowt breeches amonge the herbes and weedes, by rea: son wherof, certeyne smaule beastes or woormes (which they caule Garapates) much lyke vnto tykes, cleaue fast to theyr leg: ges. These woormes are as little as the pouder of beaten salt: And cleaue so fast that they can by no meanes be taken away except the place bee noynted with oyle. And after that the legges bee noynted awhyle with oyle, or the other partes where these lyttle tykes are fastened, they scrape the place with a knyfe and so take them away. But the Indians whi: che haue no oyle, smoke them and burne them with fyer, and abyde great peynes in takynge them awaye by this meanes. Of other lyttle beastes which trouble men and are engende: in theyr heades or other partes of theyr bodies, I saye that the Christian men which trauell into these partes, haue them but seldome tymes, and that not past one or two, and this al so very seldome. For passynge by the lyne of the Diameter where the compasse makethe difference of saylynge by the wynde cauled Greco, (that is North East) and Magistral, (that is south west) which is in the course of the Ilandes of Azori, they sayle but a lyttle way folowing owre vyage by the west, but that all the lyse which the Christians cary with them, or are engendered in theyr heades or other places of theyr bo: dies, dye and vtterly consume by lyttle and lyttle, and are not engendered in India excepte in the heades of lyttle chyl: dren in those partes alwel amonge the chyldren of the Chri:

stians

ſians which are boꝛne there, as alſo amonge the natural In=
dians who haue theym commonly in theyꝛ heades and ſume=
tymes in other partes of theyꝛ bodyes, and eſpecially they of
the pꝛouince of Cueua, which is a region conteynynge moꝛe
then a hundꝛeth leaques in length, and embꝛaſeththe one and
the other coaſt of the Moꝛth ſea and of the Eaſt. When theſe
Indians are infected with this fylthyneſſe, they dꝛeſſe and
clenſe one an other. And they that exerciſe this, are foꝛ the
moſte parte women who eate all that they take: And haue
herein ſuch dexteritie by reaſon of theyꝛ exerciſe, that owre
men can not lyghtly atteyne therunto. There is alſo another
thynge greatly to bee conſydered. And this is how the Chꝛi
ſian men beinge there cleane frome this fylthynes of India,
alwell in theyꝛ heades as the reſte of theyꝛ bodyes, yet when
they returne to coomme ageyne into Europe and begyn to ar=
ryue in that place of the Oꝛean ſea where wee ſayde befoꝛe
that the lyſe dyed and foꝛſoke them, ſuddenly in theyꝛ repaſ=
ſynge by the ſame clyme (as thoughe the lyſe had taryed foꝛ
them in that place) they can by no meanes auoyde theym foꝛ
the ſpace of certeyne dayes although they change theyꝛ ſher=
tes two oꝛ thꝛee tymes in a day. Theſe lyſe are at the fyꝛſte
as lyttle as nyttes, and growe by lyttle and lyttle vntyl they
bee of the byggeneſſe that they are in Spayne. This haue I
often tymes pꝛoued, hauynge nowe foure tymes paſſed the
Ocean ſea by this vyage.

Beſyde theſe wooꝛmes and vermyn wherof we haue ſpo=
ken, there is another lyttle miſcheuous wooꝛme, whiche we
may number amonge the kyndes of fleas, This peſtilence the
Indians caul Nigua: And is much leſſe then a flea. It perſeth
the fleſhe of a man, and ſo launſeth oꝛ cutteth the ſame (whyle
in the meane tyme it can nother bee ſeene noꝛ taken) that in
ſume it hath cutte of theyꝛ handes, and from other theyꝛ fiete
vntyll the remedy was founde to annoynt the place with oyle
and ſcrape it with a raſoure.

In the firme lande in golden Caſtyle oꝛ Beragua, there are
many vypers lyke vnto them of Spayne. They that are byt=
ten of them, dye in ſhoꝛt ſpace. Foꝛ fewe lyue to the fourthe
day except pꝛeſent remedy. Of theſe, ſume are of a leſſe kind
then other: And haue theyꝛ tayle ſumwhat rounde, and leape
in the ayer to aſſayle men. And foꝛ this cauſe, ſume caule

Nigua.

Vypers,

A A a.ii. this

this kynde of vypers Tyro. Theyr bytyng is most venemous, and for the moste parte incurable. One of theym chaunced to byte an Indian mayde whiche serued me in my house, to whome I caused the surgians to mynister theyr ordinarye cure, but they coulde doo her no good, nor yet get one droppe of bludde owt of her, but only a yelowe water, so that shee died the thyrd day for lacke of remedy as the like hath chaunced to dyuers other. This mayde was of thage of xiiij. yeares and spoke the Spanysshe toonge as yf shee had byn borne in Castyle. Shee sayde that the vyper whiche bytte her on the foote, was two spannes longe or lyttle lesse. And that to byte her shee lepte in the ayer for the space of more then syxe paces, as I haue harde the lyke of other credible persons.

Adders.

I haue also seene in the firme lande, a kynde of adders very smaule and of seuen or eyght foote longe. These are so redde that in the nyght they appeare lyke burnynge cooles, and in the day seeme as redde as bludde. These are also venemous, but not so much as the vypers. There are other much lesse and shorter and blacker. These coome owt of the ryuers and wander sumtymes farre on the lande, and are lykewyse venemous. There are also other adders of a russet coloure. These are sumwhat bygger then the vypers, and are hurtful and venemous. There are lykewyse an other sorte of manye coloures and very longe. Of these I sawe one in the yeare of Christ 1 5 15. in the Iland of Hispaniola nere vnto the sea costes at the foote of the mountaynes cauled Pedernales. When this adder was slayne, I measured her and founde her to be more then xx. foote longe, and sumwhat more then a mans fyst in byggenes. And althoughe she hadde three or foure deadely woundes with a swoorde, yet dyed shee not nor stoonke the same daye, in so much that her blude continued warme all that tyme. There are also in the marysshes and desertes of

Dragons.

the firme lande many other kyndes of lysertes, dragons, and other dyuers kyndes of serpentes wherof I entende not here to speake much, bycause I haue more particulerly entreated of these thynges in my generall historie of the Weste Jndyes.

Spyders.

There are also spiders of marueylous bygnesse. And I haue seene summe with the body and legges, bygger then a mannes hande extended euery waye, And I ones sawe one of suche bygnesse, that onely her bodye was as bygge as a
sparowe

sparowe, and full of that lanne wherof they make their web=
bes. This was of a darke russette coloure, with eyes greater
then the eies of a sparow. They are venemous and of terrible
shape to beholde. There are also scorpions and dyuers other
suche venemous wormes. Wherby we maye see, that where
as natural causes and influence of the planettes are of stron=
gest actiuitie, they cease not to engender and brynge foorthe
bothe good and badde accordynge to the disposytion of the
matter, whiche they also doo partely dispose as the phyloso
phers affyrme.

Furthermore in the fyrme lande, there are manye toades
beyng very nopous and hurtefull by reason of their great mul=
titude. They are not venemous. They are seene in greate a=
boundance in _Dariena_ where they are so bygge that when they
dye in the time of drouth, the bones of sum of them (and espe=
cially the rybbes) are of suche greatnesse that they appere too
bee the bones of cattes or of summe other beastes of the same
byggenesse. But as the waters dyminishe and the moysture
consumeth in the tyme of drouth (as I haue sayde) they also
consume therwith vntyll the yeare nexte folowing when the
rayne and moysture increase, at whiche tyme they are seene a=
gayne. Neuerthelesse, at this present, there is no such quan=
titie of them as was wonte to bee, by reason that as the land
is better cultured by the Christians, as well by the fellynge of
wooddes and shrubbes as also by the pasture of kine, horses,
and other beastes, so is it apparent that this poyson dimini=
sheth dayly, wherby that regyon becometh more holsome and
pleasaunt. These toades synge after three or foure sortes.
For summe of them synge pleasauntly: other, lyke owres of
Spayne. Summe also whistle: and other summe make an o=
ther maner of noyse. They are lykewyse of dyuers colours:
as summe greene, summe russette or grey, and summe almost
blacke. But of all sortes, they are great, and fylthye, and
nopous by reason of their great multitude: yet are they not
venemous as I haue sayde.

There are also a straunge kynde of crabbes, whiche coome   **Crabbes,**
foorthe of certeyne holes of the earth that they thrm selues
make. The head and bodye of these, make one rounde thing
muche lyke vnto the hoode of a fawkon. Hauynge foure feete
commyng owt of the one syde and as mang owt of the other.
They

They haue also two mouthes like vnto a paire of smaule pinsers, the one bygger then the other, wherwith they byte, but do no great hurte bycause they are not venemous. Their skyn and bodye is smoothe and thynne as is the skynne of a man, sauynge that it is sumwhat harder. Their colour is russette or white, or blewe, and walke sydelonge. They are very good to bee eaten: In so muche that the Christians trauayling by the fyrme lande, haue byn greatly nuryshed by them bycause they are founde in maner euery where. In shape and forme, they are muche lyke vnto the crabbe which we paynte for the sygne Cancer, and like vnto those which are found in Spaine in *Andalusia* in the ryuer *Guadalchiber* where it entereth into the sea, and in the sea coastes therabout, sauynge that these are of the water and the other of the lande. They are sumtymes hurtefull, so that they that eate of them dye. But this chaunceth onely when they haue eaten any venemous thyng, or of the venemous apples wherwith the Canibale archers poyson their arrowes wherof I wyll speake hereafter. And for this cause the Christians take hede howe they eate of these crabbes if they fynde them neare vnto the sayd apple trees.

Furthermore in these Indies, aswell in the fyrme lande as in the Ilandes, there is founde a kynde of serpentes, which they caule Y. V. *anas*, which summe caule *Iuannas*. These are terrible and fearefull to syght, and yet not hurtefull. They are very delicate to bee eaten, and it is not yet knowen whether they be beastes of the lande or fyshes, bycause they lyue in the water, and wander in the woddes and on the lande. They haue foure feete, and are commonly bigger then connies and in summe places bygger then otters, with tayles lyke lisartes or cutes. Their skynne is spotted, and of the same kynd of smothnesse or barenesse, although of dyuers colours. Upon the ridge of their backes, they haue many long prickes. Theyr teeth are very sharpe, and especially theyr fanges or Dogge teeth. Their throtes are longe and large, reachynge from their beardes to their breastes, of the lyke skynne to the resydewe of their bodyes. They are dumme, and haue no boyce or make any noyse or crye although they bee kepte tyde to the foote of a cheste or any other thynge for the space of .xx. or .xxv. dayes withowt any thyng to eate or drynke, excepte they gyue them nowe and then a lyttle of the breade of
of

of Cacabbi, oz fumme fuch other thyng. They haue foure teete,
and their foze feete as longe as a mans fynger with clawes
lyke the clawes of a byzde, but weaker, and fuche as can not
grafple oz take holde of any thynge. They are muche better
to bee eaten then to beholde. Foz fewe that fee them, wyll
haue defpze to eate of them, by reafon of their hozrible fhape
excepte fuche as haue byn accuftomed to the beaftes of thefe
regyons, whiche are moze hozrible and fearefull, as this is
not but onely in apparence. Their flefhe is of much better taft
then the flefhe of connyes and moze holfome. Foz it hurteth
none but onely fuch as haue had the frenfhe poxe. In fo much
that if they haue onely byn touched of that infyzmitie, although they haue byn hole of longe tyme, neuerthelefle they
feele hurte and complayne of the eatynge of thefe Iuannas, as
hath byn often tymes pzoued by experience.

There are founde in the fyzme lande certeyne byzdes fo lyttle that the hole body of one of theym is no bygget then the
toppe of the byggeft fynger of a mans hande: and yet is the
hare body withowt the fethers not pafte halfe fo bygge. This
byzde, befyde her lyttlenes, is of fuch velocitie and fwyftnes
in flying that who fo feeth her fleing in the ayer, can not fe her
flap oz beate her winges after any other fozt then do the doz-
res oz humble bees oz betels: fo that there is no man that feeth
her flie, that wold think her to be any other then a dozre. They
make their neftes accozdyng to the pzopoztio of their bignes.
And I haue feene that one of thefe byzdes with her neft put
in a paire of gold weights, altogether hath waid no moze the
ii. Tomini, which are in poife. 2 4. grains, with the fethers with
out the which fhe fhulde haue wayed fumwhat lefle. And doubt
lefle when I confider the fynenefle of the clawes and feete of
thefe birdes, I knowe not wherunto I may better liken them
then to the lyttle byzdes whiche the lymmers of bookes are
accuftomed to paynte on the margentes of churche bookes
and other bookes of deuine feruice. Their fethers are of many faire colours as golden yelowe and greene befide other variable colours. Their beake is verye longe foz the pzopoztion
of theyz bodies: and as fyne and fubtile as a fowyng nedle.
They are very hardye: fo that when they fee a man clyme the
tree where they haue theyz neftes, they flye at hys face and
ftryke hym in the eyes, commyng, goynge, and retournynge
with

Byzdes.

A very lyttle
byzde,

with such swyftnes, that no man wolde lightly beleue it that hath not seene it. And certenly these byrdes are so lyttle, that I durst not haue made mention hereof if it were not that diuers other which haue seene them as wel as I, can beare witnes of my saying. They make their nestes of flockes and heare of cotten wherof there is great plentie in these regions, and serueth wel for theyr purpose. But as touchyng the byrdes, foules, and beastes of these Indies, bycause they are innumerable bothe lyttle and greate, I intende not to speake muche heare, bycause I haue spoken more largely hereof in my general hystorye of the Indyes.

Beastes.

There is an other kynde of beastes seene in the firme land which seemed very straunge and marueilous to the Chrystian men to beholde, and muche differynge from all other beastes which haue byn seene in other partes of the worlde. These beastes are cauled *Bardati*: And are foure footed, hauing their tails and al the rest of theyr bodies couered onely with a skyn lyke the coperture of a barbed horse or the chekered skynne of a lysarte or Crocodyle, of coloure betwene whyte and russet, inclynynge sumwhat more to whyte. This beast, is of forme and shape much lyke to a barbed horse with his barbes and flankettes in all poyntes. And from vnder that which is the barbe and coperture, the tayle commeth foorth, and the feete in theyr place, the necke also and the eares in theyr partes, and in fyne all thynges in lyke sorte as in a barbed courser. They are of the bygnes of one of these common dogges. They are not hurtfull. They are fylthy, and haue theyr habitation in certen hillockes of earthe where digginge with there feete they make their dens very deepe & the holes therof in like maner as do connyes. They are verye excellent to be eaten, and are taken with nettes and sum also killed with crosbowes. They are lykewise taken often tymes when the husband men burie the stubble in sowyng time, or to renewe the herbage for kyne and other beastes. I haue often times eaten of theirflesshe which semeth to me of better tast then kyddes flesshe, and holsome to be eaten. And if these beastes had euer byn seene in these partes of the woorlde where the first barbed horses had their original, no man wold iudge but that the forme and fashion of the coperture of horses furnished for the warres was fyrste deuysed by the syght of these beastes.

Bardati.

They

There is also in the firme lande an other beaste called Or- *Tesreo.*
so Formigaro that is, the Ante beare. This beaste in heare and
coloure, is much lyke to the beare of Spayne, and in maner
of the same makynge saue that he hath a much longer snowt
and is of euyll syght. They are often tymes taken only with
staues without any other weapon, and are not hurtful. They
are also taken with dogges bycause they are not naturally armed althowgh they byte sumwhat. They are founde for the
moste parte about and neare to the hyllockes where are great
abundaunce of antes. For in these regions is engendered a *Antes.*
certeyne kynde of antes very lyttle and blacke, in the fyeldes
and playnes where as growe no trees, where by thinstinct of
nature these antes separate them selues to engender far from
the wooddes for feare of these beares : The whiche bycause
they are fearefull, vyle, and vnarmed (as I haue sayde) they
keepe euer in places full of trees vntyll very famen and necessitie, or the great desire that they haue to fiede of these antes,
cause them to coomme owt of the wooddes to hunte for them.
These antes make a hyllocke of earth to the heyght of a man,
or sumwhat more or lesse, and as bygge as a great chest, and
sumtymes as bygge as a butte or a hogges head, and as hard
as a stone : So that they seeme as thoughe they were stones
set vp to lymytte thendes and confines of certeyne landes.
Within these hyllockes made of most harde earth, are innumerable and infinite lyttle antes, the which may bee gathered
by busshelles when the hyllocke is broken. The which when
it is sumtymes moysted by rayne and then dryed agayne by
the heate of the soonne, it breaketh and hath certeyne smaul
ryftes as lyttle and subtyle as the edge of a knyfe. And it semeth that nature hath gyuen sense to these Antes to fynde
such a matter of earth wherwith they may make the sayde hil
locke of surhe hardenes that it may seeme a stronge pauement
made of lyme and stone. And wheras I haue proued and cau
sed sum of them to bee broken, I haue founde them of suche
hardenes as if I had not seene I coulde not haue beleaued :
In so muche that they coulde scarsely bee broken with pykes
of Iren : So stronge fortresses doo these lyttle beastes make
for theyr sauegarde agaynst theyr aduersarie the beare, who
is chiefely nuryshed by them, and gyuen them as an enemie,
accordynge to the common prouerbe which sayth, *Non e alcuna*

BBb.i. *persona*

perfona ſi libera, à chimanchi il ſuo Bargello: That is, there is no mã ſo fre that hath not his perſecutour oʒ pʒyuie enemie. And here whẽ J conſyder the maruelous pʒouidence which nature hath gyuen to theſe lyttle boddies, J cauſe to remembʒaunce the wittie ſentence of Plinie, where ſpeakyng of ſuch lyttle beaſtes, he ſayth thus. Why doo we maruayle at the towʒebearynge ſhoulders of Elephantes, and not rather where nature hathe placed ſo many ſences and ſuche induſtry in ſuche lyttle boddies? Where is hearynge, ſmellynge, ſeeinge, and feelynge, ye, where are the vaynes & arteries (without which no beaſte can lyue oʒ moue) in theſe ſo lyttle boddies whereof ſume are ſo ſmaule that theyʒ hole boddies can ſcarſely be ſene of owr eyes, what ſhall we then ſaye of the partes of the ſame? yet euen amonge theſe are there many of ſuch ſagacitie and induſtrye as the lyke is not ſeene in beaſtes of greater quantitie, no noʒ yet in man. &c. But to returne to the hyſtorie. This enemie which nature hath gyuen to theſe lyttle beaſtes, vſeth this maner to aſſayle them. When he reſoʒteth to the hyllocke where the antes lye hid as in theyʒ foʒtreſſe, he putteth his toonge to one of the ryftes whereof we haue ſpoken being as ſubtyle as the edge of a ſwooʒde, and therewith continuall lyckynge, maketh the place moyſt, the ſome and froth of his mouth beinge of ſuch pʒopertie that by continual lycking the place, it enlargeth the ryfte in ſuch ſoʒt by lyttle and lyttle, that at the length he eaſely putteth in his toonge whiche he hath very longe and thynne, and much diſpʒopoʒtionate to his bodye. And when he hath thus made free paſſage foʒ his toonge into the hyllocke to put it eaſely in and owt at his pleaſure, then he thʒuſteth it into the hole as farre as he can reache, and ſo letteth it reſte a good ſpace vntyl a great quantitie of the antes (whoſe nature reioyſeth in heate and moyſter) haue laden his tonge and as many as he can conteyne in the holowneſſe thereof: at which tyme he ſuddeynly dʒaweth it into his mouth and eateth them, and returneth agayne to the ſame pʒactiſe immediatly vntyl he haue eaten as manye as hym lyſteth, oʒ as longe as he can reache any with his tonge. The fleſhe of this beaſte, is fylthy and vnſauery. But by reaſon of thextreme ſhyftes and neceſſitie that the Chʒiſtian men were put to at theyʒ fyʒſt commynge into theſe partes, they were infoʒced to pʒoue al thynges and ſo fel to theatyng of

theſe

theſe beaſtes. But when they had founde moꝛe delycate meates, they fell into hatred with this. Theſe antes haue thap-
peraunce of the place of theyꝛ enteraunce into the hyllocke,
vnder the grounde. And this at ſo lyttle a hole that it could
hardely be founde yf certeyne of them were not ſeene to paſſe
in and owt. But by this way the beares coulde haue no ſuch
poure to hurte them as aboue at the ſayde ryſtes as I haue
ſayde. There is an other ſtrange beaſte whiche by a name of
contrary effecte, the Spanyardes caule *Cagnuolo leggiero*, that
is the lyght Dogge, wheras it is one of the ſloweſte beaſtes in
the woꝛlde, and ſo heauy and dull in mouynge that it canne
ſcarſely go fyftie paſes in a hole day. Theſe beaſtes are in the
firme lande, and are very ſtraunge to beholde foꝛ the diſpꝛopoꝛtion that they haue to all other beaſtes. They are abowte
two ſpannes in length when they are growne to theyꝛ full
byggeneſſe. But when they are very younge, they are ſumewhat moꝛe groſſe then longe. They haue foure ſubtyle fiete,
and in euery of them foure clawes lyke vnto byꝛdes, and ioyned togyther. yet are nother theyꝛ clawes oꝛ theyꝛ fiete able
to ſuſteyne theyꝛ bodyes from the grounde. By reaſon wherof and by the heauyneſſe of theyꝛ boddies, they dꝛawe theyꝛ
bellyes on the grounde. Theyꝛ neckes are hygh and ſtreyght
and all equall lyke the peſtle of a moꝛter, which is altogyther
equall euen vnto the toppe withowt makynge any pꝛopoꝛti-
on oꝛ ſimilitude of a headde, oꝛ any dyfference excepte in the
noddle. And in the toppes of theyꝛ neckes, they haue verye
rounde faces much lyke vnto owles: And haue a marke of
theyꝛ owne heare after the maner of a cyꝛcle whiche makethe
theyꝛ faces ſeeme ſumwhat moꝛe longe then large. They haue
ſmaule eyes and rounde: And noſtꝛylles lyke vnto munkeys.
They haue lyttle mouthes, and moue theyꝛ neckes frome one
ſyde to an other as thoughe they were aſtonyſſhed. Theyꝛ
chiefe deſyꝛe and delyte is to cleaue and ſtycke faſte vnto trees
oꝛ ſume other thynge whereby they may clyme alofte. And
therfoꝛe foꝛ the moſte parte, theſe beaſtes are founde vppon
trees whervnto cleaupnge faſt, they mounte vp by lyttle and
lyttle, ſtepynge them ſelues by theyꝛ longe clawes. The coloure of theyꝛ heare, is betwene ruſſet and whyte, and of the
pꝛoper coloure of the heare of a weſell. They haue no tayles,
and theyꝛ voyce is much dyſterynge frome other beaſtes: foꝛ

A ſtraunge
beaſt which
ſeemeth a
kynd of Chi-
meleon.

they

they synge onely in the nyght : And that continually frome tyme to tyme syngynge euer syre notes one hygher then ano:ther, so faulynge with the same that the fyrste note is the hyghest and the other in a baser tewne as yf a man shuld say La, sol, fa, mi, re, vt. So this beast sayth, Ha, ha, ha, ha, ha ha. And doubteleste, it seemeth vnto me, that as I haue sayde in the chapitter of the beaste cauled Bardati, that those beastes mighe bee thoriginall and document to imbarbe horses, euen so the fyrste inuenture of musycke myght sceme by the hearynge of this beast to haue the fyrst principles of that seyence rather then by any other thynge in the worlde. But nowe to returne to the hystorie : I say that in a shorte space after this beaste hath soonge and hath paused a whyle, she returneth agepne to the selfe same songe, and doth this only in the nyght and not in the day. By reason wherof and also bycause of her: uyll syght, I thynke her to bee a nyght beaste and the frende of darkenesse. Sumtymes the Christian menne fynde these beastes and brynge thepm home to theyr howses, where also they creepe all abowte with theyr naturall slowenesse, in so much that nother for threatenynge or pryckynge they wyll moue any faster then theyr natural and accustomed pase. And yf they fynde any trees, they creepe thyther immediatly, and mounte to the toppe of the hyghest braunche therof, where they remayne continually for the space of eyght, or tenne, or twentie dayes without eatynge of any thinge as farre as any man can iudge. And wheras I my selfe haue kepte thepm in my house, I coulde neuer perceaue other but that they lyue onely of ayer. And of the same opinion are in maner all men of those regions, bycause they haue neuer scene them eate any thynge, but euer turne theyr heades and mouthes towarde that parte where the wynde bloweth most : wherby may bee consydered that they take moste pleasure in the ayer. They byte not, nor yet can byte, hauyng very lyttle mouthes. They are not venemous or noyous any way: but altogyther brutishe and vtterly vnprofytable and without commoditie yet known en to men, sauynge onely to moue theyr myndes to contem: plate thinfinite poure of god, who delyteth in the varietie of creatures, wherby appeareth the poure of his incomprehen: sible wisedome and maiestie so farre to excede the capacitie of mans vnderstandynge.

In

In theſe regions there are likewiſe found certeyne foules
oꝛ byꝛdes which the Indians caule Alcatrax. Theſe are much
bygger then geeſe. The greateſt parte of theyꝛ fethers are of
ruſſet coloure, and in ſume partes yelowe. Theyꝛ bylles oꝛ
beakes are of two ſpannes in length and verye large neare to
the heade, and growynge ſmaule towarde the poynte. They
haue greate and large thꝛotes: And are much lyke to a foule
which I ſawe in Flaunders in Bꝛuſſelles in yowre maieſties
pallaice which the Flemynges caule Haina. And I remember
that when yowr maieſtie dyned one day in yowre great haule
there was bꝛought to yowre maieſties pꝛeſence a chauderne of
water with certeyne fyſſhes alyue, which the ſayde foule did
eate vp hole. And I thynke verely that that foule was a foule
of the ſea bycauſe ſhee had fiete lyke foules of the water as
haue alſo theſe Alcatrazi, which are likewyſe foules of the ſea:
and of ſuch greatneſſe that I haue ſeene a hole cote of a man
put into the thꝛoates of one of theym in Panama in the yeare
1521. And foꝛaſmuch as in that coaſte of Panama, there paſſeth and flyeth a greate multitude of theſe Alcatrazi bringe a
thynge very notable, I wyll declare the maner hereof as not
onely I, but alſo dyuers other nowe pꝛeſente in yowre maieſties courte haue often tymes ſeene.　　yowre maieſtie ſhall
therfoꝛe vnderſtande that in this place (as I haue ſayde befoꝛe) the ſea of ſur ryſeth and fauleth two leagues and moꝛe
from ſyxe houres to ſyxe houres: ſo that when it increaſeth,
the water of the ſea arryueth ſo neare to the houſes of Panama
as doth owre ſea (cauled Mare Mediterraneum) in Barzalona oꝛ in
Naples. And when the ſayd increaſyng of the ſea commeth,
there commeth alſo therwith ſuch a multitude of the ſmaule
fyſſhes cauled ſardynes, that it is ſo marueylous a thynge to
beholde, that no man wolde beleue it that hath not ſeene it.
In ſo much that the Cacique, (that is) the kynge of that land
at ſuch tyme as I dwelt there, was bounde dayly as he was
commaunded by yowre maieſties gouernour, to bꝛynge oꝛdy-
narply thꝛee canoas oꝛ barkes full of the ſayde ſardynes and
to vnlade the ſame in the markette place, whiche werr afterwarde by the ruler of the citie diuyded amonge the Chꝛiſtian
men without any coſte oꝛ charge to any of them. In ſo much
that yf the people had bin a much greater multitude then they
werr, and as many as are at this pꝛeſente in Toledo oꝛ moꝛe,
　　　　　　　　　　　　　　　　　　　　　　　　and

and had none other thynge to lyue by, they myght haue byn
sufficiently susteyned by these sardynes, bysyde thourerplus
whiche shulde haue remayned. But to returne to the foules
wherof we haue spoken. As the sea commeth, and the sardynes with the same, euen so lykewyse coome the sayde Alcatrazzi therwith: and flye continually ouer it in suche a multytude, that they appeare to couer thupper parte oꝛ floure of
the water. And thus continue in mountynge and faulynge
from the ayer to the water, and from the water to the ayer du
rynge all the tyme of theyꝛ fysshynge. And as soone as they
haue taken any of these sardynes, they flye aboue the water
and eate them incontinently, and suddeynly returne agayne
to the water foꝛ moꝛe, continuing thus course by course with
owt ceasynge. In lyke maner when the sea fauleth, they so
lowe there fysshynge as I haue sayde. There goethe also in
the company of these foules, an other kynde of foules cauled
Coda inforcata, (that is) the foꝛked tayle, wherof I haue made
mention befoꝛe. And as soone as the Alcatrax mounteth from
the water with her pꝛay of the sardynes, suddeynly this Coda
inforcata gyueth her so many strokes, and so persecuteth her,
that shee causeth her to let faule the sardynes whiche shee hath
in her mouth. The which as soone as they are faulne, and be
foꝛe they yet touch the water, the Coda inforcata catcheth them
euen in the faule, in suche soꝛte that it is a great pleasure to
beholde the combatte betwene them all the daye longe. The
number of these Alcatrazzi is such, that the Chꝛystian menne
are accustomed to send to certeyne Ilandes and rockes whiche
are neare abowte Panama, with theyꝛ boates oꝛ barkes to take
these Alcatrazzi whyle they are yet younge and can not flye:
and kyll as many of them with staues as they wyll, vntyll
they haue therwith laden theyꝛ barkes oꝛ canoas. These
younge ones are so fatte and wel fedde that they can not bee
eaten. And are taken foꝛ none other intent but only to make
grease foꝛ candels to burne in the nyght, foꝛ the whiche purpose it serueth very well: and gyueth a cleare lyght, and burneth easely. After this maner and foꝛ this purpose, innumerable of them are kylde. And yet it seemeth that the number
of them that fysshe foꝛ sardynes doo dayly increase

    There are other foules cauled Passeresempie: that is, simple
sparowes. These are sumwhat lesse then semewes: and haue
                                       theyꝛ

Passere sempie.

theyꝛ fiete lyke vnto great malardes: And ſtande in the water ſumtymes. And when the ſhyppes ſayle fyftie oꝛ a hundꝛeth leaques abowte the Ilandes, theſe foules beholdynge
the ſhyppes commyng towarde them, bꝛeake theyꝛ flyght and
faule downe vpon the ſayle yardes, maſtes, and cables therof.
And are ſo ſimple and folyſhe that they tary vntyll they maye
eaſely be taken with mens handes, and were therefoꝛe cauled
of the maryners ſimple ſparowes. They are blacke, and vppon their blacke, haue theyꝛ headde and ſhoulders of fethers
of a darke ruſſet coloure. They are not good to bee eaten, althowgh the mariners haue ſumtimes bin infoꝛced to eate thē̃.

　There is an other kynde of byꝛdes in the fyꝛme lande,
which the Chꝛiſtians caule Picuti, bycauſe they haue very great
beakes in reſpecte of the lyttleneſſe of theyꝛ boddies: Foꝛ
theyꝛ beakes are very heauy and waye moꝛe then theyꝛ hole
boddyes byſyde. Theſe byꝛdes are no bygger then quayles,
but haue a much greater buſhement of fethers, in ſo much that
theyꝛ fethers are moꝛe then theyꝛ boddies. Theyꝛ fethers are
very fayꝛe and of many variable coloures. Theyꝛ beakes are
a quarter of a yarde in length oꝛ moꝛe, and bendynge downe
towarde the earthe, and thꝛee fyngers bꝛode neare vnto the
headde. Theyꝛ tonges are very quilles, wherwith they make
a greate hyſſynge. They make holes in trees with theyꝛ beakes, in the which they make theyꝛ neſtes. And ſurely theſe
byꝛdes are maruelous to beholde foꝛ the great difference whiche they haue from all other byꝛdes that I haue ſeene, aſwel
foꝛ theyꝛ toonges (which are quylles as I haue ſayde) as alſo
foꝛ the ſtrangeneſſe of theyꝛ ſyght and diſpꝛopoꝛtion of their
greate beakes in reſpect of the reſt of theyꝛ boddies. There
are no byꝛdes founde that pꝛouyde better foꝛ the ſafegarde of
theyꝛ younge in the tyme of theyꝛ bꝛeedynge to bee withowte
daunger of wylde cattes that they enter not into theyꝛ neſtes
to deſtroye theyꝛ egges oꝛ younge. And this aſwell by the
ſtraunge maner of buyldyng theyꝛ neſtes, as alſo by theyꝛ
owne defence. And therfoꝛe when they perceaue that the cattes appꝛoche towarde them, they enter into theyꝛ neſtes: and
holdynge theyꝛ beakes towarde thentcraunce of the ſame,
ſtande at theyꝛ defence, and ſo vexe the cattes that they cauſe
them to leaue theyꝛ enterpꝛyſe.

　There are alſo other byꝛdes oꝛ ſparowes, whiche the
Chꝛiſtians

Picuti,

Chziſtians by contrary effect caule Matti, that is fooles. Wher
as neuertheleſſe there is no byzde that ſheweth moze wyt and
crafte in defendynge her younge from perell. Theſe byzdes
are lyttle and in maner blacke, and ſumewhat bygger then
owre thzuſſhes. They haue certeyne whyte fethers in theyr
tieckes, and the lyke ſagacitie oz ſharpenes of ſenſe as haue
the byzdes oz pyes cauled Gaxxuole. They ſeldome tymes light
vppon the earth. They make theyr neſſes in trees ſepara-ed
from other, bycauſe the wylde cattes (cauled Mammoni) are ac
cuſtomed to leape frome tree to tree, not deſcendynge to the
grounde foz feare of other beaſſes, excepte when they are en
fozced by thyzſſe to coomme downe to dzynke at ſuche tymes
as they are ſure not to bee moleſſed. And foz this cauſe doo
not theſe byzdes make theyr neſſes but in trees farre diuyded
from other. They make them of a cubette in length oz moze,
after the maner of bagges oz lyttle ſackes, large at the bottome, and growynge narower and narower towarde the
mouth whereby they are faſtened : hauynge the hole whereat
they enter into the ſacke, of ſuch byggenes as may onely ſuf
fice to re-eaue them. And to thende that the cattes maye not
deuoure theyr younge yf they chaunce to mounte vppon the
trees where they haue theyr neſſes, they vſe an other crafte,
which is. to make theyr neſſes in thycke bzaunches of trees,
and to defende the ſame with ſharpe and ſtronge thoznes implycate and ſet in ſuch ozder that no man is able to make the
lyke. So that the cattes can by no meanes put theyr legges
into the hole of the neſſe to take owte the younge byzdes, aſ
well foz the ſharpenes of the thoznes as alſo foz the depth of
the neſſes, in the bottome wherof, the younge birdes reſſ with
owt daunger of theyr enemie. Foz ſum of theyr neſſes beynge
thzee oz foure ſpannes in lengthe, the legge of the catte can
not reache to the bottome therof. They vſe alſo an other pol
licie : which is, to make many of theyr neſſes in one tree The
which they doo foz one of theſe two cauſes : that is, that eyther of theyr owne naturall diſpoſition they are accuſtomed
to go in great multitudes, & reioyſe in the company of theyr
owne generation as do the byzdes which we caule ſtares, oz
elles to thintent that yf it ſhoulde ſo chaunce that the cattes
ſhulde clyme the trees where they make theyr neſſes, they
might bee a greater company to reſyſſe and moleſſ the cattes,

at whoſe apꝛoch they make a fearefull and terrible cry, wher
by the cattes are put to flyght.

Furthermoꝛe, in the firme land, and in the Ilandes, there
are certeyne byꝛdes cauled Piche oꝛ Gazzuole, ſumewhat lyke
vnto thoſe which we caule woodwaules, oꝛ woodpeckes, be=
inge leſſe then owrs of Spayne. Theſe are altogither blacke,
and go hoppynge and leapyng. Theyꝛ beakes are alſo blacke
and of the ſame faſſhyon as are the popingiays beakes. They
haue longe tayles, and are ſumwhat bygger then ſtares.

There are other byꝛdes cauled Pintadelli, whiche are lyke
vnto certeyne greene byꝛdes whiche the Italyans caule Frin=
guelli: and are of ſeuen coloures. Theſe byꝛdes foꝛ feare of the
cattes, are euer woonte to make theyꝛ neſtes ouer the bankes
of ryuers oꝛ the ſea, where the bꝛaunches of trees ſo reache
ouer the water that with a lyttle weyght they maye bowe
downe to the water. Theyꝛ neſtes are made ſo neare the top=
pes of the bꝛaunches that when the cattes coome theron, the
bꝛaunches bende towarde the water, and the cattes turne
backe ageyne foꝛ feare of faulynge. Foꝛ althoughe no beaſte
in the woꝛlde bee moꝛe malicious then this, yet whereas the
moſte parte of beaſtes are naturally inclyned to ſwymme, this
catte hath no maner of apteneſſe thereunto, and is therefoꝛe
ſoone dꝛowned oꝛ ſtrangeled in the water, and by a pꝛyuie
ſenſe of nature feareth the daunger which he can not eſcape.
Theſe byꝛdes make theyꝛ neſtes in ſuche ſoꝛte, that althowgh
they bee weete and fylled with water, yet doo they ſo ſuddem
ly ryſe vp ageyne, that the younge byꝛdes are not thereby
hurte oꝛ dꝛowned.

There are alſo many nyghtyngales and other byꝛdes whi
che ſynge maruelouſly with great melodie and dyfference in
ſyngynge. Theſe byꝛdes are of maruelous dyuers coloures
the one from the other. Sum are altogither yelowe, and ſum
other of ſo excellente, delectable, and hyghe a coloure as it
weare a rubye. Other are alſo of dyuers and variable co=
loures: ſum of fewe coloures, and other ſume all of one co=
loure: beinge all ſo fayꝛe and bewtifull, that in bꝛyghtneſſe
and ſhynynge they excell all that are ſeene in Spayne, oꝛ Ita=
ly oꝛ other pꝛouinces of Europe. Many of theſe are taken
with nettes, lyme twygges, and ſpꝛynges of dyuers ſoꝛtes.

Dyuers other ſoꝛtes of greate foules lyke vnto Eagles,
and

Gazzuole.

Pintadelli.

Great fowles

and ſuche other as ſyue of pray, are founde in the firme lande
of ſuche diuerſitie, that it is in maner impoſſible to deſcrybe
them all particularly. And forasmuche as J haue more large
ly intreated hereof in my generall hyſtorie of the Jndics, J
thynke it not requyſite here to make anye further mention of
the ſame.

⁋ Of trees, fruites, and plantes.

Cocus.

Here is bothe in the firme lande and the Jſlan=
des a certeyne tree cauled Cocus, beinge a kynd
of date trees and hauynge theyr leaues of the
ſelfe ſame greateneſſe as haue the date trees
which beare dates, but dyffer much in their
growynge. For the leaues of this Cocus grow
owt of the trunkes of the tree as doo the fyngers owt of the
hande, wreathynge them ſelues one within an other and ſo
ſpreadynge abrode. Theſe trees are hygh: and are founde in
great plentie in the coaſte of the ſea of Sur, in the prouince of
Cacique Chiman. Theſe date trees bryng furth a frute after this
ſorte. Beinge altogyther bnite as it groweth on the tree, it
is of greater circumference then the heade of a man. And fró
the ſuperficiall parte to the myddeſt which is the frute, it is
inuolued and couered with many webs much lyke bnto thoſe
hyrdes of towe whiche they vſe in Andalusia. Of this towe or
webbe, the Eaſt Jndians make a certeyne kynde of clothe of
three or foure ſortes, and cordes for the ſayles of ſhyppes.
But in theſe Jndies of powr maieſtie, they paſſe not for theſe
cordes or this clothe that maye be made of the frute of Cocus,
by reaſon of the great plentie that they haue of the bombage
or cotton of the goſſampine trees. The frute which is in the
myddeſt of the ſayde towe, is (as J haue ſayde) as bygge as
a mans fyſte, and ſumtymes twyſe as bygge and more. It is
in forme, lyke bnto a walnutte, or ſum other rounde thynge
ſumwhat more longe then large, and very harde. The rynde
or barke herof, is as thycke as the epicle of letters of a riale
of plate. And within, there cleaueth faſte to the rynde of the
nutte a carnoſitie or ſubſtaunce of coornel, of the thyckeneſſe
of halfe a fynger or of the leaſt fynger of the hande : And is
verye whyte, lyke bnto a fayre Almonde, and of better taſte
and

and moꝛe pleaſaunt.　When this fruite is chewed, there re⸗
mayne certepne crummes as do the lpke of almondes. yet if it
bee ſwalowed downe, it is not vnpleaſaunt. Foꝛ althowgh
that after the iewſe oꝛ moyſture bee gonne downe the thꝛote
befoꝛe the ſapde crummes bee ſwalowed, the reſte whiche is
eaten ſeeme ſumwhat ſharpe oꝛ ſowcr, yet doth it not ſo great
ly offende the taſte as to bee caſte away. Whyle this Cocus is
yet freſhe and newly taken from the tree, they vſe not to eate
of the ſapde carnoſitie and ſrute : But fyꝛſte beatynge it very
much, and then ſtraynynge it, they dꝛawe a mylke thereof,
much better and ſweeter then is the mylke of beaſtes, and of
much ſubſtaunce : The which the Chꝛiſtian men of thoſe regi⸗
ons put in the toꝛtes oꝛ cakes which they make of the grayne
of Maizium wherof they make theyꝛ bꝛeade, oꝛ in other bꝛeade
as we put bꝛeade in poꝛrage : So that by reaſon of the ſapde
mylke of Cocus, the toꝛtes are moꝛe excellent to be eaten with
owt offence to the ſtomake.　They are ſo pleaſaunte to the
taſte, and leaue it aſwell ſatiſſyed as thowghe it had byn de⸗
lyted with many delycate dyſſhes. But to pꝛoceade further,
yowre maieſtie ſhall vnderſtand, that in the place of the ſtone
oꝛ cooꝛnell, there is in the myddeſt of the ſapde carnoſitie, a
voyde place, which neuertheleſſe is full of a moſte cleare and
excellent water, in ſuch quantitie as mape fyll a gꝛeate egge
ſhell, oꝛ moꝛe oꝛ leſſe accoꝛdynge to the byggeneſſe of the Co⸗
cus. The which water ſuerly, is the moſte ſubſtantial, excel⸗
lent and pꝛecious to be dꝛoonke, that mape bee founde in the
woꝛlde. In ſo much that in the momente when it paſſeth the
palate of the mouth and begynneth to goo downe the thꝛote
it ſeemethe that frome the ſole of the foote to the crowne of
the headde, there is no parte of the boddye but that feelethe
great cōfoꝛttherby : as it is doutleſſe one of the moſt excellent
thynges that may be taſted vppon the earth, and ſuche as I
am not able by wꝛytynge oꝛ toonge to expꝛeſſe. And to pꝛo⸗
ceade yet further, I ſay that when the meate of this fruite is
taken from the veſſell therof, the veſſell remayneth as fayꝛe
and nette as though is were pullyſhed : and is without, of co
lour inclynynge towarde blacke, and ſhyneth oꝛ glyſtereth ve⸗
ry fayꝛe. And is within of no leſſe dilicateneſſe. Suche as
haue accuſtomed to dꝛynke in theſe veſſelles, and haue bynne
trowbeled with the diſeaſe cauſed the fretinge of the guttes,

I haue ſeene
one of theſe
fruites ope⸗
ned, the whi
che when it
was hole, yf
it were ſhakē
the water
was harde
ſhogge ther⸗
in as it were
in a bottle,
but in tyme
it conſumed
and was part
ly congeled in
to a ſalte ſub⸗
ſtaunce.

say that they haue by experience founde it a marūelous remedie ageynst that disease: And that it breakethe the stone and prouoketh vrine. This frute was cauled Cocus for this cause, that when it is taken from the place where it cleaueth faste to the tree, there are seene two holes, and aboue them two other naturall holes, which altogyther, doo represent the giesture and fygure of the cattes cauled Mammone, that is, munkeys, when they crye: whiche crye the Indians caule Cocos: But in very deede, this tree is a kynd of date trees: and hath the same effecte to heale fretynge of the guttes, that Plinie descrybeth all kyndes of date trees to haue.

Great trees.

There are furthermore in the firme lande, trees of suche byggenesse that I dare not speake therof but in place where I haue so many wytnesses which haue seene the same as wel as I. I say therfore, that a leaque from Dariena or the citie of Sanctæ Maria Antiqua, there passeth a ryuer very large & diepe, which is cauled Cuti: ouer the which the Indians had layde a greate tree so trauerslinge the same that it was in the steade of a brydge, the which I my selfe with dyuers other that are at this present in yowre maiesties courte, haue often tymes passed ouer. And forasmuch as the sayde tree had lyne longe there, and by the great weight therof was so shronke downewarde and partely couered with water that none could passe ouer it but were weete to the knee, I being then in the yeare 1522. thofficial of Iustice in that citie at yowre maiesties appoyntemente, caused another greate tree to bee layde in that place whiche in lyke maner trauersed the ryuer and reached more then fyftie foote ouer the further syde. This tree was exceadynge greate, and rested aboue the water more then twoo cubytes. In the faule, it cast downe all suche other trees as were within the reache therof: And discouered certeyne vynes whiche were so laden with blacke grapes of pleasaunte taste, that they satisfyed more then fiftie persons whiche eate theyr fylle therof. This tree in the thyckest parte therof, was more then syxtene spannes thicke: And was neuerthelesse but lyttle in respect of many other trees whiche are founde in this prouince. For the Indians of the coaste and prouince of Carbagenia, make barkes or boates therof (which they caule Canoas,) of such byggenesse, beinge all of one hole tree, that sume conteyne a hundreth men, sume a hundreth and thirtie, and sum

ſume moꝛe, hauynge neuertheleſſe ſuchē voyde ſpace withiu the ſame, that there is lefte ſufficiente roome to paſſe to and fro thꝛough owte all the Canoa. Sum of theſe are ſo large by= ſyde the length, that they conteyne moꝛe then tenne oꝛ twelue ſpannes in bꝛeadth, and ſayle with twoo ſayles as with the maſter ſayle and the trinkette which they make of very good cotton. The greateſt trees that J haue ſeene in theſe partes oꝛ in anye other regions, was in the pꝛouince of Guaturo, the kynge wherof rebellynge from thobedience of powre maieſtie, was perſued by me and taken pꝛyſoner : At whiche tyme J with my company, paſſed ouer a very hygh mountayne ful of great trees, in the toppe wherof we founde one tree whiche had thꝛee rootes oꝛ rather diuiſions of the roote aboue the earth in foꝛme of a tryangle oꝛ triuette : ſo that betwene eue= ry foote of this triangle oꝛ thꝛee feete, there was a ſpace of twentie foote betwene euery foote. And this of ſuch heyght aboue the earthe, that a laden carte of thoſe wherewith they are accuſtomed to bꝛynge home coꝛne in the tyme of haruest in the kyngedome of Toledo in Spayne, myght eaſely haue paſ= ſed thꝛowgh euery of thoſe particions oꝛ wyndowes whiche were betwene the thꝛee feete of the ſayd tree. From the earth vpwarde to the trunke of the tree, the open places of the dy= uiſions betwene theſe thꝛee feete, were of ſuche heyght from the grounde, that a footeman with a iauelyn was not able to reache to the place where the ſayde feete ioyned togyther in the trunke oꝛ body of the tree which grewe of great height in one piece and one hole body, oꝛ euer it ſpꝛedde in bꝛaun= ches, which it did not befoꝛe it exceaded in heyght the towꝛe of ſaynt Romane in the citie of Toledo : from whiche heyght and vpwarde, it ſpꝛeade very greate and ſtronge bꝛaunches. Amonge certeyne Spanyardes which clymed this tree, J my ſelfe was one. And when J was aſcended to the place where u begunne to ſpꝛeade the bꝛanches, it was a maruelous thing to beholde a greate countrey of ſuche trees towarde the pꝛo= uince of Abꝛayme. This tree was eaſy to clyme, by rea on of certeyne Beſuchi (wherof J haue ſpoken befoꝛe) which grewe wꝛeathed aboute the tree in ſuche ſoꝛe that they ſeemed to make a ſcalynge ladder. Euery of the foꝛeſayde thꝛee feete which boꝛe the boddie of the tree, was twentie ſpannes in thyckeneſſe. And where they ioyned al togyther aboue in the
trunke

A maruelous tree.

trunke oʒ boddye of the tree, the principall trunke was moʒe
then foʒtie and fyue spannes in circuite. I named the mountayne where thefe trees grow, the mountayne of thʒee footed
trees. And this which I haue nowe declared, was feene of
all the companye that was there with me when (as I haue
fayde befoʒe) I tooke kynge Guaturo pʒyfoner in the yeare
1522. Many thynges moʒe myght here bee fpoken as touchynge this matter, as also howe there are many other excellent trees founde of dyuers foʒtes and dyfference, as fweete
Ceder trees, blacke date trees, and many other: of the which
fum are fo heauy that they can not flote aboue the water but
fynke immediatly to the bottome. And other ageyne as light
as a coʒke. As touchynge all which thynges I haue wʒytten moʒe largely in my generall hyftoʒie of the Indies.

And foʒafmuch as at this pʒefent I haue entered to intreate
of trees, befoʒe I paffe any further to other thynges, I wyl
declare the maner howe the Indians kyndle fyʒe, only with
wooddе and without fyʒe, the maner wherof is this. They
take a piece of woodde of two fpannes in lengthe, as bygge
as the leafte fynger of a mans hande, oʒ as an arrowe well
pullyffhed, and of a ftronge kynde of woodde whiche they
keepe onely foʒ this purpofe. And where they intende to kyndle any fyʒe, they take two other pieces of wooddе of the dry-
eft and lyghteft that they can fynde, and bynde them faft togyther one with an other as clofe as two fyngers ioyned. In
the myddeft oʒ betwene thefe, they put the poynt of the fyʒft
lytеlt ftaffe made of harde and ftronge wood which they hold
in theyʒ handes by the toppe thereof, and turne oʒ rubbe it
rounde aboute continually in one place betwene the two pieces of wooddе which lye bounde togyther vppon the earthe,
which by that vnceffant rubbynge and chafynge, are in fhoʒt
fpace kyndeled and take fyer.

I haue alfo thought good here to fpeake fumwhat of fuch
thynges as coomme to my remembraunce of certeyne trees
which are founde in this lande, and fymetyme alfo the lyke
haue bynne feene in Spayne. Thefe are certeyne putrifyed
troonkes which haue lyne fo longe rottyng on the earth that
they are verye whyte and fhyne in the nyght lyke burnynge
fyʒe bʒandes. And when the Spanyardes fynde any of this
woodde, and intende pʒiuily in the nyght to make warre and
innade

Kyndlynge of
fyʒe withowt
fyʒe,

Putrified
wooddе fhy-
nyng in the
nyght.

Inuade any prouince when caſe ſo requyreth that it ſhalbe neceſſary to go in the nyght in ſuche places where they knowe
not the way, the formoſt Chriſtian man whiche guydethe the
waye, aſſociate with an Indian to directe hym therein, taketh a lyttle ſtarre of the ſayde woodde, which he putteth in
his cappe hangynge behynde on his ſhoulders, by the lyght
wherof he that foloweth nexte to him, directeth his iourney,
who alſo in lyke maner beareth an other ſtarre behynde hym,
by the ſhynynge whereof the thyrde foloweth the ſame waye,
and in lyke maner do al the reſt, ſo that by this meanes none
are loſte or ſtragle owte of the way. And foraſmuche as this
lyght is not ſeene very farre, it is the better pollicie for the
Chriſtians bycauſe they are not thereby diſcloſed before they
inuade theyr enemies.

Furthermore as touchynge the natures of trees, one particular thynge ſeemeth woorthy to bee noted, wherof Plinie
maketh mention in his natural hyſtorye where he ſaythe that
there are certeyne trees which contynewe euer greene and neuer loſe theyr leaues, as the baye tree, the Ceder, the orange
tree, and the olyue tree with ſuch other, of the whiche in all
togyther he nameth not paſſe fyue or ſyxe. To this purpoſe,
I ſaye, that in the Ilandes of theſe Indies, and alſo in the
firme lande, it is a thynge of muche difficultie to fynde twoo
trees that loſe or caſt theyr leaues at any tyme. For althowgh
I haue diligentely ſearched to knowe the trewthe hereof, yet
haue I not ſeene any that loſe theyr leaues, eyther of theym
which we haue browght owt of Spayne into theſe regions,
as Orange trees, Limons, Ceders, Palmes, or date trees
and Pomegranate trees, or of any other in theſe regions excepte onely Caſſia, which loſeth his leaues and hath a greater
thynge appropriate to it ſelfe onely: which is, that whereas
all other trees and plantes of India ſpreade theyr rootes no-
dieper in the earthe then the depth of a mans heyght or ſumewhat more, not deſcendyng any further into the ground by
reaſon of the greate heate which is found beneth that depth,
yet doeth Caſſia pearce further into the grounde vntyl it fynd
water: whiche by the Phyloſophers opinion ſhoulde be the
cauſe of a thynne and watery radycall moyſture to ſuche thynges as drawe theyr nuryſhement therof, as fat and vnctuous
groundes with temperate heate, yelde a faſt & firme moyſture
to

to ſuche thynges as growe in them, whiche is the cauſe that
ſuche trees loſe not theyr leaues, as the ſayde thynne and wa
teryſſhe moyſture is cauſe of the contrarie, as appeareth by
the ſayde effecte which is ſcene onely in *Cagſa,* and none other
tree or plante in all theſe parties.

❡ Of Reedes or Canes.

 Haue not thought it conuenient in the chapiture before to ſpeake of that whereof I intende nowe to intreate of reedes or canes to
thintente that I woolde not mengle theym
with plantes or trees, beinge thynges of the
ſelues woorthy to bee particularly obſerued.
So it is therfore, that in the firme land there
are many ſortes of reedes, ſo that in many places they make
theyr howſes therof, coueryinge them with the toppes of the
ſame, and makynge theyr waules of them in lyke maner, as
I haue ſayde before. And amonge theſe kyndes of reedes,
there is one ſo greate, that the canes therof are as bygge as
a mans legge in the knee, and thre ſpannes in length frome
ioynt to ioynt or more: in ſo much that euery of them is of ca
pacitie to conteyne a lyttle bucket of water. In this kynde,
there are founde ſum greater and ſum leſſe, of the which ſum
they vſe to make quyuers for arrowes. There is founde an
other kynde which ſuerly is marueylous, beynge lyttle bygger then a Iauelen, the canes whereof are longer then twoo
ſpannes. Theſe reedes growe one farre from an other, as ſum
tymes twentie or thirtie paſes, and ſumetymes alſo twoo or
thre leaques. They growe in maner in all prouynces in the
Indies: And growe nere to very hygh trees whereunto they
leane, and creepe vp to the toppes of theyr braunches, which
they imbraſe and deſcende agcyne downe to the earth. Theyr
canes are full of moſte cleare water without any maner of taſſ
or ſauoure eyther of the canes or of any other thynge: And
ſuche as yf it were taken owte of the freſſheſte ſprynge in the
woꝛlde. Nor yet is it knowen that euer it hurte any that
drꝛoonke therof. For it hath oftentymes ſo chaunced that as
the Chꝛiſten men haue trauayled in theſe regions in deſolate
wayes where for lacke of water they haue byn in great daunger

ger to dye for thyrſte, they haue eſcaped that perell by reaſon
that they founde the ſayde reedes, of the water of whoſe canes they haue droonke a great quantitie withowt any hurte
thereof enſewynge. Therefore when they fynde theſe in any
place, they make water veſſelles of the canes therof, and cary
as many of them ful of water as may ſuffice for one dayes ior-
nay. And ſumtyme they cary ſo many, that they take for euery man two or three quartes of water which may ſerue them
for many dayes bycauſe it doth not corrupte, but remayneth e-
ſtyll freſſhe and good.

There are alſo certeine plantes which the Chriſtians caul
Platani. Theſe are as hygh as trees, and become as bygge in
the trunke as the knee of a man or more. Frome the foote to
the toppe, they beare certeyne longe and large leaues, beynge
more then three ſpannes in largenes, and about ten or twelue
in length: The whiche when they are broken of the wynde,
the ſtalke remayneth hole in the myddeſt. In the myddeſt of
this plant in the hygheſt parte therof, there groweth a cluſter with fortie or fyftie Platans abowt it, euery of them beinge a ſpanne and a halfe in length, and as bygge as a mans
arme in the ſmaule, or more or leſſe accordynge to the goodneſſe of the ſoyle where they growe. They haue a rynde not
very thycke, and eaſy to bee broken: being within altogither
full of a ſubſtaunce lyke vnto the marye of the bone of an oxe
as it appeareth when the rynde or barke is taken frome the
ſame. This cluſter owght to bee taken from the plant, when
any one of the Platans begynne to appere yelowe. At which
tyme they take it and hange it in their houſes where all the
cluſter wareth rype with all his Platans. This cluſter is a
very good frute: And when it is opened and the rynde taken
of, there are founde within it many good drye fygges which
beynge roſted or ſtewed in an ouen in a cloſe por or ſum ſuche
other thynge, are of pleaſaunte taſte muche lyke the conſerue
of hony. They putrifie not on the ſea ſo ſoone as ſume other
frutes do: but continue fyfteene dayes and more yf they bee
gathered ſumwhat greene. They ſeeme more delycate on the
ſea then on the lande, not for that they any thinge increaſe in
goodneſſe on the ſea, but bycauſe that whereas on the ſea o-
ther thynges are lackyng wherof is plentie on the land, thoſe
meates ſeeme of beſte taſte which ſatiſfie preſente neceſſitie.

DDd.i.   This

Platani.

Figges.

This troonke or sprygge whiche bryngeth foorth the sayde cluster is a hole yeare in growyng and brynging foorth frute, In whiche tyme it hath put foorth rounde abowte it tenne or twelue sprygges as bygge as the fyrst or pryncipall, and multiplieth no lesse then the pryncipall in bryngynge foorthe of clusters with frutes lykewyse at theyr tyme, and also in bryngynge foorth other and many sprygges as is sayde beefore. From the which sprygges or trunkes, as soone as the cluster of the frute is taken away, the plante begynneth to drye and wyther, which then they take owt of the grounde bycause it doth none other then occupie it in vayne and without profyt. They are so many and doo so maruelouslly increase and multiplie, that it is a thynge in maner incredible. They are exceadynge moyste, In so much that when they are plucked vp frõ the place wher they grow, there issueweth foorth a greate quantitie of water as well owte of the plante as owte of the place where it grewe: In suche sorte that all the moysture of the earth farre abowte, mygh seeme to bee gathered to gyther abowte the trunke or blocke of the sayde plante : with the frutes whereof, the antes are so farre in loue, that they are seene in great multitudes in the branches of the plantes. So that for the multitude thereof it sumetyme so chaunceth that men are inforced to take away the Platans frome theyr possessiion. These frutes are founde at all tymes of the yeare.

Tunas. There is also an other kynd of wyld plantes that groweth in the fyeldes : which I haue not seene but in the Ilande of Hispaniola, althowgh they be founde in other Ilandes of the Indies. These they caule Tunas. They growe of a thistle full of thornes, and brynge foorth a frute muche lyke vnto great fygges, which haue a crowne lyke medlers, and are within of a hyghe coloure, with graynes and the rynde lyke vnto a fygge. They are of good taste : And growe abundantly in the fyeldes in many places. They woorke a straunge effecte in suche as eate them. For if a manne eate twoo or three or more, they cause his vrine to bee of the verye coloure of bludde, which thynge chaunced once to my selfe. At whiche tyme as I made water and sawe the coloure of my vrine, I entered into a great suspition of my lyfe, beinge so astonyshed for feare, that I thought the same had chaunced to me vpon sum other cause. In so muche that surely my imagination mygh

myght haue doone me hurte, but that they whiche were with
me dyd conforte me immediatly, declarynge the cause therof
as they knewe by experience beinge auncient inhabitours in
those regions.

There groweth also an other plante whiche the people of
the countrey caule *Bibaos*. This putteth forth certeyne ſtreight
braunches and very brode leaues which the Indians vſe for
dyuers purpoſes. For in ſum places they couer theyr houſes
with the leaues therof cowched and layde after the maner of
ſhetche, wherunto it ſerueth very well. Sumtymes alſo whē
it rayneth, they caſt theſe ouer theyr heades to defende them
from the water.   They make alſo certeyne cheſtes whiche
they caule *Hauas*, weaued after a ſtraunge ſorte and intermixt
with the leaues of this *Bibaos*. Theſe cheſtes are wrought in
ſuch ſort, that although it rayne vpon them, or they chaunce
to faule into the water, yet are not ſuch thynges wette as are
within them.   They are made of the braunches of the ſayde
Bibaos with the leaues weaued togyther therwith. In theſe
they keepe ſalte and other ſubtyle thynges. They vſe theym
alſo for an other purpoſe, which is this: That findyng them
in the fieldes at ſuch tyme as they haue ſcarſeneſſe of vyttayles, they dygge vp the rootes of theſe plantes whyle they are
yet younge, or eate the plante it ſelfe in that parte where it is
moſte tender, which is from a foote vnder the grounde, where
it is as tender and whyte as a reede or bulruſſhe.

And foraſmuch as wee are nowe coomme to thend of this
narration, it commeth to my rememberaunce to make mention of an other thynge which is not farre from my purpoſe.
And this is howe the Indians do ſtayne or dye cloth of bombage cotton, or any other thynge which they intende to dye
of dyuers coloures: as blacke, tawny, greene, blewe, yelowe,
and redde, whiche they doo with the barkes or ryndes, and
leaues of certeyne trees, whiche they knowe by experience to
bee good for this practiſe. And by this arte they make colours
in ſuch perfection and excellencie that no better can bee deuyſed. But this ſeemeth a ſtraunge thynge, that they doo all
this in one ſelfe ſame veſſell: So that when they haue cauſed
the ſayde ryndes and leaues to boyle togyther, they make in
the ſame veſſell without any chaunge (as I haue ſayde) as
many colours as them lyſteth.   Whiche thynge I ſuppoſe to

Bibaos.

Hauas.

Dying of cot
ton.

A ſtraunge
thynge.

D D d , ii,   coomme

coomme to paſſe by the diſpoſition of the coloure whiche they
haue fyꝛſte gyuen to the thynge that they intende to dye oꝛ co
lout, whether it bee thꝛeede, webbe, oꝛ clothe, oꝛ any thynge
that they intende to coloure.

⟪ Of venemous apples wherwith they
poyſon theyꝛ arrowes.

He apples wherewith the Indian Canibales
inueneme theyꝛ arrowes, growe on certeyne
trees couered with many bꝛaunches and leaues
beinge very greene and growyng thicke. They
are laden with abundaunce of theſe euyll frutes, and haue theyꝛ leaues lyke the leaues of
a peare tree, but that they are leſſe and rounder. The frute
is much lyke the muſcadell peares of the Ilande of Sicilie oꝛ
Naples in foꝛme and byggeneſſe : And are in ſum partes ſey-
ned with redde ſpottes, and of very ſweete ſauoure. Theſe
trees foꝛ the moſte parte, growe euer by the ſea coaſtes and
neare vnto the water : And are ſo fayꝛe and of pleaſaunte ſauour, that there is no man that ſeethe theym but wyll deſyꝛe
to eate thereof.

Note.

In ſo much that if it may bee ſpoken of any frute yet grow
ynge on the earth, I wolde ſaye that this was the vnhappy
frute wherof owre fyꝛſte parentes Adam and Eue taſſed, wher
by they both loſt theyꝛ felicitie and pꝛocured death to them &
theyꝛ poſteritie. Of theſe frutes, and of the greate antes
whoſe bytynge cauſeth ſwellynge (wherof I haue ſpoken
els where) and of the cutes oꝛ lyſartes, and vypers, and ſuch
other venemous thynges, the Canibales which are the chyeſe
archers amonge the Indians, are accuſtomed to poyſon theyꝛ
arrowes wherwith they kyll all that they wounde.

Canibales ar
chiers.

wherwith
they inuenym
ther arrowes

Theſe venemes they mengle togyther and make thereof a
blacke maſſe oꝛ compoſition which appeareth lyke vnto very
blacke pytche. Of this poyſon I cauſed a great quantitie to
be burnt in *Sancta Maria Antiqua* in a place two leaques and moꝛe
within the lande, with a greate multitude of theyꝛ inuenemed
arrowes and other munition, with alſo the houſe wherein
they were reſerued. This was in the yeare. 1514. at ſuche
tyme as tharmy arriued there with capitayne *Pedrarias da villa* at
elis

Petrus de his,

the commaundemente of the Catholyke kynge Don Ferdinando.
But to returne to the hyſtory. Theſe apples (as I haue ſaid)
growe neare vnto the ſea. And wheras the Chriſtians which
ſerue yowr maieſtie in theſe parties, ſuppoſe that there is no
remedy ſo profytable for ſuch as are wounded with theſe arrowes, as is the water of the ſea if the wounde be much waſ
ſted therwith, by which meanes ſum haue eſcaped although
but fewe, yet to ſaye the trewthe, albeit the water of the ſea
haue a certeyne cauſtike qualitie ageynſt poyſon, it is not a ſuf
ficient remedy in this caſe: nor yet to this day haue the Chri
ſtians perceaued that of fiftie that haue byn wounded, three
haue recouered. But that yowr maieſtie may the better conſy
der the force of the veneme of theſe trees, yowe ſhall further
vnderſtande that yf a man doo but repoſe hym ſelfe to ſlepe
a lyttle whyle vnder the ſhadow of the ſame, he hath his head
and eyes ſo ſwolne when he ryſeth, that the eye lyddes are
ioyned with the chekes. And if it chaunce one droppe or more
of the dewe of the ſayde tree to faule into the eye, it vtterly
deſtroyeth the ſyght. The peſtilent nature of this tree is ſuch
that it can not bee declared in fewe woordes. Of theſe there
groweth greate plentie in the goulfe of Vraba, towarde the
North coaſt on the Weſte and Eaſte ſyde. The wood of theſe
trees when it burneth, maketh ſo greate a ſtynke that noo
man is able to abyde it, by reaſon it cauſeth ſo great a peyne
in the headde.

Amonge other trees which are in theſe Indies as well in
the Ilandes as in the firme lande, there is an other kynde
which they caule Xagua, wherof there is great plentie. They
are very hygh and ſtreyght, and fayre to beholde. Of theſe
they vſe to make pykes and tauelyns of dyuers lengthes and
byggeneſſe. They are of a fayre coloure betwene tulſette and
whyte. This tree bryngeth foorth a greate fruit as bygge as
Papauer or poppie, and much lyke therunto. It is very good
to be eaten when it is rype. Owte of this they gette a very
cleare water wherwith they waſhe theyr legges and ſumez
tymes all theyr boddyes when they feele theyr fleſhe weype,
fayne, or looſe. The which water, byſyde that it hath a byndynge qualitie, it hath alſo this propertie, that what ſo euer
it toucheth, it ſteyneth it blacke by lyttle and lyttle vntyll it
bee as blacke as greet, which coloure can not be taken away

iii

in leſſe ſpace then tenne oʒ twelue dayes. And if the nayle bee but touched therwith, it is ſo ſteined that it can by no meanes bee taken away vntyll it eyther faule of, oʒ growe owte and bee clypped away by lyttle and lyttle, as I my ſelfe haue oftentymes ſeene by experience.

Hobi.
Sum thynke theſe to be mirobalanes.

There is an other kynde of trees which they caule Hobi. Theſe are very great and fayʒe, & cauſe holſome ayer where they growe and a pleaſaunt ſhadow, and are founde in great abundaunce. Theyʒ frute is very good, and of good taſt and ſauoure, and much lyke vnto certeyne damſons oʒ prunes beinge lyttle and yelowe. But theyʒ ſtone is very great : by reaſon wherof they haue but lyttle meate. Theyʒ barke oʒ rynde boyled in water, maketh a holſome bathe foʒ the legges, bycauſe it bindeth and ſtepeth the looſeneſſe of the fleſſhe ſo ſenſibly that it is a marueyle to conſyder. It is ſuerly a holſome and excellent bathe agʒynſt ſuch fayntneſſe : And is the beſte tree that may bee founde in thoſe parties to ſleepe vnder. Foʒ it cauſeth no heauineſſe of the headde as doo dyuers other trees. Whiche thynge I ſpeake bycauſe the Chʒiſtians are muche accuſtomed in thoſe regions to lye in the fyeldes. It is therfoʒe a common pʒactiſe amonge them, that where ſo euer they fynd theſe trees, there they ſpʒeade theyʒ mattreſſes and beddes wherin they ſleepe.

Date trees,

There are alſo a kynde of hyghe date trees and full of thoʒnes. The wooddde of theſe is moſte excellent : beinge very blacke, and ſhynynge, and ſo heauy that no parte thereof can ſwymme aboue the water, but ſynketh immediatly to the bottome. Of this wooddde they make theyʒ arrowes and dartes : Alſo ſauelyns, ſpeares, and pykes. And I ſaye pykes, bycauſe that in the coaſtes of the ſea of Sur, beyonde Eſquegus and Vracha, the Indians vſe great and longe pykes made of the wooddde of theſe date trees. Of the ſame lykewyſe they make clubbes and ſwooʒdes and dyuers other weapons. Alſo

Thinhabitantes of the ſea of Sur.

veſſelles and houſholde ſtuffe of dyuers ſoʒtes very fayʒe and commodious. Furthermoʒe of this wooddde the Chʒiſtians vſe to make dyuers muſicall inſtrumentes, as clariſimbals, lutes, gyterns, and ſuche other, the whiche byſyde theyʒ fayʒe ſhy/ dynge coloure lyke vnto giete, are alſo of a good ſounde and very durable by reaſon of the hardeneſſe of the wooddde.

After that I haue ſayde thus much of trees and plantes,
I haue

I haue thought good alſo to ſpeake ſumwhat of herbes. You ſhall therefore vnderſtande that in theſe Indies there is an herbe much lyke vnto a yelowe lyllie, abowte whoſe leaues there growe and creepe certeyne cordes oꝛ laces, as the lyke is partly ſeene in the herbe which we caule laſed ſauery. But theſe of the Indies are muche bygger, and longer : and ſo ſtronge that they tye theyꝛ hangynge beddes thereby whiche they caule Hamacas wherof we haue ſpoken elſwhere. Theſe cordes, they caule Cabuia and Henequen, which are al one thing ſauynge that Henequen is leſſe and of a fyner ſubſtaunce as it were line : And the other is groſſer lyke the wycke oꝛ twyſte of hempe, and is imperfecte in compariſon to the other. They are of coloure betwene whyte and yelowe lyke vnto abarne, and ſum alſo whyte. With Henequen whiche is the moſte ſubtyle and fyne thꝛede, the Indians ſawe in ſunder fetters, cheynes, oꝛ barres of Iren in this maner. They moue the thꝛeede of Henequen vppon the iren which they intende to ſaw oꝛ cutte, dꝛawynge the one hande after the other as doo they that ſawe, puttynge euer nowe and then a poꝛtion of fyne ſande vppon the thꝛeede, oꝛ on the place oꝛ parte of the Iren where they continue rubbynge the ſayde thꝛeede. So that yf the thꝛeede be woꝛne, they take an other, and continewe in theyꝛ wooꝛke as before vntyl they haue cutte in ſunder the iren although it bee neuer ſo bygge : and cut it as yf it were a tender thynge and eaſye to bee ſawne.

And for aſmuch as the leaues of trees may bee counted amonge herbes, I wyll here ſpeake ſumewhat of the qualitie of the leaues of certeyne trees which are founde in the Iland of Hiſpaniola. Theſe trees are ſo full of thoꝛnes, that there is no tree oꝛ plante that ſeemeth moꝛe wylde and defoꝛmed : ſo that I can not well determyne whether they bee trees oꝛ plantes. They haue certeyne bꝛaunches full of large and defoꝛmed leaues, which bꝛaunches were fyꝛſte leaues lyke vnto the other As the bꝛaunches made of theſe leaues growe foꝛth in length, there commeth other leaues of them. So that in fine it is a dyfficult thyng to deſcrybe the foꝛme of theſe trees except the ſame ſhulde bee doone by a paynter wherby the eye myght conceaue that wherein the toonge fayleth in this behalfe. The leaues of this tree are of ſuch vertue, that beyng well beaten and ſpꝛeadde vppon a cloth after the maner of a
playſter

An herb that beareth the cordes.

Cabuia & Henequen.

A ſtraůge thinge.

Leaues.

A leafe of great vertue.

playjee, and ..o layde to a legge oz arme that is bzoken in ma
ny pieces, it healeth it in fyftene dayes, and maketh it as
hole as though it had neuer byn bzoken. Durynge the tyme
of this operation, it cleaueth so fast to the flesshe that it can
not without much difficultie bee taken away. But as soone
as it hath healed the soze and wzought his operation, it loo=
seth it selfe from the place where it was layde, as J my selfe
and dyuers other which haue pzoued it, knowe by experience

❡ Of fysshes and of the maner of fysshynge.

IN the sea coastes of the firme lande, there are
dyuers and sundzy kyndes of fysshes muche
differynge in shape and forme. And although
it be impossible to speake of all, yet wyll J
make mention of sum. And fyzst to begynne at
sardynes, yowe shall vnderstande that there
is founde a kynde of these fysshes very large and with redde
tayles, beinge a very delicate fysshe. The beste kyndes of o=
ther fysshes are these : Moxarre, Diabace, Bzettes, Dabaos, Thozn
backes, and Salmons. All these and dyuers other which J
don ot now remember, are taken in great quantitie in ryuers.
There are lykewyse taken very good creuysshes. There are
also founde in the sea, certeyne other fysshes: as soles, macke
relles, turbuttes, Palamite, Lizze, Polpi, Chieppe, Xaibas, Locustes,
Oysters, exceadynge great Toztoyses, and Tiburoni of mar=
uelous byggenesse: Also Manates, and Murene, and manye
other fysshes which haue no names in oure language. And
these of such diuersitie and quantitie as can not bee expressed
without large wzytynge and longe tyme. But to let passe to
intreate particulerly of the multitude of fysshes, J intende to
speake chiefely and sumwhat largely of thzee sozes of moste
notable fysshes: wherof the fyzst is, the great Toztoyses, the
seconde is called Tiburon, and the thyzde Manate. And to
begynne at the fyzste, J saye that in the Jlande of Cuba, are
founde great Toztoyses (which are certeyne shell fysshes) of
such byggenesse that tenne oz fyftene men are scarsely able
to lyfte one of them owt of the water, as J haue byn infoz=
med of credible persons dwellynge in the same Jlande. But
                                                        of

Tiburons.
Manates

Great Tortoy
ses,

of that which J my felfe haue feene, J can teftifie that in the
firme lande in the vyllage of Acla there are of this forte fum
taken and kylled of fuche byggenes that fire men with much
difficultie coulde fcarfely drawe them owt of the water. And
commonly the leaft fort of them are as much as two men may
cary at a burden. That which J fawe lifted vp by fyre men,
had her fhell a yarde and a quarter in length, and in breadth
more then fyue yardes. The maner of takynge them, is this.
Jt fumtymes chaunceth that in theyr greate nettes (whiche
they caule fhoote nettes) there are founde certeyne Tortoyfes
of the common forte in great quantities. And when they
coomme owt of the fea and bringe foorth theyr egges and go
togyther by coompanies from the fea to feade on the lande,
the Chriftians or Jndians folowe theyr fteppes whiche they
fynde in the fande, and foone ouertake them bycaufe they are
very heauy and flowe in goynge, although they make all the
hafte they can to returne to the fea as foone as they efpie any
boddie. When they that purfewe them haue ouertaken them,
they put a ftake or ftaffe vnder theyr legges and ouerturne the
on theyr backes as they are yet runnynge, fo that they can go
no further nor yet ryfe ageyne or turne. And thus they fuffer
them to lye ftyll whyle they folowe after the refte which they
ouerturne in lyke maner: And by this meanes take very manye at fuche tymes as they coome furth of the fea as J haue
fayde. This fyfhe is very excellent and holfome to be eaten,
and of good tafte. The feconde of the three fyfhes wherof J
haue fpoken, is the Tiburon. This is a very greate fyfhe and   Tiburons.
very quicke and fwyfte in the water, and a cruell deuourer.
Thefe are often tymes taken, afwell when the fhippes are vnder faple in the Ocean, as alfo when they lye at anker, or at
any other time, and efpecially the leafte kynd of thefe fifhes.
When the fhippes are vnder faple, the biggeft forte are taken
after this maner. When the Tiburon feeth the fhippe failinge
he foloweth it ftoppynge behynde. The which thinges the
mariners feeinge, cafte furthe all the fylthe of the fhippe into
the fea for the fyfhe to eate, who neuertheleffe foloweth the
with equal pafe although they make neuer fuche hafte wyth
full wynd and failes, and waloweth on euery fyde and about
the fhyppe: And thus foloweth it fumetyme for the fpace of
a hundreth and fyftie leaques and more. And when the mariners

EE e, i.

riners are disposed to take them, they cast downe by the sterne
of the shippe, a hoke of yren as bigge as the biggest finger of
a mans hande of thre spannes in lengthe and crooked like a
fysshe hooke with beardes accordinge to the bignesse therof,
and fastened to an iren chayne of fyue or syre linkes neare vnto thende, and from thense tyed with a greate rope, fastening
also on the hooke for a bayte, a piece of sum fisshe, or hogges
flesshe, or sum other flesshe, or the bouwelles and intralles of
an other Tiburon whiche they haue taken before, whiche may
easely bee doone, for I haue seene nyne taken in one day.
And if they wold haue taken more, they myght also. Thus
when the Tiburon hath pleasauntly folowed the ship a longe
viage, at the lengthe he iswaloweth the baite with the hocke.
And aswell by his stryuinge to flye or escape, as also by the
swyfte passage of the shyppe, the hooke ouerthwarteth and
catcheth hold of his chappes. The which fisshe whē it is takē,
it is of suche huge biggenesse that twelue or fyfteene men
are scarsely able to drawe it owt of the water and lifte it into
the shyppe: Where one of the mariners gyueth it many knoc-
kes on the headde with a clubbe or beetle vntil he haue slaine
it. They are sumtymes founde of tenne or twelue foote long,
and of fyue, syre, or seuen spannes in breadth where they are
brodest. They haue very greate and wyde mouthes to the proportion of the reste of theyr boddies, and haue two rowes of
teethe the one sumewhat separate from the other, of cruell
shape & standing very thicke. When they haue slayne this
fysshe, they cutte the boddy therof in smaule pieses, and put
it to drye, hangynge it thre or foure dayes at the cordes of
the sayle clothes to drye in the wynde, and then eate it. It
is doubtlesse a good fysshe and of greate commoditie to serue
the shippes for viralles for many dayes. The leaste of these
fysshes are moste holsome and tender. It hath a skinne much
like to the skynne of a sole, wherunto the sayde Tuberon is
like in shape. Which I saye bycause Plinie hath made mention of none of these thre fisshes among the number of them
wherof he wryeth in his natural historie. These Tiburons
coomme furth of the sea and enter into the ryuers, where they
are no lesse perelous then greate lisartes or Crocodiles wherof I haue spoken largely before. For they deuoure men, kine,
and horses, euen as doo the Crocodiles. They are very daun
                                                    gerous

Plinie.

Crocodyles.

gerous in certepne waſſhpnge places oʒ pooles by the ryuers
ſpdes, and where they haue deuoured at other tymes. Dy:
uers other fyſſhes both greate and ſmaule, of ſundʒy ſoʒtes
and kyndes are accuſtomed to folowe the ſhyppes goynge vn:
der ſaple, of the which J wyl ſpeake ſumwhat when J haue
wʒytten of Manate which is the thyʒde of the thʒee whereof   Manates.
J haue pʒompſed to entreate. Manate therefoʒe, is a fyſſhe
of the ſea, of the byggeſt ſoʒte, and muche greater then the
Tiburon in length and bʒeadth : And is very bʒutyſſhe and
vyle, ſo that it appeareth in foʒme lyke vnto one of thoſe
great beſſelles made of goates ſkynnes wherin they vſe to ca
ry newe wyne in *Medina de Campo* oʒ in *Areualo*. The headde of
this beaſt is lyke the head of an ore, with alſo lyke eyes. And
hath in the place of armes, two great ſtumpes wherwith he
ſwymmeth. Jt is a very gentle and tame beaſte : And cōmeth
oftētymes owt of the water to the next ſhoʒe where if he find
ny herbes oʒ graſſe, he feedeth therof. Owre men are accuſto
med to kyl many of theſe and dyuers other good fyſſhes with
theyʒ croſſebowes, purſuinge them in barkes oʒ Canoas, by:
cauſe they ſwymme in maner aboue the water. The whiche
thynge when they ſee, they dʒawe them with a hooke tyde at
a ſmaule coʒde, but ſumwhat ſtronge. As the fyſſhe flyeth a:
way, the archer letteth go and pʒolongeth the coʒde by lyt:
tle and lyttle vntyll he haue lette it go many fathams. At the
ende of the coʒde, there is tyde a coʒke oʒ a piece of lyght
woodde. And when the fyſſhe is goone a lyttle way, & hathe
coloured the water with his bludde, and feeleth hym ſelfe to
faynt and dʒawe towarde thende of his lyfe, he reſoʒtethe to
the ſhoʒe, and the archer foloweth gatherynge vp his coʒde:
wherof whyle there yet remaine ſixe oʒ eyght fathams oʒ ſum
what moʒe oʒ leſſe, he dʒaweth it towarde the lande, and
dʒaweth the fyſſhe therwith by little and lyttle as the waues
of the ſea helpe hym to doo it the moʒe eaſely. Then with
the helpe of the reſte of his companie he lyftethe this greate
beaſt owt of the water to the lande, beinge of ſuch bygneſſe
that to conuey it from thenſe to the citie, it ſhalbe requiſite to
haue a carte with a good yoke of oren, and ſumtymes moʒe,
accoʒdyng as theſe fyſſhes are of byggeneſſe, ſum being much
greater then other ſum in the ſame kynde as is ſeene of other
beaſtes. Sumtymes they lyft theſe fyſſhes into the Canoa oʒ

EEe.ii.   barke

barke, withowt drawynge them to the lande as before. For as soone as they are slayne, they flote aboue the water. And I beleue verely that this fyshe is one of the best in the world to the taste, and the lykest vnto fleshe. Especially so lyke vnto biefe, that who so hath not seene it hole, can iudge it to bee none other when he seethe it in pieces then verye biefe or veale. And is certeynly so lyke vnto fleshe, that all the men in the worlde may herein bee deceaued. The taste lykewyse, is lyke vnto the tast of very good veale, and lasteth longe yf it bee poudered. So that in fine, the base of these parties, is by no meanes lyke vnto this. This Manate, hath a certeine stone or rather bone in his headde within the brayne, which is of qualitie greatly appropriate agaynste the disease of the stone, if it bee burnte and grounde into smaule pouder, and taken fastynge in the mornynge when the payne is felte, in such quantitie as may lye vppon a penye with a drawght of good whyte wyne. For beynge thus taken three or foure mornynges, it acquieteth the grefe as dyuers haue toulde me whiche haue proued it trewe. And I my selfe by testimonie of sight, doo wytnesse that I haue seene this stone sought of dyuers for this effecte.

The fysshe Manate.

A remedy agaynst the stone.

There are also dyuers other fysshes as bygge as this Manate: Emonge the which there is one cauled Vihuella. This fyshe beareth in the toppe of his headde, a swoorde beinge on euery syde full of many sharpe teeth. This swoorde is naturally very harde & stronge, of foure or fyue spannes in length and of proportion accordynge to the same byggenes. And for this cause is this fyshe cauled Spada: that is the swoord fyshe. Of this kynde summ are found as lyttle as sardines: and other so greate, that two yokes of oxen are scarsely able to drawe them on a carte. But whereas before, I haue promysed to speake of other fysshes which are taken in these seas whyle the shyppes are vnder sayle, I wyl not forget to speake of the Tunnye which is a great and good fyshe, and is oftentymes taken and kylde with troute speares and hookes caste in the water when they play and swymme aboute the shyppes. In lyke maner also are taken many turbuts which are very good fysshes as are lyghtly in all the sea.

The swoorde fyshe.

Tunnye.

Turbut.

And here is to bee noted, that in the greate Ocean sea, there is a straunge thynge to bee considered, whiche all that haue

haue byn in the Indies affirme to bee trewe. And this is, that lyke as on the lande there are sum prouinces fertile and frutefull, and sum barren, euen so dooth the lyke chaunce in the sea : So that at sum wyndes the shyppes sayle fiftie or a hundreth, or two hundreth leaques and more, withowt takyng or seinge of one fysshe. And ageyne in the selfe same Ocean, in sum places, all the water is seene tremble by the mouynge of the fysshes, where they are taken abundauntly.

It commeth further to my rememberaunce to speake sumwhat of the flyinge of fysshes, which is doubtlesse a straunge thynge to beholde, and is after this maner. When the shyppes sayle by the greate Ocean folowynge theyr vyage, there ryseth sumtymes on the one syde or on the other, many coompanies of certeyne lyttle fysshes, of the which the byggest is no greater then a sardyne : and soo diminisshe lesse and lesse from that quantitie that sum of them are very lyttle. These are caulled *Volatori* : that is, flyinge fysshes. They ryse by great coompanies and flockes in such multitudes that it is an astonysshement to beholde them. Sumtymes they ryse but lyttle from the water : &(as it chaunceth) continew one flyght for the space of a hundreth pases and sumtymes more or lesse before they faule ageyne into the sea. Sumtymes also they faule into the shyppes. And I remember that on an euenyng when all the company in the shippe were on theyr knees syngynge *salue regina* in the highest parte of the Castel of the poope, and sayled with a full wynde, there passed by vs a flocke of these flyinge fysshes : and came so neare vs that many of them fell into the shyppe, amonge the which, two or thre fell hard by me which I tooke alyue in my hande : so that I myght well perceaue that they were as bigge as sardynes and of the same quantitie, hauynge two wynges or quylles growyng owt of theyr fynnes, lyke vnto those wherwith all fysshes swymme in ryuers. These wynges are as longe as the fysshes theym selues. As longe as theyr wynges are moyste, they beare them vp in the ayer. But as soone as they are drye, they can continew theyr flyght no further then as I haue sayde before, but faule immediatly into the sea, and so ryse ageyne, and flye as before from place to place.

In

Note.

Flyinge fysshes.

In the yeare A thouſand fyue hundꝛeth fiftene.when I
came fyꝛſt to infoꝛme your maieſtye of the ſtate of the thynges
Indya, and was the yeare folowynge in Flaunders in the
tyme of youre moſte foꝛtunate ſucceſſe in theſe youre kynge=
domes of Aragonie and Caſtyle,wheras at that vyage I ſay
led aboue the Iland *Bermuda* otherwyſe cauled *Garza,* beynge
the furtheſte of all the Ilandes that are founde at thys daye
in the woꝛlde, and arryuynge there at the deapthe of eight
peardes of water, and dyſtant from the land as farre as the
ſhotte of a piece of oꝛdynaunce, I determined to ſende ſume of
the ſhyppe to lande as well to make ſearche of ſuche thynges
as were there, as alſo to leaue in the Ilande certayne hogges
foꝛ increaſe. But the tyme not ſeruyng my purpoſe by reaſon
of contrarye wynde, I could bꝛyng my ſhyppes no nearer the
Ilande beinge twelue leaques in lengthe and ſyre in bꝛeadth
and about thyꝛty in circuite, lying in the thyꝛtie thꝛe ꝑ degre
of the noꝛthe ſyde. Whyle I remayned here, I ſawe a ſtryfe
and combatte betwene theſe flyinge fyſhes and the fyſhes na=
med gylte heades, and the foules cauled ſeamewes and coꝛ=
moꝛauntes, whych ſuerlye ſeemed vnto me a thynge of as
greate pleaſure and ſolace as coulde bee deuyſed, whyle the
gylte heades ſwamme on the bꝛymme of the water and ſum=
tymes lyfted their ſhulders aboue the ſame to rayſe the ſwym
mynge fyſſhes owt of the water to dꝛyue them to flyght, and
folowe them ſwymming to the place where they faule to take
and eate them ſodaynlye. Agayne on the other ſyde, the ſea=
mewes and coꝛmoꝛautes, take manye of theſe flying fyſſhes:
ſo that by thys meanes theye are nother ſafe in the ayre noꝛ
in the water. In the ſelfe ſame perrell and daunger doo men
lyue in thys moꝛtall lyfe wherin is no certayne ſecurytye ne=
ther in hygh eſtate noꝛ in lowe. Which thynge ſuerlye ought
to put vs in remembraunce of that bleſſed and ſafe reſtynge
place whych god hath pꝛepared foꝛ ſuch as loue hym, who
ſhall acquyete and fynyſhe the trauayles of thys troubelous
woꝛlde wherin are ſo manye daungyours, and bꝛynge them
to that eternall lyfe where they ſhall fynde eternall ſecurytye
and reſte. But to returne to the hyſtoꝛye: theſe byꝛdes and
foules whych I ſawe, were of the Ilande of *Bermuda* nere vn=
to the whych I ſawe theſe flyinge fyſſhes. Foꝛ they coulde
bee of no other lande, foꝛaſmuche as they are not accuſtomed
to

The Iland of
Bermuda.

Not to hye foꝛ
the pye,noꝛ to
lowe fꝛoꝛ the
crowe.

to wander farre frome the coaſtes where they are bredde.

¶ Of thincreaſe and decreaſe, (that is) ryſynge and faullynge of our Ocean ſea and Southe ſea caulled the ſea of Sur.

Wyll nowe ſpeake of certeayne thynges whiche are ſeene in the Prouynce, or at the leaſte in the citie of golden Caſtyle otherwyſe cauled Beragua, and in the coaſtes of the North ſea and of the South ſea caulled the ſea of Sur. Not omittyng to note one ſynguler and meruelous thynge which I haue conſydered of the Ocean ſea. wherof hytherto no coſmographer, pylote or maryner or any other haue ſatiſfyed me. I ſay therfore as it is well knowen to your maieſtye and all ſuch as haue knowlege of the Ocean ſea, that this greate Ocean caſteth from it ſelfe the ſea Mediterraneum by the mourhe of the ſtrayght of Gibilterra: in the which the water from thend and furtheſte parte of that ſea, euen vnto the mouth of the ſayde ſtraight, eyther in the Eaſt towarde the coaſte common lye caulled Leuante, or in any other parte of the ſayde ſea Mediterraneum, the ſea doothe not ſo faule nor increaſe as reaſon wolde iudge for ſo greate a ſea. But increſethe verye lyttle and a ſmaule ſpace. Neuertheleſſe, withoute the mouthe of the ſtraight in the mayne Ocean, it increaſeth and fauleth verye muche and a great ſpace of grounde from ſyxe houres to ſyxe houres, as in all the coaſtes of Spayne, Britannye, Flanders, Germanye and England. The ſelfe ſame Ocean ſea in the fyrme lande newly founde, in the coaſtes of the ſame lypyng towarde the Northe, dothe neyther ryſe nor faule, nor lykewiſe in the Ilandes of Hiſpaniola and Cuba and all the other Ilandes of the ſame ſea lyinge towarde the northe, for the ſpace of thre thouſande leaques, but onelye in lyke maner as doothe the ſea Mediterraneum in Italye: whiche is in maner nothynge in reſpecte to that increaſe and decreaſe whiche the ſayde Ocean hath in the coaſtes of Spayne and Flaunders. But this is yet a greater thynge, that alſo the ſelfe ſame Ocean in the coaſtes of the ſayde fyrme lande lyinge towarde the Southe in the citie of Panama, and alſo in the coaſte of that land

Beragua.

The weſt Ocean.
The ſea mediterraneum.

Hiſpaniola.
Cuba.

lande whiche lyethe towarde the Eaſte and Weſte from that citie, as in the Jlande of pearles oʒ Margarites whiche the Jn=dians caule Tarrarequi, and alſo in Tabogs and Otoque, and in all other Jlandes of the ſouthe ſea of Sur, the water ryſeth and fauleth ſo much, that when it fauleth it goth in maner owt of ſyghte, which thynge J my ſelfe haue ſeene oftentymes.

The South ſea.

And here youre maieſtie may note an other thynge, that from the noʒthe ſea to the ſouthe ſea beynge of ſuche dyfference the one from the other in ryſynge and faulynge, yet is the lan=de that deuydeth theym not paſt eyghteene oʒ twentye lea=ques in bʒeadthe frome coaſte to coaſte. So that bothe the ſayde ſeas beynge all one Ocean this ſtraunge effecte is a thynge woʒthy greately to bee conſidered of al ſuche as haue inclination and deſyre to knowe the ſecreate wooʒkes of na=ture wherin the infinite powre and wyſedome of god is ſeene

The power and wiſdome of god is ſene in his creatures

to bee ſuch as may allure all good natures to reuerence and loue ſo diuine a maieſtie. And wheras by the demonſtrations of lerned men J am not ſatiſfyed of the natural cauſe hereof, J content my ſelfe to knowe and beleue that he which hathe made theſe thynges, dooth knowe this and many other whi=che he hath not granted to the reaſon of man to compʒehend, much leſſe to ſo baſe a wyt as myne is. They therefoʒe that are of greater vnderſtandynge, ſhall ſearche the cauſe hereof, foʒ them and foʒ me, foʒaſmuch as J haue onely put the mat=ter in queſtion as a wytneſſe that haue ſeene thexperience of the thynge.

❡ Of the ſtrayght oʒ narowe paſſage of the lande lyinge be=twene the Noʒth and South ſea, by the whiche ſpyces way much ſooner and eaſſyer be bʒought from the J=landes of Molucca into Spayne by the Weſt Oce=an then by that way wherby the Poʒtugales ſayle into Eaſt Judia.

IT hath byn an opinion amonge the Coſmogra=phers and Pylottes of late tyme, and other which haue had pʒactiſe in thynges touchynge the ſea, that there ſhulde bee a ſtraygh[t] of wa=ter paſſynge from the Noʒth ſea of the firme, in=to the South ſea of Sur, whiche neuertheleſſe hath

hath not byn seene nor founde to this daye. And suerlye yⁱ
there be any suche strayght, we that inhabite those partes do
thynke the same shulde bee rather of lande then of water. For
the fyrme lande in sum partes therof is so strayght and narrowe that the Indyans saye that frome the monutaynes of
the prouynce of *Esquegua* or *Vrraca*, (whych are betwene the one
sea and the other) If a man assend to the toppe of the mountaynes and looke towarde the Northe, he maye see the water of the North sea of the Prouynce of *Beragua*. And ageyne
lookynge the contrarye waye, may on the other syde towarde
the Southe, see the sea of *sur* and the prouynces whyche
consyne with it, as doo the terrytoryes of the twoo Lordes
or kynges of the sayde prouynces of *Vrraca* and *Esquegua*. And I
beleue that if it bee as the Indyans saye, of al that is hetherto knowen, this is the narowest strayght of the fyrme lande,
whiche sume affyrme to bee full of rough mountaynes. Yet
doo I not take it for a better waye, or so shorte as is that
whyche is made from the porte cauled *Nomen dei* (whiche is in
the Northe sea) vnto the newe citye of *Panama* beynge in the
coaste and on the banke of the sea of *sur*. Whiche waye is likewyse very rough ful of thicke wods, mountaines, ryuers, valleys, and verye diffyculte to passe through, and can not bee
doone withowt greate laboure and trauayle. Sum measure
this waye in this part, to bee from sea to sea . xviii. leaques,
whych I suppose to bee rather. xx. not for that it is any more
by measure, but bicause it is rough and dyffyculte as I haue
sayde, and as I haue founde it by experyence hauynge nowe
twyse passed that way by foote: countyng from the porte and
vyllage of *Nomen Dei* vnto the dominion of the *Cacique* of *Iuana*
ga otherwyse cauled *Capira*. viii. leaques: And frome thense
to the ryuer of *Chagre*, other . viii . leaques. So that at this
ryuer beinge . xvi . leaques from the sayde porte, endeth the
roughnesse of the way. Then from hense to the maruelous
brydge are two leaques: And beyonde that, other twoo vnto
the port of *Panama*: So that all togyther in my iudgemente,
make . xx . leaques. And if therfore this nauigation may bee
founde in the South sea for the trade of spices (as we trust in
God) to bee brought from thense to the sayde porte of *Panama*
(as is possible enough) they may afterwarde easy passe to the
Northe sea notwithstandynge the difficultie of the waye of

Esquegua
and vrrace.

Nomen Dei.

Panama.

The ryuer of
Chagre.

Fff, i. the

the .xx. leagues aforesayde. Whiche thynge I affirme as a
man well trauayled in these regions, hauynge twyse on my
feete passed ouer this strayght in the yeare .1521. as I haue
sayde. It is furthermore to bee vnderstode, that it is a maruelous facilitie to bryng spices by this way which I wil now
declare. From Panama to the ryuer of Chagre, are foure leagues
of good and fayre way by the which cartes may passe at pleasure by reason that the mountaynes are but fewe and lyttle,
and that the greateste parte of these foure leagues is a playne
grounde voyde of trees. And when the cartes are coomme to
the sayde ryuer, the spices may bee caryed in barkes and pin-
nesses. For this ryuer entereth into the North sea fyue or vi
leagues lower then the port of Nomen dei; and emptieth it selfe
in the sea nere vnto an Ilande cauled Bastimento, where is a very good and safe port. Yowr maiestie may now therfore consyder howe great a thynge and what commoditie it maye bee to
conuey spices this way, forasmuch as the ryuer of Chagre hauyng his originall only two leagues from the South sea, con-
tineweth his course & emptieth it selfe into the other North
sea. This ryuer runneth fast and is very greate, and so commodious for this purpose as may be thowght or desyred. The
maruelous bridge made by the worke of nature, being two
leagues beyonde the sayd ryuer, and other twoo leagues on
this syde the porte of Panama, so lyinge in the mydde way betwene them both, is framed naturally in such sort that none
which passe by this viage see any such bridge or thynke that
there is any such buyldyng in that place vntyll they bee in the
toppe therof in the way toward Panama. But as soone as they
are on the brydge, lookynge towarde the ryght hande, they
see a lyttle ryuer vnder them which hath his chanell distante
from the feete of them that walke ouer it, the space of twoo
speares length or more. The water of this ryuer is very shalowe, not passyng the depth of a mans legge to the knee: and
is in breadth betwene thyrtie and fortie paces: and fauleth
into the ryuer of Chagre. Towarde the ryght hand standyng
on this brydge, there is nothyng seene but great trees. The
largenesse of the brydge, conteyneth .xv. paces: and the
length therof about threescore or fourescore paces. The arche
is so made of moste harde stone, that no man can beholde it
without admiration, beinge made by the hyghe and omnipotent

The Ilande
Bastimento.

The marue-
lous bridge.

tent createur of all thynges. But to returne to speake sum=
what moze of the conueping of spices, I say that when it shal
please almyghty god that this nauigation afozesayde shal bee
founde by the good foztune of powre maiestie, and that the
spices of the Flandes of the South sea (which may also bee
otherwyse cauled the Ocean of the East India in the whiche
are the Flandes of Molucca) shalbe bzowght to the sayd coaste
and the pozte of Panama, and bee conueyed from thense (as we
haue sayde) by the firme lande with cartes vnto the ryuer of
Chagre, and from thense into this or other sea of the Mozth,
from whense they may afterward bee bzowght into Spayne,
I say that by this meanes the vyage shall bee shoztened moze
then seuen thousande leaques, with muche lesse daunger then
is by the viage nowe vsed by the way of Commendatoz of Ay=
sa capitayne vnder powre maiestie, who this pzesent yeare at=
tempted a vyage to the place of the sayde spyces. And not on=
ly the way is thus much shoztened, but also a thyzde parte of
the tyme is abbzeuiate. To conclude therfoze, if any had he=
therto attempted this vyage by the sea of Sur, to seeke the Fi=
landes of spyces, I am of firme opinion that they shuld haue
byn founde longe sence, as doubtelesse they maye bee by the
reasons of Cosmographie.

The Flandes
of Molucca.

The commo=
ditie of this
viage.

⟪ Howe thynges that are of one kynde, dyffer in fozme
and qualitie, accozdynge to the nature of the place
where they are engendzed oz growe. And of the
beastes cauled Tygers.

IN the firme lande are fownde many terryble
beastes which sum thinke to be Tigers. Which
thynge neuerthelesse, I dare not affirme, con=
sydcrynge what auctoures doo wzyte of the
lyghtnes and agilitie of the Tyger, whereas
this beast beynge other wyse in shape very like
vnto a Tyger, is notwithstandynge very slowe. yet trewe it
is, that accozdynge to the maruayles of the wozlde and diffe=
rences which naturall thynges haue in dyuers regions vnder
heauen and dyuers constellations of the same vnder the whi=
che they are created, wee see that sum suche plantes and her=
bes as are hurtfull in one countrey, are harmelesse and hol=

Tigers.

plantes and
herbes.

FFf.ii. some

Birdes.

Men.

Sheepe.

Bulles.

Iucca.

Battes.

Plinie.

the Tiger.

some in other regions. And byrdes which in one prouince are of good taste, are in other so vnsauery that they may not bee eaten. Men likewyse which in sum countreys are blacke, are in other places whyte: and yet are both these and they men.

Euen so may it bee that Tygers are lyght in sum region as they wryte, and maye neuerthelesse bee slowe and heauy in these Indies of yowr maiestie wherof we speake. The sheepe of Arabie drawe theyr tayles longe and bigge on the ground, and the bulles of Egypt haue theyr heare growynge towarde theyr headdes: yet are those sheepe and these bulles. Men in sum countreys are hardy and of good courage, and in other naturally fearefull and brutyshe. All these thynges and many moe which may bee sayde to this purpose, are easy to bee proued and woorthy to bee beleued of suche as haue redde of the lyke in autours or trauayled the worlde, whereby theyr owne syght may teache theym thexperience of these thynges wherof I speake. It is also manifest, that Iucca wherof they make theyr breade in the Ilande of Hispaniola, is deadely poyson yf it bee eaten greene with the iuse: And yet hathe it no suche propertie in the firme land where I haue eaten it many tymes & found it to bee a good frute. The bats of Spayne although they bite, yet are they not venemous. But in the firme lande many dye that are bytten of them. And in this fourme may so many thynges bee sayde that tyme shall not suffice to wryte, wheras my intent is only to proue that this beast may be a Tiger or of the kind of Tigers although it be not of suche lyghtnesse and swiftnes as are they wherof Plinie and other autours speake, discrybynge it to bee one of the swyftest beastes of the lande, and that the ryuer of Tigris for the swift course therof was cauled by that name. The first Spaniardes which sawe this Tyger in the firme lande, dyd so name it. Of the kynde of these was that which Don Diego Columbo the Admirall sent yowre maiestie owte of newe Spayne to Toledo. Theyr heades are lyke to the heades of Lyons or Lionesses, but greater. The reste of all theyr boddies and theyr legges, are full of blacke spottes one nere vnto an other and diuided with a circumference or frynge of redde colour shewinge as it were a fayre woorke and correspondent picture. Abowt theyr croopes or hynder partes, they haue these spots byggest: and lesse and lesse towarde theyr bellies, legges, and

heades

headdes. That which was brought to Toledo, was younge and but lyttle, and by my estimation, of thage of three yeares But in the firme lande there are many founde of greater quantitie. For I haue seene sum of three spannes in heyght, and more then fyue in length. They are beastes of great force, with stronge legges, and well armed with nayles and fanges which we caule dogge teeth. They are so fierce that in my iudgement no reall lyon of the byggest sorte is so stronge or fierce. Of these, there are many founde in the firme land whiche deuour many of the Indians & do much hurte otherwyse. But syns the comming of the Christians, many haue byn kyld with Crossebowes after this maner. As soone as the archer The hunting of tigers. hath knowlege of the haunt of any of these Tygers, he gothe searchynge theyr trase with his crossebowe and with a lyttle hounde or bewgle and not with a grehounde, bycause this beast wolde soone kyll any dogge that wolde venter on hym. When the hounde hath founde the Tyger, he runneth about hym bayinge continually, and approcheth so neare hym snappynge and grynnynge with so quicke flyinge and returnyng, that he hereby so molesteth this fierce beaste that he dryueth hym to take the next tree, at the foote whereof he remayneth styl baping and the Tyger grynnyng and shewyng his teeth, whyle in the meane tyme the archer commeth neare, and . xii. or . riiii . pases of, stryketh hym with the quereel of his crossebowe in the breste, and flyeth incontinent, leauynge the Tyger in his trauaple for lyfe and death, bytynge the tree and eatynge earth for fiercenesse. Then within the space of twoo or three houres or the day folowynge, the archer returneth thyther, and with his dogge fyndeth the place where he lyeth deade.

In the yeare. 1522. I with the other rulers & magistrates of the citie of *Sancta Maria Antiqua* in *Dariena*, toke order in owr A reward for kyllinge of tigers. counsayle, A rewarde of foure or fyue pieces of golde to bee giuen to euery man that kylde any of these Tygers: by reason wherof many were kylde in shorte space both with crossebowes and also with dyuers snares and ingens. But to conclude, I wyll not obstynately stand in opinyon whether these beastes bee Tygers or Panthers, or of the number of any other such beastes of spotted heare , or also peraduenture sum other newe beaste vnknowen to the owlde wryters as were

many

many other wherof I haue spoken in this booke. Of which thynge, I doo not greatly meruayle, for asmuche as vnto owre tyme thys greate parte of the worlde was vnknowen to the antiquitie: In so muche that none of the wryters of that age, nor yet Ptolomie in his Cosmographie, or any other sence hym, haue made any mention herof, vntill the fyrst Admyrall Don Chrystopher Colonus discouered the same.

A thynge doutelesse without comparyson muche greater then that whyche is sayd of Hercules, that he fyrst gaue thentrance of the sea *Mediterraneum* into the Ocean, whiche the Grekes coulde neuer doo before hym. And herof rysethe the fable that the mountaynes of Calpe and Abila (which are directly one agaynst an other in the strayght of *Gibilterra*, the one beyng in Spayne and the other in Affryke) were ioyned togither before they were opened by Hercules, who erected those hys pyllers whiche your maiestye gyue in token of prehemynence and lyke enterpryses with lykewyse these hys wordes PLVS VLTRA: wordes doutelesse worthy for so greate an vnyuersall an Emperoure, and not conuenyent for any other Prynce. Forasmuche as your holy Catholyke Maiestye haue spredde them in so straunge and remote regyons, so manye thousande leaques further than euer dyd Hercules. And certeynlye syr, If there had byn an Image of golde made in the prayse and fame of *Colonus*, He had as well deserued it as any of those men to whom for theyr noble enterpryse the antiquitie gaue deuyne honoure, if he had byn in their tyme. But to returne to the matter wherof I began to speake: I neede say no more of the forme of thys beaste, for as muche as your Maiestye haue seene that whych is yet alyue in Tolledo. And suerly the keper of your Maiesties lyons, who hath taken vppon hym the charge to tame this beaste, myght better haue bestowed his paynes in an other thynge that myght haue bynne more profitable for the safegarde of his lyfe bycause this Tyger beinge yet but younge, wyl dayly bee stronger and fiercer and increase in malyce. The Indians (and especially they of the firme lande in the prouince whiche the Catholyke Kynge Don Ferdinando commaunded to bee cauled golden Castyle) caule this beaste *Ochi*. This thynge is straunge that chaunced of late: that wheras the Tiger wherof we haue made mention before, wolde haue kylde his keper that then kept hym in a cage

Marginal notes:

Colocus compared to Hercules.

The pillers of Hercules

the straightes of Gibilterra.

Note.

PLVS VLTRA.

Howe farre Themperous maiestie excelleth Hercules.

A tyger made tame.

cage, was in fewe dayes after made so tame that he ledde her
tyed only with a smaule coꝛde and playde with her so family=
arly that I maruayled greatly to see it, yet not without cer=
teyne belefe that this frendshyp wyll not laste longe without
daunger of lyfe to the keeper, foꝛasmuch as suerly these bea=
stes are not meete to bee amonge men foꝛ theyꝛ fiercenes and
cruell nature that can not bee tamed.

**Of the maners and customes of the Indians of the
firme lande, and of theyꝛ women.**

He maners and customes of these Indians, are
dyuers in diuers pꝛouinces. Sum of them take
as many wyues as them lyste, and other lyue
with one wyfe whome they foꝛsake not with=
out consent of both parties, which chauncethe
especially when they haue no chyldꝛen. The no The Indian women.
bilitie aswel men as women, repute it infamous to ioyne with
any of base parentage oꝛ strangers, except Chꝛistians, whom
they count noble men by reason of theyꝛ valientnes, although
they put a difference betwene the common soꝛte and the other
to whom they shewe obedience, countynge it foꝛ a great mat=
ter and an honoꝛable thyng yf they bee beloued of any of thē.
In so much that yf they knowe any Chꝛistian man carnally,
they keepe theyꝛ fayth to hym, so that he bee not longe ab=
sent farre from them. Foꝛ theyꝛ intent is not to bee widowes
oꝛ to lyue chast lyke religious women. Many of theym haue
this custome, that when they perceaue that they are with
chylde, they take an herbe wherwith they destroy that is con
ceaued. Foꝛ they say that only wel aged women shulde beare
chyldꝛen, and that they wyl not foꝛbeare theyꝛ pleasures and
defoꝛme theyꝛ boddies with bearynge of chyldꝛen, wherby
theyꝛ teates becoome loose and hangynge which thynge they
greatly dispꝛayse. When they are delyuered of theyꝛ chyldꝛen
they go to the ryuer and washe them. Whiche doone, theyꝛ
bludde and purgation ceaseth immediatly. And when after
this they haue a few days absteyned frō the company of men,
they becoomme so strayght as they say which haue had carnall
familiaritie with them, that such as vse them, can not with=
out much difficultie satisfie theyꝛ appetite. They also whiche
neuer had chyldꝛen, are euer as bꝛgins. In sum partes they The men of India.
weare

weare certeyne lyttle apern s rounde about them before and behynde as lowe as to theyr knees and hammes, wherwith they couer theyr pryuie partes, and are naked all theyr boddie bysyde. The principal men beare theyr pryuities in a holowe pype of golde : but the common sorte haue theym inclosed in the shelles of certeyne great welkes, and are bysyde vtterly naked. For they thynke it no more shame to haue theyr cods seene then any other parte of theyr boddies. And in many prouinces borthe the men and women go vtterly naked without any such couerture at al. In the prouince of *Cucus* they caul a man *Chuy*, and a woman *Ira* : which name is not greately diſagreeable to many both of theyr women and of owres.

These Indians gyue great honour and reuerence to theyr *Cacique* (that is) theyr kynges and rulers. The principall *Cacique*, hath twelue of his most strange Indians appoynted to

The kynge is borne on mēs backes.

beare hym when he remoueth to any place, or gothe abrod for his pleasure. Two of them cary hym syttyng vppon a longe piece of woodde which is naturally as lyght as they can fynd The other tenne folowe nexte vnto hym as foote men. They keepe continually a trottynge pase with hym on theyr shulders. When the twoo that cary hym are wery, other twoo coomme in theyr places without any disturbance or stey. And thus if the way bee playne, they cary hym in this maner for the space of .rb. or. rr. leaques in one day. The Indians that are assigned to this office, are for the most parte slaues or *Naborii*, that is, such as are bounde to continuall seruce.

Lettinge of bludde.

I haue also noted that when the Indians perceaue them selues to bee troubled with to much bludde, they lette theym selues blud in the calfes of theyr legges & brawnes of theyr armes. This doo they with a very sharpe stone, and sumtymes with the smaule toothe of a vyper, or with a sharpe reede or thorne

They haue no beardes .

All the Indians are commonly without beardes : In so much that it is in maner a maruayle to see any of them eyther men or women to haue any downe or heare on theyr faces or other partes of theyr boddies. Albeit, I sawe the *Cacique* of the prouince of *Caturapa* who had heare on his face and other partes of his boddie, as had also his wyfe in suche places as

They paynte theyr bodies.

women are accustomed to haue. This *Cacique* had a great part of his body paynted with a blacke colour which neuer fadeth : And is much lyke vnto that wherwith the Mores payut them

selues

selues in Barberie in token of nobilitie. But the Moores are
paynted specially on theyr vysage and throte and certeyne
other partes. Likewyse the principall Indians vse these
payntynges on theyr armes and brestes, but not on theyr vy-
sages, bycause amonge them the slaues are so marked. When
the Indians of certeyne prouinces go to the battayle (especially the Caniball archers) they cary certeyne shelles of greate
welkes of the sea which they blowe and make therwith great
sounde muche lyke the noyse of hornes. They carye also certeyne tymbrels which they vse in the steade of drummes. Also
very fayre plumes of fethers, and certeyne armure of golde:
especially great and rounde pieces on theyr brestes, and splin-
tes on there armes. Lykewyse other pieces whiche they put
on theyr heades and other partes of theyr bodyes. For they
esteeme nothynge so much as to appeare galante in the wars,
and to go in most coomely order that they can deuyse, glyste-
rynge with precious stones, iewelles, golde, and fethers. Of
the leaste of these welkes or perewincles, they make certeyne
lyttle beades of diuers sortes and colours. They make also
little braslelets whiche they mengle with gaudies of golde.
These they rowle about there armes frome the elbowe to the
wreste of the hande. The lyke also doo they on theyr legges
from the knee to the soles of theyr feete in token of nobilitie.
Especially theyr noble women in dyuers prouinces are accustomed to weare such Jewelles, and haue theyr neckes in maner laden therwith. These beades and Jewels and such other
trynkettes, they caule *Caquiras*. Bisyde these also, they weare
certeyne rynges of golde at theyr eares and nostrelles which
they bore ful of holes on both sides, so that the ringes hange
vppon theyr lyppes. Sum of these Indians, are poulde and
rounded. Albeit, commonly both the men and women take it
for a decent thynge to weare longe heare, which the women
weare to the myddest of theyr shulders and cut it equally, especially aboue theyr browes. This doo they with certeyne
harde stones which they keepe for the same purpose. The principall women when theyr teates faule or becoome loose, beare
them vp with barres of golde of the length of a spanne and a
halfe, wel wrought, and of such byggenesse that sum of them
way more then two hundreth Castilians or ducades of golde.
These barres haue holes at both thendes, whereat they tye

The Canibal-les.

Armure of golde.

Their galant-nes in the warres.

Their Juells

howe the wo-men beare vp their teates, wych barres of golde.

two fmaul cordes made of cotton at euery ende of the barres. One of thefe cordes goth ouer the fhulder, and the other vnder the arme holes where they tye both togyther, fo that by this meanes the barre beareth vp theyr teates. Sum of thefe chiefe women go to the battaple with theyr hufbandes, or when they them felues are regentes in any prouinces, in the which they haue all thynges at commaundement and execute thoffice of generall capitaynes, and caufe them felues to bee caryed on mens backes in lyke maner as doo the Catiques of whom J haue fpoken before.

The ftature and coloure of the Indians.

Thefe Jndians of the firme lande are muche of the fame ftature and coloure as are they of the Jlandes. They are for the moft part of the colour of an olyue. Jf there bee any other difference, it is more in byggeneffe then otherwyfe. And efpecially they that are cauled Coronati, are ftronger and bygger then any other that J haue feene in thefe parties, except thofe of the Jlande of giantes whiche are on the fouth fyde of the Jlande of Hifpaniola nere vnto the coaftes of the firme lande: And lykewyfe certeyne other which they caule Yucatos which are on the north fyde. All which chiefely, although they bee no giantes, yet are they doubteleffe the byggefte of the Jndyans that are knowen to this day, and commonly bygger then the Flemynges : and efpecially many of them afwell women as men, are of very hyghe ftature, and are all archiers bothe men and women. Thefe Coronati inhabite thirtie leaques in length by thefe coaftes from the poynt of Canoa to the greate ryuer which they caule Guadalchibir nere vnto Sancta Maria de gratia. As J trauerfed by thofe coaftes, J fylled a butte of freffe water of that ryuer fyxe leaques in the fea frome the mouthe therof where it fauleth into the fea. They are cauled Coronati (that is crowned) bycaufe theyr heare is cutte round by theyr eares, and poulde lower a great compafe abowte the crowne much lyke the fryers of faynt Auguftines order. And bycaufe J haue fpoken of theyr maner of wearynge theyr heare, here commeth to my rememberaunce a thynge which J haue oftentymes noted in thefe Jndians. And this is, that they haue the bones of the fculles of theyr heades foure tymes thycker and much ftronger then owres. So that in commyng to hand ftrokes with them, it fhalbe requifite not to ftrike them on the heades with fwoordes. For fo haue many fwoordes bynne broken

The Jndians cauled Coronati.
The Jlande of giantes.
Iucatos.

The fculles of the Jndias heades.

bꝛoken on theyꝛ heades with lyttle hurt doone. And to haue
ſayde thus much of theyꝛ cuſtomes and maners, it ſhal ſuffice
foꝛ this tyme, bycauſe I haue moꝛe largely intreated herof in
my generall hyſtoꝛie of the Indies. yet haue I nother there
noꝛ here ſpoken much of that parte of the firme lande whiche
is cauled Noua Hiſpania (that is, newe Spayne whereof the I-
lande of Iucatana is part) foꝛaſmuche as Ferdinando Coꝛteſe
hath wꝛytten a large booke t,ereof.

New Spaine

Of the houſes of theſe Indians, I haue ſpoken ſufficient
ly elſwhere. yet haue I thought good to infoꝛme poꝮr ma
ieſtie of the buyldynge and houſes which the Chꝛiſtians haue
made in dyuers places in the firme lande. They buylde them
nowe therefoꝛe with two ſolars oꝛ loftes, and with loopes and
wyndowes to open and ſhutte. Alſo with ſtronge tymber and
very fayꝛe boꝛdes. In ſuche ſoꝛte that any noble man maye
wel and pleaſauntly bee lodged in ſum of them. And amonge
other, I my ſelfe cauſed one to bee builded in the citie of Sancta
Maria Antiqua in Dariena whiche coſte me moꝛe then a thouſande
and fyue hundꝛeth Caſtelians : being of ſuch ſoꝛt that I may
well interteyne and commodiouſly lodge any Loꝛde oꝛ noble
man, reſeruynge alſo a parte foꝛ my ſelfe and my famelie. Foꝛ
in this may many houſeholdes bee kepte both aboue and benethe. It hath alſo a fayꝛe garden with many oꝛange trees
bothe ſweete and ſowꝛe : Ceders alſo, and Lemondes, of the
which there is nowe great plentie in the houſes of the Chꝛy-
ſtians. On one ſyde of the gardeyne, there runneth a fayꝛe ry
uer. The ſituation is very pleaſaunte, with a good and holſome ayer, and a fayꝛe pꝛoſpecte abowte the ryuer. In fine,
owre truſte is that in fewe yeares al thynges in theſe regions
ſhall growe to a better ſtate accoꝛdynge to the holy intention
of poꝮr maieſtie.

The houſes
of the Chriſti
ans in India

Darien.

Gardens.

Of the chiefe Ilandes Hiſpaniola and Cuba.

He Indians which at this pꝛeſent inhabite the
Ilande of Hiſpaniola, are but fewe in number, and the Chꝛyſtyans not ſo many as they
ought to bee foꝛaſmuche as many of them that
were in this Ilande, are gonne to other Ilandes and to the fyꝛme lande. Foꝛ beynge foꝛ the
　　　　　G G g. ii.　　　　　　moſte

Men are desirous of newe thynges.

The commodities of Hispaniola, Englande and Sicilie.

Golde mines.

Cotton.

Cassia.

Suger.

Plantes and herbes.

Greate thynges hyndered by respecte of presente gaynes.

moste parte younge men vnmaried, and desirous dayly to see newe thyngs wherin mans nature deliteth, they were not willyng to continewe longe in on place: especially seeing dat lie other newe landes discouered where they thowght they might sooner fylle there purses by beinge present at the firste spoyle. Wherin neuerthelesse their hope deceaued many of them, and especially suche as had houses and habitations in thys Ilande, For I certeynly beleue, confyrmynge my selfe herein with the Iudgement of many other, that if any one Prynce had no more signiores then only this Ilande, it shuld in shorte tyme bee suche as not to giue place eyther to Sicilie or Englande: wheras euen at this present there is nothynge wherfore it shulde malice their prosperitie not beinge inferi oure to them in any filicite that in maner the heauens can graunte to any lande: beinge furthermore suche as maye in riche many prouinces and kyngedomes by reason of many riche golde mynes that are in it of the beste golde that is founde to this day in the worlde, and in greatest quantitie.

In this Ilande, nature of her selfe bryngeth furthe suche a boundance of cotton that if it were wrought and maynteyned there shuld be more and better then in any parte of the world. There, is so greate plentie of excellent Cassia that a greate qua titie is brought from thense into Spayne: from whense it is caried to dyuers partes of the worlde. It increaseth so muche that it is a meruelous thynge to consider. In this are many ryche shoppes wher suger is wrought: and that of such perfectenes and goodnes, and in suche quantitie that shippes come laden therwith yearly into Spayne. All suche sedes, settes, or plantes, as are brought out of Spayne and planted in this Ilande, becoomme muche better, bygger, and of grea ter increase then they are in any parte of owre Europe. And if it chaunce otherwyse that sumetymes they prosper not so well, the cause is that they which shulde tyll and husband the grounde, and sowe and plant in dewe seasons, haue no respect hereunto, being impacient whyle the wheate and vynes ware rype, beinge gyuen to wanderynge and other affayres of pre sent gaynes (as I haue sayd) as searchynge the gold mines, fyshynge for pearles, and occuppyinge marchaundies, with such other trades, for the greedy folowyng wherof, they neglecte and contempne both sowynge and plantynge. Suche frutes as are brought owt of Spayne, into this Ilande, prosper

per marueloufly and waxe rype all tymes of the yeare: as her
bes of all fortes very good and pleafaunt to bee eaten. Alſo
many pomegranates of the beſt kynde, and oranges bothe
ſweete and ſower. Lykewyſe many fayre lymones & ceders:
and a great quantitie of all ſuch as are of ſharpe, ſowre, and
bytter taſte. There are alſo many fygge trees whiche brynge
furth theyr frute all the hole yeare. Lykewyſe thoſe kynd of
date trees that beare dates: and dyuers other trees and plan
tes which were brought owt of Spayne thyther.

Beaſtes doo alſo increaſe in lyke abundaunce: and eſpeci
ally the heardes of kyne are ſo augmented both in quantitie
and number, that there are nowe many patrones of cattayle
that haue more then two thouſand heades of neate: and ſum
three or foure thouſande, and ſum more. Byſyde theſe, there
are very many that haue heardes of foure or fyue hundrethe.
And trewth it is, that this Iland hath better paſture for ſuch
cattayle then any other countrey in the worlde: alſo holſome
ond cleare water and temperate ayer, by reaſon whereof the
heardes of ſuch beaſtes are much bygger, fatter, and alſo of
better taſte then owres in Spayne bycauſe of the ranke pa=
ſture whoſe moyſture is better digeſted in the herbe or graſſe
by the continuall and temperate heate of the ſoonne, wherby
being made more fatte and vnctuous, it is of better and more
ſtedfaſt nuryſhement. For continuall and temperate heate,
dooth not only drawe muche moyſture owt of the earth to the
nuryſhement of ſuch thynges as growe and are engendered in
that clyme, but dooth alſo by moderation preſerue the ſame
from reſolution and putrefaction, digeſtynge alſo and conden
ſatynge or thyckenynge the ſayde moyſte nuryſhemente into a
gummie and vnctuous ſubſtaunce as is ſeene in all ſuche thin
ges as growe in thoſe regions. And this is the only naturall
cauſe aſwell that certeyne great beaſtes and of longe lyfe (as
the Elephante and Rhinoceros with ſuch other) are engende
red only in regions nere vnto the Equinoctiall, as alſo that
the leaues of ſuch trees as growe there, doo not wyther or
faule, vntyll they bee thruſte owt by other, accordynge to the
verſe of the poete which ſayth: Et nata pira piris, et ficus in ficubus ex-
tant. That is in effecte: peares growynge vppon peares, and
fygges vppon fygges. Plinie alſo wryteth, that ſuche trees
are neuer infected with the diſeaſe of trees that the Latines
cauſe

Oranges.
pomegran=
tes.

Figges al the
yeare.
Dates.

Beaſtes.

Greate hear=
des of cattail.

good paſture.

The effecte of
continuall and
moderate
heate.

The cauſe of
fatte nuriſſhe
mente.

Beaſtes of
longe lyfe in
reg ons a
bowte the E=
quinoctiall
line
Trees whoſe
leaues doo
not wither

The cancar of the tree

caule *Carles*, which we may caule the worme or canker, being but a certeyne putrifaction by reaſon of a wateryſhe nuryſhement not well conſolidate. The ſame thynge hath bynne the cauſe that certeyne Phyloſophers conſiderynge aſwell that man is the hotteſt and moyſteſt beaſt that is (which is the beſt complexion) as alſo that men lyue longeſte in certeyne partes of India nere the Equinoctiall (where yet to this day ſumme liue to thage of a hundreth and fiftie yeares) were of opinion that yf mankynde had any begynnynge on the earthe, that place owght by good reaſon to be vnder or not farre from the Equinoctiall lyne for the cauſes aforeſayde. Sum of the diuines alſo vppon lyke conſideration haue thought it agreable that theyr Paradyſe ſhulde bee about the ſame within the precincte of thoſe ryuers which are named in the booke of Geneſis. But to lette paſſe theſe thynges and to returne to the hyſtorie.

Longe lyuide men in India.

Paradiſe neare the e quinoctiall line

Shepee and hogges

In this Ilande furthermore, are many ſheepe and a great number of hogges: of the which (as alſo of the kyne) manye are becoome wyld: And lykewyſe many dogges and cattes of thoſe which were brought owt of Spayne. Theſe (and eſpecially the dogges) doo much hurte amonge the cattayle by reaſon of the negligence of the hearde men.

Dogges and cattes becom wylde

There are alſo many horſes, mares, and mules, and ſuche other beaſtes as ſerue thuſe of men in Spayne, and are much greater then they of the fyrſte brode brought thether owt of Spayne. Sum places of the Ilande are inhabyted, although not ſo many as were requiſite: Of the which I wyll ſaye no more but that all the regions of the Ilande are ſo well ſituate that in the courſe of tyme all thynges ſhall coomme to greater perfection by reaſon of the rychneſſe and pleaſauntneſſe of the countrey and fertilitie of the ſoile.

The ſituation of hiſpaniola.

But nowe to ſpeake ſumwhat of the principall and chiefe place of the Ilande, which is the citie of *San Domenico* : I ſaye that as touchynge the buildynges, there is no citie in Spaine ſo muche for ſo muche (no not *Barſalona* whiche I haue oftentymes ſeene) that is to bee preferred before this generallye. For the houſes of *San Domenico*, are for the moſte parte of ſtone as are they of Barſalona: or of ſo ſtronge and well wrought earth that it maketh a ſinguler & ſtronge byndyng. The ſituation is muche better the that of Barſalona by reaſon that the

The citie of ſandomenico

streates are

are much larger and playner, and without comparyſon moꝛe
directe and ſtreyght furth. Foꝛ beinge buylded nowe in owr
tyme, byſyde the commoditie of the place of the foundation,
the ſtreates were alſo directed with coꝛde, compaſe and mea-
ſure, wherin it excelleth al the cities that I haue ſene. It hath
the ſea ſo nere, that of one ſyde there is no moꝛe ſpace betwen
the ſea and the citie then the waules. And this is about fyftie
paſes where it is furtheſt of.   On this ſyde, the waters of
the ſea beate vppon the naturall ſtones and fayꝛe coaſte. On
the other parte, harde by the ſyde and at the foote of the hou
ſes, paſſeth the ryuer Ozama whiche is a marueylous poꝛte
wherin laden ſhyppes ryſe very nere to the lande and in maner vnder the houſe wyndowes, & no further from the mouth
of the ryuer where it entereth into the ſea, then is frome the
foote of the hyll of Monyuye to the monaſtery of ſaynt Frances
oꝛ to the lodge of Barſalona. In the myddeſt of this ſpace in
the citie, is the foꝛtreſſe and caſtle, vnder the which and twen
tie paſes diſtant from the ſame, paſſe the ſhippes to aryſe ſum
what further in the ſame ryuer. From the enteraunce of the
ſhyppes vntyll they caſt anker, they ſayle no further from the
houſes of the citie then thyꝛtie oꝛ foꝛtie paſes, bicauſe of this
ſyde of the citie the habitacion is nere to the ryuer. The poꝛt
oꝛ hauen alſo, is ſo fayꝛe and commodious to defraight oꝛ vnlade ſhyppes, as the lyke is founde but in fewe places of the
woꝛlde. The chymineis that are in this citie, are abowt ſyxe
hundꝛeth in number, and ſuch houſes as I haue ſpoken of be
foꝛe: Of the which ſum are ſo fayꝛe and large that they maye
well receaue and lodge any loꝛde oꝛ noble manne of Spayne
with his trayne and famelie. And eſpecially that which Don
Diego Colon viceroy vnder your maieſtie hath in this citie, is
ſuche that I knowe no man in Spayne that hath the lyke by
a quarter in goodneſſe conſyderynge all the commodities of
the ſame.   Lykewyſe the ſituation thereof, as beinge
aboue the ſayde poꝛte and altogyther of ſtone and hauynge
many fayꝛe and large roomes with as goodly a pꝛoſpect of the
lande and ſea as may be deuyſed, ſeemeth vnto me ſo magni-
ficall and pꝛincelyke that yowr maieſtic maye bee as well lodged therin as in any of the mooſte exquiſite builded houſes of
Spayne. There is alſo a Cathedꝛall churche buylded of late
where aſwell the byſhop accoꝛdyng to his dignitie, as alſo the
canones are wel indued. This church is wel buylded of ſtone
and

The riuer ỏ
zama

The hauen

A cathedrall
churche and
monaſteris in
Hiſpaniola.

and lyme, and of good woorkemanſhyppe. There are further:
moe thee monaſteries bearyng the name of ſaynt Dominike,
ſaynt Frances, and ſaynt Marie of Mercedes : The whiche
are all well buylded althoughe not ſo curiouſlye as they of
Spayne. But ſpeakynge without peiudice of any other reli
gious monaſterie, yowre maieſtie may bee well aſſured that in
theſe thee monaſteries, god is as wel ſerued as in any other
religious houſe with men of holy lyuynge and vertuous exem
An hoſpitale. ple. There is alſo a very good hoſpitall for the ayde and ſuc
cour of poe people, whiche was founde by Michaell Paſſa=
ment theaſurer to yowr maieſtie. To conclude, this citie from
day to day increaſeth in welth and good oder, aſwel for that
the ſayde Admyall and viceroy with the lorde Chaunceloure
and counſayle appoynted there by yowr maieſtie, haue they
continuall abydynge here, as alſo that the rycheſt men of the
Ilande reſot hyther for they moſte commodious habitation
and trade of ſuch marchaundies as are eyther bought owt of
Spayne o ſent thyther from this Iland which nowe ſo abun
deth in many thynges that it ſerueth Spayne with many com
modities, as it were with vſury requityng ſuch benefites as
it fyſt receaued from thenſe.

The people of this Ilande are commonlye of ſumewhat
leſſe ſtature then are the Spanyardes, and of a ſhynynge o
cleare bowne coloure. They haue wyues of they owne, and
abſteyne from they dowghters, ſyſters, and mothers. They
The people haue large foheades, longe blacke heare, and no beardes o
heare in any other parts of they bodies aſwel mē as women,
except very fewe as perhaps ſcarſely one amonge a thouſand.
They go as naked as they were borne, excepte that on the
partes which may not with honeſtie bee ſeene, they weare a
certeyne leafe as bode as a mans hande, which neuertheleſſe
is not kepte cloſe with ſuche diligence but that ſumtymes a
man may ſee that they thynke ſufficiently hydde.

In this Iland are certeyne glo woozmes that ſhyne in the
Glo wormes nyght as doo owles. But are muche bygger and gyue a grea
ter lyght : In ſo much that when the men of the Ilande goo
any iorneys in the nyght, they beare ſumme of theſe woozmes
made faſt abowt they fiete and heade, in ſuche ſoe that he
that ſhulde ſee them a farre and ignoant of the thinge, wolde
bee greatly aſtonyſhed therat. By the lyght of theſe alſo, the

women

women woozke in theyz houses in the night. These woozmes they caule Cicuas.   Theyz lyght lasteth foz the space of thzee dayes, and diminissheth as they begynne to dzye vp.

There is also a kynd of crowes whose breath stynketh in the moznynge and is sweete at after noone. The excremente which they anoyde, is a lynynge woozme.

As touchynge other thynges of this Jlande whereof Peter Martyz hath moze largely intreated in his Decades, J haue thought it superfluous to repeate the same ageyne owte of this hystozie of Gonzalus Ferdinandus : but haue here gathered only suche thynges as eyther are not touched of Peter Martyz oz not so largely declared : as J haue doone the lyke in all other notable thynges which J haue collected owt of this Summarie of Gonzalus.

❧ Of the Jlande of Cuba and other.

F the Jlande of Cuba and the other, as the Jlandes of Sancti Iohannis and Iamaica, the same maye bee sayde in maner in all thynges as befoze of Hispaniola although not so largely. Yet in lesse quantitie doo they bzynge foozth the lyke thynges : as gold, copper, cattayle, trees plantes, fysshes, and such other of the whiche wee haue spoken there.

In Cuba, is a certeyne kynde of Partyches beinge verye little, with theyz fethers much of the colour of turtle dooues: but are of muche better taste to bee eaten. They are taken in great number.   And beinge bzought wylde into the houses, they becoome as tame within the space of thzee oz foure dayes as though they had byn hatched there. They becoomme exceadynge fatte in shozt space, and are doubtelesse the most delicate and pleasaunt meate that euer J haue eaten. But to let passe many other thynges that myght here bee sayde, and to speake of two maruelous thynges which are in this Jland of Cuba : wherof the one is, that a valley conteynynge twoo oz thzee leaques in length betwene two mountaynes, is full of a kynde of very harde stones of suche perfecte roundenesse and lyke vnto pellettes of gunnes that no arte can make better oz moze exactly polysshed. Of these, sum are as smaule

Crowes stynkynge and sweete.

Saynt John his Jlande. Iamaica.

Partriches.

Pellettes for gunnes wrought by nature.

as pellettes for handegunnes : and other so increasynge bygger and bygger from that quantitie, that they may serue for
all sortes of artyllerie althoughe they bee of byggenesse to receaue one or two or more quintales of pouder, euery quintale
conteynyng one hundreth weyght : or of what other quantitie so euer they bee. These pelletes are founde through owte
al the valley within the earth as in a myne, which they digge
and take owte such as they neede of all sortes.

The other marueylous thinge of this Jland is this : That
farre from the sea, there issheweth owt of a mountayne a certeyne lycour much lyke the cley of Babilon cauled *Bitumen* or
lyke vnto pytche in great quantitie and such as is very commodious for the calkynge of shyppes. This fauleth continually from the rocke and runneth into the sea in suche abundaunce that it is seene flotynge aboue the water on euery side
of the sea there abowt as it is dryuen froms place to place by
the wynde or course of the water.

Quintus Cursius wryteth in his hystorie, that great Alexander
came to the citie of *Memi* where is a great caue or denne in the
which is a sprynge or fountayne that continually auoydethe
a great quantitie of *Bitumen* in such sort that it is an easy thing
to beleue that the stones of the walles of Babilon myght bee
layde therwith accordynge as the sayde auctoure wryteth. I
haue seene this myne of *Bitumen*, not only in the Jland of Cuba, but also such an other in new Spayne, which was found
of late in the prouince of *Panuco* where it is much better then
the other of Cuba, as I haue seene by experience in calkynge
of shyppes.

**A fountayne
of the pytche
of Bitumen.**

Quintus Cursius

**Bitumen of
Babilon.**

Panuco

¶ Of the lande of *Baccaleos* cauled *Terra Baccalearum,* situate on the North syde of the firme lande.

Hortly after that your Maiestie came to the citie of Toledo, there arryued in the moneth of
Nouember, Steuen Gomes the pylot who the
yeare before of 1524. by the commaundement
of your maiestie sayled to the Northe partes
and founde a greate parte of lande continu-
ate from that which is cauled *Baccaleos* discourynge towarde
the West to the .xl. and .xli. degree, fro whense he brought
certeyn

Baccaleos.

certeyne Indians (for so caule wee all the nations of the new
founde landes) of the whiche he brought sum with hym from
thense who are yet in Toledo at this present, and of greater
stature then other of the firme lande as they are commonlye.
Theyr coloure is much lyke thother of the firme lande. They
are great archers, and go couered with the skinnes of dyuers
beastes both wylde and tame. In this lande are many excel=
lent furres, as marterns, sables, and such other rych furres
of the which the sayde pilote brought summe with hym into
Spayne. They haue syluer and copper, and certeyne other
metalles. They are Idolaters and honoure the soonne and
moone, and are seduced with suche superstitions and errours
as are they of the firme.

   And to haue wrytten thus muche, it maye suffice of suche
thinges as haue semed to me most woorthy to be noted in the
Sumarie of *Gonzalus Ferdinandus* wrytten to Thēperours maiestie

Indians.

Ryche furres and syluer.

Idolaters.

¶ Of other notable thynges gathered owte of dyuers autours : And fyrste of the vniuersal carde and newe woorlde.

He hole globe or compase of the earth was dy=
uyded by the auncient wryters into three par=
tes, as *Europa, Affrica,* and *Asia:* whiche partes
conteyne in longitude .180. degrees, begyn=
nynge the fyrst degree at the Ilandes of Cana
rie. And conteyne in latitude towarde the
North. 63. degrees, begynnynge the fyrste degree frome the
Equinoctiall: And .10. degrees towarde the South. All the
reste of the longitude which conteyneth other .180. degrees,
is discouered of late tyme, as the West India cauled the newe
woorlde, bycause none of the owlde autoures had any knowe=
lege or made any mention therof. All that therfore is cauled
newe which is Westwarde from the Ilandes of Canaric. And
thus accomptynge these .180. degrees towarde the East disco
uered in owlde tyme, with the other .180. degrees disco=
uered of late dayes, they make, 360. degrees, which is al the
circle of the Equinoctiall in the sphere. Also the part aboue
the .63. degrees of the North latitude, was founde by men of
late tyme, as Norway and Grutlande with many other pro=
uinces

West India the newe woorlde.

The circums=ference of the Equinoctiall lyne.

The North regions.

          HHh, ii.

The South regions.

uinces. Lykewise the part moſt ſouth then .16. degrees of la titude, was diſcouered of late dayes, althonghe Ariane and Plinie ſay that it was knowen in owlde tyme : whiche yf it were, yet had they no ſuche particular deſcription thereof as we haue in theſe dayes.

¶ A diſcourſe of the vyage made by the Spanyardes rounde abowte the worlde.

He vyage made by the Spanyardes rownde abowt the worlde, is one of the greateſt and moſte marueylous thynges that hath bynne knowen to owre tyme. And althoughe in ma ny thynges we excell owre aunciente predi ceſſours, in this eſpeciallye wee ſo farre ex ceade all theyr inuentions, that the lyke hath not heretofore byn knowen to this day. This viage was wryt ten particularly by Don Peter Martyr of Angleria being one of the counſayle of Themperours Indies, to whom alſo was committed the wrytyng of the hyſtorie and examination of al ſuche as returned from thenſe into Spayne to the citie of Si uile, in the yeare. M. D. xxii. But ſendynge it to Rome to bee prynted in that miſerable tyme when the citie was ſacked it was loſt and not founde to this day or any memory remay nynge therof, ſauynge ſuche as ſum that redde the ſame haue borne in mynde. And amonge other notable thynges by hym wryrten as touchynge that vyage, this is one, that the Spa nyardes hauynge ſayled abowt thre yeares and one moneth, and the moſt of them notynge the dayes, day by day (as is the maner of all them that ſayle by the Ocean) they founde when they were returned to Spayne, that they had loſte one daye. So that at theyr arryuall at the porte of Siuile beinge the ſe uenth day of September, was by theyr accompt but the ſixth day. And where as Don Peter Martyr declared the ſtrange effecte of this thynge to a certeyne excellente man who for his ſingulet lernynge was greately aduaunced to honoure in his common welthe and made Themperours ambaſſadoure, this wooethly gentelman who was alſo a greate Philoſopher and Aſtronomer, anſwered that it coulde not otherwyſe chaunce unto them hauynge ſayled thre yeares continrally, euer fo lowynge

Don Peter Martyr.

Rome ſacked

A day loſt in thre yeares and one mo neth.

folowynge the foonne towarde the Weſt. And ſayde furthermore
that they of owlde tyme obſerued that all ſuche as ſayled be=
hinde the foonne towarde the Weſt, dyd greatly lengthen the
day. And albeit that the ſayde booke of Peter Martyr is pe
ryſſhed, yet hath not fortune permitted that the memorie of
ſo woozthy and marueylous an enterpzyſe ſtulde vtterly bee
extincte : forafmuch as a certeyne noble gentleman of the cy=
tie of Uincenza in Italie, cauled maſter Antonie Pigafetta   **Antonie Pi=**
(who beinge one of the coompanie of that vyage and after   **gafetta.**
his returne into Spayne in the ſhyppe Uictoria, was made
knyght of the Rhodes) wzote a particular and large booke
therof which he gaue to Thempcrours Maieſtie, and ſente a
coppie of the ſame into Fraunce to the lady Regente moother
vnto the frenche kynge, who committed it to an excellent phi   **Iacobus Faber.**
loſopher cauled maſter *Iacobus Faber*, hauyng longe ſtudyed in
Italy, wyllynge him to tranſlate it into the Frenche toonge.
This booke therefore was pzinted fyzſt in the frenche toonge
and then in the Italien, with alſo an epiſtle to the Cardinall
of Salſepurge as touchynge the ſame viage, wzitten by Max   **Maximilien**
imiliane Tranſiluane ſecretarie to Thempcrours Maieſtie, in   **Tranſiluane**
the yeare , 1522. And doubteleſſe amonge al the cities of I=
talie, the citie of Uicenza may herein much glozie, that beſide
the ancient nobilitie and many excellent and rare wyttes whi
che it hath bzowght furth aſwell in learnynge as diſcipline
of warre, it hath alſo had ſo woozthy and valiaunt a gentle
man as was the ſayde maſter Antonie Pigafetta, who hauing
compaſed abowte the ball oz globe of the wozlde, hath lyke=
wyſe deſcribed that vyage particularly. Foz the whiche his   **The rewarde**
ſo noble and woonderfull an enterpziſe ſo happily atchiued,   **of noble cō=**
if the ſame had byn doone in the owlde tyme when thempyze   **terpzyſes.**
of the Grekes and Romans flozyſſhed, he ſtulde doubteleſſe
haue byn rewarded with an Image of marble oz golde erec=
ted in a place of honoure in perpetuall memozie and foz a ſin=
gular exemple of his vertue to the poſteritie. In fine, this may
we bouldly affirme, that the antiquitie had neuer ſuch know= **The antiqui**
lege of the wozlde whiche the foonne coompaſeth abowte in   **tie had no**
xxiiii. houres, as we haue at this pzeſente by thinduſtrye of   **ſuche know=**
men of this owne age. But befoze I ſpeake any thynge of the   **lege of the**
viage, I haue thought it good fyzſt to adde hereunto, the E=   **wozlde as**
piſtle of Maximilian Tranſiluane which he wzote to the Car= **we haue.**
                                          diwall

dinall of Salsepurge as a preface to his sayde booke.

❡ The Epistle of Maximilian Transiluane, secretarie to The Emperours maiestie: wzytten to the ryght honozable and reuerende lozde, the lozde Cardinall of Salsepurge, of the marueylous and woonderfull nauigation made by the Spanyardes rounde abowt the wozlde in the yeare of Chzist. M. D. xix.

The Ilandes of Molucca.

Aures Cherso-nesus.

Malaccha.

Spyces.

IN these dales my most honozable and reuerend lozde, returned one of those fiue shippes which the yeare befoze Themperours beinge at Sara-gosa in Spayne, were at his maiesties com-maundement sent to the newe wozlde. hereto-foze vnknowen vnto vs, to seeke the Ilandes of spices. Foz albeit the Poztugales bzynge vs great quanti-tie of spyces from that parte of Easte India whiche in owlde tyme was cauled *Aures Chersonesus* (where is nowe thought to bee the greate and ryche citie of *Malaccha*) yet in Easte India growe none of those spices excepte pepper. Foz other spices, as Sinamome, cloues, nutmegges, and mase. (whiche is the huske that couereth the shell of the nutte) are bzought frome other farre contreys & frō Ilandes scarsely knowen by theyz names. From the whiche Ilandes they are bzought in shyps oz barkes made withowt any iren tooles, and tyed togyther with cozdes of date trees: with rounde sayles lykewise made of the smaule twigges of the bzanches of date trees weaued togyther. These barkes they caule *Giunche*: with the whiche barkes and sayles, they make theyz vyages with onely one wynde in the stearne oz contrarywyse.

The Ilandes of Spyces vn knowen in owlde tyme.

Neyther yet is it a thynge greatly to bee marueyled at that these Ilandes where the spyces growe haue byn vnknowen so many wozldes past vnto owre tyme, fozasmuch as all such thynges as vnto this day haue byn wzytten of owld autours of the places where spices growe, are all fabulous and false: In so muche that the countreys where they affirme theym to growe, are nowe certeynely founde to bee further frome the place where they growe in deede, then we are from them. Foz lettynge passe many other thynges that are wzytten, I wyll
speake

speake only of this which Herodotus (otherwise a famous auc‑
tour) affirmeth that Sinamome, is founde in the toppes of
the nestes of certeyne byrdes and foules that bzynge it frome
farre countreys, & especially the Phenyr, the which I knowe
no man that euer hath seene.   But Plinie who myght moze
certeynely affirme thynges by reason that befoze his tyme ma
ny thynges were knowen and discouered by the nauigations
of great Alexander and other, sayth that Sinamome groweth
in that parte of Ethiope which the people inhabite cauled Tro‑
gloditi. Neuerthelesse itis nowe founde that Sinamome grow
eth very farre from all Ethiope and muche further frome the
Trogloditi whiche dwell in caues vnder the grounde. But to
owre men which are nowe returned from those partes and the
Jlandes of spices, hauynge also good knowlege of Ethiope, it
was necessarie to passe farre beyonde Ethiope beefoze they
coome to these Jlandes, and to coompasse abowte the whole
wozlde, and many tymes vnder the greatest circumference of
heauen. The which nauigation made by them, being the most
maruevlous thynge that euer was doone by man vppon the
earth sence the fyzst creation of the wozlde, and neuer founde
befoze, oz knowen, oz attempted by any other, I haue delibe‑
rated faythfully to wzyte to yowre honozable lozdshippe and
to declare the hole successe therof. As touchynge which mat‑
ter, I haue with all diligence made inquisition to knowe the
trewth aswell by relation of the Capitayne of that shyppe as
also by conference with euery of the maryners that returned
with hym. All which gaue the selfe same infozmation both
to Themperours matestie and dyuers other : And this with
such faythfulnesse and sinceritie, that not only they are iud‑
ged of all men to haue declared the trewth in all thynges, but
haue thereby also gyuen vs certeyne knowlege that all that
hath hytherto byn sayde oz wzitten of owlde autours as tou‑
chynge these thynges, are false and fabulous. Foz who wyll
beleue that men are found with only one legge. Oz with such
feete whose shadowe couereth theyz bodyes? Oz men of a cu‑
bite heyght, and other such lyke, beinge rather monsters then
men? Of the which, neyther the Spanyardes who in owre
tyme saylyng by the Occan sea, haue discouered al the coastes
of the lande toward the West both vnder and aboue the Equi
noctiall, noz the Poztugales who compassynge abowt al Af‑
frykc haue passed by all the Easte and lykewyse discouered all
thosc

Herodotus.
Sinamome.

The Phenyr.

Plinie.

The nauigati
ons of greate
Alexander.
Ethiope.
Trogloditi.

The nauigati
on abowte the
wozlde.

The owlde
autours re‑
proued.

Monsters.
The vyages
of the Spany
ardes and
Poztugales.

Sinus Magnus.

those coastes vnto the great goulfe cauled *Sinus Magnus*, nor yet the Spanyardes in this theyr laste nauigation, in the which they compased abowt the hole earth, dyd neuer in any of their vyages wryte of such monsters : which doubtelesse they wold not haue omytted if they myght haue had certeyne knowlege therof. But nowe intendynge to speake of the whole world, I wyll not bee longe in my preface, but begynne my narration as foloweth.

❧ A briefe declaration of the vyage or nauigation made abowte the worlde. Gathered owt of a large booke wrytten herof by master Antonie Pygafetta Vincentine, knyght of the Rhodes and one of the coompanye of that vyage in the which, *Ferdinando Magaliawes* a Portugale (whom sum caule *Magellanus*) was generall Capitayne of the nauie.

Sebastian Munster.

The Ilandes of Molucca.

Lthowgh Sebastian Munster in his vniuersall Cosmographie in the fyfthe booke of the landes of the greater Asia (which I translated into Englyshe abowte two yeares sence) hath wrytten of the vyage of *Magellanus*, declarynge therein howe the Spanyardes by the West, and the Portugales by the Easte, saylyng to the Ilandes of *Molucca*, compased the hole globe of the worlde betwene them, yet haue I here thought it good to make a briefe repeticion of this vyage, addynge hereunto dyuers notable thynges which were not touched of Munster, as I haue gathered them owt of the bookes of Antonie Pigafetta and Transiluanus wrytten of the same vyage. For albeit in deede it was a straunge and woonderful thynge that the Spanyardes and Portugales compased the hole circumference of the worlde betwene them, yet is it more marueylous that the same was doone with one shippe and one coompanie of men as dyd the Spanyardes in this vyage, who keepynge theyr contiuuall course by the Weste, returned into Spayne by the Easte. A thynge doubtlesse so muche more woonderfull and strange then yf they had returned from the halfe circumference by the same way they went. In howe muche they were ignorante

Ignorante in the vyage neuer attempted beefore, belyde the thoulande daungiours and perylles whiche they were daylye lyke to faule into, alwell by wanderynge in vnknowen coaltes as allo by faulynge into the handes of the Portugales by whole dominions in the Eafte, they fhulde needes paffe of neceffitie, not trultynge to theyr gentelneffe for the controuerfie which had byn longe betwene them for the flandes of *Molucca*. I wyll therefore (as I haue fayde) make a briefe rehearfall of this vyage from the begynnynge to the endynge: Omyttynge neuertheleffe many notable thynges whiche are more largely deferibed in the bookes of *Maximilianus Transiluanus* and *Antonius Pigafetta*.

Controuerfie berwene the Spanyardes and Portugales.

The tenthe day of August, in the yeare of owre lorde M. D. rir. Ferdinando Magalianes departed from the porte of Siuile in Spayne with a nauie of fyue fhyppes and two hundreth thirtie and feuen men, wel furnyffhed with all thynges neceffarie. And faylynge fyrfte downe by the ryuer of *Guadalchiber* which runneth from the fayde porte into the fea, they came fyrfte to a place named *Giouan Dulfarax* where are manye vyllages of the Moores: And from thenfe arryued at a caftel of the Duke of *Medina Sidonia*, where is the porte from whiche they enter into the fea and to the cape faynte Vincent beinge diftant from the Equinoctiall. rrrbii. degrees, and frome the fayde port .r. leagues, and is from thenfe to Siuile betwene rbii. and .rr. leagues. Here they remayned certeyne dayes to make newe prouiffon of fuch thynges as they lacked.

Ferdinando Magalianes.

The Cape of faynt Uincent

Departynge from henfe the .rr. daye of September, they arryued the .rrbi. day of the fame moneth at one of the flandes of Canarie cauled *Tenerife*, beinge. rrb. degrees aboue the Equinoctiall. In one of thefe flandes is none other water but that is continually engendered of a clowde which appeareth dayly at noone tyde as though it defcended from heauen and compafeth abowt a certeyne great tree from whofe branches difilleth greate abundaunce of water, and faulethe in freames from the roote of the fame into certeine trenches and ceftarnes made and placed to receaue it. This water ferueth fufficiently all thinhabitauntes and cattayle of the flande. The lyke thinge is alfo feene in the fland of faynt Thomas, lyinge directly vnder the Equinoctiall lyne.

The flandes of Canarie.

water engendered of a clowde.

The fland faynt Thomas.

The thyrde day of October abowt mydnyght, the capytayne

tayne commaunded theym to lyght fyzebzandes and to hoyfe vp theyz layles directynge theyz courfe towarde the South, faylynge betwene Capo Verde of Affryke and the Jlandes lyinge abowt the fame, beinge from the Equinoctiall .riiii. degrees and a halfe. They fayled thus, manye dayes in the fyght of the coafte of Guinea, of Ethioe, where is the mountayne cauled Serra Lions beinge .viii. degrees aboue the Equinoctiall. Jn this coaft they had no maner of contrary wynde but a great calme and fayze wether foz the space of thzeefcoze and tenne dayes, in the which they came vnder the Equinoctiall lyne. Jn this vyage they fawe manye ftraunge fyfhes and monfters of the fea belyde an other ftraunge thynge whiche appeared vnto them. Foz there appeared in theyz fhyppes certeyne flames of fyze burnynge very cleare, which they caul faynt Helen and faynt Nicolas. Thefe appeared as thoughe they had byn vppon the maft of the fhyppes, in fuche cleauenelfe that they tooke away theyz fight foz the space of a quarter of an houre : by reafon wherof, they fo wandered owte of theyz courfe and were difparfed in funder, that they in maner difpayzed to meete ageyne. But as God wolde, the fea and tempeft beinge quieted, they came fafely to theyz determyned courfe. And befoze J fpeake any further of the vyage, J haue here thought good to faye fumewhat of thefe ftraunge fyers, which fum ignozant folkes thynke to bee fpirites oz fuche other phantafies wheras they are but natural thynges pzoccadynge of naturall caufes and engendered of certeyne erhalations. Of thefe therefoze, the greate Philofopher of owre tyme Hieronimus Cardanus in his feconde booke de Subtilitate, wzyteth in this maner.

There are two maner of fyers engendered of erhalations wherof the one is hurtfull and the other without hurte. That which is hurtful, is fyer in deede, engendered of malicious & venemous vapours which in fuccelfe of time take fyer as apt matters to be kyndeled. The other kynd, is no trewe fyer, but lyke the matter that is in such owlde puttrified wod as giueth the fhynynge of fyer without the fubftaunce oz qualitie therof. Of the kynde of trewe fyer, is the fyer baule oz ftarre commonly cauled faynt Helen which is fumtyme feene abowt the maftes of fhyppes, beinge of fuche fyery nature that it fumetyme melteth bzafen velfelles, and is a token of dzownyng.

fol

Capo verde.

Fylhes and monfters of the fea.

The fyers of faintc Helene & S. Nicolas. A tempeft.

The naturall caufe of fuch fiers as faule in the fhyps

Cardanus.

Two kyndes of fyers engendered of erhalations.

Trewe fyer & falfe fyer.

forafmuch as this chaunceth only in great tempeftes. For the
vapoure or exhalation whereof this fyre is engendered, can
not bee dryuen togyther or compacte in forme of fyre, but of
a groffe vapoure and by a great poure of wynde, and is ther=
fore a token of imminent perell : As on the contrary parte, the
lyke fyers cauled in owlde tyme *Caftor* and *Pollux* and nowe na
med the two lyghtes of faynt Peter and faynt Nycolas whi=
che for the moft parte faule on the cables of the shyppes, lea=
pynge from one to an other with a certeyne flutterynge noyfe
lyke byrdes, are a token of fecuritie and of the tempefte ouer=
paffed. For they are but vapoures cleauynge to the cables :
which in fucceffe of tyme, the fyer paffynge from one to an o=
ther, appere in the fimilitude of a lyght candell. They are a
token of fecuritie bycaufe they are lyttle, not flowe or groffe,
wherby they myght haue ioyned altogyther in one, and byn
therby more malicious and lafted longer, wheras beinge ma
ny and but lyttle, they are the fooner confumed.   Hetherto
Cardanus. But let vs nowe returne to the vyage.

Caftor and Pollux.
The lyghtes of faynt Pe=ter and faynte Nycolas.

When they had fayled paste the Equinoctiall lyne, they
loft the fyght of the north ftarre, and fayled by fouthwefte
vntyll they came to a lande named the lande of *Brefil* whiche
fum caule *Brafilia,* beinge .xxii. degrees and a halfe toward the
fouth pole or pole Antartyke. This lande is continuate and
one firme lande with the cape of faynte Augustine whiche is
vii. degrees from the Equinoctiall. In this lande they were
refreffhed with many good frutes of innumerable kindes, and
founde here alfo very good fugar canes and diuers kyndes of
beaftes and other thynges which I omitte for breuitie. They
entered into this hauen on faynt Lucies day : where the fonne
beinge there *Zenith* (that is the poynt of heauen directly ouer
theyr heades) they felte greater heate that daye then when
they were vnder the Equinoctiall line. This lande of Brafile
is very large and great : and bygger then all Spayne, Portu=
gale, Fraunce, and Italie : and is moste abundaunte in all
thynges. The people of this countrey praye to noo maner of
thinge : but liue by thinftincte of nature, and to thage of .C.xx
and .C. xl. yeares. Bothe the men and women go naked, and
dwell in certeyne longe houses. They are very docible, and
prone enough to the Chriftian fayth.

Fowrtene dayes after that they arryued at the fayd port,

They loft the fyght of the North ftarre.
The lande of Brefile.
The South pole.

Sugar.

The greate=neffe of the land of Bra=file.

J.i.ii.   they

they departed from this lande and sayled to the .xxxiiii. degree and a halfe toward the pole Antartike where they found
a great ryuer of freſhe water and certeyne Canibales. Of
theſe they ſawe one owt of theyr ſhyppes, of ſtature as bigge
as a giante, hauynge a voyce lyke a bul. Owre men purſued
them, but they were ſo ſwyfte of foote that they coulde not
ouertake them. Abowt the mouth of this ryuer, are ſeuen I-
landes, in the byggeſt wherof, they founde certeyne precious
ſtones, and cauled it the cape of ſaynt Marie. The Spanyardes thought that by this ryuer they might haue paſſed into
the ſouth ſea. But they were deceaued in theyr opinion. For
there was none other paſſage then by the ryuer which is .xvii.
leaques large in the mouth.

Thus folowynge this coaſte by the tracte of the lande towarde the pole Antartyke, they came to a place where were
two Ilandes replenyſhed with gieſe and woolues of the ſea
which ſum thynke to bee thoſe fyſſhes that wee caule pikes.
Theſe were in ſuch number that in an houre all the fyue ſhippes myght haue byn lade with gieſe beinge all of blacke coloure, and ſuch as can not flye. They lyue of fyſſhe and are ſo
fatte that they coulde ſcarſely fle theym. They haue noo fethers but a certeyne downe : and theyr byls like rauens byls.
Theſe woolues of the ſea are of dyuers coloures, and of the
byggeneſſe of calues, with theyr heades of golden coloure.
Here were they in great daungiour by tempeſt. But as ſoone
as the thre fyers cauled ſaynte Helen, ſaynte Nycolas, and
ſaynt Clare, appered vppon the cabels of the ſhyppes, ſuddeynely the tempeſte and furye of the wyndes ceaſed.

Departynge frome henſe, they ſayled to the. 49. degree
and a halfe vnder the pole Antartyke: where beinge wynte-
red, they were infoꝛced to remayne there foꝛ the ſpace of two
monethes, all which tyme they ſawe no man except that one
daye by chaunce they eſpyed a man of the ſtature of a giante,
who came to the hauen daunſyng and ſyngynge, and ſhortly
after ſeemed to caſt duſt ouer his heade. The capitayne ſente
one oꝛ his men to the ſhoꝛe with the ſhyppe boate, who made
the lyke ſigne of peace. The which thynge the giante ſeinge,
was owt of feare and came with the capitaynes ſeruaunte to
his pꝛeſence into a lyttle Ilande. When he ſawe the capitayne with certeyne of his coompany abowte hym, he was
greatly

Cauilaſes.

Giantes.

Inſulæ gemma-
rum.
Cap.S. Marie.

The pole En
artike.
Geeſe:
Sea woolues

The. Xix. de-
gree of the
ſouth pole.

Giantes.

greatly amafed and made fignes beldynge vppe his hande to
heauen, fignifyinge therby that owre men came from thenfe.
This giante was fo bygge, that the heade of one of owr men
of a meane ftature, came but to his wafte. He was of good
cozpozature and well made in all partes of his bodie, with a
large vyfage paynted with dyuers coloures, but foz the moft
parte yelowe. Vppon his cheekes were paynted two hartes,
and redde circles abowt his eyes. The heare of his headde
was coloured whyte, and his apparell was the fkynne of a
beafte fowde rogyther. This beafte (as feemed vnto vs) had
a large heade and great eares lyke vnto a mule, with the body
of a camel and tayle of a hoyfe. The feete of the giant were
foulded in the fayde fkynne after the maner of fhoos. He had
in his hande, a bygge and fhozte bowe, the ftrynge whereof
was made of a fynewe of that beafte. He had alfo a bundell
of longe arrowes made of reefes fethered after the maner of
owrs, typte with fharpe ftones in the fteade of iren heades.
The Capitayne caufed him to eate and dzynke, and gaue him
many thynges, and amonge otherz greate lookynge glaffez
In the which as foone as he fawe his owne lykeneffe, was fud
deynely afrayde and ftarted backe with fuch violence that he
ouerthzewe two that ftoode neareft abowte hym. When the
Capitayne had thus gyuen hym certeyne haukes belles and
other great belles, with alfo a lookynge glaffe, a combe, and
a payze of beades of glaffe, he fente hym to lande with foure
of his owne men well armed.

Shozely after, they fawe an other giaunte of fumewhat
greater ftature, with his bowe and arrowes in his hande, As
he drewe neare vnto owre menne, he layde his hande on his
heade and poynted vp towarde heauen, and owr men dyd the
lyke. The Capitayne fente his fhyppe boate to bzynge him to
a lyttle Ilande beinge in the hauen. This giante was verye
tractable and pleafaunt. He foonge and daunfed: and in his
daunfynge lefte the pzinte of his feete on the grownde. Here
mayned longe with owre men who named hym Iohan. He
coulde wel fpeake and playnely pzonounce thefe wozdes: Iefuz,
Aue Maria, Iohannes, euen as we doo, but with a bygger boyce.
The capitayne gaue hym a fhert of lynnen clothe, and a coate
of whyte woollen clothe: Alfo a cappe, a combe, a lookynge
glaffe, with dyuers fuche other thynges, and fo fente hym to
his coompany. The day folowyng, he refozted agayne to the
                                            fhyppes

The bygnes
of the giants.

An other
giante.

ſhyppes, and bʒought with hym one of thoſe greate beaſtes, which he gaue the capitayne. But after that daye they neuer ſawe hym moʒe, ſuppoſynge hym to bee ſlayne of his owne coompany foʒ the conuerſation he had with owre men.

After other.rb. dayes were paſte, there came foure other **Foure other giantes.** giantes without any weapons, but had hydde theyʒ bowes and arrowes in certeyne buſſhes. The capitayne reteyned two of theſe whiche were youngeſt and beſte made. He tooke them by a deceyte in this maner, that gyuynge them kniues, **Two giantes are taken by a pollicie.** ſheares, lookynge glaſſes, belles, beadʒs of cryſtall, & ſuche other tryfels, he ſo fylled theyʒ handes that they coulde hold no moʒe. Then cauſed two payʒe of ſhacſels of iren to bee put on theyʒ legges, makynge ſignes that he wold alſo gyue them thoſe chaynes: which they lyked very wel bycauſe they were made of bʒyght and ſhynynge metal. And wheras they could not cary them bycauſe theyʒ handes were full, the other gyauntes wolde haue caryed them: but the Capitayne wolde not ſuffer them. When they felte the ſhackels faſte about theyʒ legges, they begunne to doubte: but the Capitayne dyd put them in comfoʒte and badde them ſtande ſtyll. In fine when they ſawe how they were deccaued they roʒed lyke bulles and **The deuyll Setebos.** cryed vppon theyʒ greate deuyll Setebos to helpe them. Being thus taken, they were immediatly ſeperate and put in ſundʒy ſhyppes. They coulde neuer bynde the handes of the other two, yet was one of them with much difficultie ouerthʒowne by nyne of owre men, and his handes bownde: but he ſuddeynely looſed hym ſelfe and fledde, as dyd alſo the other that came with them. In theyʒ flying, they ſhot of theyʒ arrowes **Deuyls appere to the gyaunces when they dye.** and ſlewe one of owre men. They ſay that when any of them dye, there appere.r. oʒ.rii. deuyls leappynge and daunſynge a bout the bodye of the deade, and ſeeme to haue theyʒ boddyes paynted with dyuers colours. And that amonge other, there is one ſeene byggʒer then the reſidue, who maketh great mirth and reioyſynge. This greate deuyll they caule Setebos, and caule the leſſe Cheleule. One of theſe giantes which they toke, declared by ſignes that he had ſeene deuyls with two hoʒnes aboue theyʒ heades, with longe heare downe to theyʒ feete: And that they caſt furth fyʒe at theyʒ thʒotes both befoʒe and **Patagoni.** behynde. The Capitayne named theſe people Patagoni. The moſt part of them weare the ſkynnes of ſuche beaſtes wherof I haue ſpoken befoʒe: And haue no houſes of coutinuaunce but,

but make certeyne cotages which they couer with the sayde
skynnes, and cary them from place to place. They lyue of raw
fleſhe and a certeyne ſweete roote which they caule *Capar*.
One of theſe which they had in theyr ſhyppes, dyd eate at one
meale a baſket of byſkette, and dzunke a bowle of water at a
dzaught.

The gyantes feedynge.

They remayned fyue monethes in this pozte of ſaint Juli-
an, where certeyne of the vnder capitaynes conſpirynge the
death of theyr general, were hanged and quartered: Amonge
whom the treaſurer Luigo of Mendozza was one. Certeyne
of the other conſpiratours, he left in the ſayd land of *Patogoni*

They coſpire agcynſt theyr Capitayne.

Departyng from hense to the .52. dcgree toward the pole
Artartike lackynge a thyzde parte, where they founde a ryuer of freſſhe water and good fyſſhe. Theyr ſhyppes were
here in great daungiour. They remayned twoo monethes in
this pozte where they made newe pzouiſion of freſſhe water,
fuell, and fyſſhe. Here the Capitayne cauſed all his men to
bee confeſſed.

Confeſſion.

Appzochynge to the.52. degrees, they founde the ſtraight
nowe cauled the ſtraight of Magellanus, beinge in ſum place
C.r.leaques in length: and in bzeadth ſumwhere very large
and in other places lyttle moze then halfe a leaque in bzedth.
On both the ſydes of this ſtrayght, are great and hygh moun
taynes couered with ſnowe, beyonde the whiche is the enteraunce into the ſea of *Sur*. This enteraunce the Capitayne na
med *Mare Pacificum*. Here one of the ſhyppes ſtole away pziui
lie and returned into Spaine. Jn this was one of the giantes
who dyed as ſoone as he felt the heate that is abowte the E-
quinoctiall lyne.

The ſtraight of Magella-nus.

The South ſea. Mare pacificum.

When the Capitayne *Magalianes* was paſt the ſtraight and
ſawe the way open to the other mayne ſea, he was ſo gladde
therof that foz ioy the teares fell from his eyes, and named
the poynt of the lande from whenſe he fyzſt ſawe that ſea, *Ca-po Deſiderato*.

The giantes died foz heat.

Capo Deſideato

Suppoſing that the ſhyp which ſtole away had byn loſte, they
reered a croſſe vppon the top of a hyghe hyll to directe their
courſe in the ſtraighe yf it were theyr chaunce to coome that
way. They founde that in this ſtrayght in the moneth of Oc
tober the nyght was not paſt foure houres longe. They found
in this ſtrayght at euery thzee myles, a ſafe hauen and excel:
lent

Short nights in the moneth of October.

Flying fysshes

cellent water to dzynke: woodde also and fysshe, and greate plentie of goodherbes. They thynke that there is not a fayrer strayght in the wozlde. Here also they sawe certeyne flyinge fysshes.

The gyantes language.

The other giante which remayned with them in the shyp, named bzeade Capar: water, Oli: redde clothe, Cherecauted colour, Cheiche: blacke colour, Amel: And spoke al his wozdes in the throte. On a tyme, as one made a crosse befoze him and kyssed it, shewynge it vnto hym, he suddeynely cryed Setebos, and declared by signes that if they made any moze crosses, Setebos wold enter into his body and make him bzust. But when in fine he sawe no hurte coome thereof, he tooke the crosse and imbzased and kyssed it oftentymes, desyzinge that he myght bee a Chzystian befoze his death. He was therfoze baptyzed and named Paule.

The gyant is badtised.

Departynge owt of this strayght into the sea cauled Mare Pacificum the .xxviii. day of Nouember in the yeare. 1520. they sayled thzee moonethes and. xx. dayes befoze they sawe any lande. And hauynge in this tyme consumed all theyz byskct and other vyttayles, they fell into suche necessitie that they were inforced to eate the pouder that remayned therof beinge nowe full of woozmes and stynkynge lyke pysse by reason of the salte water. Theyz freshe water was also putrifyed and become yelowe. They dyd eate skynnes and pieces of lether which were foulded abowt certeyne great ropes of the shyps. But these skynnes beinge made verye harde by reason of the soonne, rayne and wynde, they hunge them by a cozde in the sea foz the space of foure oz fiue dayes to mollifie them, and sodde them and eate them. By reason of this famen and vncleue feedynge, summe of theyz gummes grewe so ouer theyz teethe, that they dyed miserably foz hunger. And by this occasion dyed. xix. men, and also the giante with an Indian of the lande of Bzasile otherwyse cauled Terra de papagalli, that is the lande of popingiayes. Besyde these that dyed. xxv. oz. xxx. were so sicke that they were not able to doo any seruice with theyz handes oz armes foz feeblenesse: So that there was in maner none without sum disease. In these thzee monethes x xx. dayes, they sayled foure thousande leaques in one goulfe by the sayde sea cauled Pacificum (that is) peaceable, whiche may well bee so cauled fozasmuch as in all thys tyme hauyng

Three monethes sayt lyng without the syght of lande. Extreme famen.

Diseases of famen.

no

no fyght of any lande, they had no miffoztune of wynde oz
any other tempeft. Durynge this tyme alfo, they difcoucred
only two little Jlandes vnhabited, where they fawe nothing
but birdes and trees, and therefoze named thepm infoztunate
Jlandes, beinge one from the other abowte two huzdzeth lea
ques diftante. The firfte of thefe Jlandes is from the Equi=
nocttal toward the pole Antartike. xb. degrees, and the other
fyue. Theyz failinge was in fuche foze that they failed dai=
ly betweene. l. lx. to .lxx. leaques. So that in fine, if god of
his mercy had not gyuen them good wether, it was neceffary
that in this foo greate a fea they fhuld all haue dyed foz hun=
ger. Whiche neuertheleffe they efcaped foo hardely, that it
may bee doubted whether euer the like biage may be attemp=
ted with fo good fucceffe.

They confydered in this nauigation that the pole Antar=
tike hath no notable ftarre after the foze of the pole Artike.
But they fawe many ftarres gathered togyther, whyche are
like two clowdes one feparate a little from an other, and fum
what darke in the myddeft. Betweene thefe, are two ftarres
not very bigge, noz muche fhynninge, whiche moue a little:
And thefe two are the pole Antartike. The needell of theyz
compaffe varyed fumwhat, and turned euer towarde the pole
Artike. Neuertheleffe, had no fuche foze as when it is in
thefe partes of the pole Artike. In fo muche that it was
neceffarie to helpe the needle with the lode ftone (com=
monly cauled the adamant) befoze they could faile ther=
with, bycaufe it moued not as it doothe when it is
in thefe owre partes. When they were in the
myddeft of the goulfe, they fawe a croffe of
fiue cleare ftarres directly toward the
Weft, eand of equall diftance the
one from the other.

B. B. k.t. The

The vyage rounde

⸿ The order of the ſtarres abowt the pole Antartike, ſumme haue figured
in this maner.

☸ The pole Antartike.   B. The Croſſe.

In these dayes they sayled betwene the West and South
so farre that they approched to the Equinoctiall line, & were
in longitude from the place from whense they fyrst departed,
a hundreth and twentie degrees. In this course they sayled
by two Ilandes of exceadynge height, wherof the one named
Cipanghu, is. xp. degrees from the pole Antartike: And the o=
ther named Sumbdit. xb. degrees. When they were past the
Equinoctiall line, they sayled betwene the West and South=
west at the quarter of the West towarde the Southwest more
then a hundreth leaques, changinge theyr sayles to the quar=
ter of the Southwest vntyll they came to the .xiii. degrees a=
boue the Equinoctial towarde the pole Artyke, intentyng as
much as were possible, to approche to the cape cauled of the
owlde wryters Cattigara: The whiche is not founde as the
owlde Cosmographers haue discribed it, but is towarde the
north aboue.xii. degrees as they afterwarde vnderstode.

When they had thus sayled.lxx. leaques of this vyage in
the.xii. degree aboue the Equinoctial, and.C.xlvi. degrees of
longitude (as I haue sayde) the fyrst day of March they dis=
couered a lyttle Ilande towarde the northwest, and two o=
ther towarde the southwest: but the one was hygher and
bygger then the two other. In the byggest of these, the gene
rall capitayne wolde haue rested hym selfe a whyle: but he
coulde not by reasen the people of these Ilands resorted con
tinually to the shippes with theyr canoas, and stole nowe one
thynge and nowe an other, in such sorte that owr men could
take no reste, and therfore demaunded of the capitayne that
they mygh stryke theyr sayles to brynge the shyppes to land.
But the Capitayne beinge prouoked to anger, wente alande
with fortie armed men, and burnte about fiftie of theyr hou=
ses with many of theyr Canoas: And slewe also abowt seuen
men, and recouered a shyppe boate whiche the Barbarians
had stolne, and so departed folowynge his vyage. The Capi
tayne named these Ilands Insulæ Latronum, that is, the Ilands
of theeues. When owr men had so wounded summe of th ym
with arrowes that they were stryken throughe bothe syd s,
they pulled furth the arrowes not ceasyng to matuerle at thē
tyll they fell downe deade: And yet coulde not the other so de
part, but styll folowed the shyppes with more then two hun=
dreth of theyr boates, approchynge as nere to the shyppes as
they

The Equi=
noctial line.

The Ilandes
of Cipanghu
and Sumbdit

Insulæ Latronū.

they coulde, and proferynge owre men certeyne fysshes. As the shyppes passed with full sayle in the myddefte of they boates, they sawe in sum of them certeyne women lamenting and tearynge they heare, which owre men thought they dyd for the death of they hufbandes. As farre as they could perceaue, thefe people lyue at they owne libertie without anye ruler or gouernour. They go naked and haue blacke beardes and blacke heare on they heades whiche they weare longe downe to they waftes. They are of the fame ftature that we are, and well made, of coloure lyke vnto an olyue. They wo men are well fauored with blacke and thicke heare on they heades reachynge to the grownde. The menne coloure they teeth redde and blacke, which they efteeme a coomely thynge. They annoynt they bodies and heare with the oyle of Cocus. They boates are sum all blacke, sum whyte, and sum redde, and haue fayles made of the broade leaues of date trees sowd togyther. In the fteade of a rudder, they vfe a certeyne brode boorde with a ftaffe in the toppe, and maye when they wyll, make the fterne the forecaftell, or the forecaftell the fterne. They fayle fo fwyftely that they feeme a farre of, lyke Delphyns fwymmynge aboue the water.

The tenth day of March, in the yeare. 1521. they wente alande vppon a lyttle Iland named Zamal, xxx. leaques dyftant from the Ilande of theeues. Bycaufe this Ilande was not inhabyted, they refted here a whyle, where the capitayne caufed a pauilion to bee pytched for the ficke and crafed men, and a hogge to bee kylde.

The. xviii. day of Marche, they fawe a boate with nyne men commynge towarde them, fhewynge theim felues ioyfull and relopfynge of they commynge. They brought many prefentes with them, and feemed to bee people of much humanitie. They gaue the capitayne a great fyfhe, and a great veffel of the wyne of thofe date trees whiche beare the frute Cocus. They made alfo fignes that within the fpace of foure dayes, they wolde brynge ryffe and dyuers foules and beafts as they dyd in deede.

This Cocus is a frute of certeyne date trees wherof they make breade, wyns, oyle, and vineger. They make wyne in this maner. They cutte a bygge braunche of the tree, & hange there at a reede as bigge as a mans legge, into the which drop peth

People with longe heare

They coloure they teethe.

The Ilande of Zamall

Wyne of date trees.

The marueilous frute Cocus.

peth a sweete licour from the tree lyke vnto newe whyte wine sumwhat tart, & let the reede continewe there from mozninge tyll euenynge, and from euenynge to mozninge. The frute of this tree cauled Cocus, is as bygge as the head of a man oz moze. The fyzste rynde of this, is greene and of the thicke= nesse of two fyngers, hauynge in it certeyne threedes wherof they make cozdes with the which they rye theyz boates. Vn= der this rynde, there is a thicke shell whiche they burne and make pouder therof and vse it as a remedie foz certeyne disea= ses. Vnder this shell, is a whyte substaunce lyke the carnell of a nutte being a synger in thicknesse, which they eate with flesshe and fysshe as wee doo bzeade. It hath the taste of an almonde, and is vsed in the steade of bzeade when it is dzyed. In the myddest of this carnell, is a cleare and sweete water, beinge very holsome and cozdiale. This water sumtyme con= geleth and lyeth within the shell lyke an egge. When they in= tende to make oyle hereof, they ley it to putrifie in water, and boyle it vntyll it bee lyke oyle oz liquide butter.   When they intende to make vineger, they suffer only the water to putri= fie, and then set it to the soonne where it becommeth vineget lyke vnto that which is made of whyte wyne. And when they mengle the carnell with the water which is in the myddest of the frute, and strayne it thozowe a cloth, they make a mylke therof lyke vnto goates mylke. These date trees are lyke vn= to them that beare dates, but are not so full of knottes. With the iuise of two of these date trees, a hole famelie of tenne per= sons may bee maynteyned with wyne bfynge one viii. dayes, and the other, other. viii. dayes: foz they shulde els bee dzyed and wythered. These trees continue foz the space of a hun= dzeth yeares. This Jlande where they founde this humane and gentell people, is cauled Zuluan, and is not verye bygge. Abowt this Jlande they founde manye other Jlandes, and therefoze named this sea Archipelsgo di San Lazaro, that is, the great sea of saynte Lazarus, beinge tenne degrees aboue the Equinoctiall towarde thre pole, and. C. lzi. frome the place from whense they departed.   The people of this Jlande are Caphraxite (that is gentyles. They go naked sauynge that they couer theyz pziuie partes with a clothe made of the rynde of a certeyne tree. The chiefest men, haue abowte theyz heades a sylken cloth of needle woozke. They are grosse and bzode set

The Jland of zuluan.

The sea cau= led Archipe= lago di san Lazaro.

Gentyles.

and

and of the coloure of an oliue. They annoynte theyr bodies with the oyle of *Coeus* to defend them agaynst the heate of the soonne and dryneste of the wynde. The xxb. day of Marche, they departed from hense aid directed theyr course betwene the Weste and Southwest, and sayled betwene foure Ilandes named *Cenilo, Huinanghan, Hibusson,* and *Abarien.* &c.

Foure Ilands

The Iland of Buthuan.

The xxviii. daye of Marche, they came to the Ilande of *Buthuan* where they were honorably interteyned of the Kynge and the Prynce his soonne who gaue theim muche golde and spices. The capitayne gaue the kynge a vesture of red clothe and an other of yelowe made after the Turkysshe faſhyon, and also a red cappe. And gaue likewise to other that came with hym, certeyne knyues, glasses, and beades of cristalle. After that, the capitayne had shewed the Kynge the secreates of his shippe and suche marchaundies as he had therin, he caused a piece of ordinaunce suddenly to bee shote of, whereat the kyng was greately amased vntil the capitayne comforted hym. Then the Capitaine commaunded one of his men to be armed from the heade to the foote, and caused three other to strike hym with theyr swoordes, whereat the Kynge maruayled greately, and sayde to thinterpretoure (who was a slaue borne in Malacha) that one of those armed men was able to encounter with a hundreth of his men. But he maruayled muche more when the capitaine toulde hym by thinterpretoure howe he founde the straight by the compasse and lode stone, and howe many dayes they were without sight of any lande. Then askynge licence to departe, the capitayne sente two of his men with hym, of the whiche Antonie Pigafetta was one. When the kynge sawe Antonie Pigafetta write the names of many thinges, and afterwarde rehearse them agayne, he maruayled yet more, makynge sygnes that suche men descended from heauen. The Kynge brought them firste to his pallaice where he interteyned them honorably and gaue them manye gyftes, as dyd also the Prince in his pallaice beynge in another Ilande named *Caleghan.*

The Iland of Caleghan.

Plentie of golde.

As they spyed a certeyne myne of earthe in the Kynges Ilande, they founde pieces of golde, sum as bigge as nuttes and other as bigge as egges. All the kynges vessells were of golde, and his house well furnysshed. In all the hole nation there was no man of coomlier personage then the kinge.

De

He had his heare long downe to his shulders, and very blake, with a vaile of silke rowled abowte his head, and two greate ringes of golde hanginge at his eares. He had abowte hys myddle, a clothe wroughte of cotton and silke impaled wyth golde, and reacheinge downe to his knees. On his one syde, he had a long dager with a hafte of golde, and the shethe of a fayre kynde of carued woodde. He had on euery finger, three ringes of golde, and had his bodie annoynted with oyle of storax and Beniamin. The natural coloure of his face was like vnto the coloure of an oliue: And all his bodye bysyde paynted with diuers colours. The kynges name was Raia Colambu, and the Prince was called Raia Siagu.

The laste day of Marche neare vnto Easter, the capitaine caused his preeste to say masse, and sente to the kinge by thin∣terpretoure, that his commyng a lande at that tyme was not to dyne with hym, but only to heare masse. The Capitayne came alande with fyftie of his men in theyr best apparel with∣owte weapons or harnesse, and all the residue well armed. Before the boates came to lande, he caused sixe pieces of or∣dinaunce to be shotte of in token of peace, and so came aland, where the two kinges embrased hym, and accompanyed hym to the place appoynted for masse to be sayde not farre frome the sea syde. Sumwhat before the beginnynge of masse, the Capitayne sprinkeled the Kynges with damaske water. When the preeste was at mid masse at the offitorie, the kings profered them selues to go to kysse the crosse with the cappy∣tayne, but offered nothynge. At the tyme of sacringe when the preeste lifted vppe the bodie of Christ, and the Christians kneeled downe and helde vppe their handes ioyned togither, the kinges dyd the like also wyth greate reuerence. In the meane tyme, whyle certeyne of the Christians were at the com∣munion, a handegunne was shotte of to signifie vnto theym that were in the shyppes, to discharge all theyr ordnaunce. When masse was fynysshed, the Capitaine caused certeyne of his men to put on theyr harnesse and to make a combat with theyr naked woordes, wherat the kynges tooke great plea∣sure. This doone, the Capitaine caused a crosse to be broughte furth, with nayles and a crowne of thornes, gyuynge com∣maundement to all his men to gyue reuerence therunto, and signifyinge to the kynges by thinterpretour that that banner was

Was gyuen hym by Themperoure his lozde and master, with commaundement to leaue the same in al places where he came to the great commoditie and profits of all such as wolde reuerendly receaue it as an assured token of frendshyp: And that he wold therfoze leaue it there alwel to accomplyshe his lozds commaundement, as also that if at any tyme any shyppes of Chzistians shulde chaunce to coome that way, shulde by seing that crosse perceaue that other men had byn well enterteyned there, and wolde therfoze not onely abstepne from doing them any hurte oz displeasure, but also helpe to ayde them agepnste theyz enemies. And that therfoze it shulde bee requisite to erecte that crosse bnpon the toppe of the hyghesse mountayne that mygbt bee scene from the sea on euery syde. Also to pzay bnto it reuerently. And that in so doinge, they shulde not bee burie with thunder, lygbtnynge, oz tempestes. When the kynges harde these woozdes, they gaue the Capitayne great thankes, pzomysinge gladly to obserue and fulfyll all suche thynges as he required.   Then the Capitayne demaunded whether they were Moozes oz gentyles. They answered that they had none other kynde of religion, but that lyftynge bppe theyz handes ioyned together and theyz faces toward heauen, they caused bppon theyz god *Abba*. Whiche answere lyked the Capitayne berz well, bycause the gentyles are sooner persuaded to owre fayth then the Moozes. &c.

Moores and gentyles.

Departynge frome hense, they came to the Ilandes of *Zeilon*, *Zubuth*, *Messana*, and *Calaghan*, by the conducte of certepne pylottes of the sayde kynges.   Of these, *Zubuth* is the beste, and hath the trade of beste traffique. In the Ilande of *Messana*, they founde dogges, cattes, hogges, hennes, goates, ryce, ginger, Cocus, myrke, panyke, barlye, frgges, ozanges, waxe, and golde in greate quantitie. This Ilande is aboue the Equinoctiall towarde owre pole. ix. degrees twoo thyzde partes: and .162. degrees frome the place frome whense they departed. They remayned in this Iland foz the space of .viii. dayes, and then directed theyz bpage towarde the nozthwest, and passed betwene these fyue Ilandes, *Zeilon*, *Bohol*, *Canghu*, *Barkai*, and *Catighan*. In this Ilande of *Catighan*, are certepne great battes as bygge as Eagles, of the which they toke one. They are good to bee eaten, and of taste muche lyke a henne. There are also stocke dooues, turtle dooues, popingiayes, and certepne foules as bygge as hennes. These foules haue lyttle

many Ilands

The Iland of Messana.

Battes as bygge as Eagles. Fowles with hoznes.

hoznes

hoznes, and lay great egges, which they couer a cubet depthe
in the sande, by the heate whereof and vertue of the soonne,
they are hatchid, and the younge byzdes creepe owte of the
sande by them selues. From the Jlande of Meſſana to Catighan
are,xx. leaques saplynge towarde the Weſt. And bycauſe the
kynge of Meſſana coulde not folowe the ſhyppes, they taryzed foz him about the Jlandes of Polo, Ticobon, and Pozon, where
the Capitayne tooke hym into his ſhippe with certeyne of his
pzincipall men, and ſo folowed theyz byage towarde the Jzlande of Zubut, whiche is abowte fiftie leaques diſtaunt from Catighan.

Egges hatched in sand.

The Jlande of Zubut.

The.bii. day of Apzyll abowte noone, they entered into
the pozte of Zubut: And paſſynge by many byllages and habitecions in trees, they came to the citie, where the Capitayne
gaue commaundement to the maryners to ſtryke theyz ſayles
t to ſet them ſelues in ozder in maner of battayle ray, cauſing
all the ozdinaunce to bee ſhotte of, wherewith all the people
were put in greate feare. After this, the Capitayne ſent an
ambaſſadoure with thinterpzetoure to the kynge of Zubut.
When they appzoched nere to the citie, they founde the kyng
with a great company of men ſoze aſtonyſhed at the noyſe of
the gunnes. But thinterpzetour aduertiſed them that it was
the cuſtome of owre men in al ſuche places where they coome,
to diſcharge theyz ozdinaunce in token of frendeſhyppe and to
honoue the lozde of the citie. With which woozdes the kyng
and his coompany were well quieted. After this, thinterpzetour declared that his maſter was the Capitayne of the ſhips
of the greateſt Pzince in the wozlde, and that they wente to
diſcouer the Jlandes of Molucca: And further, that hearyng
of his good name and fame by the repozte of the kyng of Meſſana, they determyned to biſite hym and to haue byttayles
foz epchaunge of theyz marchaundies. The kynge anſwered
that he was well contented therwith, and that they were hartely welcoome. Neuertheleſſe, that it was a cuſtome in that
place, that all ſuch ſhyppes as entered into that hauen, ſhuld
pay tribute: And that there were not many dayes paſte, ſence
a ſhyppe laden with golde and ſlaues dyd ſo paye. In token
wherof, he cauſed to coome befoze hym certeyne marchauntes
of that coompany whiche yet remayned with hym. To this
thinterpzetour anſwered, that foz aſmuch as his lozde was
the Capitayne of ſo myghtie a Pzince, he neuer payde tribute

The kynge of Zubut.

A ſhyp laded with gold and ſlaues.

to any kynge in the woolde, and wold not nowe begynne. He prayinge hym to take this foz a resolute answere, that if he wolde accepte the peace that was profered hym, he shulde enjoy it, And if he rather desyzed warre, he shoulde haue his handes full. When thinterpzetour had sayde these woozdes, one of the sayde marchauntes (who was a Mooze) spake to the kynge in this maner. CATACAIA Chine: that is, Take hede ye sy?, Foz these men are they that haue conquered Calicut, Malaca, and all the greater India: and are of suche poure that of powe intreate them otherwyse then well, powe may to late knowe what they are able to doo moze then they haue dvone at Calicut and Malaca. When thinterpzetoure harde these woozdes, he sayde that the kynge his loze was of much greater puissaunce and moze dominions, and lozde of moze shyppes then was the kynge of Poztugale: declarynge further that he was kynge of Spayne and Emperour of all Chzistendome Addynge hereunto that yf he wolde not bee his frende, he wolde hercafter sende thyther suche a poure of armed men as shulde destroy his contrey. The Moore conferred all these woozdes with the kynge, who sayde that he wolde further deliberate with his counsayle, and gyue theym a full answere the daye folowynge. In the meane tyme he sente theym certeyne vyttayles and wyne. When all these thynges were declared to the kynge of Messana who was the chiefest the a towne nexte vnto hym, and lozde of many Ilandes, he wente alande and repayzed to the kynge of Zubu and declared vnto hym the great humanitie and curtesie of the generall Capitayne. Shoztely after, the Capitayne sente certeyne of his men with thinterpzetour to the kynge of Zubu to knowe his pleasure and what aunswere he wolde make them. As they wente towarde the courte, they mette the kynge commyng in the streete accompanied with many of his chiefe men. He caused owr men to sit downe by hym, and demaunded of them if there were any moze then one Capitayne in theyz coompanie : And whether it were theyz requeste that he shulde pay tribute to themperour. They answered that they desyzed none other thynge but that they myght exercise marchaundies with them, and to barter ware foz ware. The kynge made answere that he was well content therwith ; wyllynge the Capitayne in token of frendshippe to sende him a little of the blud of his ryght arme, affirmyng that he wold do the lyke. &c.

After

Calicut.
Malacha.

Sheadyng of bludde is a token of frendshyppe

After this the kynge of Megeana with the kynge of Zubu his neuie (who was the prince) and certeyne other of his gen tylmen, came to the shyppes and brought the Capitayne ma= ny goodly presentes. They entered into greate amitie, and had large communication of many thynges. The Capitayne perfuaded them to the Chriſtian faythe, which they gladly em braſed, and tooke ſuche pleaſure in hearynge the articles of owre beliefe, that the teares fell from theyr eyes for ioye. They were baptiſed, and ſhortly after all the people of the Ilande. They eſteeme nothyng more precious then drynkyng glaſſes of Uenice wooʒke.

When they came to the citie, they founde the kyng in his pallaice ſittynge vppon a floure or flooʒe made of the leaues of date trees wʒought after a curious diuiſe lyke a certeyne kynde of mattes. He had vppon his body, none other appa= rell but only a cloth of bombaſine cotton hangyng befoʒe his priuie partes. On his heade, he had a vayle of needle wooʒke: and abowre his necke a chaine of greate price. At his eares, hunge two rynges of golde wherein were incloſed many pre= cious ſtones. He was but of ſmaule ſtature, but ſumewhat groſſe, and had the reſidue of his body paynted with dyuers coloures whereof ſum were lyke vnto ſtampynge fyʒe. Befoʒe hym, he had two veſſelles made of the fine earth cauled Por= cellana, with ſodden egges. Alſo four veſſels of Porcellana full of wyne made of date trees, and couered with many odoʒife= rous herbes. The prince bʒoughr them to his houſe, where he had foure doughters verye well fauoured and whyte lyke owres. He cauled them to daunce all naked, and therwith to ſynge, and play on certeyne tymbrelles made of metall.

At this tyme it ſo chaunced that one of the Spanyardes dyed in one of the ſhyppes. And when certeyne of theyr coom panye deſyred the kynge to gyue them leaue to burie hym on the land, he anſwered that foʒaſmuch as he and all his, were at the commaundement of theyr kynge and maſter, how much moʒe ought the grounde ſo to bee.

They greatly marueyled at the cerimonies perteynyng to the maner of owre funeralles, and honoured the croſſes whi= che were ſet at bothe thendes the graue.

They pyne with iuſtice, and vſe waightes and meaſures. Theyr houſes are made of timber and ſawne boozdes, and

The kynge of Zubu is bap= tiſed.

The kynge of Zubu his ap= parell.

Well fauored women.

are so buylded aboue the grownde vppon proppes and pyles, that they ascende to the same by certeyne stayers. Under theyr houses, they keepe theyr hoggts and hennes.

When they came to batterynge, they gaue golde, ryse, hogges, hennes, and dyuers other thynges for sume of owre

tryfels of smaule value. They gaue tenne Pesos of golde for xvi. poundes weyght of iren. One pesus is in value a ducate and a halfe. The sunday folowynge, the kynge was baptysed with great solemnitie. At which tyme, the Capitayne admonysshed him before not to bee afrayde at the shootyng of of the ordinaunce, bycause it was theyr custome so to doo at such solemne feastes.

After this, the Capitayne caused theym to breake all theyr Idoles, and to set vppe the crosse in dyuers places, prayinge to the same bothe mornynge and euenynge kneelynge on theyr knees and holdynge vp theyr handes ioyned togyther. The kinge in his baptisme, was named Charles after the Emperours name, and the Prince, Ferdinando after the name of his maiesties brother. The kynge of Messana was named John, and the Moore Christopher. To all other they gaue such names as are commonly vsed in Christendome. And thus beefore masse was begunne, were fiue hun-

dreth men baptised. When masse was fynysshed, the Capitayne inuited the kynge to dyne with him in his shyppe, and at his commynge, caused the ordinaunce to bee discharged.

The queene was also baptised with fortie of her gentlewomen, and her doughter the Princes wife. The queene was very younge and fayre, hauynge her body couered with a white cloth. Her lyppes were redde, and she had on her head a hat, on the toppe wherof was a triple crowne much lyke the popes. This crowne & the hat, were made of the leues of dates trees.

Within the space of viii. dayes, th'inhabitauntes of the Ilande were baptised, excepte one vyllage of Idolaters who wolde not herein obey the kynges commaundement. Wherupon the Capitayne sent certayne of his menne, thyther, who burnt the towne and erected a crosse in that place bycause the people of the vyllage were gentyles (that is) Idolaters. But if they had byn Moores (that is Mahumetistes) they wold haue erected a pyller of ston, bycause the Moores are more stooberne and harder to bee conuerted then are the gentyles.

When the queene came to the place where shee shuld heare masse

masse, thee came furth with great pompe and solemnitie, ha=
uynge goinge befoze her thzee younge damoselles and thzee
men with theyz cappes in theyz handes, whom thee folowed
apparelled in whyte and blacke, with a great bayle of sylke
vppon her heade fringed abowte with golde, whiche couered
her hatte and hunge downe to her shoulders. Shee had also
a great trayne of women folowynge her, beinge all barefoo=
ted and naked, excepte that vppon theyz heades and pziuie
partes, they woze certeyne bayles of silke, and hadde theyz
heare spzedde.

Befoze the kynge of Zubut was baptised, he was named
Raia Humabuon. When the Capitayne demaunded of hym
why all the Idoles in the Ilande were not burnt accozdynge
to his pzomesse, he answered that they esteemed the no moze
as goddes, but only made sacrifice to theym foz the Pzinces
bzother who was very sycke, and as noble and wyttie a
man as was in the Ilande. The Capitayne answered that if
he wolde burne al his Idoles and beleue faythfully in Chzist,
and bee baptised, he shulde be immediatly restozed to health,
and that he wolde els gyue them leaue to stryke of his heade.
By these woozdes and persuasions of the Capitayne, he con=
ceaued such hope of health, that after he was baptised he felt
no moze greefe of his disease. And this was a manifest myza
cle wzought in owre tyme wherby dyuers infidels were con=
uerted to owre fayth, and theyz Idoles destroyed, and also
theyz altares ouerthzowen on the whiche they were accusto=
med to eate the sacrifyced fleshe. The people of the Ilande
pay the kynge a poztion of vittaylles foz theyz tribute by all
theyz cities and byllages.

Not farre from this Ilande of Zubut, is the Iland of Ma=
than, whose inhabitauntes vse maruelous cerimonies in theyz
sacrifices to the soonne and burying the deade. They weare
rynges of golde abowt theyz pziuie members. The Ilande is
gouerned by two Pzinces wherof the one is named Zula, and
the other Cilapulapu. And wheras this Cilapulapu refused to pay
tribute to the kynge of Spayne, the Capitayne went ageynst
hym in his owne person with .ir. of his menne armed with
coates of mayle and helmettes. Cilapulapu diuided his army
into thzee battayles, hauynge in euery battaile two thousand
and fiftie men armed with bowes, arrowes, dartes and iaue=
lins

lins hardened at the poyntes with fyer. This contineued longe and sharpe. But the Capitayne beinge a valient man and presynge hym selfe in the brunte of the battayle, was sore wounded and slayne, forasmuch as the moste of the Barbarians directed all theyr force ageynst hym. Besyde the Capitayne, were slayne of owre men abowt. viii. or. ix. Of the Barbarians, were. xv. slayne and many sore wounded. After the death of the Capitayne, they chose two other in his place, of the which one was Odoardo Barbesa a Portugale, and the other John Serrano who was shortely after betrayde by thinterpretour and taken prisoner with dyvers other.

The capitaine Magellauus is slayne.

Certeyne dayes before the Capitaynes death, they hadde knowleage of the Ilandes of Molucca whiche they chiefely sought. Departynge therfore from the Ilande of Mathan, they sayled farre and came to the cape of an other Ilande named Bohol. In the myddest of this mayne sea (whiche they named *Archipelagus*) they consulted to burne the shyppe named Conception, bycause they were nowe fewe in number, and to furnyshe the other two shyppes with thartillerie therof. Thus direccynge theyr course towarde Southewest, they came to an other Ilande named *psuiloghon*, where they founde blacke men lyke vnto the Sarasins. Shortly after, they arryued at an other great Iland, whose kyng named Raia Calauar, intreated them very frendely in all thynges as dyd the kyng of Messana. This Ilande is ryche in golde, and hath plentie of ryse, gynger, hoggs, goates, hennes, and dyuers other thynges. It is named Chippit, and is. viii. degrees aboue the Equinoctiall line towarde owr pole: And in longitude from the place from whense they first departed.170. degrees: And abowt.50. leaques from Zubut.

The J'and of Bohol.

They burnte one of theyr shyppes.

Blacke men.

The Ilande of Chippit.

Departinge frome hense they came to an other Iland named Caghaian beinge 40. leaques frome Chippit as they sayled betwene the weste and Southe weste. This Ilande is very greate, and in maner vnhabited. The people are moores, and were banysshed owt of the Ilande of Burnei whiche sum caule Porne.

The Iland of Caghaian.

Frome this Ilande aboute xxv. leaques betwene the west and northe weste, they founde a maruelous frutefull Ilande named Pulaoan, beinge towarde owre pole aboue the Equinoctiall ix. degrees and a thirde parte: And C.lxxix. degrees and a thyrde

The Iland of Pulaoan.

a thyrd parte in longitude frome the place of theyr departing. Frome this Jlande.r. leaques towarde the South weste, they sawe an other Jlande whiche seemed to them sumtymes to mounte as they sayled by the coastes therof. As they were entringe into the porte, there arose a boystious and darke tempeste which ceased as soone as the fiers of the three sayntes (wherof we haue spoken before) appeared vppon the cabells. Frome the begynninge of this Jlande to the porte, are fyue leaques. This Jlande is greate and riche: and the chiefe citie therof conteyneth. r. rv. thousande houses. The kynge intertepned owre men very frendlye, and sent them bysyde many other presentes, two elephantes trapped with silke to bring them to his pallaice that brought the presentes which the Capytaynes sent hym.   He hath a magnyfycalle courte and a greate garde. Also a multitude of concubynes. He is a moore, and is named Raia Siripada.   He is a kynge of great poure, and hath vnder hym many other kynges, Jlandes, and cities. This Jlande of Burnei is aboue the Equinoctiall toward owre pole fyue degrees and a quarter.   And in longitude frome the place of theyr departing. C. lrrvi. degrees and two thirde partes.

The Jland of Burnei or Porne.

A great citie.

Elephantes

Departinge frome Burnei, they came to an Jlande cauled Cimbubon, beinge. viii. degrees aboue the Equinoctiall lyne Here they remayned. rl. dayes to calke theyr shyppes and furnysshe them with fresshe water and fuell whiche was to them great payne and trauayle becauce they were in maner all bare footed, theyr shooes and in maner theyr other apparell being worne by reason of the longe vyage. In the wooddes of this Jlande, they founde a tree whose leaues as soone as they faule on the grounde, doo stirre and remoue frome place to place as though they were alyue. They are muche lyke the leaues of a mulbery tree: And haue on euery syde as it were two short and blunt fiere. When they are cut or broken, there is no blud be seene come furth of them. yet when any of them are touched, they suddeynely moue and starte away. Antonie Pigafetta kepte one of them in a platter for the space of. viii. dayes. And euer when he touched it, it ranne rounde about the platter. He supposeth that they liue only by ayer.

The Jland of Cimbulon.

Leaues of trees which seeme to lyue

Departynge from hense, they directed theyr coarse by the weste quarter towarde the Southeaste, to fynde the Jlandes of of Molucca, and sayled not farre from certeyne mountaynes where they founde the sea full of great weedes and herbes.

From hense, they came to the Ilandes of Zolo and Taghima, in the which are founde perles of exceadyng biggenesse.

Folowyng theyr course toward the north East, they came to a great citie named Mingdando, lyinge aboue the Ilandes of Buthuan and Calaghan, where they tooke a canoa of certeyne of thinhabitauntes: by whome being informed of the Ilandes of Molucca, they lefte theyr course towarde the north East, and folowed the South caste nere vnto a cape of the Iland of Buthuan, they were aduertised for certentie that on the bankes of a certeyne ryuer, there dwelte men ouergrowen with heare, and of high stature.

Folowyng still theyr course by the south caste, and passyng by many smaule Ilandes, they came to the Ilandes of Molucca the syxte daye of Nouember and the xxvii. monethe after theyr departure owt of Spayne. Beinge therfore ioyfull and gyuyng thankes vnto god, they discharged all theyr ordynaunce. In the coaste of all these Ilandes, euen vnto the Ilandes of Molucca, soundyng with theyr plummet, they founde the deapthe of the sea to bee no lesse then a hundreth and two yardes, which is contrary to the saying of the Portugales who affyrme that no shyppe can passe that way with out great daungioure by reason of the shalownes and rockes or shelues: and for the darkenesse which the clowdes cause in the heauen. All which thyngs they fayned to thintent that none other shulde haue knowelcage of theyr vyagies.

The viii. day of Nouember in the yeare, 1521, before the rysinge of the soonne, they entered into the porte of the Ilande of Tidore, being one of the chiefe Ilandes of Molucca, where they were honorably interteyned of the kynge who declared that he had louge before seene a sygne in heauen that certeyne shyppes shuld comme from a farre contrey to the Ilandes of Molucca: And that wheras for the better certificat therof he consydered the stations of the moone, he sawe there in the commyng of owre shyppes, and that we were the men whome he seemed to see in the same. Wherupon he profered hym selfe to enter into leaque of frendshyppe with the kynge of Spayne, and to accepte owre men as his brotherne and chyldren: wyllyng them to come alande as into theyr owne houses.

Marginal notes:

A sea full of weedes.

Perles.

Men ouergrowen with heare.

The Ilandes of Molucca.

The portugales are reproued.

Tidore one of the Ilandes of Molucca.

A vision in the planettes

houses. Also that for theyr commynge, that Islande shulde
no more bee cauled Tidore, but Castile for the greate loue whi
che he bore to theyr kynge whom he reputed as his lorde and
master. This kynge is a Moore, and is named Raia Sultan
Mauzor.

The Ilandes of Molucca are fiue in number, & are thus
named: Tarenate, Tidore, Mutir, Macchian, and Bacchian. Of these,
Tarenate is the chiefest.

Directly agaynste the Ilande of Tidore, there is an other
great Ilande named Gilolo, inhabited of Moores and Gentyles. The Moores haue two kynges, of the which one hath
syre hundreth chyldren, & the other sire hundreth and fiftie.
The Gentyles kepe not so many women as doo the Moores
nor yet lyue in suche superstitions. They praye to the fyrste
thynge that they meete in the mornynge when they go furth
of theyr houses, and honoure that as theyr god for that day.
The kynge of the gentyles is very rythe in golde. In the
sayde Ilande of Gilolo, are reedes as bygge as a mans legge,
and full of cleare water holsome to bee drunke.

The .xii. daye of Nouember, the kynge of Tidore appoynted owre men a ware house in the citie where they might
sell theyr marchaundies. Theyr maner of exchange was in
this sort. For tenne yardes of good redde cloth, they had one
Bahar of cloues, whiche amounteth to foure Cantari and
syre pounde weight: And one Cantar is a hundreth pounde
weight. For .xv. yardes of cloth sumwhat woorse then the
other, they receaued in Cambie, one Bahar. For .xxxv. drynkynge cuppes of glasse, they had one Bahar. For .xvii. Ca-
thyls of quicke syluer, one Bahar. They came dayly to the
shyppes with many of theyr barkes full of goates, hennes,
fygges of a spanne longe, also the frute cauled Cocus, with dy
uers other kyndes of vyttayles in such quantitie that it was
a marueylous thynge to beholde. They furnyshed also theyr
shyppes with fresshe water which is hotte as it isheweth owt
of the sprynge, but is very coulde when it hath stoode a while
in an other place. It spryngeth from the mountaynes on the
which the cloue trees growe. They sawe a cloude ryse in ma
ner dayly, which compaseth about the sayde mountaynes.

The kynge of the Ilande of Bacchian, sente the kynge of
Spayne two deade byrdes of straunge forme. They were of
the byggenes of turtle doones, with lyttle heades and longe

Mm.i.   bylles;

The fyue I-
landes of mo-
lucca.
Tarenate.
The Iland of
Gilolo.

Moores & gen
tyles.

Golde.
water in
reedes.

Theyr maner
of barterings.

water of a
straunge qua-
litie.

Byrdes of
a straunge
forme.

bylles : also longe and smaule legges and no wynges, but in
the steade therof certeyne longe fethers of diuers colours, and
tayles lyke turtle dooues. All the other fethers are of one co=
loure much lyke vnto tawny, except those of the wynges.
They flye not but when the wynde bloweth. These Moores
are of opinion that these byrdes coomme frome the heauenlye
Paradyse, and therfore caule them Manucodiata, that is the
byrdes of god.

When they were determyned to depart from the Ilandes
of Molucca, certeyne kynges of the Ilandes accompanied the
with theyr canoas, and conducted them to an Ilande cau=
led Mare where they refresshed theyr shyppes with fresshe wa
ter and fuell. The kynges sent Themperours maiestie many
presentes : and embrasynge owre menne, departed with the
teares in theyr eyes : And owre men for theyr laste farewell,
shotte of all theyr ordinaunce. When in the Ilande of Mare,
they perceaued that one of theyr shyppes leaked and toke wa
ter very sore : wherby they were inforced to tary there three
dayes. But seinge that they coulde fynde no remedie for the
same but in longe tyme, they determined to leaue it, gyuynge
order that if afterwarde it coulde bee reparyd, they shulde re
turne into Spayne as well as they coulde.

In all the Ilandes of Molucca is founde cloues, ginger,
breade of the roote of Sagu, ryse, goates, sheepe, hennes,
fygges, almendes, sweete pomegranates and sowre, oran=
ges, lemendes, and hony which is made of certeyne flyes lesse
then antes : Also canes of suger, oyle of Cocus, mellons,
gourdes, and a maruellous coulde frute which they name Ca=
mulicai and dyuers other frutes. Furthermore whyte and
redde pepingiayes, and other of variable colours. It is not
passe fiftie yeares sence the moores fyrste inhabited anye of
these Ilands, which were before inhabited only with getyles.

The Ilande of Tidore, is aboue the Equinoctiall line to=
warde owre pole, at wt .27. minutes : And in longitude fro
the place from whense they departed, 171. degrees. And from
the Archipelagus in the which is the Iland of Zamal which our
men named the Iland of theeues, is. degrees and a halfe, and
runneth to the quarter of south southwest, and north north=
east. Terenate, is vnder the Equinoctial line foure minutes vn
der the pole Antartike. Mutir, is directly vnder the Equinoc=
tiall line, Macchian is, xv, minutes toward the pole Antartike,
and

They leaue
one of theyr
shyppes be=
hynd them.

The Ilandes
of Molucca.

Hony of flyes.

Popingiayes.

The Iland of
Tidore.

Terenate,
Mutir,

Macchian,

and Bacolan one degree. Thele Jlandes are lyke foure tharpe mountaynes, except Macchian which is not tharpe. The byggeſt of all theſe, is Bacchian.

Departyng from the Jland of Mare and directyng theyr courſe towarde the ſouthweſt, with onely. xlbi. men in theyr thyppe and. riii. Indians, they paſſed by the Jlandes of Chacouan, Lagoma, Sico, Gioghi, Caphi, Sulacho, Lumatola, Tenetum, Buru, Ambon, Budia, Celaruti, Benaia, Ambalao, Bandan, zorobua, zolot, Moceuamor, Galian, and Mallua, with dyuers other Jlandes both great and ſmaule, of Moores, Gentyles, and Canibales. Owre men remayned rb. dayes in the Jlande of Mallua to repayre theyr thyppe in certepne places where it tooke water. All the fieldes of this Jlande is full of longe and rounde pepper, and is ſituate towarde the pole Antartike vnder the Equinoctiall line. biii. degrees and a halfe, and is in the longitude of, 169. degrees and 40. minutes.

The piloて which owre men brought owt of the Jlandes of Molucca, toulde them that not farre from thenſe, was an Jland named Arucetto in the which are men and women not paſt a cubite in height, hauynge eares of such byggeneſſe that they lye vppon one and couer them with the other. But owr men wolde not ſayle thyther, bothe bycauſe the wynde and courſe of the ſea was ageynſte theym, and alſo for that they gaue no credite to his reporte.

The. rrb. day of January in the yeare. 1522. they departed from Mallua, and the day folowyng, arryued at a greate Jland named Timor, beinge fiue leaques diſtante from Mallua betwene the ſouth and ſouthweſt. In this Jlande is founde the woodde of whyte ſanders and ginger, and dyuers kindes of frutes. Alſo ſundry kyndes of beaſtes, and plentie of vyttaple and galde. They of the Jlandes of Giaua, Moluca, and Loxon, reſort to this Jlande for ſanders. Thinhabitauntes are gentyles. They ſay that when they go to cut the woodde of ſaunders, the deuyll appeareth to them in dyuers formes and aſketh theym what they haue neede of : And that after this biſion, many of them are longe ſicke. In al the Jlandes of this Archipelagus, rayneth the diſeaſe of ſaynt Job (whiche wee caule the frenche pore) more then in any other place in the worlde.

M M m. ii.   Farre

Side notes:
Bacchian,
many Jlands
The Jland of Mallua.
Pepper.
Lyttle men with longe eares.
The Jland of Timor.
Whyte ſanders and ginger.
The deuyll appeareth.
Saynt Job his diſeaſe.

Farre from this Jlande betwene the west and northwest they came to an Jlande named Eude, in the whiche groweth great plentie of Sinamome. In this tracte are founde many Jlandes lying in order as it were one directly behynde, another, euen vnto the Jlande of the greater Giaua, named Giaua maior, and vnto the cape of Malaccha, beinge in East Jndia. Giaua the lesse, is as bygge as the Jlande of Madera, and is but halfe a leaque distante from Giaua maior. Here they were infor med that aboue Giaua maior toward the north, is a great goulfe cauled the goulfe of China, in the which are trees of exceadyng byggenesse, inhabyted with foules of suche, greatenes that they cary great beastes in the ayer. The frutes of these trees are as bygge as cucummers.

The cape of Malaccha is one degree and a halfe aboue the Equinoctiall line towarde the pole Artike. On the East side of this cape, runneth a very longe coaste in the which are ma ny regions and cities wherof sum are cauled by these names, Cingaporla which is the cape. Also Pahan, Calantan, Patani, Braulin, Beneu, Longon, and Odia wherin is the citie in the which dwel leth the kynge of Sian named Zacabeders. Theyr cities are buil ded as owres are, and subiecte to the kynge of Sian. After the realme of Sian, are the regions of Iamgoma & Campaa where Reubarbe groweth, of the which are dyuers opinions, sum supposynge it to bee a roote, and other a putrifyed tree, affir mynge that yf it were not putrified, it shulde not haue so great a sauour. They caule it Calama. Next vnto this, is found the great China, whose kyng is thought to bee the greatest prince in the worlde, and is named Santoa Raia. Furthermore, al that is written hereafter of this kyng and these regions, they lerned by thinformation of a Moore that was in the Jlande of Timor. He affirmed that the sayde kynge hathe threescore and tenne crowned kynges vnder his empyre, and hathe a porte in the sea named Canthan: And two principal cities na med Nauchin and Connulaha where he remayneth hym selfe, and hath euer foure of his chiefe princes lying abowt his pallace on euery syde, towarde the Easte, Weste, Northe, and South giuinge dylygente attendaunce what is doone in euerye of theyr quarters. All the pryncees of the greater Jndia (cau led Indaa Maior,) and of that wherof J haue spoken before, are obedient to this kynge. And in token that they are trewe

subiectes

Cinamome

The Jlandes of Siaua.

Malaccha.

The greate goulfe of Chins.

The cape of Malaccha.

The names of many regi ons.

Reubarbe.

The greate kynge of Chi na.

The greater Jndia.

ſubiectes, they keepe in theyr pallaices which are in the middeſt of theyr cities, the beaſte cauled Linx, being fayrer then a
lyon, And is the great kynges ſignette, whiche all ſuche as
intende to go to China, beare with them ſealed in waxe or on a
piece of Iuerye for theyr ſafe conducte, withowt the which
they may not enter into the hauen.

When any of his kyngs rebell or are diſobedient, he cauſeth them to bee flene, and ſalted and dryed at the ſoonne:
Then to bee ſtuffed with chaffe, and ſette vppe on ſum hygh
thyng in the myddeſt of the chiefe ſtreate of the citie where al
the people may ſee it. He neuer ſuffereth his owne perſon
to bee openly ſeene to any man. But when his noble men of
the courte are deſyrous to ſee hym, he commeth downe frome
hys pallaice into a ryche pauylyon accompanyed with ſyxe of
hys principall concubynes apparcyled with lyke veſtures as
is he hym ſelfe. All thys way he is not ſeene by reaſon of
the pauylyon. When he hath paſſed through the pauylyon,
he entereth into a ſerpent named Nagha, being the moſt marueylous and ryche woozke of the woorlde, and placed in the
greateſt courte of the pallaice. When the kynge entereth in
to this with the wome, to thintent that he may not be knowē
among them, he cauſeth the ſayd noble men only to looke in
at a glaſſe which is in the breſt of the ſerpente, where they
ſee the kynge amonge the women, but cannot diſcerne which
is he. He ioyneth in mariage with hys ſyſter that the blud
royall bee not myxte with any other. His pallaice is enuironed with ſeuen large walles, the one being farre dyſtante frō
the other: And hath in euery ſuch circuite tenne thowſande
men for the garryſon of hys pallaice, who haue theyr waytinge dayes appoynted them courſe by courſe with freſſhe mē
in theyr places, and thus keepe theyr watch continually both
daye and nyght. In this pallaice are lxxix. haules, in the
which is an infinite number of women that ſerue the kynge
hauyng euer lyght torches in theyr handes for the greater
magnyfycence. He that wolde ſee all the pallaice, ſhulde
ſpend a hole day therin. Amonge other, there are foure
principal haules where ſumtymes the kynge gyueth audience
to hys noble men. Of theſe, one is couered both aboue and
beneth with metall, an other all ouer with ſyluer, the thyrde
with gold, and the fourth with pearles and precious ſtones.

Theſe

Marginal notes:

The beaſt cauled a lint.

The puniſhe-
ment of re-
belles.

The kynge is
not ſeene but
at a glaſſe.

A thyng of
ſtrange woork-
manſhyppe.

The kynge
maryeth his
ſyſter.
his pallaice.

A marueilous
garde.

women ſerue
the kynge.

Foure mar-
uelous haules

The people of China, are whyte menne, appareled as we are, and eate theyr meate on tables as wee doo. They haue the croſſe in ſum eſtimation, but knowe not the cauſe whye. Beyonde the coaſte of China, are dyuers other nations and people as Chenchii where pearles and cynamon are founde. Alſo the people named Lichii, where reyneth the great kynge of men, hauyng vnder hym .xxii. kynges, and is ſubiecte to the kyng of China. Here is alſo founde the great citie of CATHAY in the Eaſt, and dyuers other nations in the ſayd firme land, of the which ſum are brutyſſhe and beſtiall which vſe to kyll and eate theyr parentes when they are owld, thinking therby that they ſhall reuyue in them. All theſe people are gentyles.

The .xi. day of February in the yeare. 1522, they departed from the Iland of Timor and were ingulfed by chance in the great ſea cauled Lantchidol, and tooke theyr courſe betwene the weſte and ſouth weſte, leauynge the northe coaſtes on theyr ryght hand, fearyng leaſt if they ſhuld ſayle toward the firm land, they myght bee ſeene of the portugales who are of great power in Malaccha: and therfore dyrected theyr cours withowt the Iland of Sumatra cauled in owld tyme Taprobana: Leauyng alſo on theyr ryght hand vpon the fyrm land, the prouinces and regions of Pegu, Bongala, Calicut, Canonor, Goa, Cambaia, the goulfe of the Ilande of Ormus, and all the coaſtes of the greater India. And more ſafely to paſſe the cape of Buona Speranza being aboue Affrike, they ſayled about .xlii. degrees toward the pole Antartike, and remayned ſeuen weekes abowte that cape with many fetches compaſſyng the wynd with theyr ſayles contynually alofte, becauſe they had a weſt and north weſte wynd in the proos of theyr ſhyppe which wolde not ſuffer them to paſſe. The cape of Buona Speranza, is toward the pole Antartik beneth the Equinoctiall line .xxxiiii. degrees and a halfe: and .1600. leaques from the cape of Malaccha: And is the greateſte and moſte daungerous cape that is founde at thys day in al the worlde.

When they had by theſe perels ouerpaſſed thys cape, certeyne of them alwell for lacke of vytayles as alſo by reaſon of ſyckeneſſe, were mynded to ſayle to a hauen of the Portugales named Monzambique aboue Affryke. But the other anſwered that they wold rather dye then go to any other place then directly to Spayne. They folowed theyr courſe therfore ſaylynge

Margin notes:
- The people of China.
- The Croſſe.
- The greate kyng of men CATHAY.
- The ſea of Lantchidol.
- Malaccha.
- The Iland of Sumatra.
- Pegu,
- Bengala,
- Calicut.
- Canonor.
- Goa.
- Cambaia.
- Ormus.
- Eaſt India.
- Cap. de Buona Speranza.
- The port of Monzambique.

faylynge towarde the Southwest two monethes continuallp
without touchynge at anp porte: In whiche tyme there dyed
abowte. xri. of thepr coempany, whom thep cast into the sea.
And suerlp if god of his infinite mercie had not preserued the
residue in tyme, thep hadde all dyed of samen.

In fine, beinge inforced of necessitie, and halfe of thepr com-
panpe deade, thep saylid to one of the Ilandes of *Capo verde*
cauled *Insula Sancti Iacobi*, that is, sapnte James Ilande, par-
teyning to the kyng of Portugale. Where, as soone as thep
arryued, thep sent certepne alande in the shippe boate for vit-
tayles, declarynge to the Portugales with all loue and fauour what necessitie thep were dryuen to and what miseries
and trauaples thep had sustepned, informynge them further
if thepr marueylous biage and suche thynges as thep hadde
scene in both the East and West India, with such other gin-
til woordes wherby thep obtepned certepne measure of rise.
But when afterwarde. xiii. of thepm returned for more rpse,
thep were dcrepned: Whereuppon the reste whiche remapned
in the shippe, fearynge the lyke chaunce, departed with full
sayles, and the. vii. day of September with the help of god
entered into the hauen of *San Lucar* nere vnto Siuile, where
dischargynge all thepr ordinaunce for iop, thep wente im mediatly to the greate churche in thepr shertes and barefooted
with a torche before them to gyue thankes to almpghtie god
who had brought them safe to thepr owne countrey, and restored them to thepr wyues and chyldren.

As touchynge thende of this biage, Transiluanus wryteth sumwhat more largely as foloweth.

The other shyppe which thep left behynde them to bee re-
papred, returned afterwarde by the Archipelagus aforesapde
and by the great sea to the coastes of the firme of the west India, and arryued at a region of the same being ageynst *Dariena*,
where the South sea of *Sur* is seperate but by a lyttle space
of lande from the West Ocean in the which are the Ilandes
of *Hispaniola* and *Cuba*, and other Ilandes of the Spanyardes.
The other shyppe which returned into Spayne by compasing
abowt the hole bowle of the worlde by the coastes of East India and Affrike, departynge from the Iland of *Tidore*, and saylynge euer on this syde the Equinoctiall, dyd not fynde the
cape of *Cattigara* beinge aboue Asia, and (by the description

of

Famen.

Capo Verde.
S. James
Ilande.

The ingrati-
tude of the
portugales.

The port of
sapnt Lucas
nere vnto
Siuile.

what became
of the other
shyppe.
Dariena

The cape of
Cattigara.

The vyage rounde

Ptolome.

of Ptolome) rechynge many degrees beyonde the Equinoctial,
But hauynge sapled many dayes by the mayne sea, they came
to the cape of *Buona Speranza* and frome thence to the Ilandes
of *Capo verde*, where their shyppe beinge soore broofed by reason of the longe viage, leaked and tooke water, in suche sorte
that the mariners being nowe but fewe in number, and those

The vyage hardly performed.

also weake and feeble by reason of longe sickenesse and hunger, were not able both todrye the poompe continually and
otherwyse gouerne the shippe: and were therfore of necessitie
inforced to goo alande at the Ilande of saynte James to bye

They bye slaues for lacke of helpe

theym certeyne slaues to helpe them. But beinge destitute of
mony, accordynge to the custome of the mariners, they profered
them cloures for theyr slaues. The which thyng when it came
to the eares of the Portugale that was Capitayne of that I-
lande, he cast .xiii. of them in prison. Wherby the residue that
remayned in the shippe (beinge nowe but .xviii. in number)
were put in such feare that they departed immediatly without
rescuing theyr felowes, and sapled continually both by daye
and by nyght by the coastes of Affrike, and came in fine to
Spayne the .vi. day of September in the yeare. 1522. and arryued at the porte nere bnto Siuile the .xvi. moneth after they
departed from the Ilande of *Tidore*. Mariners doubtlesse more

Maryners woorthy immortall fame.
Argonauti.
The viage of Jason to wyn the golden fleese.

woorthy to bee celebrate with eternall memorie then they whiche in owlde tyme were cauled *Argonauti* that sapled with Jason to win the golden fleese in the region of *Cholchis* and the riuer of Phasis in the greate sea of *Pontus*. And the shyppe it
selfe, more woorthye to bee placed amonge the starres then

The shyppe more woorthy fame then owlde Argo of Grecia.
The vyage

that owlde Argo which departynge owt of Grecia, sapled to
thends of that great sea. For this owre marueylous shyppe,
takynge her byage from the straightes of Gibilterra and saplynge by the greate Ocean towarde the South and pole Antartike, and turnynge from thense to the Weste, folowed that
course so farre that passynge bnder the great circumference of
the worlde, shee came into the Easte, and frome thense ageyne
into the Weste, not by returnynge backewarde, but styll saplynge forwarde, so compasynge abowt the baule of the world
bnder the hole circumference of heauen bntyll shee were my-
raculously restored to her natiue region of Spayne and house
of Siuile.